VOICE MOTION

Melodic movement within three-part harmony

A WORKBOOK FOR GUITAR

and other harmonic instruments

JOHANNES HAAGE

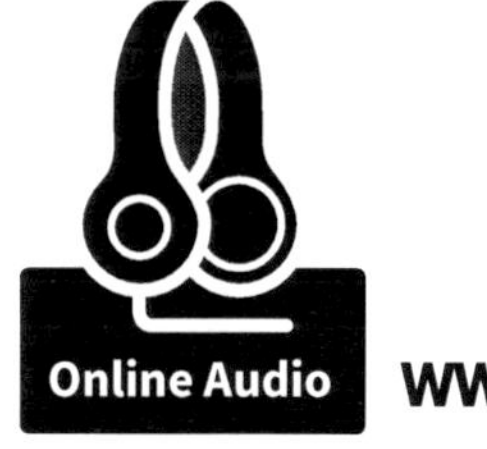

www.melbay.com/30903MEB

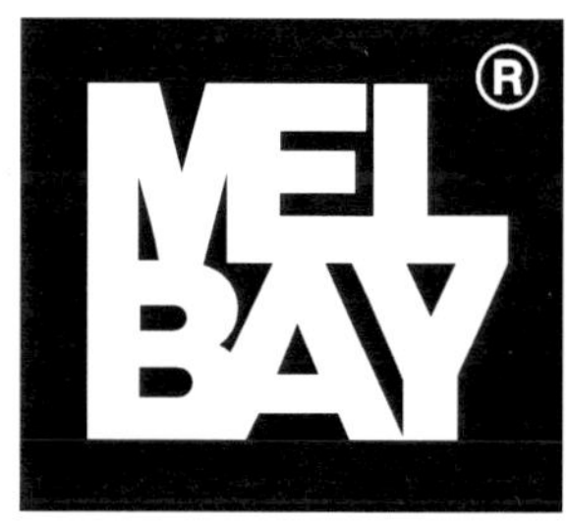

WWW.MELBAY.COM

INTRODUCTION

by Ben Monder

In the great tradition of Mick Goodrick and George Van Eps, this invaluable book is systematic in presentation and exhaustive in scope.
It will lead the student toward a view of harmony that is based less on discrete vertical structures and more the result of independently moving lines.

This approach opens vast new possibilities to the improvisor, and illuminates a path toward the goal of spontaneous composition.

Jump almost anywhere in this book and one will be able to play through examples that sound great, have instant practical applicability, and that most likely have not been heard before. Most importantly, they will inspire the student to create his or her own interpretations of the concepts within, and to work towards the pursuit of developing a personal vocabulary.

While these exercises are presented in terms of three-part chords, by "melting" the verticalities there is huge potential for a linear application as well.

Happy practicing!

PREFACE

This book focuses on the intersection of melody and harmony. Specifically, it explores how to move melodic voices independently within three-part harmony on the guitar.

The world of harmony has always fascinated me as a listener and musician - I admire those colleagues who play the most interesting chords but also seem to have figured out how to freely move the voices around within them.

As with any other topic, when you get deeper into it and start exploring, it usually becomes even more interesting - but it can also overwhelm you with the seemingly infinite possibilities it contains, making it difficult to systematically work on it without feeling lost.

In these cases I find it helpful to zoom in on a specific part of that infinity, set practical limits, figure out all possibilities within them, and put these possibilities in a clear and comprehensive order, so they can be practiced systematically.

Many invaluable books have been written that touch upon the subject, presenting endless voice leading exercises and harmonic mechanisms to keep anyone busy for many lifetimes. Nevertheless, in my personal studies over the years I could not find a condensed and conclusive list of all possible ways to move any or all voices within three-part harmony, in steps of 2nds and/or 3rds, within the context of common seven-note scales.

So I set out to figure out these possibilities myself, to delimit and tame this looming three-voiced infinity - which ultimately led to writing this book.

It contains not only the essential list of all possible moves, but far beyond that. It is a conclusive exploration of all relevant heptatonic scales, its modes and three-part chord structures as well. It also presents many examples, exercises and etudes to demonstrate their application.

Hopefully, there will be as many ways of using this material as there are individual readers. It is written by and from the view of a guitarist, primarily with the needs of the serious guitar student in mind - but it claims to be non-guitaristic enough to also be valuable for anyone who plays or composes for a harmonic instrument, and who has a basic understanding of both diatonic harmony and the common western music notation system.

Johannes Haage
Berlin, February 2022

TABLE OF CONTENTS

ABOUT THIS BOOK

This book presents a unique harmonic toolbox which can be used at any stage of a musicians personal artistic development.
It starts with a complete course on diatonic three-part chords, and moves on to a structured presentation of all possible ways to move any or all voices within them.
The reader gets a conclusive overview of heptatonic harmony and all its possible melodic movement which he or she can use when writing for or playing three distinct, simultaneous voices.
This will not only vastly expand ones chord vocabulary - it also shows a clear method for practicing to move any harmonic voice independently, in any inversion.

The book is divided into three main parts:

Part 1 teaches all available diatonic three-part chord structures in the key of C, and introduces the full list of all possible voice motion moves in close voicing.

Part 2 shows the same for open, drop-2 voicings.

Part 3 presents a complete course on basic heptatonics, and offers concepts and etudes to effectively practice the material of parts 1 and 2 in all keys and harmonic situations.
Furthermore, it expands the scope of application to larger step sizes, and all other playable voicing types on the guitar.

Each main part concludes with a guitar solo piece written specifically for this book to showcase melodic independence within the context of three-part harmony.

Throughout the book, numerous exercises are included for practicing the various voice motion moves. These movements can easily be applied to any style of music.

To keep a clear focus, this book does not include purely technical or genre-specific guitar exercises, nor does it teach basic functional harmony, chord-scale theory or counterpoint.
The student is encouraged to study these and other related topics with outside sources parallel to working with this book, as this knowledge will greatly enhance the learning experience.

HOW TO USE THIS BOOK

While its material is presented in a progressive and logical order, this book is not necessarily meant to be read from cover to cover.
Depending entirely on your current personal skill level, pick whatever seems interesting and valuable, play with it, jump around at will, and start exploring it in your own way.
Apply yourself, control the level of complexity, and customize any exercise or etude to fit your personal taste and musical goals.

The only requirements for a guitarist to successfully start working with this book are a basic understanding of the diatonic scale, and a good knowledge of where to find the notes of the common western notation system on the fretboard.
The "Appendix for Guitarists" presents a clear method to acquire these skills; refer to it at any point if you encounter difficulties navigating the fretboard.

Beginners/Intermediate Students:
Start with triads, take them up and down the diatonic scale, and begin exploring the melodic moves within any chord structure you are already familiar with - then progress to 4ths and other non-triadic structures to build up a more varied harmonic pallette.

Advanced Students:
Enhance your three-part chord knowledge and build up maximum independence of individual voices and fingers, learning to apply unfamiliar sounds and moves in all keys and inversions.

Soloists:
Use the material to harmonize and add extra dimensions to your linear melodies.

Accompanists:
Add movement to static chords, free up the individual voices, and acquire more flexibility to respond with counterpoint to any melody.

Arrangers:
Discover new tools to harmonize melodies, or add complexity and independence to all three voices.

Pianists:
All of the material in this book is easily accessible on the piano keyboard.
Although the material is presented within the sonic range of a regular 22-fret guitar, play through all or any of it with both hands, and expand it to the higher and lower registers, making use of the greater range of the piano.
Strict three-part harmony may not be so common to some pianists, but is a field well worth exploring, and a great base to work from when adding more voices.
The Appendix for Pianists at the end of the book presents concepts and ideas to adapt the material to the keyboard and apply it to piano-specific playing situations.

PRELIMINARY TOPICS

On Playability:

Depending on the instrument you play, some chord structures or melodic movements in this book might be uncomfortable to play at first, others may even seem to be impossible to play. On the guitar, try moving the respective material up an octave, take it to a higher register, or different keys... please use caution and stop immediately if you experience any pain. Especially for root position clusters in close voicing or other structures involving minor 2nd intervals, look for open strings to make some of these seemingly impossible chords playable. Throughout most of the book, not many indications of guitar fingerings are given, as they tend to differ depending on too many factors like range, octave, key, personal taste, etc. Fingerings might also compromise the clarity of the presentation. Explore any applicable string sets; as a rule of thumb, keep any voice movement on the same string if possible.

On Categorization:

One of the most basic vital skills of our brain is to form cognitive categories in which it can place events and objects the moment our senses perceive them. Without our category-learning mind, we would not be able to build upon our experiences; in fact, we would not be able to interact with our environment, or even survive.
In an actual playing situation, a musician should be in the moment, fully focused on listening and creating sound. The mind normally can not and should not be occupied with consciously identifying and naming all of the musical elements being used.
To stay in the flow of creation, the unconscious, implicit brain system needs a solid base of pre-formed categories of the tools it wants to use at any given moment; then it can work effortlessly and the mind can focus on creating.
When practicing, a musician can use his conscious, analytical, explicit brain system to form clearly defined categories for the tools he needs (like three-part chord structures, voicing types, guitar chord forms etc.) and work thoroughly on them until they become deeply engrained. The more solid the base of categories, the better the mind can effortlessly use these tools in a creative situation and stay focused. If a tool it wants to use is not readily available, the mind becomes self-conscious and the explicit, analytical system kicks in, making it impossible to stay in the moment.

On Style:

Although this material obviously tends to lend itself more to some genres of music than others, this book is not about any specific style.

On Rhythm/Time:

This book is mainly about harmony and melody. The topic of rhythm is not entirely ignored, but left out of most discussions deliberately to keep a clear focus.
A good sense of rhythm and the ability to play in time is arguably more important for your playing than anything in this book though; so if you feel you lack something there, set the book down immediately and turn on your metronome.

PART ONE: Close Voicing

OVERVIEW

This chapter will teach you to identify and categorize all diatonic 3-part chord types and structures in close voicing, and how to practice them on your instrument ascending and descending the scale.

Some useful rules, terms and definitions are introduced for moving any or all voices melodically departing from these chord structures, as well as basic principles for practicing them.

The full list of all possible voice motion moves in close voicing is presented in two ways:
First, in the order of motion type (1A)
and then in the order of the chord structures the moves may start off from (1B).

A short solo guitar piece composed strictly in close three-part harmony ends the section, showcasing independent voice movement created by applying the moves.

CONTENTS

IDENTIFYING ALL THREE-PART CHORD STRUCTURES

Before you can start to seriously study the entire potential of melodic voice movement within three-part harmony, it is necessary to know and name all possible three-part chord structures. In a seven-note (heptatonic) scale like the diatonic there are only five different possible chord types which can be built on any scale degree:

1. Triads (two 3rds stacked on top of each other / scale degrees 1-3-5)
2. 4ths (two 4ths stacked / scale degrees 1-4-7)
   The symbols used in this book to describe the chords of this type show the specific kind of 4th intervals as they are stacked to form the root position of the respective chord.
3. 7th no5 (a 7th chord without its 5th degree, or a 3rd and a 5th stacked / scale degrees 1-3-7)
4. 7th no3 (a 7th chord without its 3rd degree, or a 5th and a 3rd stacked / scale degrees 1-5-7)
5. Clusters (two 2nds stacked/ scale degrees 1-2-3 or any 3 adjacent notes played simultaneously)

Any three-part chord structure using only notes of the diatonic scale will fall into one of these five categories. Here are all five chord types built up from the note C' in close voicing, and their two inversions.

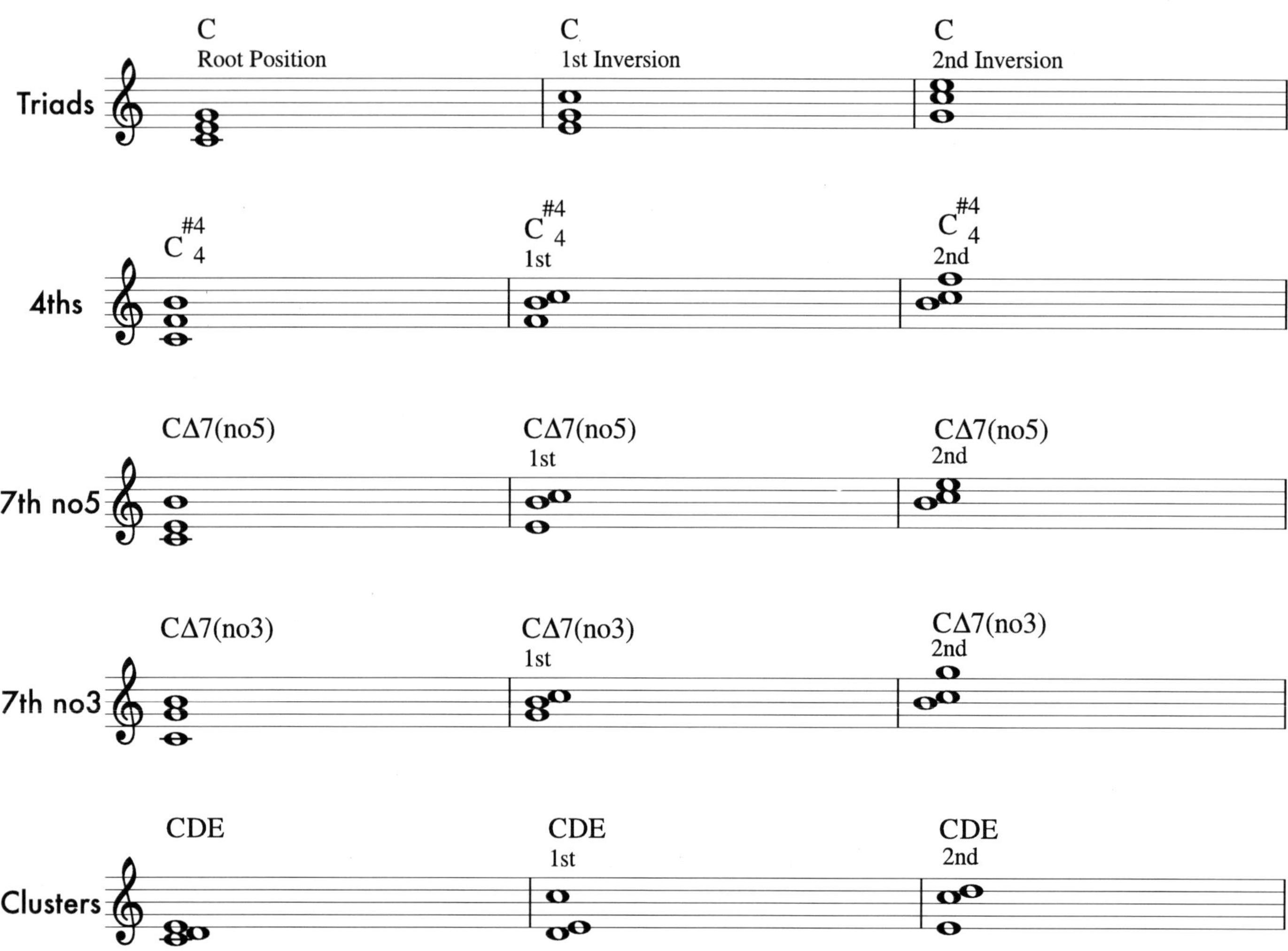

These are the 15 possible three-part "C"- chord structures within the diatonic scale in the key of C. You can build 15 similar chords on any of the seven scale degrees, which means there is a grand total of 105 different three-part chord structures (15x7=105) within the diatonic scale or any other balanced heptatonic; see Part 3A "Heptatonics".

Throughout Part 1 and the rest of the book these 15 chord structures will be used to show all possible close-voiced starting points for melodic voice motion within the diatonic scale.

For better comparability and clarity, we now move them into the same range, so each has the note C" as the top note:

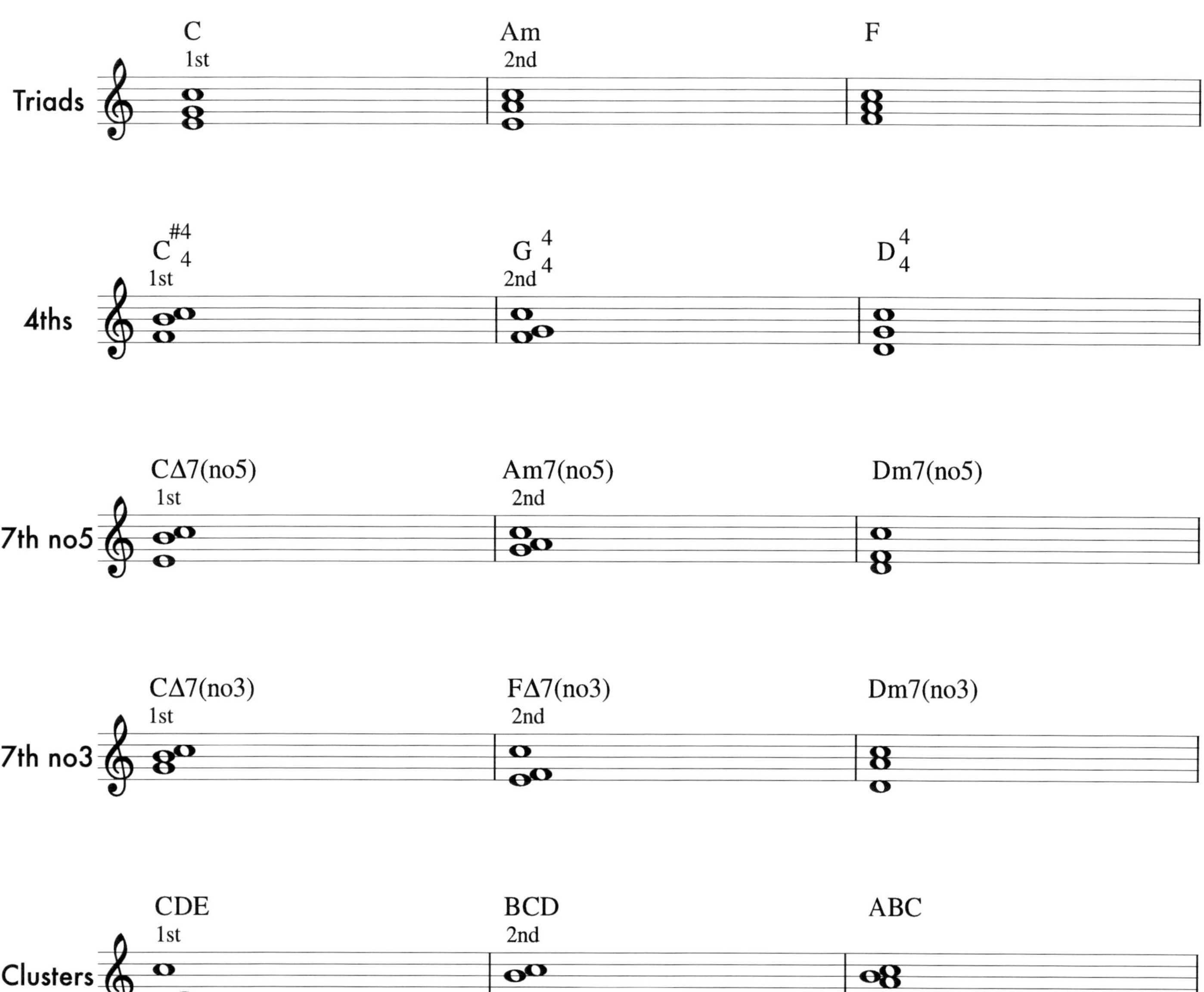

As preparation for the main part of this book, practice playing and identifying all 15 of these chords.

Then take each one up and down the C major diatonic scale for the full range of your instrument. (See the the next page for examples.)
Make sure to be able identify and name each chord on any scale degree.

All chords in the main part of this book will be presented with chord names in the way shown above. No labelling below the chord symbols indicates root position, while the 1st and 2nd inversions are marked 1st/2nd.

VOICE MOTION PREPARATORY EXERCISES
for Part One

This page shows some basic ways of taking the 1st inversion C major triad up and down the diatonic scale in seconds (+/- 1 scale degree) and/or thirds (+/-2 scale degrees), moving all three voices in parallel.

Apply these exercises to all of the 15 chords on the previous page and play them on your instrument.

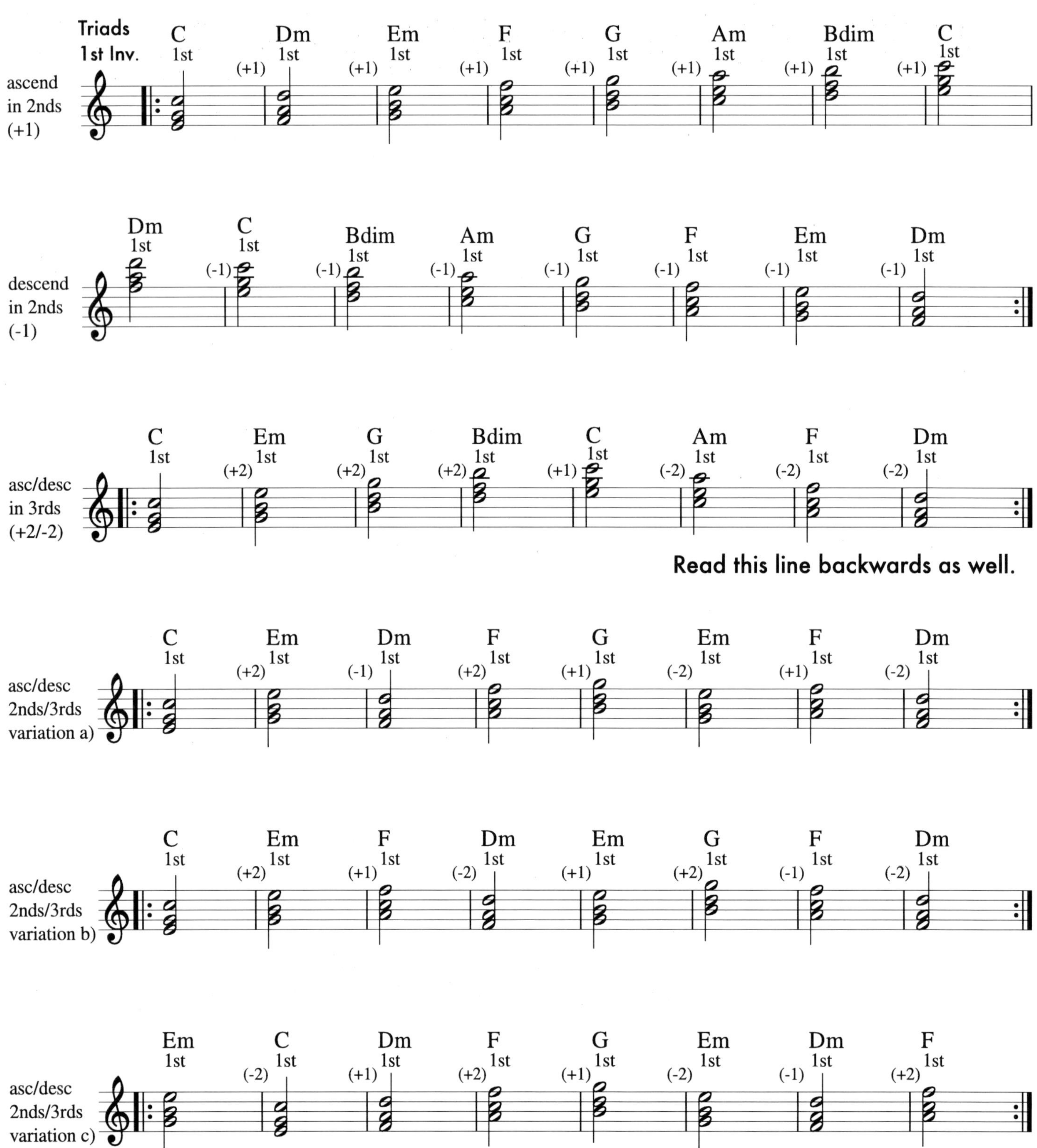

Play the last 3 lines throughout the full range of your instrument and then read them in reverse order as well.

To prepare for Part 1 of this book, we re-arrange the 15 close-voiced chords with the top note C'' in the order of their intervallic range, from wide (spanning an interval of a 7th) to close (spanning a 3rd).

Read and play through the chords line by line (horizontally), column by column (vertically), and from top right to bottom left (diagonally) and back.

Take note of common tones between chords and of any resulting voice movement.

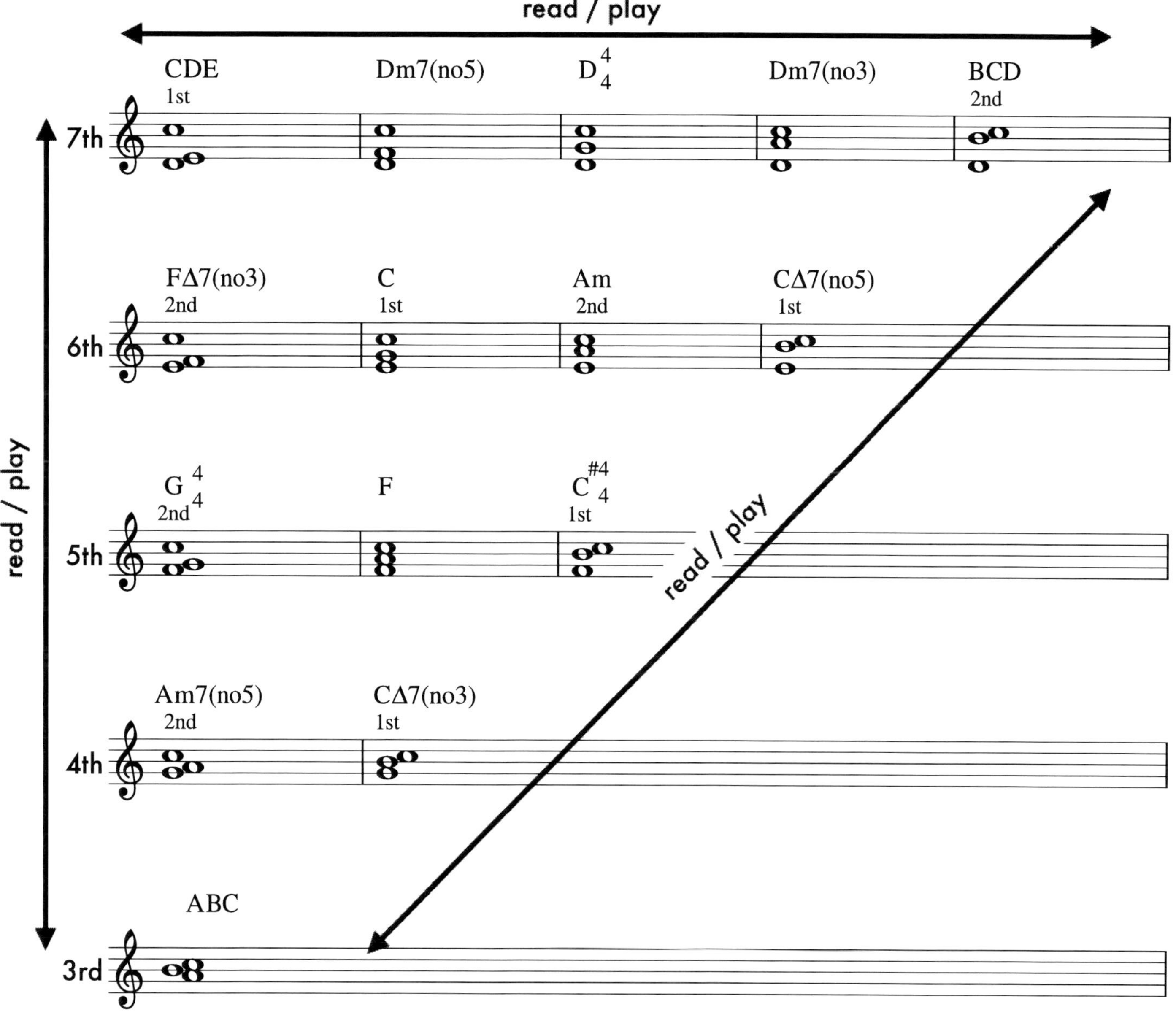

On Chord Names:
Throughout large parts of this book, the three-note structures will have names above them so you can clearly place them in one of the five chord categories and identify their inversions.

The goal is to learn to identify any three-part structure in an isolated way, regardless of musical situation or context. When adding more notes to it or playing it over a different bassnote, it might become part of a new sound with a different name - yet the identity of the three-note structure itself will not change.

VOICE MOTION
Rules, Terms & Definitions

One main goal of this book is to methodically examine all possible ways to move any or all voices within harmonic three-part structures, in steps of 2nds and/or 3rds.

To get only useful results, we need to establish a few rules or criteria which all moves have to meet in close voicing. These three rules are:

1. No meeting of the voices on the same note.
   This would result in a chord structure with only two different notes, leaving the sphere of three-part harmony.

2. No crossing of voices.

3. No voice motion beyond the maximum range of the 7th interval.
   The resulting structure would not be a chord in close voicing, but a rather spread, open voicing of some kind.

Any move which starts from a close-voiced three-part chord and which meets these three criteria will inevitably lead into some other close-voiced, three-part chord.

There are a total of 108 such possible moves within three-part harmony of a diatonic scale. Building upon the 15 close-voiced chords with the top note C", Part 1 will show all of them in a clear and methodical way.

The 108 possible moves will be presented grouped into five voice motion types. They differ in the number of moving voices, and how these voices move in relationship to one another:

1. Single-Voice Motion

2. Double-Voice Parallel Motion

3. Double-Voice Contrary Motion

4. Triple-Voice Parallel Motion

5. Triple-Voice Contrary Motion

On the next page you will find one particular move with Single-Voice Motion as an example of how all 108 moves will be presented in Part 1A.

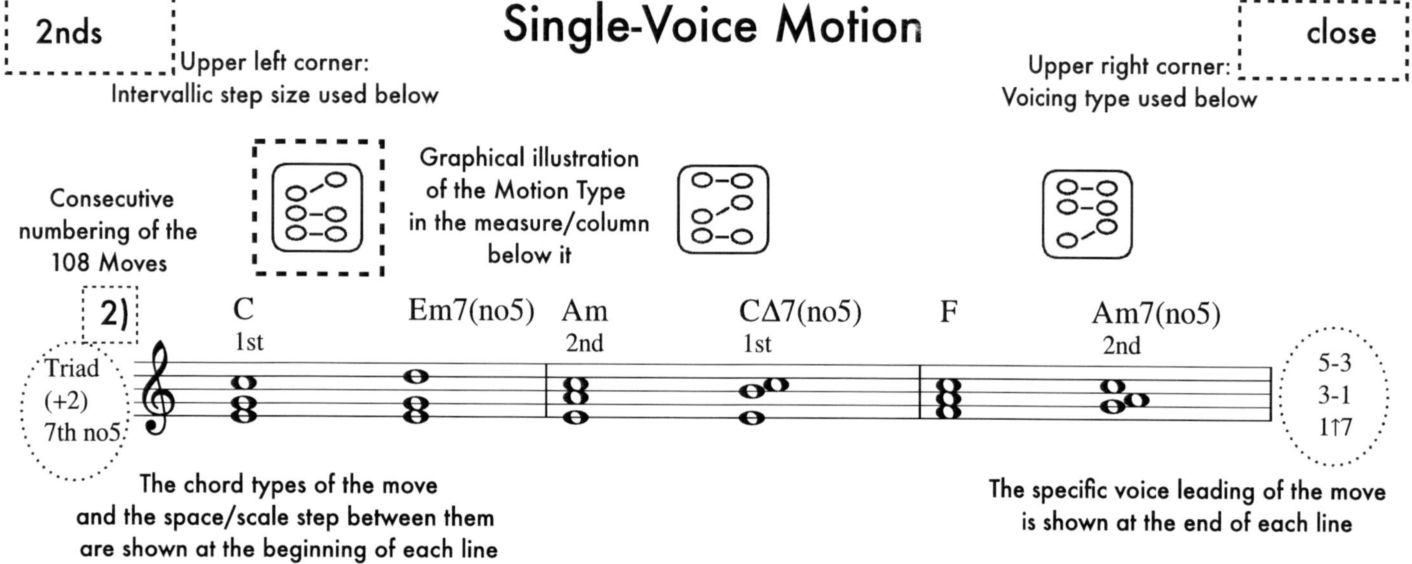

The example above shows the second of the 108 possible moves in its three inversions.

Reading any of the two-chord measures regularly from left to right (reg.) will produce an ascending motion; reading then in reverse from right to left (rev.) will produce a descending one.

Together with their inversions, the 108 moves produce a total of 324 chord pairs. Each measure represents a unique motion between two close-voiced three-part chords. Each of these motions can be performed on any of the seven scale degrees with their different chord qualities.

Out of the 324 motions:
146 have the top note moving up/down a 2nd.
105 motions have the top note moving up/down a 3rd.
73 motions have one of the two lower voices leading, moving up/down a 2nd (45) or a 3rd (28), while the top note stays the same.

Voice Motion Examples in 2nds

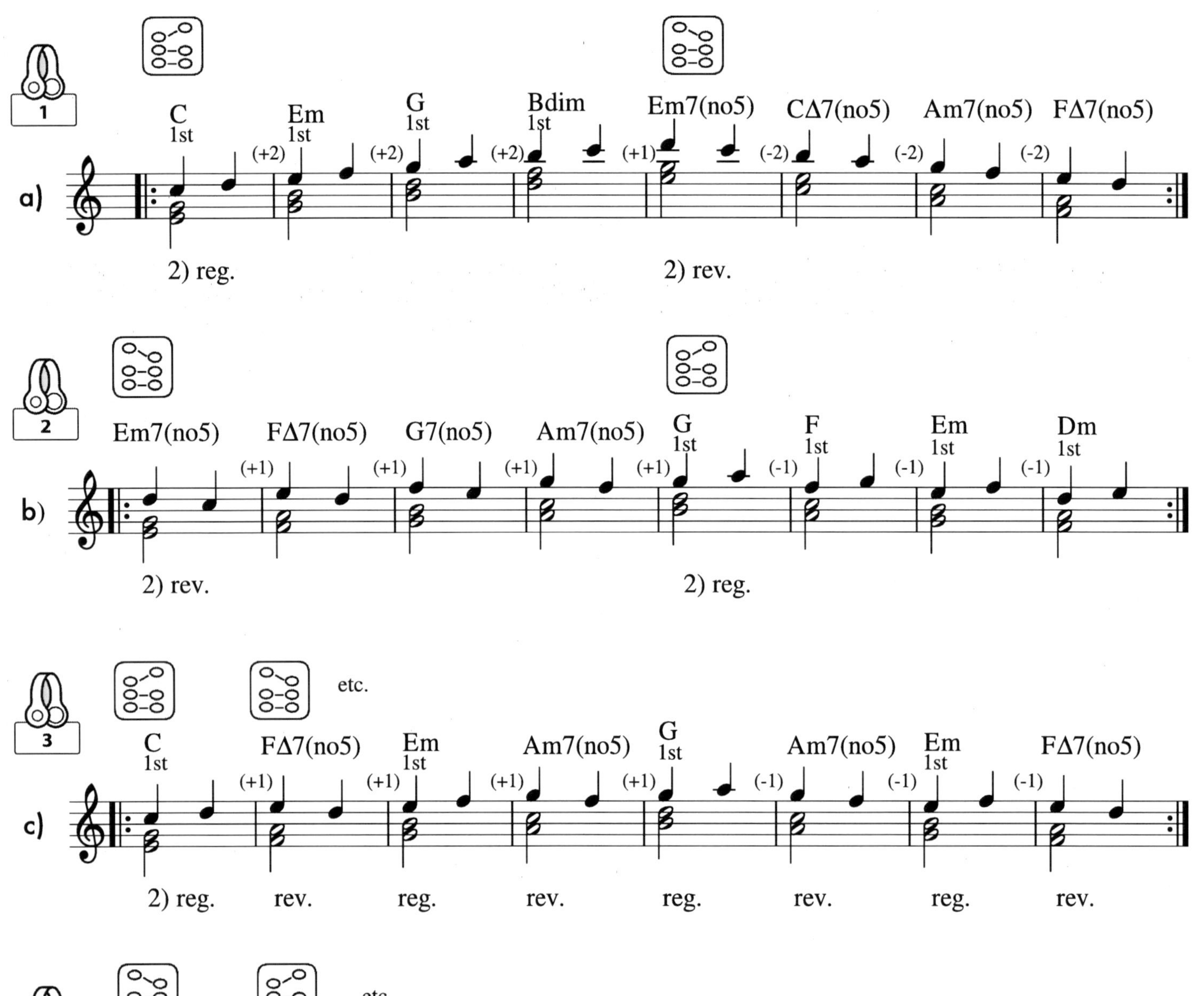

This page shows some basic ways of practicing the move 2) shown on the previous page, taking the first measure - with an upper voice motion of a 2nd - up and down the scale in four different ways.

Practice all motions with the top note moving up/down a 2nd as in variations a) to d) above, in all keys, for the full range of your instrument, memorizing the principles of the variations.

Combine the four different principles to create melodies made up of intervals of a 2nd, or use them to harmonize simple diatonic melodies that you already know.

Single-Voice Motion

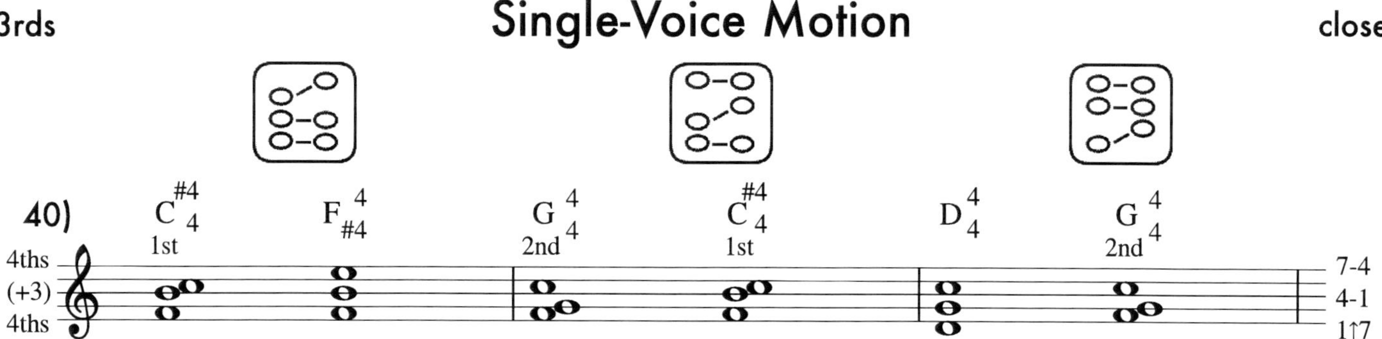

The example above shows move number 40, with a single voice moving in 3rds, all inversions.

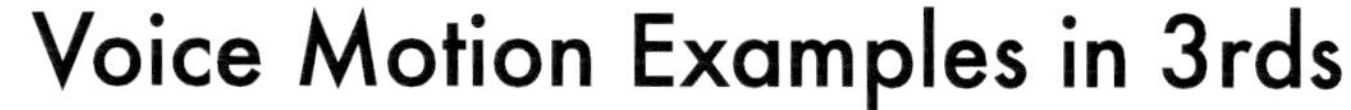

Voice Motion Examples in 3rds

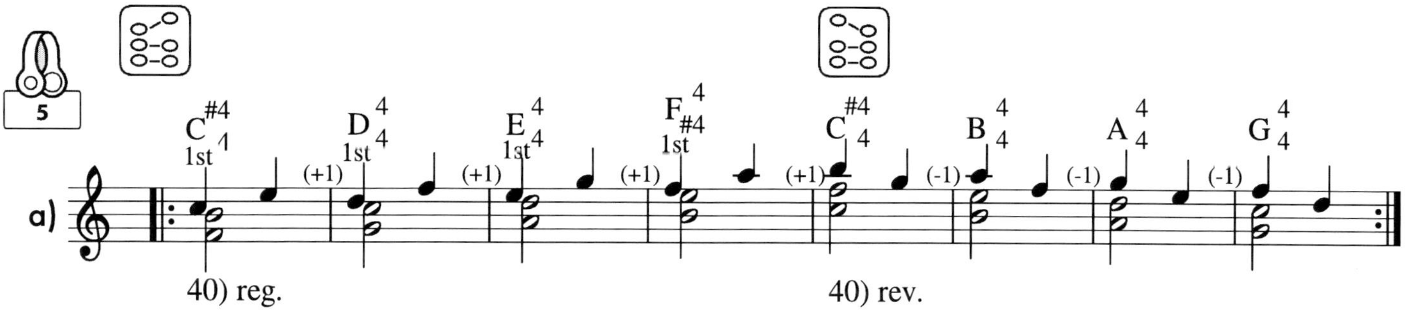

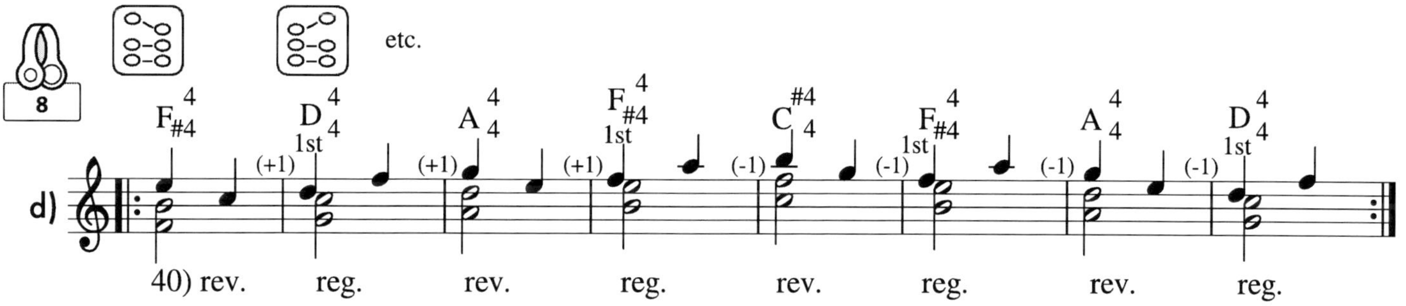

5

a) 40) reg. 40) rev.

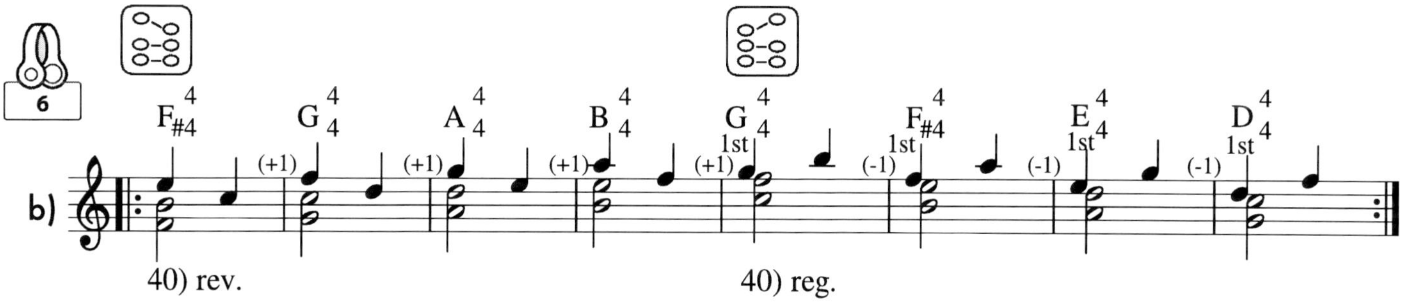

6

b) 40) rev. 40) reg.

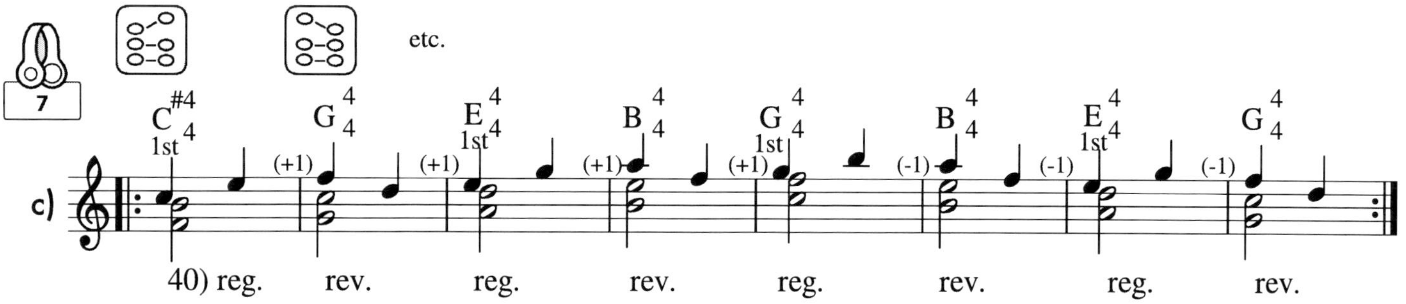

7

etc.

c) 40) reg. rev. reg. rev. reg. rev. reg. rev.

8

etc.

d) 40) rev. reg. rev. reg. rev. reg. rev. reg.

Practice all motions with the top note moving up/down a 3rd as in variations a) to d) above, in all keys, throughout the full range of your instrument. Memorize the four different principles of combining regular and reverse motion ascending and descending the scale.

2nds

Voice Motion Examples (cont.)

close

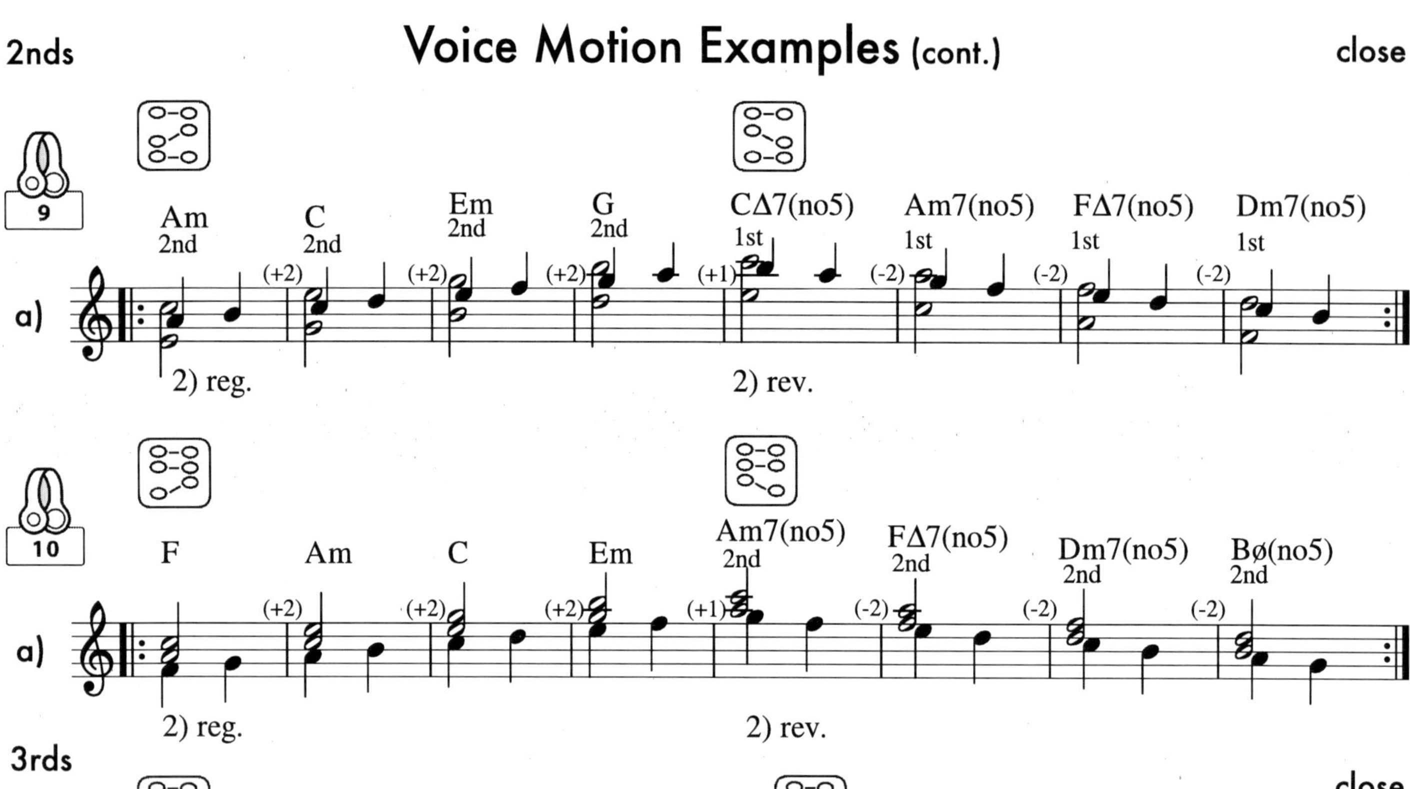

3rds

close

11

G 4 4 2nd — A 4 4 2nd — B 4 4 2nd — C #4 4 2nd — G 4 4 1st — F 4 #4 1st — E 4 4 1st — D 4 4 1st

a) (+1) (+1) (+1) (+1) (-1) (-1) (-1)

40) reg. 40) rev.

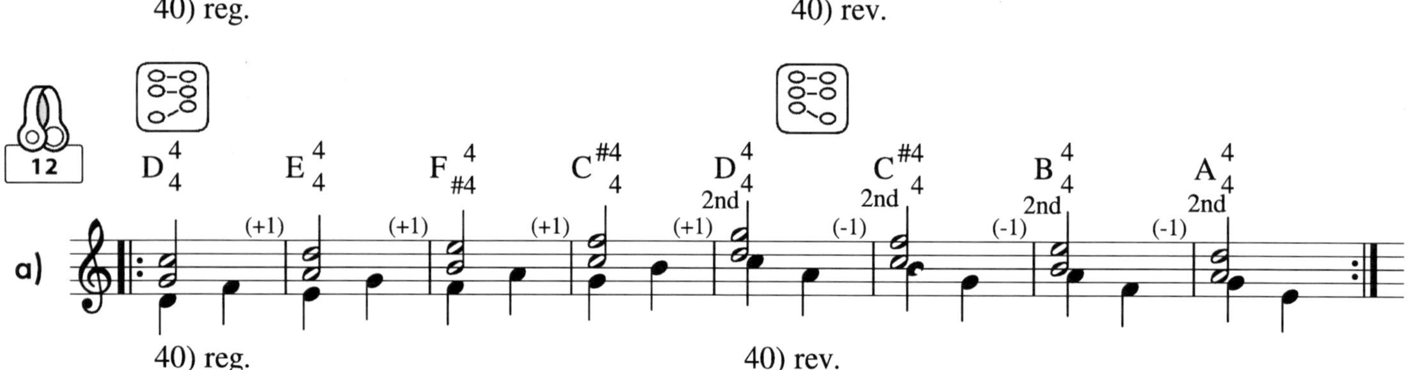

This page shows the previous exercise variations a) applied to the other inversions of the moves 2) and 40), with Single-Voice Motion in the middle or low voice.
Practice like variation b) to d) as well, in all keys, throughout the full range of your instrument.
All motions with one of the two lower voices leading up/down a 2nd or 3rd can be practiced this way.

PART 1A

The 108 Possible Moves in Close Voicing

Read every page of this section both horizontally (lines) and vertically (columns).

Apply all of the exercises of the introduction throughout the full range of your instrument, in all keys.

GRAPHICAL OVERVIEW OF ALL MOTION TYPES in PART ONE

(close voicing)

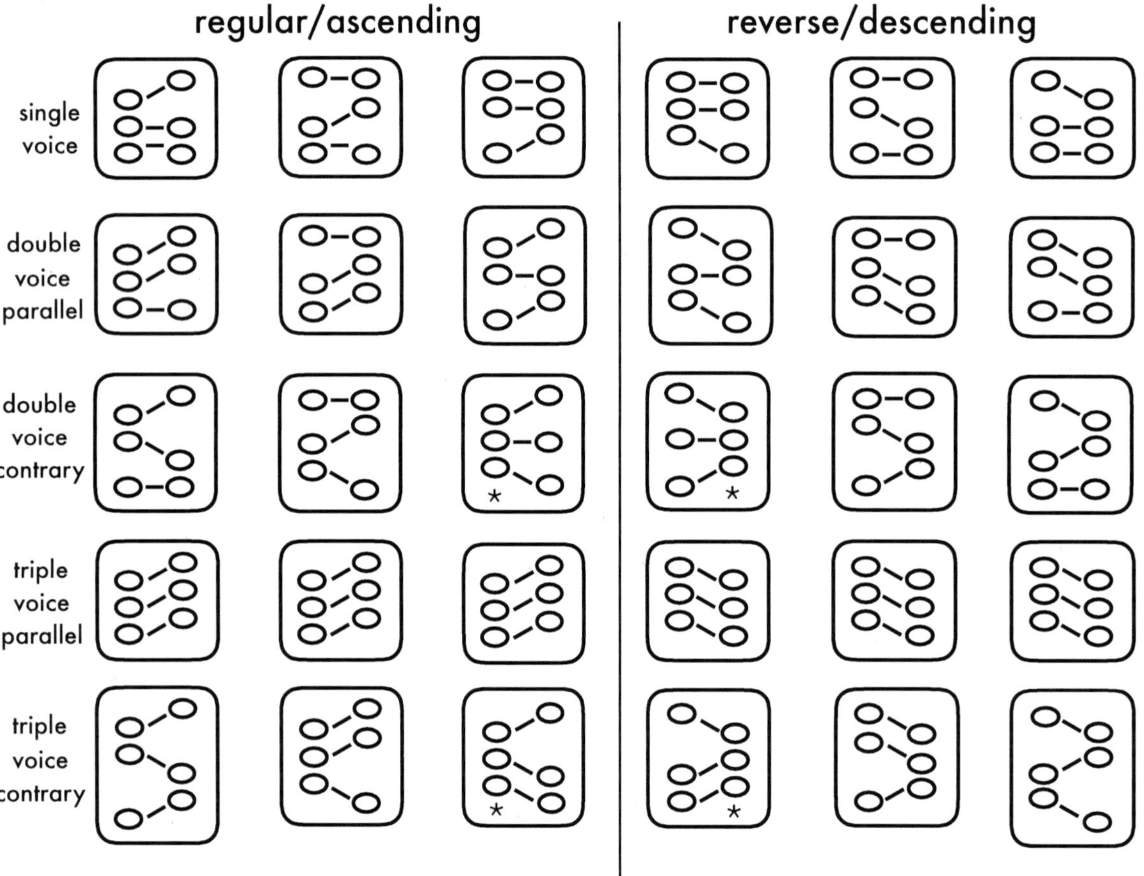

When two or three voices move in contrary motion, the direction of the highest moving (or leading) voice determines how our ears perceive the direction of that motion. For this reason, some ascending moves with contrary motion produce inversions which we hear as descending. In these cases, the order of chords is reversed to consistently present only ascending motions. This chord reversal is indicated by an asterisk (*) in the graphical representation of the motion above the respective move.

Single-Voice Motion

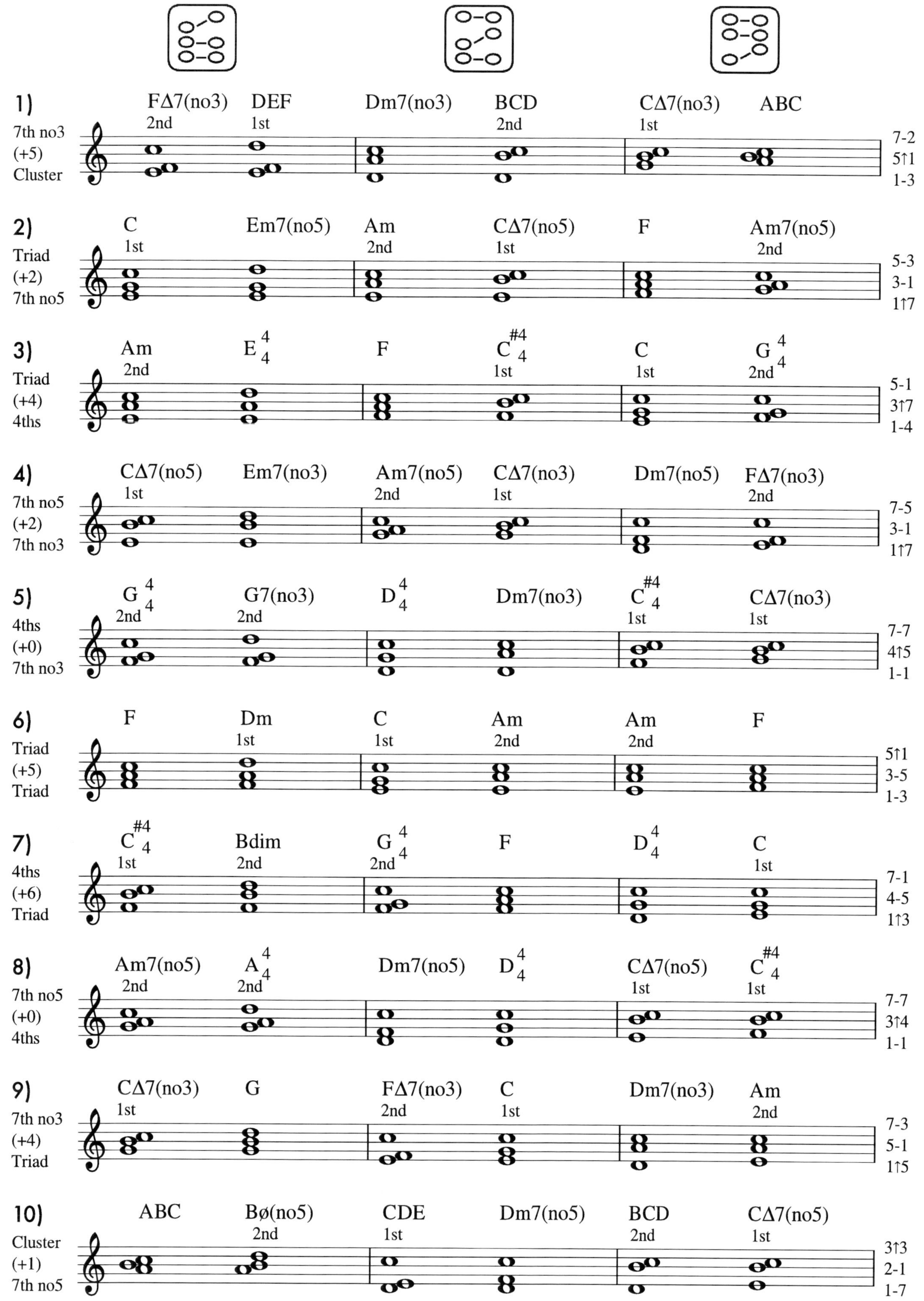

1) 7th no3 (+5) Cluster

FΔ7(no3) 2nd | DEF 1st | Dm7(no3) | BCD 2nd | CΔ7(no3) 1st | ABC

7-2 / 5↑1 / 1-3

2) Triad (+2) 7th no5

C 1st | Em7(no5) | Am 2nd | CΔ7(no5) 1st | F | Am7(no5) 2nd

5-3 / 3-1 / 1↑7

3) Triad (+4) 4ths

Am 2nd | E^{4}_{4} | F | $C^{\#4}_{4}$ 1st | C 1st | G^{4}_{4} 2nd

5-1 / 3↑7 / 1-4

4) 7th no5 (+2) 7th no3

CΔ7(no5) 1st | Em7(no3) | Am7(no5) 2nd | CΔ7(no3) 1st | Dm7(no5) | FΔ7(no3) 2nd

7-5 / 3-1 / 1↑7

5) 4ths (+0) 7th no3

G^{4}_{4} 2nd | G7(no3) 2nd | D^{4}_{4} | Dm7(no3) | $C^{\#4}_{4}$ 1st | CΔ7(no3) 1st

7-7 / 4↑5 / 1-1

6) Triad (+5) Triad

F | Dm 1st | C 1st | Am 2nd | Am 2nd | F

5↑1 / 3-5 / 1-3

7) 4ths (+6) Triad

$C^{\#4}_{4}$ 1st | Bdim 2nd | G^{4}_{4} 2nd | F | D^{4}_{4} | C 1st

7-1 / 4-5 / 1↑3

8) 7th no5 (+0) 4ths

Am7(no5) 2nd | A^{4}_{4} 2nd | Dm7(no5) | D^{4}_{4} | CΔ7(no5) 1st | $C^{\#4}_{4}$ 1st

7-7 / 3↑4 / 1-1

9) 7th no3 (+4) Triad

CΔ7(no3) 1st | G | FΔ7(no3) 2nd | C 1st | Dm7(no3) | Am 2nd

7-3 / 5-1 / 1↑5

10) Cluster (+1) 7th no5

ABC | Bø(no5) 2nd | CDE 1st | Dm7(no5) | BCD 2nd | CΔ7(no5) 1st

3↑3 / 2-1 / 1-7

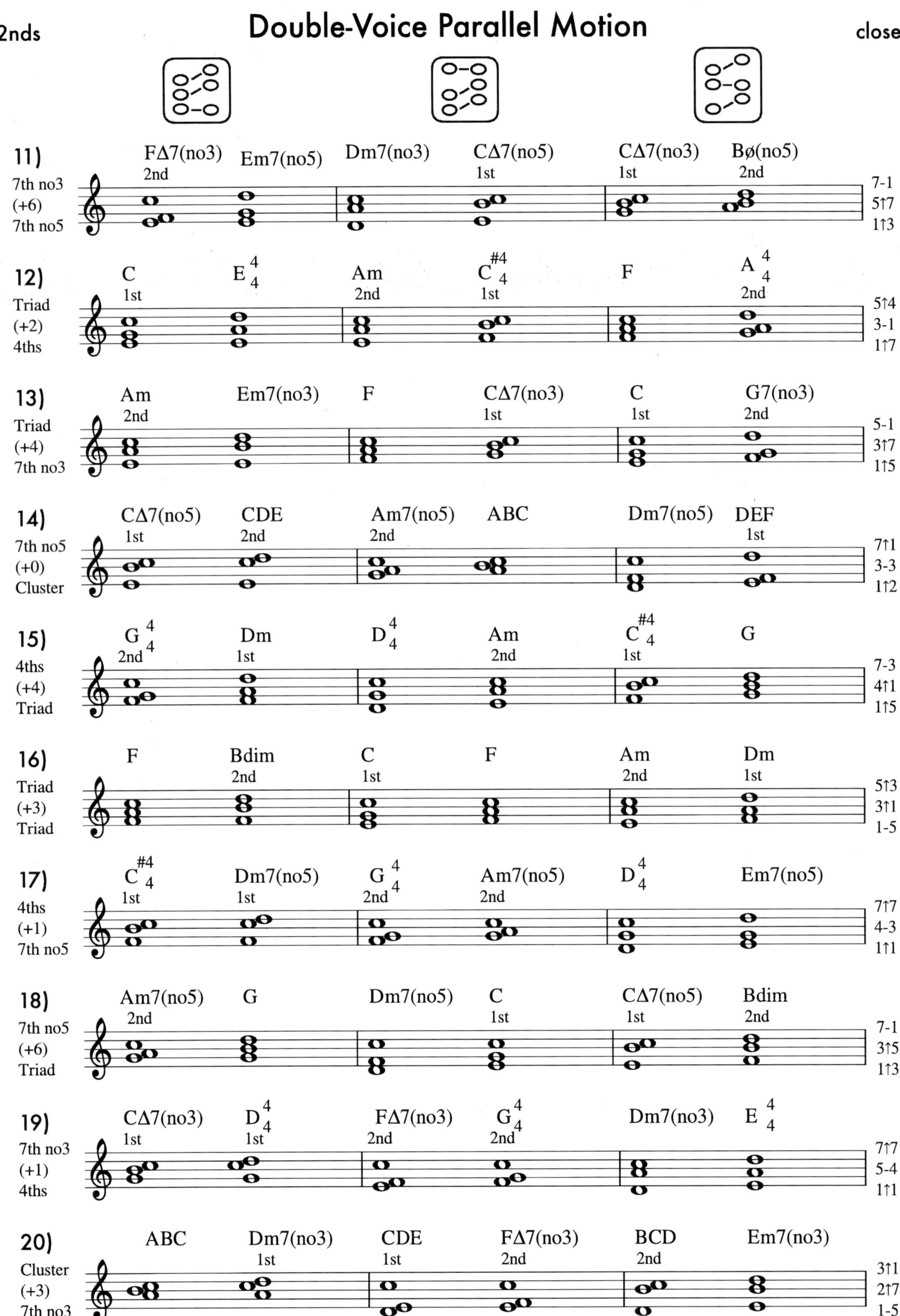
2nds
Double-Voice Parallel Motion
close
11)
7th no3
(+6)
7th no5
FΔ7(no3) 2nd
Em7(no5)
Dm7(no3)
CΔ7(no5) 1st
CΔ7(no3) 1st
Bø(no5) 2nd
7-1
5↑7
1↑3
12)
Triad
(+2)
4ths
C 1st
E 4 4
Am 2nd
C #4 4 1st
F
A 4 4 2nd
5↑4
3-1
1↑7
13)
Triad
(+4)
7th no3
Am 2nd
Em7(no3)
F
CΔ7(no3) 1st
C 1st
G7(no3) 2nd
5-1
3↑7
1↑5
14)
7th no5
(+0)
Cluster
CΔ7(no5) 1st
CDE 2nd
Am7(no5) 2nd
ABC
Dm7(no5)
DEF 1st
7↑1
3-3
1↑2
15)
4ths
(+4)
Triad
G 4 4 2nd
Dm 1st
D 4 4
Am 2nd
C #4 4 1st
G
7-3
4↑1
1↑5
16)
Triad
(+3)
Triad
F
Bdim 2nd
C 1st
F
Am 2nd
Dm 1st
5↑3
3↑1
1-5
17)
4ths
(+1)
7th no5
C #4 4 1st
Dm7(no5) 1st
G 4 4 2nd
Am7(no5) 2nd
D 4 4
Em7(no5)
7↑7
4-3
1↑1
18)
7th no5
(+6)
Triad
Am7(no5) 2nd
G
Dm7(no5)
C 1st
CΔ7(no5) 1st
Bdim 2nd
7-1
3↑5
1↑3
19)
7th no3
(+1)
4ths
CΔ7(no3) 1st
D 4 4 1st
FΔ7(no3) 2nd
G 4 4 2nd
Dm7(no3)
E 4 4
7↑7
5-4
1↑1
20)
Cluster
(+3)
7th no3
ABC
Dm7(no3) 1st
CDE 1st
FΔ7(no3) 2nd
BCD 2nd
Em7(no3)
3↑1
2↑7
1-5

Double-Voice Contrary Motion

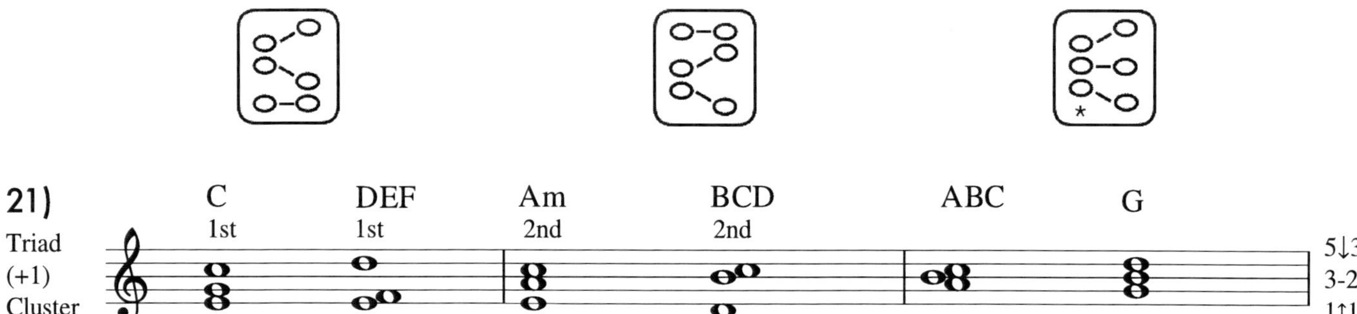

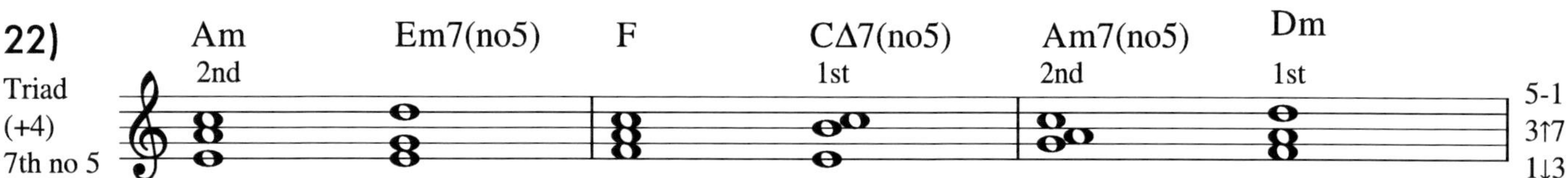

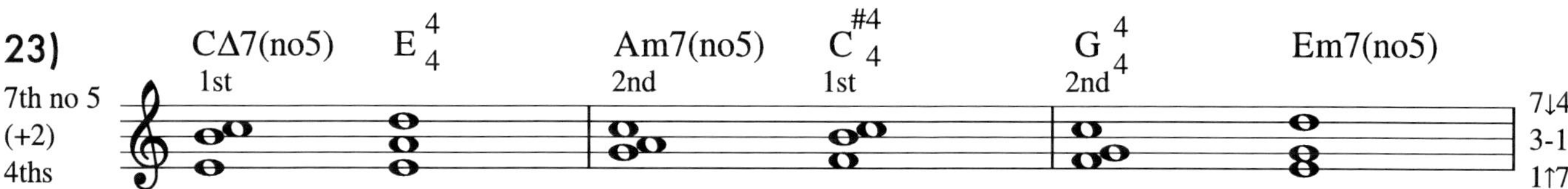

24)
Triad
(+1)
7th no 3

F
G7(no3) 2nd
C 1st
Dm7(no3)
CΔ7(no3) 1st
Bdim 2nd

5↑5
3↓1
1-7

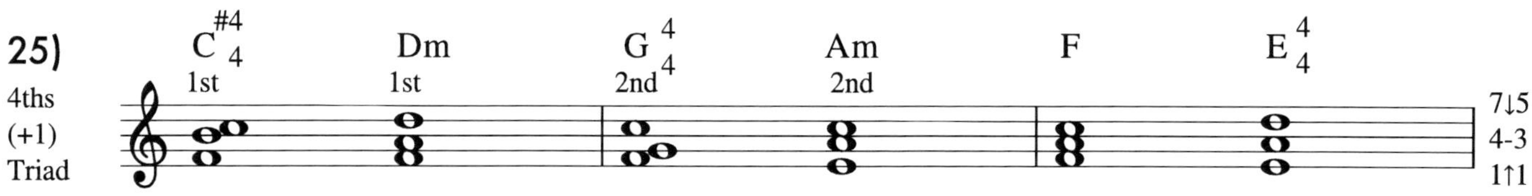

26)
7th no 3
(+5)
4ths

CΔ7(no3) 1st
A 4 4 2nd
FΔ7(no3) 2nd
D 4 4
C #4 4 1st
Em7(no3)

7↓1
5-7
1↑4

Triple-Voice Parallel Motion

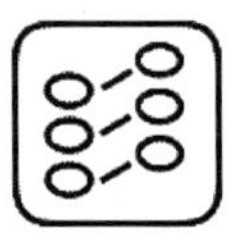

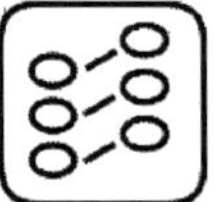

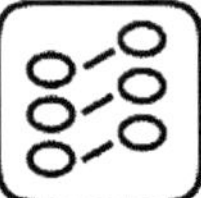

27)
Triad
(+1)
Triad

C 1st | Dm 1st | Am 2nd | Bdim 2nd | F | G

5↑5
3↑3
1↑1

28)
4ths
(+1)
4ths

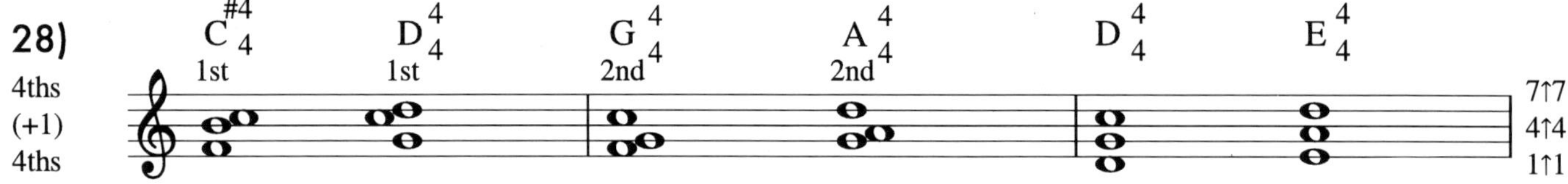

29)
7th no 5
(+1)
7th no 5

CΔ7(no5) 1st | Dm7(no5) 1st | Am7(no5) 2nd | Bø(no5) 2nd | Dm7(no5) | Em7(no5)

7↑7
3↑3
1↑1

30)
7th no 3
(+1)
7th no 3

CΔ7(no3) 1st | Dm7(no3) 1st | FΔ7(no3) 2nd | G7(no3) 2nd | Dm7(no3) | Em7(no3)

7↑7
5↑5
1↑1

31)
Cluster
(+1)
Cluster

CDE 1st | DEF 1st | BCD 2nd | CDE 2nd | ABC | BCD

3↑3
2↑2
1↑1

Triple-Voice Contrary Motion

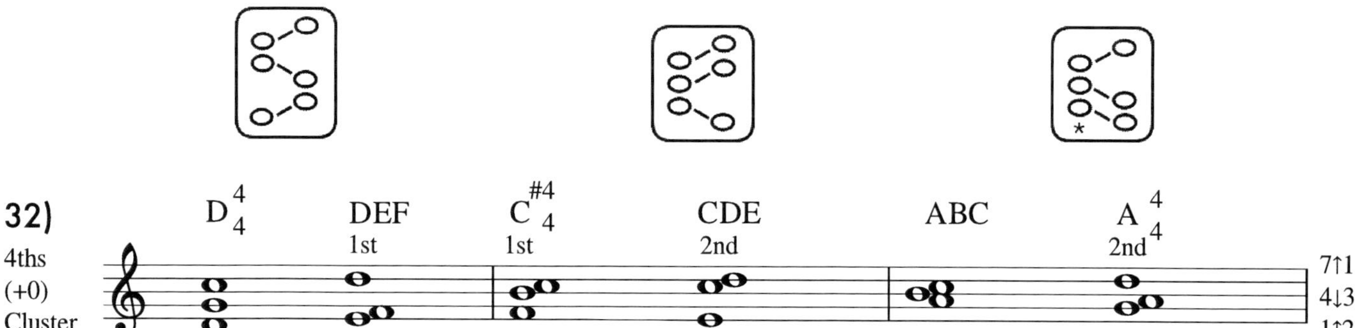

33)
7th no 3
(+1)
7th no 5
Dm7(no3)
Em7(no5)
CΔ7(no3)
1st
Dm7(no5)
1st
Am7(no5)
2nd
G7(no3)
2nd
7↑1
5↓7
1↑3

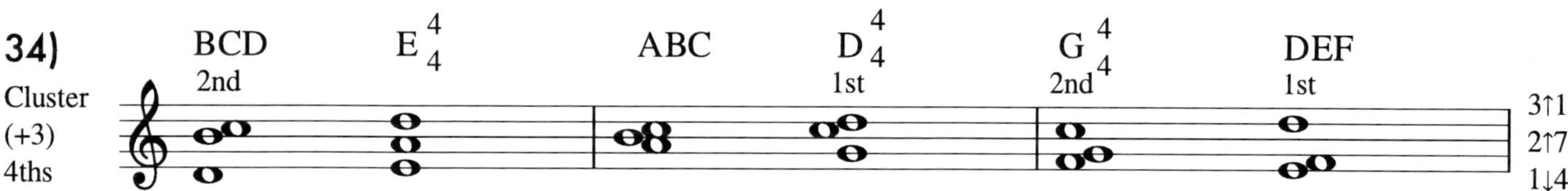

35)
Triad
(+6)
7th no 3
Am
2nd
G7(no3)
2nd
F
Em7(no3)
CΔ7(no3)
1st
Dm
1st
5↑7
3↑5
1↓1

36)
7th no 5
(+1)
Triad
CΔ7(no5)
1st
Dm
1st
Am7(no5)
2nd
Bdim
2nd
F
Em7(no5)
7↓5
3↑3
1↑1

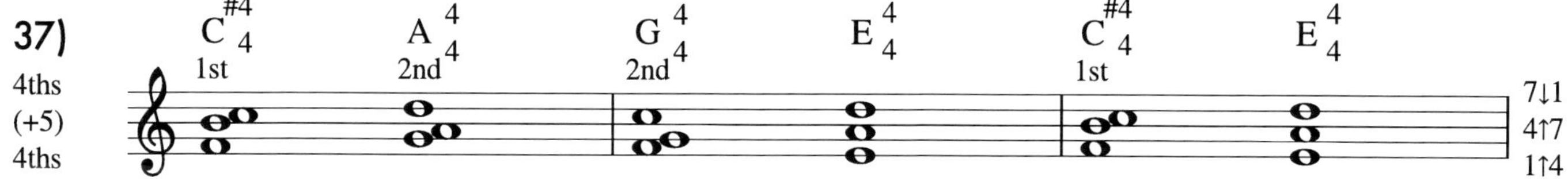

Single-Voice Motion

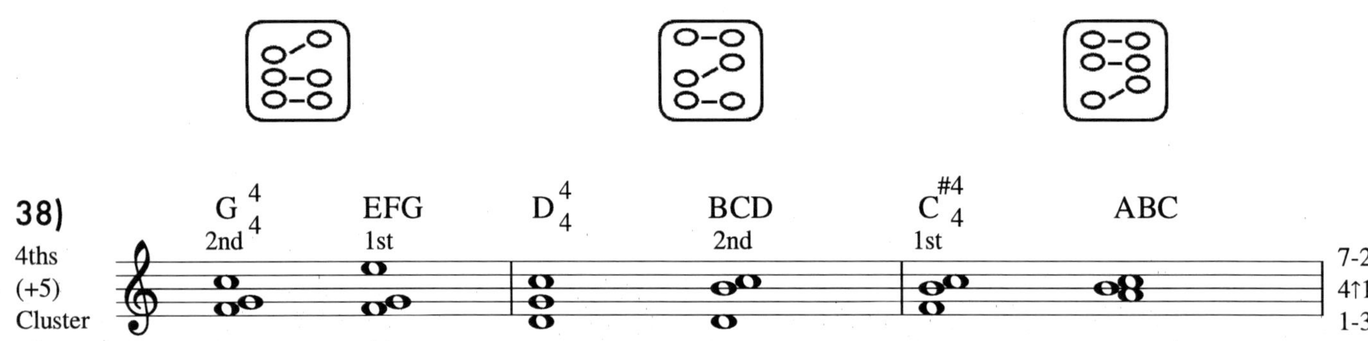

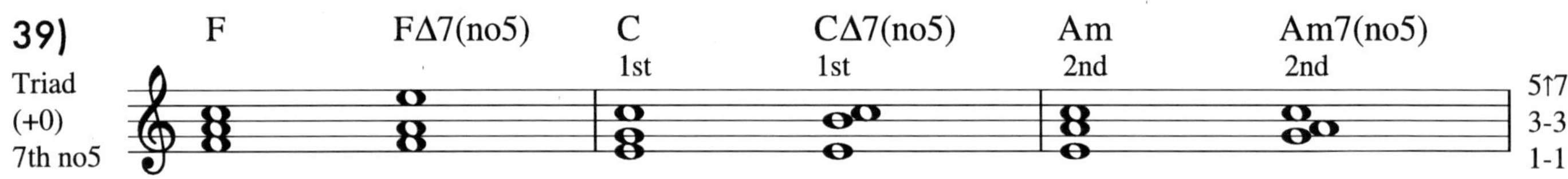

40)
4ths
(+3)
4ths

C #4 4 1st | F 4 #4 | G 4 4 2nd | C #4 4 1st | D 4 4 | G 4 4 2nd

7-4
4-1
1↑7

41)
7th no5
(+0)
7th no3

Am7(no5) 2nd | Am7(no3) 2nd | Dm7(no5) | Dm7(no3 | CΔ7(no5) 1st | CΔ7(no3) 1st

7-7
3↑5
1-1

42)
7th no3
(+2)
Triad

CΔ7(no3) 1st | Em 1st | FΔ7(no3) 2nd | Am 2nd | Dm7(no3) | F

7-5
5-3
1↑1

43)
Cluster
(+1)
4ths

ABC | B 4 4 2nd | CDE 1st | D 4 4 | BCD 2nd | C #4 4 1st

3↑4
2-1
1-7

Double-Voice Parallel Motion

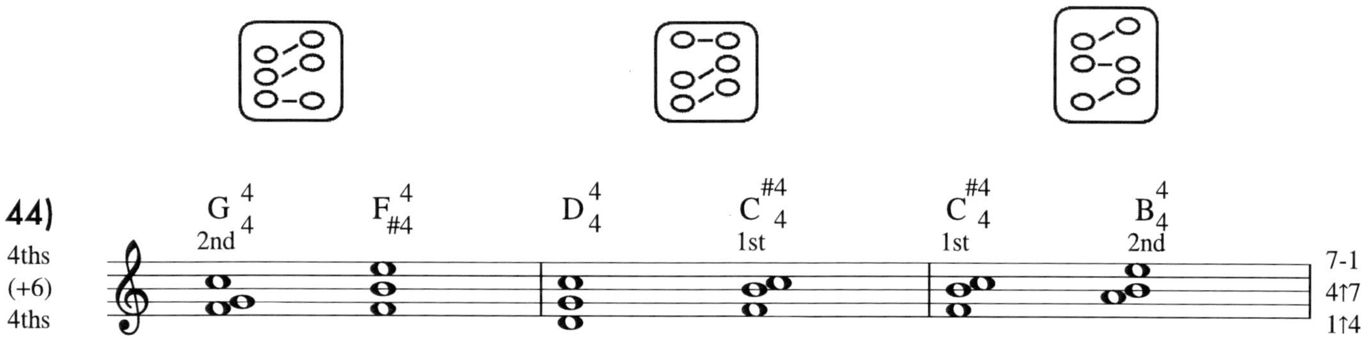

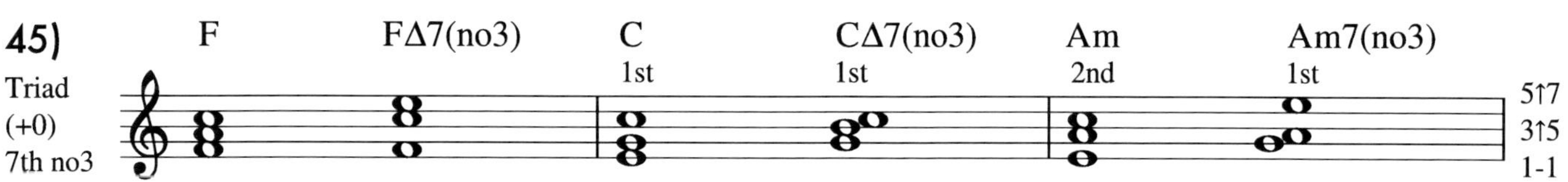

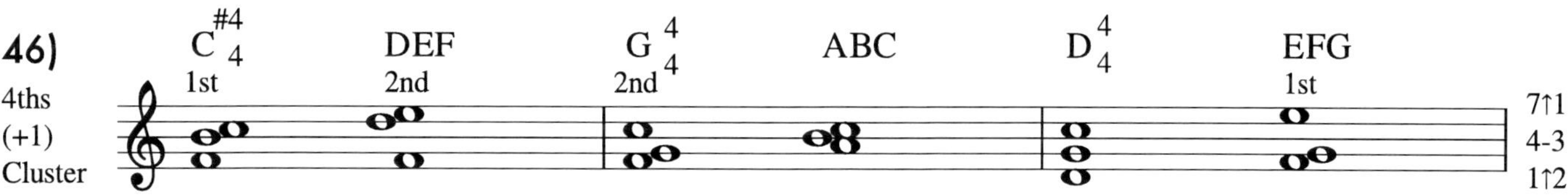

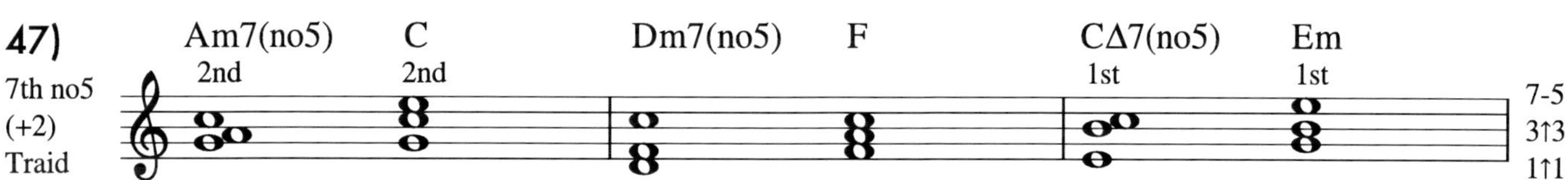

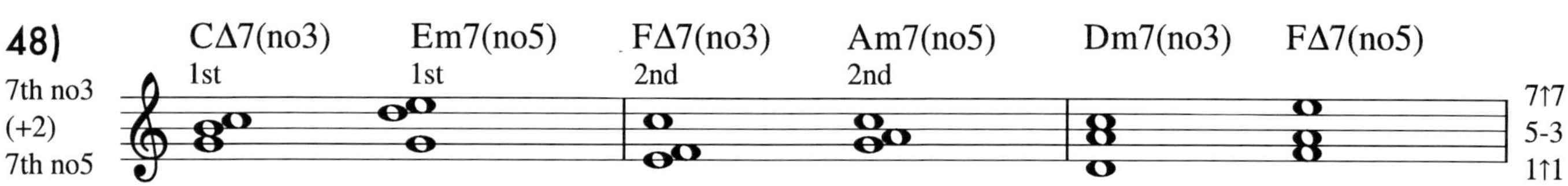

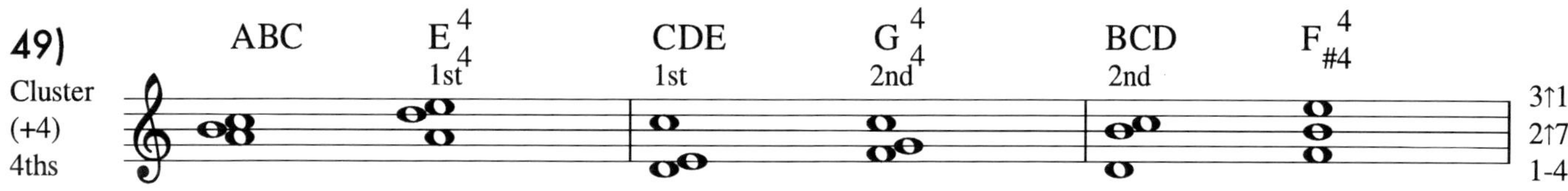

Double-Voice Contrary Motion

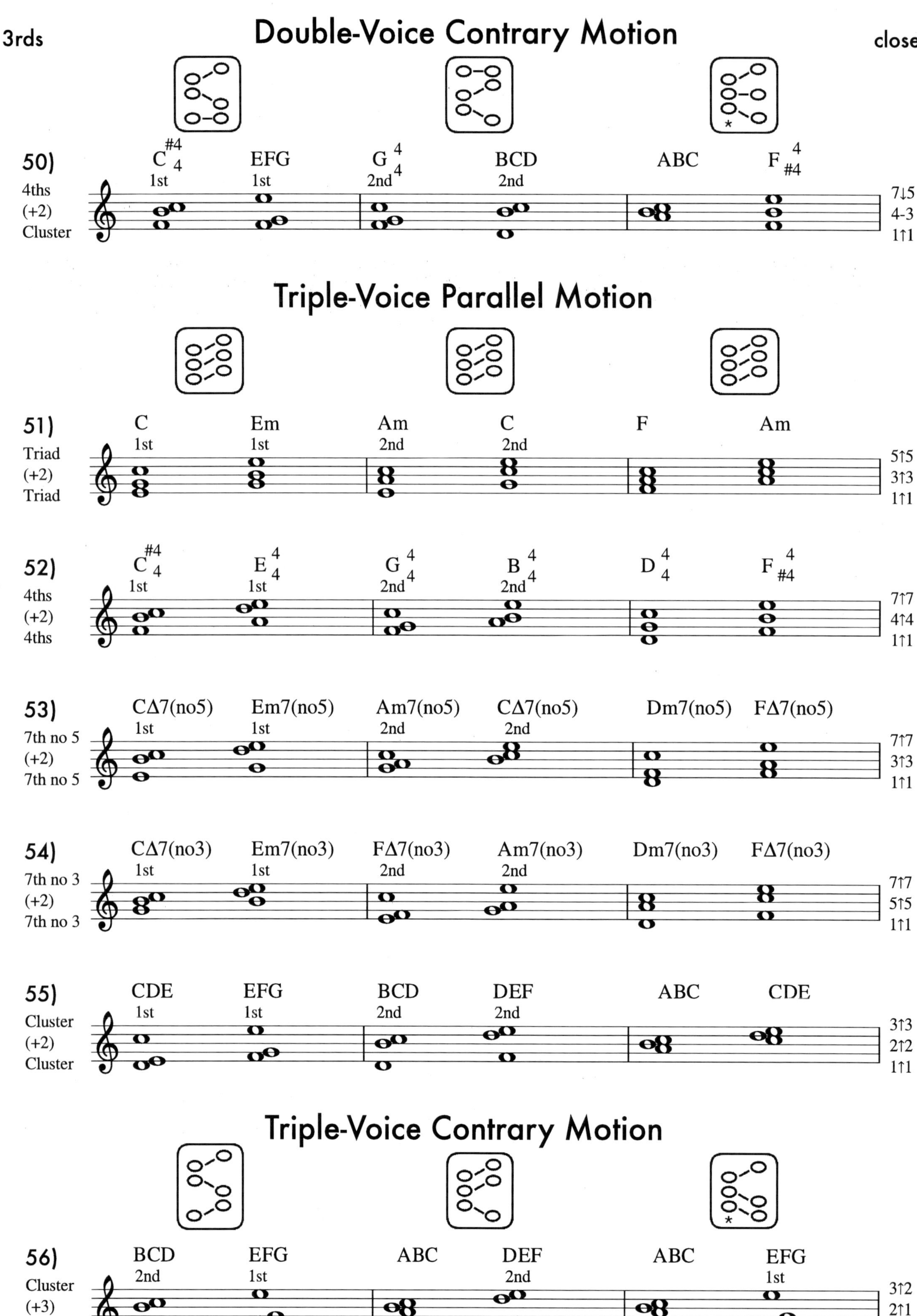

VOICE MOTION MOVES USING A MIX OF 2nds AND 3rds

The remaining voice motion moves 57) to 108) on the following pages each use melodic movement in intervals of 2nds and 3rds at the same time. The graphic voice motion icon above each column indicates which one of the voices moves in an interval of a 2nd (2) or a 3rd (3).

In the triple-voice motion of move 75) and onwards, there are two possible intervallic combinations of 2nds and 3rds:
a move can either have one voice moving in an interval of a 3rd, while the remaining two voices move in intervals of 2nds (322);
or only one of the voices moving in an interval of a 2nd, while the two remaining voices move in intervals of 3rds (233).
On each respective page, this specific intervallic combination within the moves below is displayed numerically (322 or 233) in the upper left corner.

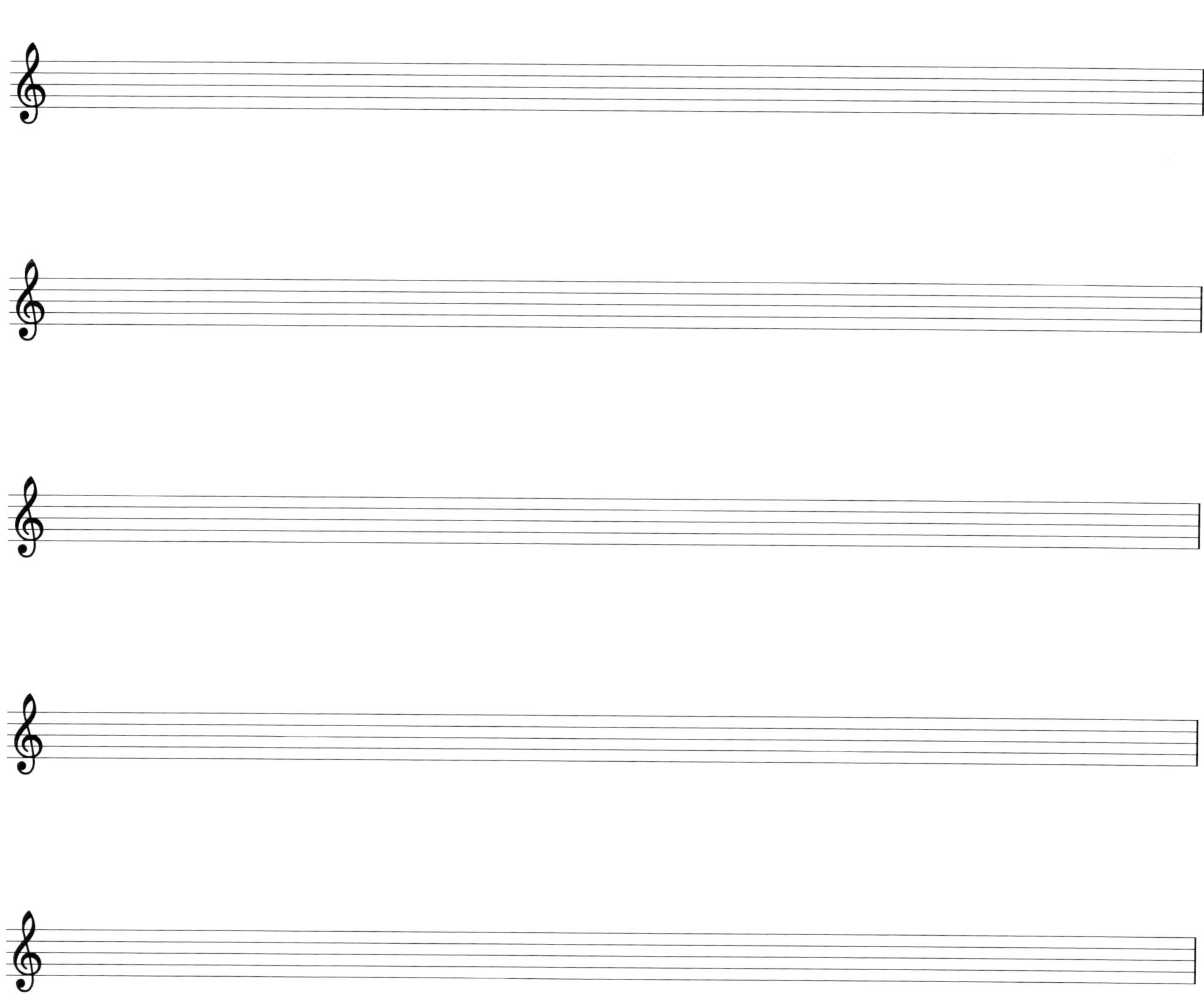

Use blank lines for your personal notes and ideas

Double-Voice Parallel Motion 1

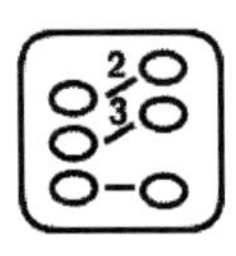

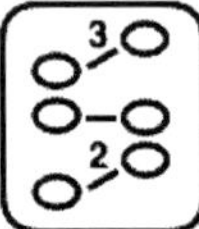

57)
7th no3
(+6)
4ths

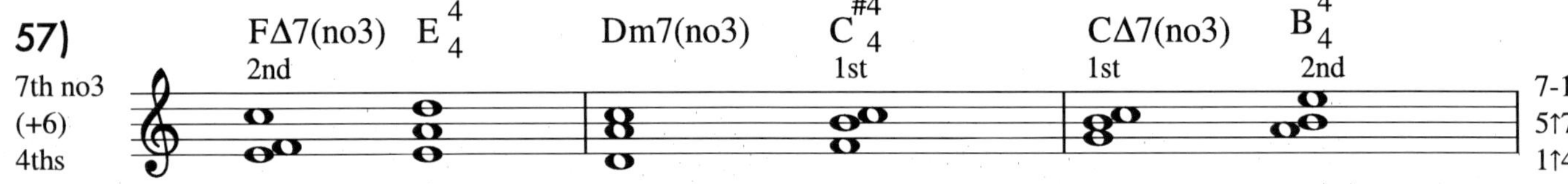

58)
Triad
(+2)
7th no3

C (1st) | Em7(no3) | Am (2nd) | CΔ7(no3) (1st) | F | Am7(no3) (2nd)

5↑5
3-1
1↑7

59)
Triad
(+2)
Cluster

Am (2nd) | CDE (2nd) | F | ABC | C (1st) | EFG (1st)

5-3
3↑2
1↑1

60)
4ths
(+2)
Triad

G 4 4 (2nd) | Bdim (2nd) | D 4 4 | F | C #4 4 (1st) | Em (1st)

7-5
4↑3
1↑1

61)
Triad
(+5)
7th no5

F | Dm7(no5) (1st) | C (1st) | Am7(no5) (2nd) | Am (2nd) | FΔ7(no5)

5↑1
3↑7
1-3

62)
7th no5
(+3)
4ths

Am7(no5) (2nd) | D 4 4 (1st) | Dm7(no5) | G 4 4 (2nd) | CΔ7(no5) (1st) | F 4 #4

7-4
3↑1
1↑7

Double-Voice Parallel Motion 2

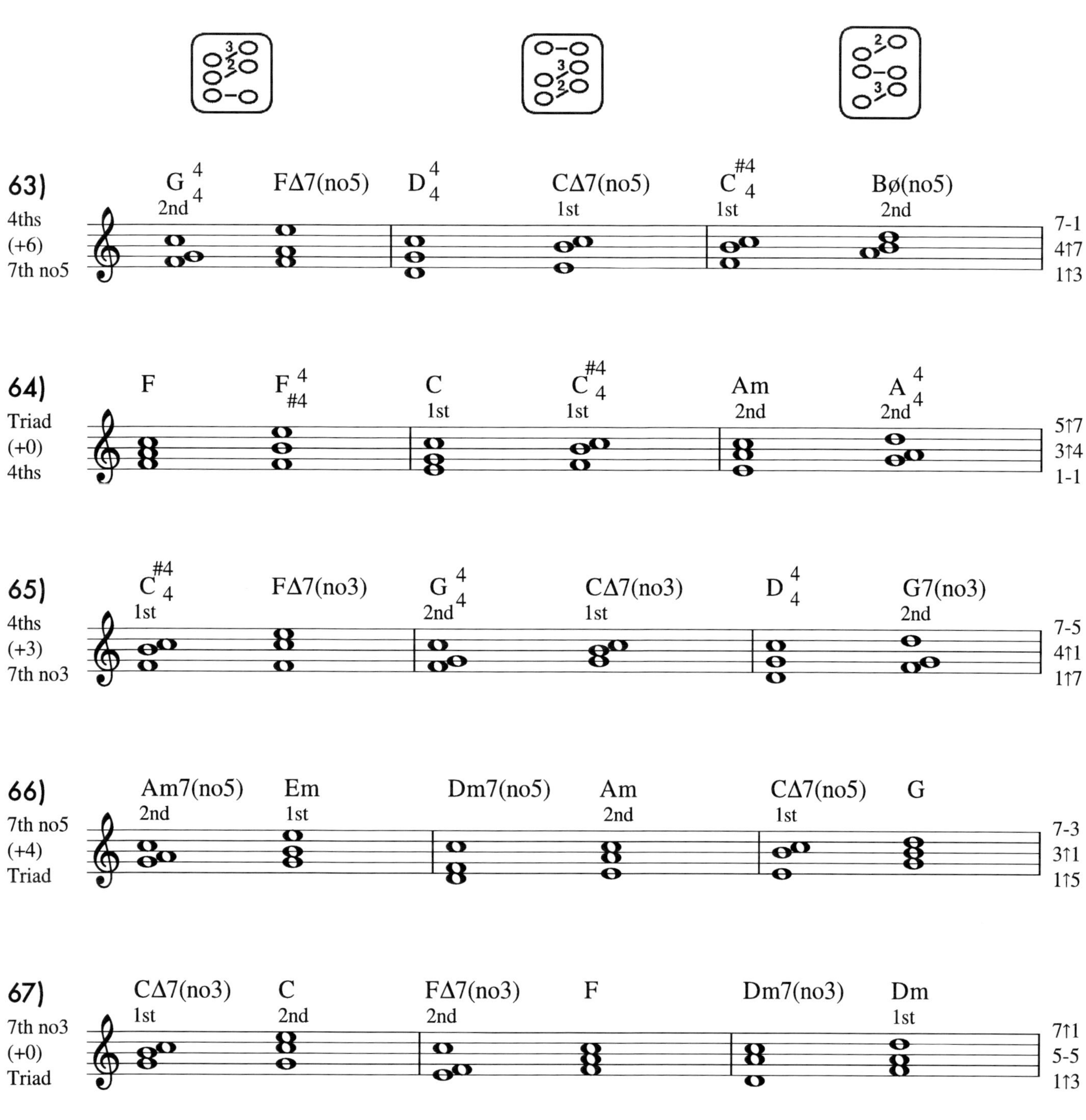

Double-Voice Contrary Motion 1

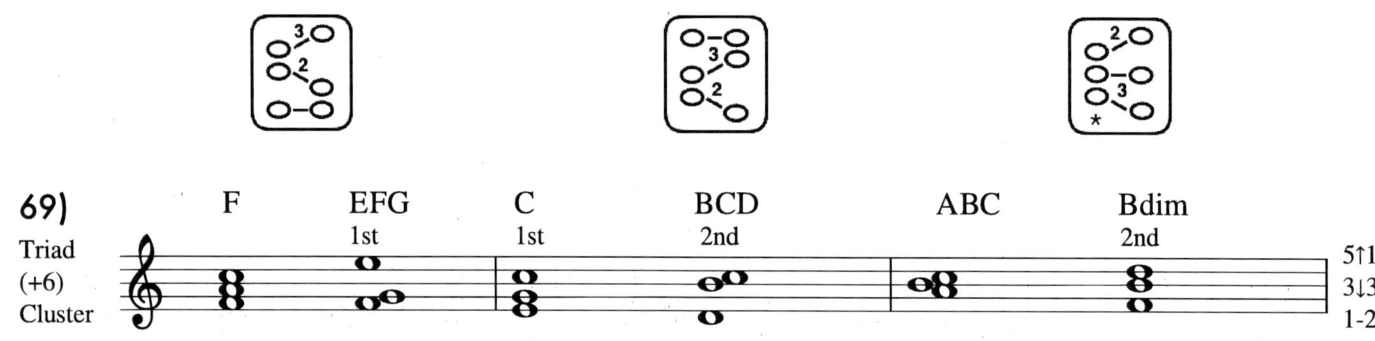

70)
4ths
(+3)
7th no 5
C #4 4
1st
FΔ7(no5)
G 4 4
2nd
CΔ7(no5)
1st
Am7(no5)
2nd
E 4 4
7↓3
4-1
1↑7

71)
7th no 3
(+5)
7th no 3
CΔ7(no3)
1st
Am7(no3)
2nd
FΔ7(no3)
2nd
Dm7(no3)
CΔ7(no3)
1st
Em7(no3)
7↓1
5-7
1↑5

Double-Voice Contrary Motion 2

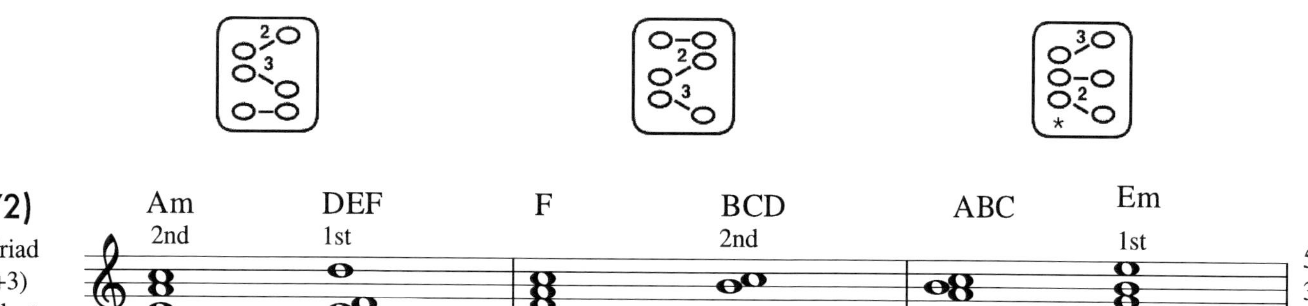

72)

Triad (+3) Cluster

Am 2nd | DEF 1st | F | BCD 2nd | ABC | Em 1st

5-2
3↑1
1↓3

73)

7th no 5 (+2) 7th no 5

CΔ7(no5) 1st | Em7(no5) | Am7(no5) 2nd | CΔ7(no5) 1st | Am7(no5) 2nd | FΔ7(no5)

7↓3
3-1
1↑7

74)

4ths (+4) 7th no 3

C #4 4 1st | G7(no3) 2nd | G 4 4 2nd | Dm7(no3) | CΔ7(no3) 1st | F 4 #4

7↓1
4-7
1↑5

2nds/3rds

322*

Triple-Voice Parallel Motion 1

close

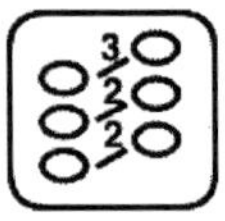

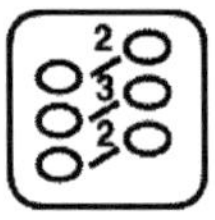

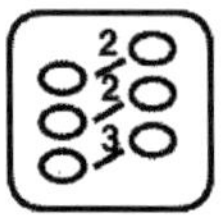

75) 7th no3 (+6) Cluster

FΔ7(no3) 2nd | EFG 1st | Dm7(no3) | CDE 2nd | CΔ7(no3) 1st | BCD

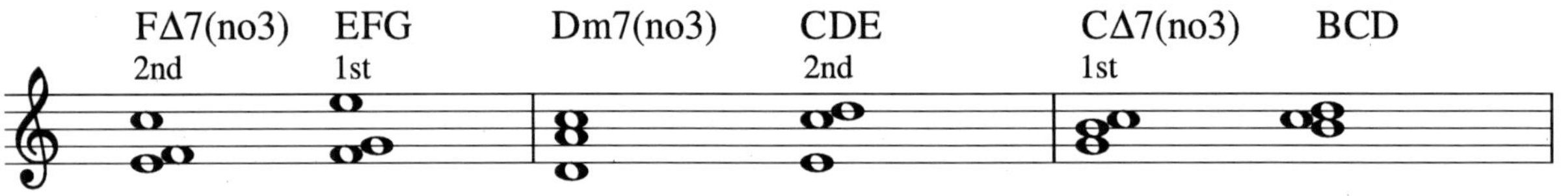

7↑2 / 5↑1 / 1↑3

76) Triad (+3) 7th no5

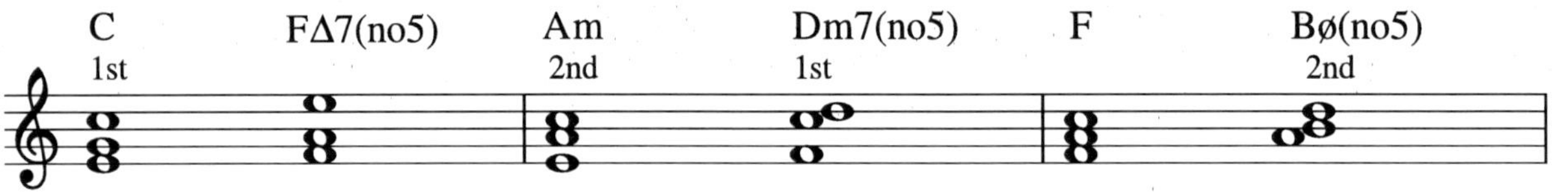

C 1st | FΔ7(no5) | Am 2nd | Dm7(no5) 1st | F | Bø(no5) 2nd

5↑3 / 3↑1 / 1↑7

77) Triad (+5) 4ths

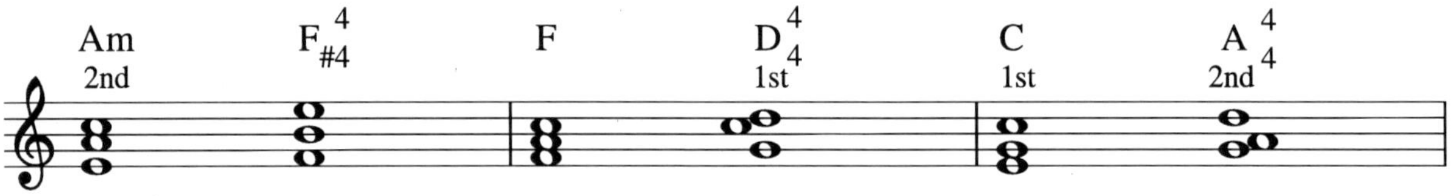

Am 2nd | $F^{4}_{\#4}$ | F | D^{4}_{4} 1st | C 1st | A^{4}_{4} 2nd

5↑1 / 3↑7 / 1-4

78) 7th no5 (+3) 7th no3

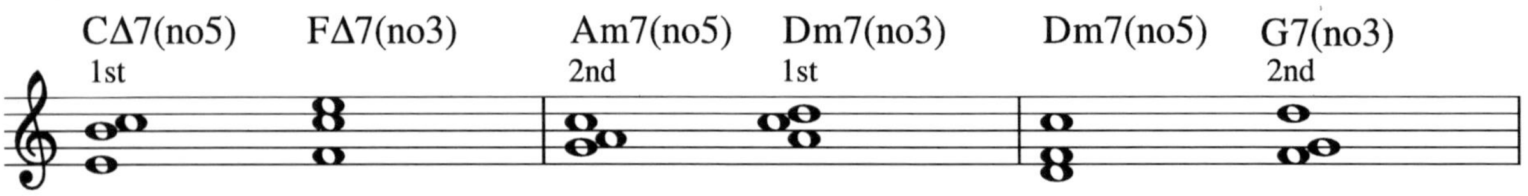

CΔ7(no5) 1st | FΔ7(no3) | Am7(no5) 2nd | Dm7(no3) 1st | Dm7(no5) | G7(no3) 2nd

7↑5 / 3↑1 / 1↑7

79) 4ths (+1) 7th no3

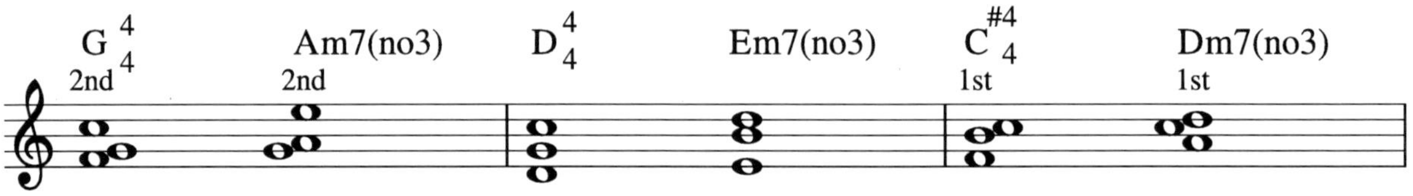

G^{4}_{4} 2nd | Am7(no3) 2nd | D^{4}_{4} | Em7(no3) | $C^{\#4}_{4}$ 1st | Dm7(no3) 1st

7↑7 / 4↑5 / 1↑1

80) Triad (+6) Triad

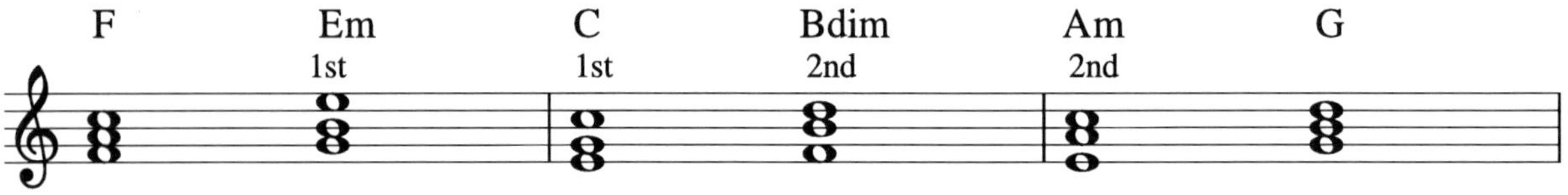

F | Em 1st | C 1st | Bdim 2nd | Am 2nd | G

5↑1 / 3↑5 / 1↑3

81) 4ths (+0) Triad

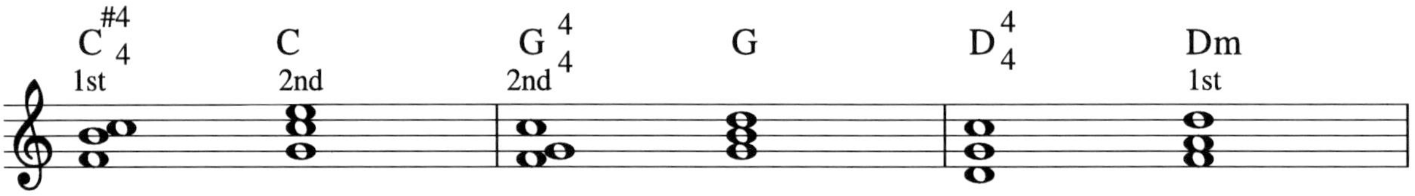

$C^{\#4}_{4}$ 1st | C 2nd | G^{4}_{4} 2nd | G | D^{4}_{4} | Dm 1st

7↑1 / 4↑5 / 1↑3

82) 7th no5 (+1) 4ths

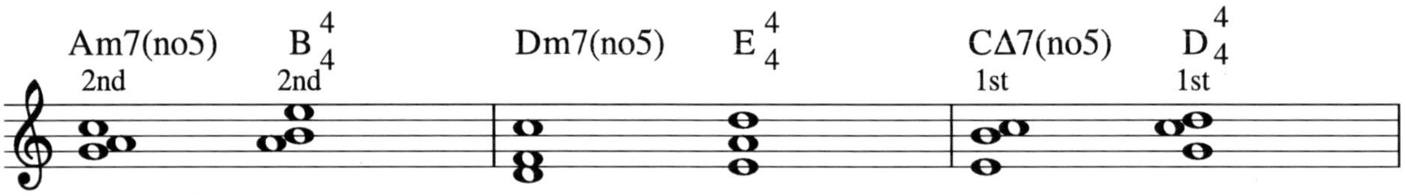

Am7(no5) 2nd | B^{4}_{4} 2nd | Dm7(no5) | E^{4}_{4} | CΔ7(no5) 1st | D^{4}_{4} 1st

7↑7 / 3↑4 / 1↑1

83) 7th no3 (+5) Triad

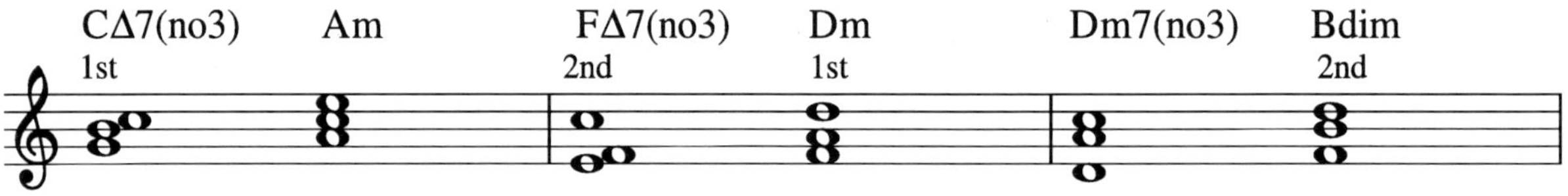

CΔ7(no3) 1st | Am | FΔ7(no3) 2nd | Dm 1st | Dm7(no3) | Bdim 2nd

7↑3 / 5↑1 / 1↑5

84) Cluster (+2) 7th no5

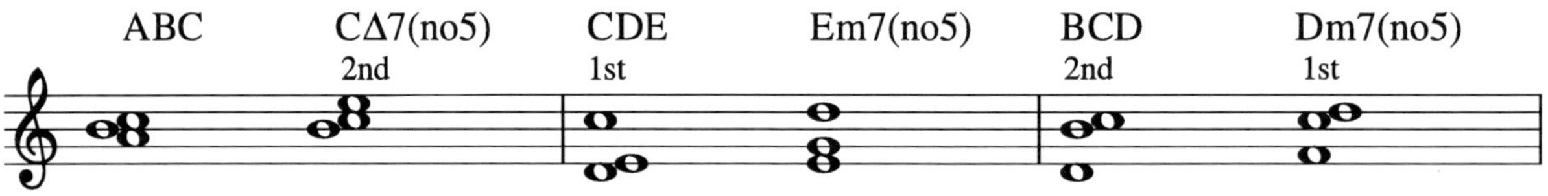

ABC | CΔ7(no5) 2nd | CDE 1st | Em7(no5) | BCD 2nd | Dm7(no5) 1st

3↑3 / 2↑1 / 1↑7

* See page 29 for an explanation of this number.

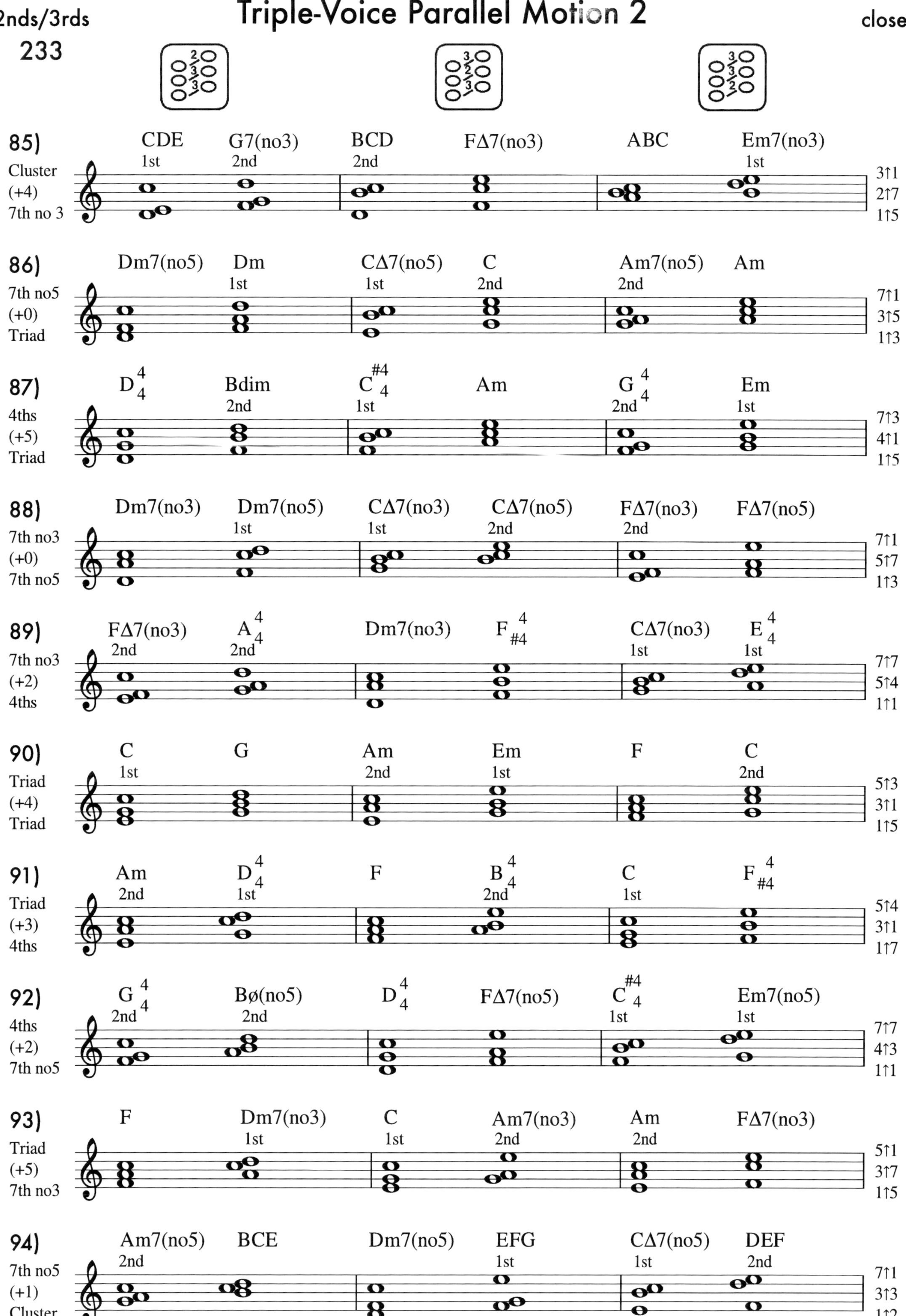
2nds/3rds
233
Triple-Voice Parallel Motion 2
close
85) Cluster (+4) 7th no 3
CDE 1st G7(no3) 2nd BCD 2nd FΔ7(no3) ABC Em7(no3) 1st
3↑1 2↑7 1↑5
86) 7th no5 (+0) Triad
Dm7(no5) Dm 1st CΔ7(no5) 1st C 2nd Am7(no5) 2nd Am
7↑1 3↑5 1↑3
87) 4ths (+5) Triad
D 4 4 Bdim 2nd C #4 4 1st Am G 4 4 2nd Em 1st
7↑3 4↑1 1↑5
88) 7th no3 (+0) 7th no5
Dm7(no3) Dm7(no5) 1st CΔ7(no3) 1st CΔ7(no5) 2nd FΔ7(no3) 2nd FΔ7(no5)
7↑1 5↑7 1↑3
89) 7th no3 (+2) 4ths
FΔ7(no3) 2nd A 4 4 2nd Dm7(no3) F 4 #4 CΔ7(no3) 1st E 4 4 1st
7↑7 5↑4 1↑1
90) Triad (+4) Triad
C 1st G Am 2nd Em 1st F C 2nd
5↑3 3↑1 1↑5
91) Triad (+3) 4ths
Am 2nd D 4 4 1st F B 4 4 2nd C 1st F 4 #4
5↑4 3↑1 1↑7
92) 4ths (+2) 7th no5
G 4 4 2nd Bø(no5) 2nd D 4 4 FΔ7(no5) C #4 4 1st Em7(no5) 1st
7↑7 4↑3 1↑1
93) Triad (+5) 7th no3
F Dm7(no3) 1st C 1st Am7(no3) 2nd Am 2nd FΔ7(no3)
5↑1 3↑7 1↑5
94) 7th no5 (+1) Cluster
Am7(no5) 2nd BCE Dm7(no5) EFG 1st CΔ7(no5) 1st DEF 2nd
7↑1 3↑3 1↑2

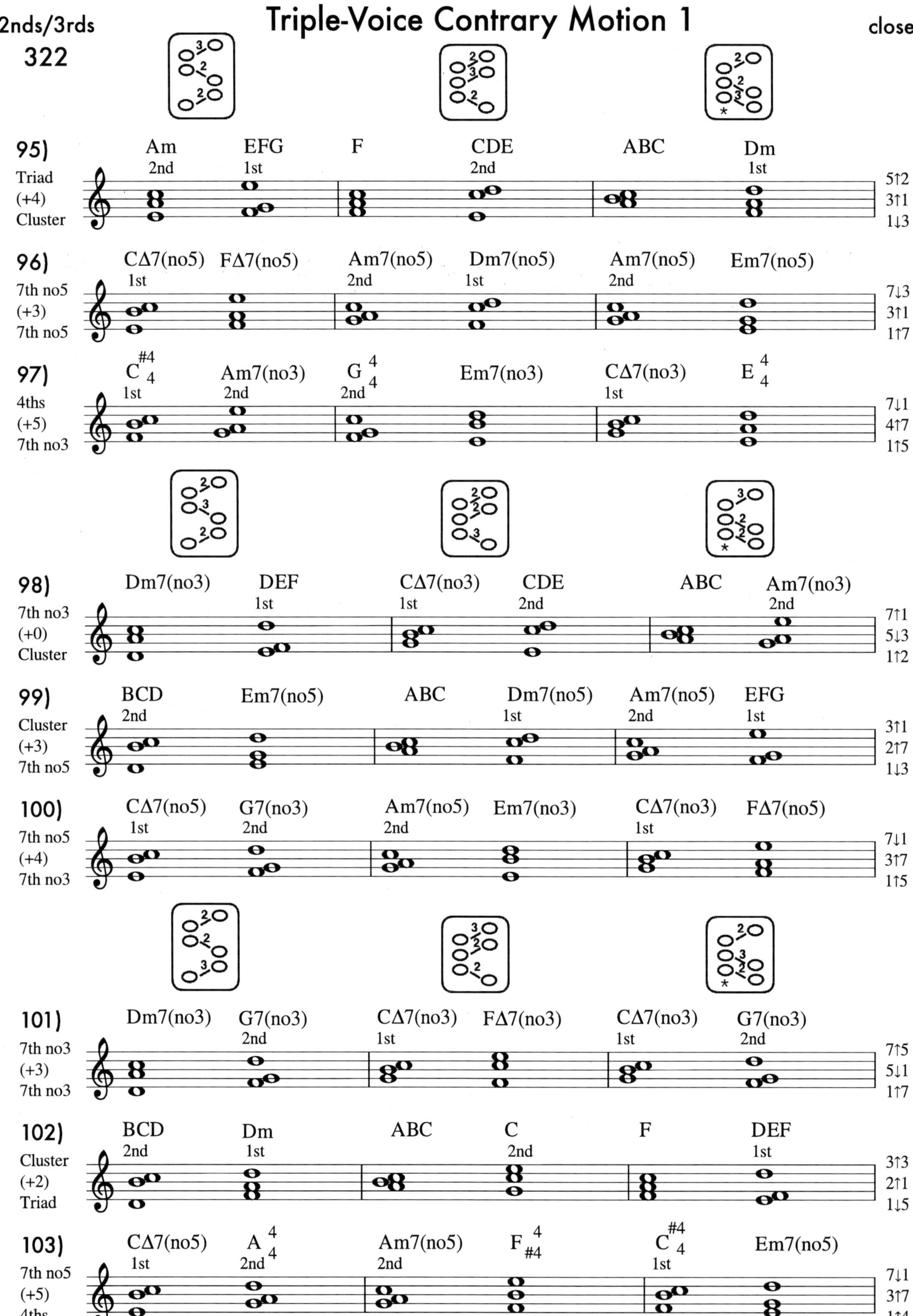
2nds/3rds
322
Triple-Voice Contrary Motion 1
close
95)
Triad
(+4)
Cluster
Am 2nd
EFG 1st
F
CDE 2nd
ABC
Dm 1st
5↑2
3↑1
1↓3
96)
7th no5
(+3)
7th no5
CΔ7(no5) 1st
FΔ7(no5)
Am7(no5) 2nd
Dm7(no5) 1st
Am7(no5) 2nd
Em7(no5)
7↓3
3↑1
1↑7
97)
4ths
(+5)
7th no3
C #4 4 1st
Am7(no3) 2nd
G 4 4 2nd
Em7(no3)
CΔ7(no3) 1st
E 4 4
7↓1
4↑7
1↑5
98)
7th no3
(+0)
Cluster
Dm7(no3)
DEF 1st
CΔ7(no3) 1st
CDE 2nd
ABC
Am7(no3) 2nd
7↑1
5↓3
1↑2
99)
Cluster
(+3)
7th no5
BCD 2nd
Em7(no5)
ABC
Dm7(no5) 1st
Am7(no5) 2nd
EFG 1st
3↑1
2↑7
1↓3
100)
7th no5
(+4)
7th no3
CΔ7(no5) 1st
G7(no3) 2nd
Am7(no5) 2nd
Em7(no3)
CΔ7(no3) 1st
FΔ7(no5)
7↓1
3↑7
1↑5
101)
7th no3
(+3)
7th no3
Dm7(no3)
G7(no3) 2nd
CΔ7(no3) 1st
FΔ7(no3)
CΔ7(no3) 1st
G7(no3) 2nd
7↑5
5↓1
1↑7
102)
Cluster
(+2)
Triad
BCD 2nd
Dm 1st
ABC
C 2nd
F
DEF 1st
3↑3
2↑1
1↓5
103)
7th no5
(+5)
4ths
CΔ7(no5) 1st
A 4 4 2nd
Am7(no5) 2nd
F 4 #4
C #4 4 1st
Em7(no5)
7↓1
3↑7
1↑4

Triple-Voice Contrary Motion 2

close

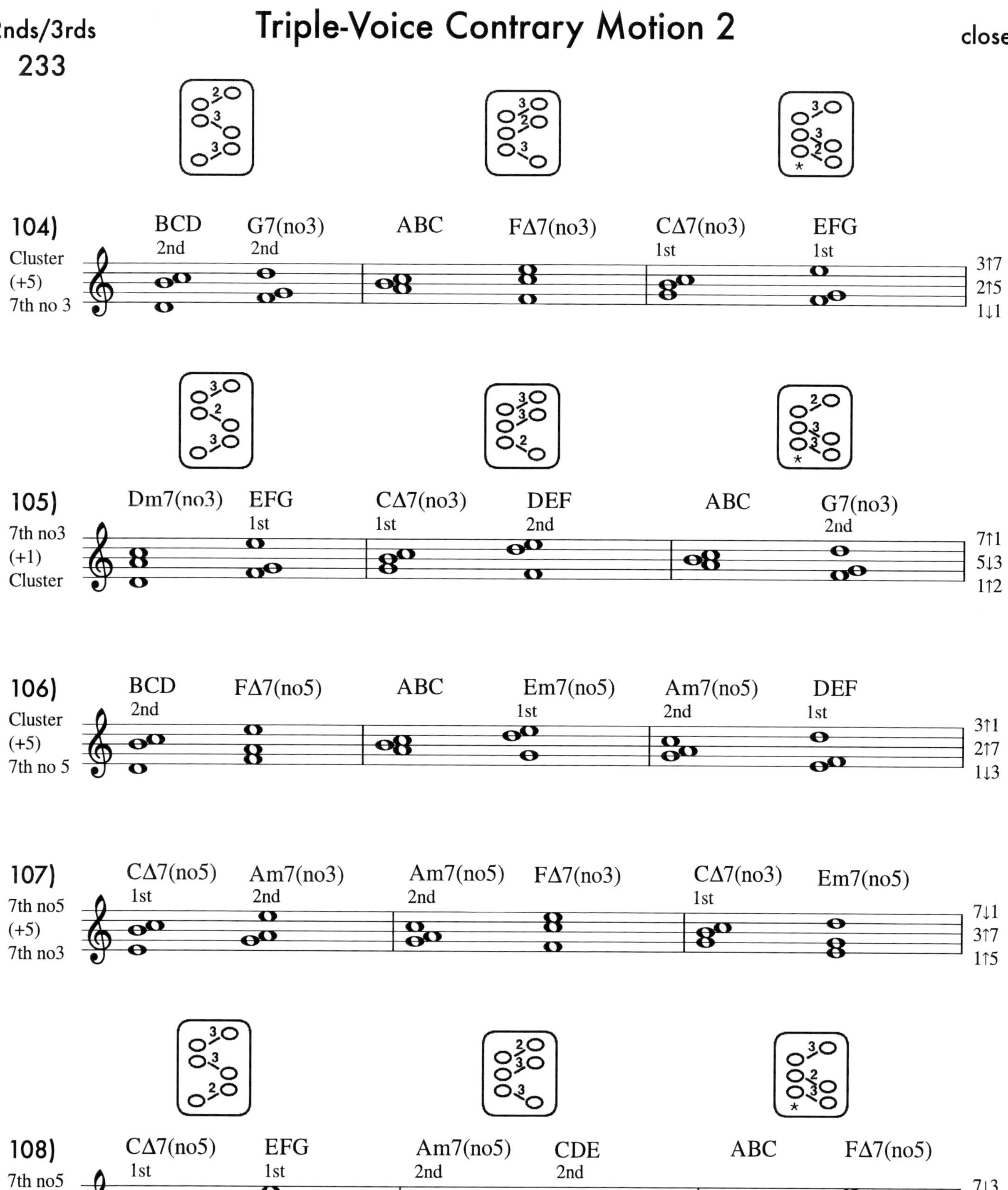

PART 1B

The 15 Chord Structures with the Top Note C
with All Possible Departing Motion in Close Voicing

There is an average of 21.6 moves per chord in each direction, ascending and/or descending.

Apply all voice motion exercises from the introduction using the full range of your instrument in all keys.

Triads in 1st Inversion

Using regular/ascending motion

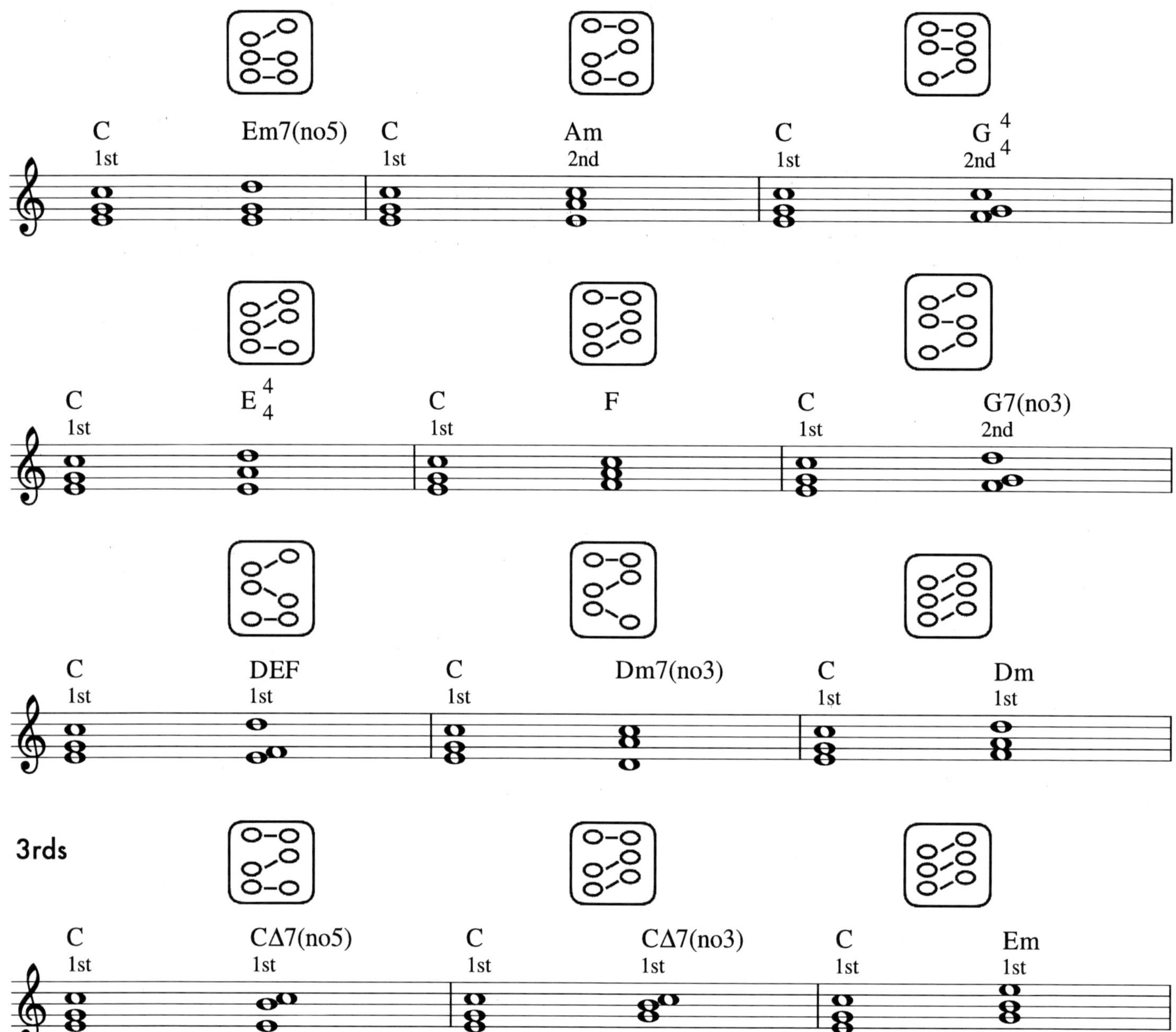

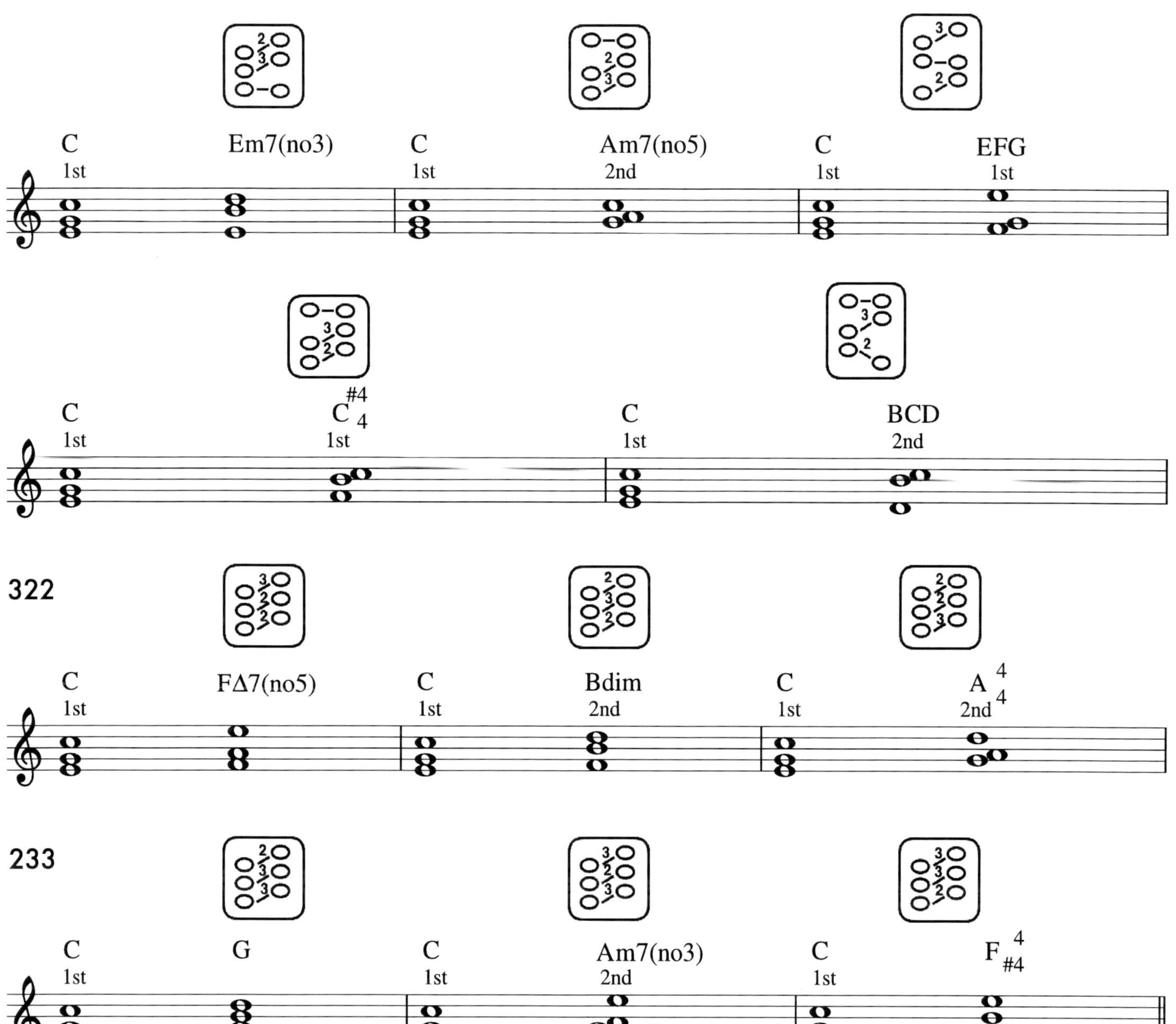
C
1st
Em7(no3)
C
1st
Am7(no5)
2nd
C
1st
EFG
1st
C
1st
C #4 4
1st
C
1st
BCD
2nd
322
C
1st
FΔ7(no5)
C
1st
Bdim
2nd
C
1st
A 4 4
2nd
233
C
1st
G
C
1st
Am7(no3)
2nd
C
1st
F 4 #4

2nds

Triads in 1st Inversion

close

Using reverse/descending motion

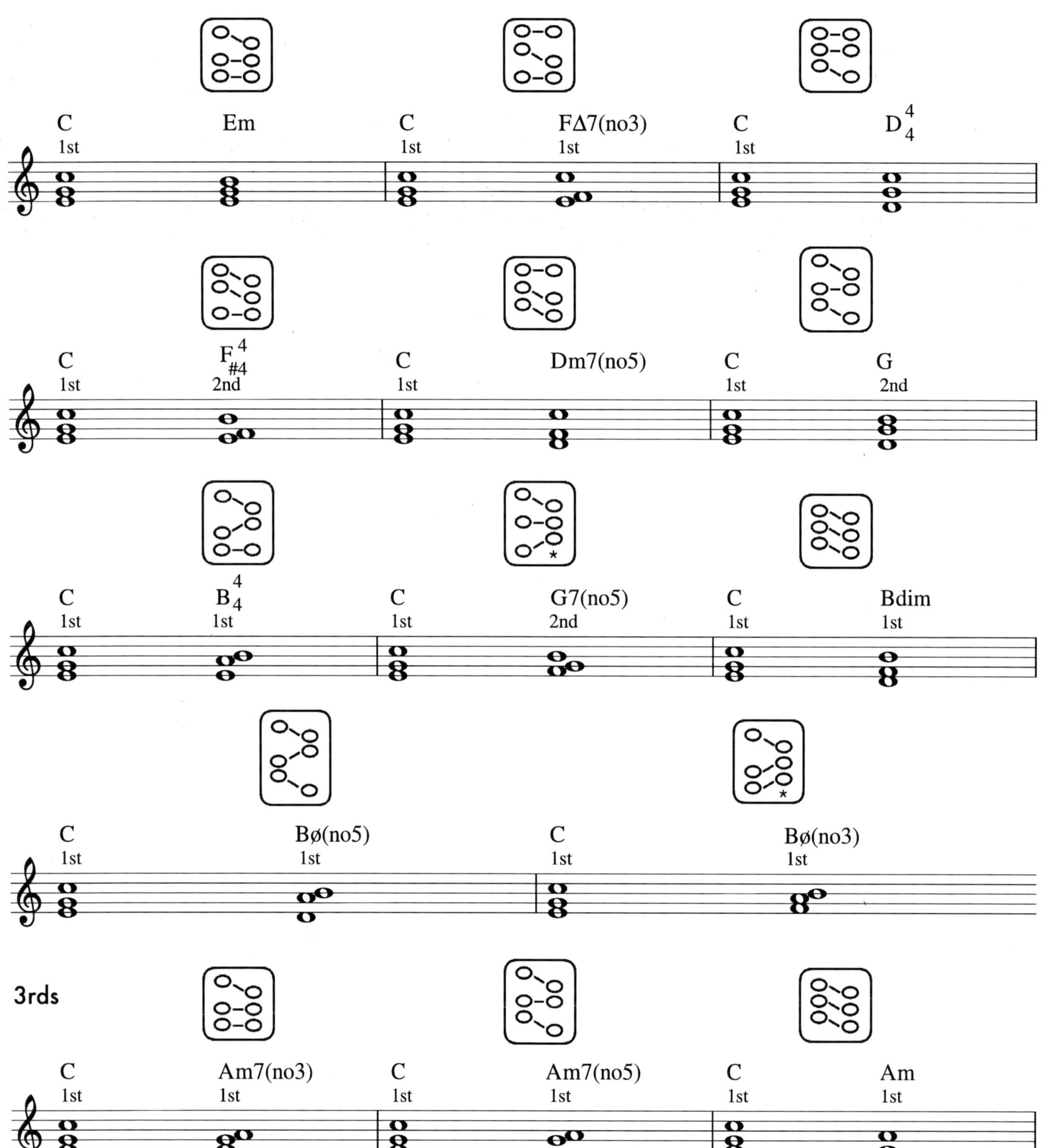

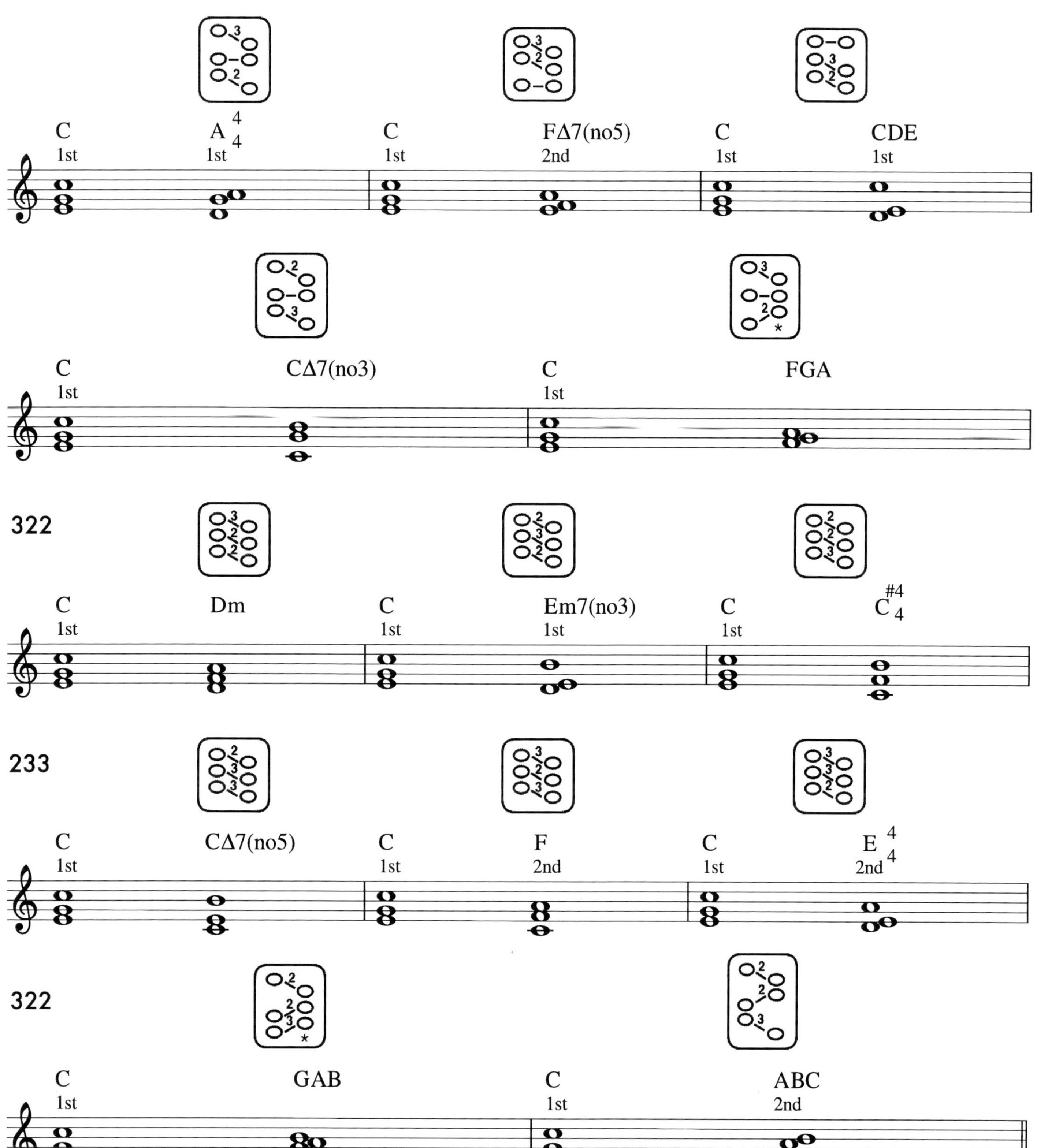
C
1st
A 4 4
1st
C
1st
FΔ7(no5)
2nd
C
1st
CDE
1st
C
1st
CΔ7(no3)
C
1st
FGA
322
C
1st
Dm
C
1st
Em7(no3)
1st
C
1st
C #4 4
233
C
1st
CΔ7(no5)
C
1st
F
2nd
C
1st
E 4 4
2nd
322
C
1st
GAB
C
1st
ABC
2nd

2nds

Triads in 2nd Inversion

close

Using regular/ascending motion

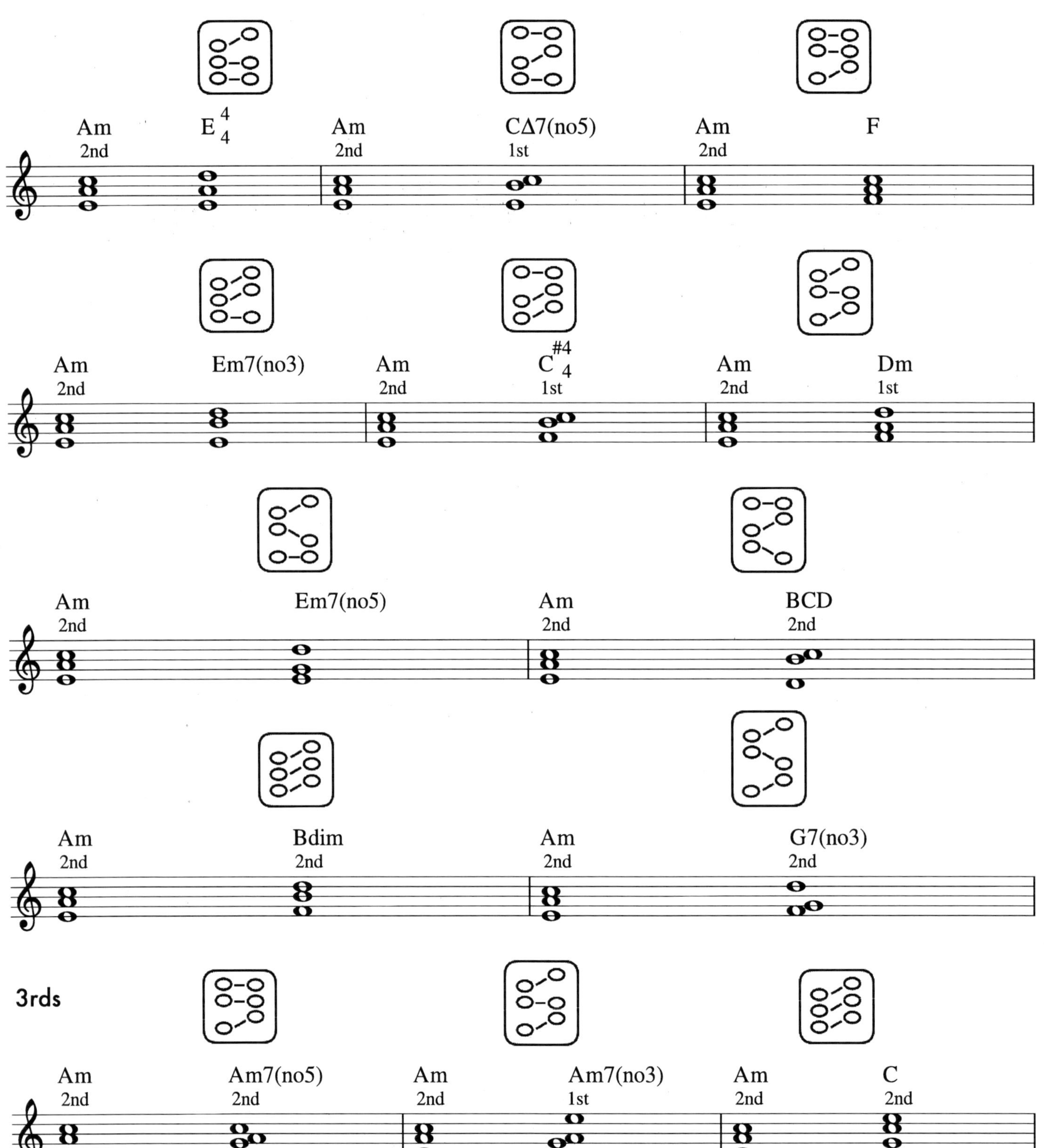

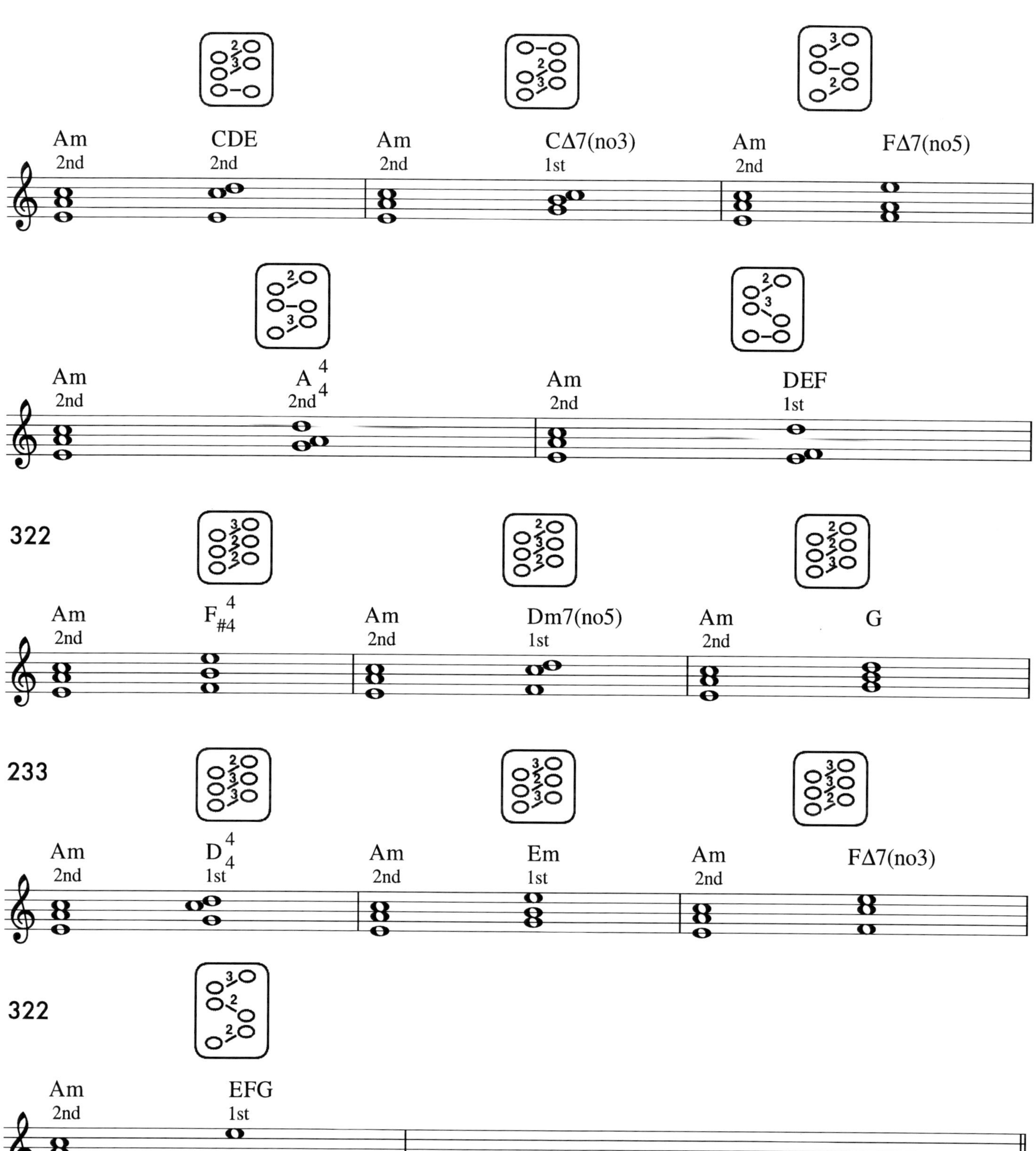
Am
2nd
CDE
2nd
Am
2nd
CΔ7(no3)
1st
Am
2nd
FΔ7(no5)
Am
2nd
A 4 4
2nd
Am
2nd
DEF
1st
322
Am
2nd
F 4 #4
Am
2nd
Dm7(no5)
1st
Am
2nd
G
233
Am
2nd
D 4 4
1st
Am
2nd
Em
1st
Am
2nd
FΔ7(no3)
322
Am
2nd
EFG
1st

Triads in 2nd Inversion

Using reverse/descending motion

2nds   close

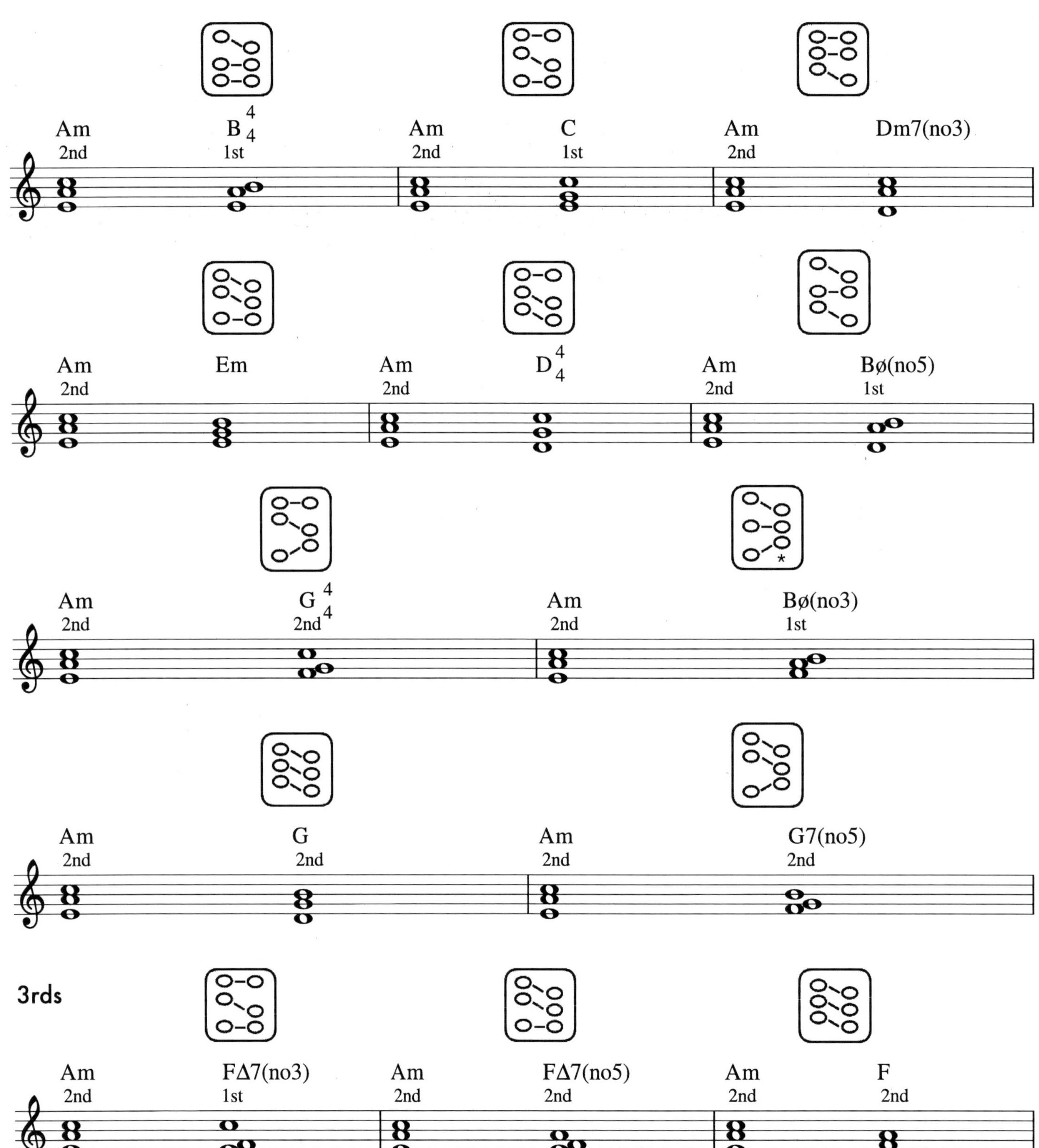

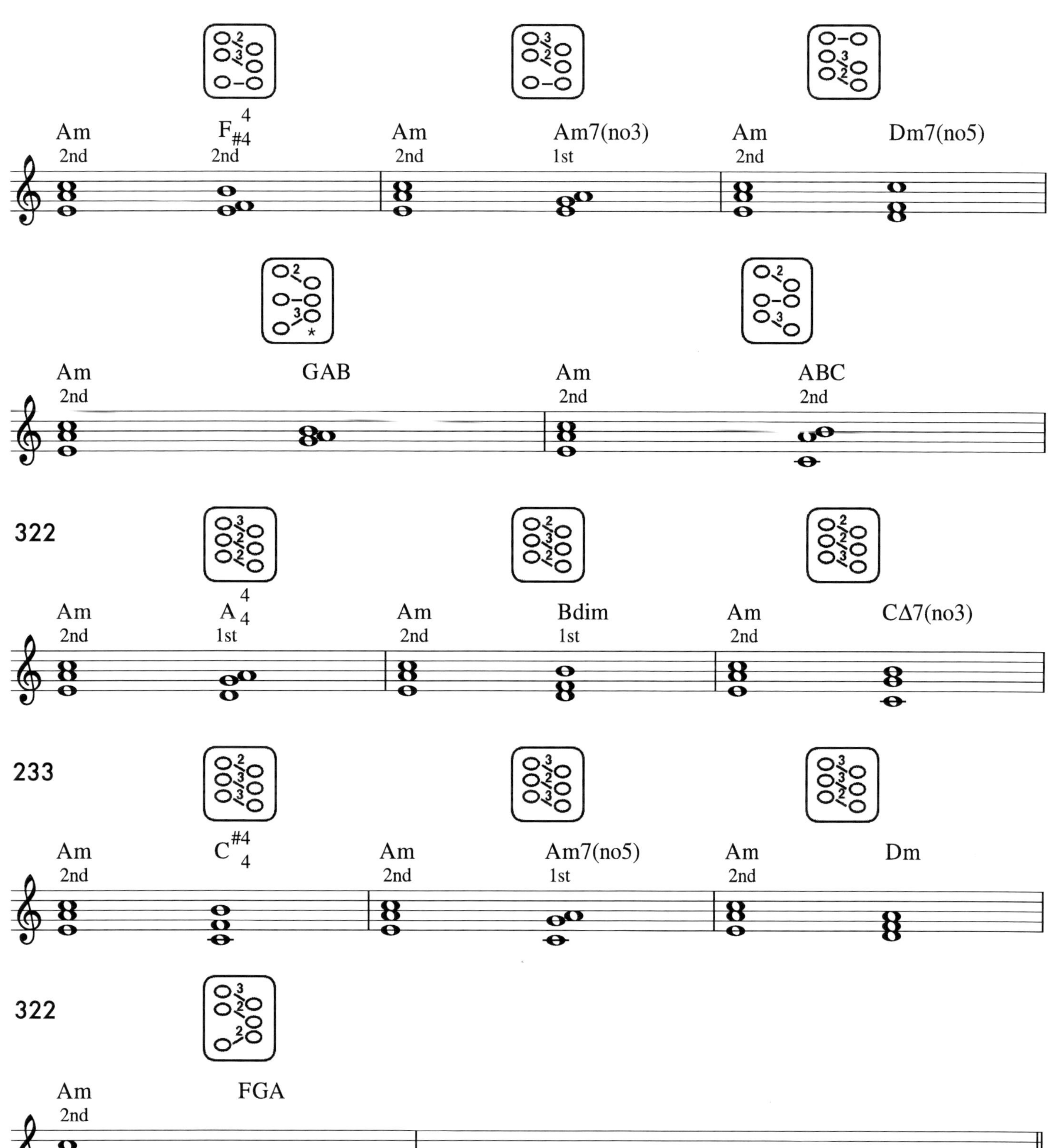
Am
2nd
F #4 4
2nd
Am
2nd
Am7(no3)
1st
Am
2nd
Dm7(no5)
Am
2nd
GAB
Am
2nd
ABC
2nd
322
Am
2nd
A 4 4
1st
Am
2nd
Bdim
1st
Am
2nd
CΔ7(no3)
233
Am
2nd
C #4 4
Am
2nd
Am7(no5)
1st
Am
2nd
Dm
322
Am
2nd
FGA

Triads in Root Position

Using regular/ascending motion

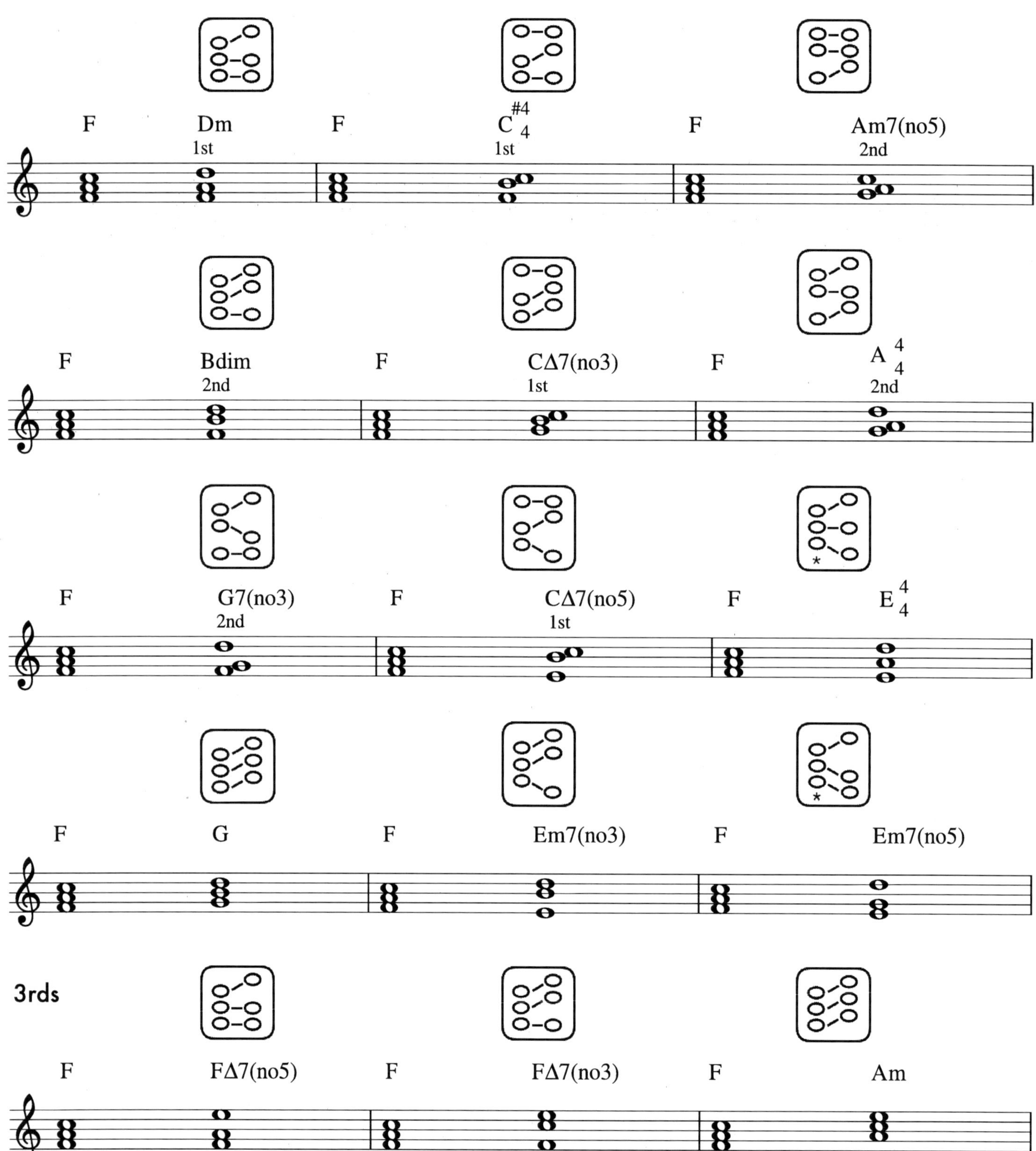

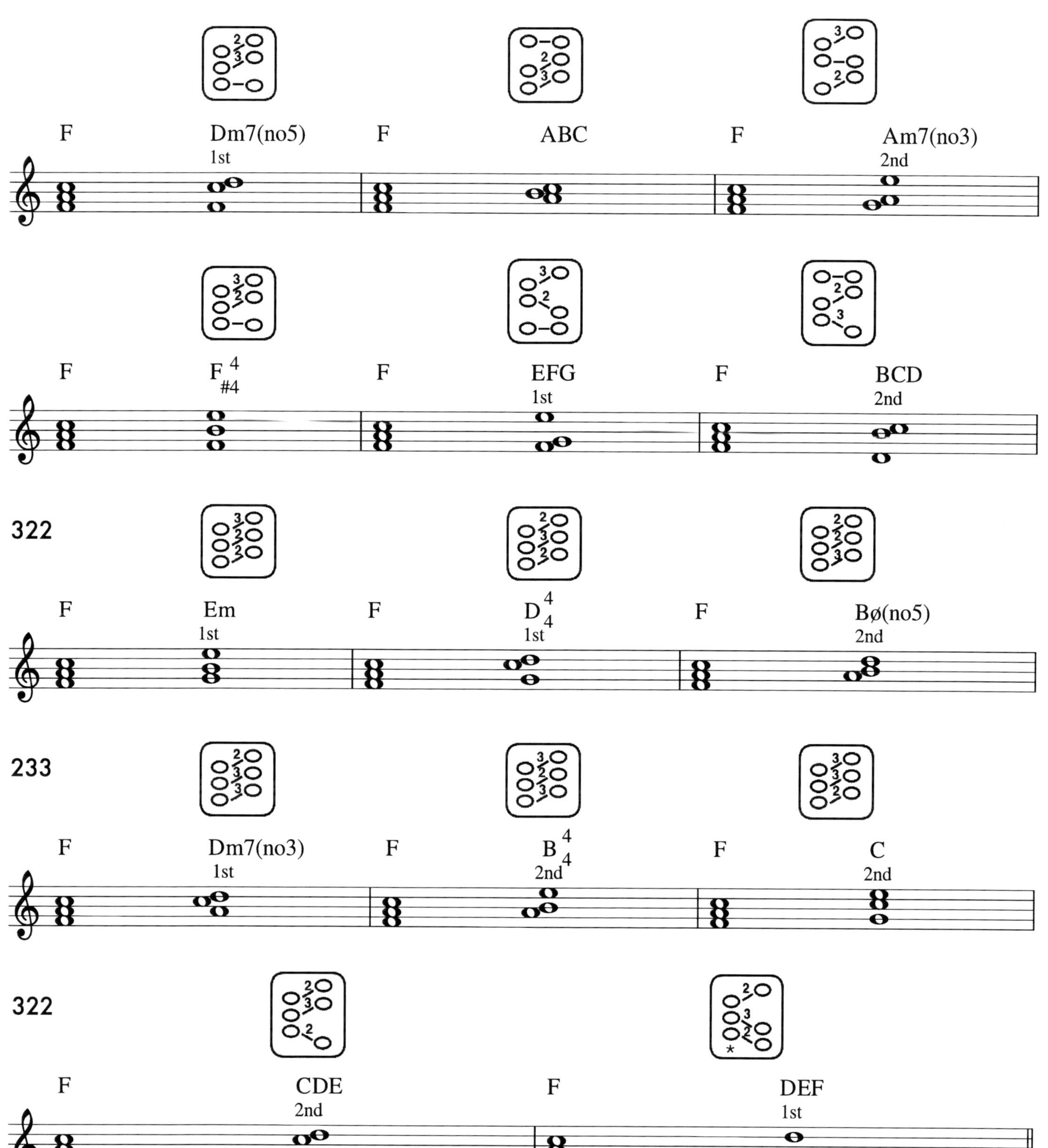
F
Dm7(no5)
1st
F
ABC
F
Am7(no3)
2nd
F
F 4 #4
F
EFG
1st
F
BCD
2nd
322
F
Em
1st
F
D 4 4
1st
F
Bø(no5)
2nd
233
F
Dm7(no3)
1st
F
B 4 4
2nd
F
C
2nd
322
F
CDE
2nd
F
DEF
1st

2nds

Triads in Root Position

Using reverse/descending motion

close

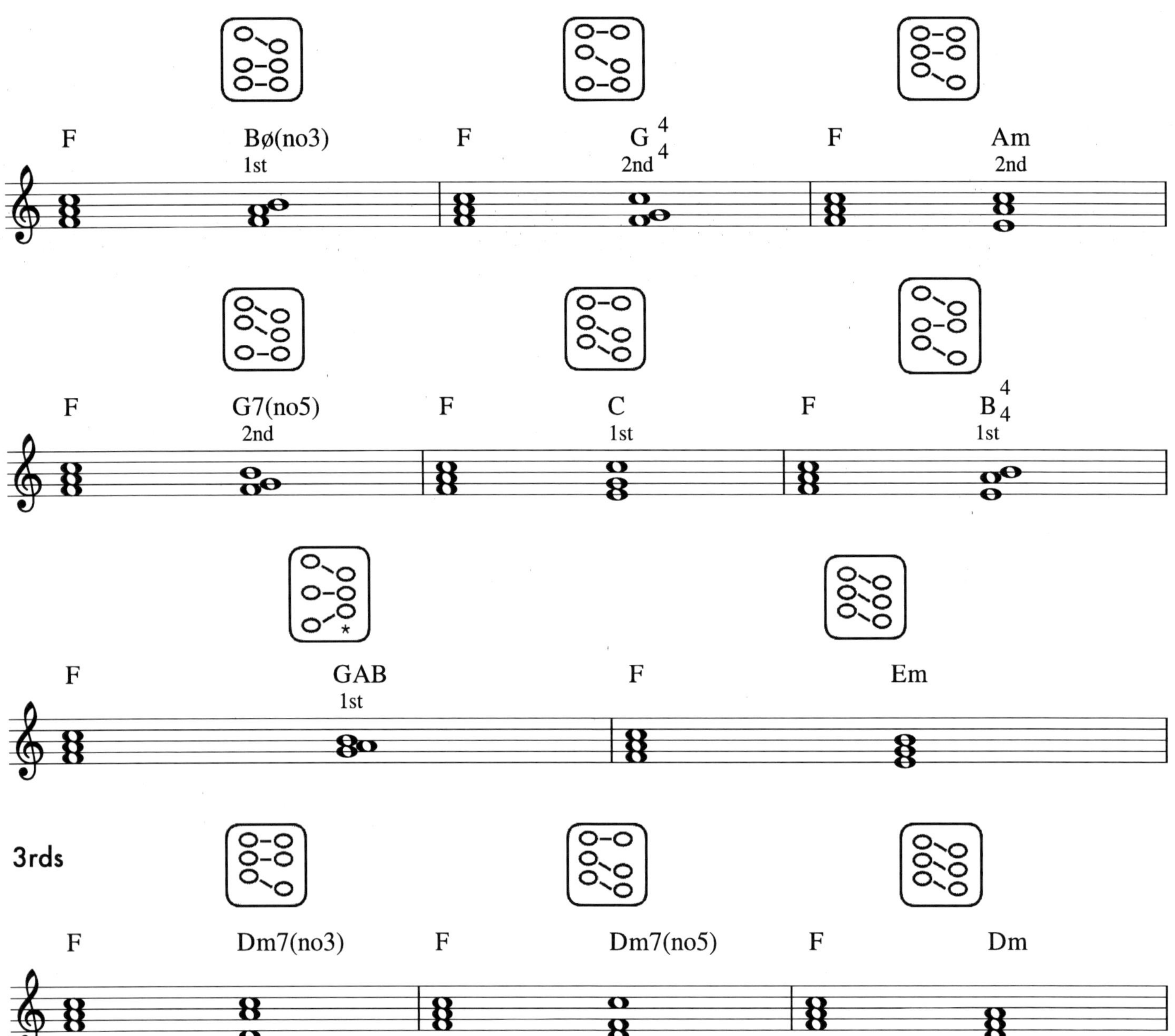

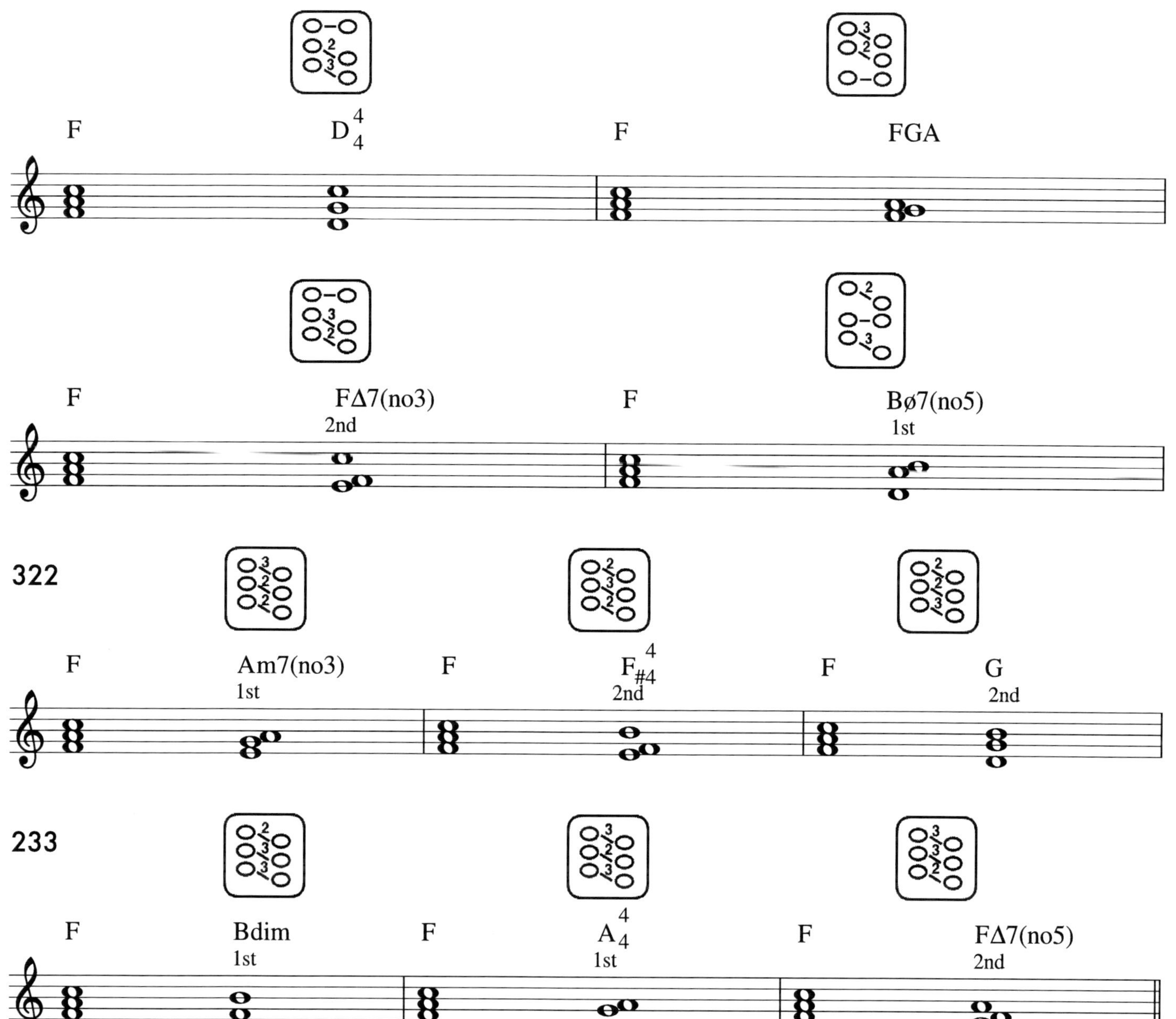
F
D 4 4
F
FGA
F
FΔ7(no3)
2nd
F
Bø7(no5)
1st
322
F
Am7(no3)
1st
F
F 4 #4
2nd
F
G
2nd
233
F
Bdim
1st
F
A 4 4
1st
F
FΔ7(no5)
2nd

4ths in 1st Inversion

Using regular/ascending motion

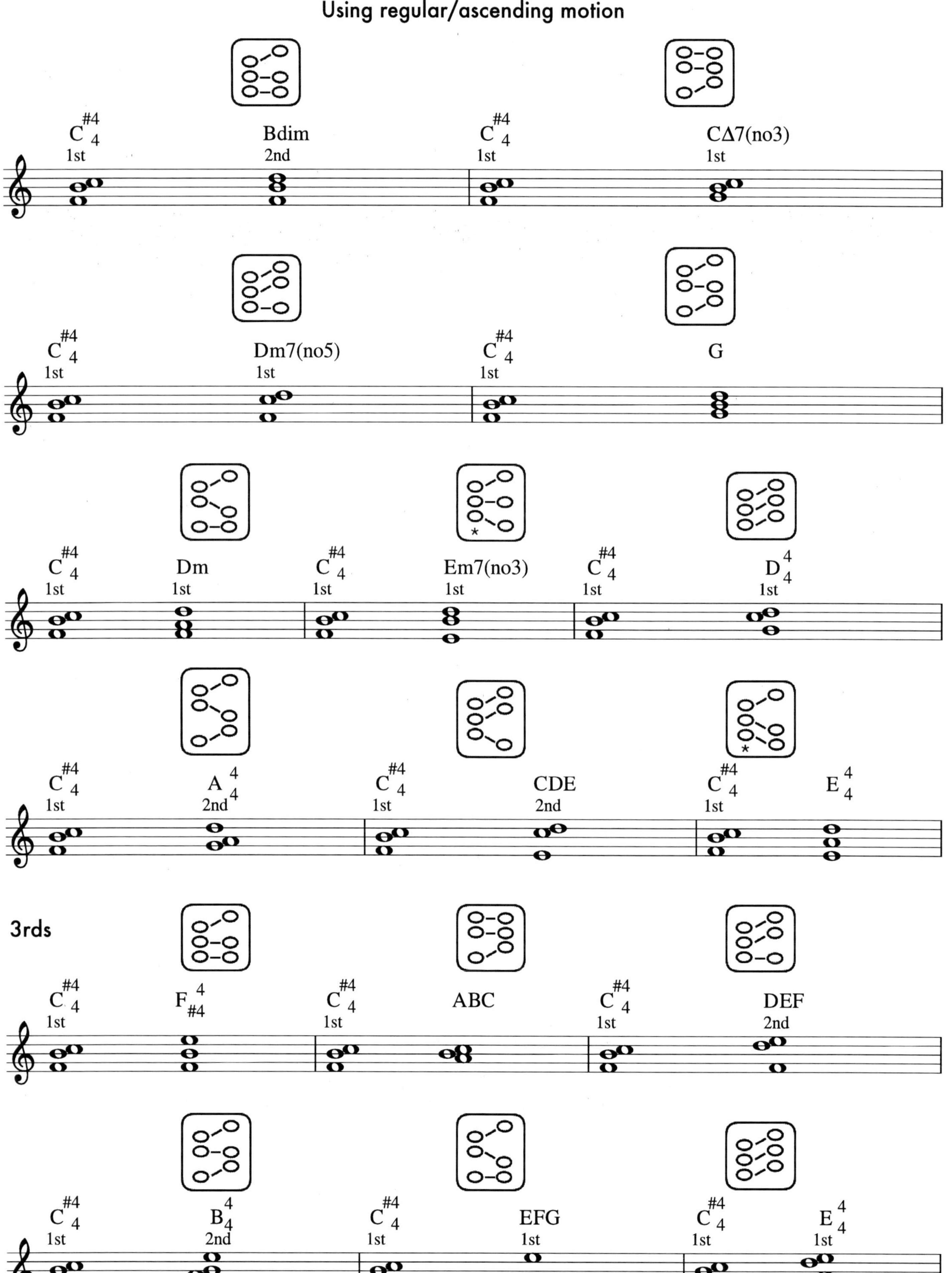

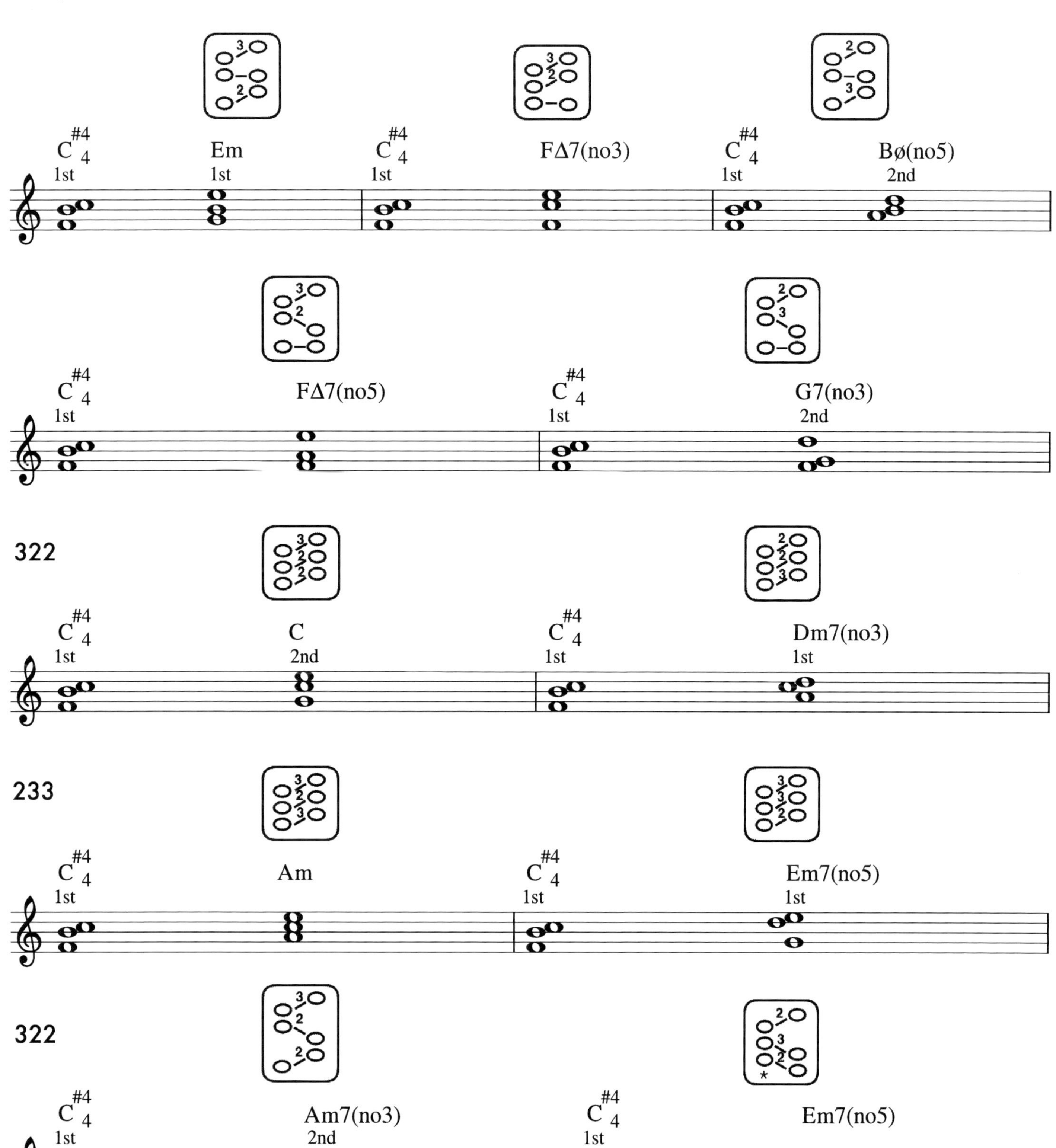
C#4 4
1st
Em
1st
C#4 4
1st
FΔ7(no3)
C#4 4
1st
Bø(no5)
2nd
C#4 4
1st
FΔ7(no5)
C#4 4
1st
G7(no3)
2nd
322
C#4 4
1st
C
2nd
C#4 4
1st
Dm7(no3)
1st
233
C#4 4
1st
Am
C#4 4
1st
Em7(no5)
1st
322
C#4 4
1st
Am7(no3)
2nd
C#4 4
1st
Em7(no5)

4ths in 1st Inversion

Using reverse/descending motion

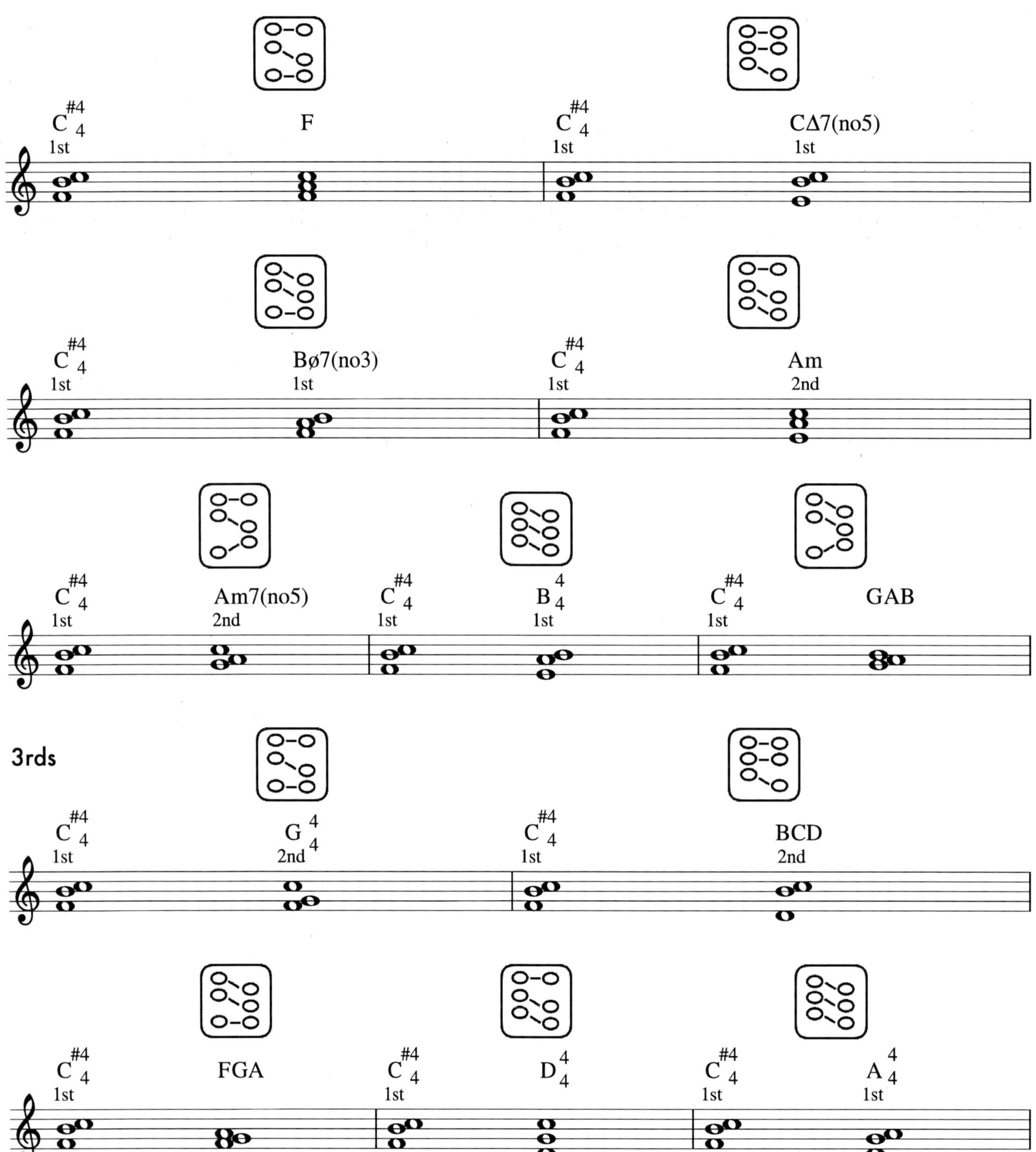

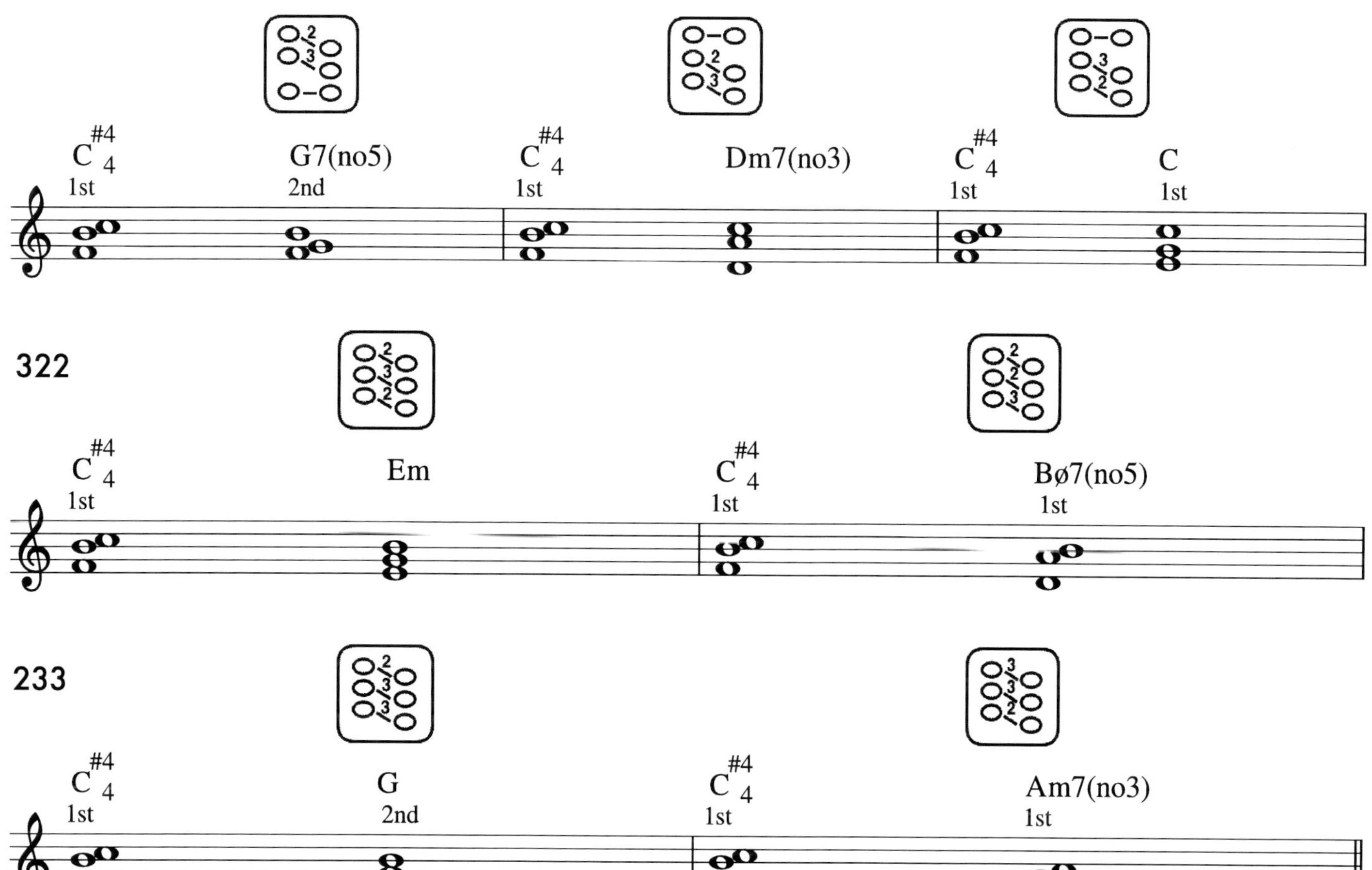
C #4 4
1st
G7(no5)
2nd
C #4 4
1st
Dm7(no3)
C #4 4
1st
C
1st
322
C #4 4
1st
Em
C #4 4
1st
Bø7(no5)
1st
233
C #4 4
1st
G
2nd
C #4 4
1st
Am7(no3)
1st

2nds

4ths in 2nd Inversion

close

Using regular/ascending motion

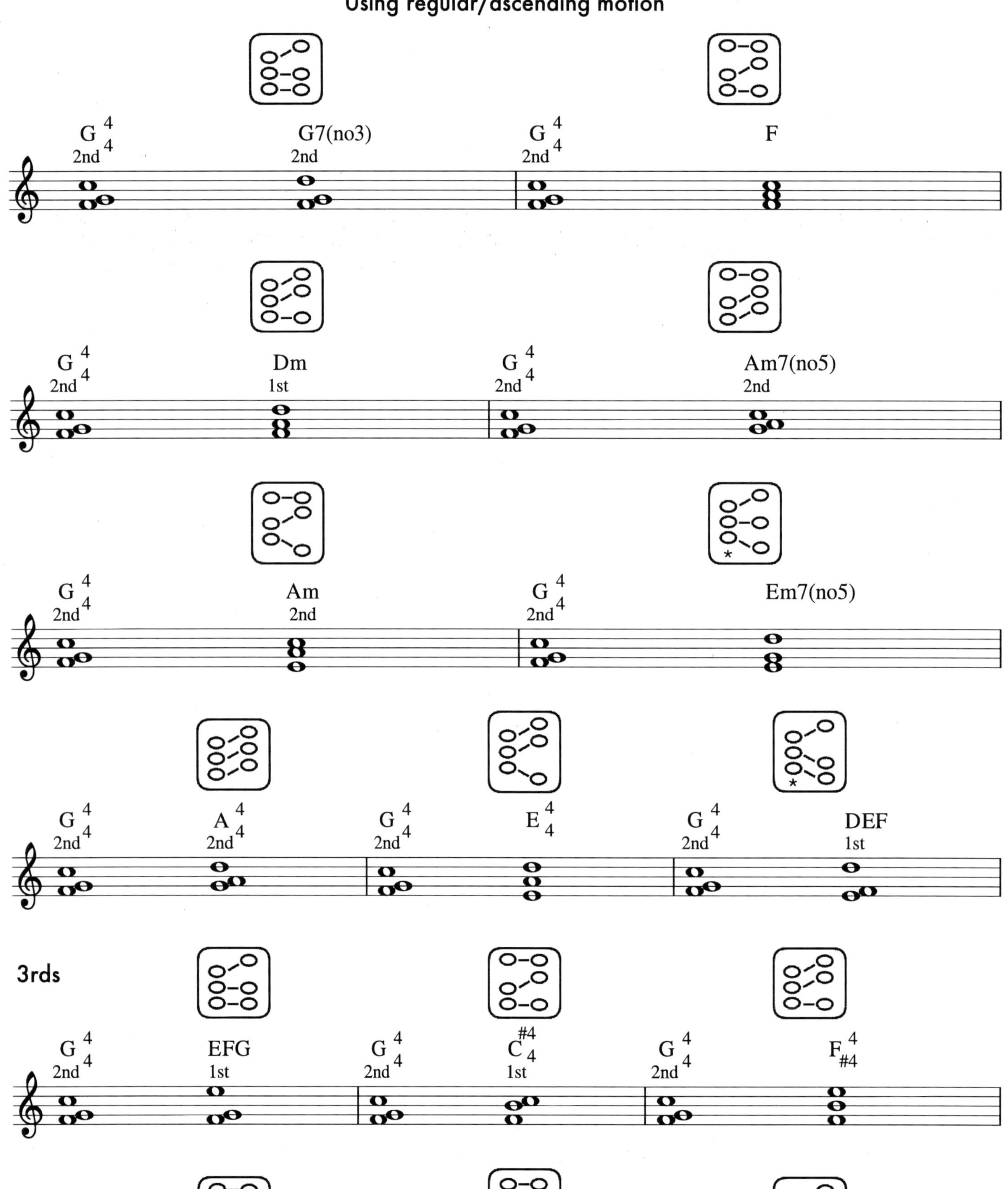

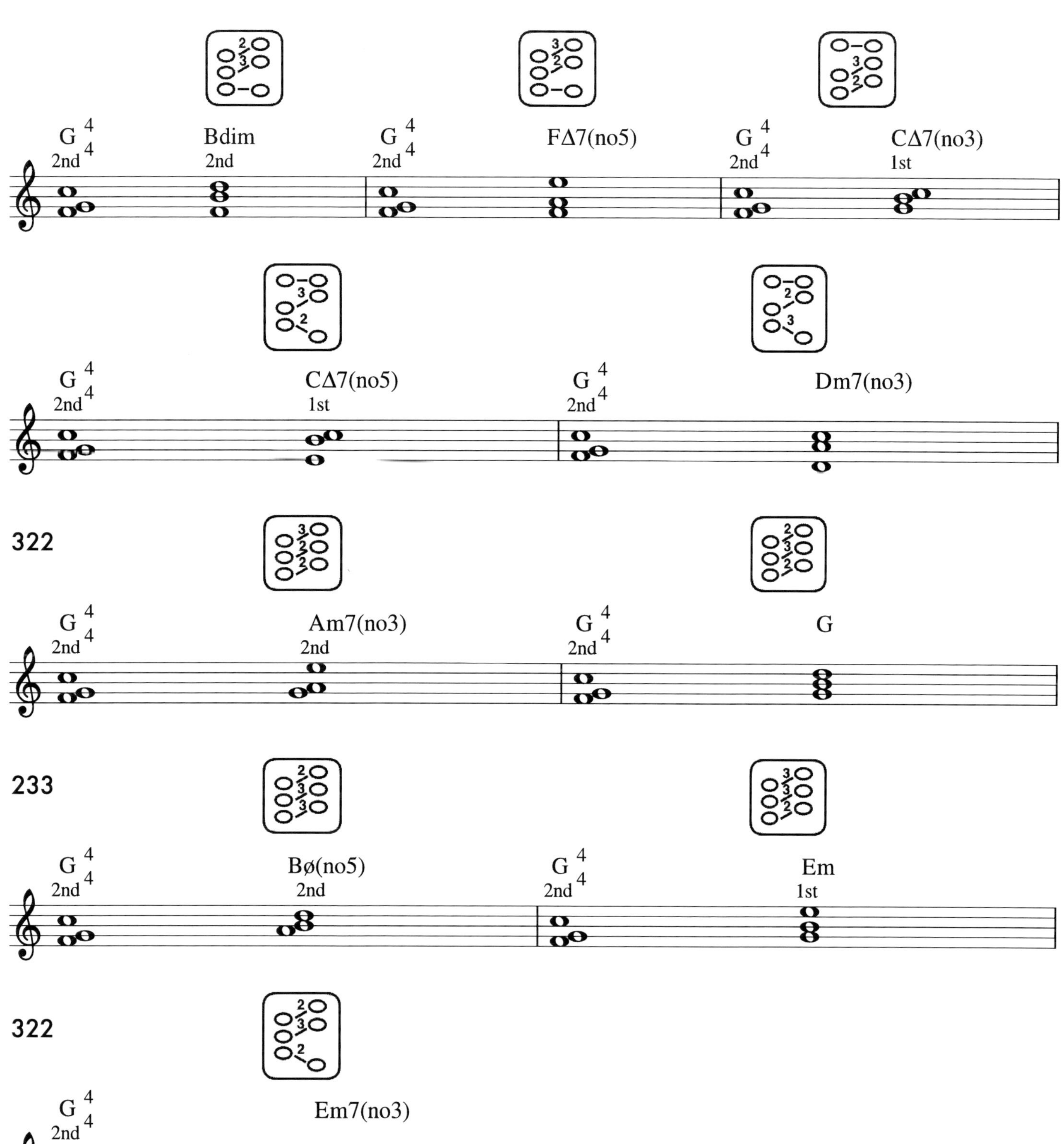
G 4/4 2nd
Bdim 2nd
G 4/4 2nd
FΔ7(no5)
G 4/4 2nd
CΔ7(no3) 1st
G 4/4 2nd
CΔ7(no5) 1st
G 4/4 2nd
Dm7(no3)
322
G 4/4 2nd
Am7(no3) 2nd
G 4/4 2nd
G
233
G 4/4 2nd
Bø(no5) 2nd
G 4/4 2nd
Em 1st
322
G 4/4 2nd
Em7(no3)

4ths in 2nd Inversion

Using reverse/descending motion

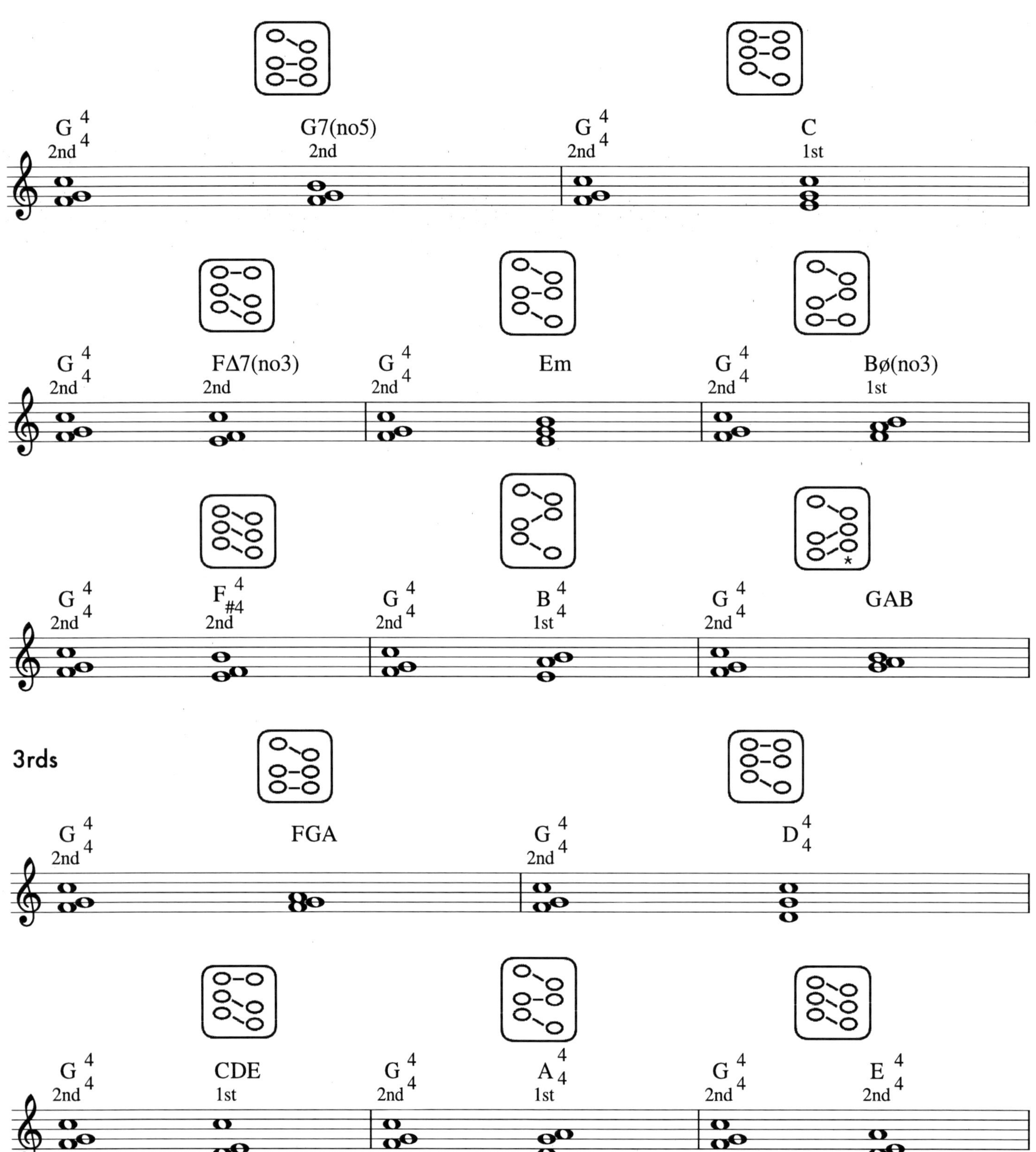

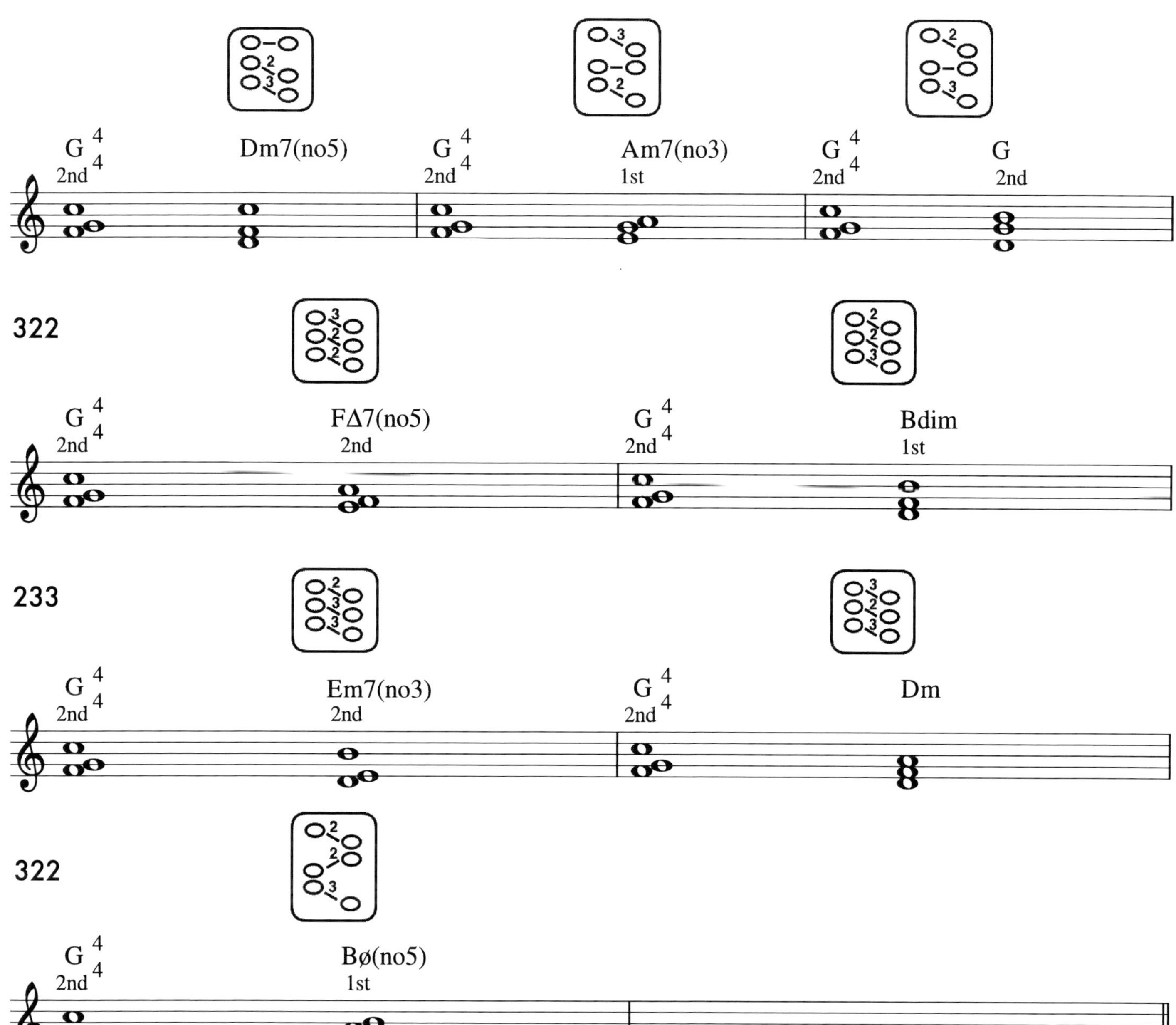
G 4/4 2nd
Dm7(no5)
G 4/4 2nd
Am7(no3) 1st
G 4/4 2nd
G 2nd
322
G 4/4 2nd
FΔ7(no5) 2nd
G 4/4 2nd
Bdim 1st
233
G 4/4 2nd
Em7(no3) 2nd
G 4/4 2nd
Dm
322
G 4/4 2nd
Bø(no5) 1st

2nds

4ths in Root Position

Using regular/ascending motion

close

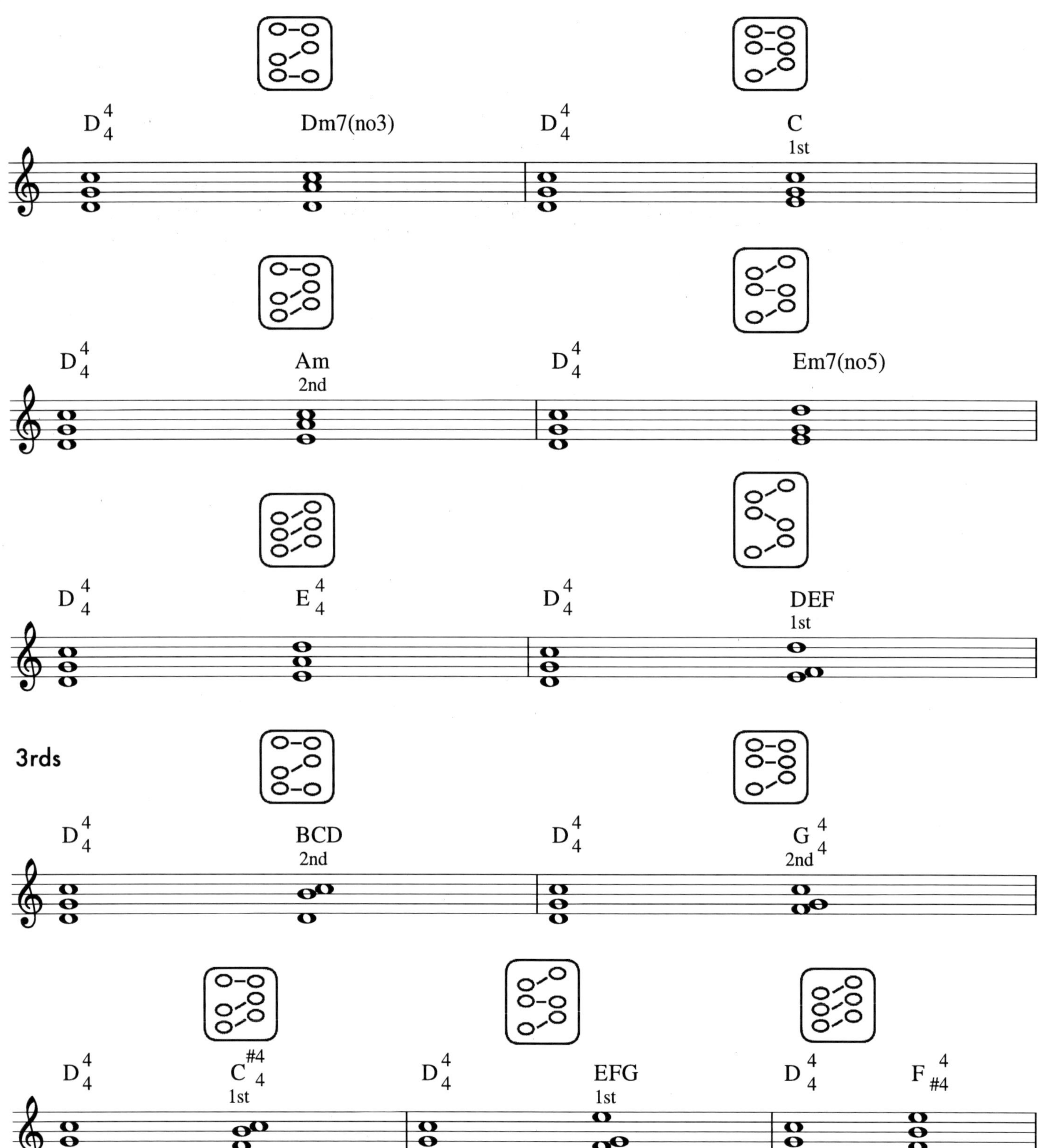

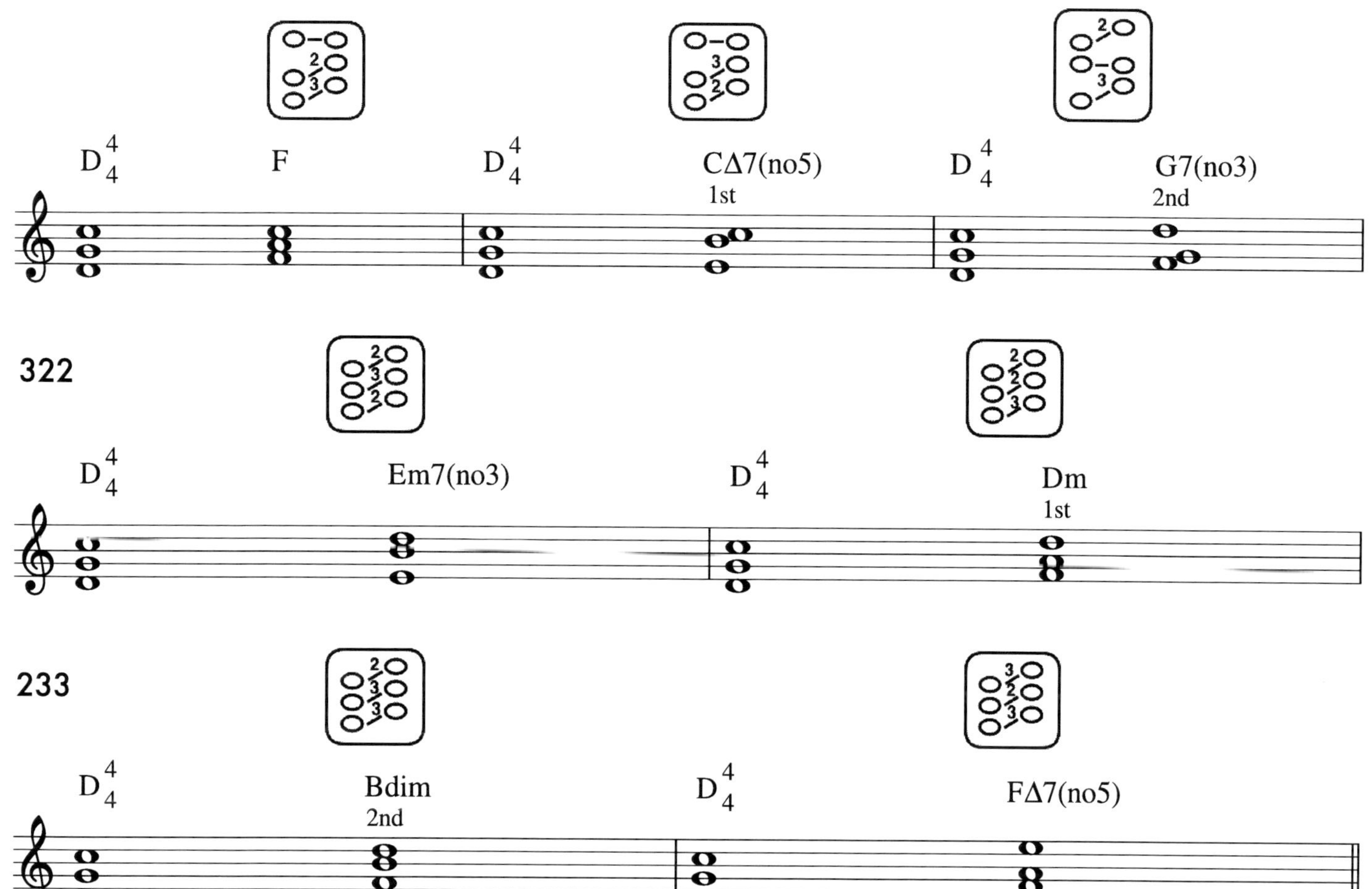
D 4/4
F
D 4/4
CΔ7(no5)
1st
D 4/4
G7(no3)
2nd
322
D 4/4
Em7(no3)
D 4/4
Dm
1st
233
D 4/4
Bdim
2nd
D 4/4
FΔ7(no5)

2nds

4ths in Root Position

Using reverse/descending motion

close

D 4/4 — G 2nd | D 4/4 — Dm7(no5) | D 4/4 — Bdim 1st

D 4/4 — CΔ7(no3) | D 4/4 — Bø(no5) 1st | D 4/4 — FΔ7(no3) 2nd

D 4/4 — Em | D 4/4 — C #4/4

D 4/4 — ABC 2nd | D 4/4 — F 4/#4 2nd | D 4/4 — B 4/4 1st

3rds

D 4/4 — A 4/4 1st | D 4/4 — CDE 1st | D 4/4 — E 4/4 2nd

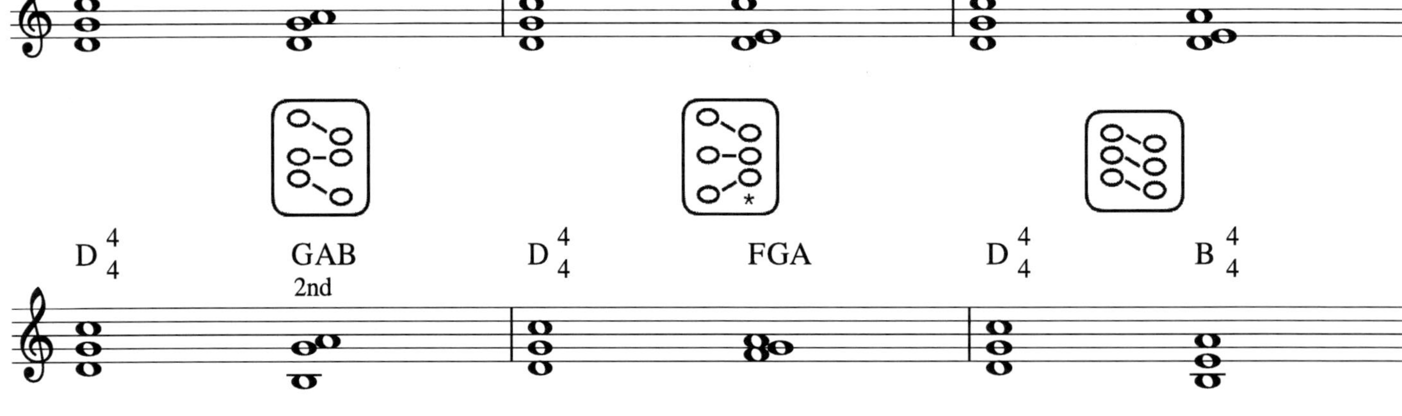

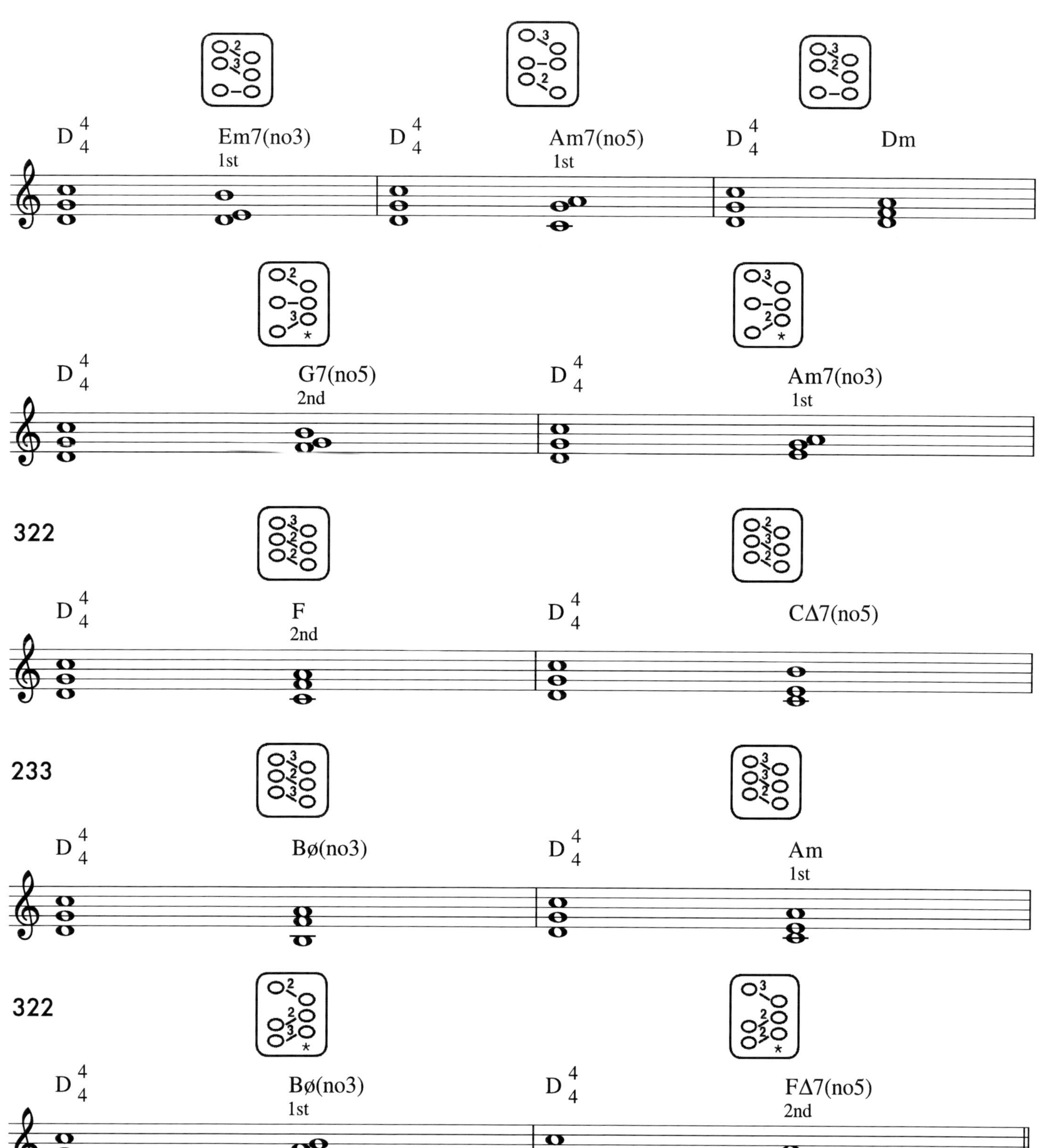
D 4/4
Em7(no3)
1st
D 4/4
Am7(no5)
1st
D 4/4
Dm
D 4/4
G7(no5)
2nd
D 4/4
Am7(no3)
1st
322
D 4/4
F
2nd
D 4/4
CΔ7(no5)
233
D 4/4
Bø(no3)
D 4/4
Am
1st
322
D 4/4
Bø(no3)
1st
D 4/4
FΔ7(no5)
2nd

2nds

7th no 5 in 1st Inversion

close

Using regular/ascending motion

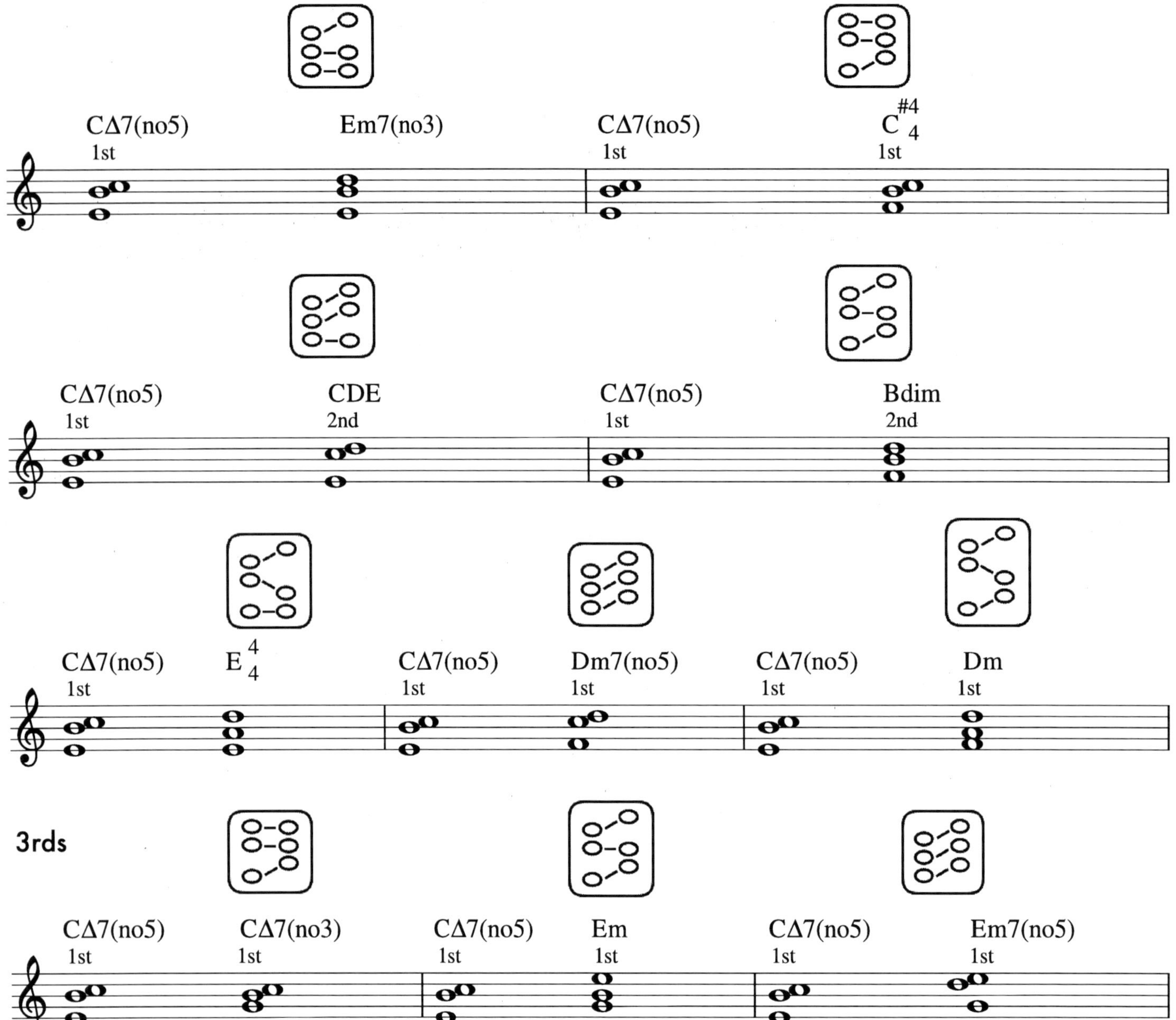

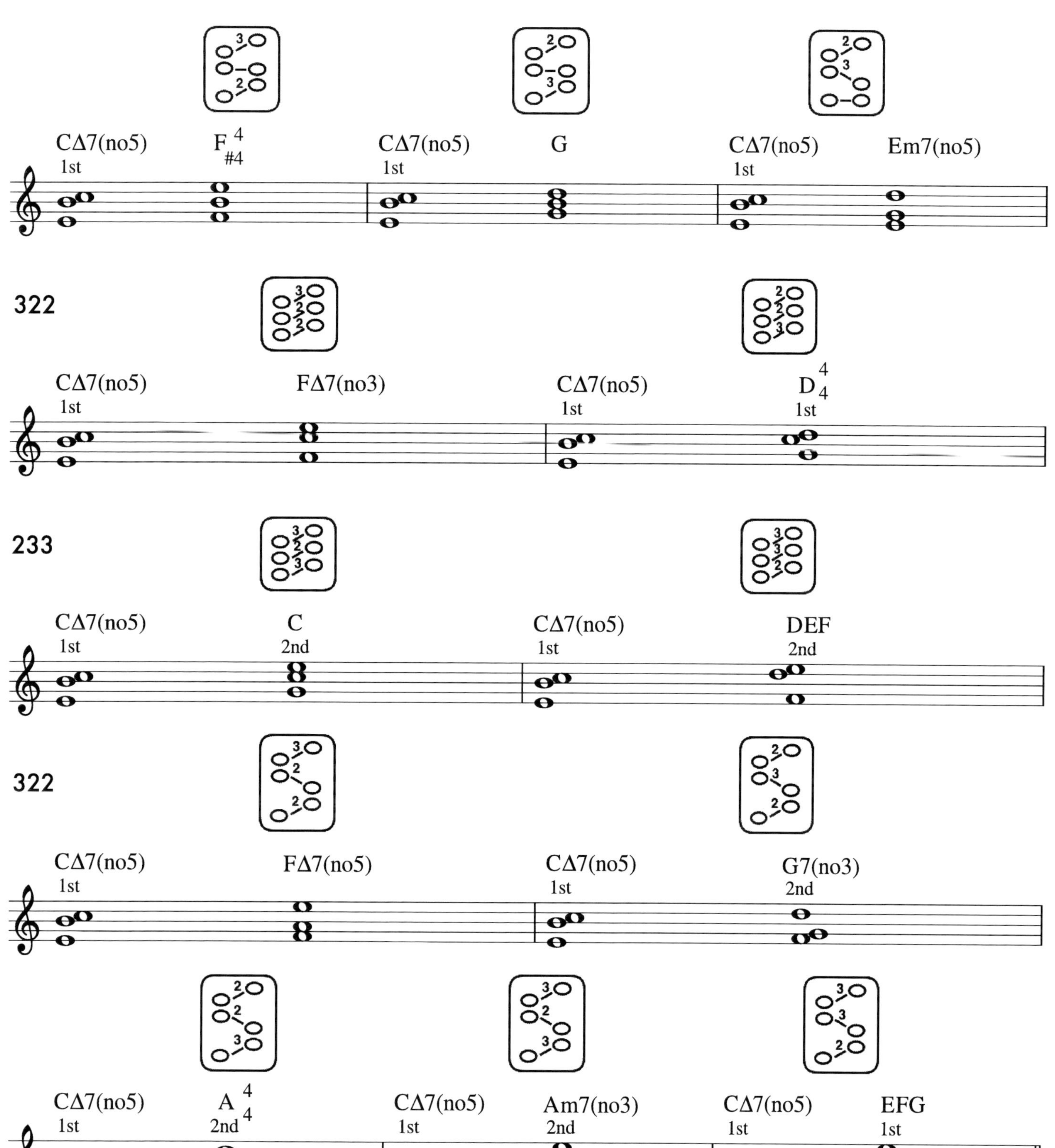
CΔ7(no5)
1st
F 4 #4
CΔ7(no5)
1st
G
CΔ7(no5)
1st
Em7(no5)
322
CΔ7(no5)
1st
FΔ7(no3)
CΔ7(no5)
1st
D 4 4
1st
233
CΔ7(no5)
1st
C
2nd
CΔ7(no5)
1st
DEF
2nd
322
CΔ7(no5)
1st
FΔ7(no5)
CΔ7(no5)
1st
G7(no3)
2nd
CΔ7(no5)
1st
A 4 4
2nd
CΔ7(no5)
1st
Am7(no3)
2nd
CΔ7(no5)
1st
EFG
1st

2nds

7th no 5 in 1st Inversion

close

Using reverse/descending motion

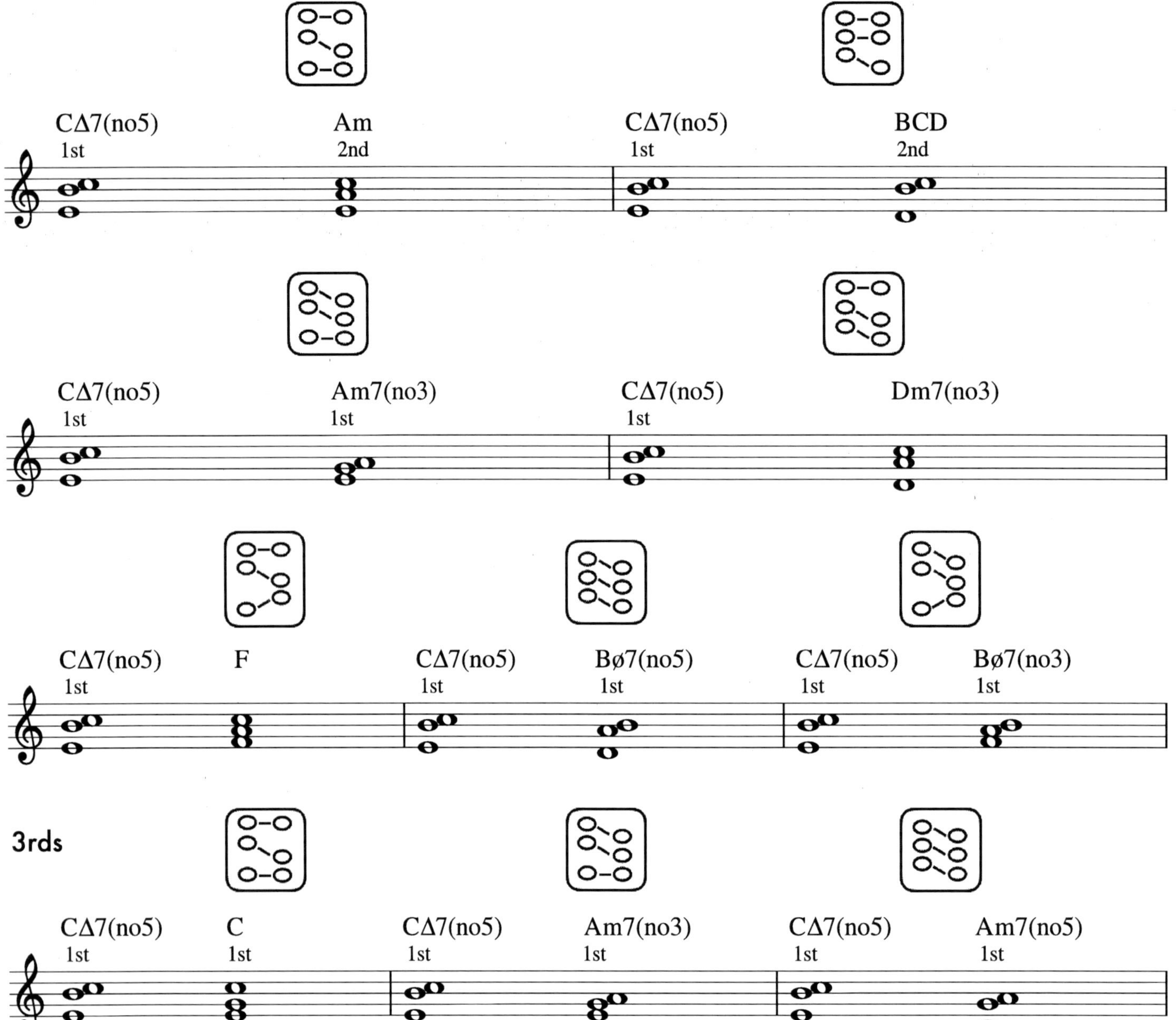

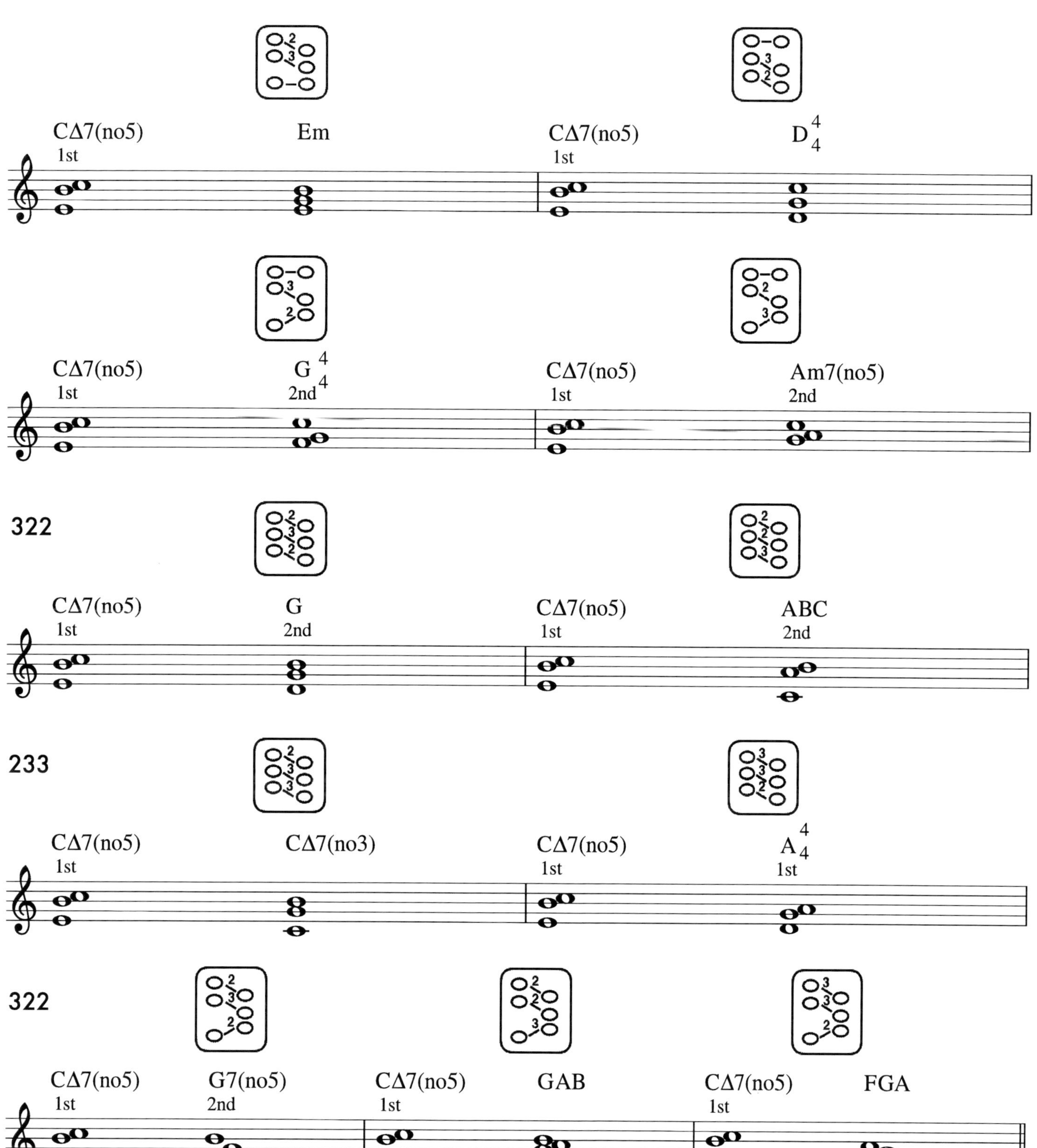
CΔ7(no5)
1st
Em
CΔ7(no5)
1st
D 4 4
CΔ7(no5)
1st
G 4 4
2nd
CΔ7(no5)
1st
Am7(no5)
2nd
322
CΔ7(no5)
1st
G
2nd
CΔ7(no5)
1st
ABC
2nd
233
CΔ7(no5)
1st
CΔ7(no3)
CΔ7(no5)
1st
A 4 4
1st
322
CΔ7(no5)
1st
G7(no5)
2nd
CΔ7(no5)
1st
GAB
CΔ7(no5)
1st
FGA

2nds

7th no 5 in 2nd Inversion

close

Using regular/ascending motion

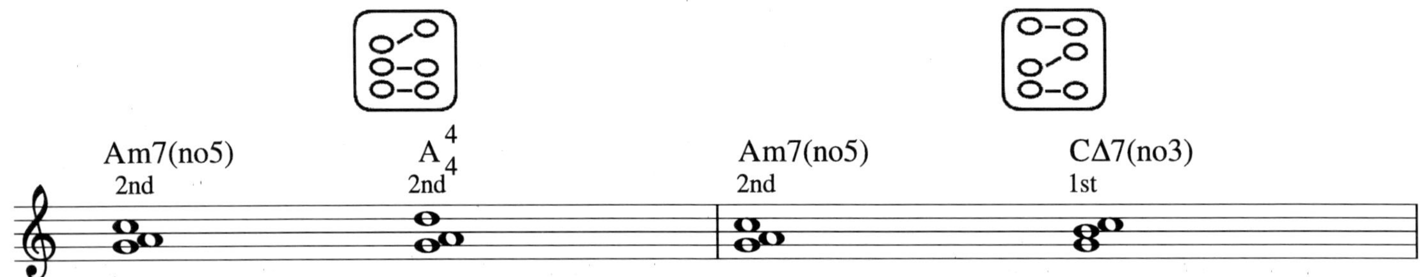

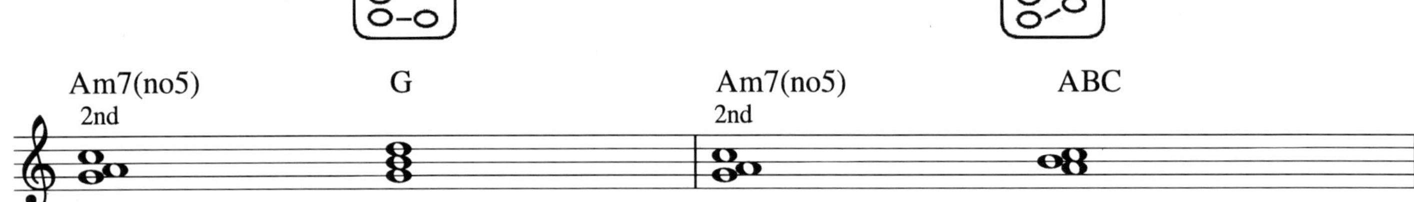

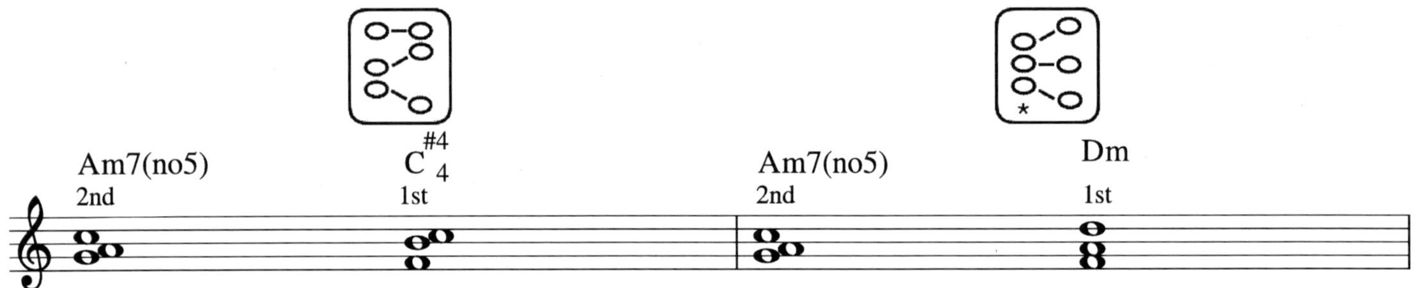

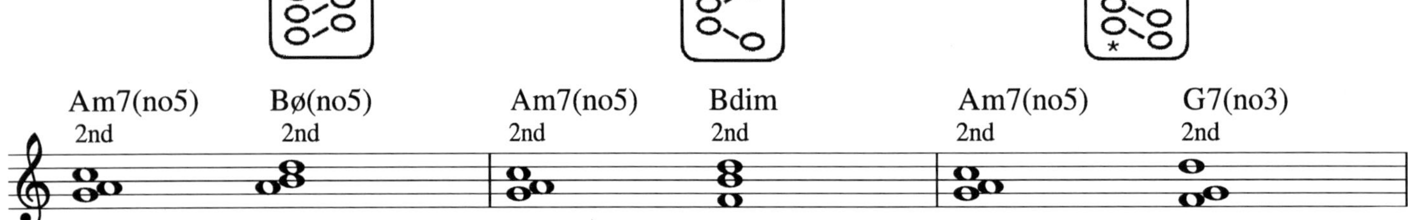

3rds

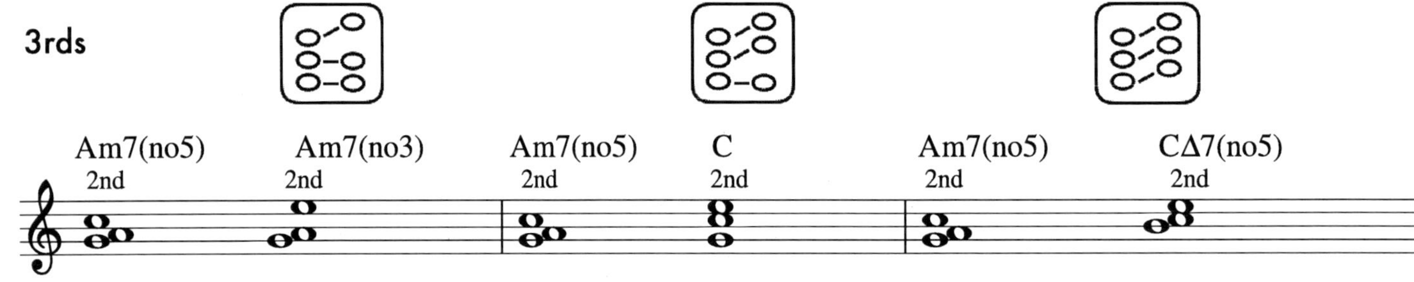

2nds/3rds

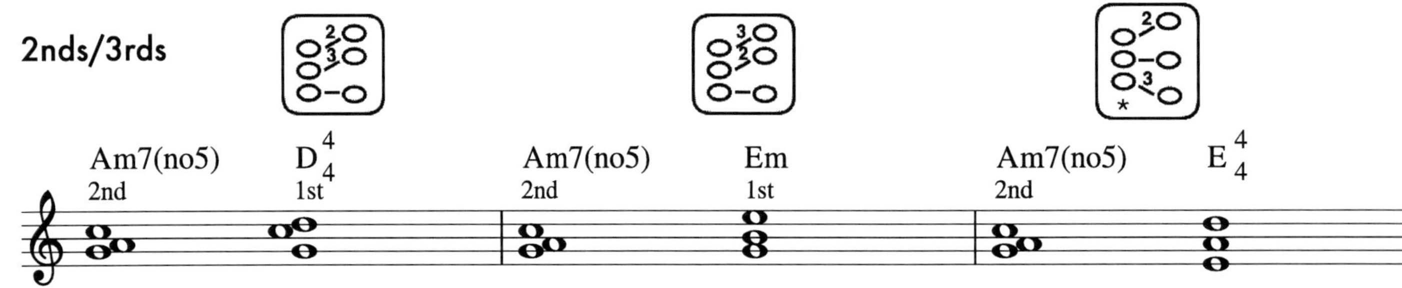

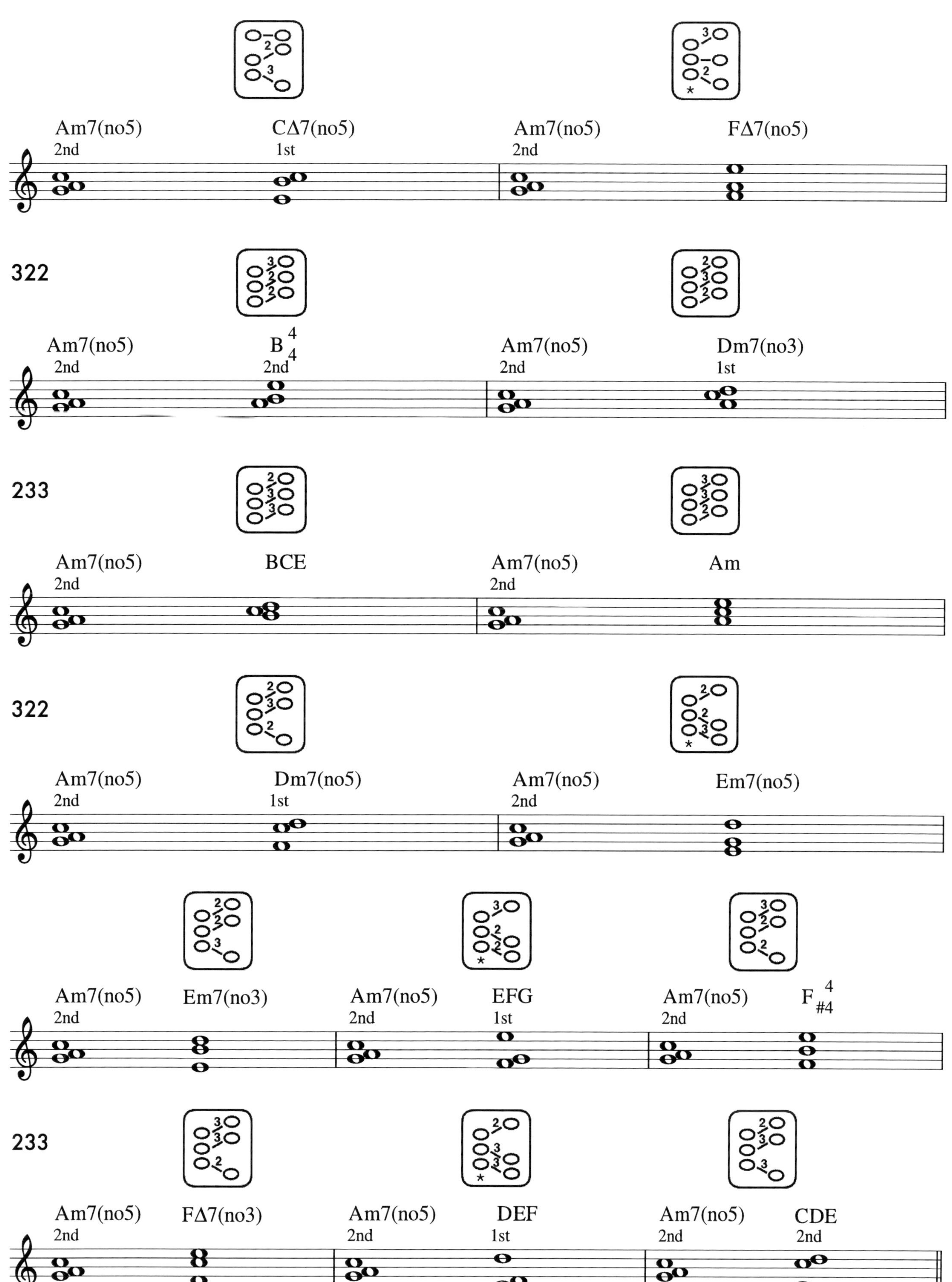
Am7(no5)
2nd
CΔ7(no5)
1st
Am7(no5)
2nd
FΔ7(no5)
322
Am7(no5)
2nd
B 4 4
2nd
Am7(no5)
2nd
Dm7(no3)
1st
233
Am7(no5)
2nd
BCE
Am7(no5)
2nd
Am
322
Am7(no5)
2nd
Dm7(no5)
1st
Am7(no5)
2nd
Em7(no5)
Am7(no5)
2nd
Em7(no3)
Am7(no5)
2nd
EFG
1st
Am7(no5)
2nd
F 4 #4
233
Am7(no5)
2nd
FΔ7(no3)
Am7(no5)
2nd
DEF
1st
Am7(no5)
2nd
CDE
2nd

2nds

7th no 5 in 2nd Inversion

close

Using reverse/descending motion

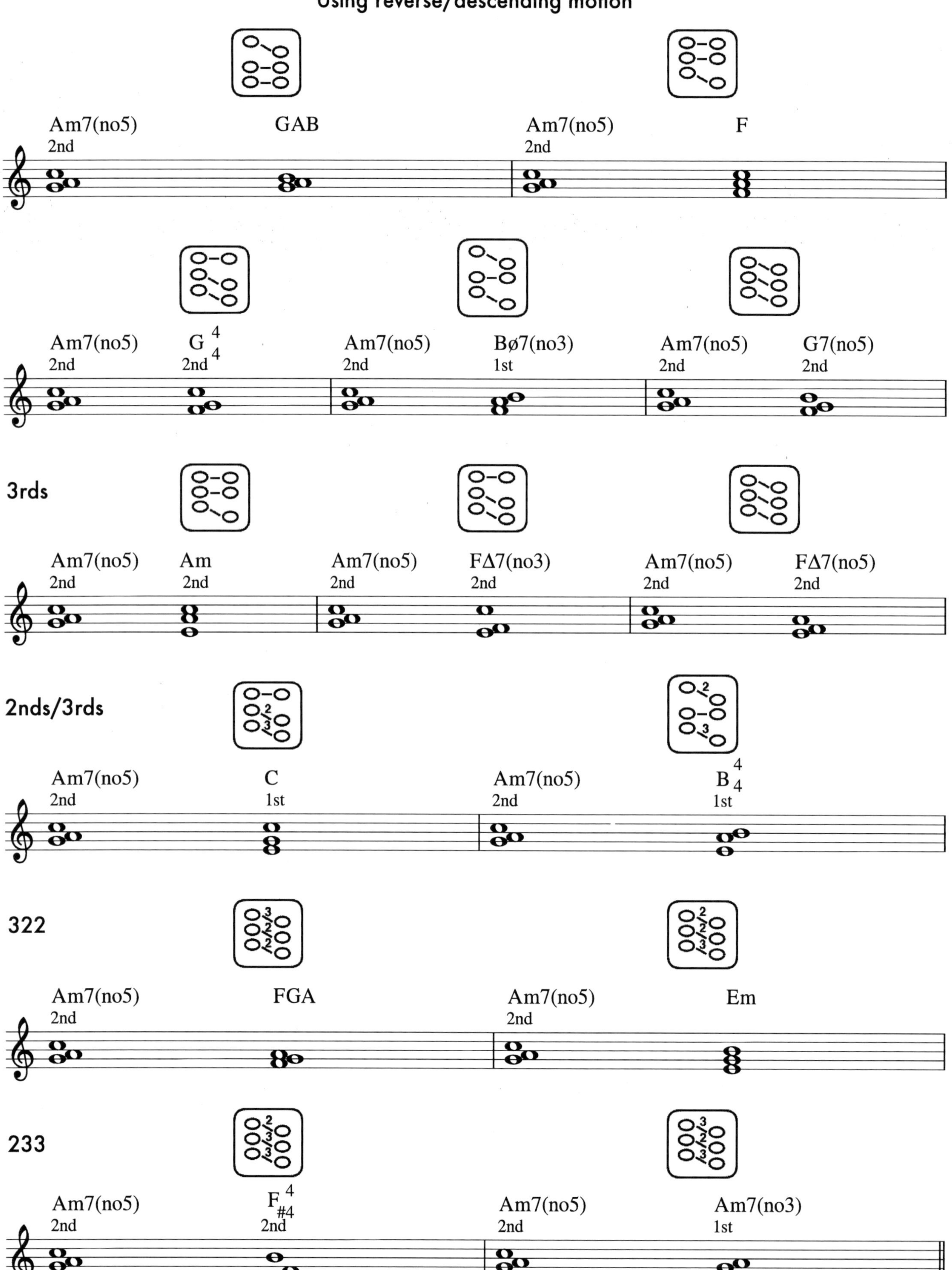

7th no 5 in Root Position

Using regular/ascending motion

close

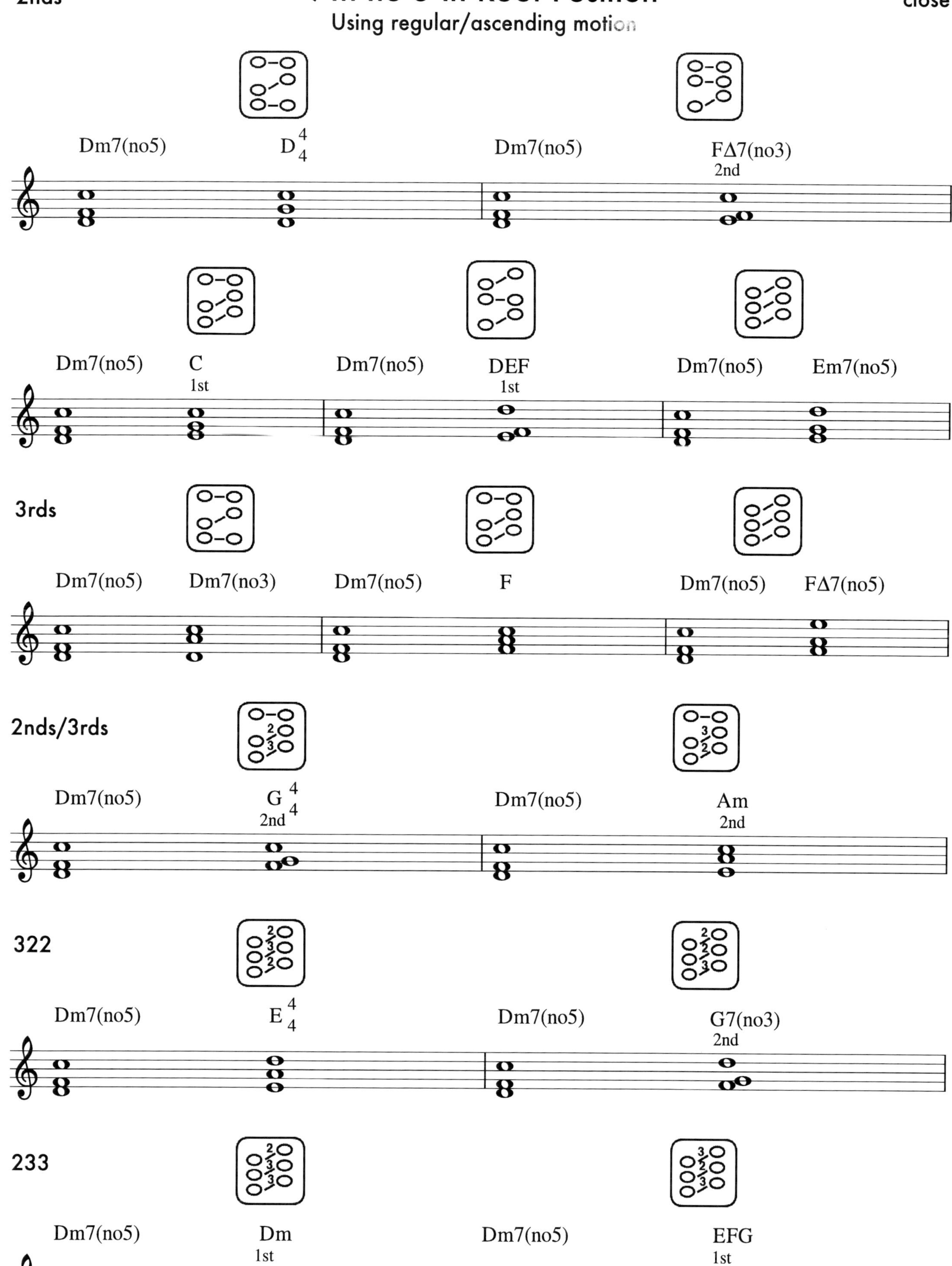

2nds

7th no 5 in Root Position

Using reverse/descending motion

close

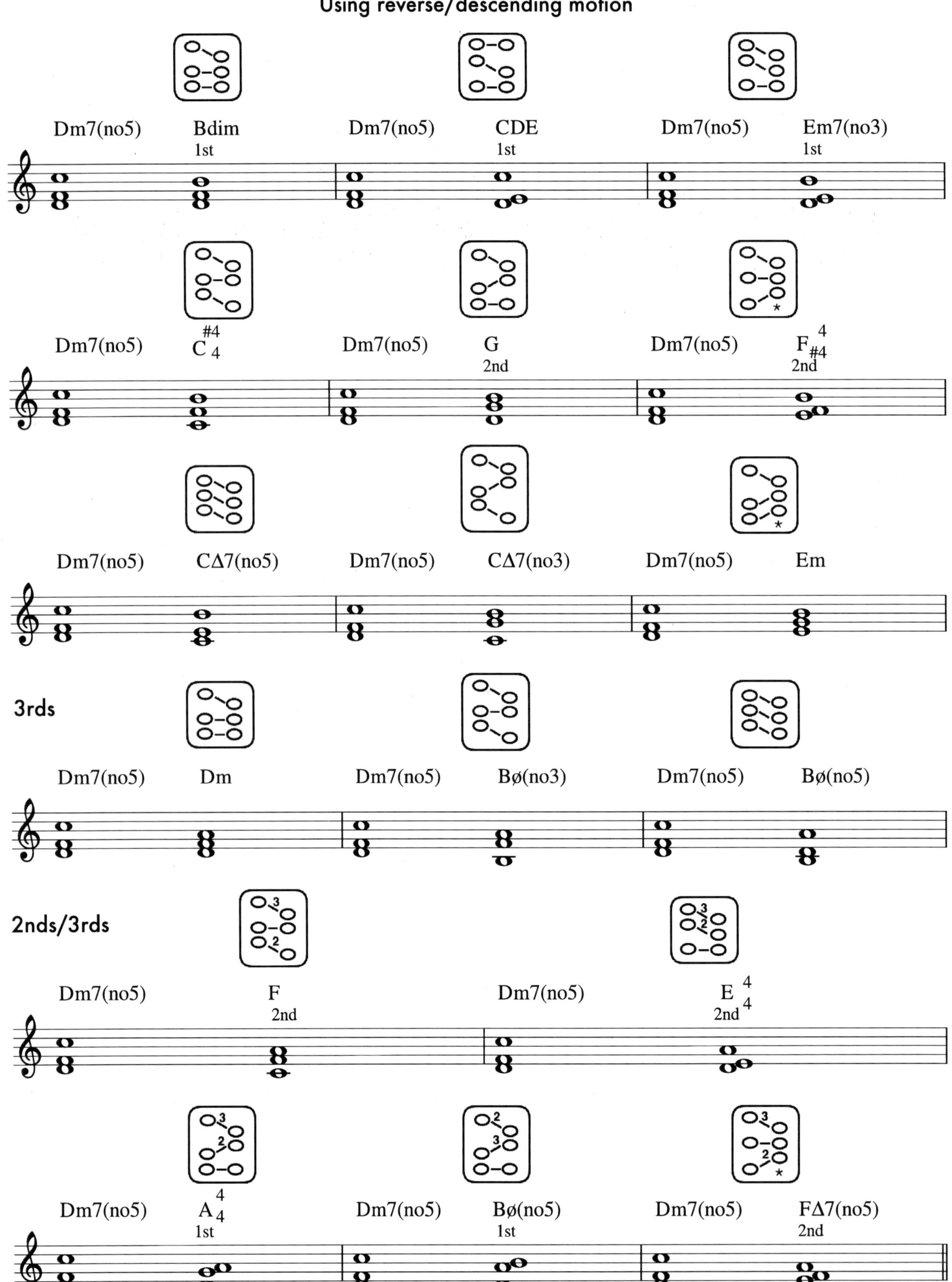

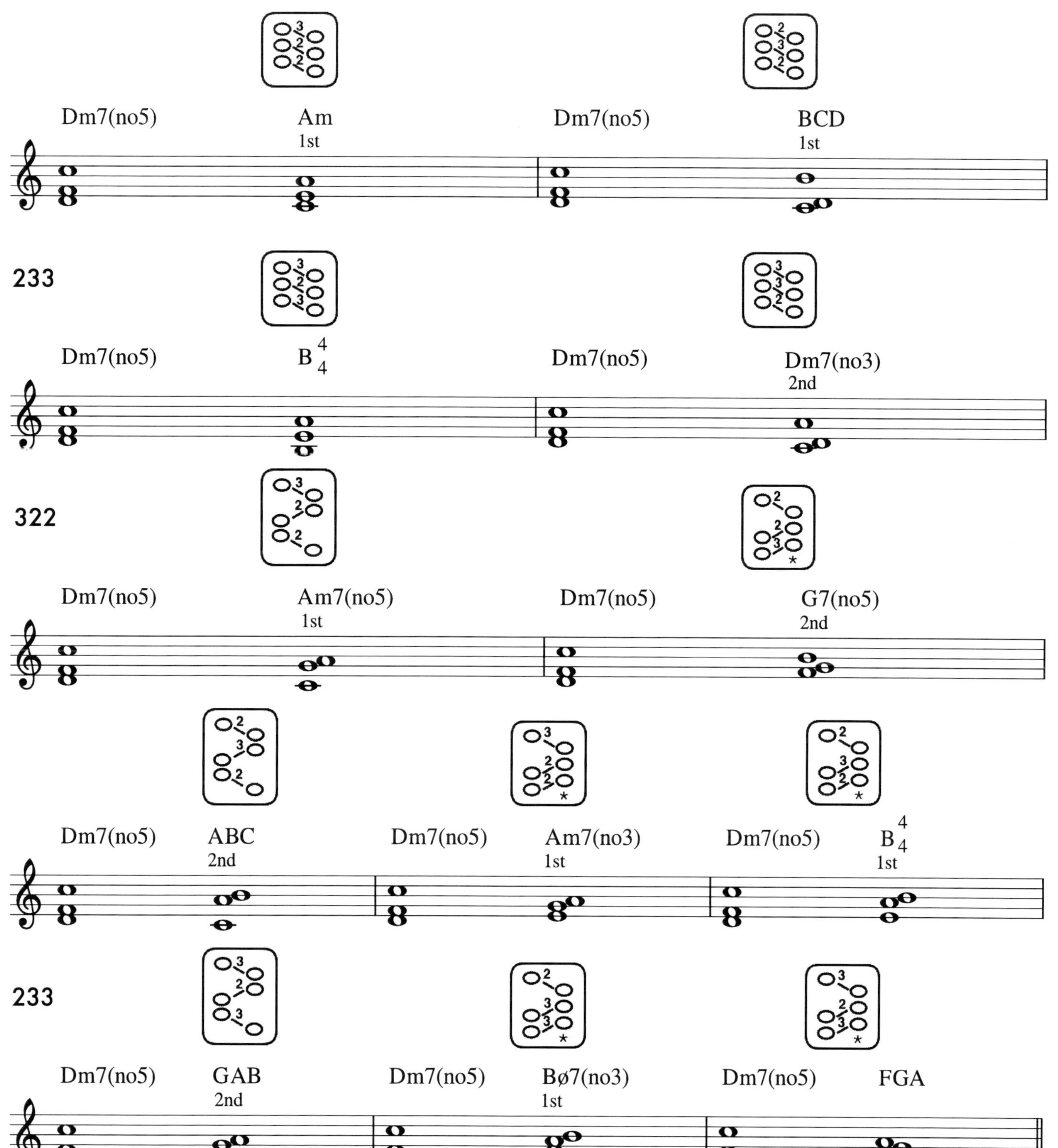
Dm7(no5)
Am
1st
Dm7(no5)
BCD
1st
233
Dm7(no5)
B 4 4
Dm7(no5)
Dm7(no3)
2nd
322
Dm7(no5)
Am7(no5)
1st
Dm7(no5)
G7(no5)
2nd
Dm7(no5)
ABC
2nd
Dm7(no5)
Am7(no3)
1st
Dm7(no5)
B 4 4
1st
233
Dm7(no5)
GAB
2nd
Dm7(no5)
Bø7(no3)
1st
Dm7(no5)
FGA

2nds

7th no 3 in 1st Inversion

close

Using regular/ascending motion

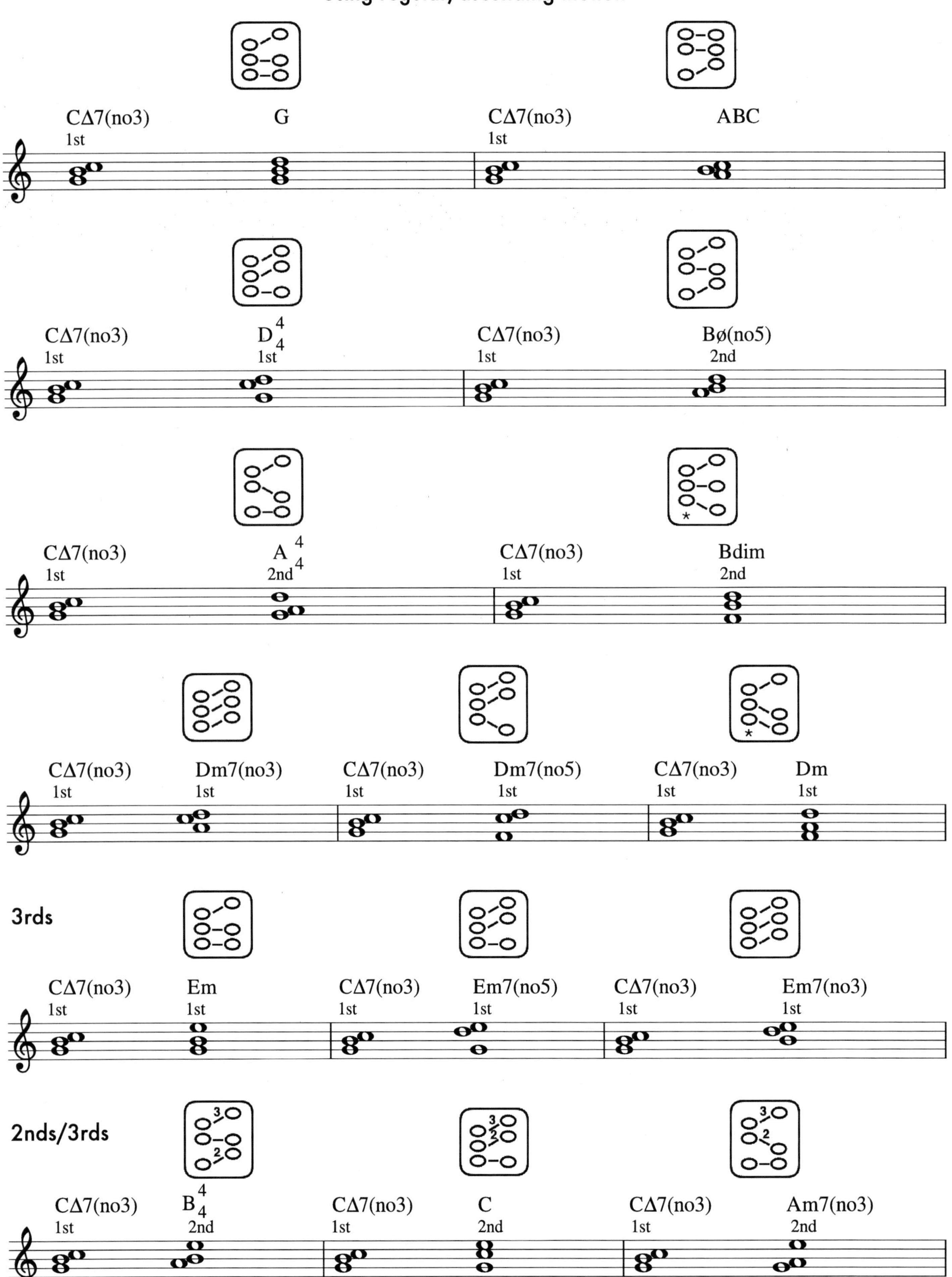

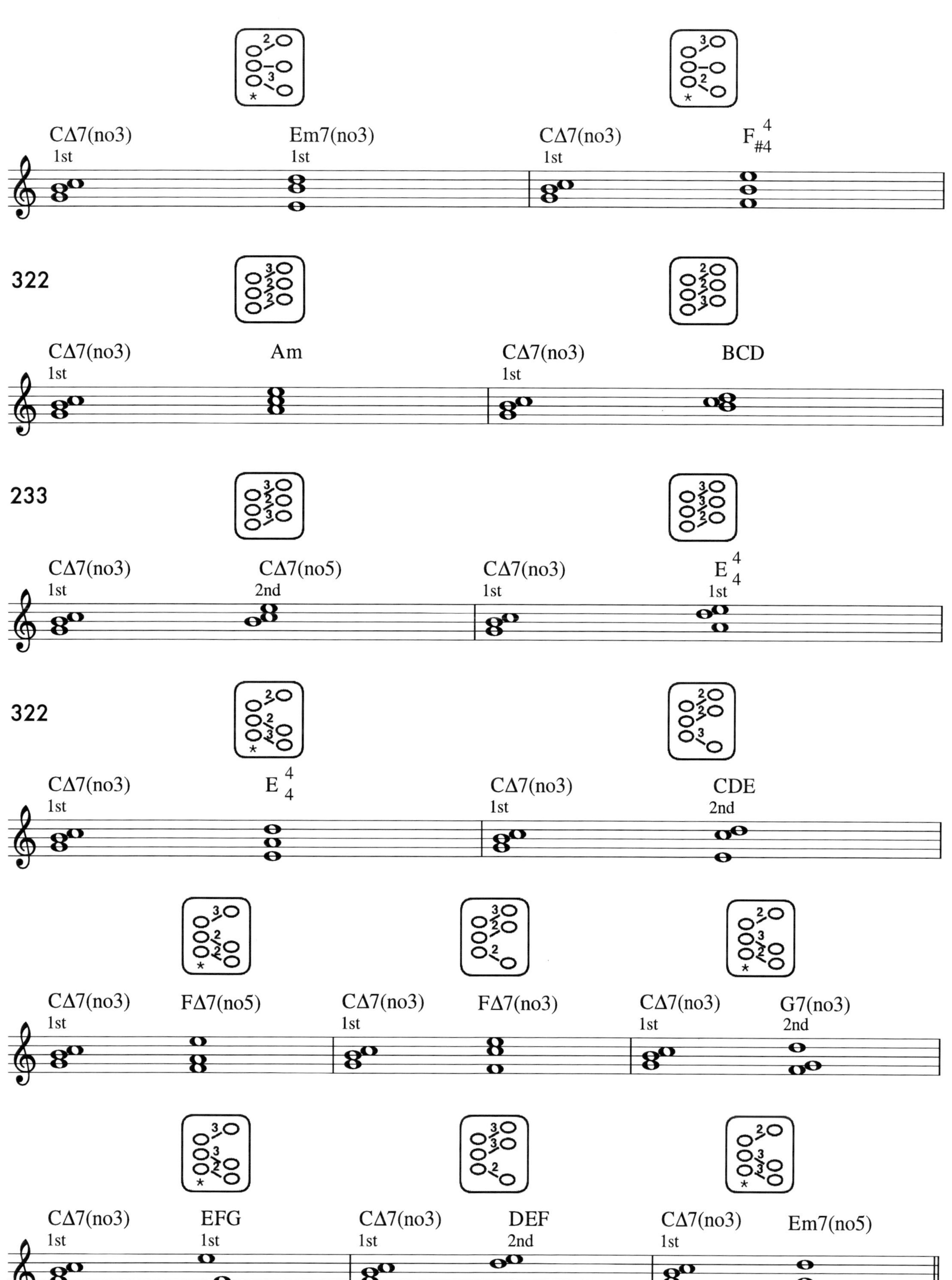
CΔ7(no3)
1st
Em7(no3)
1st
CΔ7(no3)
1st
F 4 #4
322
CΔ7(no3)
1st
Am
CΔ7(no3)
1st
BCD
233
CΔ7(no3)
1st
CΔ7(no5)
2nd
CΔ7(no3)
1st
E 4 4
1st
322
CΔ7(no3)
1st
E 4 4
CΔ7(no3)
1st
CDE
2nd
CΔ7(no3)
1st
FΔ7(no5)
CΔ7(no3)
1st
FΔ7(no3)
CΔ7(no3)
1st
G7(no3)
2nd
CΔ7(no3)
1st
EFG
1st
CΔ7(no3)
1st
DEF
2nd
CΔ7(no3)
1st
Em7(no5)

7th no 3 in 1st Inversion

Using reverse/descending motion

2nds close

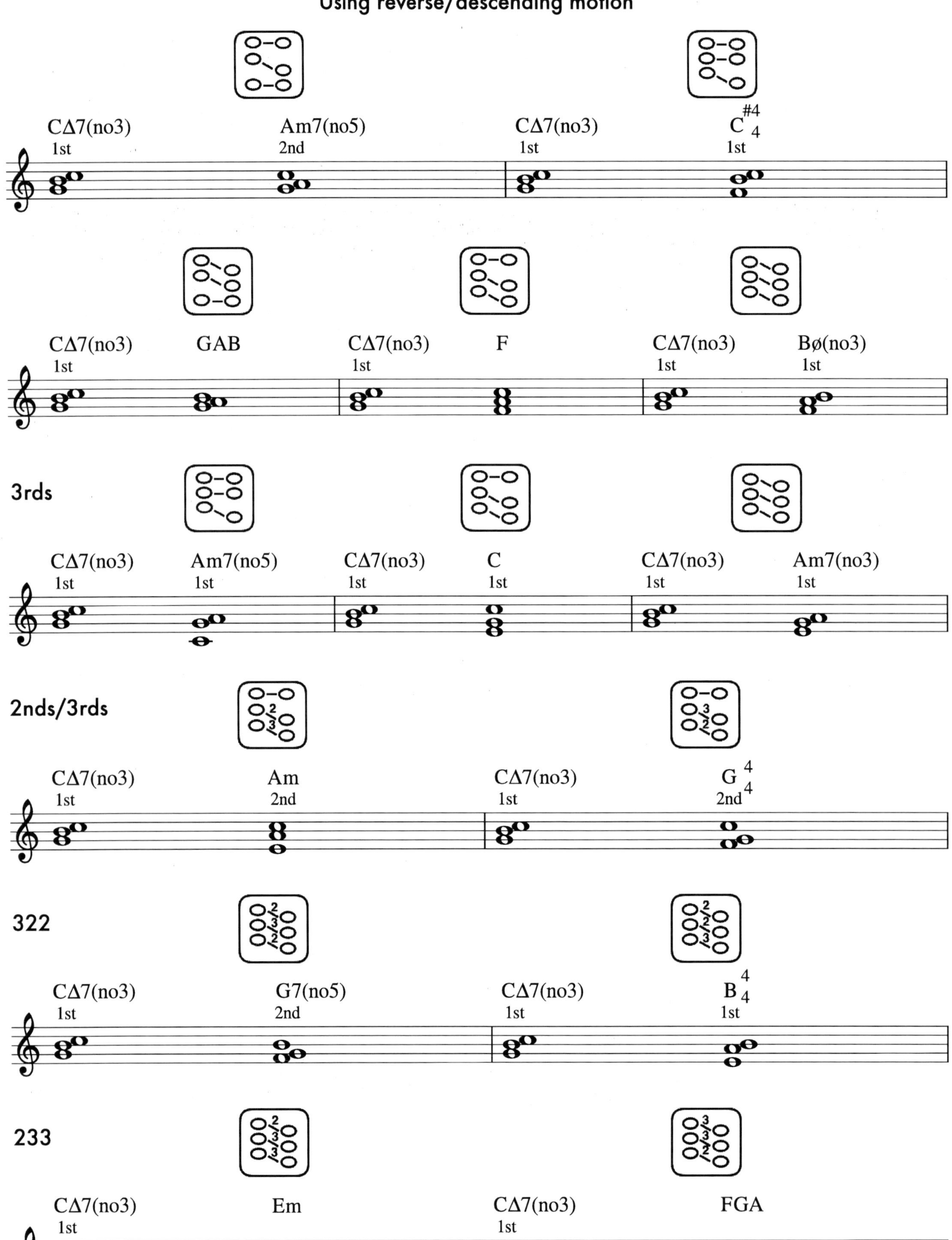

2nds

7th no 3 in 2nd Inversion

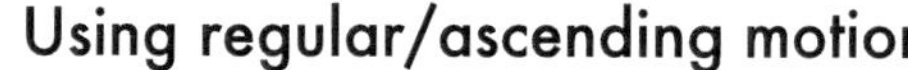

Using regular/ascending motion

close

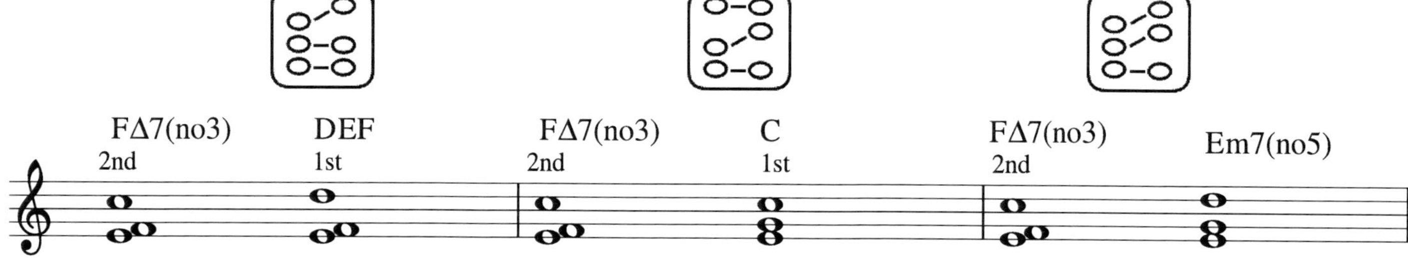

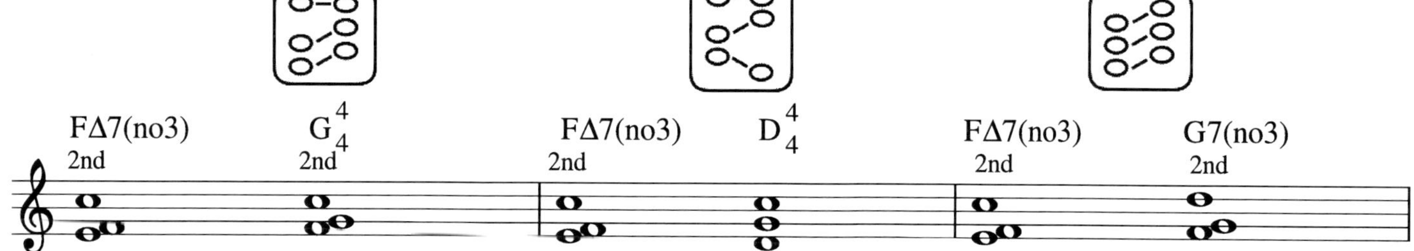

3rds

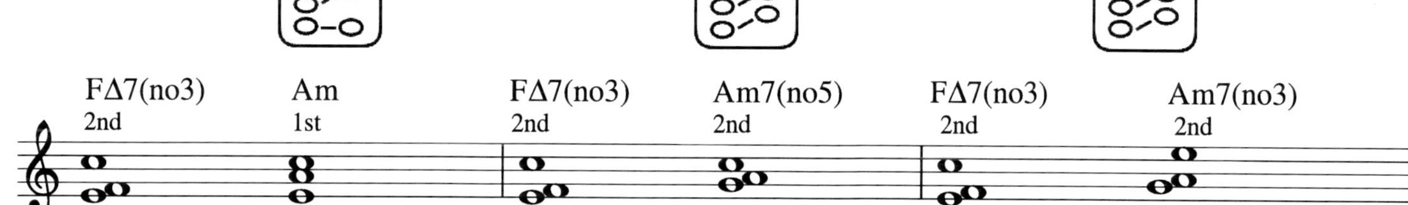

2nds/3rds

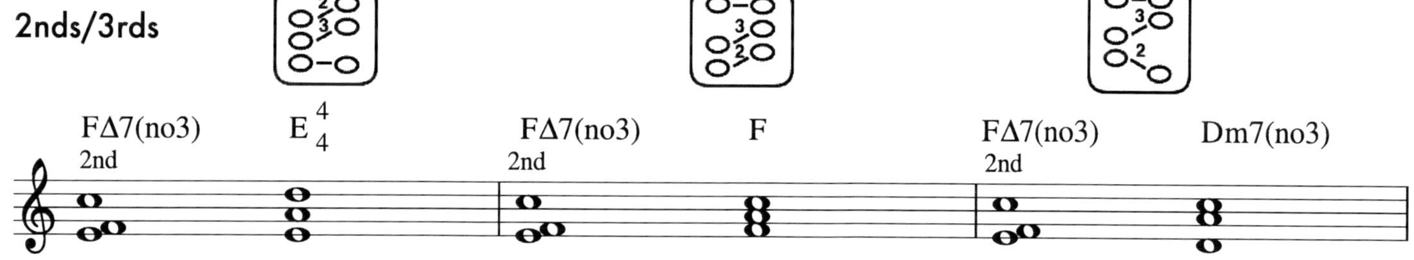

322

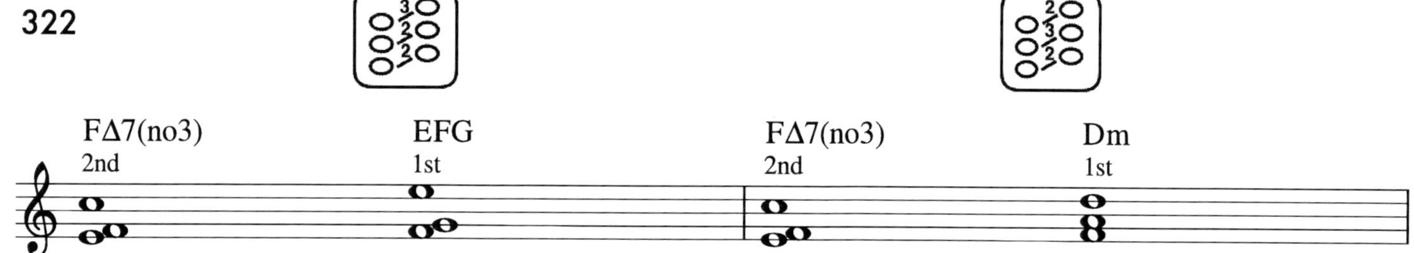

233

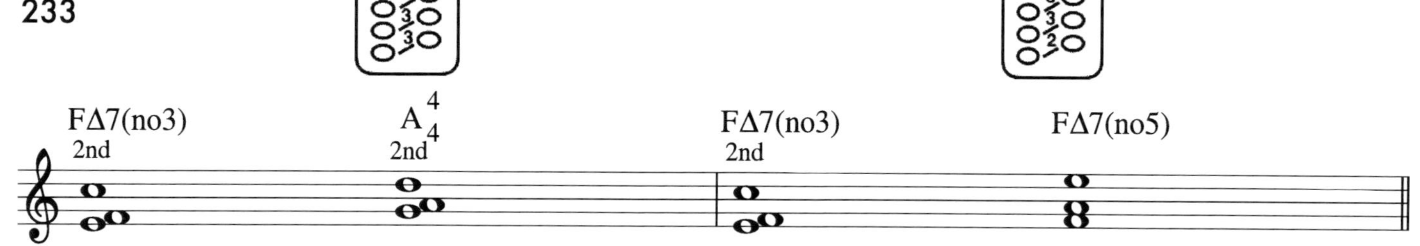

7th no 3 in 2nd Inversion

Using reverse/descending motion

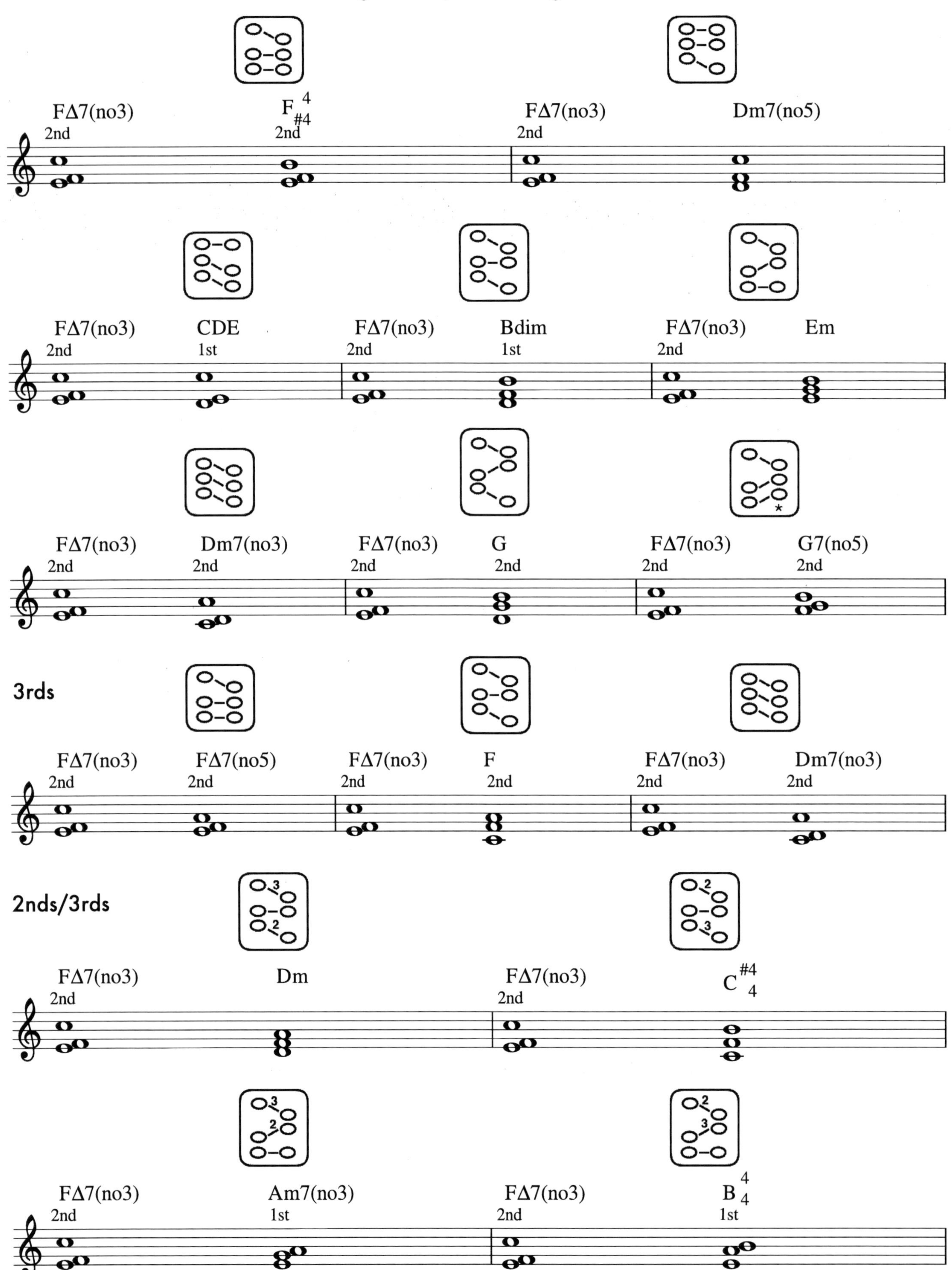

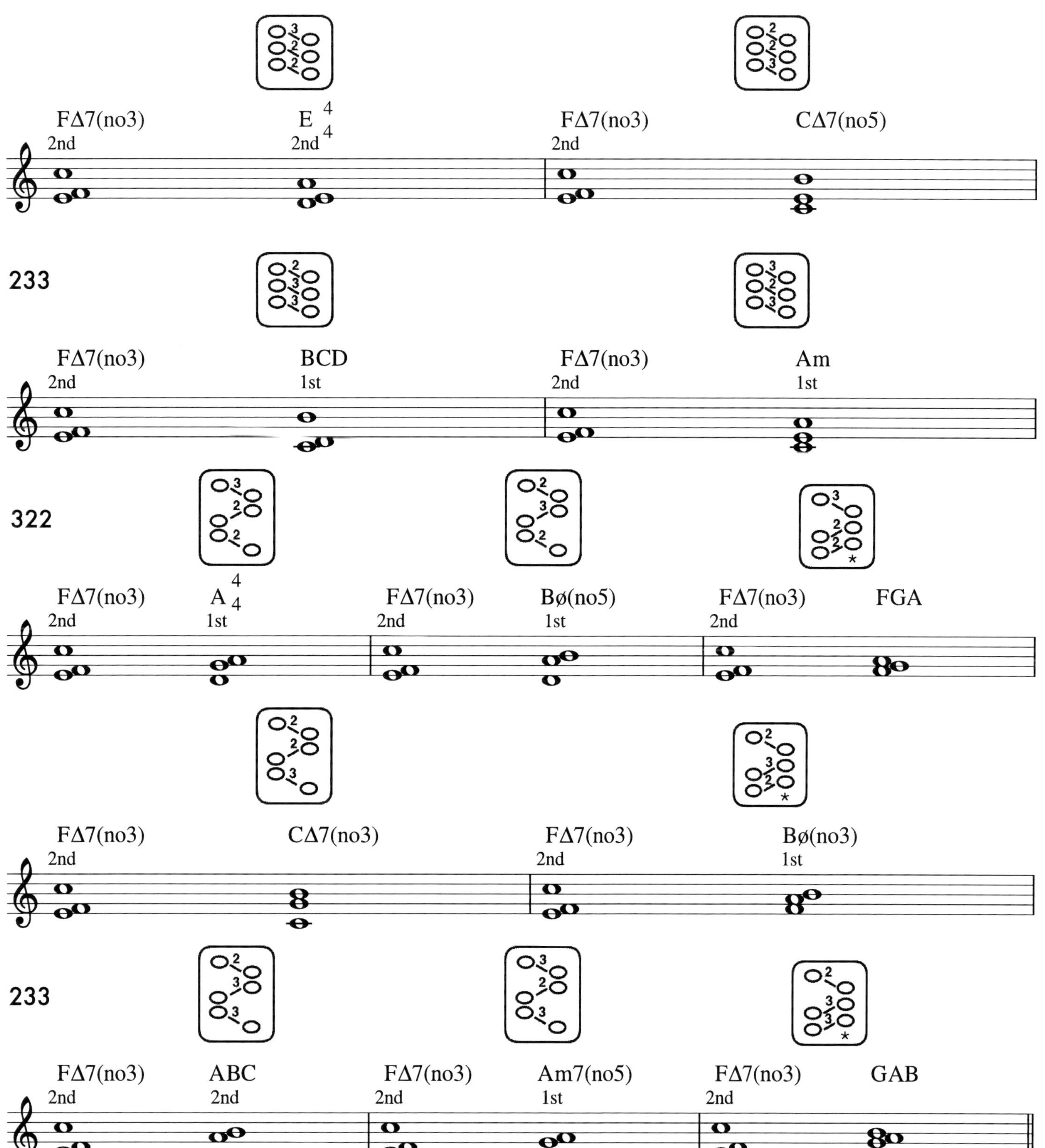
FΔ7(no3)
2nd
E 4 4
2nd
FΔ7(no3)
2nd
CΔ7(no5)
233
FΔ7(no3)
2nd
BCD
1st
FΔ7(no3)
2nd
Am
1st
322
FΔ7(no3)
2nd
A 4 4
1st
FΔ7(no3)
2nd
Bø(no5)
1st
FΔ7(no3)
2nd
FGA
FΔ7(no3)
2nd
CΔ7(no3)
FΔ7(no3)
2nd
Bø(no3)
1st
233
FΔ7(no3)
2nd
ABC
2nd
FΔ7(no3)
2nd
Am7(no5)
1st
FΔ7(no3)
2nd
GAB

2nds

7th no 3 in Root Position

Using regular/ascending motion

close

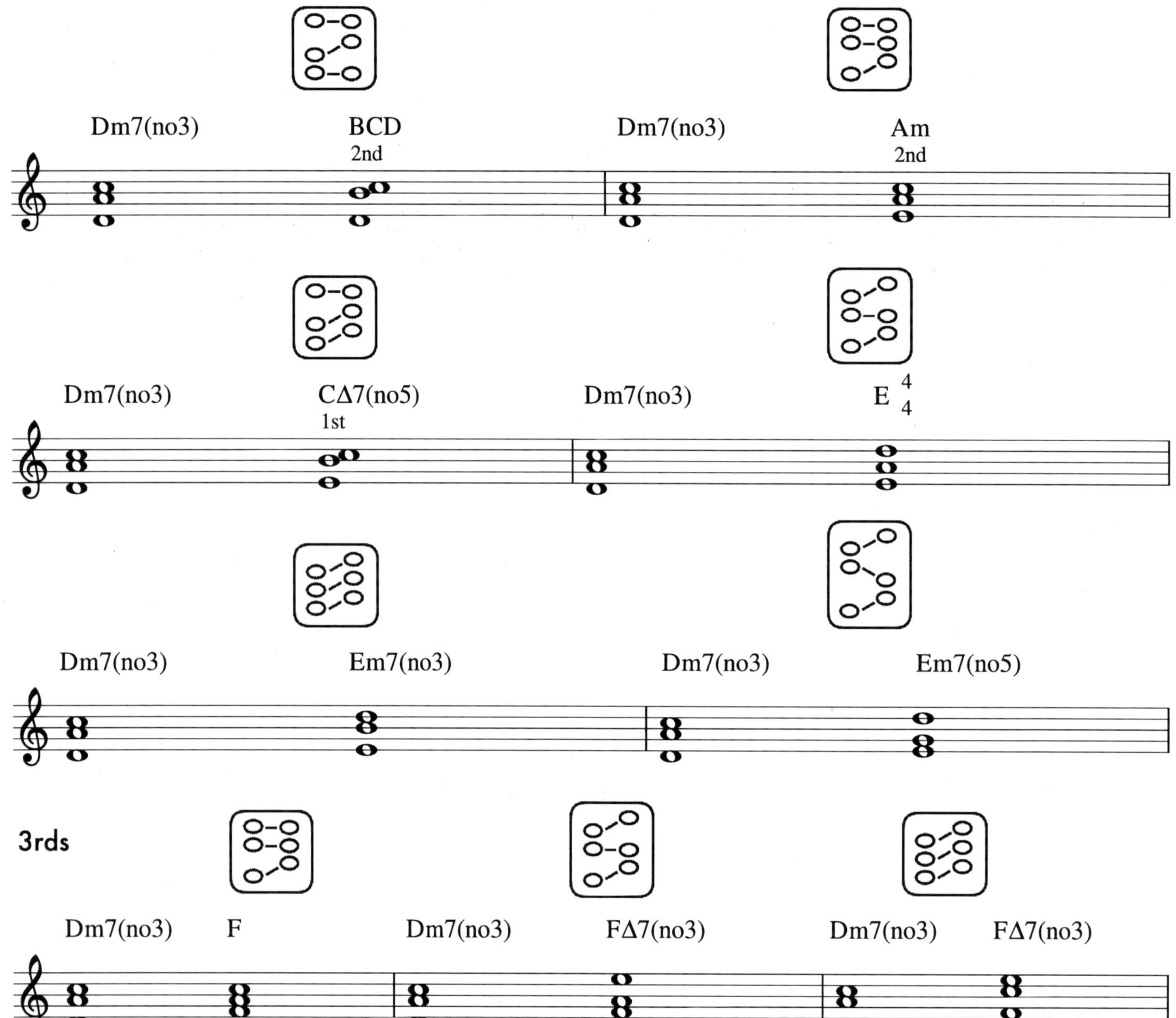

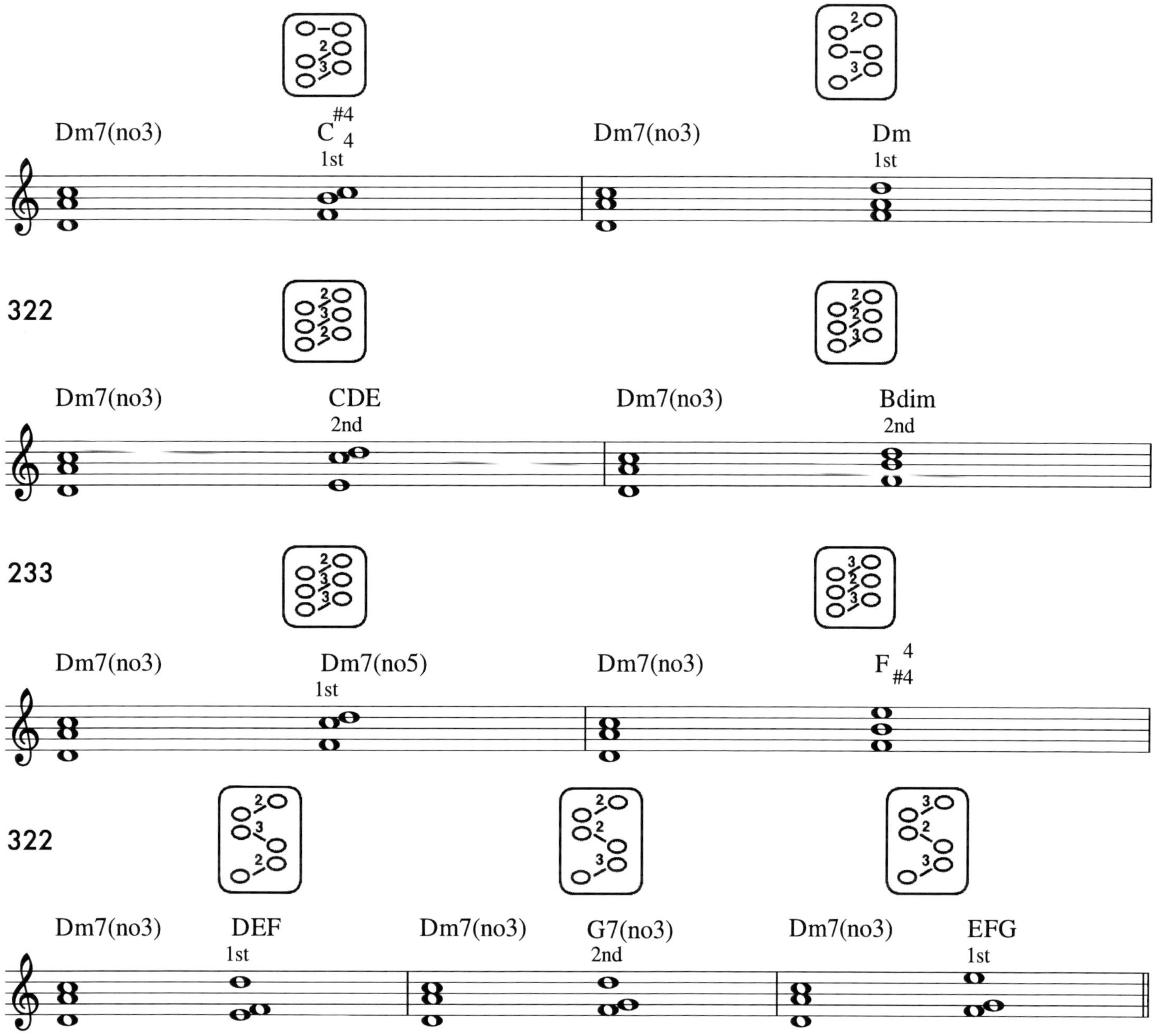

Dm7(no3) C#4 4 1st Dm7(no3) Dm 1st

322

Dm7(no3) CDE 2nd Dm7(no3) Bdim 2nd

233

Dm7(no3) Dm7(no5) 1st Dm7(no3) F 4 #4

322

Dm7(no3) DEF 1st Dm7(no3) G7(no3) 2nd Dm7(no3) EFG 1st

7th no 3 in Root Position

Using reverse/descending motion

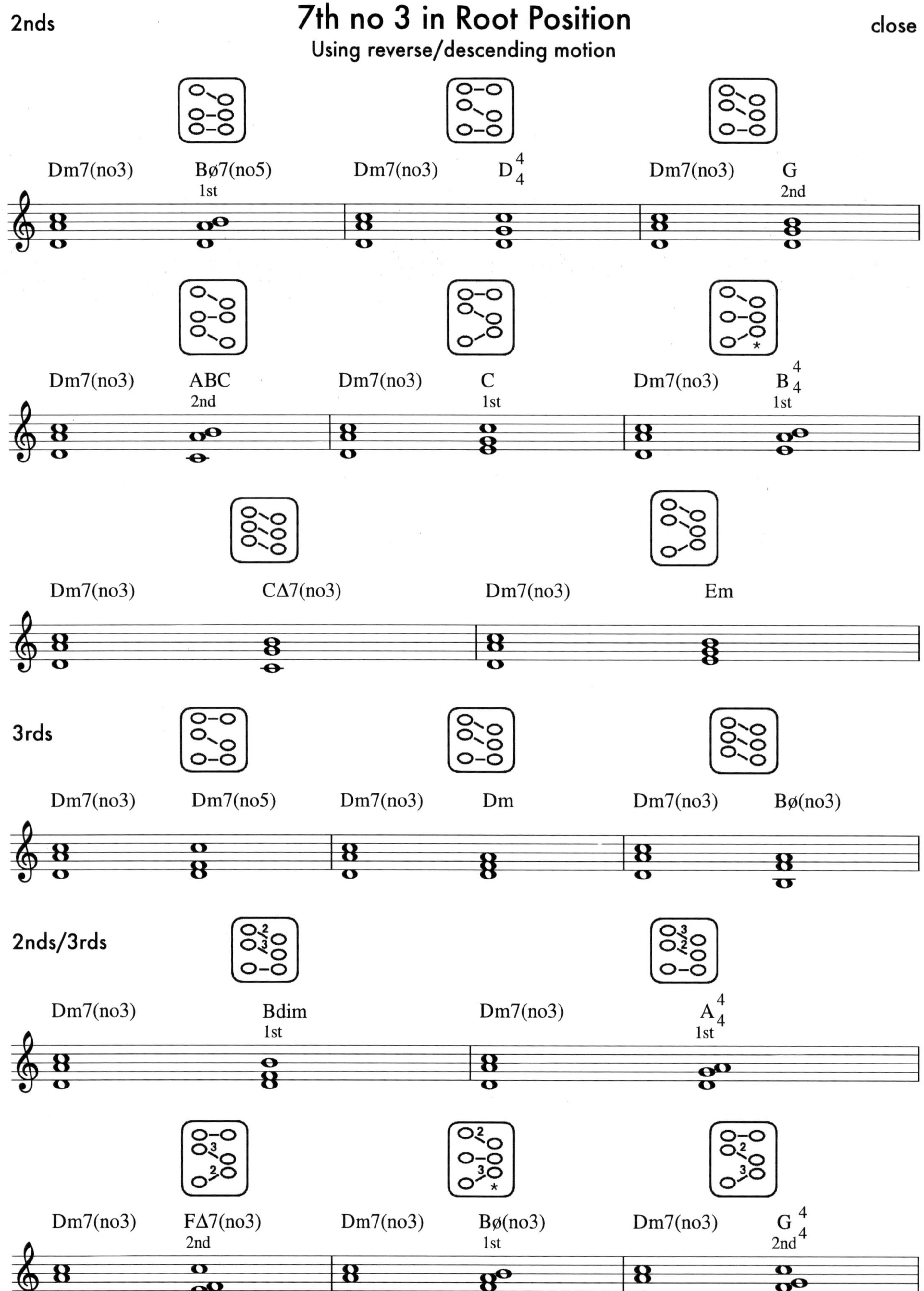

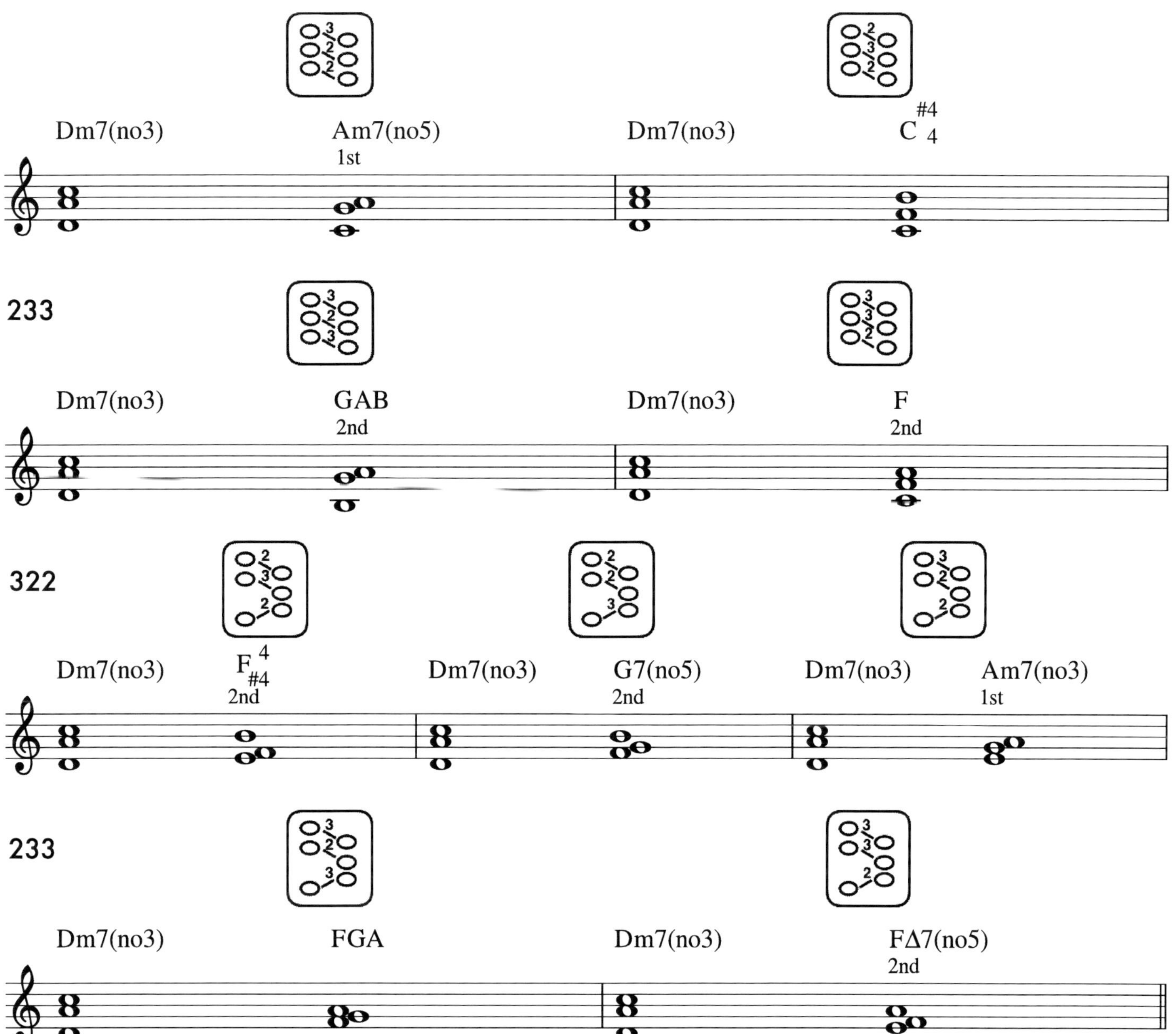
Dm7(no3)
Am7(no5)
1st
Dm7(no3)
C #4 4
233
Dm7(no3)
GAB
2nd
Dm7(no3)
F
2nd
322
Dm7(no3)
F 4 #4
2nd
Dm7(no3)
G7(no5)
2nd
Dm7(no3)
Am7(no3)
1st
233
Dm7(no3)
FGA
Dm7(no3)
FΔ7(no5)
2nd

Clusters in 1st Inversion

Using regular/ascending motion

2nds close

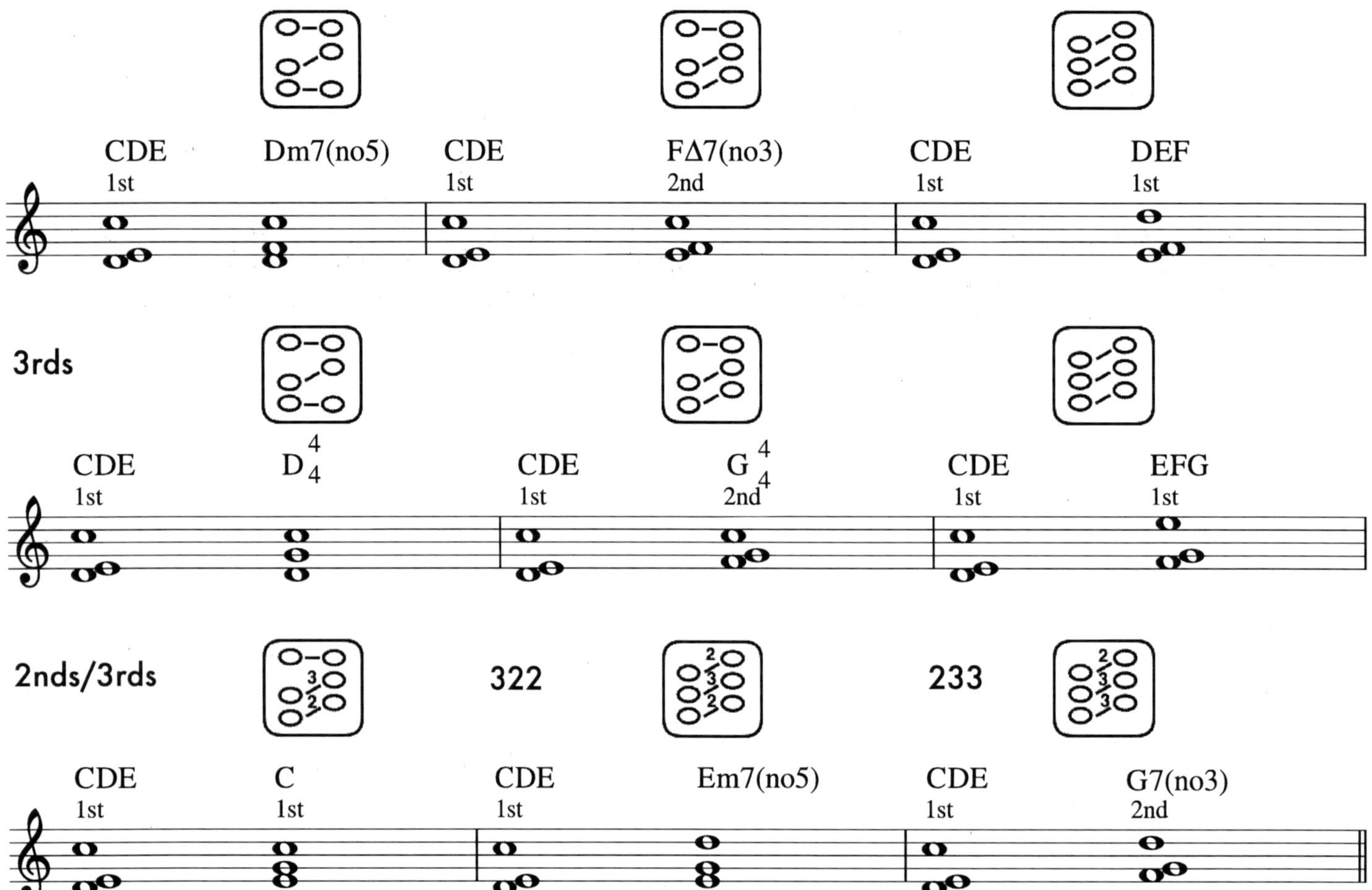

2nds

Clusters in 1st Inversion

Using reverse/descending motion

close

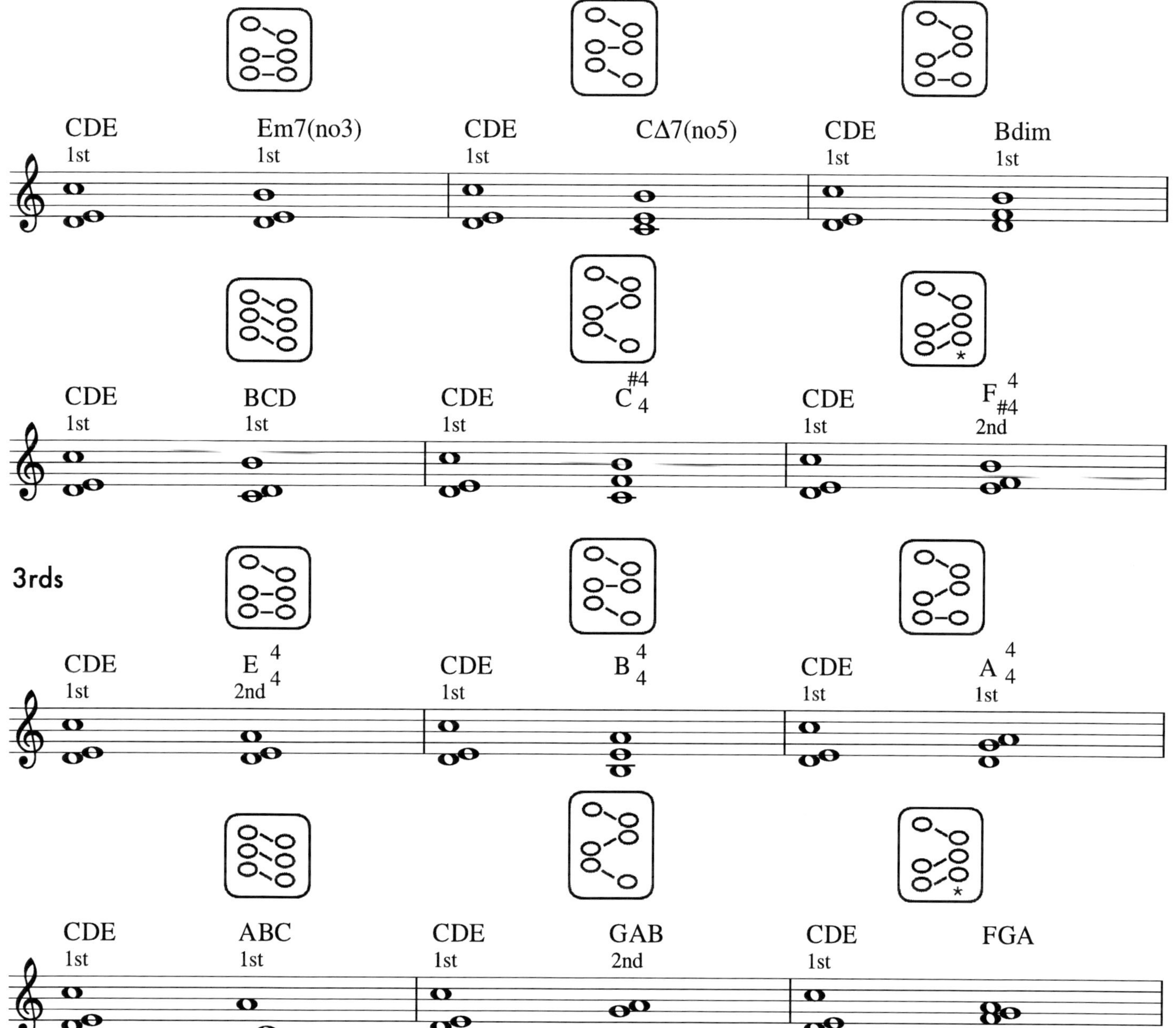

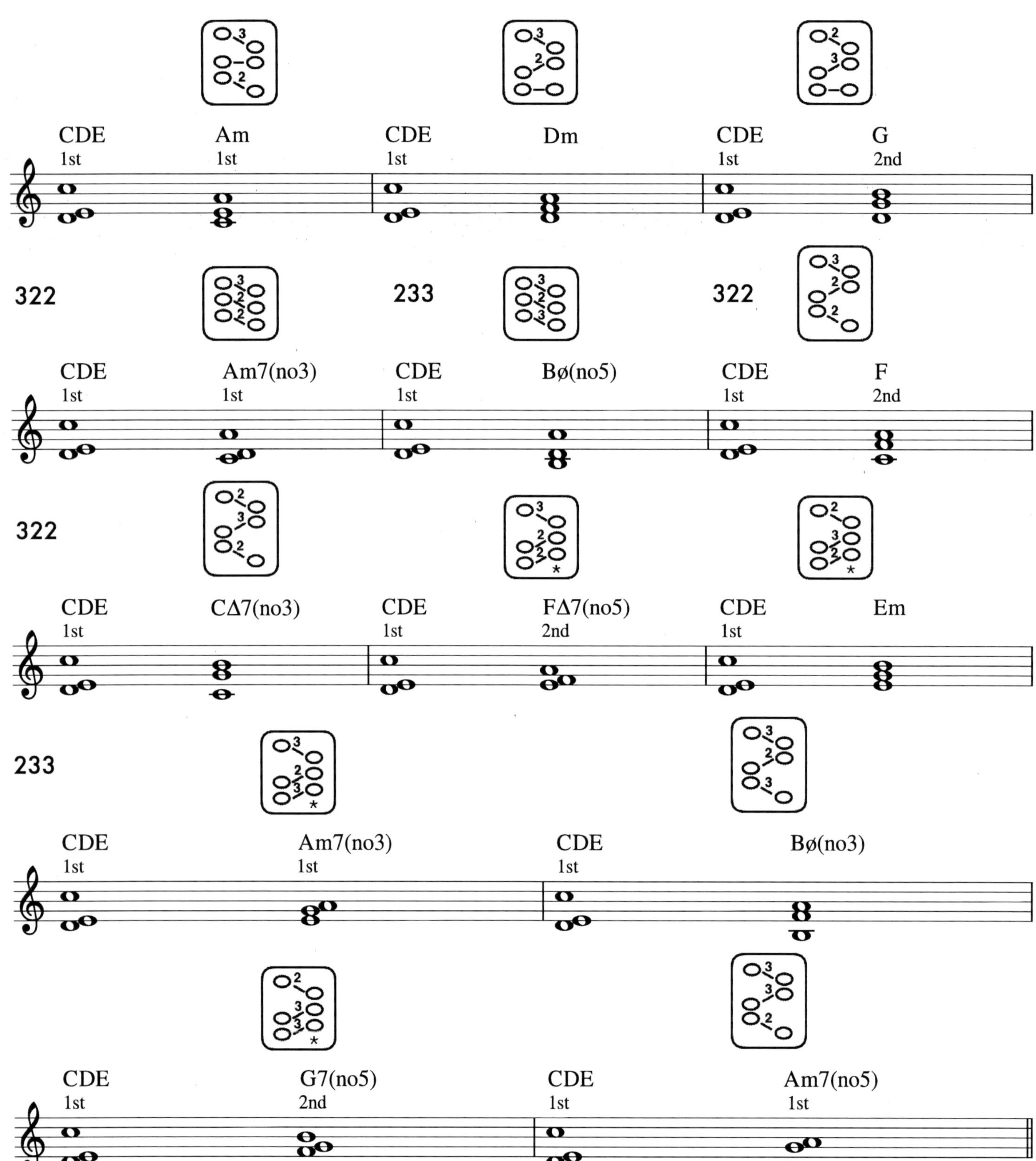
CDE
1st
Am
1st
CDE
1st
Dm
CDE
1st
G
2nd
322
233
322
CDE
1st
Am7(no3)
1st
CDE
1st
Bø(no5)
CDE
1st
F
2nd
322
CDE
1st
CΔ7(no3)
CDE
1st
FΔ7(no5)
2nd
CDE
1st
Em
233
CDE
1st
Am7(no3)
1st
CDE
1st
Bø(no3)
CDE
1st
G7(no5)
2nd
CDE
1st
Am7(no5)
1st

2nds

Clusters in 2nd Inversion

Using regular/ascending motion

close

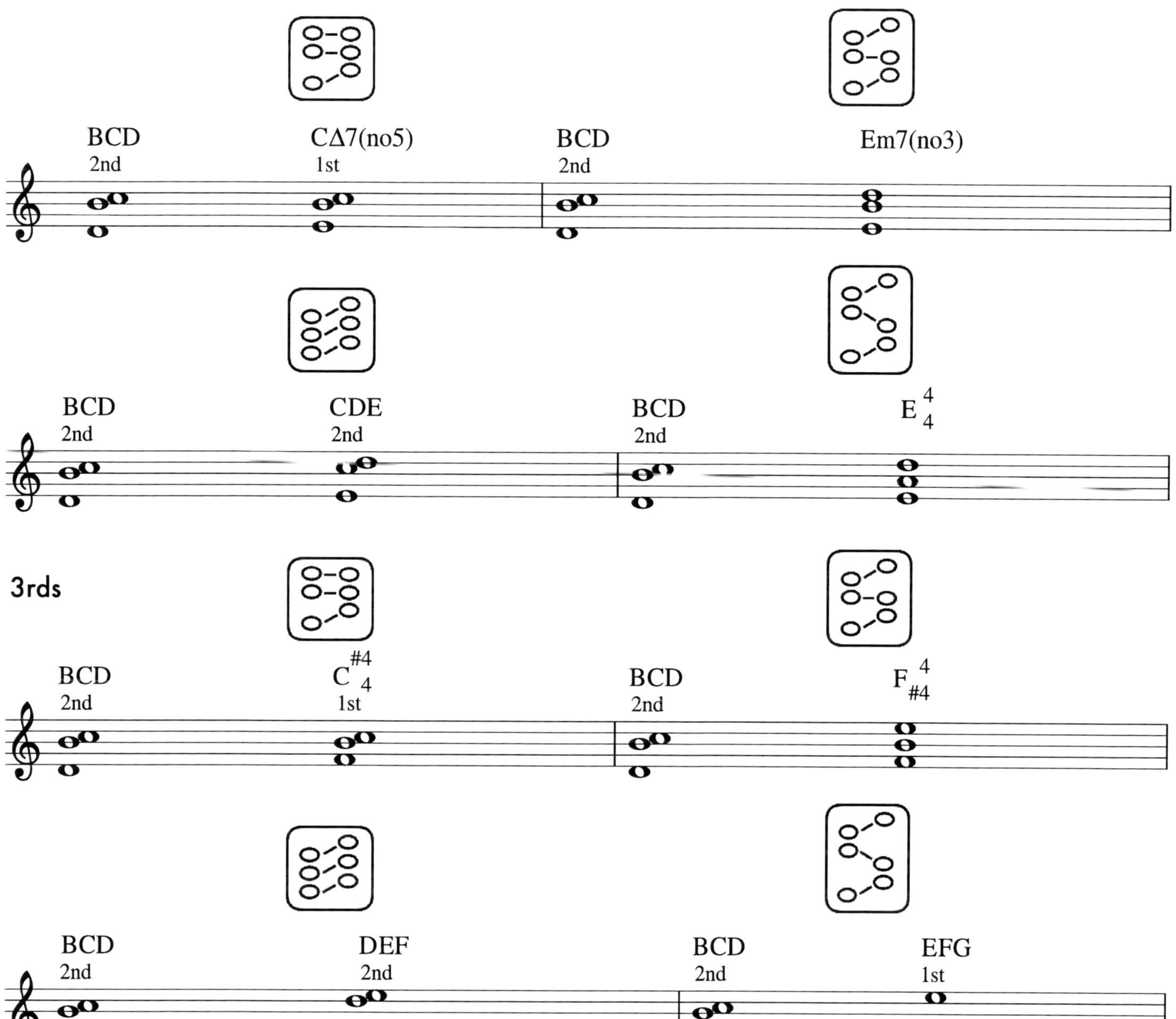

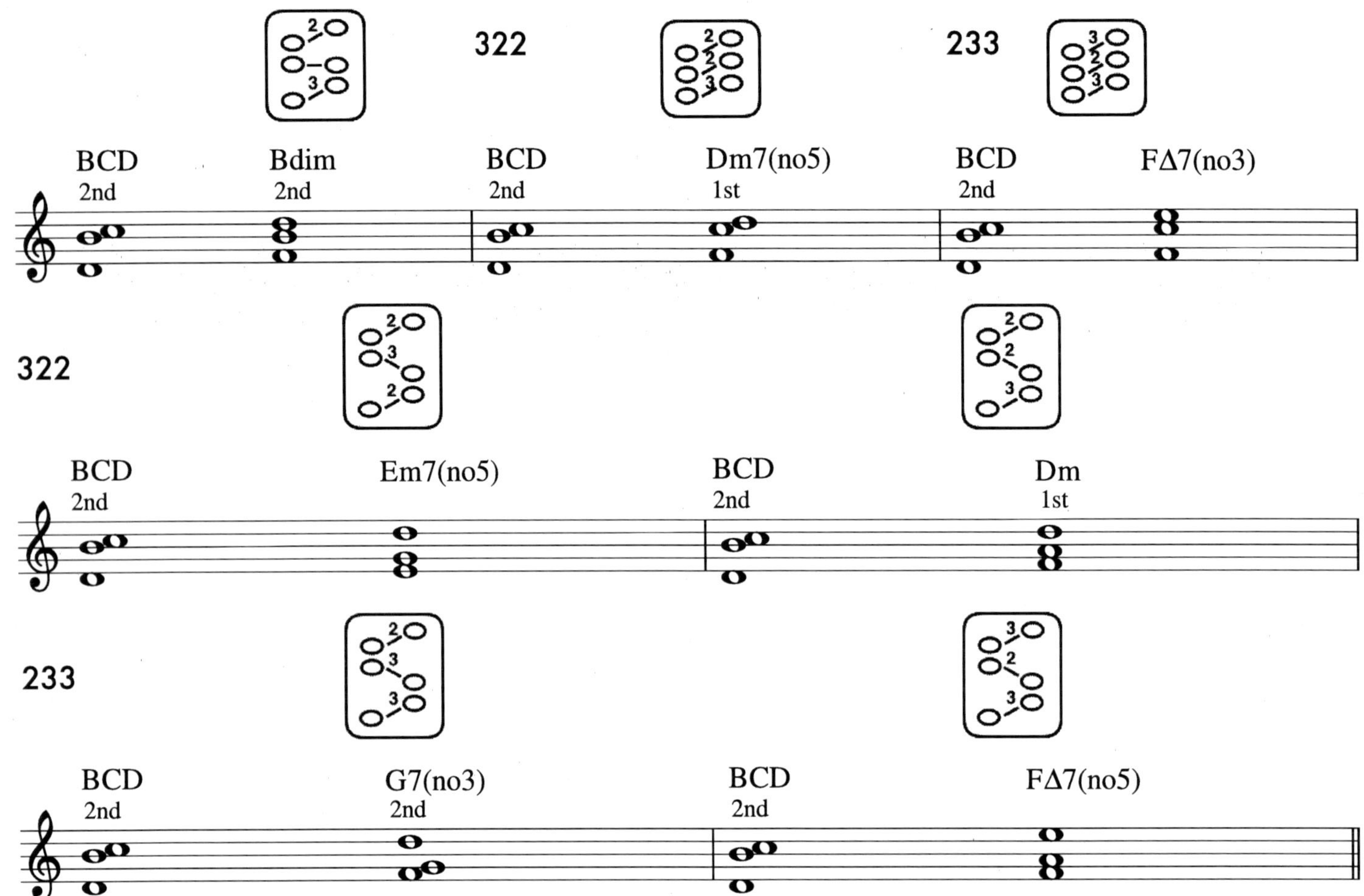
322
233
BCD
2nd
Bdim
2nd
BCD
2nd
Dm7(no5)
1st
BCD
2nd
FΔ7(no3)
322
BCD
2nd
Em7(no5)
BCD
2nd
Dm
1st
233
BCD
2nd
G7(no3)
2nd
BCD
2nd
FΔ7(no5)

2nds

Clusters in 2nd Inversion

Using reverse/descending motion

close

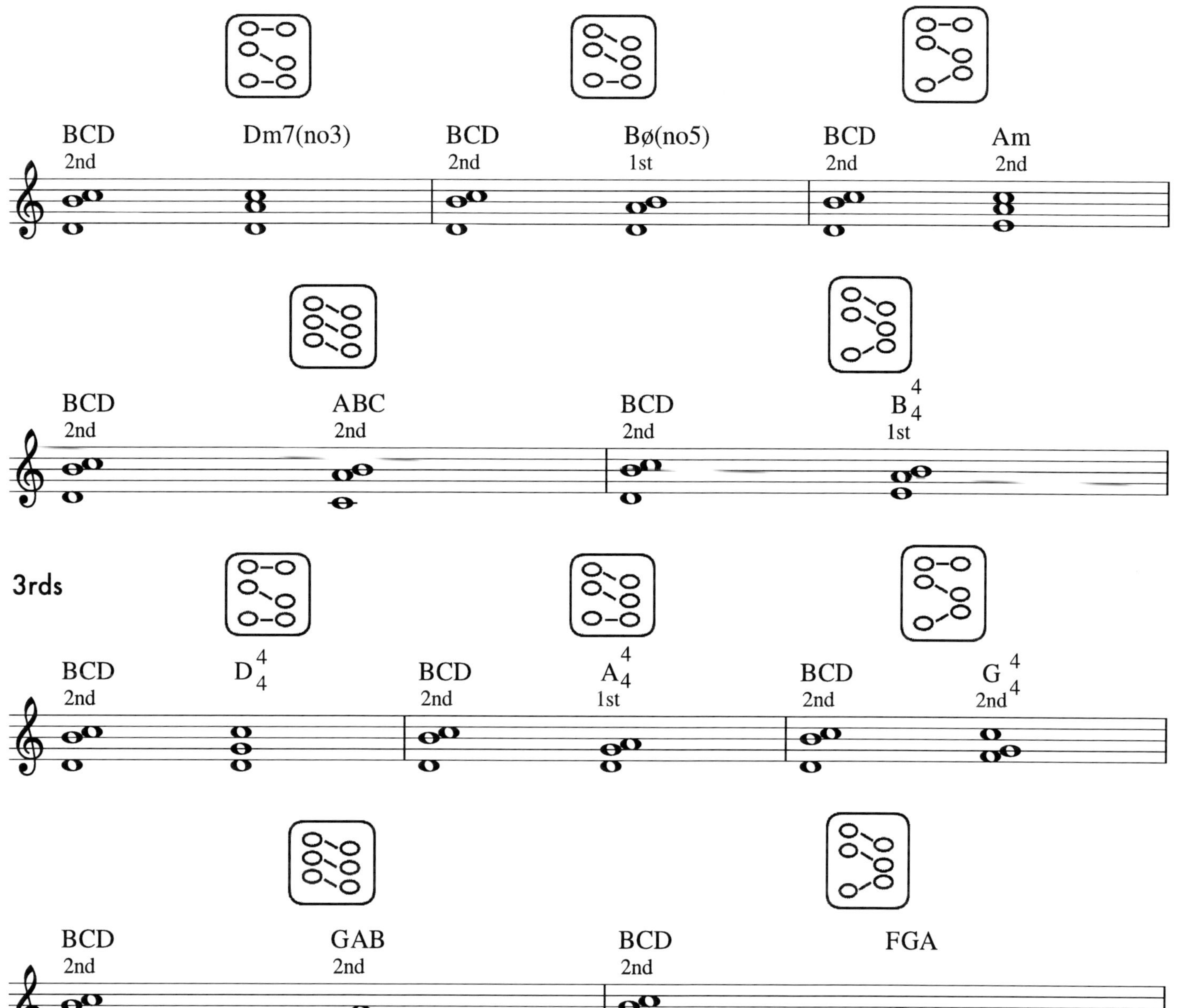

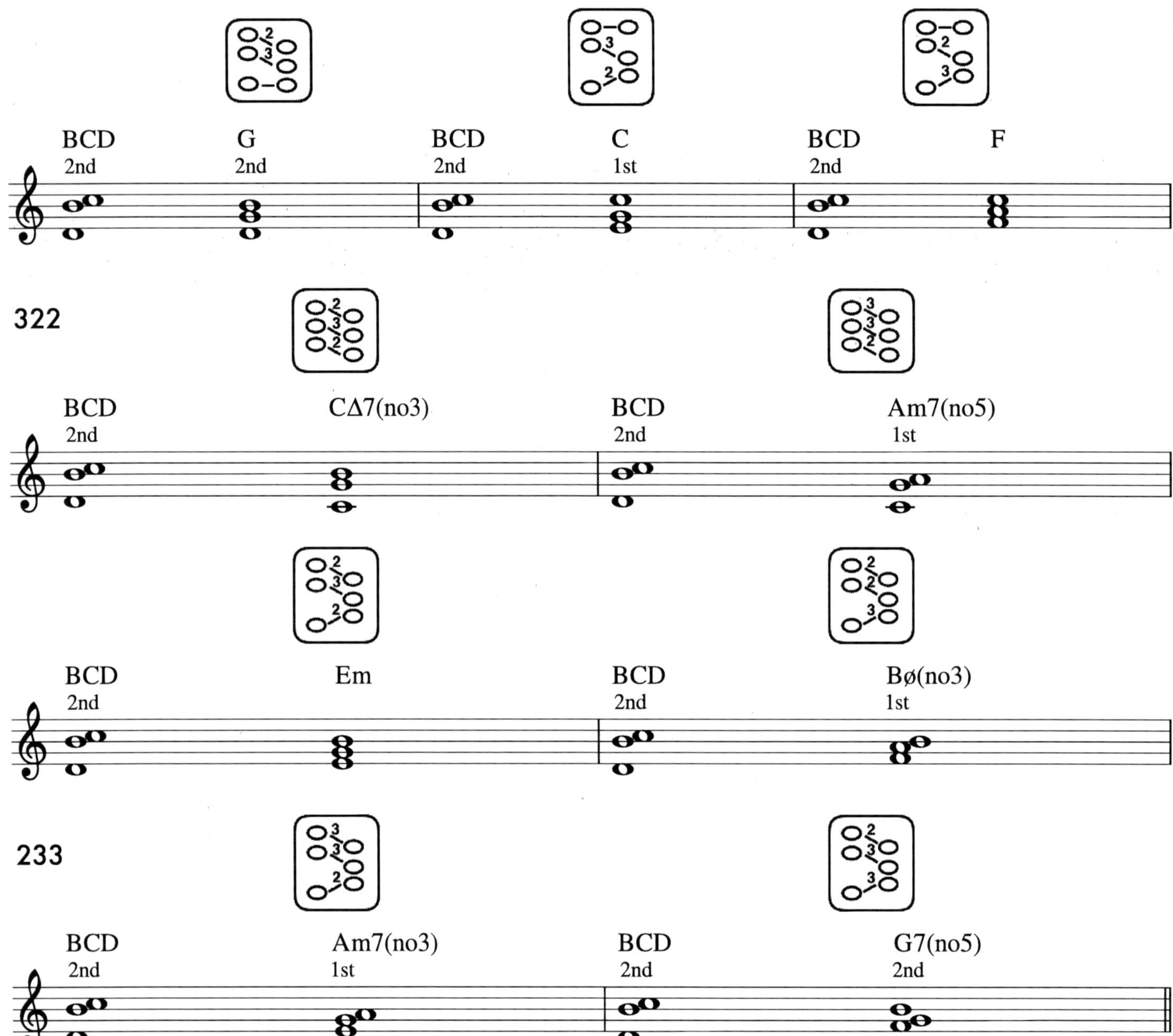
BCD
2nd
G
2nd
BCD
2nd
C
1st
BCD
2nd
F
322
BCD
2nd
CΔ7(no3)
BCD
2nd
Am7(no5)
1st
BCD
2nd
Em
BCD
2nd
Bø(no3)
1st
233
BCD
2nd
Am7(no3)
1st
BCD
2nd
G7(no5)
2nd

2nds

Clusters in Root Position

close

Using regular/ascending motion

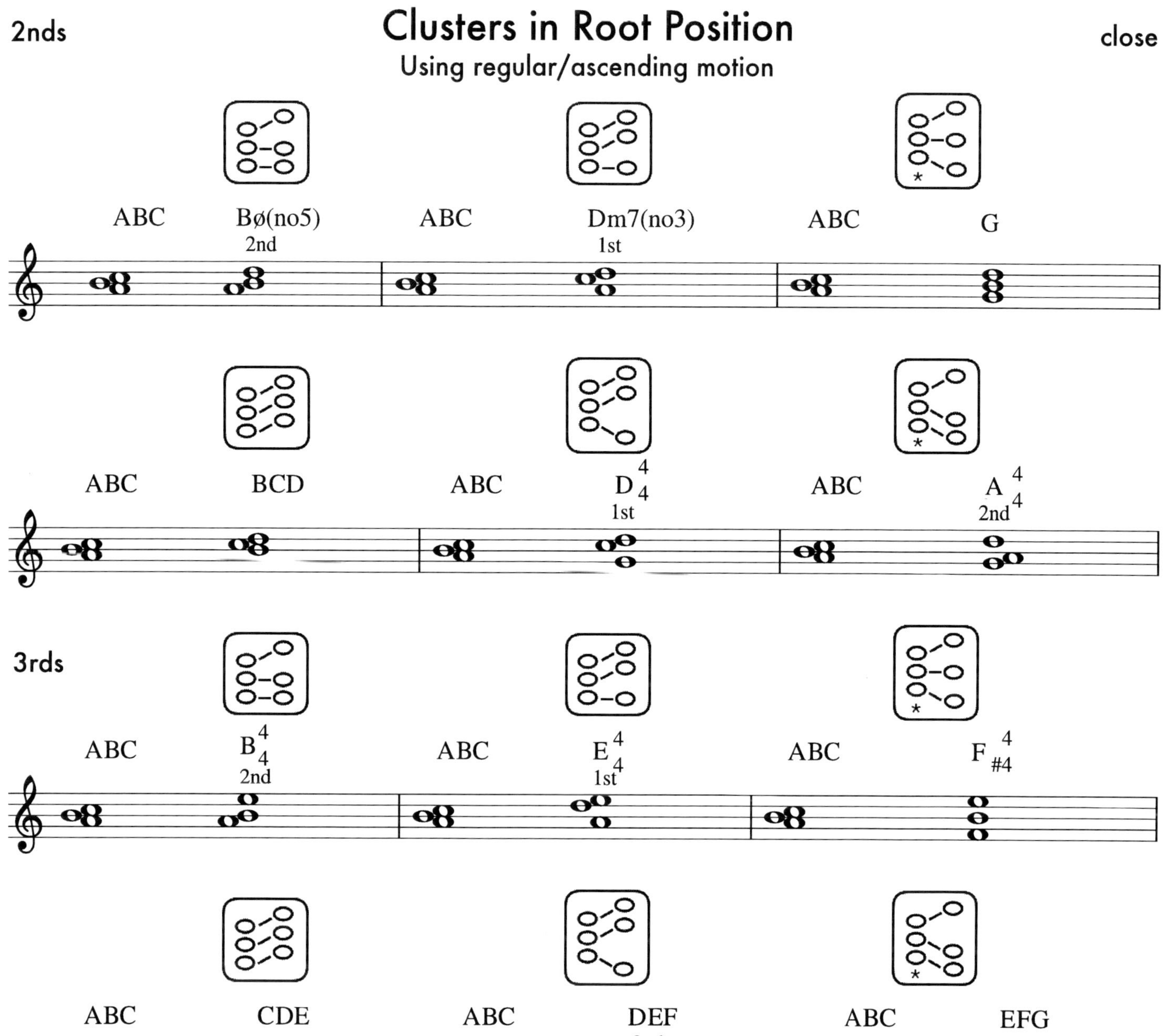

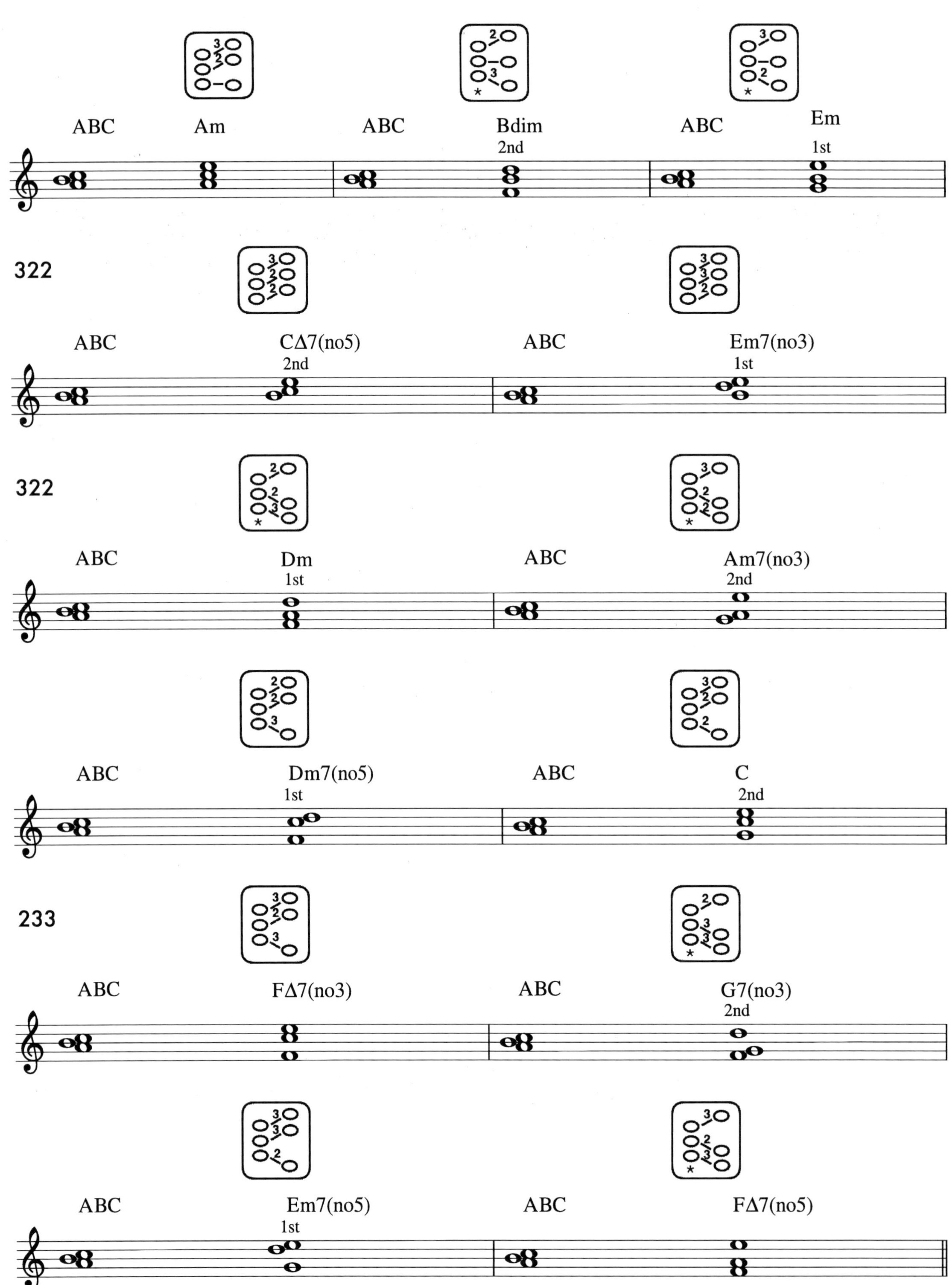
ABC
Am
ABC
Bdim
2nd
ABC
Em
1st
322
ABC
CΔ7(no5)
2nd
ABC
Em7(no3)
1st
322
ABC
Dm
1st
ABC
Am7(no3)
2nd
ABC
Dm7(no5)
1st
ABC
C
2nd
233
ABC
FΔ7(no3)
ABC
G7(no3)
2nd
ABC
Em7(no5)
1st
ABC
FΔ7(no5)

2nds

Clusters in Root Position

close

Using reverse/descending motion

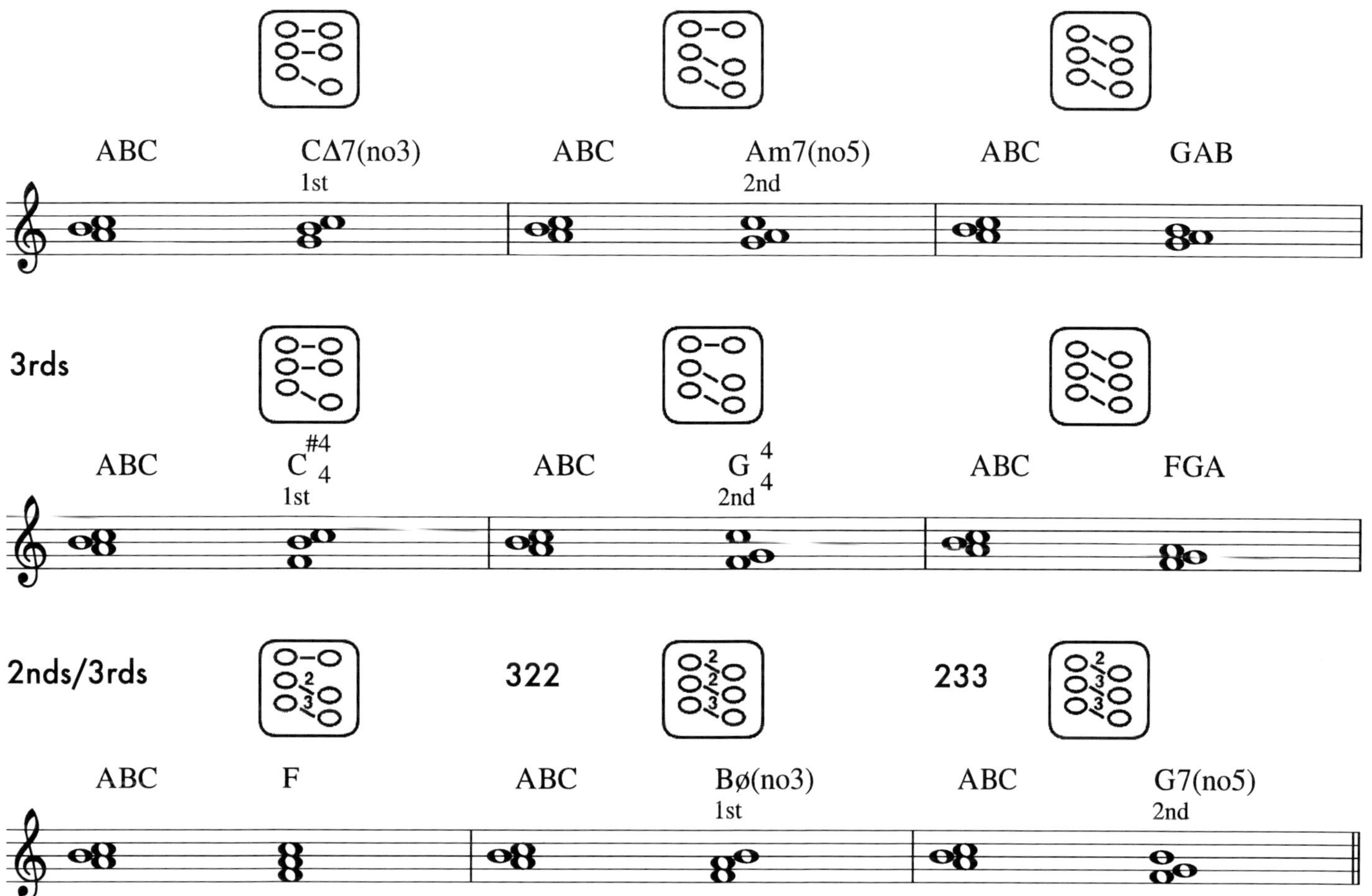

The short guitar solo piece on the next page brings Part 1 to a close.
Composed in strictly close-voiced, three-part harmony with the intermediate to advanced student in mind, it shows the application of various voice motion moves presented on the previous pages.
The voice motion gets progressively more polyphonic throughout the piece.
Depending on your interest, analyze the specific moves, chord structures, scales and keys used in the composition.

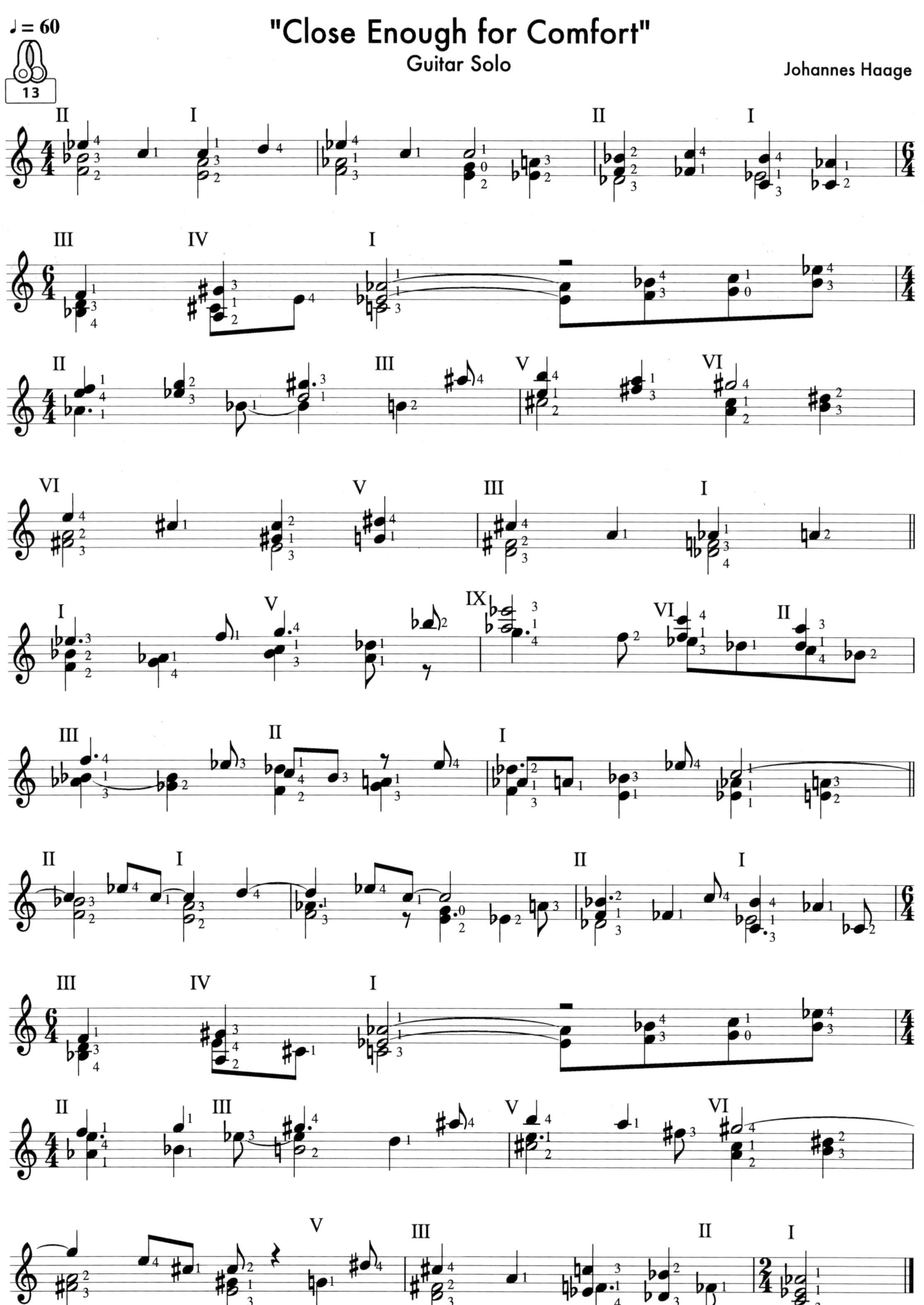
♩ = 60
13
"Close Enough for Comfort"
Guitar Solo
Johannes Haage

PART TWO: Open Voicing

OVERVIEW

This chapter will teach you how to create wider ranging open voicings on the basis of the previously learned close-voiced chord structures by dropping the middle voice down one octave (drop-2), and how to identify, categorize and practice these new chord structures on your instrument.

The full list of all possible voice motion moves in open (d2) voicing is presented
in two ways, parallel to Part 1:
First, in the order of motion type (2A)
and then ordered by their harmonic point of departure (2B).

Another short solo guitar piece composed strictly in three-part open (d2) harmony ends the section, applying the moves to create melodic voice movement.

CONTENTS

INTRODUCTION: OPEN VOICINGS

Part 2 essentially presents the same material as the Part 1, but all chord structures are in open voicing (drop-2).
The middle voices (or second ones from the top) of the close-voiced chords of Part 1 are dropped down one octave (thus, drop-2 or d2), producing a wider intervallic range of the chord structures.

Notice that after dropping the middle voice of a close-voiced chord, its name/inversion changes: For example, dropping the third of a close voiced root position triad down an octave makes it an open-voiced 1st inversion triad (drop-2).

In this book, the inversions are always named after the lowest sounding note, regardless of the type of voicing:
The 1st inversion always has the second lowest (middle) voice of the close-voiced root position chord structure as the bottom note, whereas the 2nd inversion will always have the upper voice of the close-voiced root position chord structure in the bottom.

Here is an example with all three inversions of the C major triad, close-voiced and open (d2):

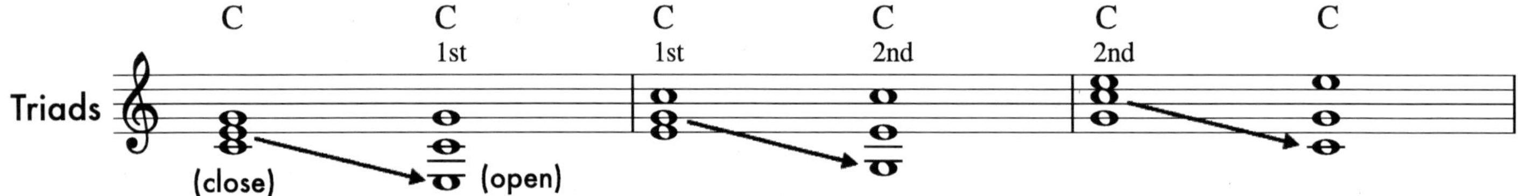

"Drop-2" is the most common, and arguably the most applicable and versatile type of three-note open voicing.

There are other possible open voicing types which can be derived from the close-voiced material in Part 1 as well, by dropping other or more voices; like drop-3 or drop 2&3, etc.
They yield many interesting sounds and possibilites. Do explore them depending on your personal interest. (See Part 3E "The Big Picture")

The order of the pages of Part 2 are analogous to Part 1, so all individual chords, motions etc. can be compared directly.

Some of the open voicings shown will go down as far as the low D.
On the guitar, use drop-D tuning, or take the chord/motion higher up the scale so the voicings get into the playable range of your instrument.

Parallel to Part 1, here are all five chord types and its two inversions in open voicing (d2), built from the note C'.

open

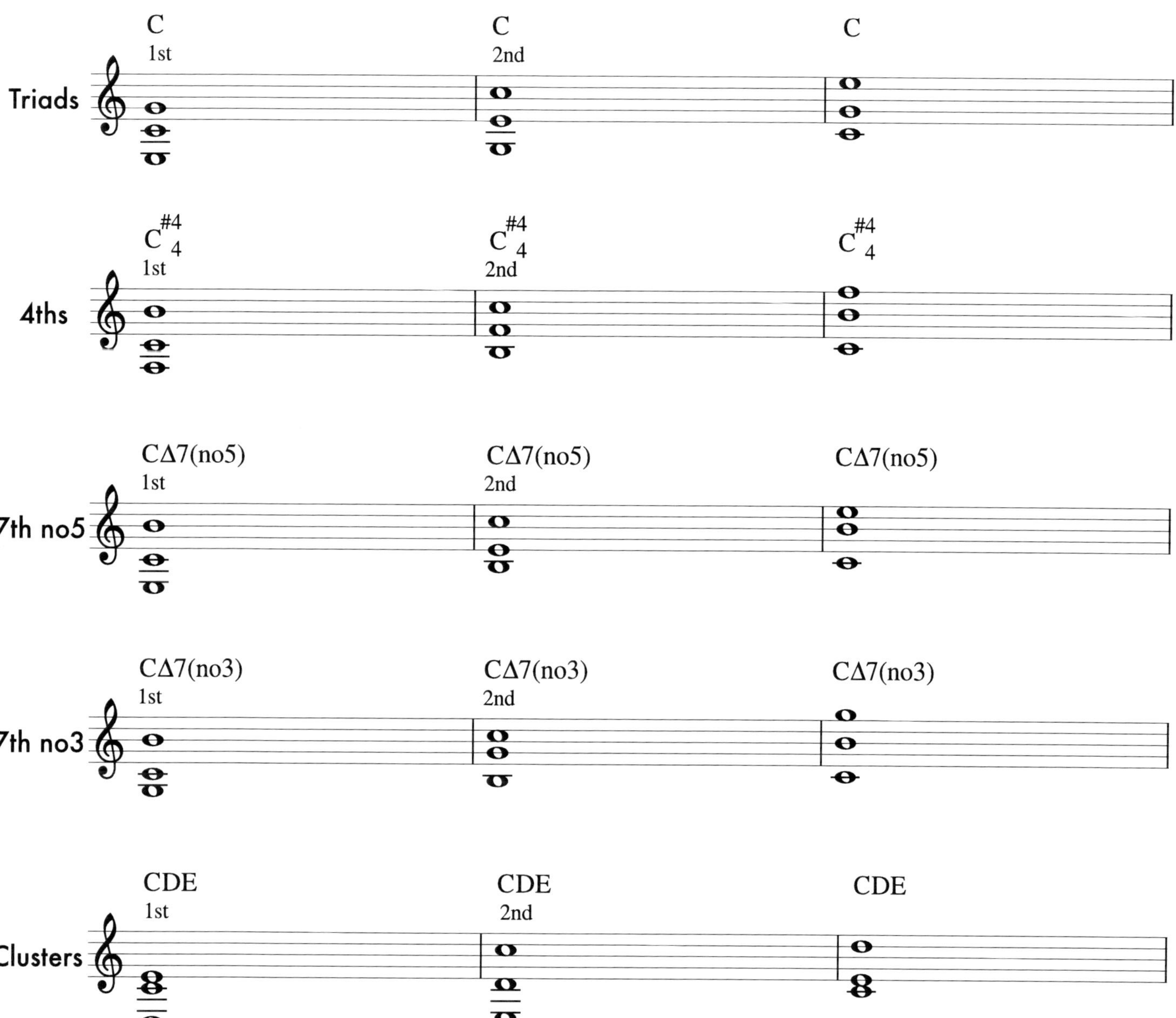

These are the 15 possible three-part, open-voiced "C"- chord structures contained within the C major diatonic scale.

Write the 15 similar voicing changes based on the other six scale degrees; then play all 105 different three-part chord structures (15x7=105) within the C major diatonic scale, or any other balanced heptatonic, see Part 3A "Heptatonics".

Throughout Part 2 and the rest of the book, these 15 chord structures will be used to show all possible open-voiced starting points for various melodic voice motions within the diatonic scale.

For better comparability and clarity, we now move the 15 structures into the same range, so each has the note C" as its upper voice:

open

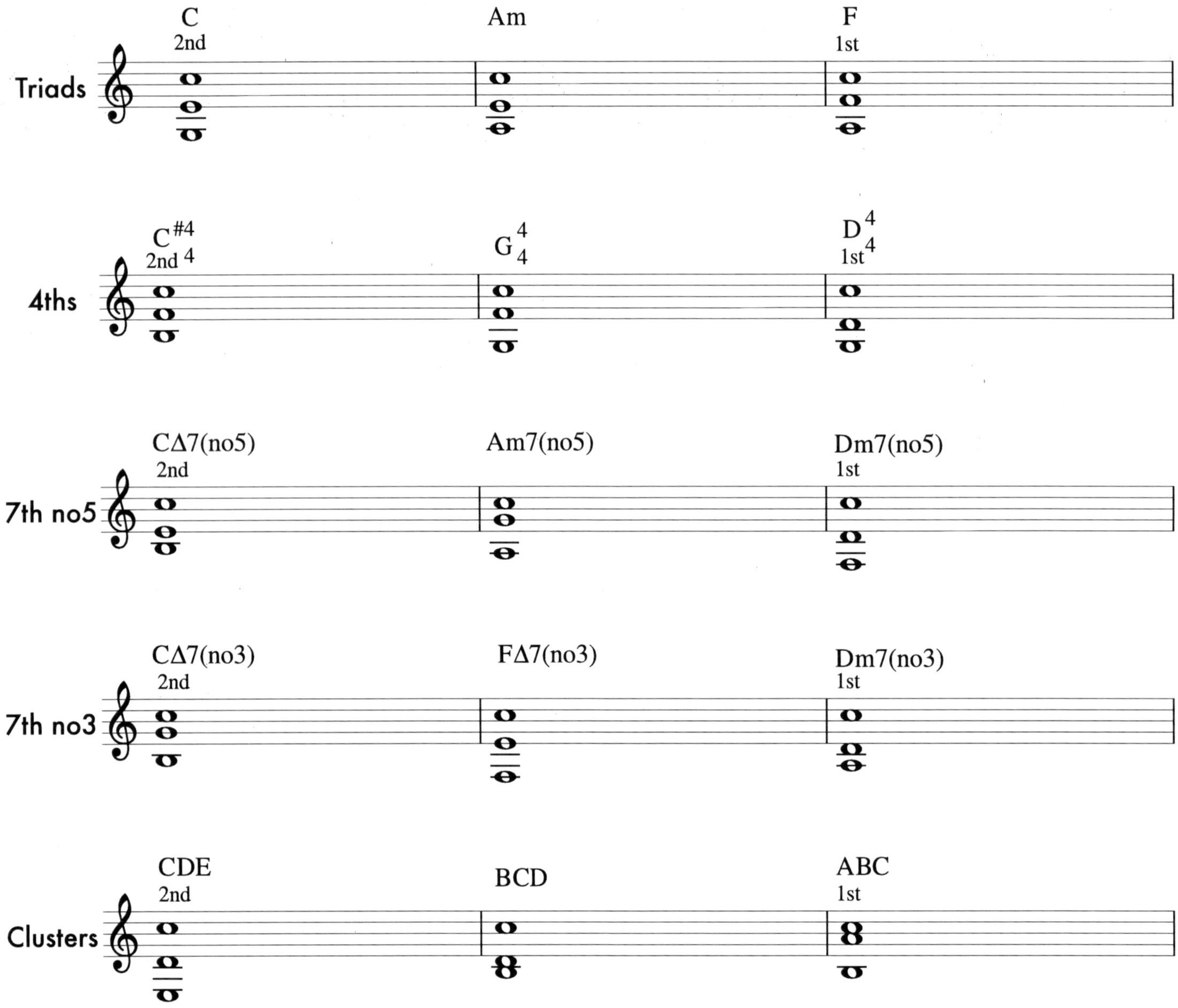

Triads: C 2nd | Am | F 1st

4ths: C#4 2nd 4 | G 4 4 | D 4 1st 4

7th no5: CΔ7(no5) 2nd | Am7(no5) | Dm7(no5) 1st

7th no3: CΔ7(no3) 2nd | FΔ7(no3) | Dm7(no3) 1st

Clusters: CDE 2nd | BCD | ABC 1st

As preparation for Part 2 of this book, practice playing and identifying each of these 15 chords.

Then take each one up and down the C major diatonic scale throughout the full range of your instrument; see the next page for examples.

Make sure you are able to identify and name each chord on any scale degree at all times. Also refer to Part 3A "Heptatonics" for this ability.

VOICE MOTION PREPARATORY EXERCISES for Part Two

open

This page shows some basic ways to take the open-voiced 2nd inversion C major triad (d2) up and down the diatonic scale in seconds and/or thirds, moving all three voices in parallel.

Apply these exercises to all of the 15 chords on the previous page, in all keys.

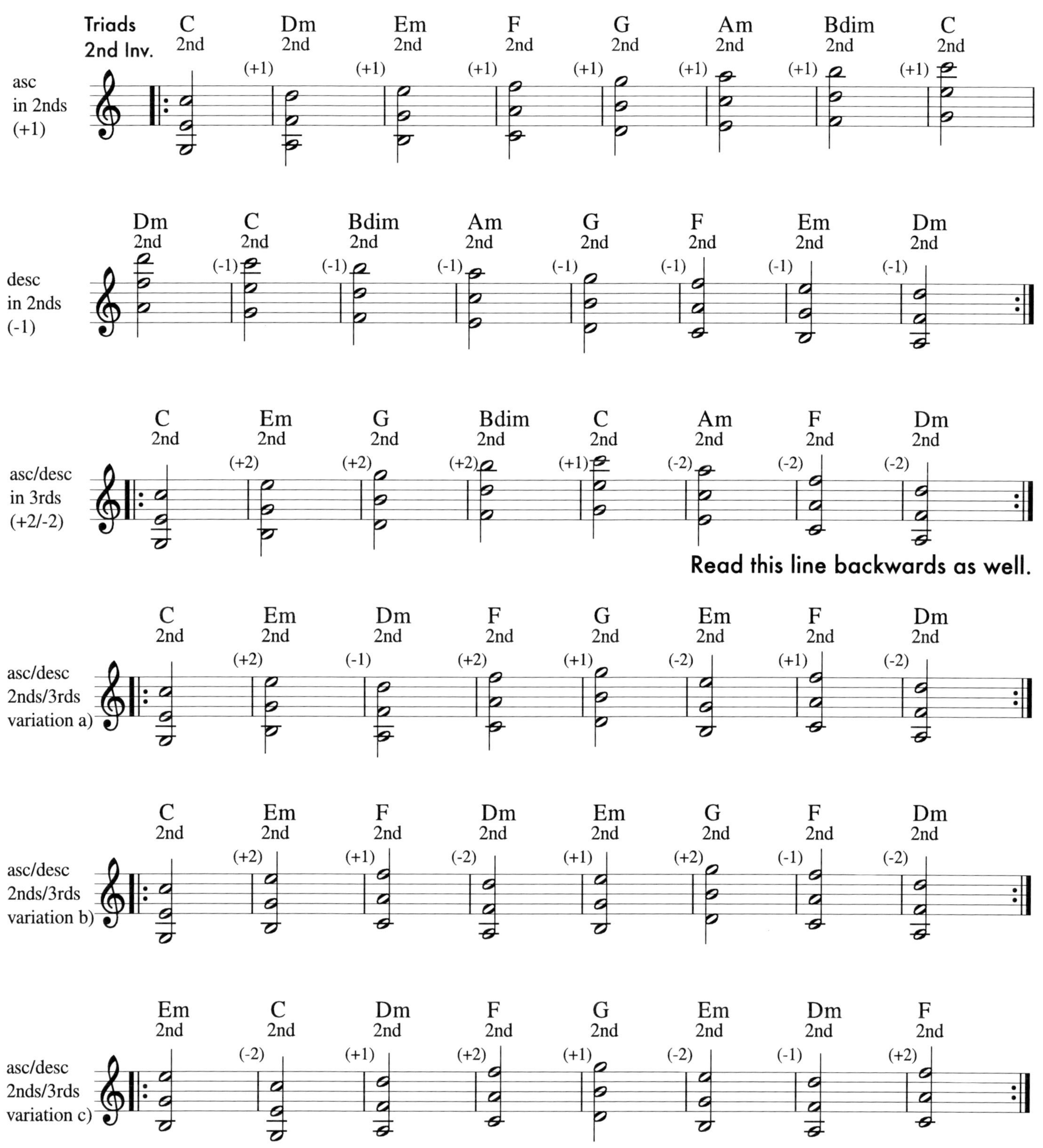

Play the last 3 lines throughout the full range of your instrument and then read them in reverse order as well.

To further prepare for Part 2 of this book, we re-arrange the 15 open-voiced chord structures with the top note C" in the order of their intervallic range, analogous to Part 1, from widest (spanning an interval of a 13th or an octave +5 steps) to closest (spanning a 9th/octave +1).

Read and play through the chords line by line (horizontally), column by column (vertically), and from top right to bottom left (diagonally) and back.

Take note of common notes between each chord, and of any resulting voice movement.

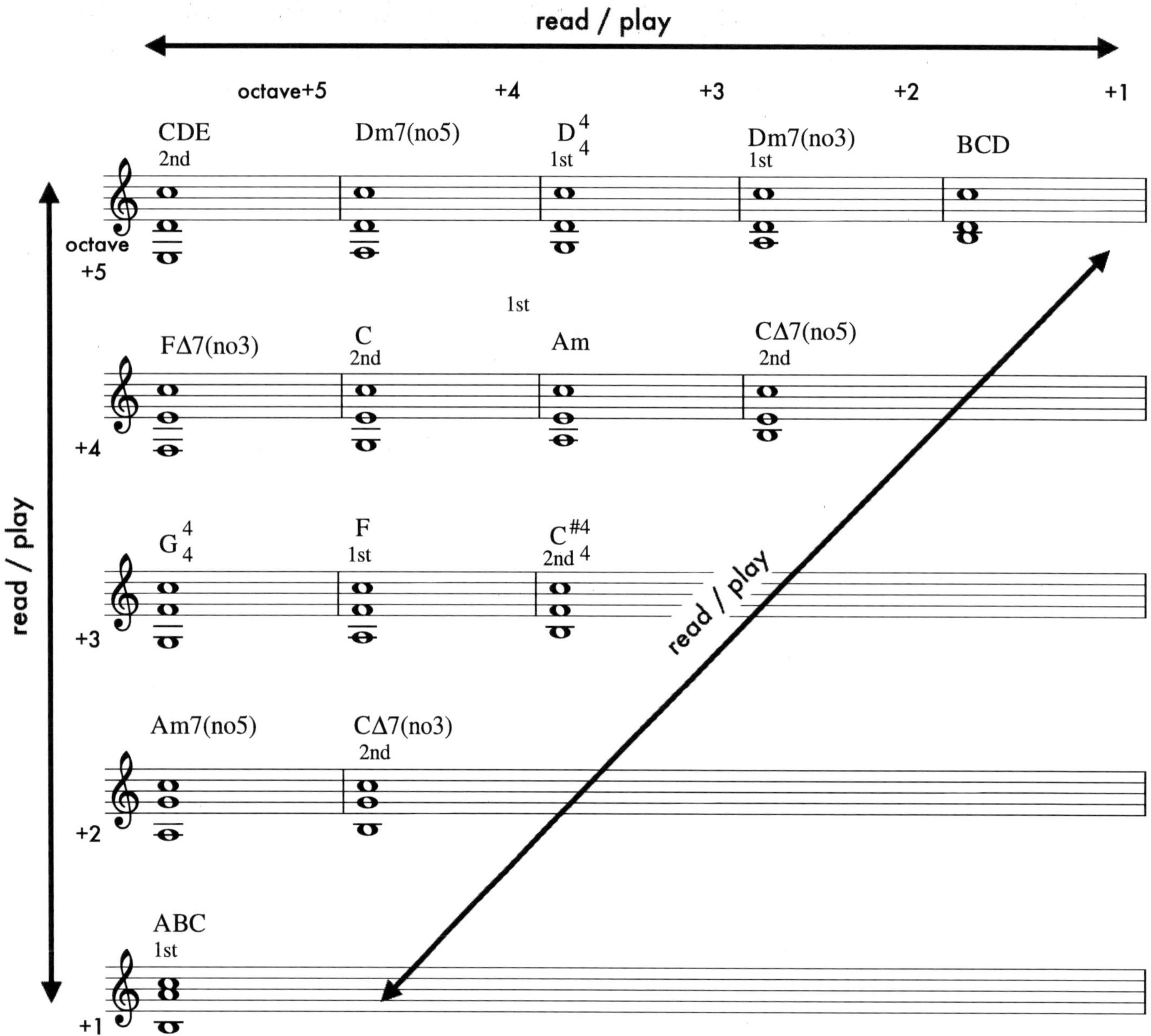

Part 2 will show the same 108 moves that were introduced in Part 1, but in open (d2) voicing.

Compare all chords, moves and motions of both parts, taking note of the differences and/or similarities in playability, sound, aesthetics, applicability, etc.
Refer to the Introduction of Part 1 for exercises to practice all motions with the leading voice moving up/down a 2nd or 3rd, and apply them to the open voicings.

Practice all moves of Part 2 that way, in all inversions and keys.

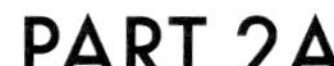

PART 2A

The 108 Possible Moves in Open Voicing
(Drop-2)

Read every page of this section both horizontally (lines) and vertically (columns).

Apply all of the exercises of the introduction throughout the full range of your instrument, in all keys.

GRAPHICAL OVERVIEW OF ALL MOTION TYPES in PART TWO

(open voicing)

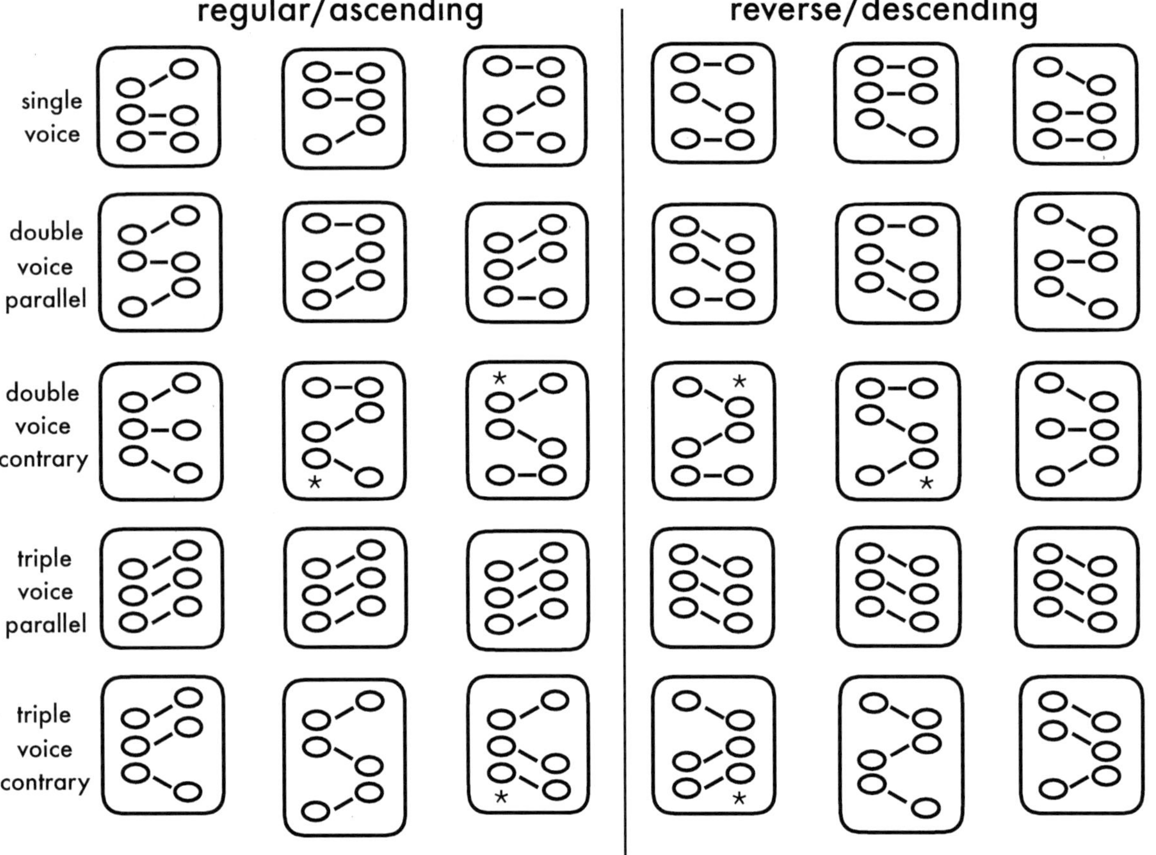

Single-Voice Motion

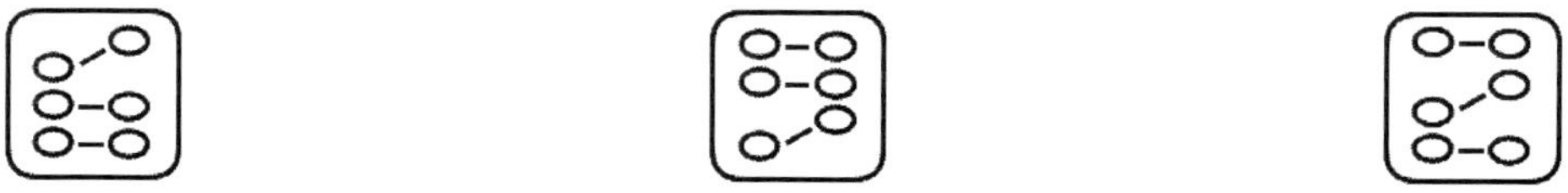

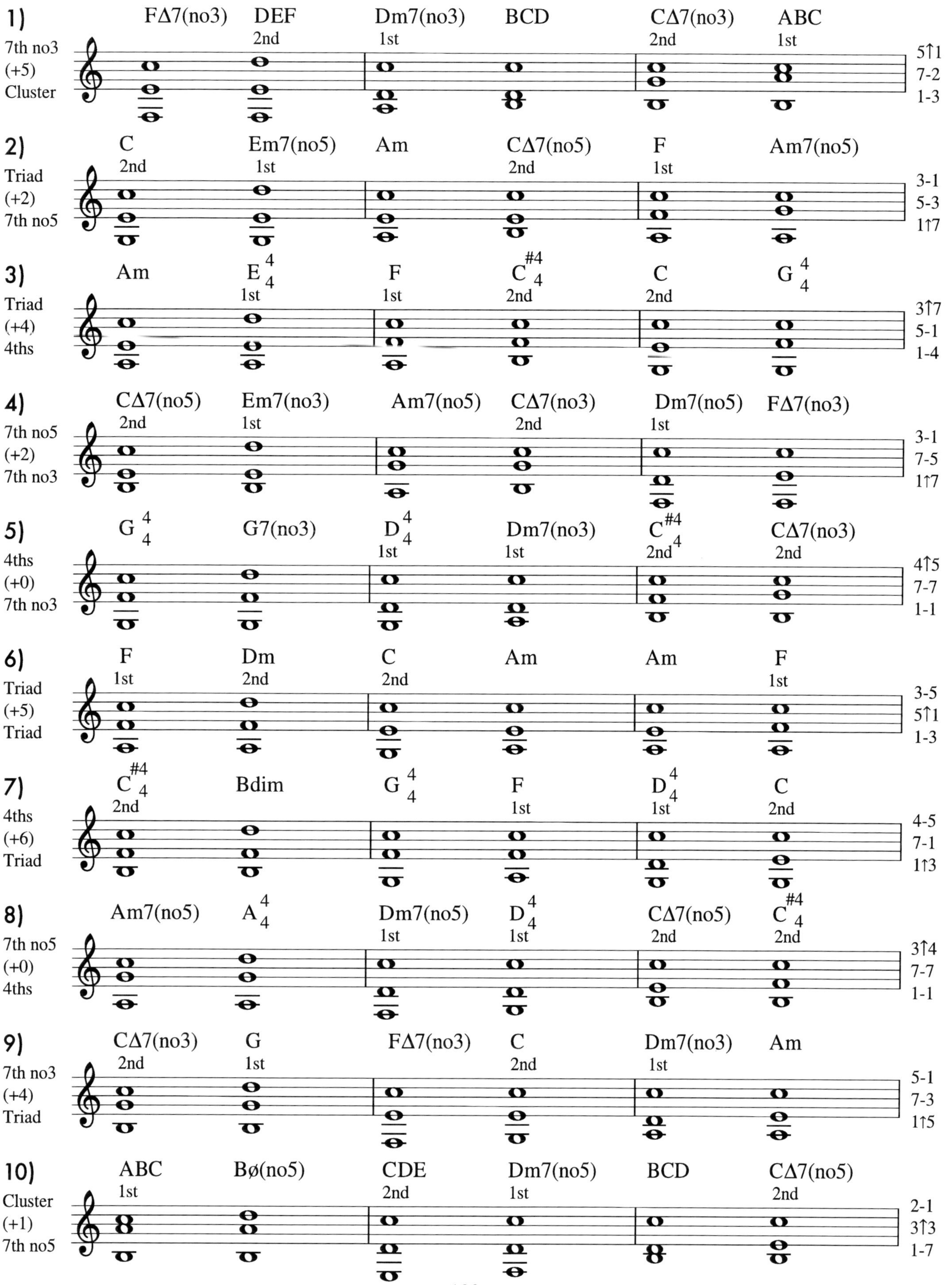

1)

7th no3
(+5)
Cluster

FΔ7(no3)	DEF	Dm7(no3)	BCD	CΔ7(no3)	ABC
	2nd	1st		2nd	1st

5↑1
7-2
1-3

2)

Triad
(+2)
7th no5

C	Em7(no5)	Am	CΔ7(no5)	F	Am7(no5)
2nd	1st		2nd	1st	

3-1
5-3
1↑7

3)

Triad
(+4)
4ths

Am	E^{4}_{4}	F	$C^{\#4}_{4}$	C	G^{4}_{4}
	1st	1st	2nd	2nd	

3↑7
5-1
1-4

4)

7th no5
(+2)
7th no3

CΔ7(no5)	Em7(no3)	Am7(no5)	CΔ7(no3)	Dm7(no5)	FΔ7(no3)
2nd	1st		2nd	1st	

3-1
7-5
1↑7

5)

4ths
(+0)
7th no3

G^{4}_{4}	G7(no3)	D^{4}_{4}	Dm7(no3)	$C^{\#4}_{4}$	CΔ7(no3)
		1st	1st	2nd	2nd

4↑5
7-7
1-1

6)

Triad
(+5)
Triad

F	Dm	C	Am	Am	F
1st	2nd	2nd			1st

3-5
5↑1
1-3

7)

4ths
(+6)
Triad

$C^{\#4}_{4}$	Bdim	G^{4}_{4}	F	D^{4}_{4}	C
2nd			1st	1st	2nd

4-5
7-1
1↑3

8)

7th no5
(+0)
4ths

Am7(no5)	A^{4}_{4}	Dm7(no5)	D^{4}_{4}	CΔ7(no5)	$C^{\#4}_{4}$
		1st	1st	2nd	2nd

3↑4
7-7
1-1

9)

7th no3
(+4)
Triad

CΔ7(no3)	G	FΔ7(no3)	C	Dm7(no3)	Am
2nd	1st		2nd	1st	

5-1
7-3
1↑5

10)

Cluster
(+1)
7th no5

ABC	Bø(no5)	CDE	Dm7(no5)	BCD	CΔ7(no5)
1st		2nd	1st		2nd

2-1
3↑3
1-7

Double-Voice Parallel Motion

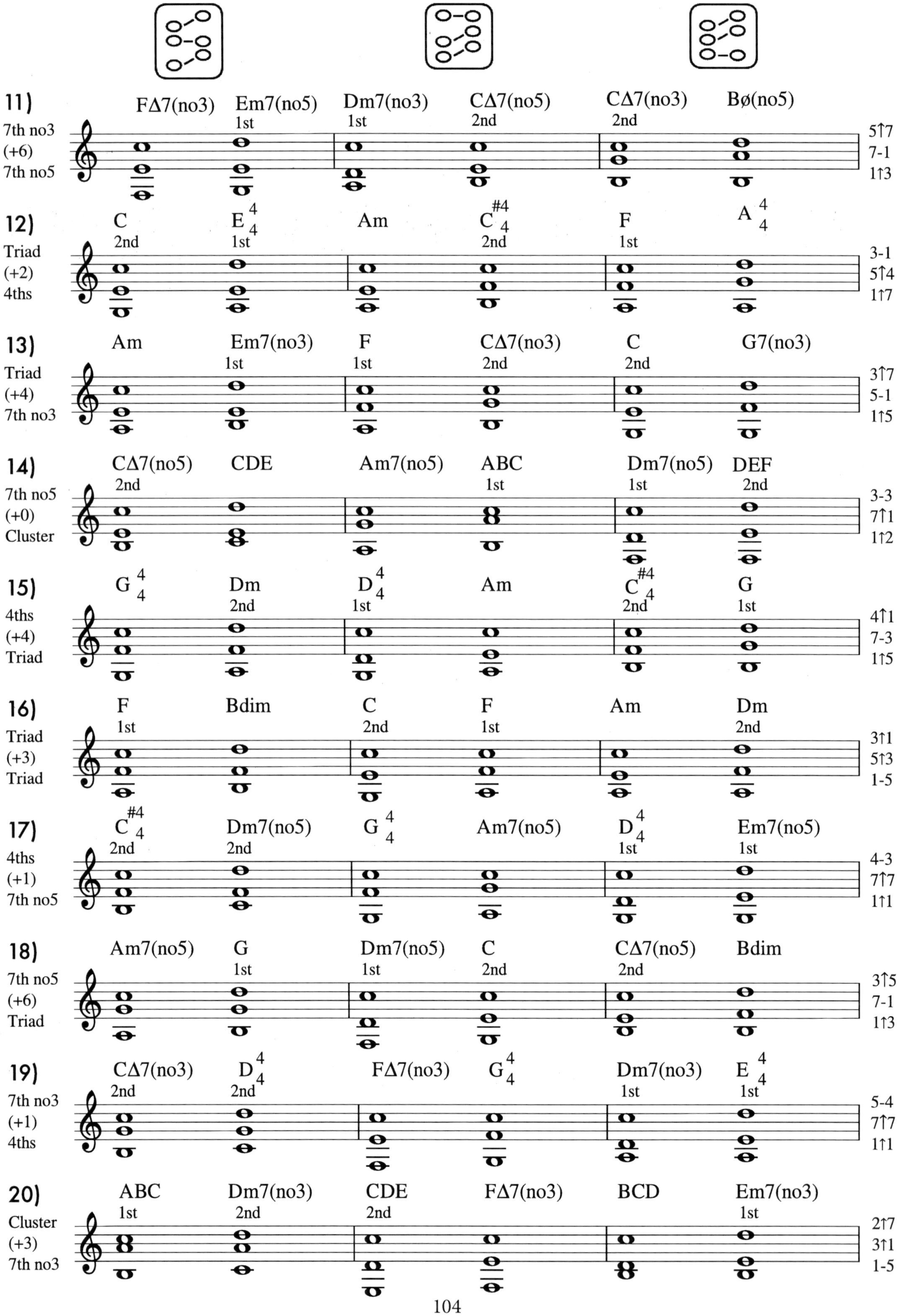

11) 7th no3 (+6) 7th no5

FΔ7(no3) — Em7(no5) 1st — Dm7(no3) 1st — CΔ7(no5) 2nd — CΔ7(no3) 2nd — Bø(no5)

5↑7, 7-1, 1↑3

12) Triad (+2) 4ths

C 2nd — E $^{4}_{4}$ 1st — Am — C $^{\#4}_{4}$ 2nd — F 1st — A $^{4}_{4}$

3-1, 5↑4, 1↑7

13) Triad (+4) 7th no3

Am — Em7(no3) 1st — F 1st — CΔ7(no3) 2nd — C 2nd — G7(no3)

3↑7, 5-1, 1↑5

14) 7th no5 (+0) Cluster

CΔ7(no5) 2nd — CDE — Am7(no5) — ABC 1st — Dm7(no5) 1st — DEF 2nd

3-3, 7↑1, 1↑2

15) 4ths (+4) Triad

G $^{4}_{4}$ — Dm 2nd — D $^{4}_{4}$ 1st — Am — C $^{\#4}_{4}$ 2nd — G 1st

4↑1, 7-3, 1↑5

16) Triad (+3) Triad

F 1st — Bdim — C 2nd — F 1st — Am — Dm 2nd

3↑1, 5↑3, 1-5

17) 4ths (+1) 7th no5

C $^{\#4}_{4}$ 2nd — Dm7(no5) 2nd — G $^{4}_{4}$ — Am7(no5) — D $^{4}_{4}$ 1st — Em7(no5) 1st

4-3, 7↑7, 1↑1

18) 7th no5 (+6) Triad

Am7(no5) — G 1st — Dm7(no5) 1st — C 2nd — CΔ7(no5) 2nd — Bdim

3↑5, 7-1, 1↑3

19) 7th no3 (+1) 4ths

CΔ7(no3) 2nd — D $^{4}_{4}$ 2nd — FΔ7(no3) — G $^{4}_{4}$ — Dm7(no3) 1st — E $^{4}_{4}$ 1st

5-4, 7↑7, 1↑1

20) Cluster (+3) 7th no3

ABC 1st — Dm7(no3) 2nd — CDE 2nd — FΔ7(no3) — BCD — Em7(no3) 1st

2↑7, 3↑1, 1-5

Double-Voice Contrary Motion

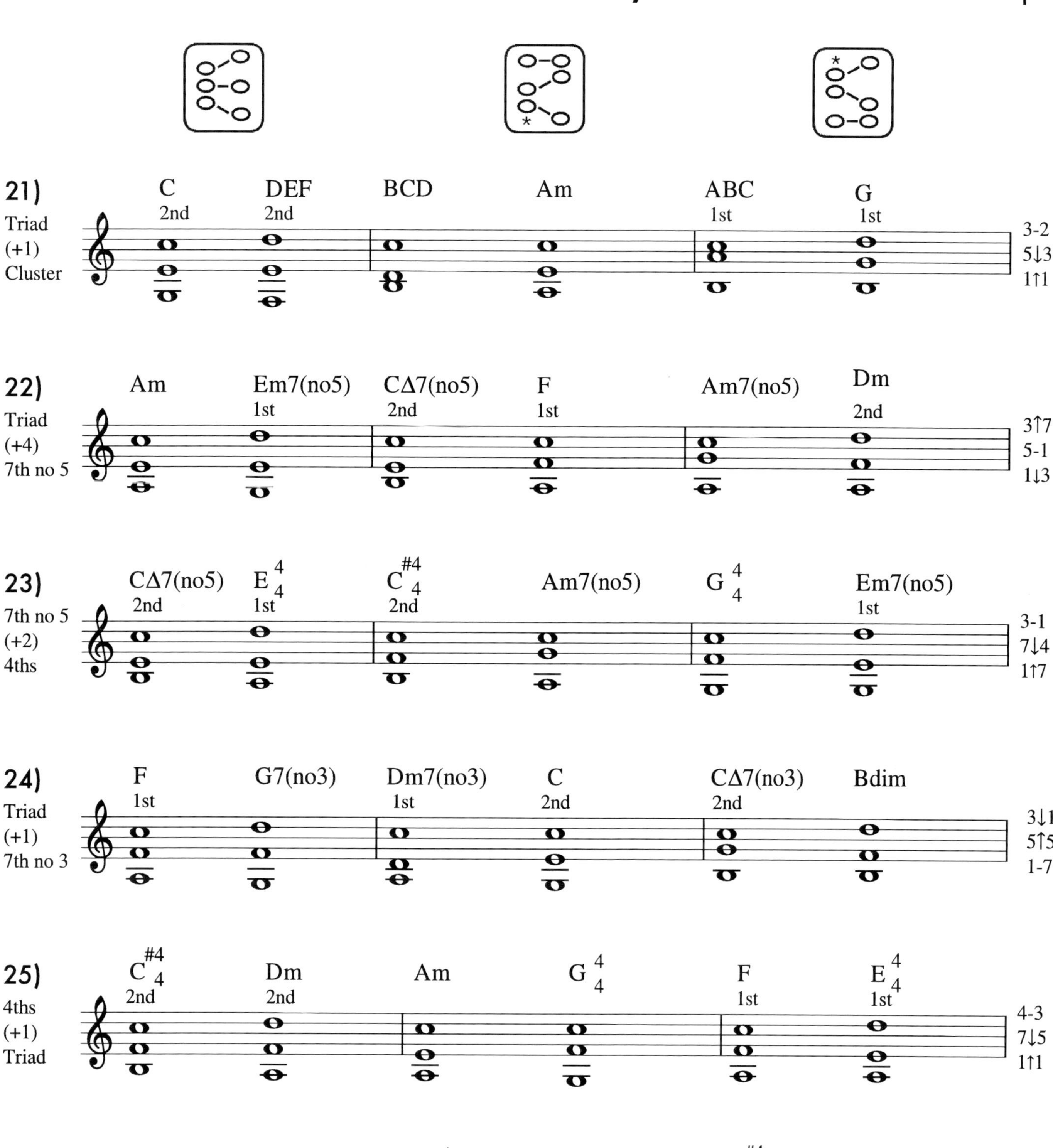

Triple-Voice Parallel Motion

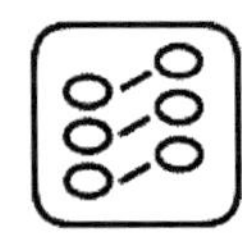
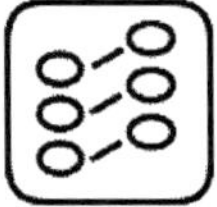
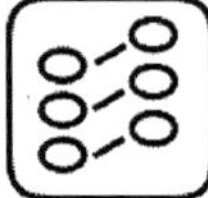

27)

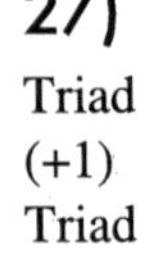

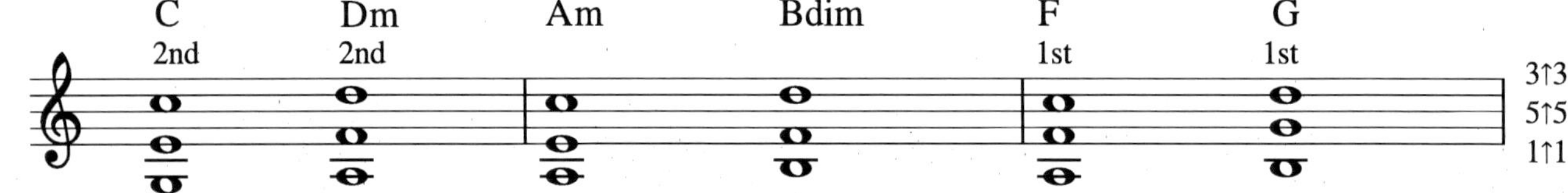

28)

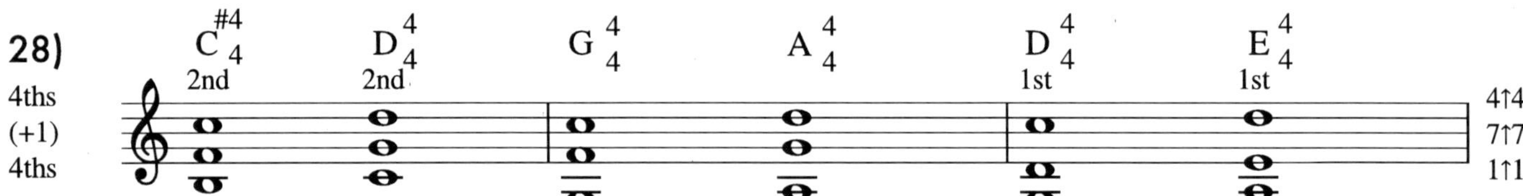

29)

7th no 5
(+1)
7th no 5

CΔ7(no5)	Dm7(no5)	Am7(no5)	Bø(no5)	Dm7(no5)	Em7(no5)
2nd	2nd			1st	1st

3↑3
7↑7
1↑1

30)

7th no 3
(+1)
7th no 3

CΔ7(no3)	Dm7(no3)	FΔ7(no3)	G7(no3)	Dm7(no3)	Em7(no3)
2nd	2nd			1st	1st

5↑5
7↑7
1↑1

31)

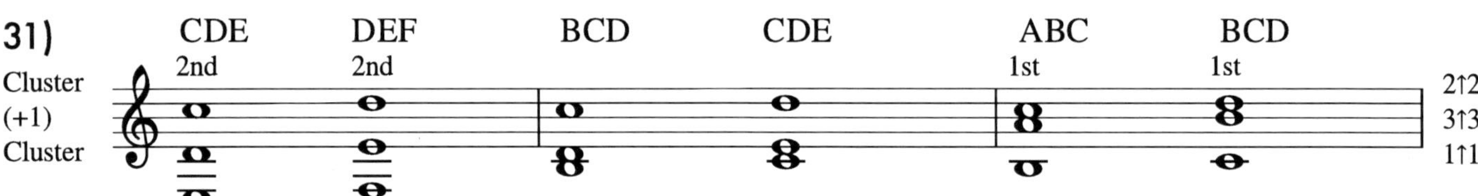

Triple-Voice Contrary Motion

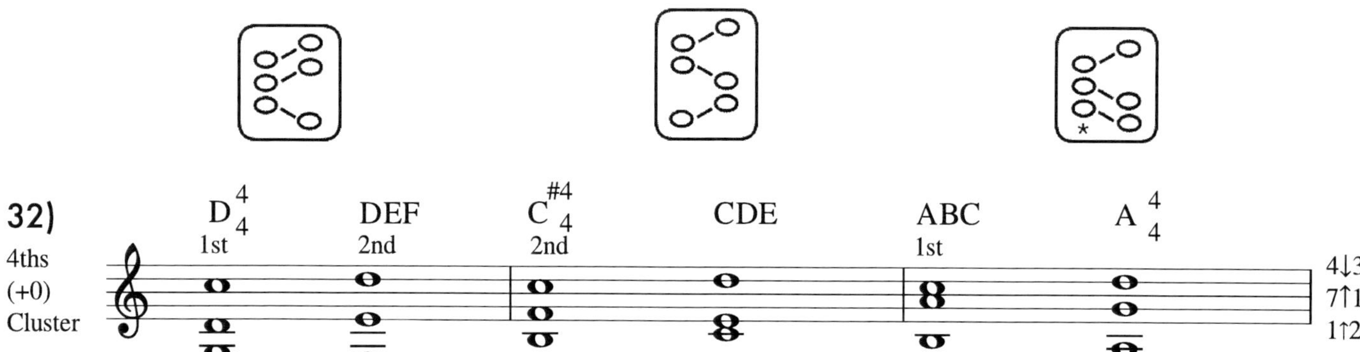

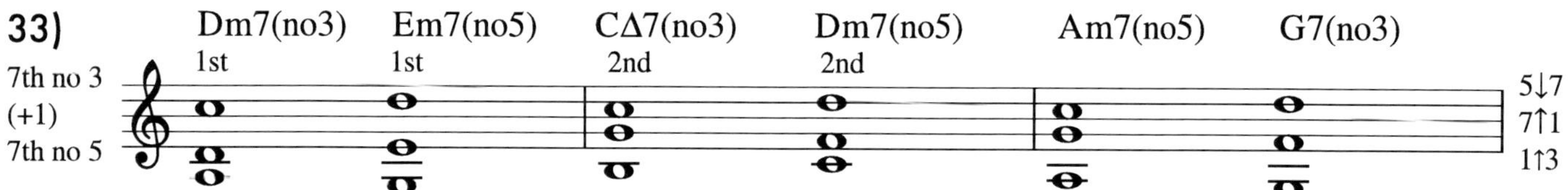

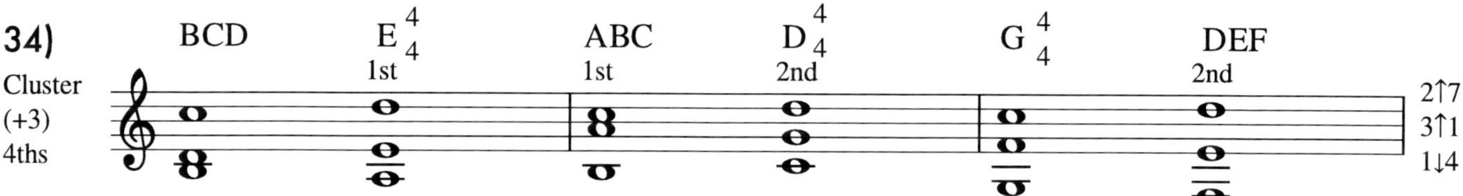

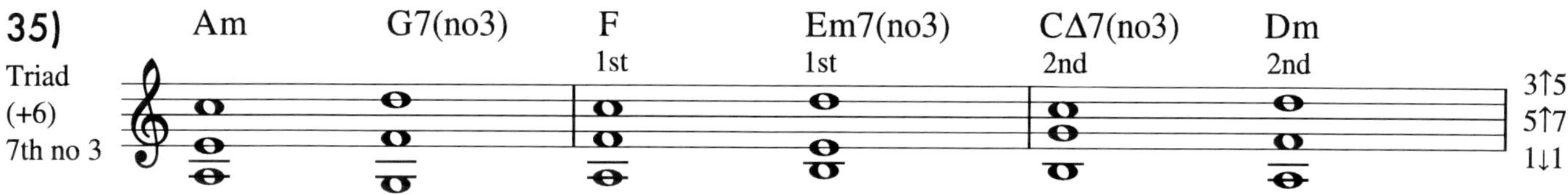

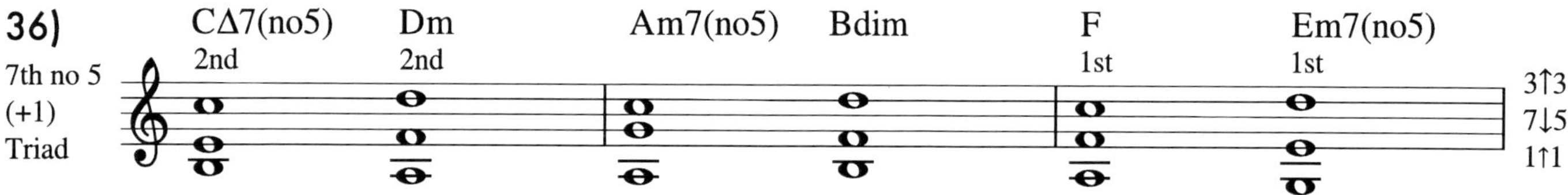

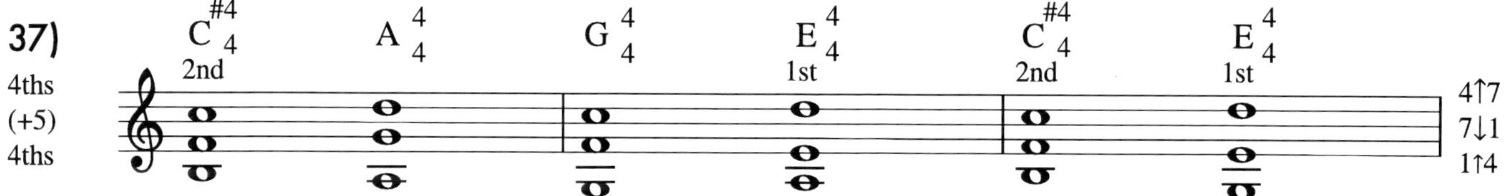

3rds

Single-Voice Motion

open

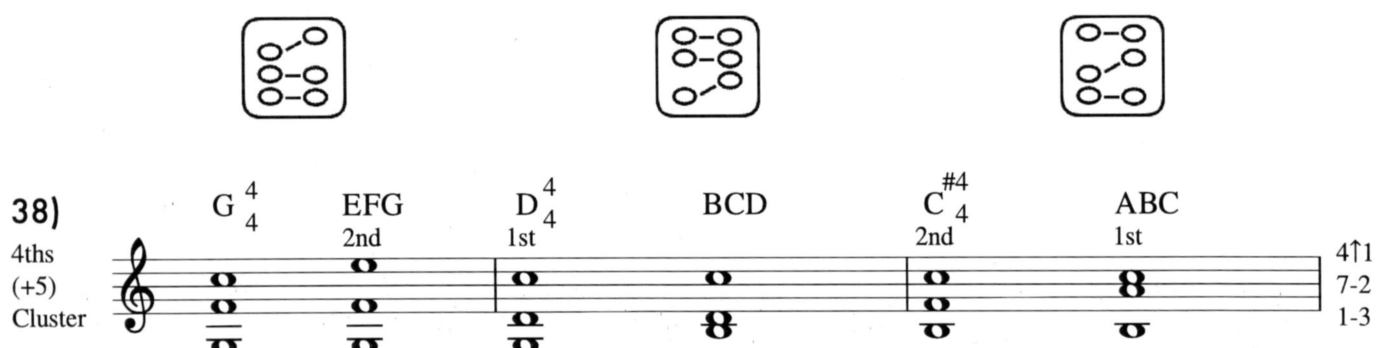

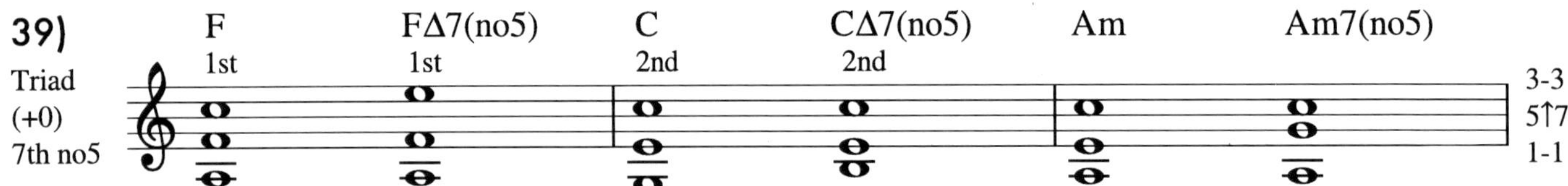

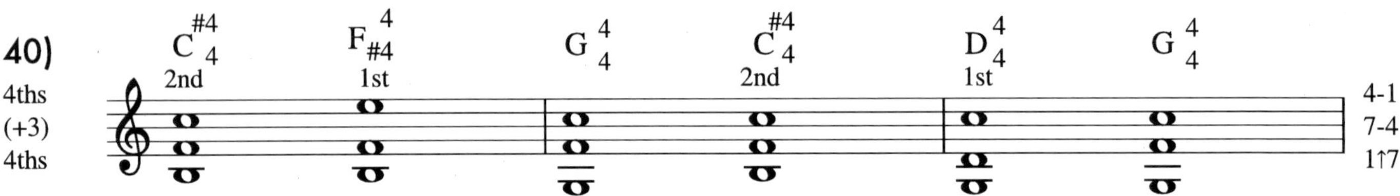

41)
7th no5
(+0)
7th no3
Am7(no5)
Am7(no3)
Dm7(no5)
1st
Dm7(no3
1st
CΔ7(no5)
2nd
CΔ7(no3)
2nd
3↑5
7-7
1-1

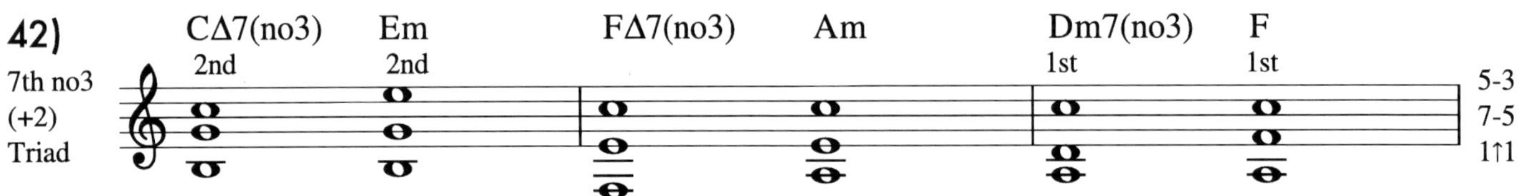

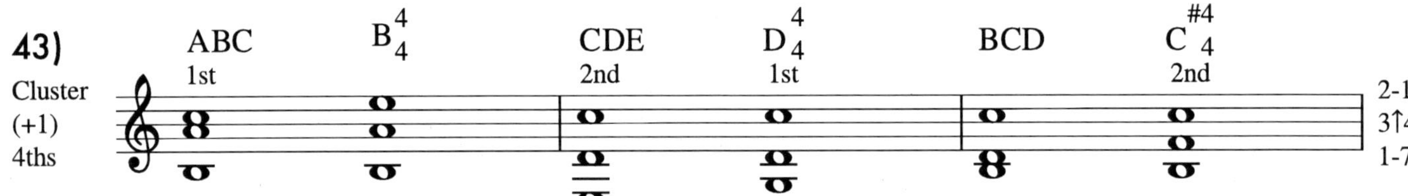

3rds

Double-Voice Parallel Motion

open

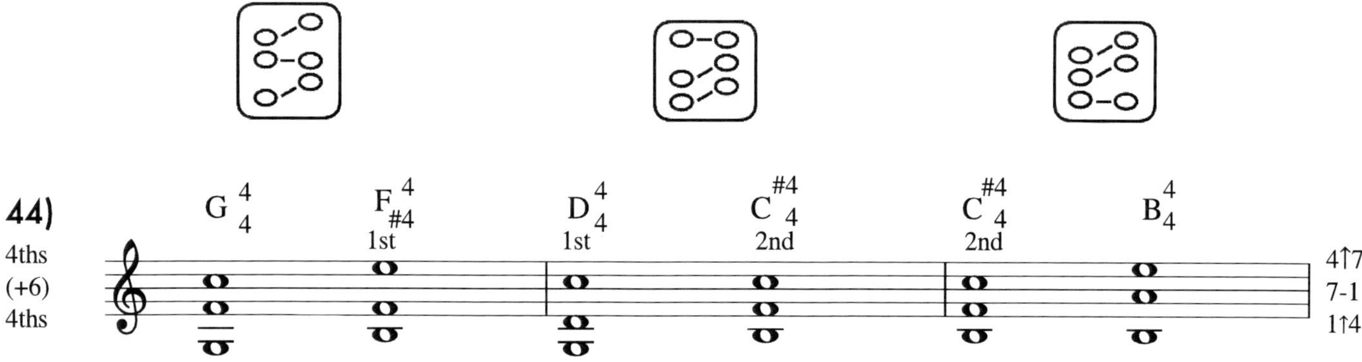

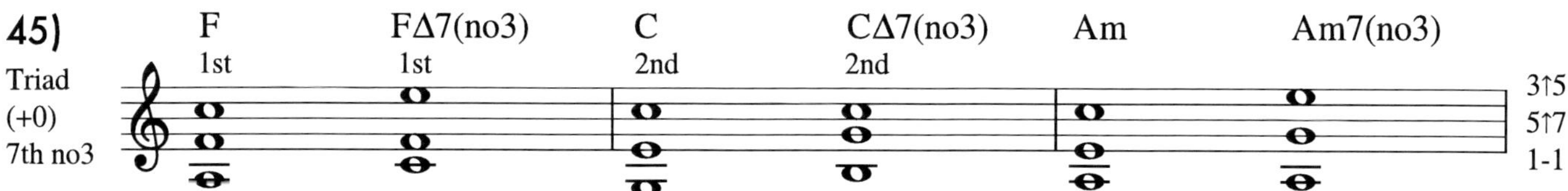

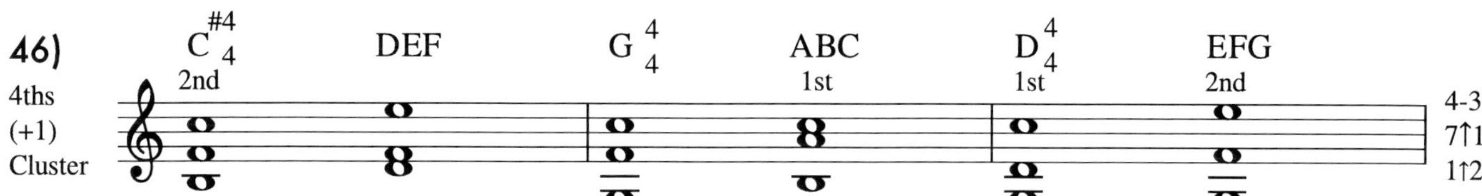

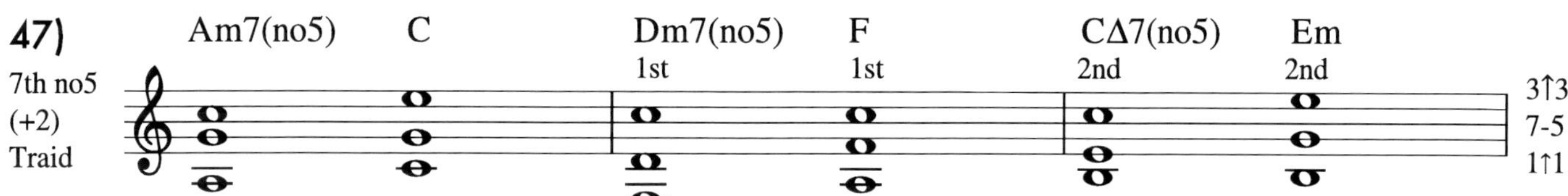

48)
7th no3
(+2)
7th no5

CΔ7(no3) 2nd | Em7(no5) 2nd | FΔ7(no3) | Am7(no5) | Dm7(no3) 1st | FΔ7(no5) 1st

5-3
7↑7
1↑1

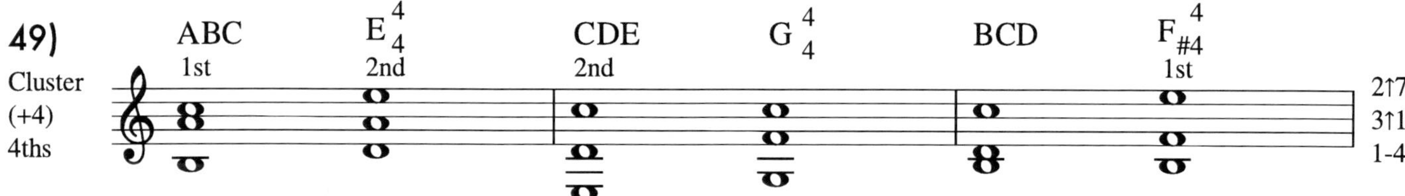

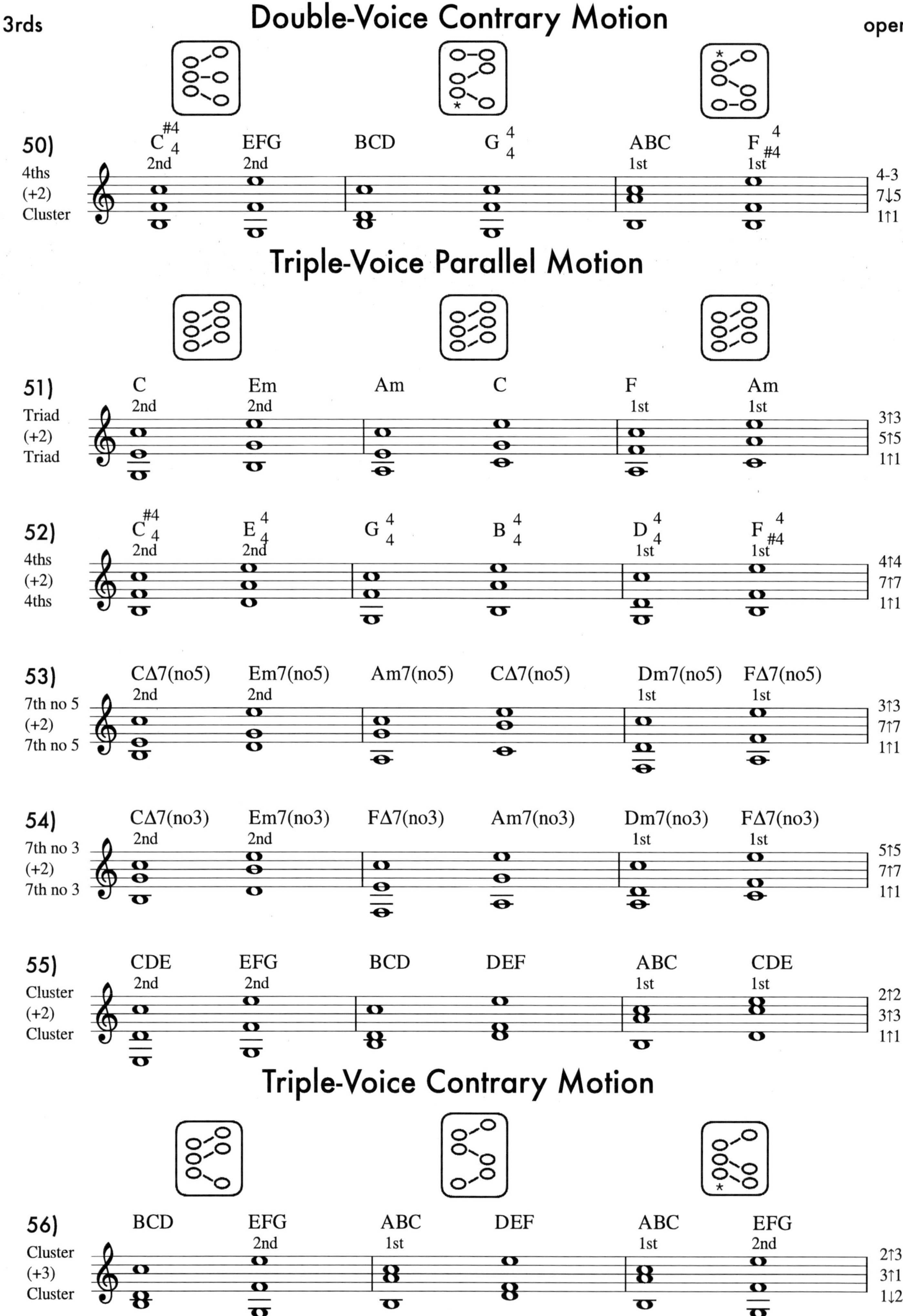
3rds
Double-Voice Contrary Motion
open
50)
4ths
(+2)
Cluster
C #4 4
2nd
EFG
2nd
BCD
G 4 4
ABC
1st
F 4 #4
1st
4-3
7↓5
1↑1
Triple-Voice Parallel Motion
51)
Triad
(+2)
Triad
C
2nd
Em
2nd
Am
C
F
1st
Am
1st
3↑3
5↑5
1↑1
52)
4ths
(+2)
4ths
C #4 4
2nd
E 4 4
2nd
G 4 4
B 4 4
D 4 4
1st
F 4 #4
1st
4↑4
7↑7
1↑1
53)
7th no 5
(+2)
7th no 5
CΔ7(no5)
2nd
Em7(no5)
2nd
Am7(no5)
CΔ7(no5)
Dm7(no5)
1st
FΔ7(no5)
1st
3↑3
7↑7
1↑1
54)
7th no 3
(+2)
7th no 3
CΔ7(no3)
2nd
Em7(no3)
2nd
FΔ7(no3)
Am7(no3)
Dm7(no3)
1st
FΔ7(no3)
1st
5↑5
7↑7
1↑1
55)
Cluster
(+2)
Cluster
CDE
2nd
EFG
2nd
BCD
DEF
ABC
1st
CDE
1st
2↑2
3↑3
1↑1
Triple-Voice Contrary Motion
56)
Cluster
(+3)
Cluster
BCD
EFG
2nd
ABC
1st
DEF
ABC
1st
EFG
2nd
2↑3
3↑1
1↓2

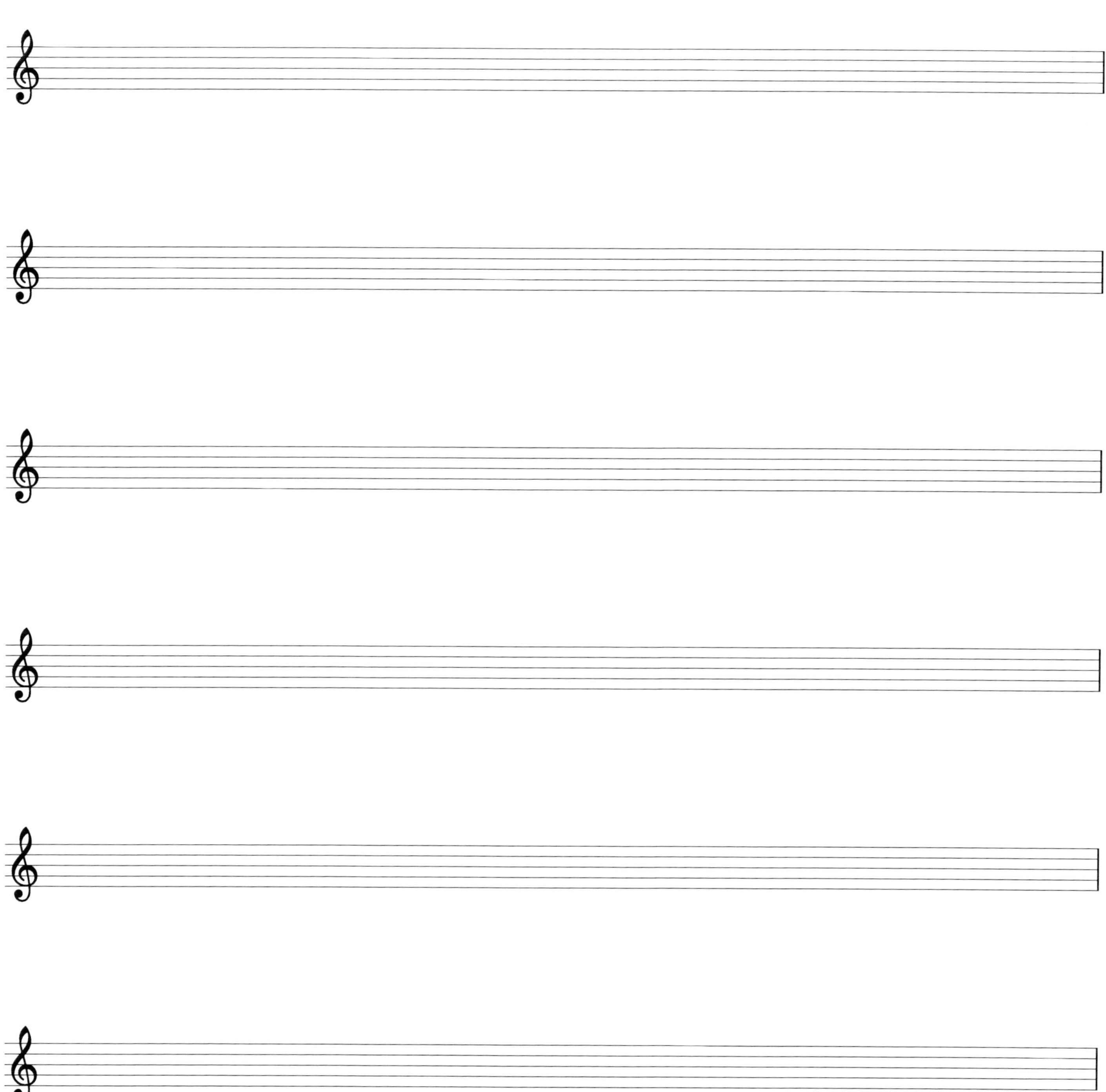

Page left blank for your personal notes and ideas

Double-Voice Parallel Motion 1

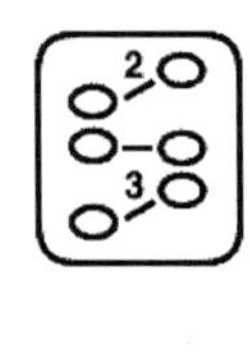

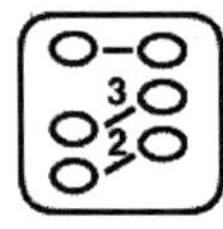

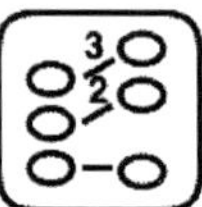

57)

7th no3
(+6)
4ths

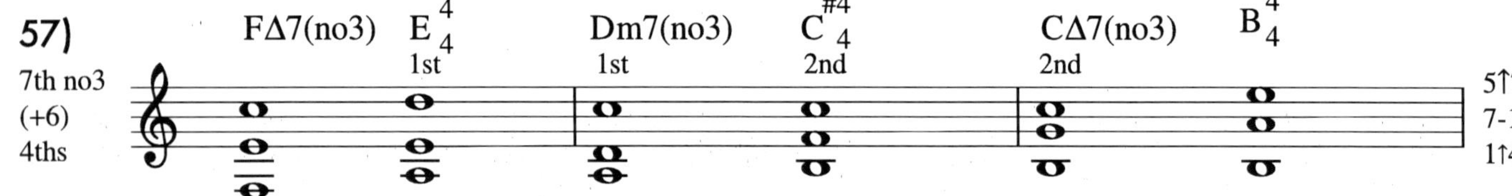

58)

Triad
(+2)
7th no3

C 2nd | Em7(no3) 1st | Am | CΔ7(no3) 2nd | F 1st | Am7(no3)

3-1
5↑5
1↑7

59)

Triad
(+2)
Cluster

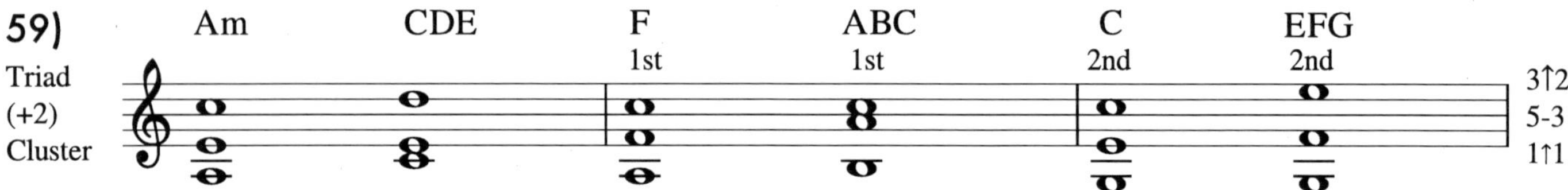

60)

4ths
(+2)
Triad

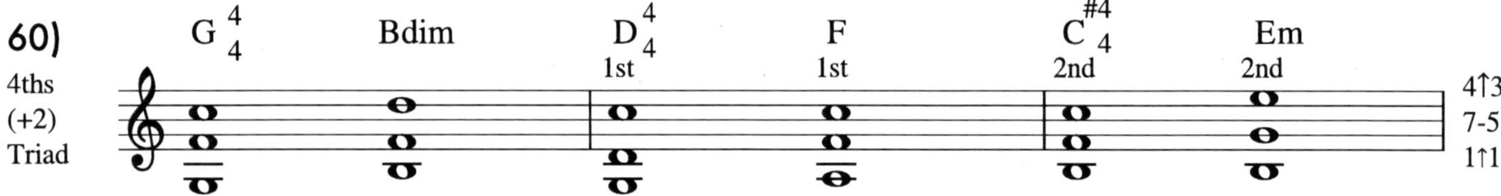

61)

Triad
(+5)
7th no5

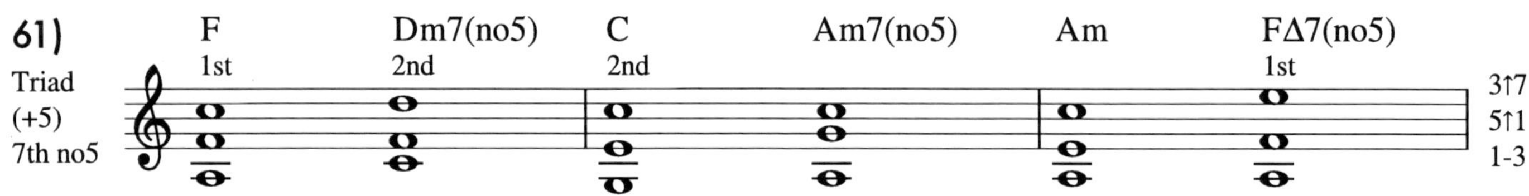

62)

7th no5
(+3)
4ths

Am7(no5) | D 4 4 2nd | Dm7(no5) 1st | G 4 4 | CΔ7(no5) | F 4 #4 1st

3↑1
7-4
1↑7

Double-Voice Parallel Motion 2

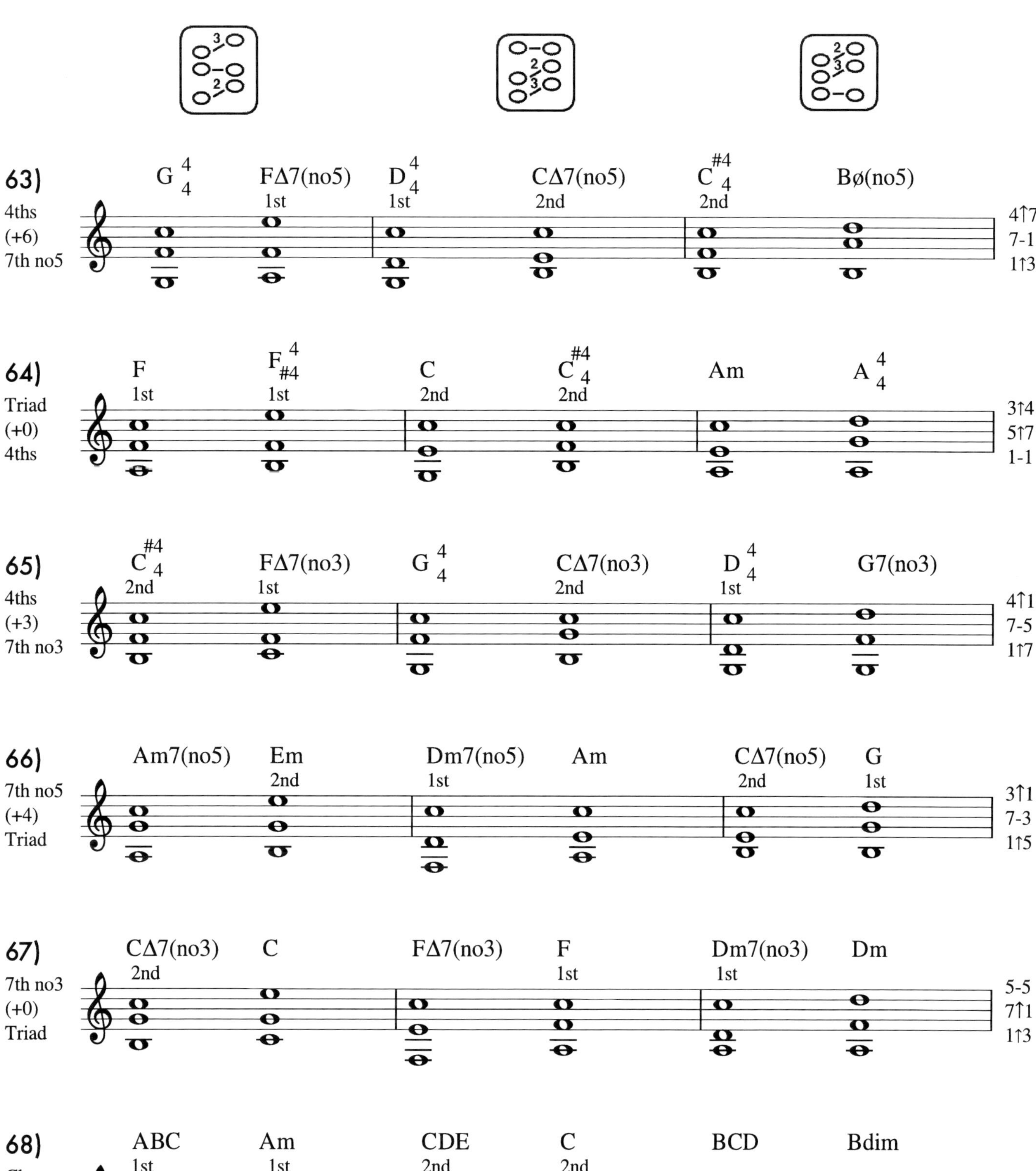

Double-Voice Contrary Motion 1

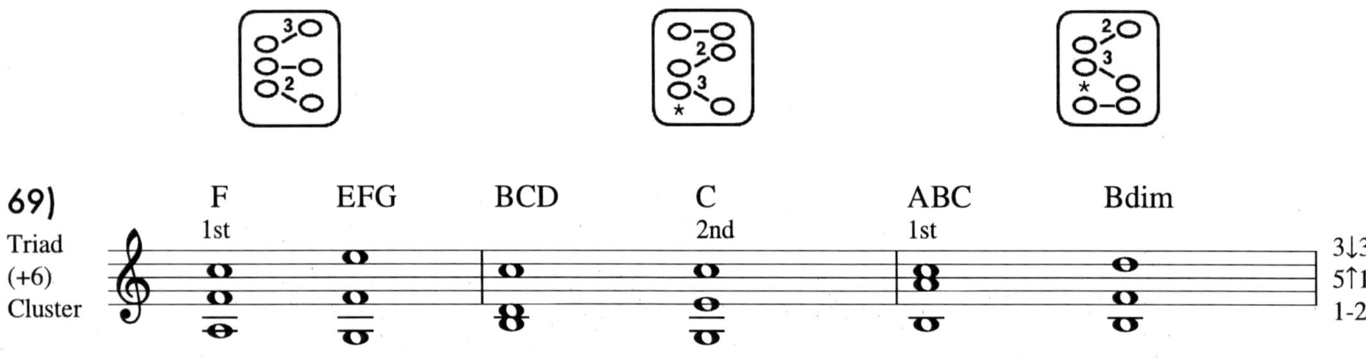

70)
4ths
(+3)
7th no 5

C #4 4 (2nd) | FΔ7(no5) (1st) | CΔ7(no5) (2nd) | G 4 4 | Am7(no5) | E 4 4 (1st)

4-1
7↓3
1↑7

71)
7th no 3
(+5)
7th no 3

CΔ7(no3) (2nd) | Am7(no3) | Dm7(no3) (1st) | FΔ7(no3) | CΔ7(no3) (2nd) | Em7(no3) (1st)

5-7
7↓1
1↑5

Double-Voice Contrary Motion 2

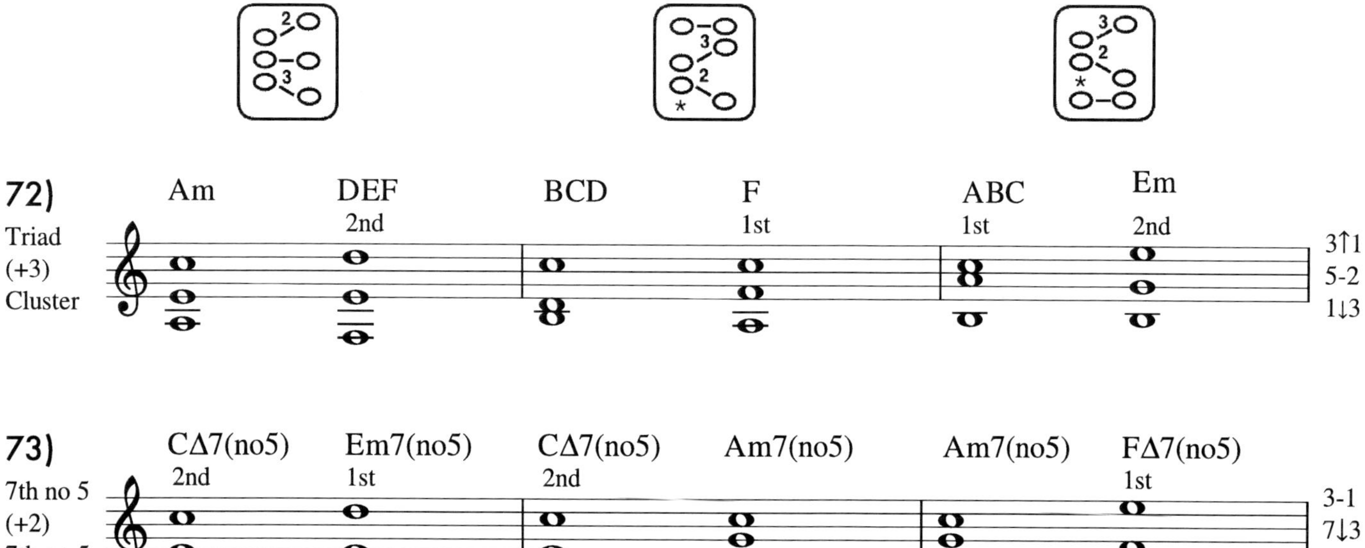

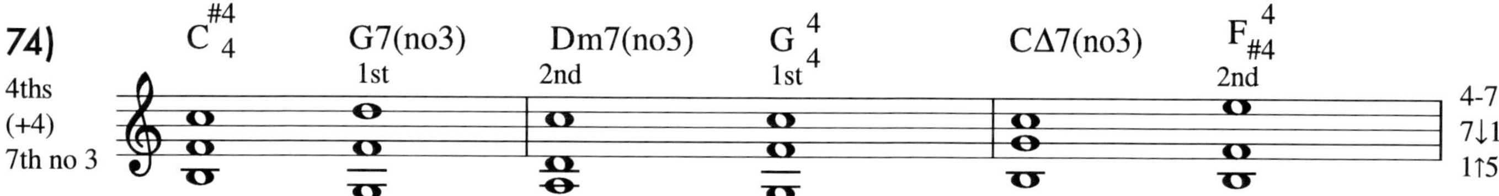

74)

4ths
(+4)
7th no 3

C #4 4 | G7(no3) 1st | Dm7(no3) 2nd | G 4 4 1st | CΔ7(no3) | F 4 #4 2nd

4-7
7↓1
1↑5

2nds/3rds

Triple-Voice Parallel Motion 1

open

322*

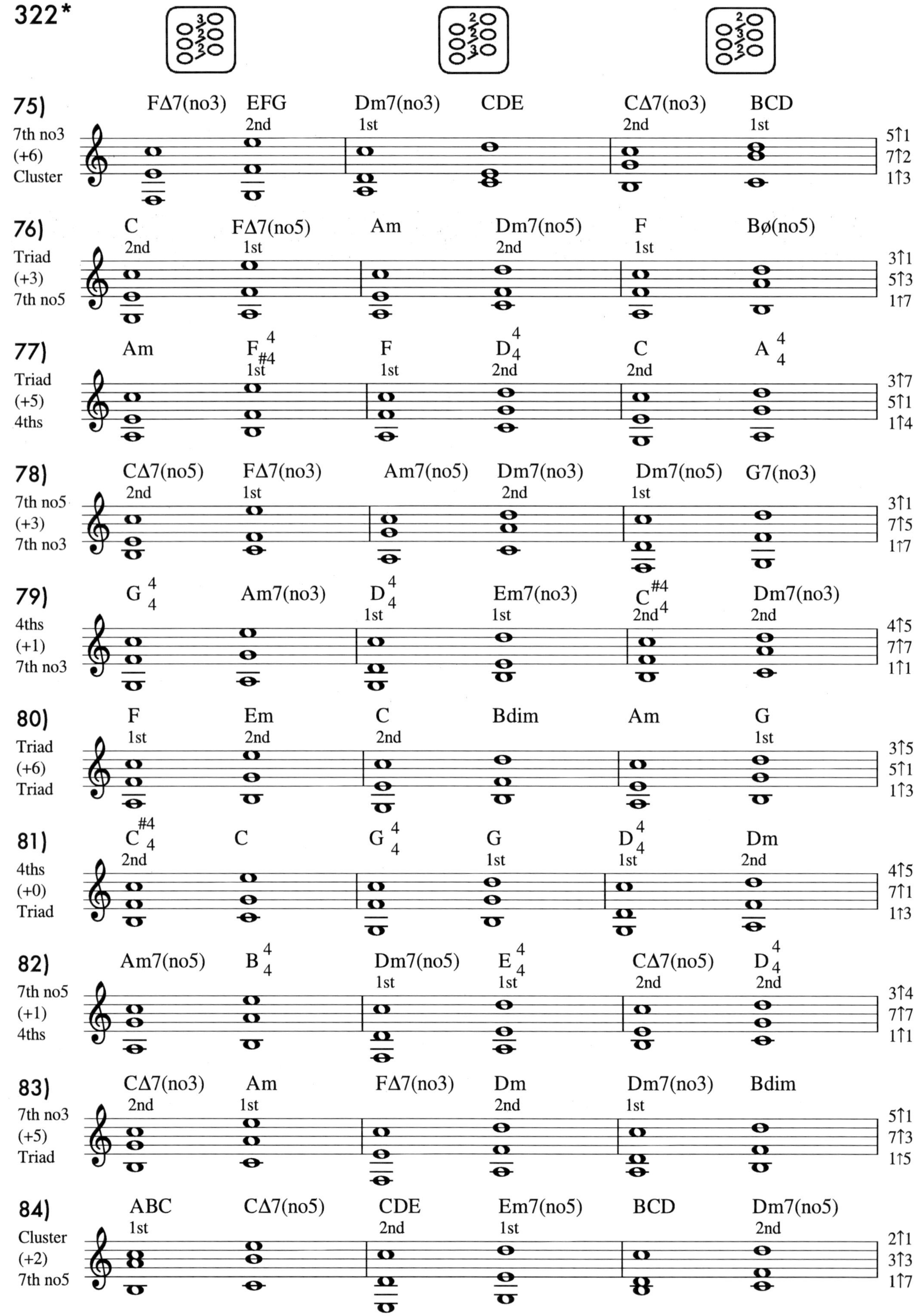

75) 7th no3 (+6) Cluster

FΔ7(no3) — EFG (2nd) — Dm7(no3) (1st) — CDE — CΔ7(no3) (2nd) — BCD (1st)

5↑1 / 7↑2 / 1↑3

76) Triad (+3) 7th no5

C (2nd) — FΔ7(no5) (1st) — Am — Dm7(no5) (2nd) — F (1st) — Bø(no5)

3↑1 / 5↑3 / 1↑7

77) Triad (+5) 4ths

Am — $F^{4}_{\#4}$ (1st) — F (1st) — D^{4}_{4} (2nd) — C (2nd) — A^{4}_{4}

3↑7 / 5↑1 / 1↑4

78) 7th no5 (+3) 7th no3

CΔ7(no5) (2nd) — FΔ7(no3) (1st) — Am7(no5) — Dm7(no3) (2nd) — Dm7(no5) (1st) — G7(no3)

3↑1 / 7↑5 / 1↑7

79) 4ths (+1) 7th no3

G^{4}_{4} — Am7(no3) — D^{4}_{4} (1st) — Em7(no3) (1st) — $C^{\#4}_{4}$ (2nd) — Dm7(no3) (2nd)

4↑5 / 7↑7 / 1↑1

80) Triad (+6) Triad

F (1st) — Em (2nd) — C (2nd) — Bdim — Am — G (1st)

3↑5 / 5↑1 / 1↑3

81) 4ths (+0) Triad

$C^{\#4}_{4}$ (2nd) — C — G^{4}_{4} — G (1st) — D^{4}_{4} (1st) — Dm (2nd)

4↑5 / 7↑1 / 1↑3

82) 7th no5 (+1) 4ths

Am7(no5) — B^{4}_{4} — Dm7(no5) (1st) — E^{4}_{4} (1st) — CΔ7(no5) (2nd) — D^{4}_{4} (2nd)

3↑4 / 7↑7 / 1↑1

83) 7th no3 (+5) Triad

CΔ7(no3) (2nd) — Am (1st) — FΔ7(no3) — Dm (2nd) — Dm7(no3) (1st) — Bdim

5↑1 / 7↑3 / 1↑5

84) Cluster (+2) 7th no5

ABC (1st) — CΔ7(no5) — CDE (2nd) — Em7(no5) (1st) — BCD — Dm7(no5) (2nd)

2↑1 / 3↑3 / 1↑7

* See page 29 for an explanation of this number.

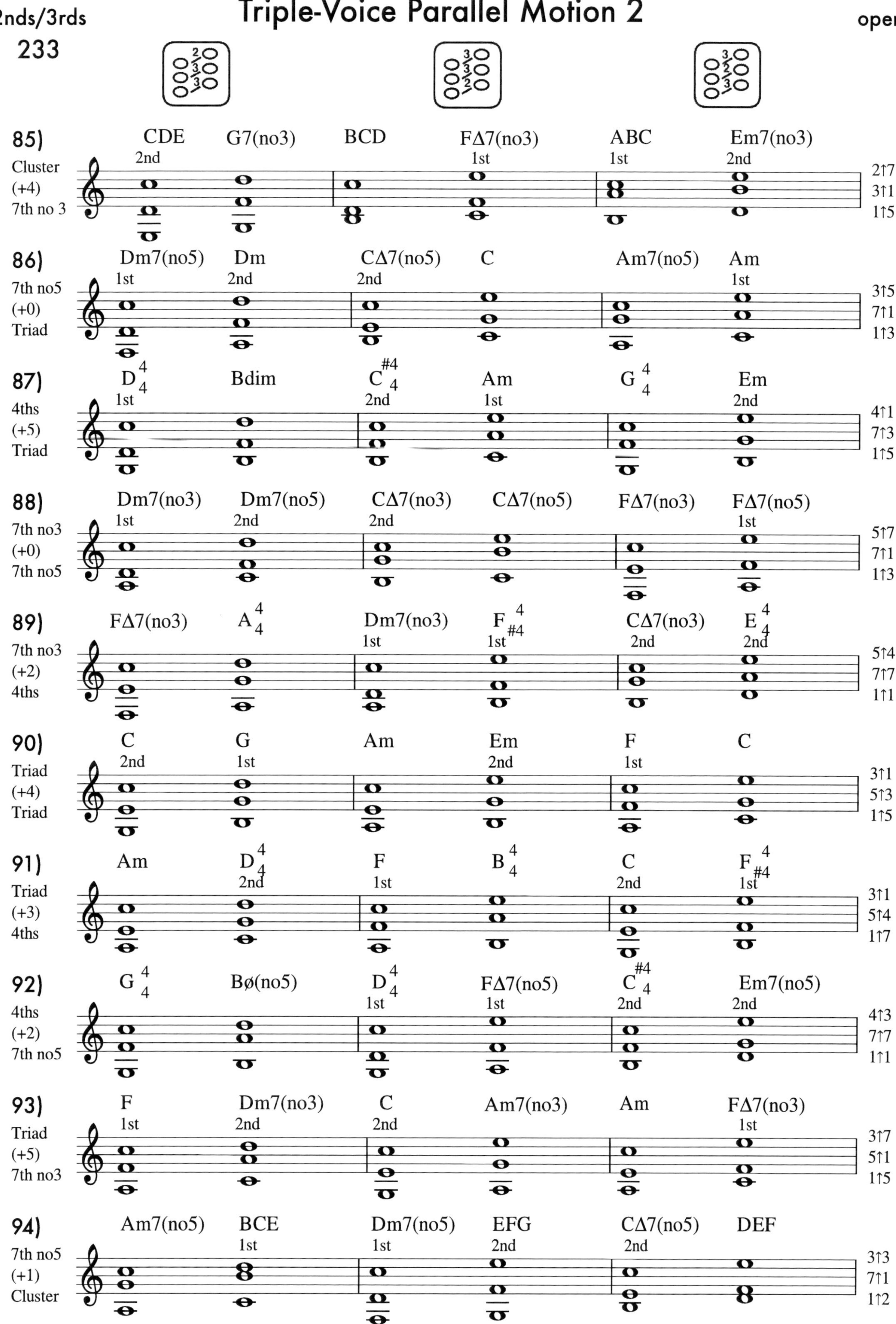
2nds/3rds
233
Triple-Voice Parallel Motion 2
open
85) Cluster (+4) 7th no 3
CDE 2nd | G7(no3) | BCD | FΔ7(no3) 1st | ABC 1st | Em7(no3) 2nd
2↑7 3↑1 1↑5
86) 7th no5 (+0) Triad
Dm7(no5) 1st | Dm 2nd | CΔ7(no5) 2nd | C | Am7(no5) | Am 1st
3↑5 7↑1 1↑3
87) 4ths (+5) Triad
D 4 4 1st | Bdim | C #4 4 2nd | Am 1st | G 4 4 | Em 2nd
4↑1 7↑3 1↑5
88) 7th no3 (+0) 7th no5
Dm7(no3) 1st | Dm7(no5) 2nd | CΔ7(no3) 2nd | CΔ7(no5) | FΔ7(no3) | FΔ7(no5) 1st
5↑7 7↑1 1↑3
89) 7th no3 (+2) 4ths
FΔ7(no3) | A 4 4 | Dm7(no3) 1st | F 4 #4 1st | CΔ7(no3) 2nd | E 4 4 2nd
5↑4 7↑7 1↑1
90) Triad (+4) Triad
C 2nd | G 1st | Am | Em 2nd | F 1st | C
3↑1 5↑3 1↑5
91) Triad (+3) 4ths
Am | D 4 4 2nd | F 1st | B 4 4 | C 2nd | F 4 #4 1st
3↑1 5↑4 1↑7
92) 4ths (+2) 7th no5
G 4 4 | Bø(no5) | D 4 4 1st | FΔ7(no5) 1st | C #4 4 2nd | Em7(no5) 2nd
4↑3 7↑7 1↑1
93) Triad (+5) 7th no3
F 1st | Dm7(no3) 2nd | C 2nd | Am7(no3) | Am | FΔ7(no3) 1st
3↑7 5↑1 1↑5
94) 7th no5 (+1) Cluster
Am7(no5) | BCE 1st | Dm7(no5) 1st | EFG 2nd | CΔ7(no5) 2nd | DEF
3↑3 7↑1 1↑2

Triple-Voice Contrary Motion 1

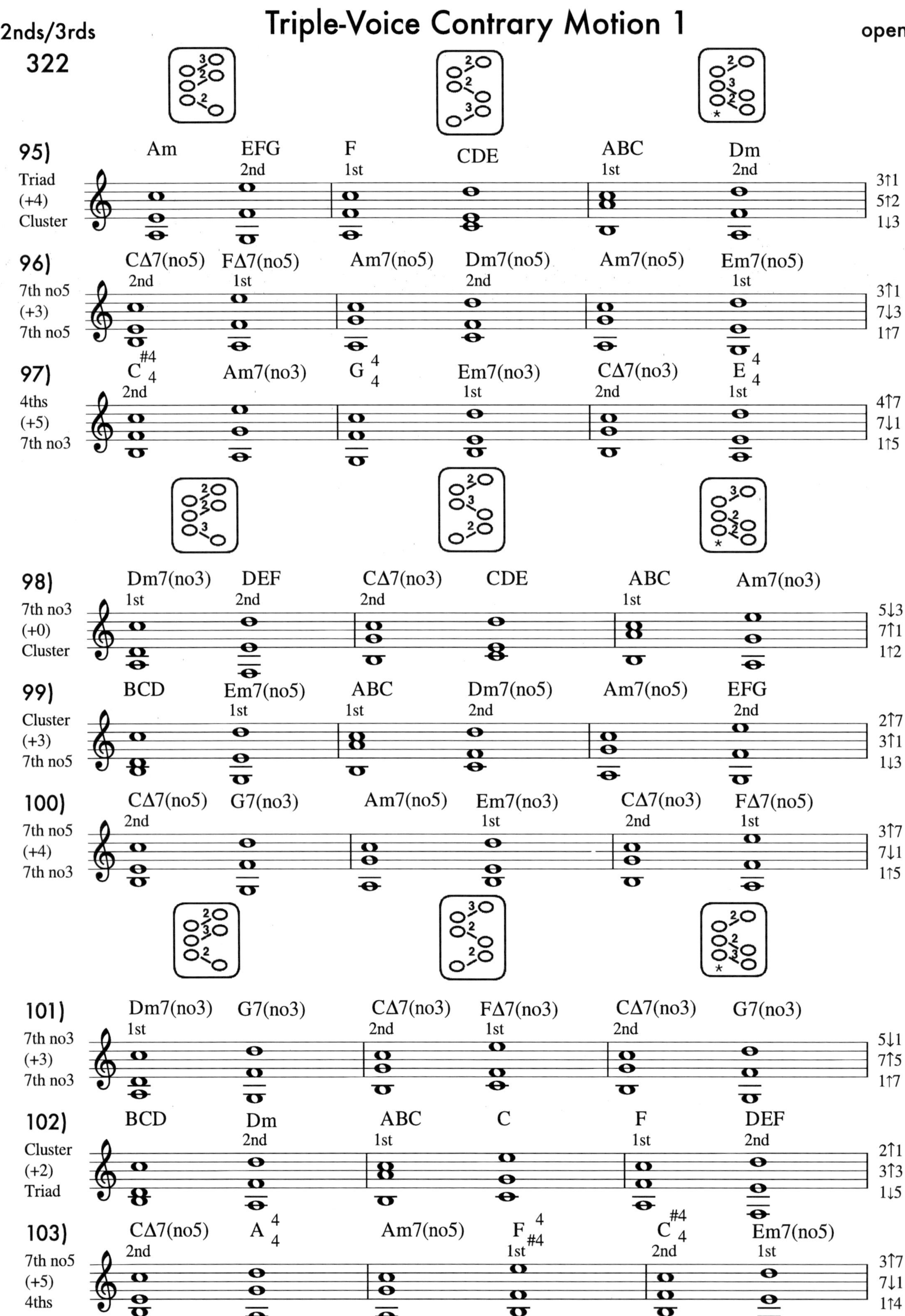

2nds/3rds
233

Triple-Voice Contrary Motion 2

open

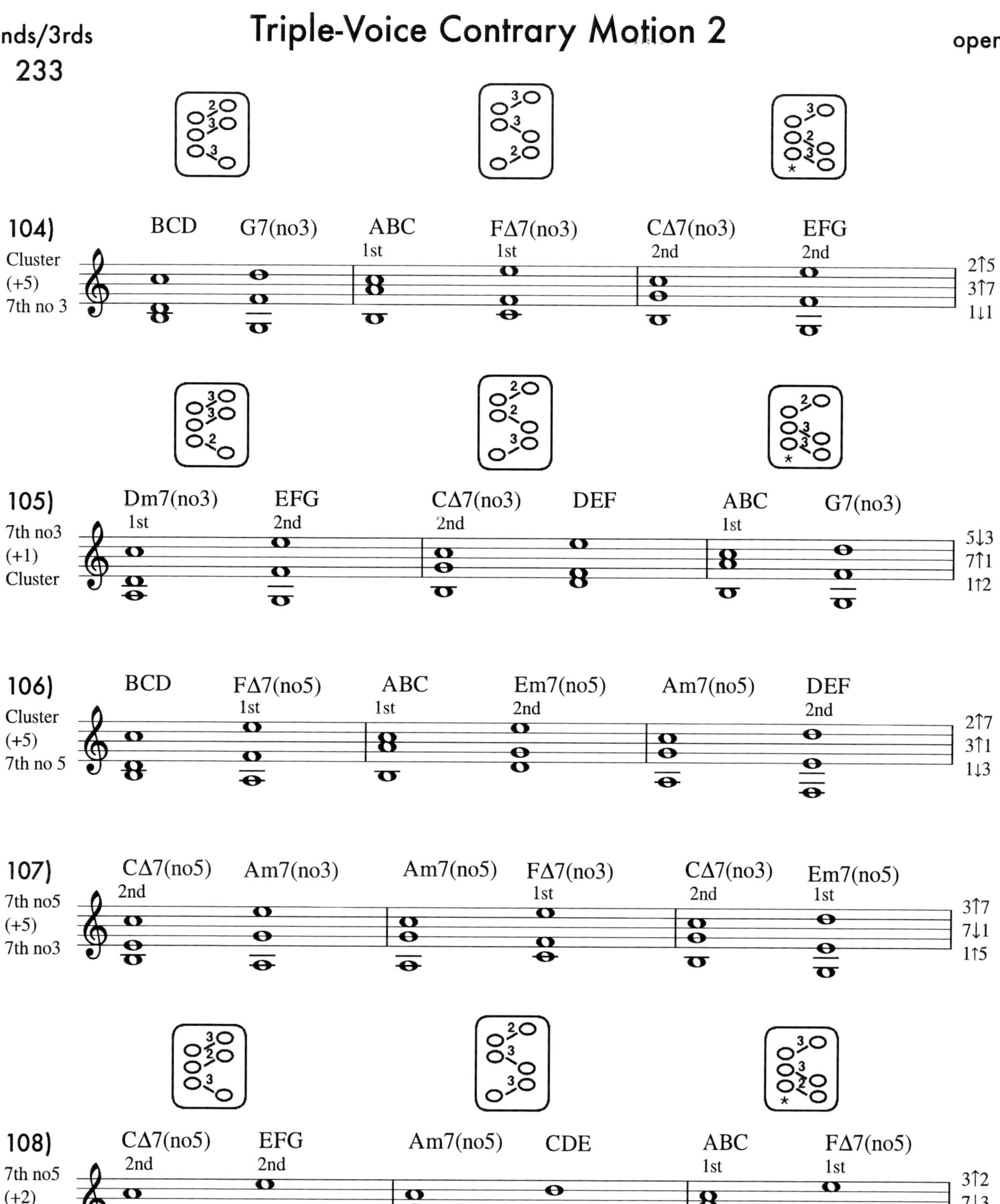

PART 2B

The 15 Chord Structures with the Top Note C with All Possible Departing Motion in Open Voicing (Drop-2)

There is an average of 21.6 moves per chord in each direction, ascending and/or descending.

Apply all voice motion exercises from the introduction to all keys throughout the full range of your instrument.

Triads in 2nd Inversion

Using regular/ascending motion

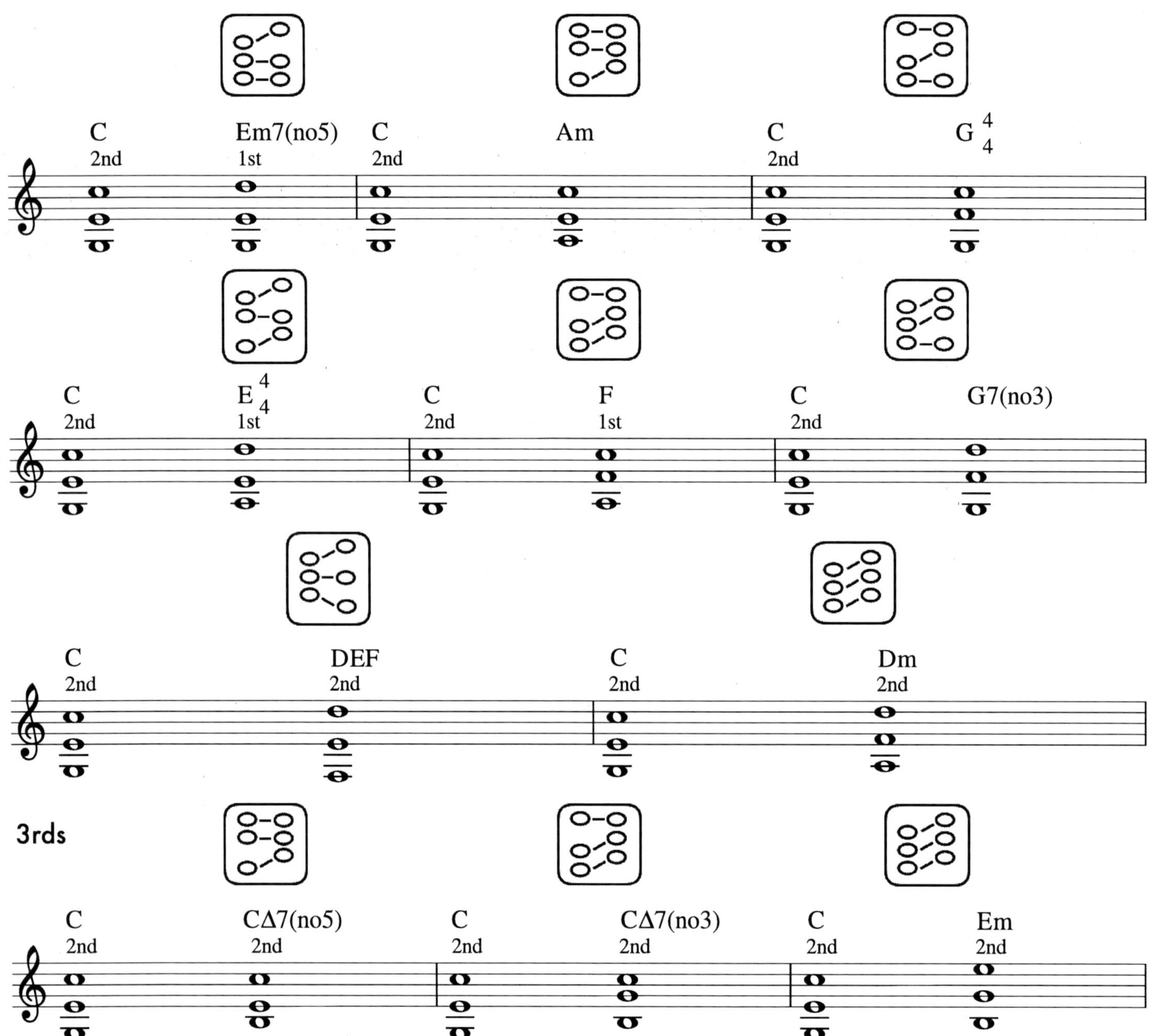

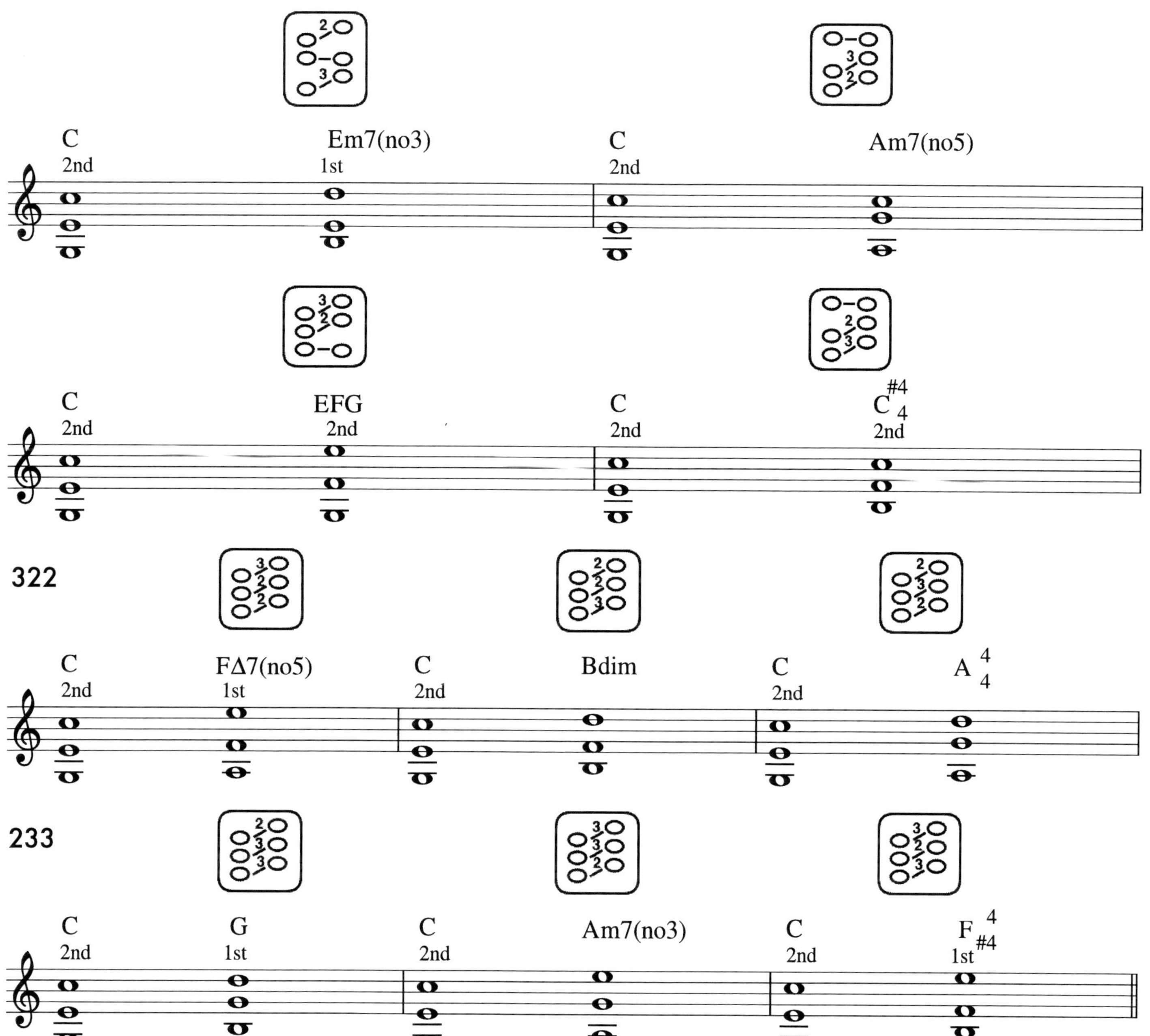
C
2nd
Em7(no3)
1st
C
2nd
Am7(no5)
C
2nd
EFG
2nd
C
2nd
C #4 4
2nd
322
C
2nd
FΔ7(no5)
1st
C
2nd
Bdim
C
2nd
A 4 4
233
C
2nd
G
1st
C
2nd
Am7(no3)
C
2nd
F 4 #4
1st

2nds

Triads in 2nd Inversion

Using reverse/descending motion

open

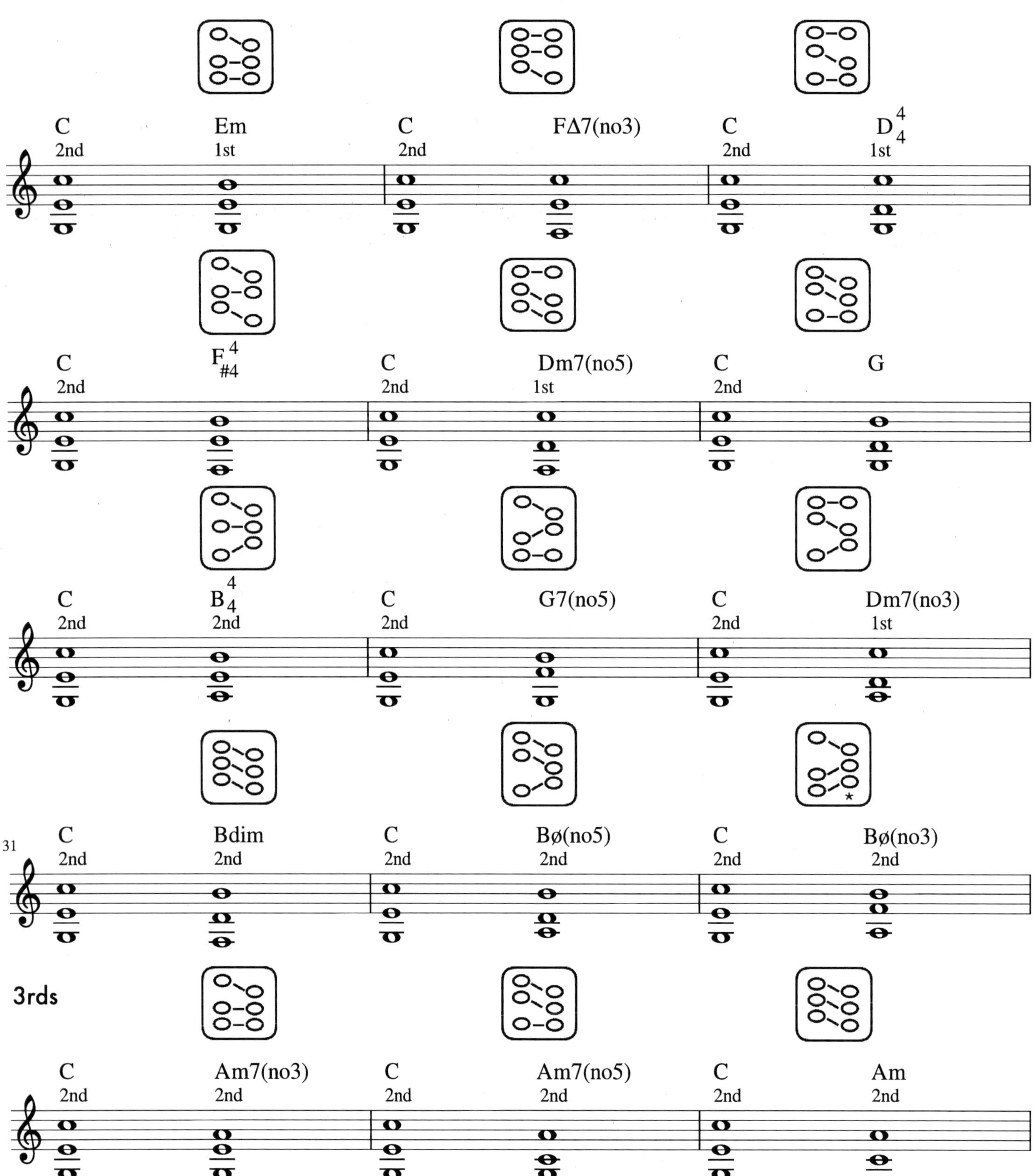

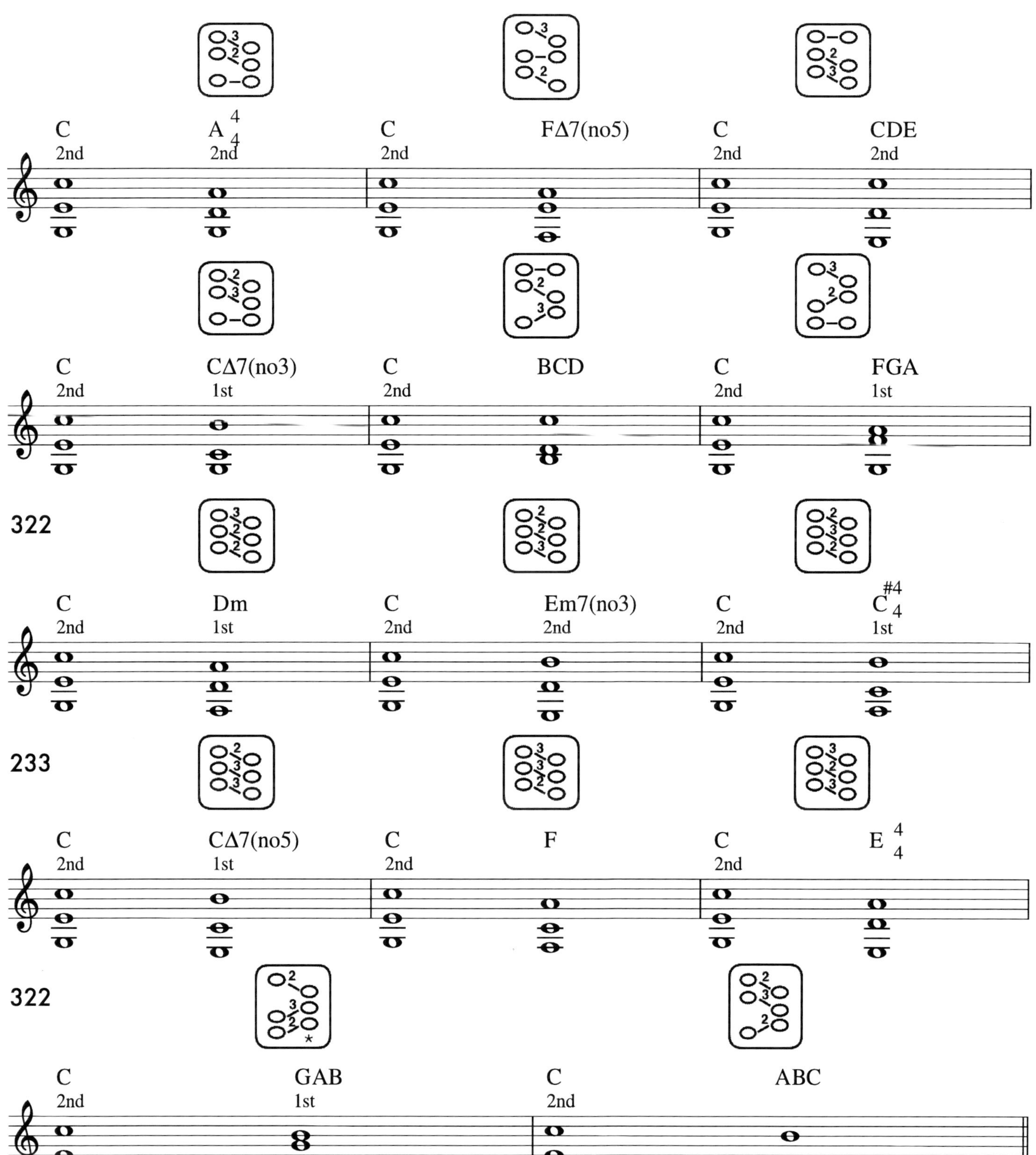
C
2nd
A 4 4
2nd
C
2nd
FΔ7(no5)
C
2nd
CDE
2nd
C
2nd
CΔ7(no3)
1st
C
2nd
BCD
C
2nd
FGA
1st
322
C
2nd
Dm
1st
C
2nd
Em7(no3)
2nd
C
2nd
C #4 4
1st
233
C
2nd
CΔ7(no5)
1st
C
2nd
F
C
2nd
E 4 4
322
C
2nd
GAB
1st
C
2nd
ABC

2nds

Triads in Root Position

Using regular/ascending motion

open

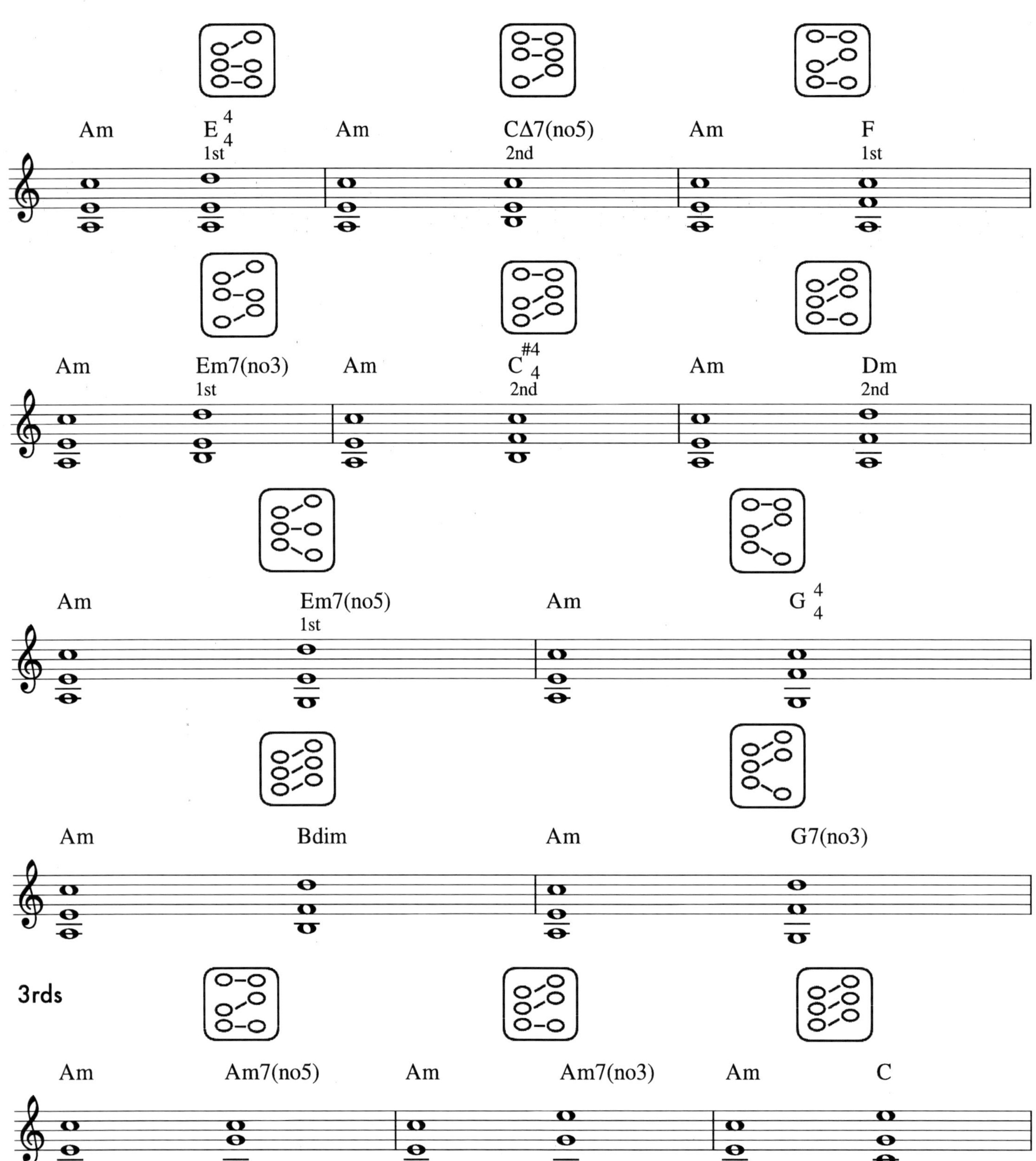

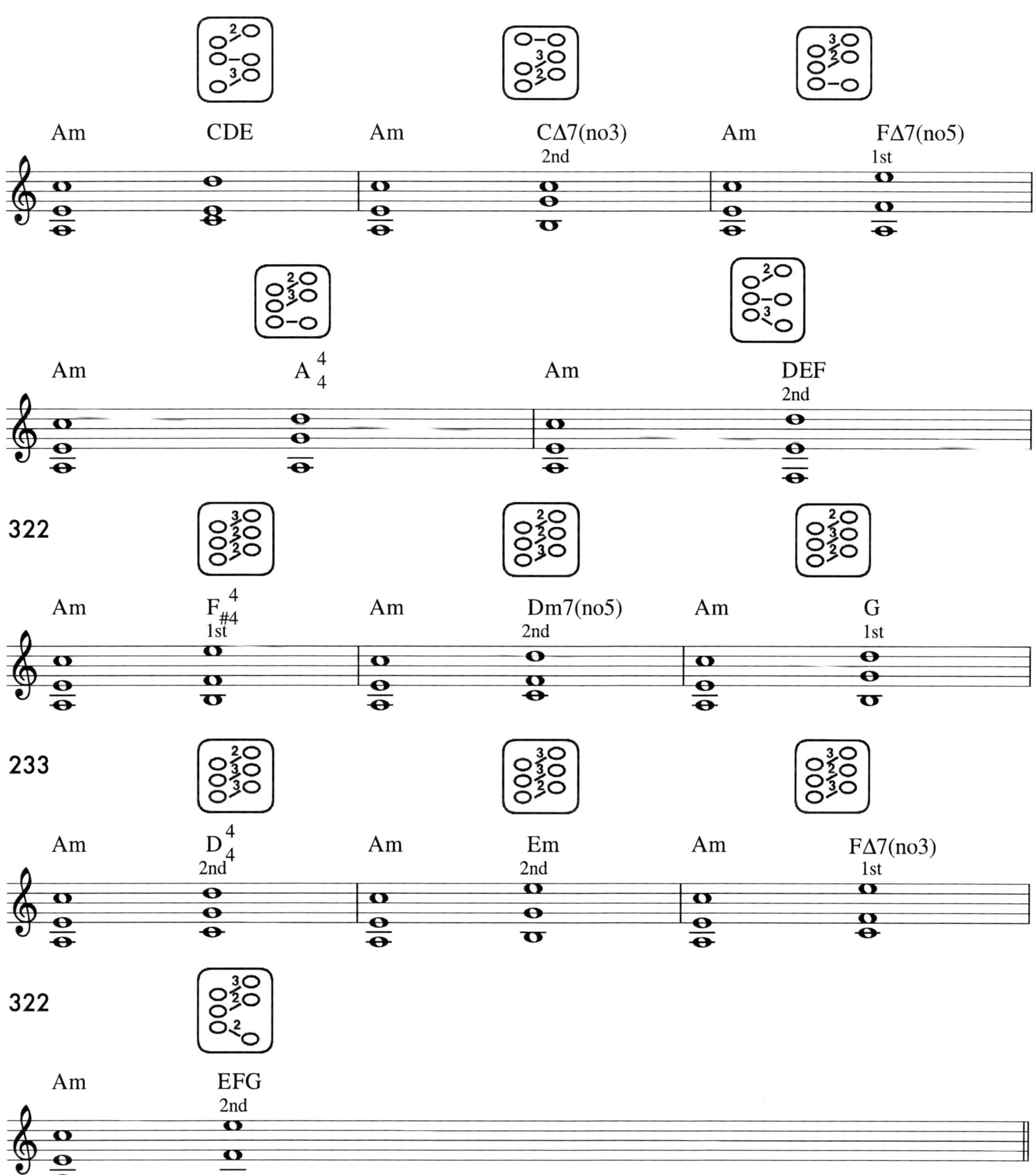
Am
CDE
Am
CΔ7(no3)
2nd
Am
FΔ7(no5)
1st
Am
A 4 4
Am
DEF
2nd
322
Am
F 4 #4
1st
Am
Dm7(no5)
2nd
Am
G
1st
233
Am
D 4 4
2nd
Am
Em
2nd
Am
FΔ7(no3)
1st
322
Am
EFG
2nd

2nds

Triads in Root Position

Using reverse/descending motion

open

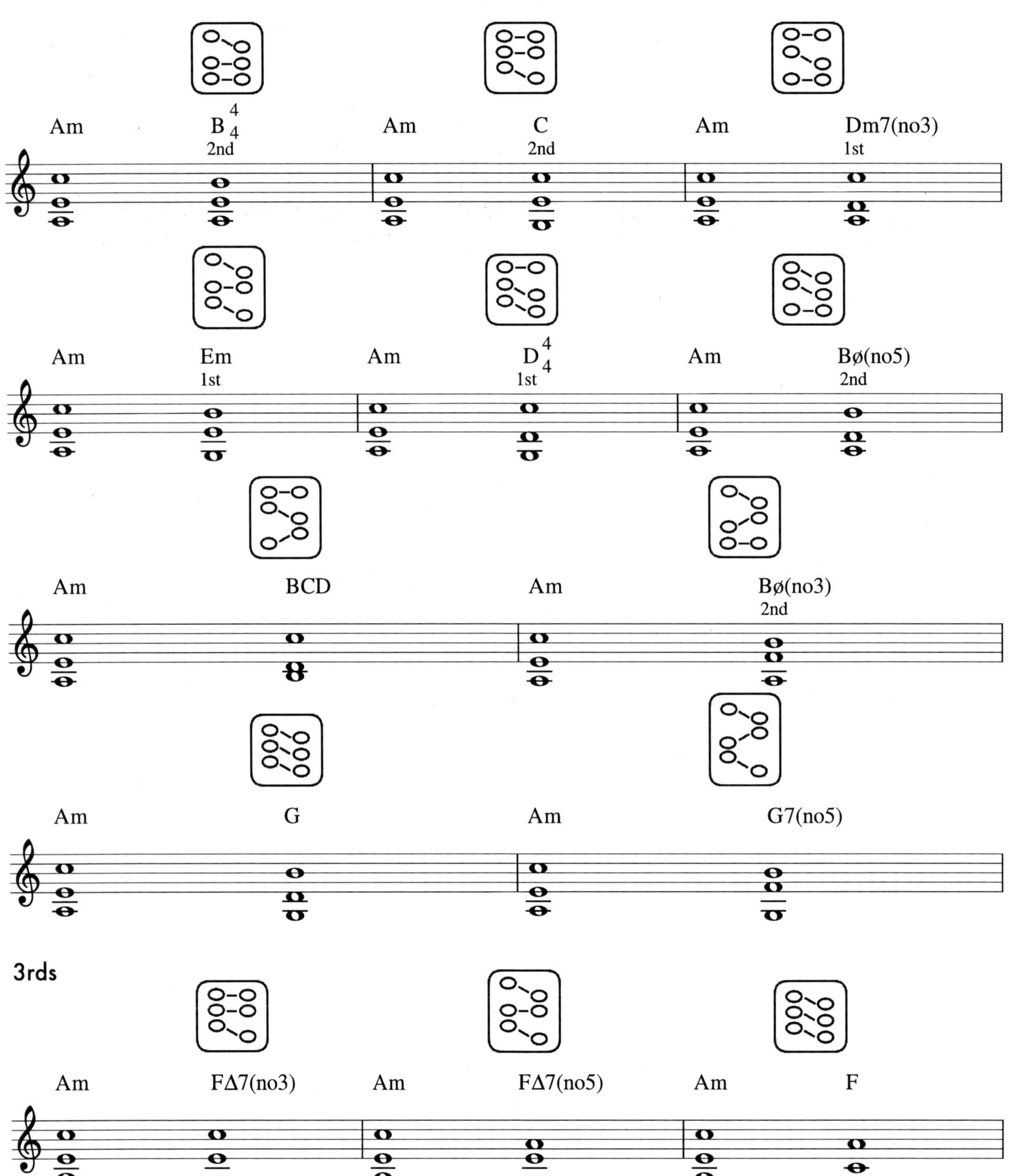

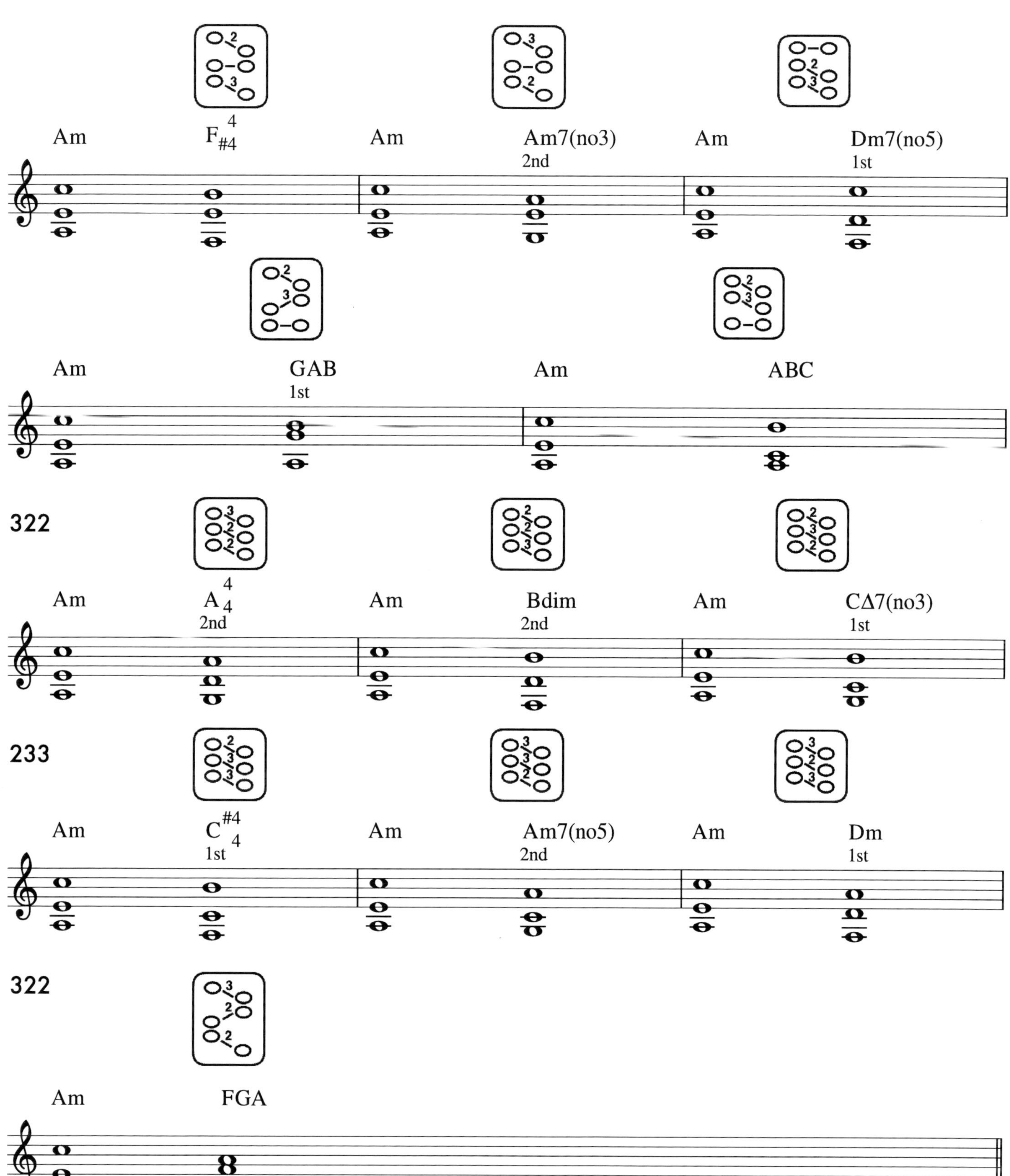
Am
F 4 #4
Am
Am7(no3)
2nd
Am
Dm7(no5)
1st
Am
GAB
1st
Am
ABC
322
Am
A 4 4
2nd
Am
Bdim
2nd
Am
CΔ7(no3)
1st
233
Am
C #4 4
1st
Am
Am7(no5)
2nd
Am
Dm
1st
322
Am
FGA

2nds

Triads in 1st Inversion

Using regular/ascending motion

open

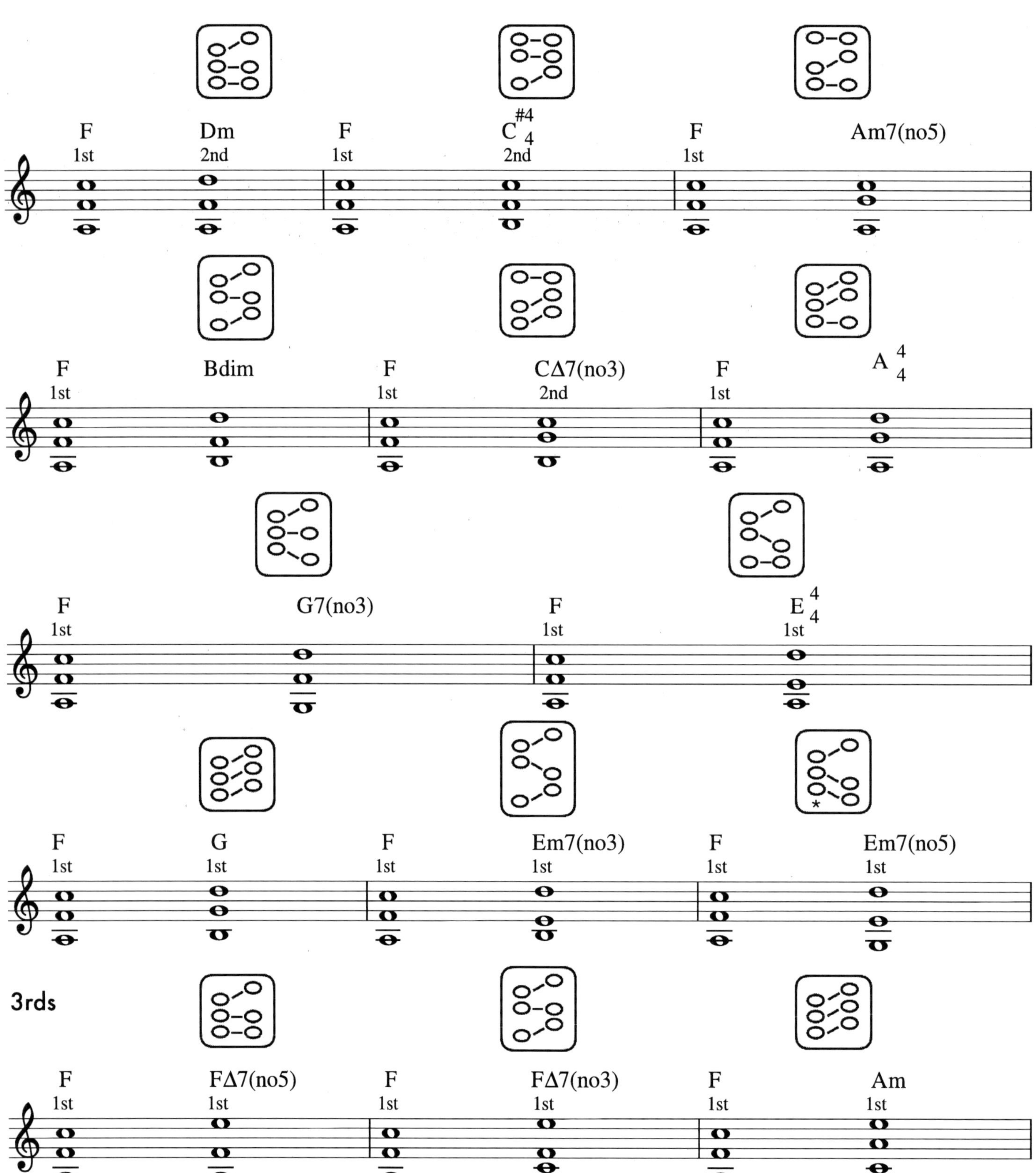

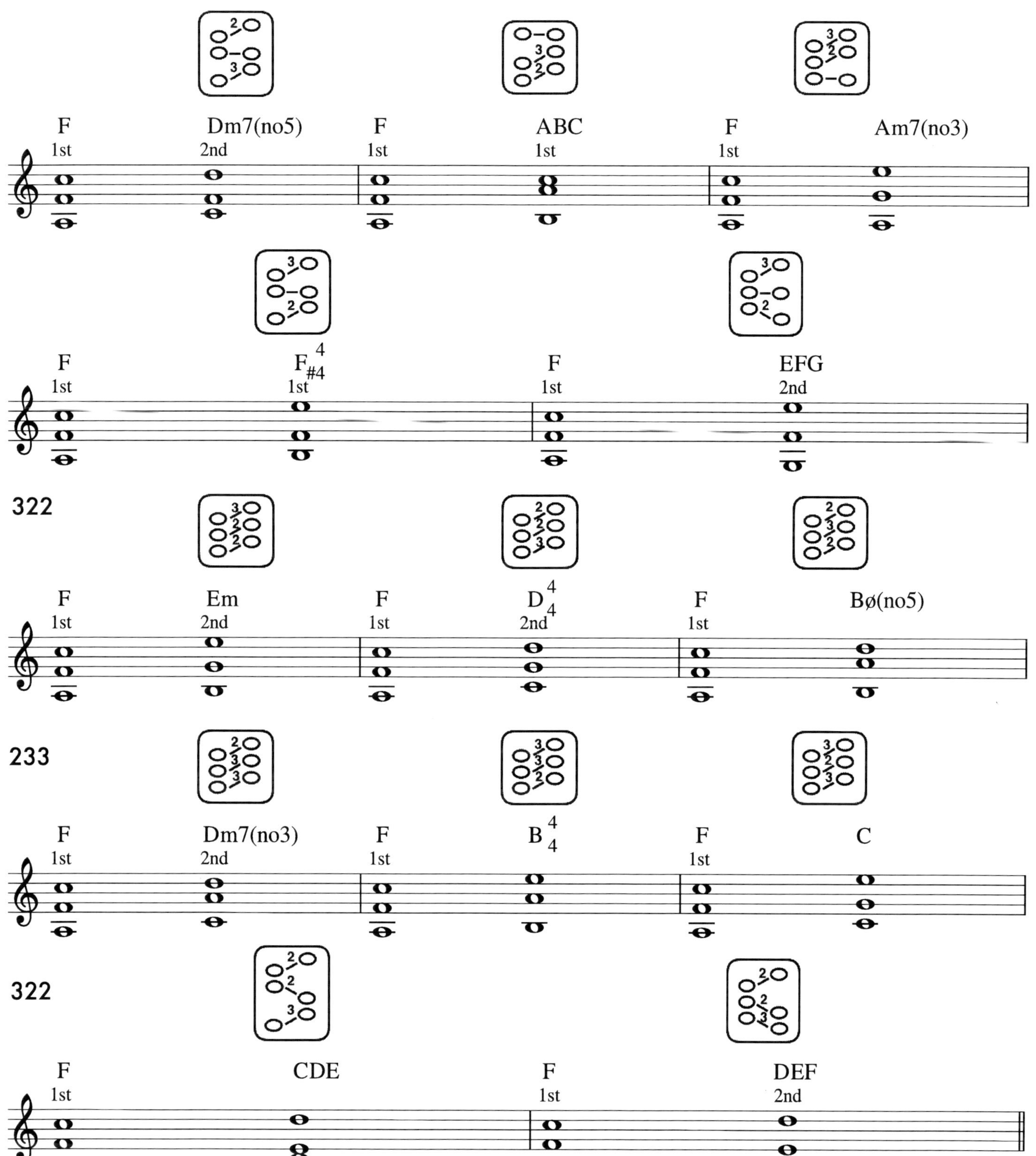
F
1st
Dm7(no5)
2nd
F
1st
ABC
1st
F
1st
Am7(no3)
F
1st
F#4 4
1st
F
1st
EFG
2nd
322
F
1st
Em
2nd
F
1st
D 4 4
2nd
F
1st
Bø(no5)
233
F
1st
Dm7(no3)
2nd
F
1st
B 4 4
F
1st
C
322
F
1st
CDE
F
1st
DEF
2nd

2nds

Triads in 1st Inversion

Using reverse/descending motion

open

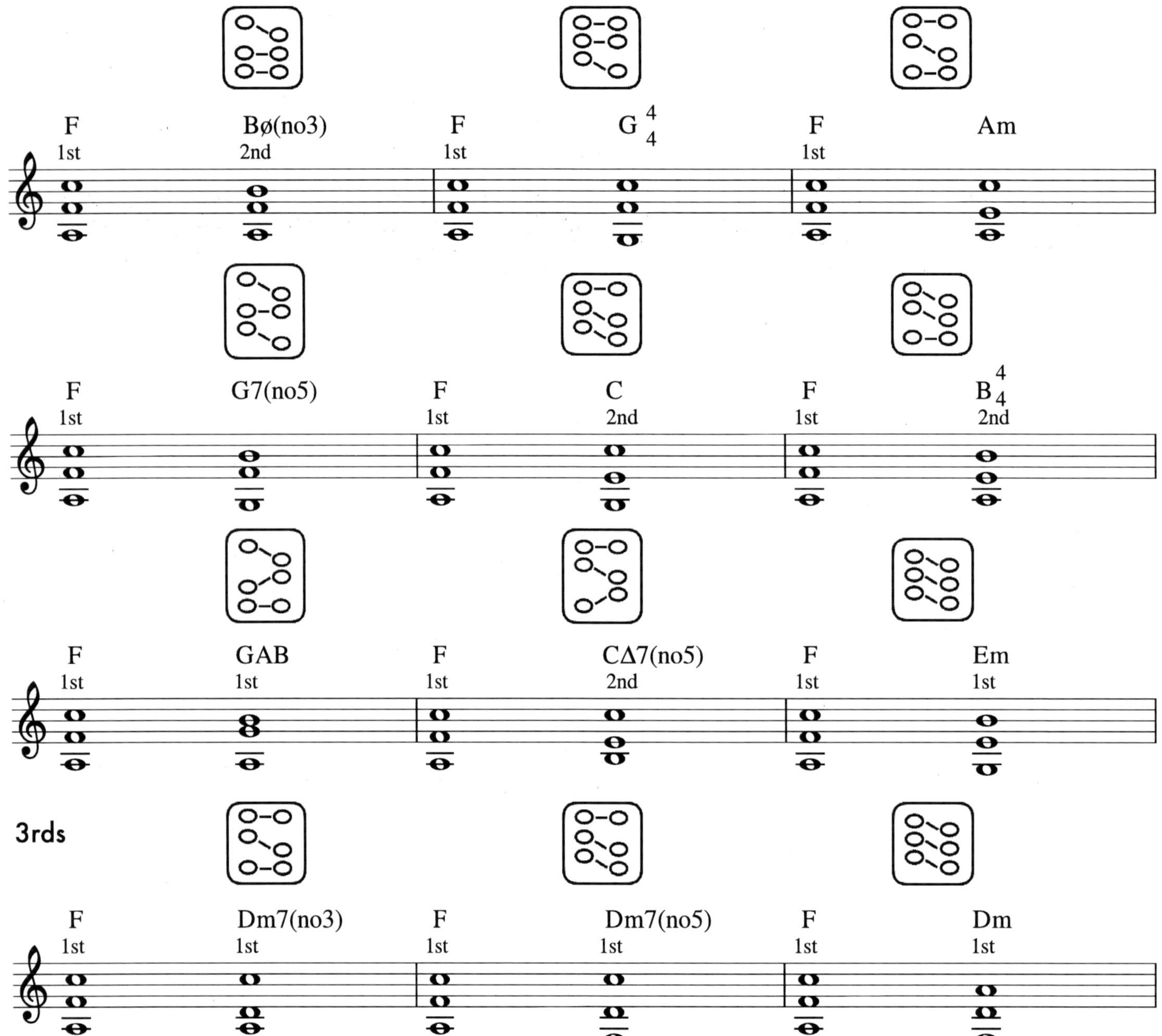

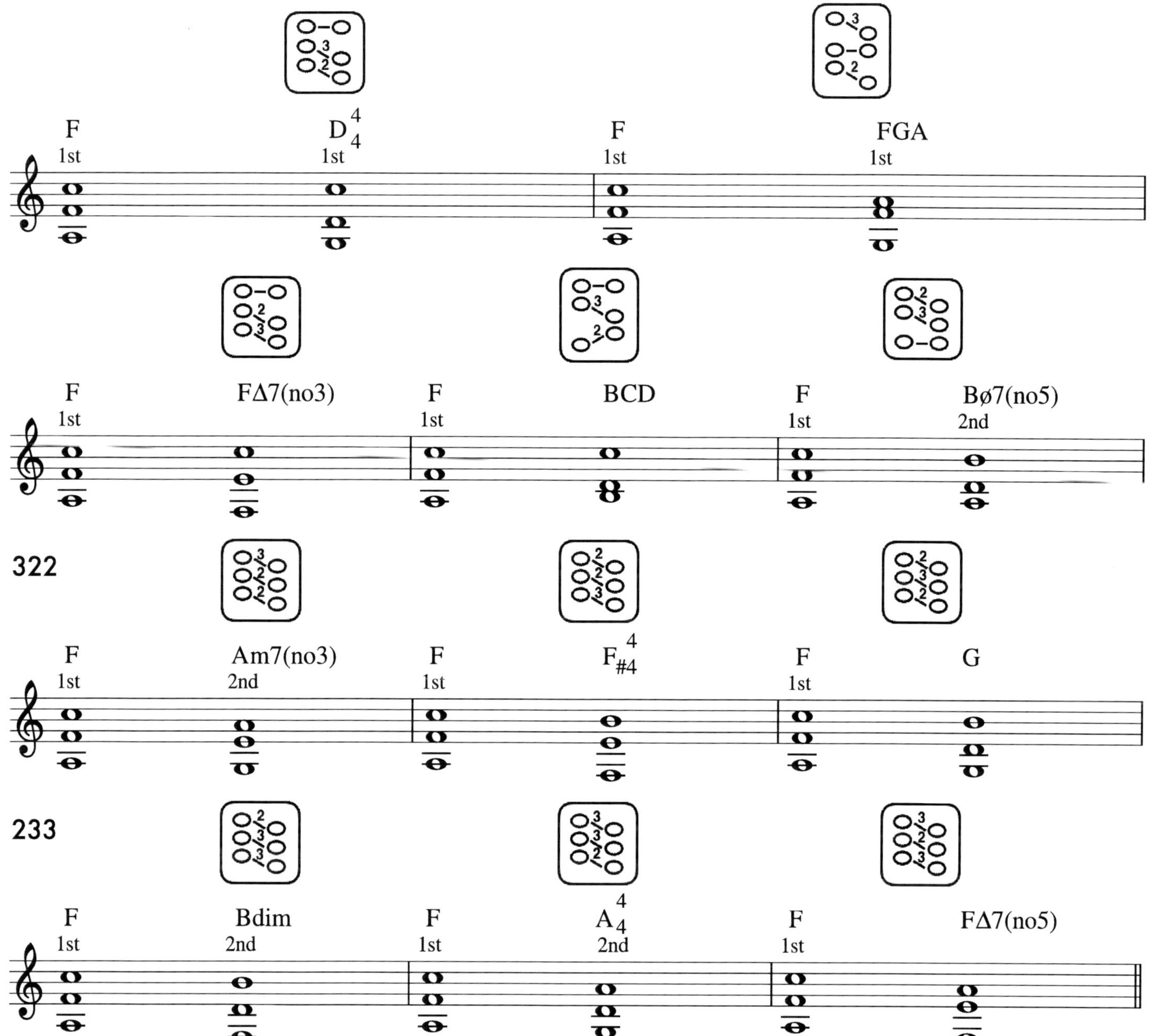
F
1st
D 4 4
1st
F
1st
FGA
1st
F
1st
FΔ7(no3)
F
1st
BCD
F
1st
Bø7(no5)
2nd
322
F
1st
Am7(no3)
2nd
F
1st
F 4 #4
F
1st
G
233
F
1st
Bdim
2nd
F
1st
A 4 4
2nd
F
1st
FΔ7(no5)

2nds

4ths in 2nd Inversion

Using regular/ascending motion

open

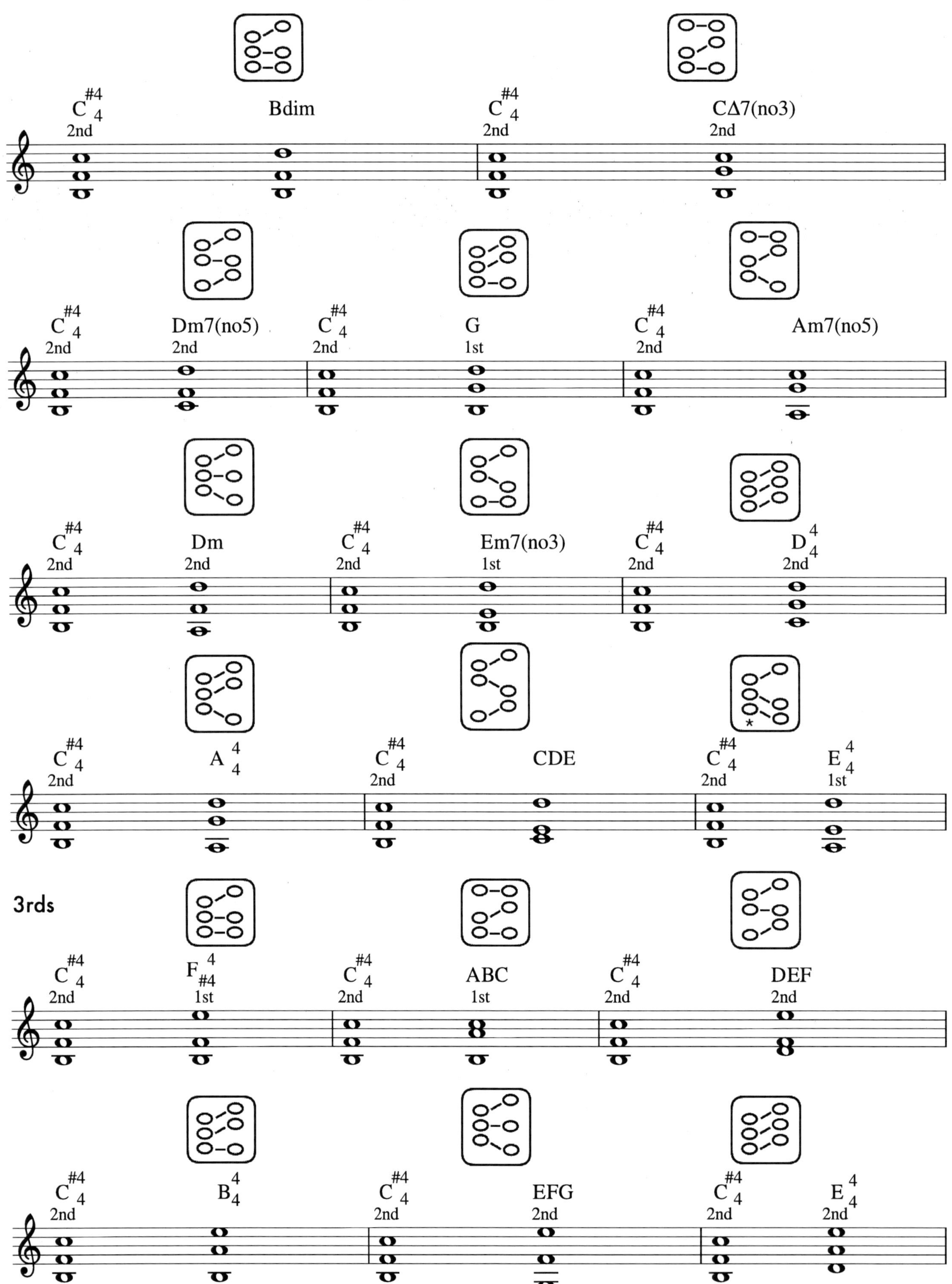

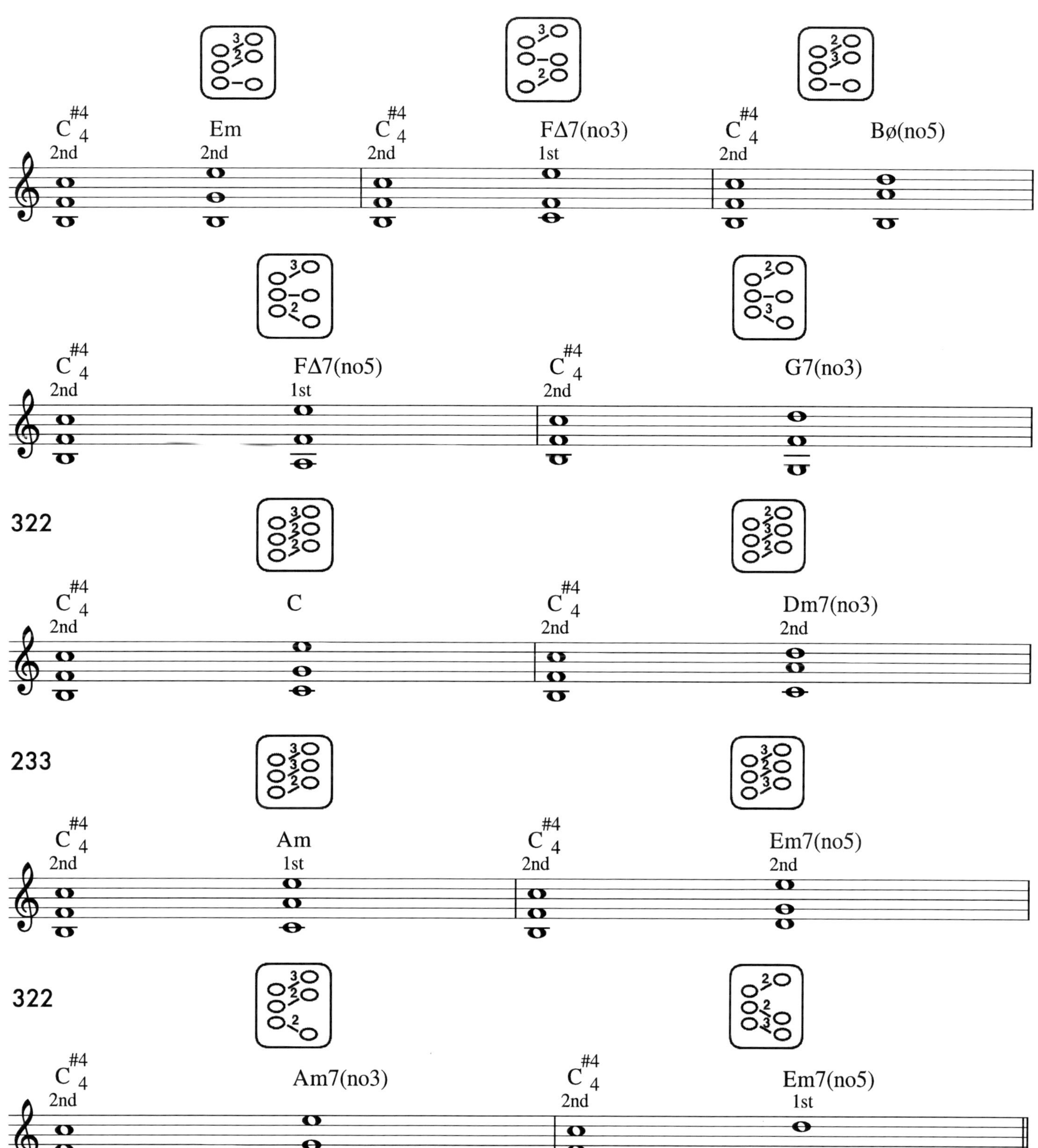
C#4 4 2nd
Em 2nd
C#4 4 2nd
FΔ7(no3) 1st
C#4 4 2nd
Bø(no5)
C#4 4 2nd
FΔ7(no5) 1st
C#4 4 2nd
G7(no3)
322
C#4 4 2nd
C
C#4 4 2nd
Dm7(no3) 2nd
233
C#4 4 2nd
Am 1st
C#4 4 2nd
Em7(no5) 2nd
322
C#4 4 2nd
Am7(no3)
C#4 4 2nd
Em7(no5) 1st

2nds

4ths in 2nd Inversion

Using reverse/descending motion

open

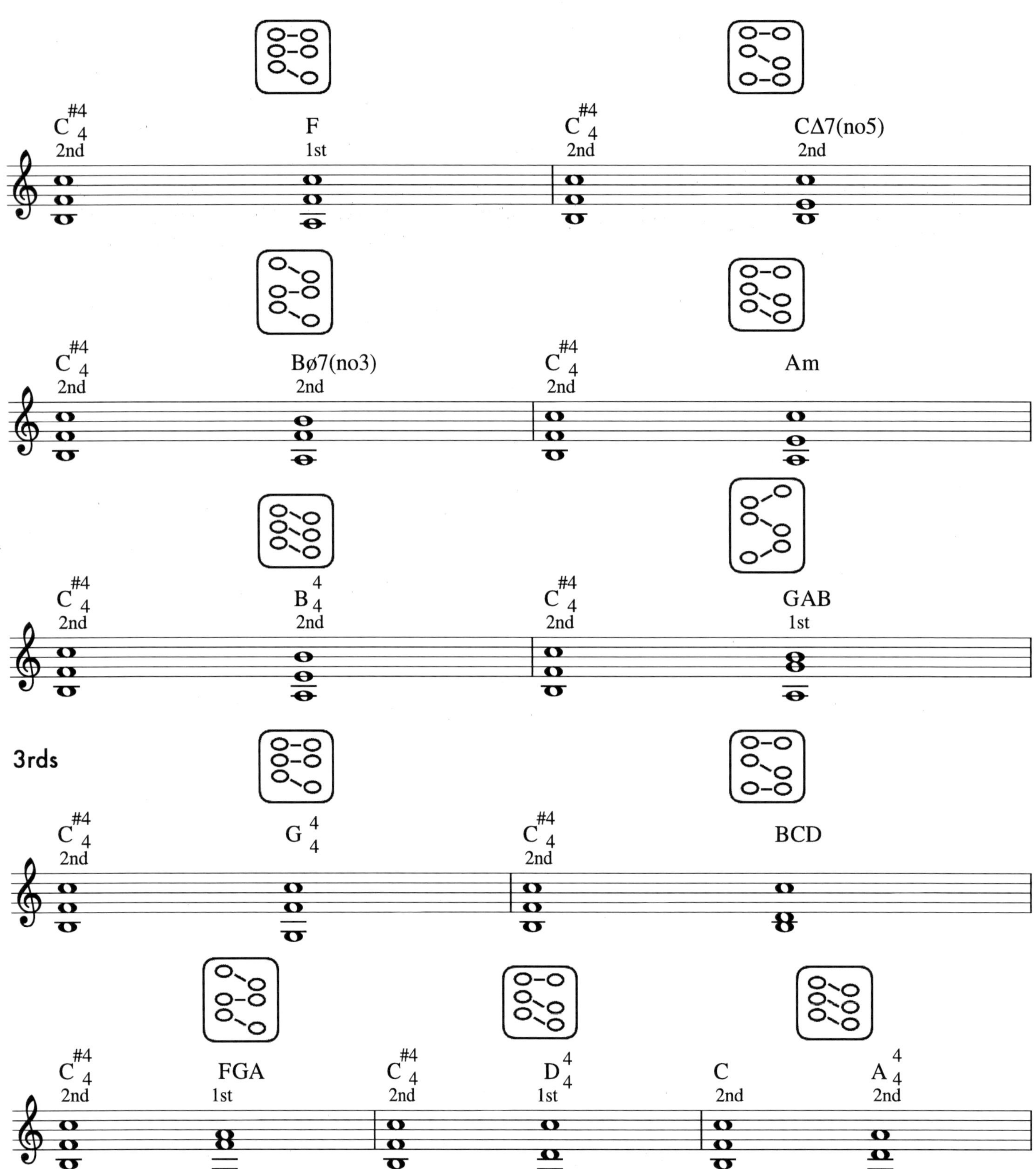

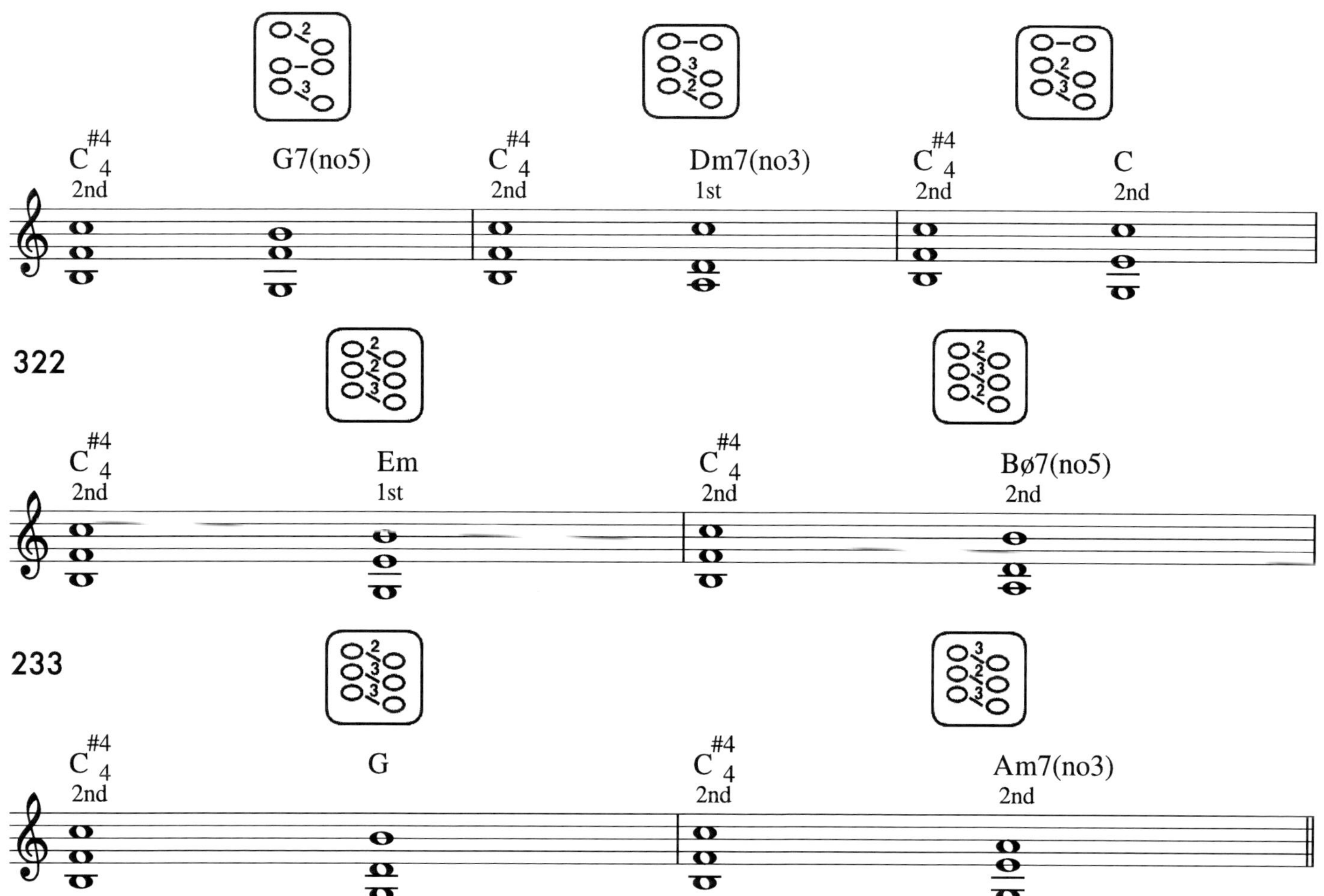
C#4 4 2nd
G7(no5)
C#4 4 2nd
Dm7(no3) 1st
C#4 4 2nd
C 2nd
322
C#4 4 2nd
Em 1st
C#4 4 2nd
Bø7(no5) 2nd
233
C#4 4 2nd
G
C#4 4 2nd
Am7(no3) 2nd

2nds

4ths in Root Position

open

Using regular/ascending motion

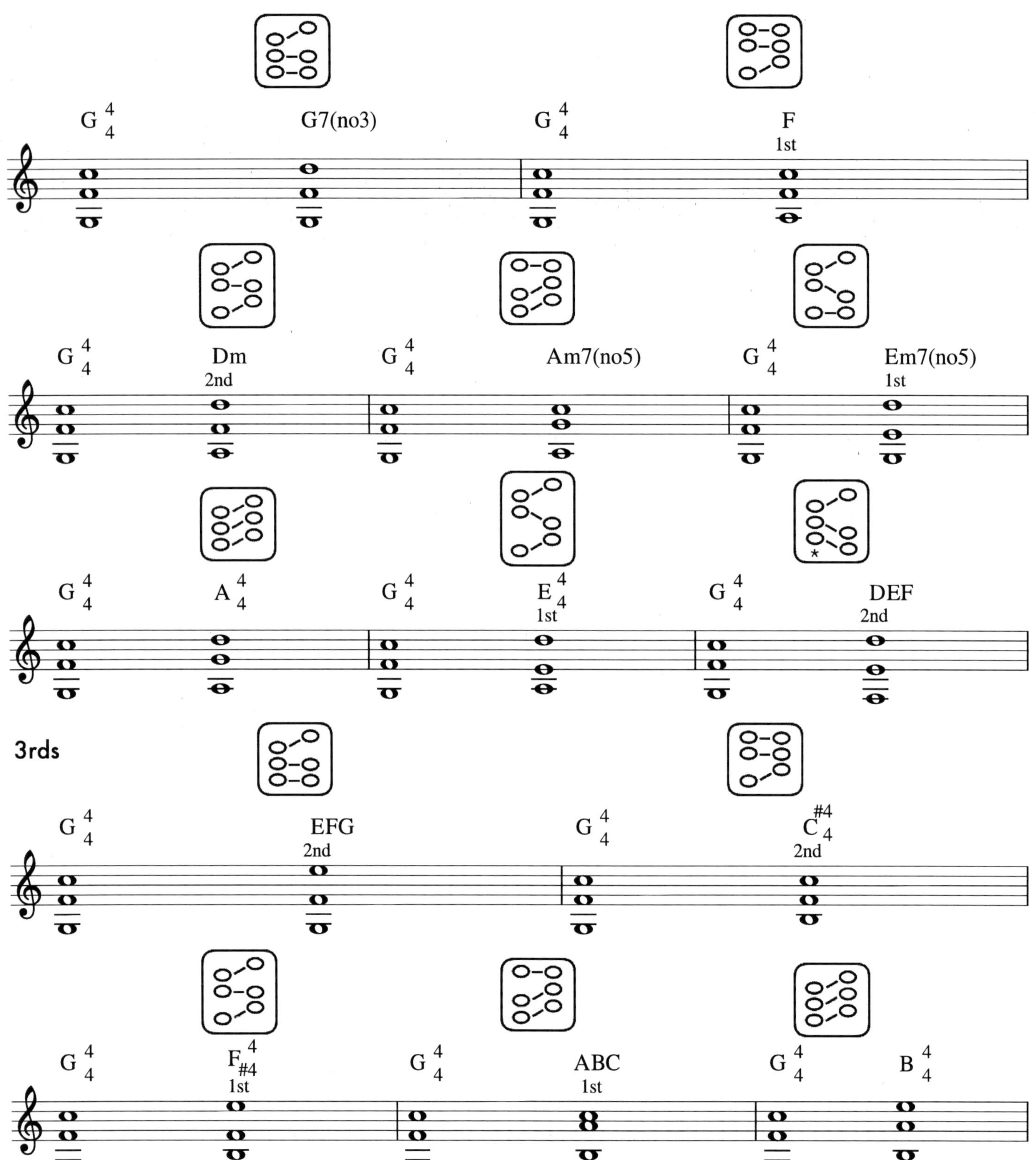

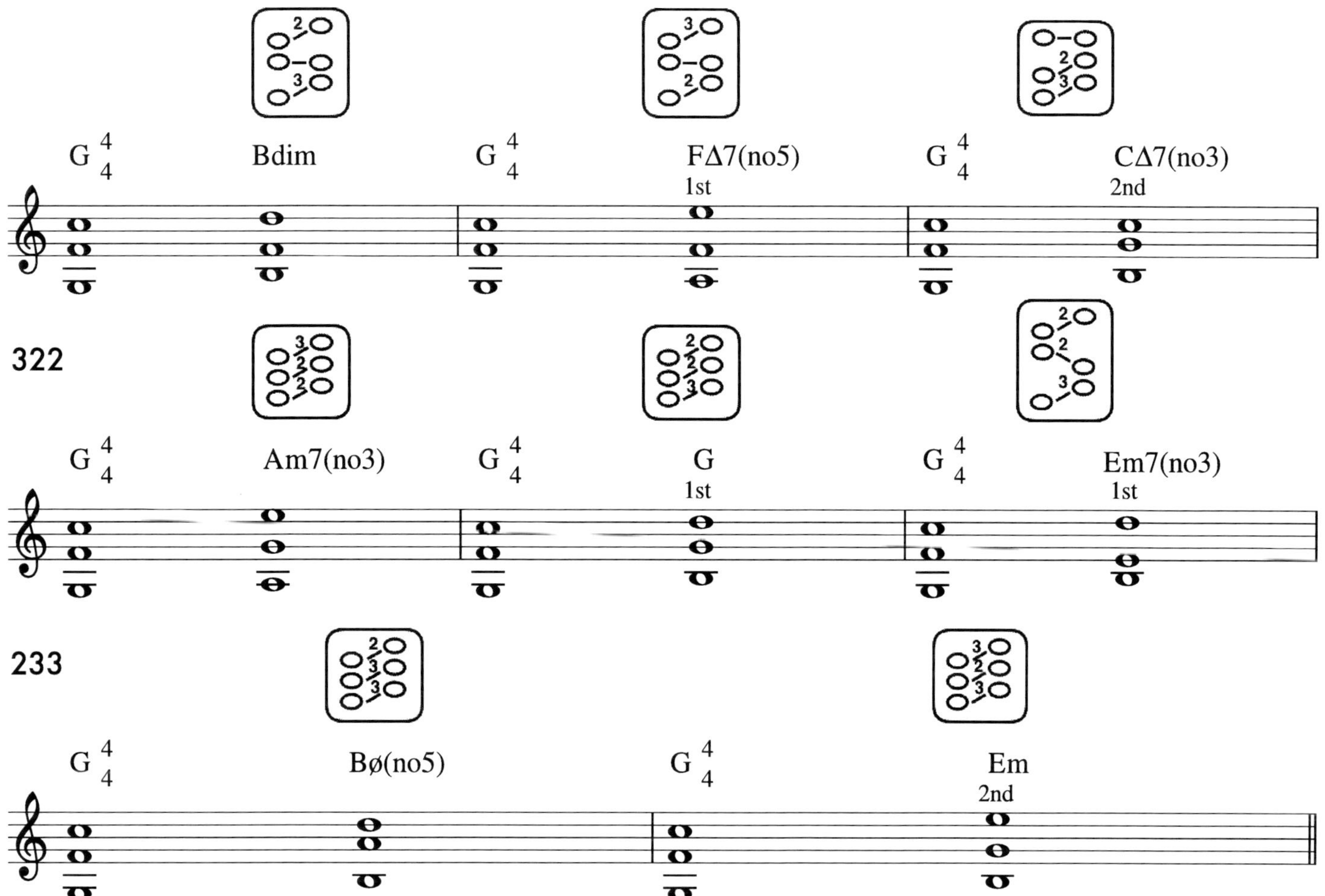
G 4/4
Bdim
G 4/4
FΔ7(no5)
1st
G 4/4
CΔ7(no3)
2nd
322
G 4/4
Am7(no3)
G 4/4
G
1st
G 4/4
Em7(no3)
1st
233
G 4/4
Bø(no5)
G 4/4
Em
2nd

2nds

4ths in Root Position

Using reverse/descending motion

open

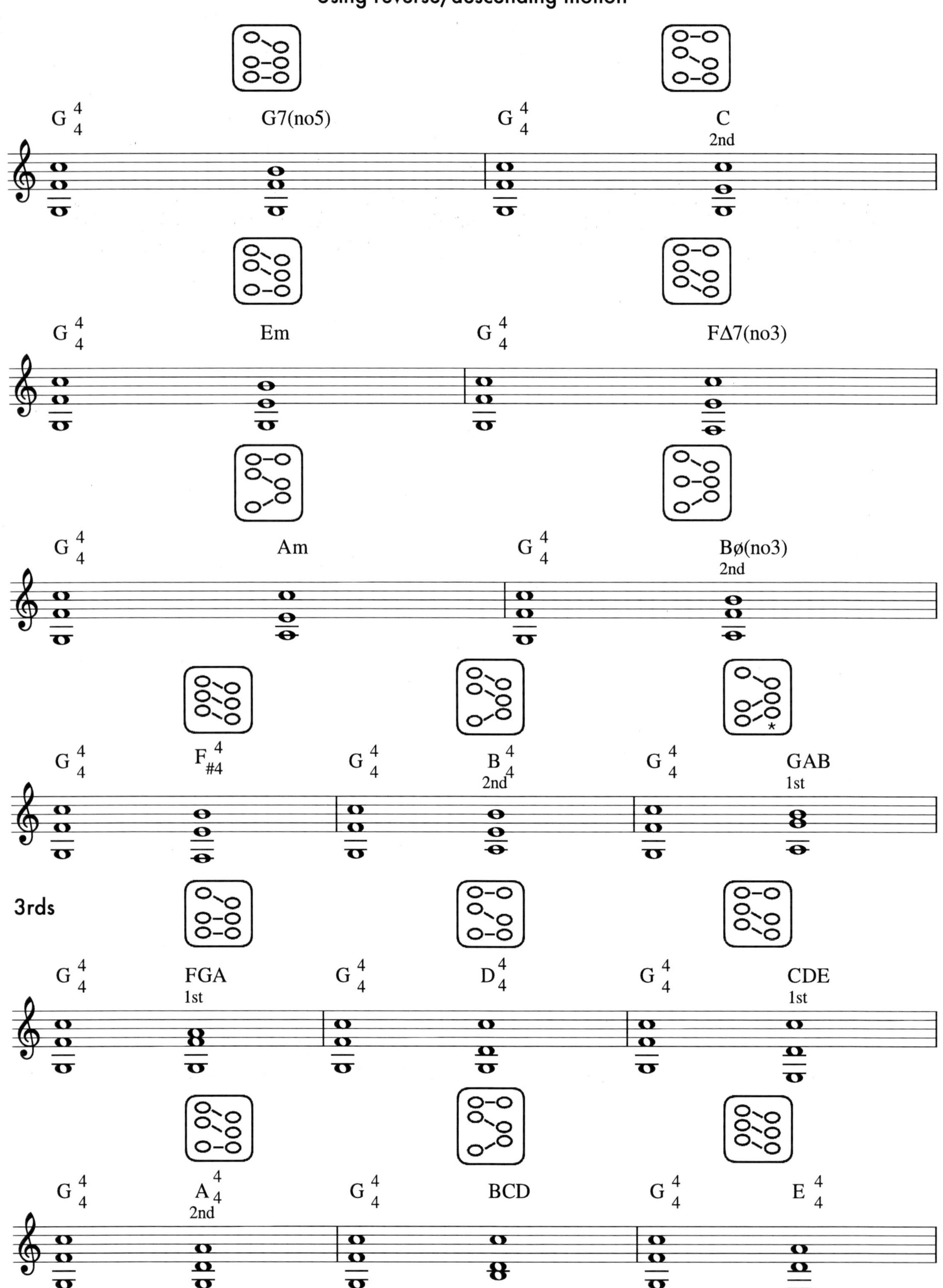

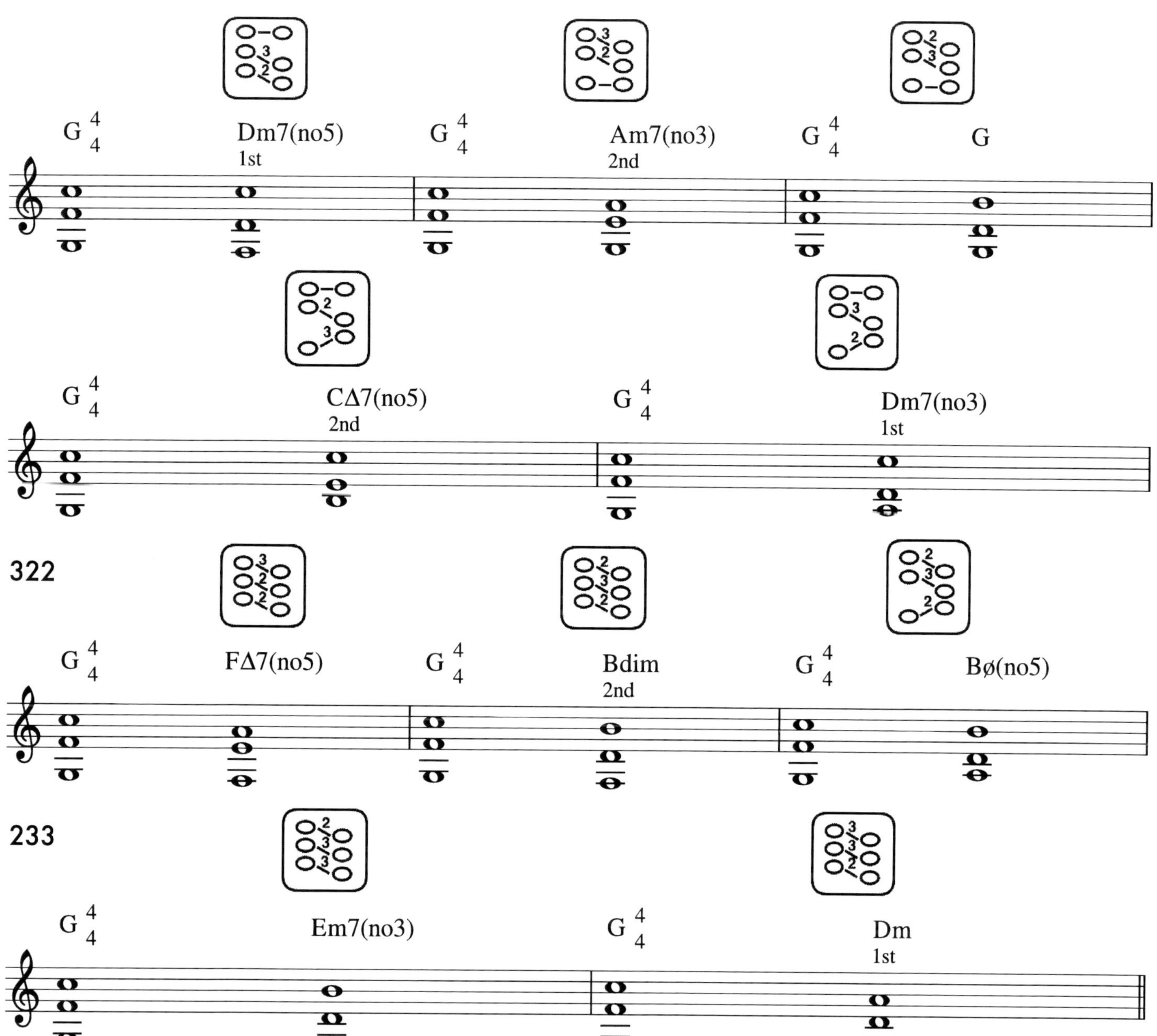
G 4/4
Dm7(no5)
1st
G 4/4
Am7(no3)
2nd
G 4/4
G
G 4/4
CΔ7(no5)
2nd
G 4/4
Dm7(no3)
1st
322
G 4/4
FΔ7(no5)
G 4/4
Bdim
2nd
G 4/4
Bø(no5)
233
G 4/4
Em7(no3)
G 4/4
Dm
1st

2nds

4ths in 1st Inversion

Uisng regular/ascending motion

open

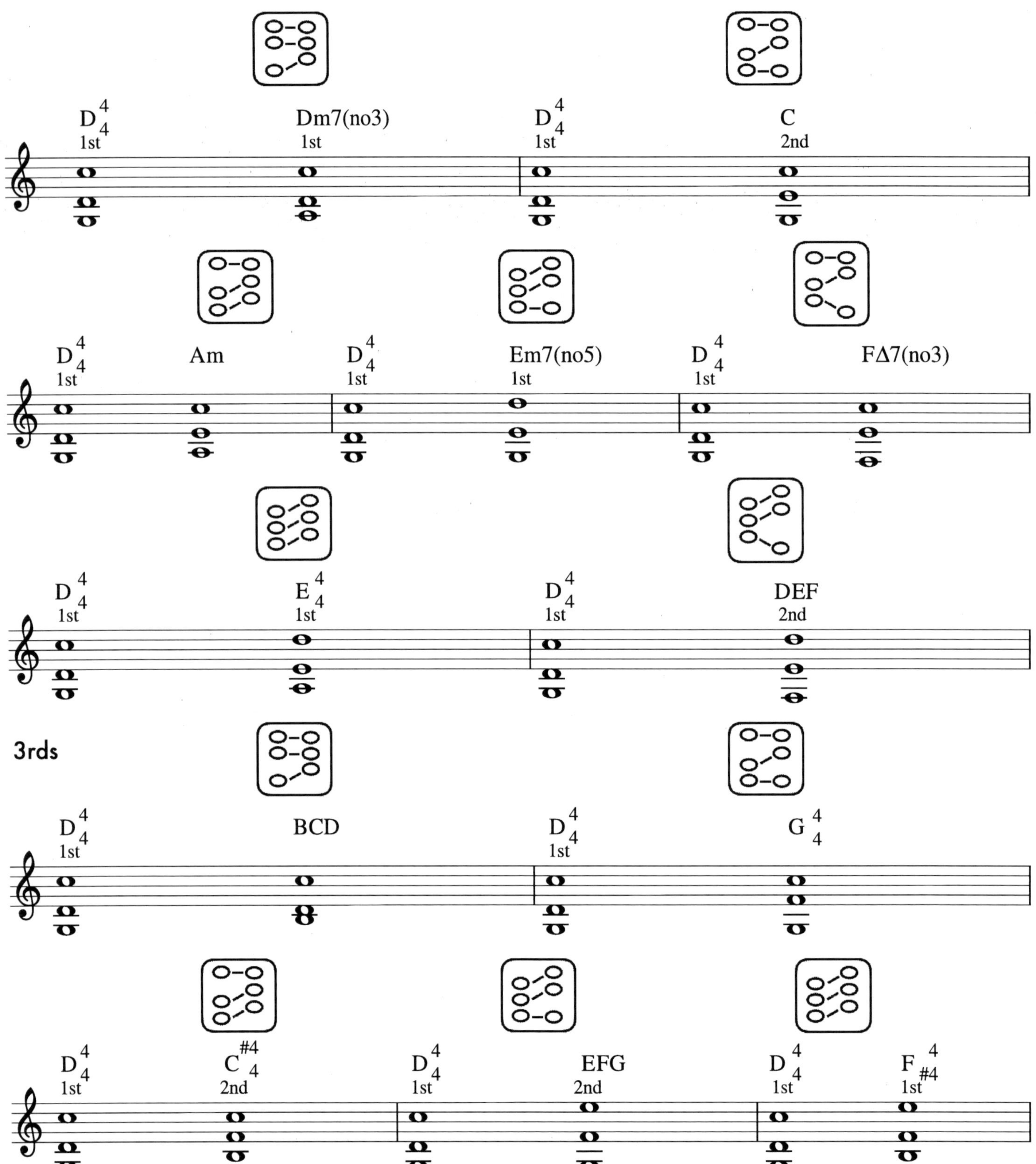

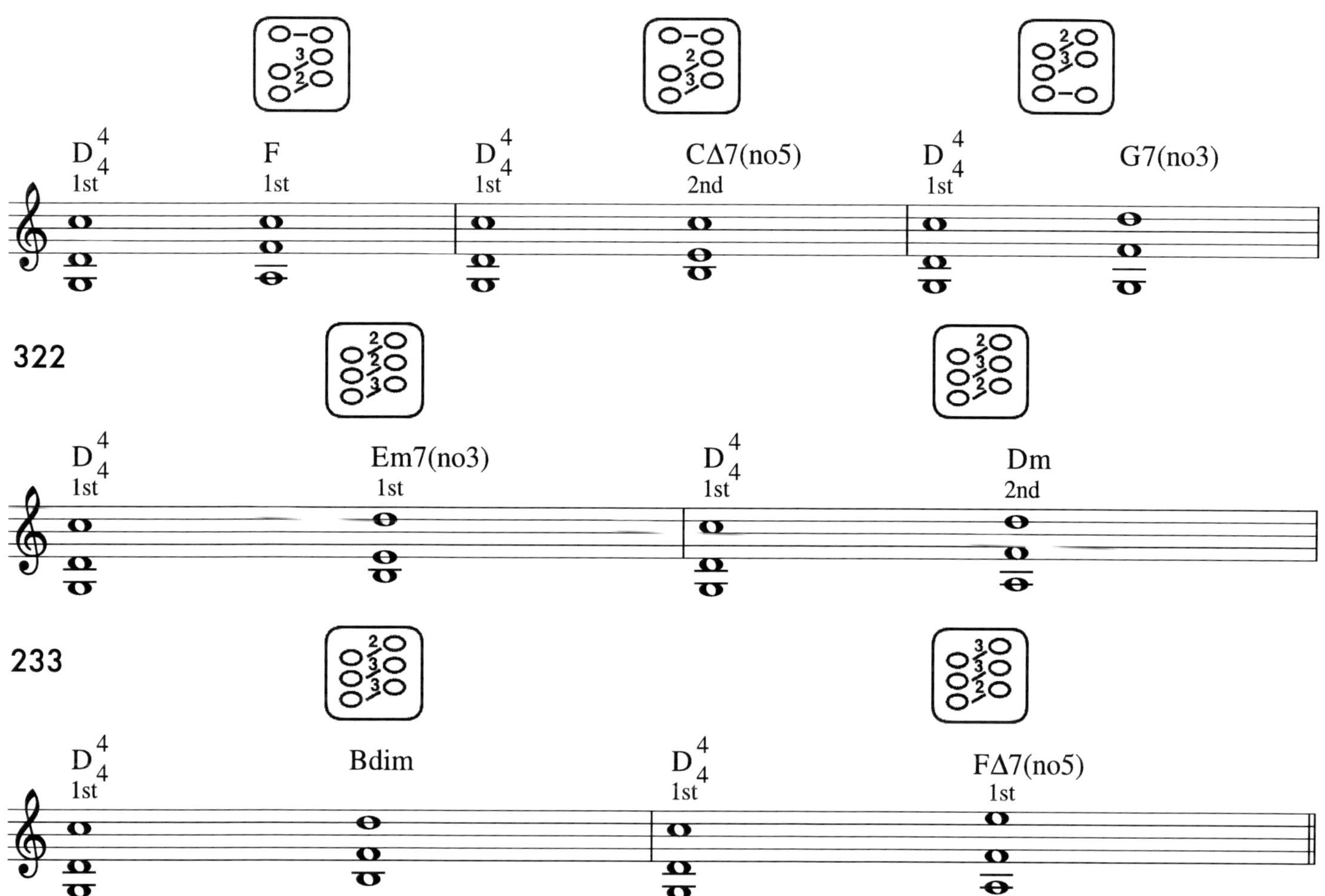
D 4 4 1st
F 1st
D 4 4 1st
CΔ7(no5) 2nd
D 4 4 1st
G7(no3)
322
D 4 4 1st
Em7(no3) 1st
D 4 4 1st
Dm 2nd
233
D 4 4 1st
Bdim
D 4 4 1st
FΔ7(no5) 1st

2nds

4ths in 1st Inversion

open

Using reverse/descending motion

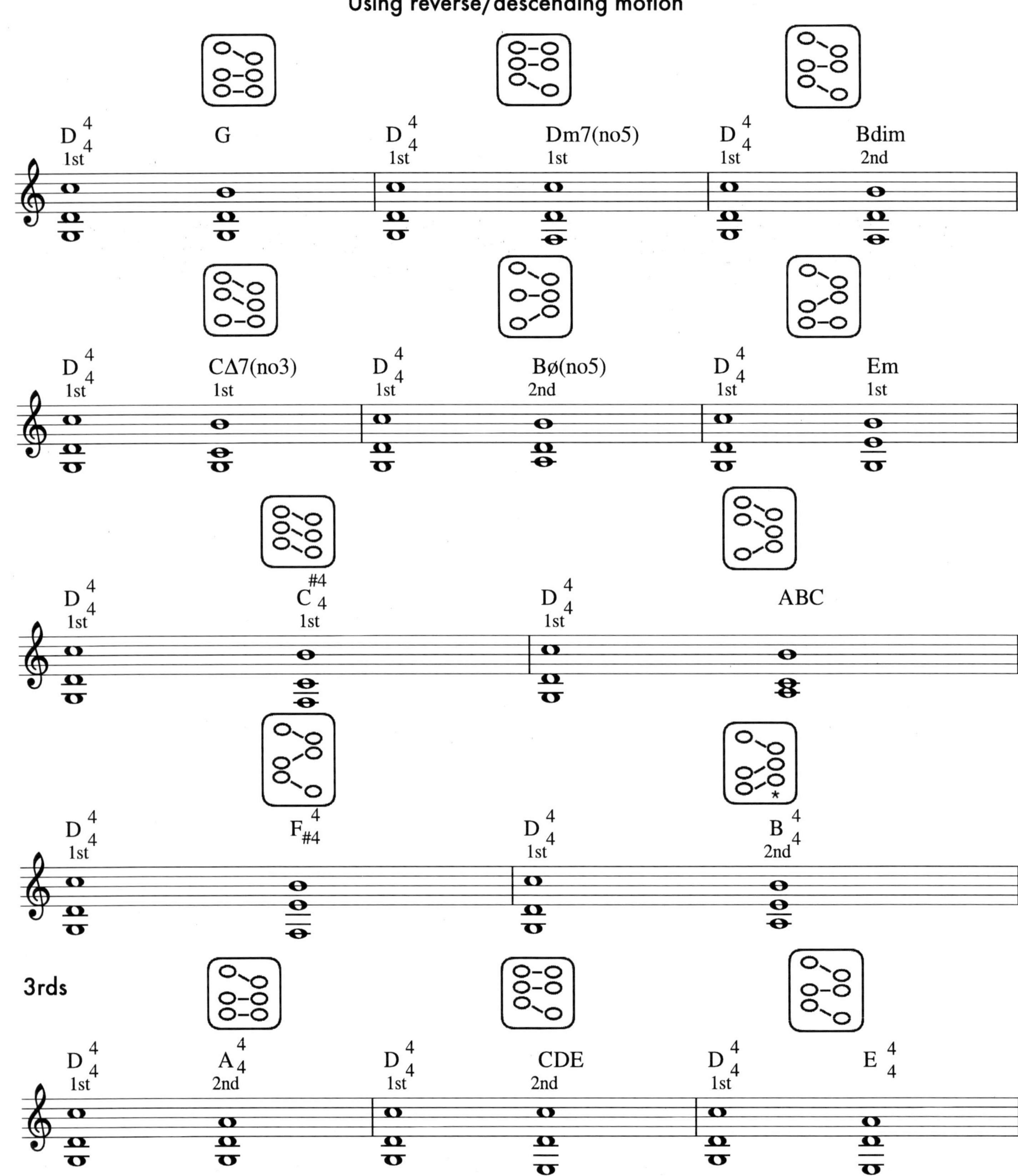

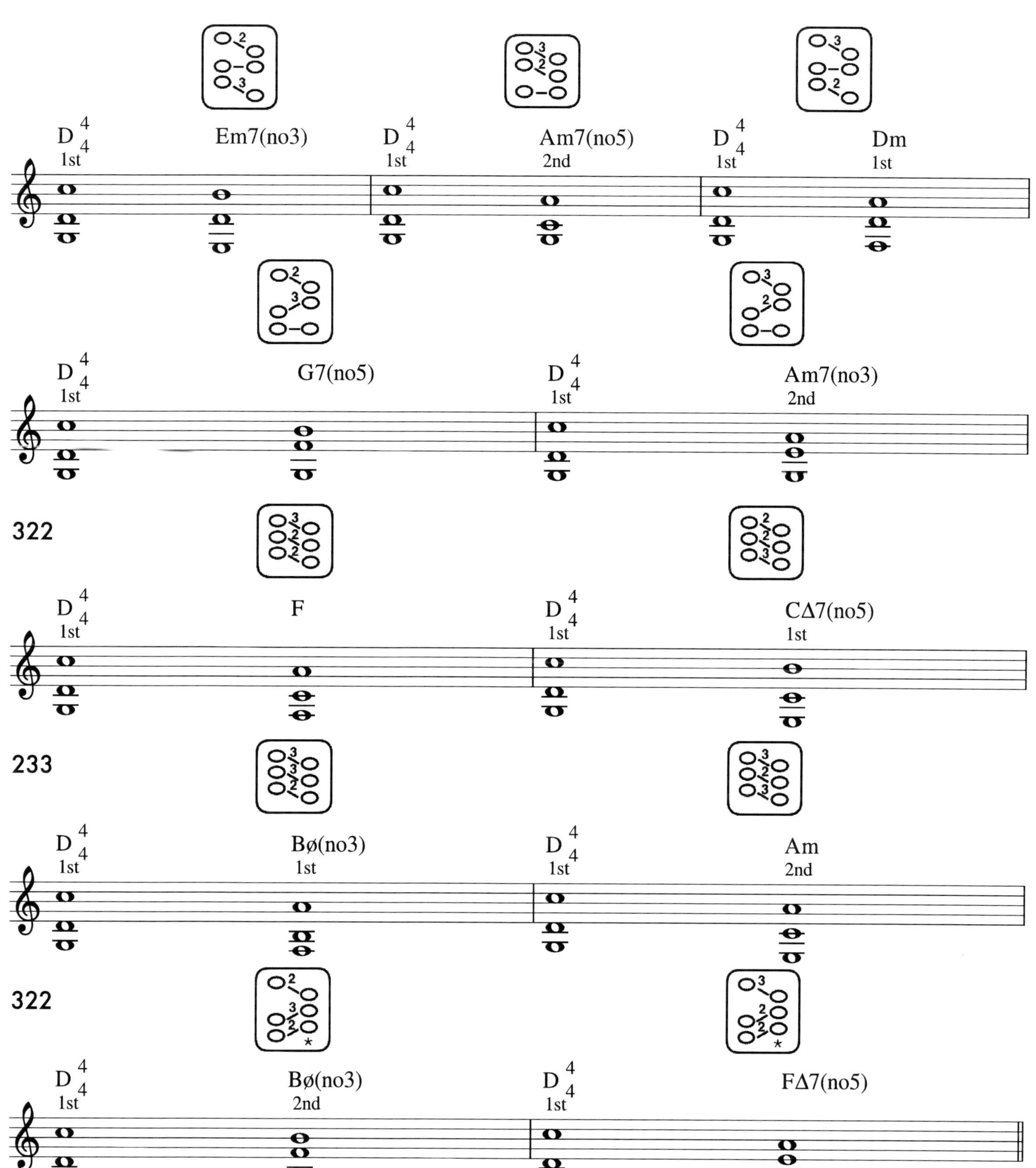
D 4 4 1st
Em7(no3)
D 4 4 1st
Am7(no5) 2nd
D 4 4 1st
Dm 1st
D 4 4 1st
G7(no5)
D 4 4 1st
Am7(no3) 2nd
322
D 4 4 1st
F
D 4 4 1st
CΔ7(no5) 1st
233
D 4 4 1st
Bø(no3) 1st
D 4 4 1st
Am 2nd
322
D 4 4 1st
Bø(no3) 2nd
D 4 4 1st
FΔ7(no5)

2nds

7th no 5 in 2nd Inversion

open

Using regular/ascending motion

CΔ7(no5) 2nd — Em7(no3) 1st | CΔ7(no5) 2nd — C$^{\#4}_{4}$ 2nd

CΔ7(no5) 2nd — CDE | CΔ7(no5) 2nd — Bdim

CΔ7(no5) 2nd — E$^{4}_{4}$ 1st | CΔ7(no5) 2nd — F 1st

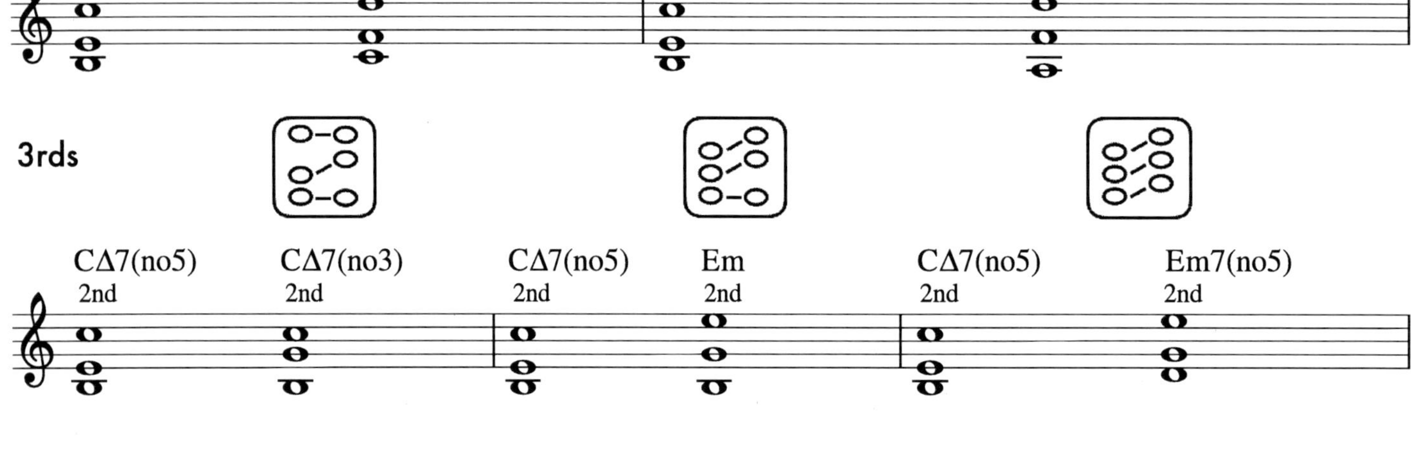

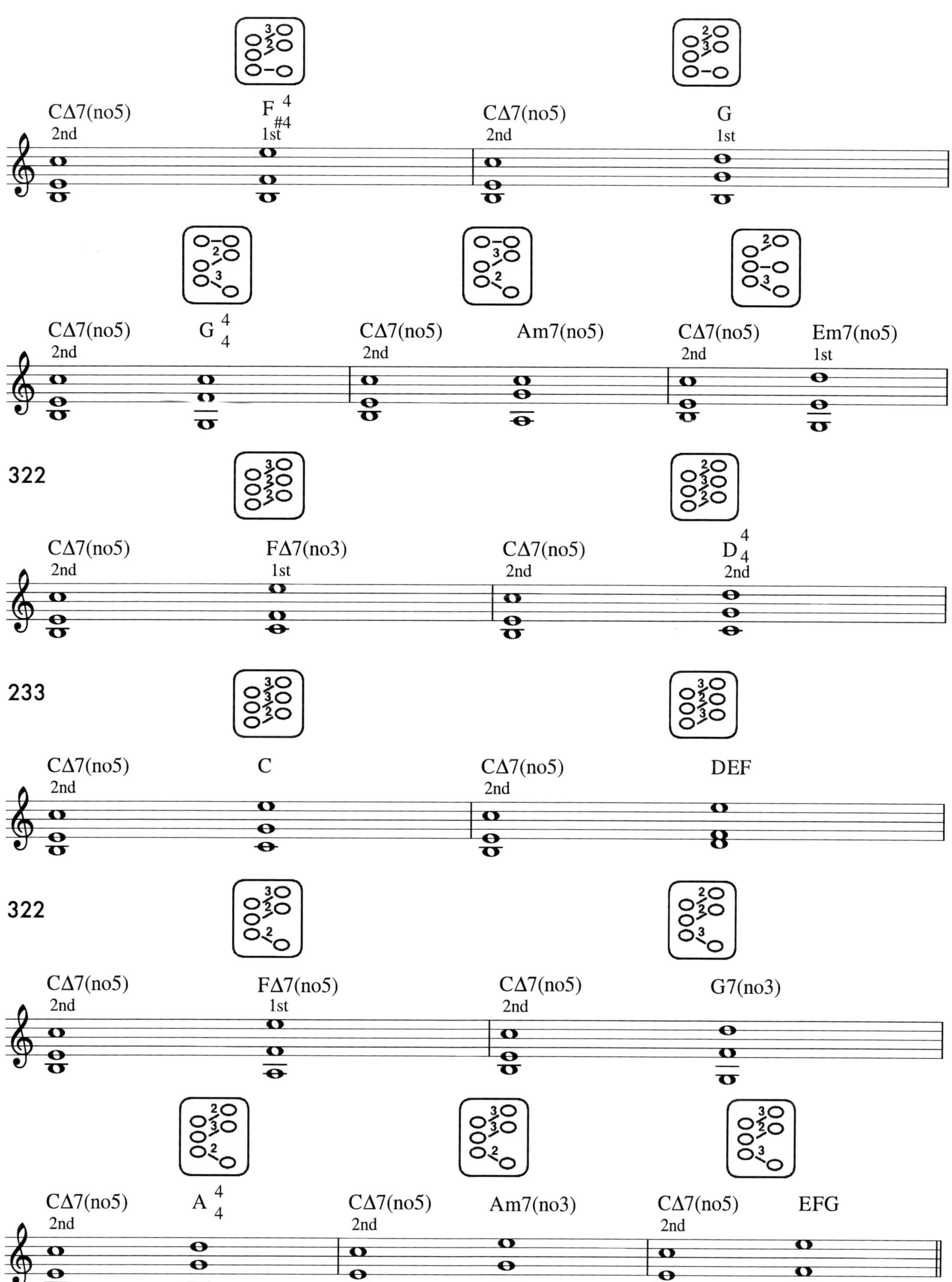
CΔ7(no5) 2nd
F 4 #4 1st
CΔ7(no5) 2nd
G 1st
CΔ7(no5) 2nd
G 4 4
CΔ7(no5) 2nd
Am7(no5)
CΔ7(no5) 2nd
Em7(no5) 1st
322
CΔ7(no5) 2nd
FΔ7(no3) 1st
CΔ7(no5) 2nd
D 4 4 2nd
233
CΔ7(no5) 2nd
C
CΔ7(no5) 2nd
DEF
322
CΔ7(no5) 2nd
FΔ7(no5) 1st
CΔ7(no5) 2nd
G7(no3)
CΔ7(no5) 2nd
A 4 4
CΔ7(no5) 2nd
Am7(no3)
CΔ7(no5) 2nd
EFG

7th no 5 in 2nd Inversion

Using reverse/descending motion

2nds | open

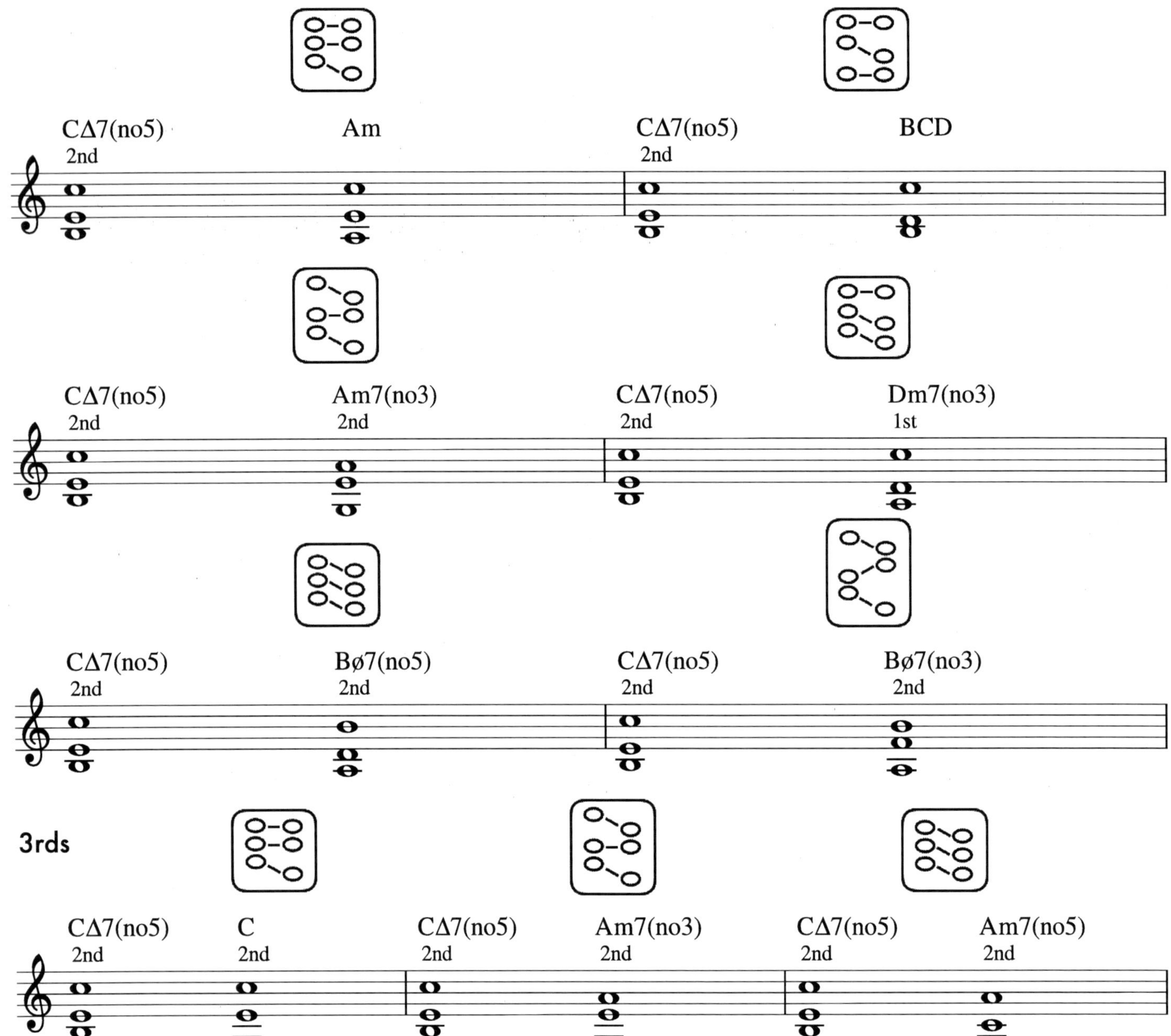

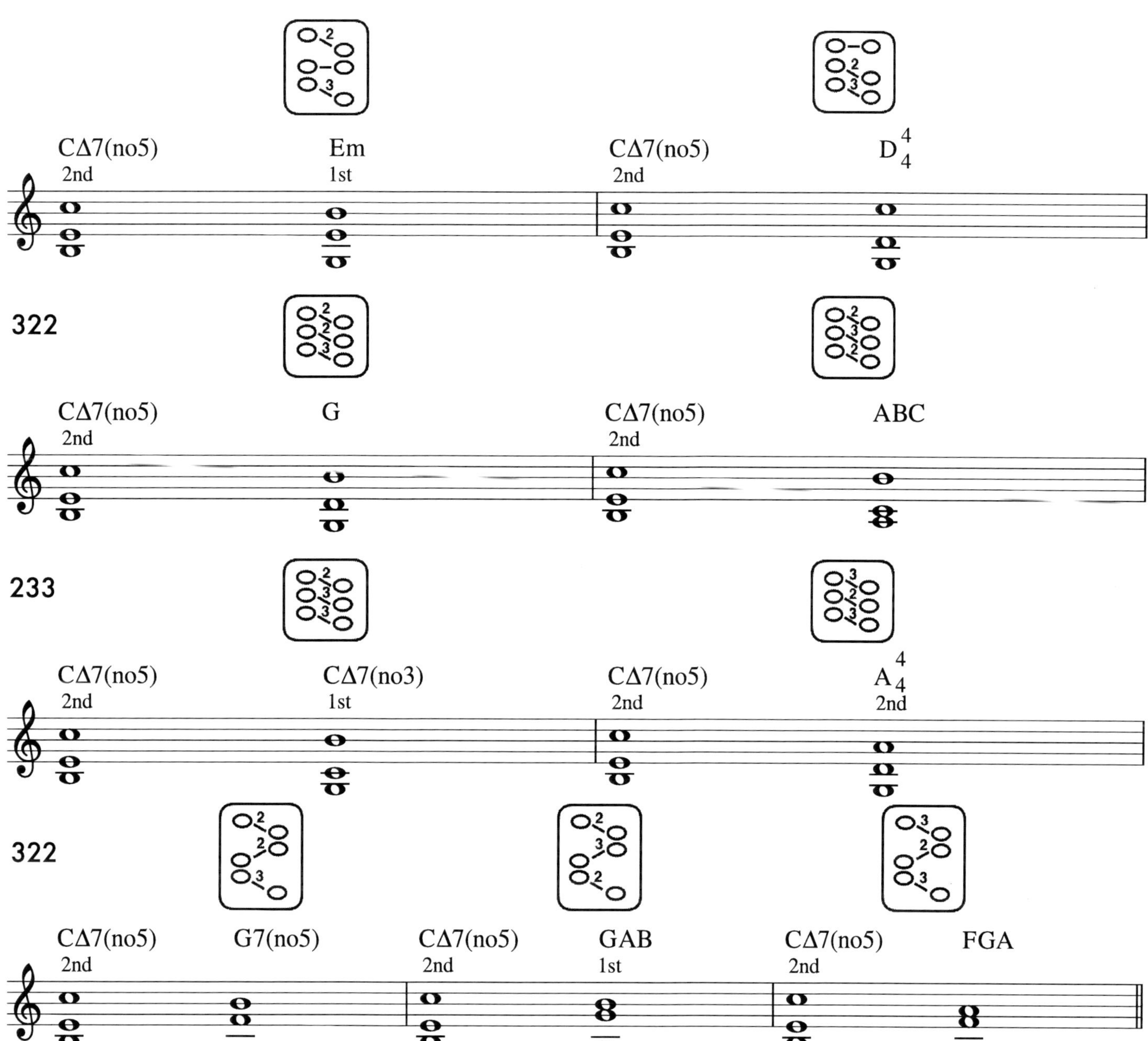

322
233
322
CΔ7(no5)
2nd
Em
1st
D 4 4
G
ABC
CΔ7(no3)
1st
A 4 4
2nd
G7(no5)
GAB
1st
FGA

2nds

7th no 5 in Root Position

Using regular/ascending motion

open

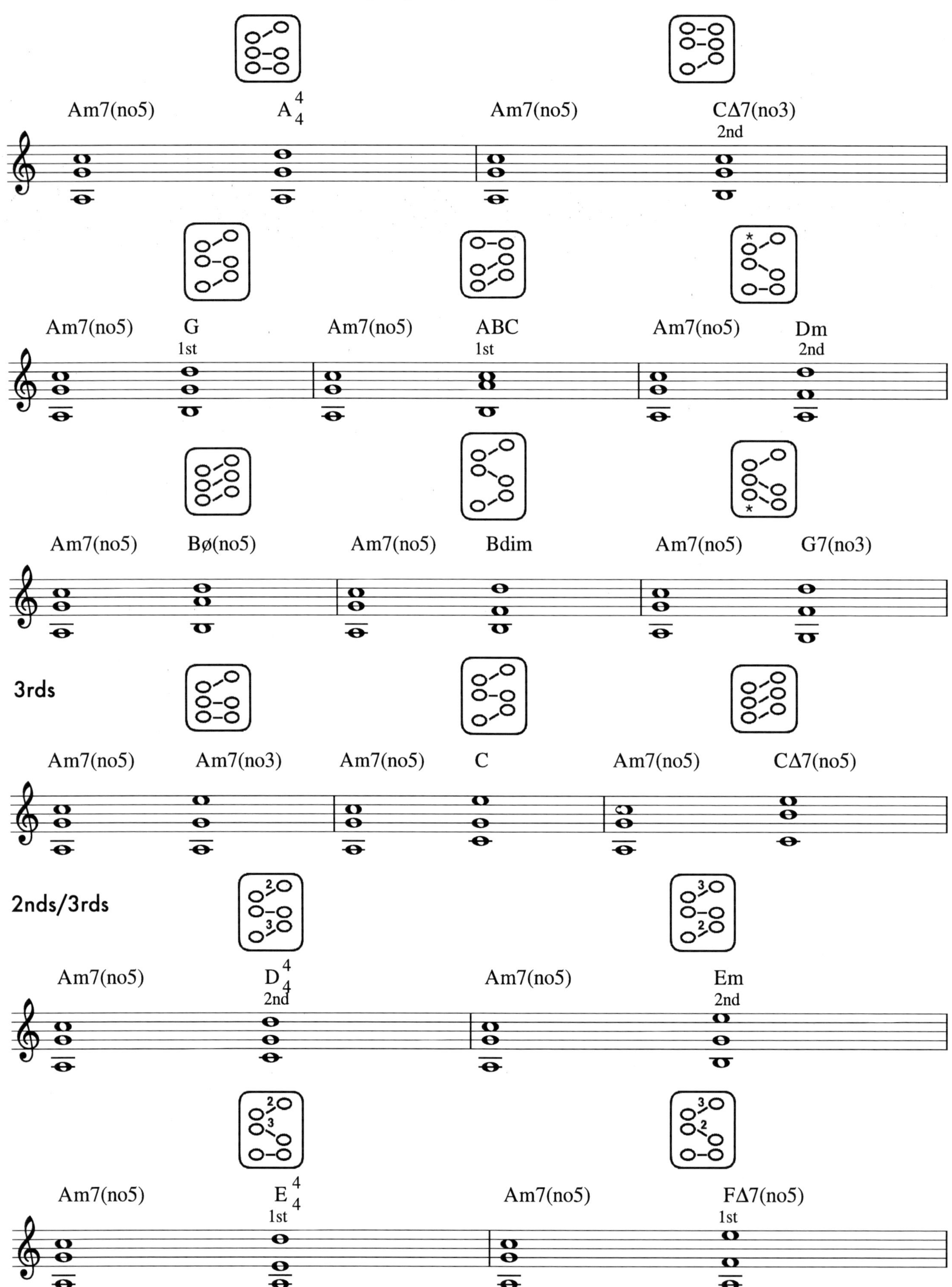

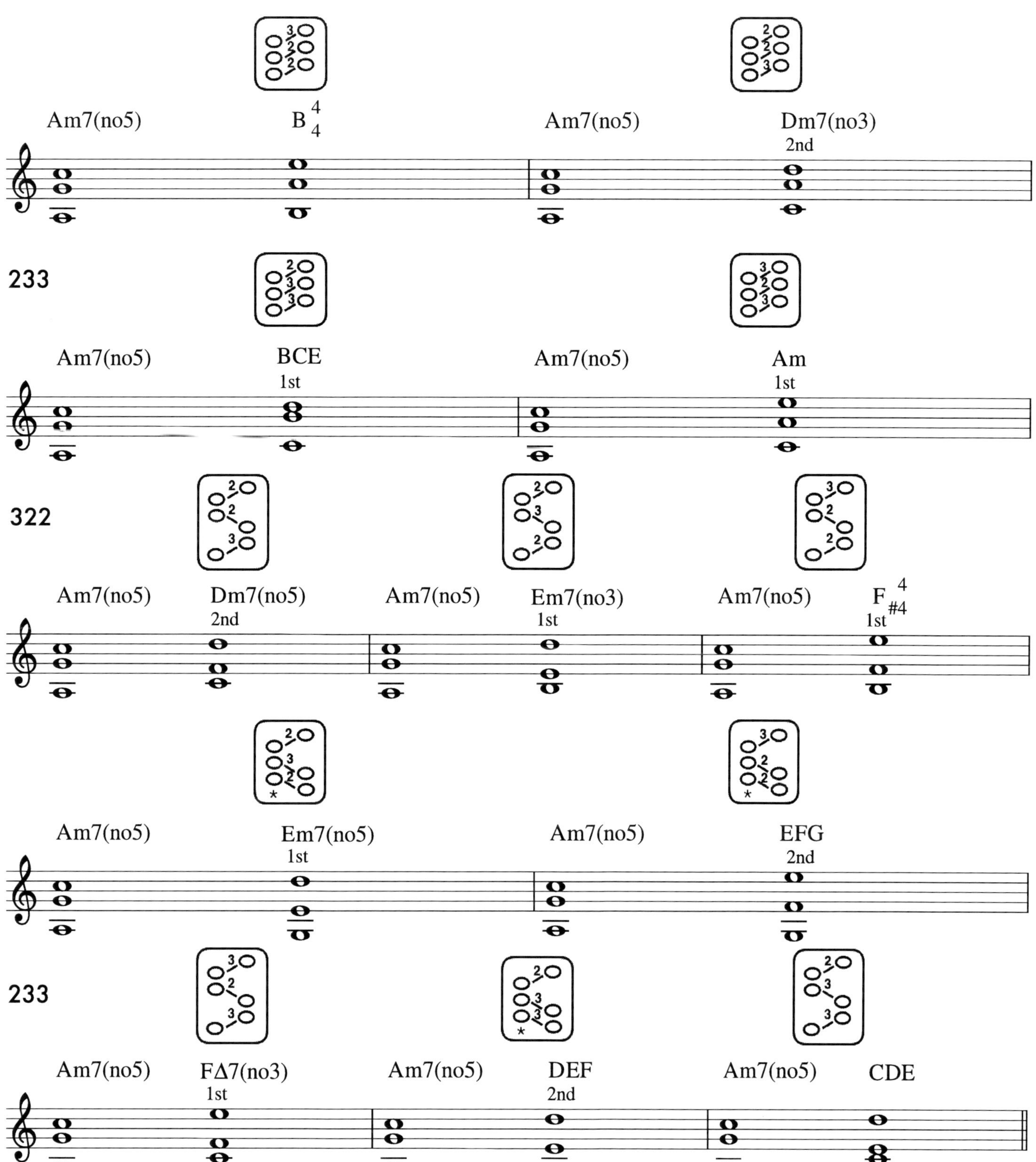
Am7(no5)
B 4 4
Am7(no5)
Dm7(no3)
2nd
233
Am7(no5)
BCE
1st
Am7(no5)
Am
1st
322
Am7(no5)
Dm7(no5)
2nd
Am7(no5)
Em7(no3)
1st
Am7(no5)
F 4 #4
1st
Am7(no5)
Em7(no5)
1st
Am7(no5)
EFG
2nd
233
Am7(no5)
FΔ7(no3)
1st
Am7(no5)
DEF
2nd
Am7(no5)
CDE

2nds

7th no 5 in Root Position

open

Using reverse/descending motion

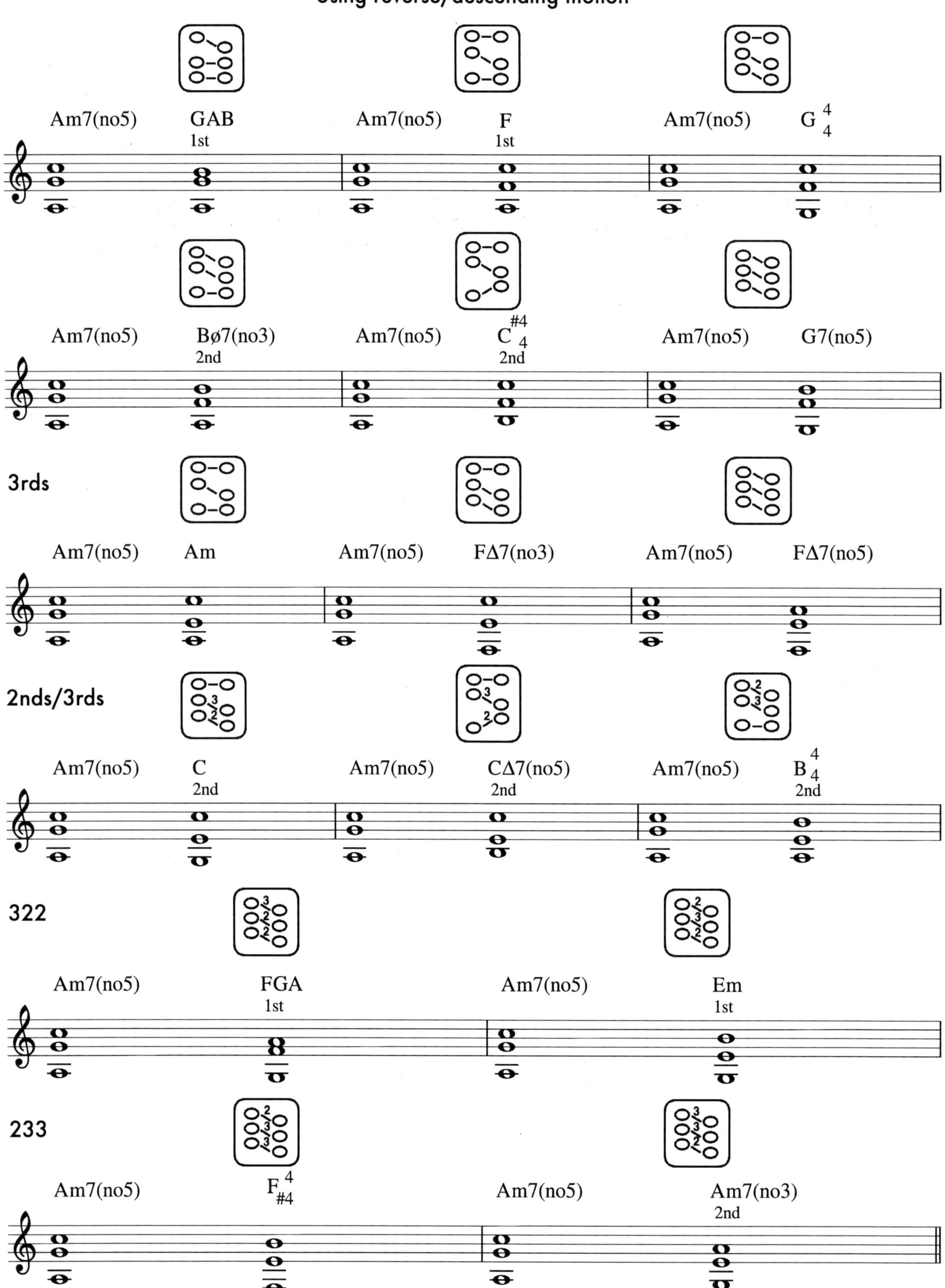

7th no 5 in 1st Inversion

Using regular/ascending motion

2nds | open

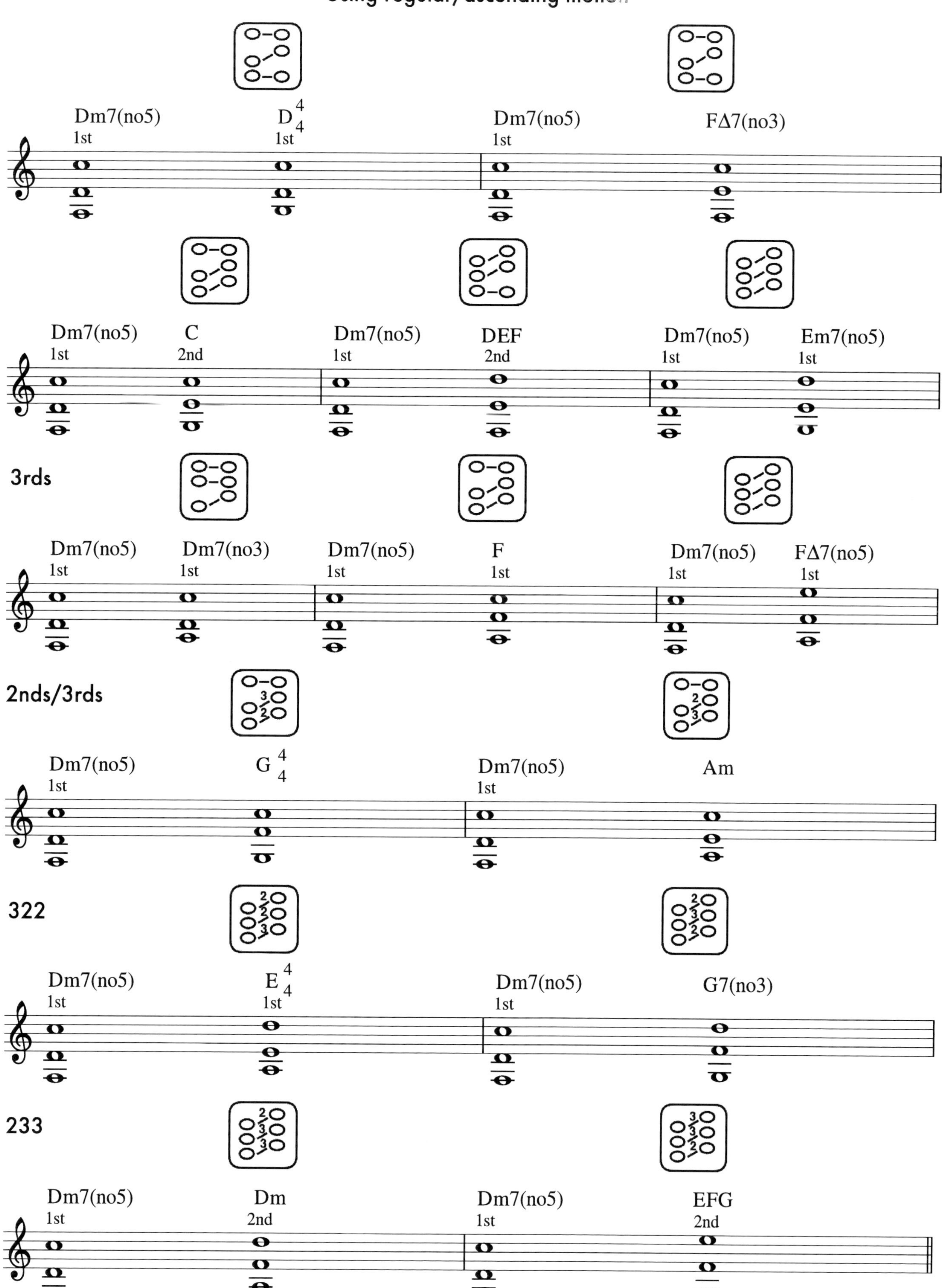

2nds

7th no 5 in 1st Inversion

open

Using reverse/descending motion

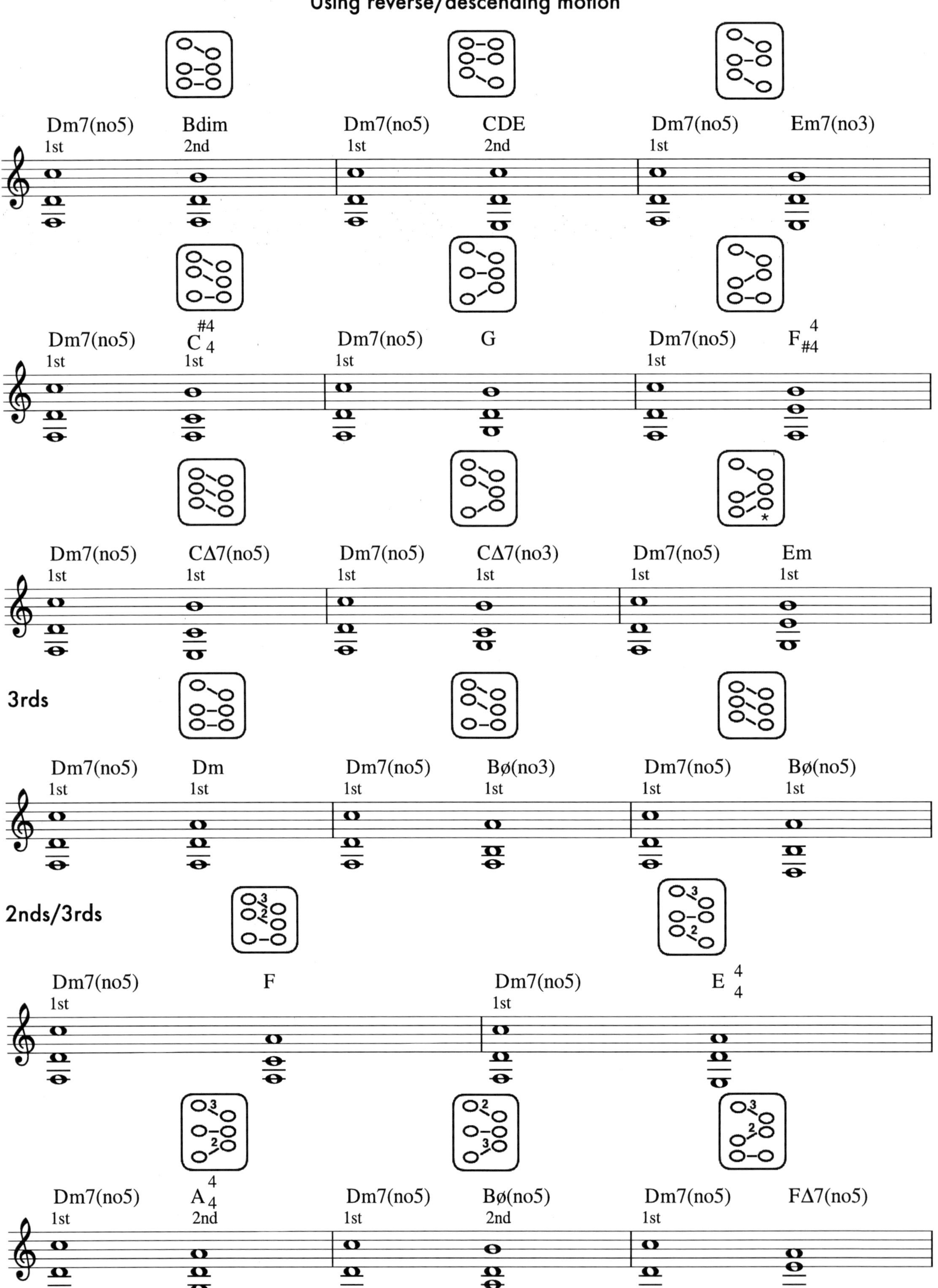

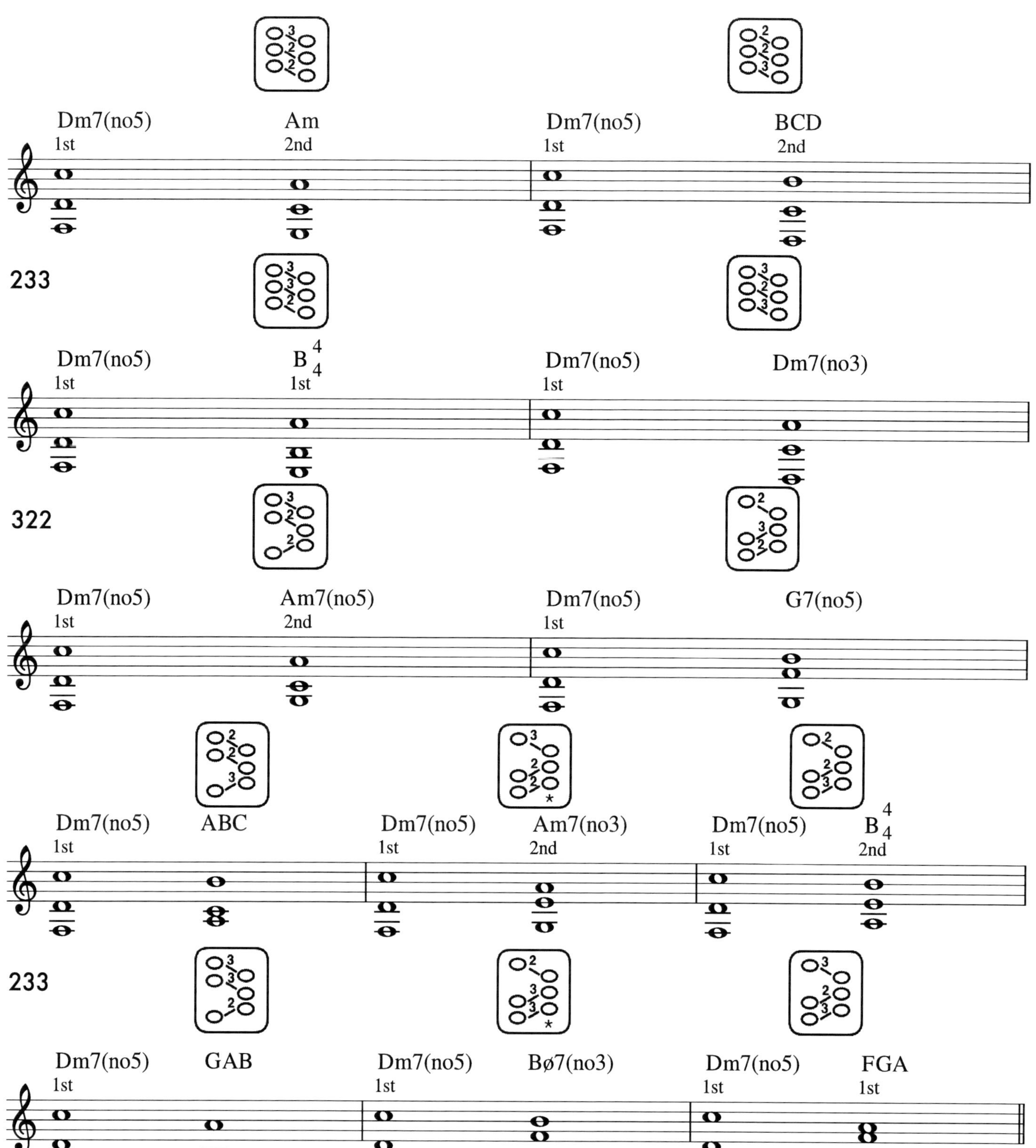
Dm7(no5)
1st
Am
2nd
Dm7(no5)
1st
BCD
2nd
233
Dm7(no5)
1st
B 4 4
1st
Dm7(no5)
1st
Dm7(no3)
322
Dm7(no5)
1st
Am7(no5)
2nd
Dm7(no5)
1st
G7(no5)
Dm7(no5)
1st
ABC
Dm7(no5)
1st
Am7(no3)
2nd
Dm7(no5)
1st
B 4 4
2nd
233
Dm7(no5)
1st
GAB
Dm7(no5)
1st
Bø7(no3)
Dm7(no5)
1st
FGA
1st

2nds

7th no 3 in 2nd Inversion

open

Using regular/ascending motion

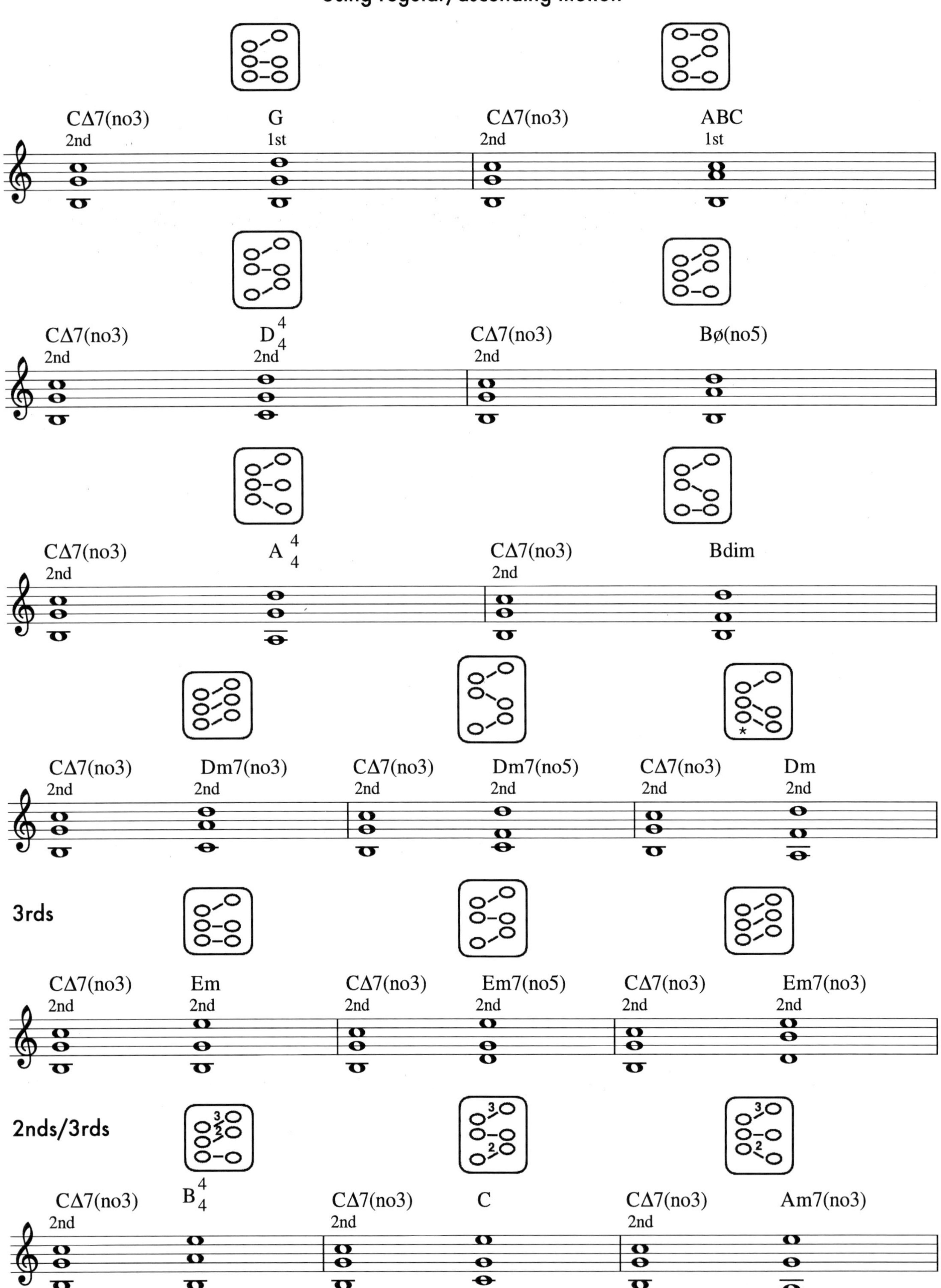

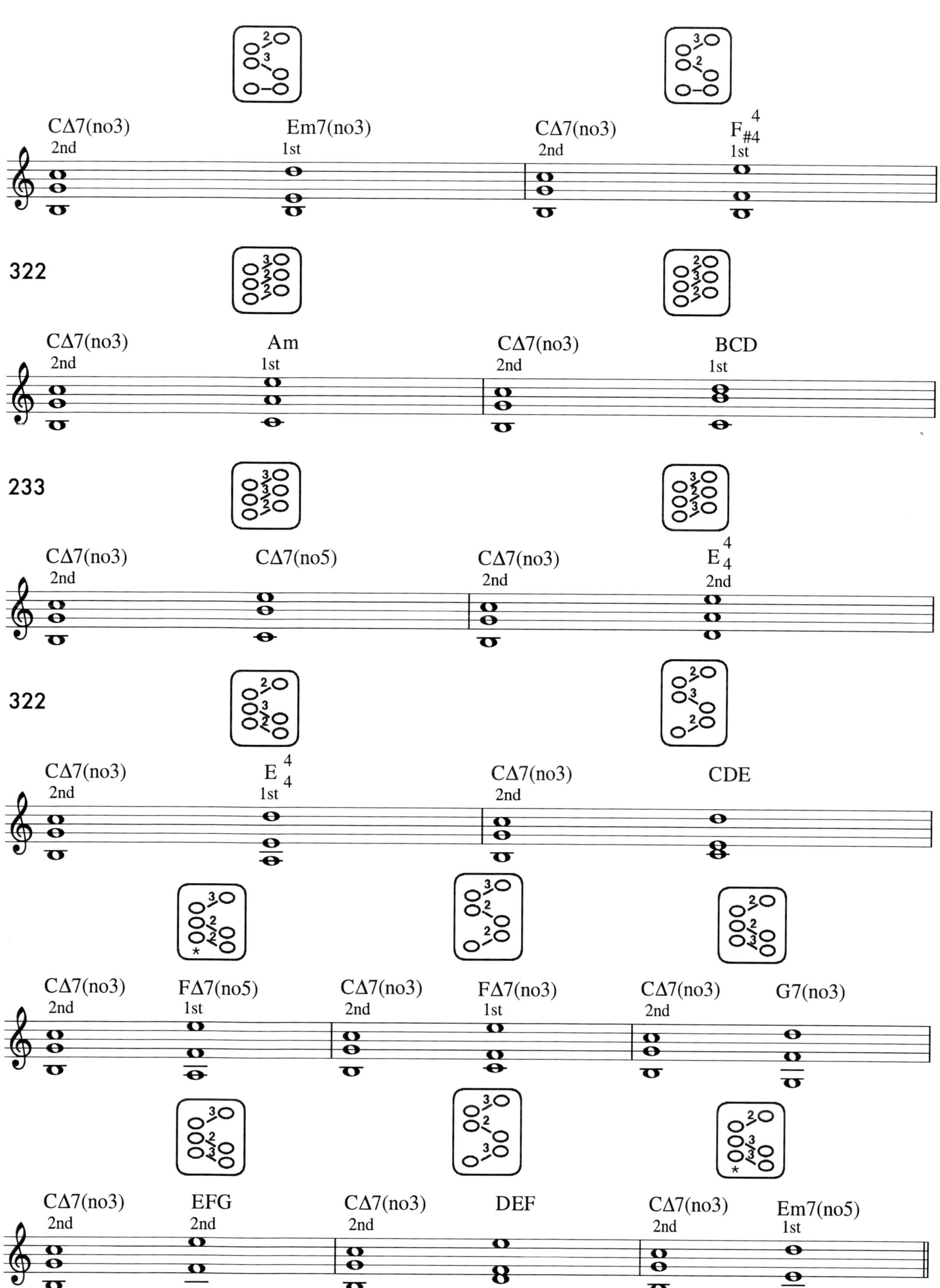

CΔ7(no3) 2nd
Em7(no3) 1st
CΔ7(no3) 2nd
F#4 4 1st
322
CΔ7(no3) 2nd
Am 1st
CΔ7(no3) 2nd
BCD 1st
233
CΔ7(no3) 2nd
CΔ7(no5)
CΔ7(no3) 2nd
E 4 4 2nd
322
CΔ7(no3) 2nd
E 4 4 1st
CΔ7(no3) 2nd
CDE
CΔ7(no3) 2nd
FΔ7(no5) 1st
CΔ7(no3) 2nd
FΔ7(no3) 1st
CΔ7(no3) 2nd
G7(no3)
CΔ7(no3) 2nd
EFG 2nd
CΔ7(no3) 2nd
DEF
CΔ7(no3) 2nd
Em7(no5) 1st

2nds

7th no 3 in 2nd Inversion

Using reverse/descending motion

open

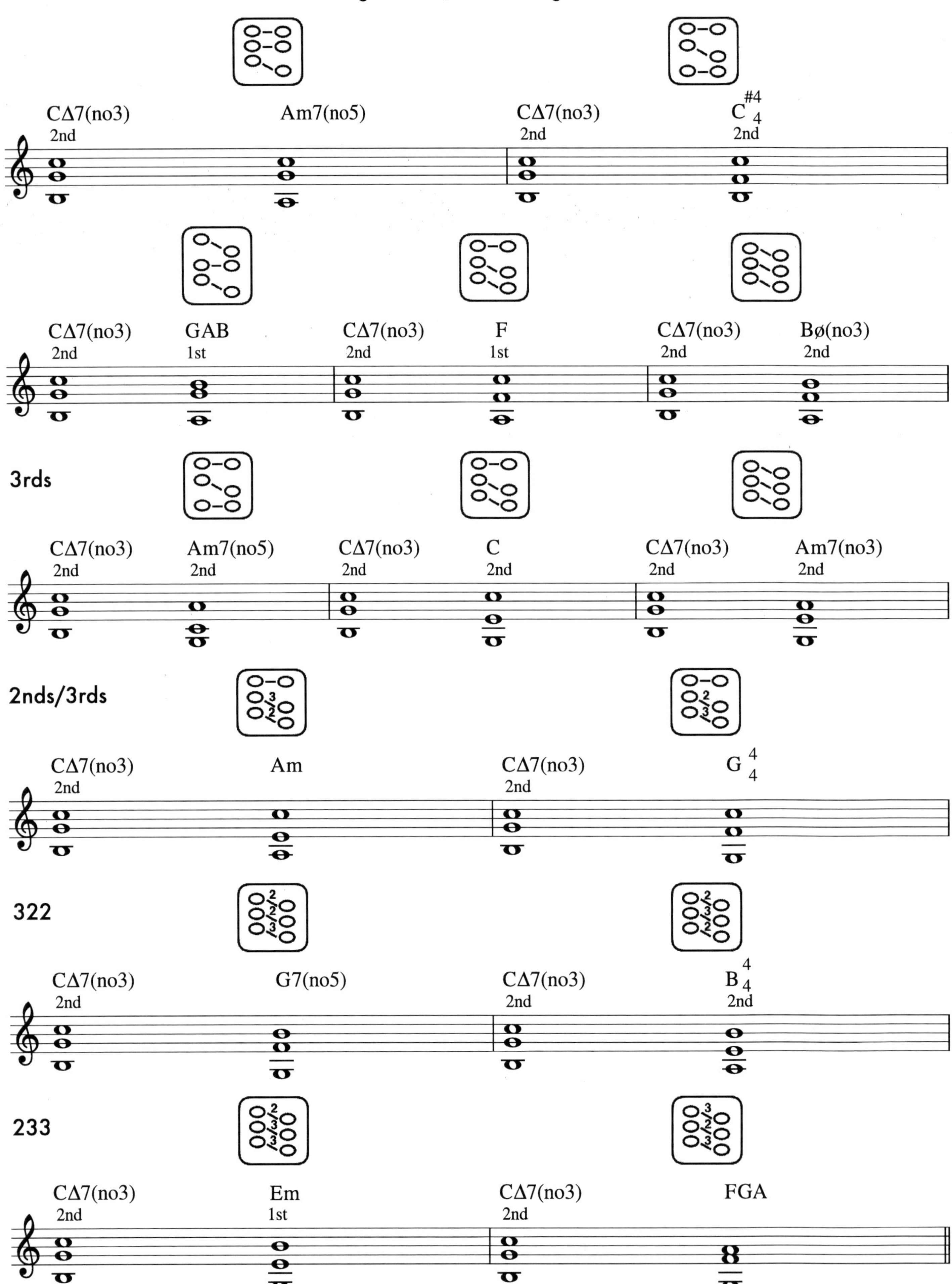

2nds

7th no 3 in Root Position

Using regular/ascending motion

open

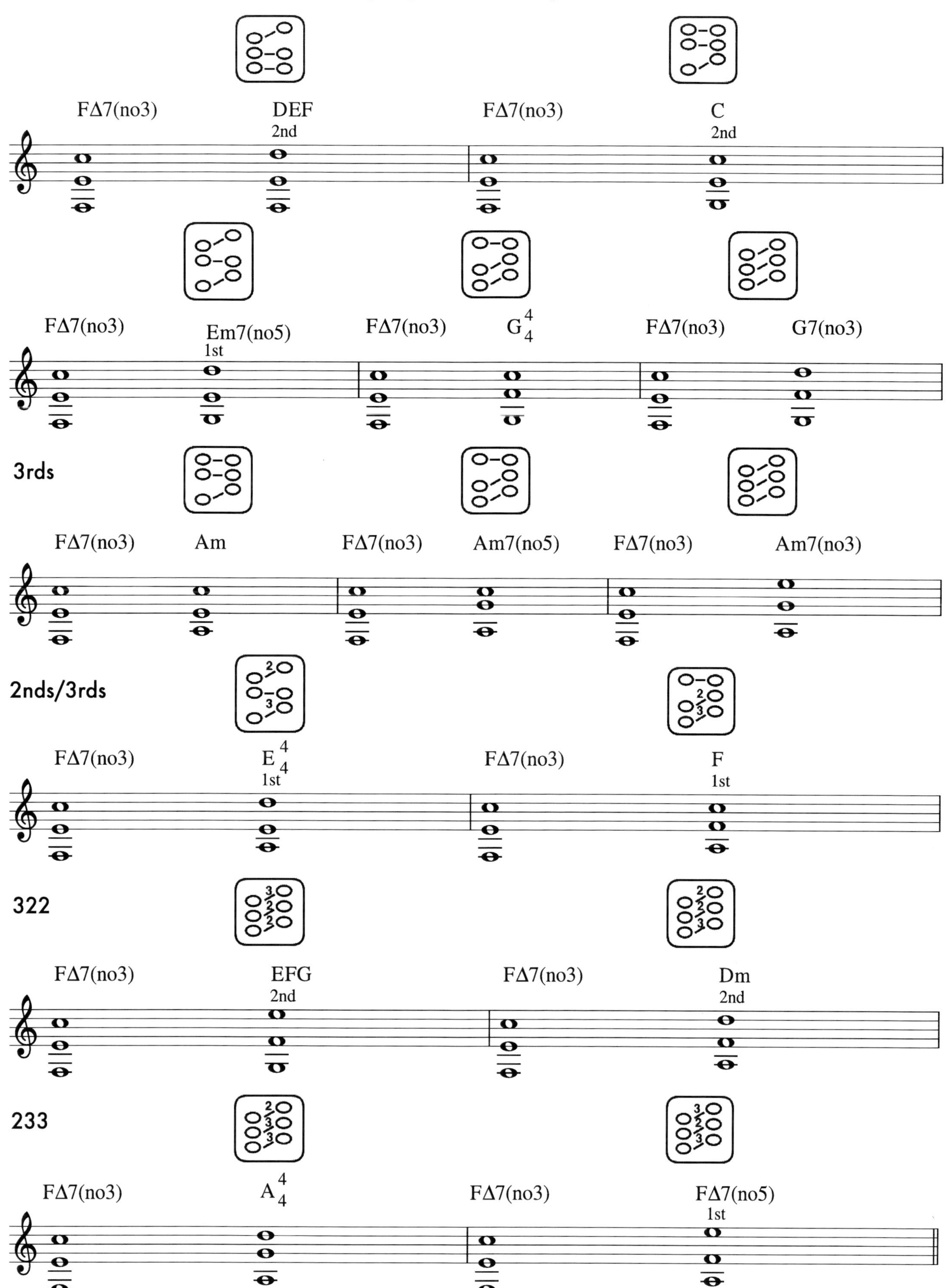

2nds

7th no 3 in Root Position

Using reverse/descending motion

open

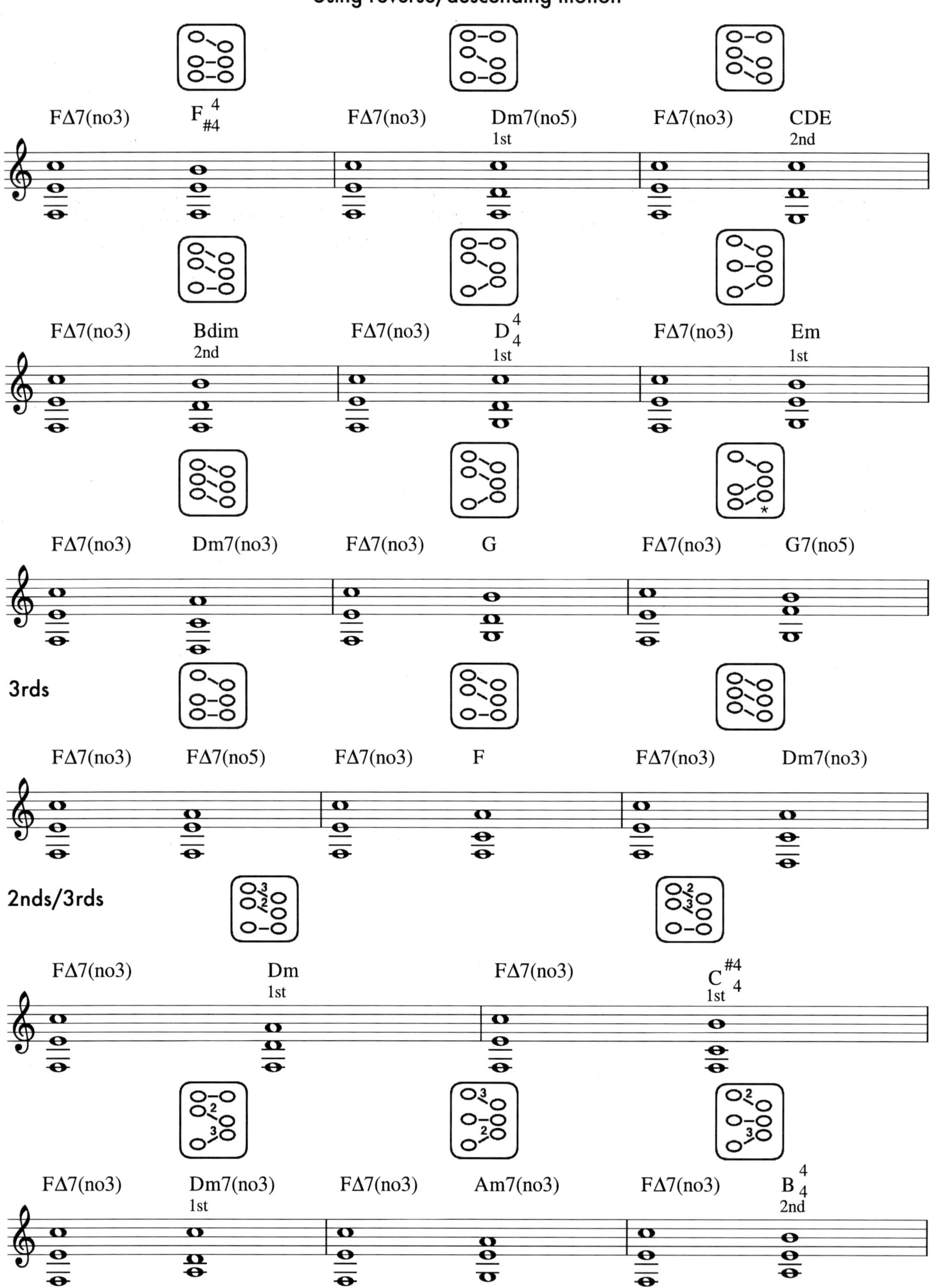

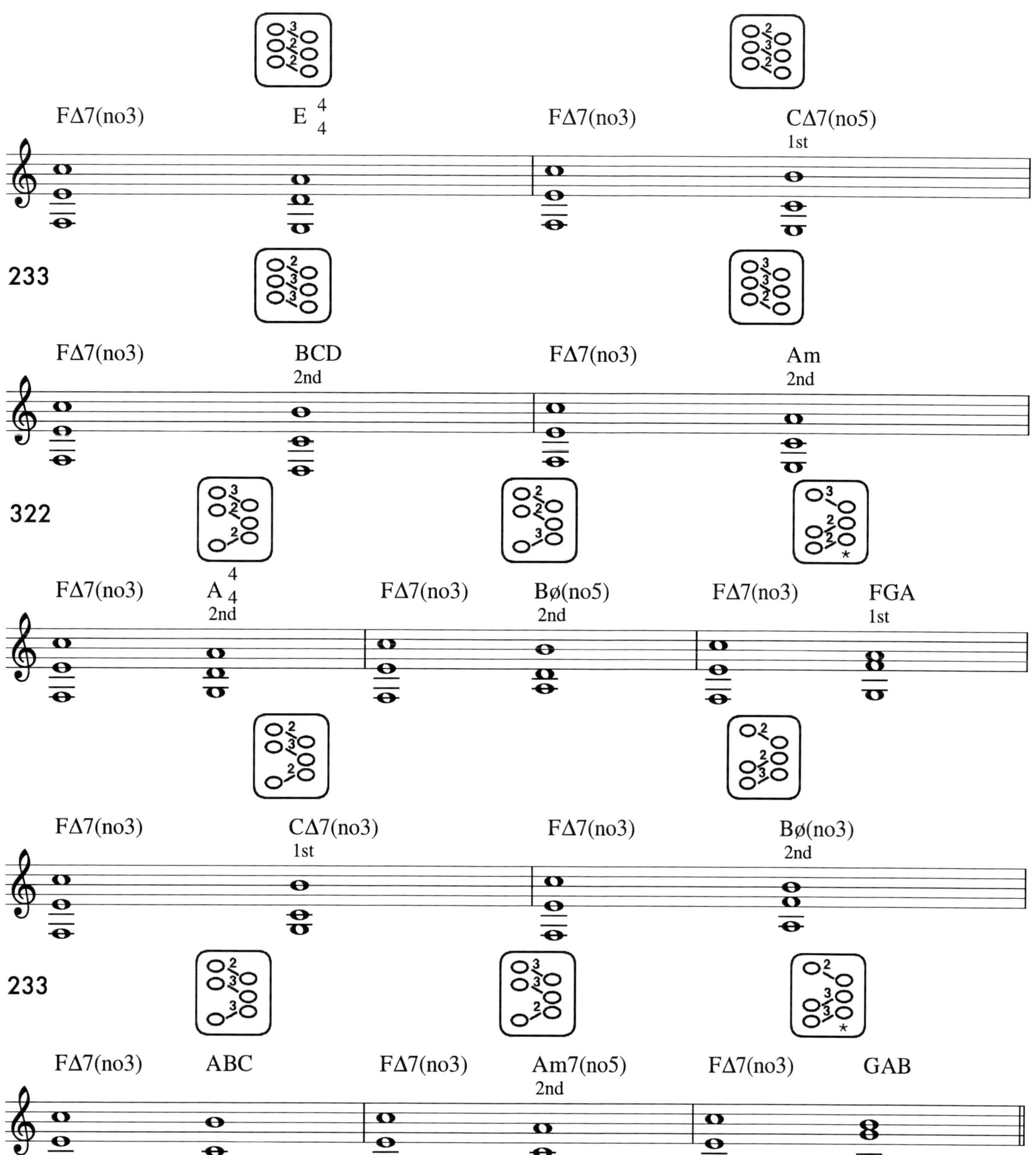
FΔ7(no3)
E 4 4
FΔ7(no3)
CΔ7(no5)
1st
233
FΔ7(no3)
BCD
2nd
FΔ7(no3)
Am
2nd
322
FΔ7(no3)
A 4 4
2nd
FΔ7(no3)
Bø(no5)
2nd
FΔ7(no3)
FGA
1st
FΔ7(no3)
CΔ7(no3)
1st
FΔ7(no3)
Bø(no3)
2nd
233
FΔ7(no3)
ABC
FΔ7(no3)
Am7(no5)
2nd
FΔ7(no3)
GAB

2nds

7th no 3 in 1st Inversion

Using regular/ascending motion

open

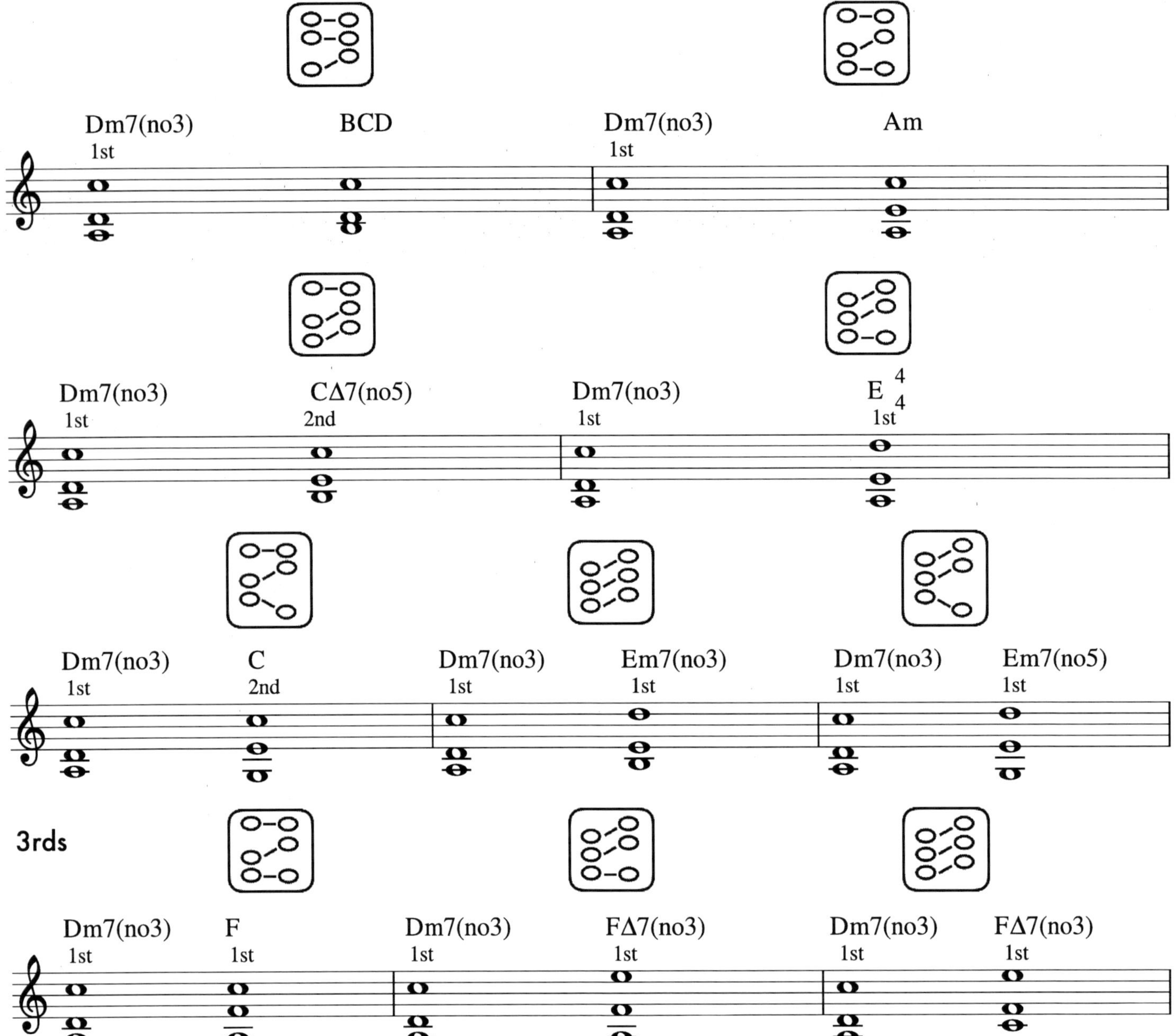

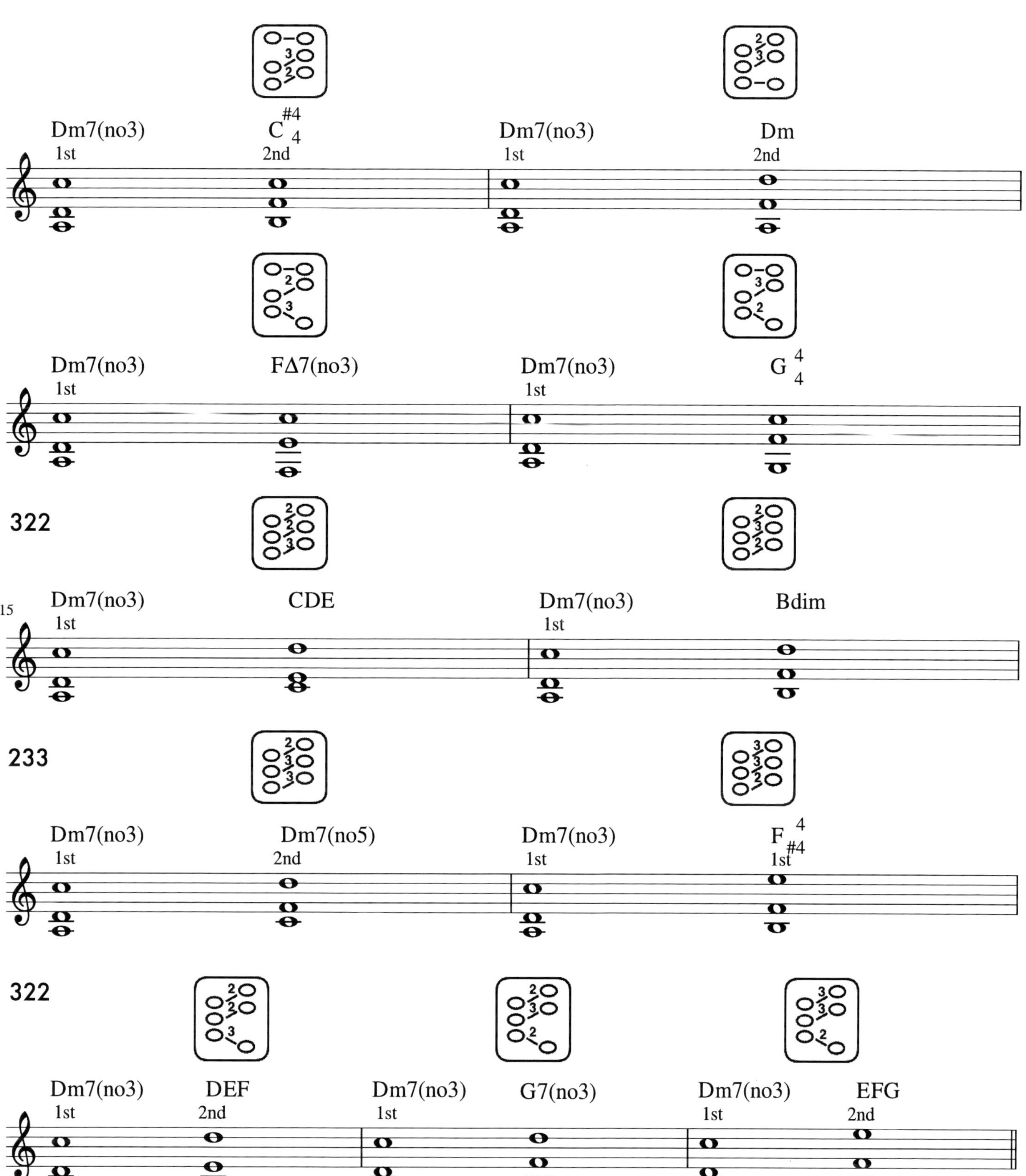
Dm7(no3)
1st
C #4 4
2nd
Dm7(no3)
1st
Dm
2nd
Dm7(no3)
1st
FΔ7(no3)
Dm7(no3)
1st
G 4 4
322
15
Dm7(no3)
1st
CDE
Dm7(no3)
1st
Bdim
233
Dm7(no3)
1st
Dm7(no5)
2nd
Dm7(no3)
1st
F 4 #4
1st
322
Dm7(no3)
1st
DEF
2nd
Dm7(no3)
1st
G7(no3)
Dm7(no3)
1st
EFG
2nd

2nds

7th no 3 in 1st Inversion

Using reverse/descending motion

open

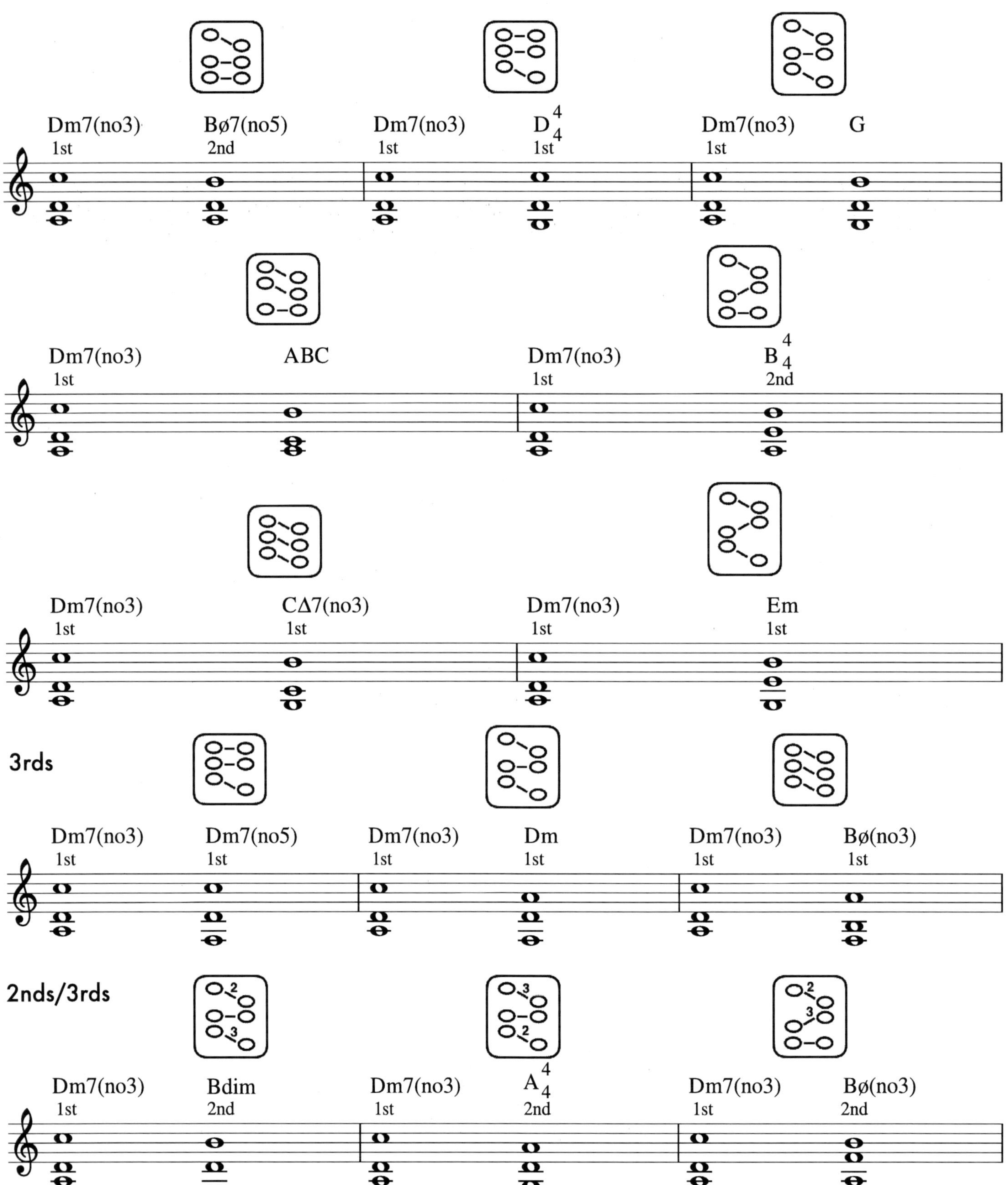

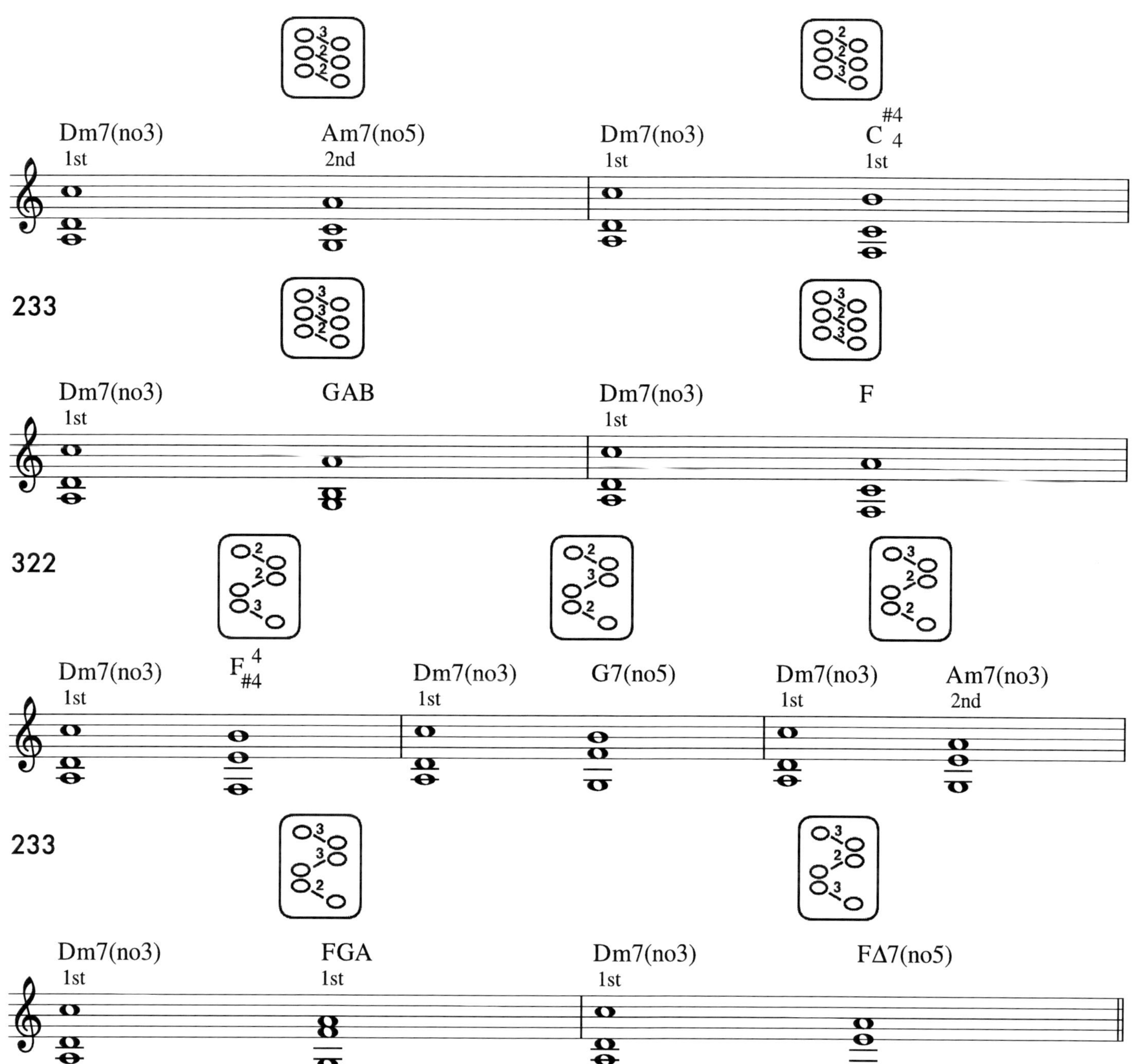
Dm7(no3)
1st
Am7(no5)
2nd
Dm7(no3)
1st
C #4 4
1st
233
Dm7(no3)
1st
GAB
Dm7(no3)
1st
F
322
Dm7(no3)
1st
F 4 #4
Dm7(no3)
1st
G7(no5)
Dm7(no3)
1st
Am7(no3)
2nd
233
Dm7(no3)
1st
FGA
1st
Dm7(no3)
1st
FΔ7(no5)

Clusters in 2nd Inversion

2nds | open

Using regular/ascending motion

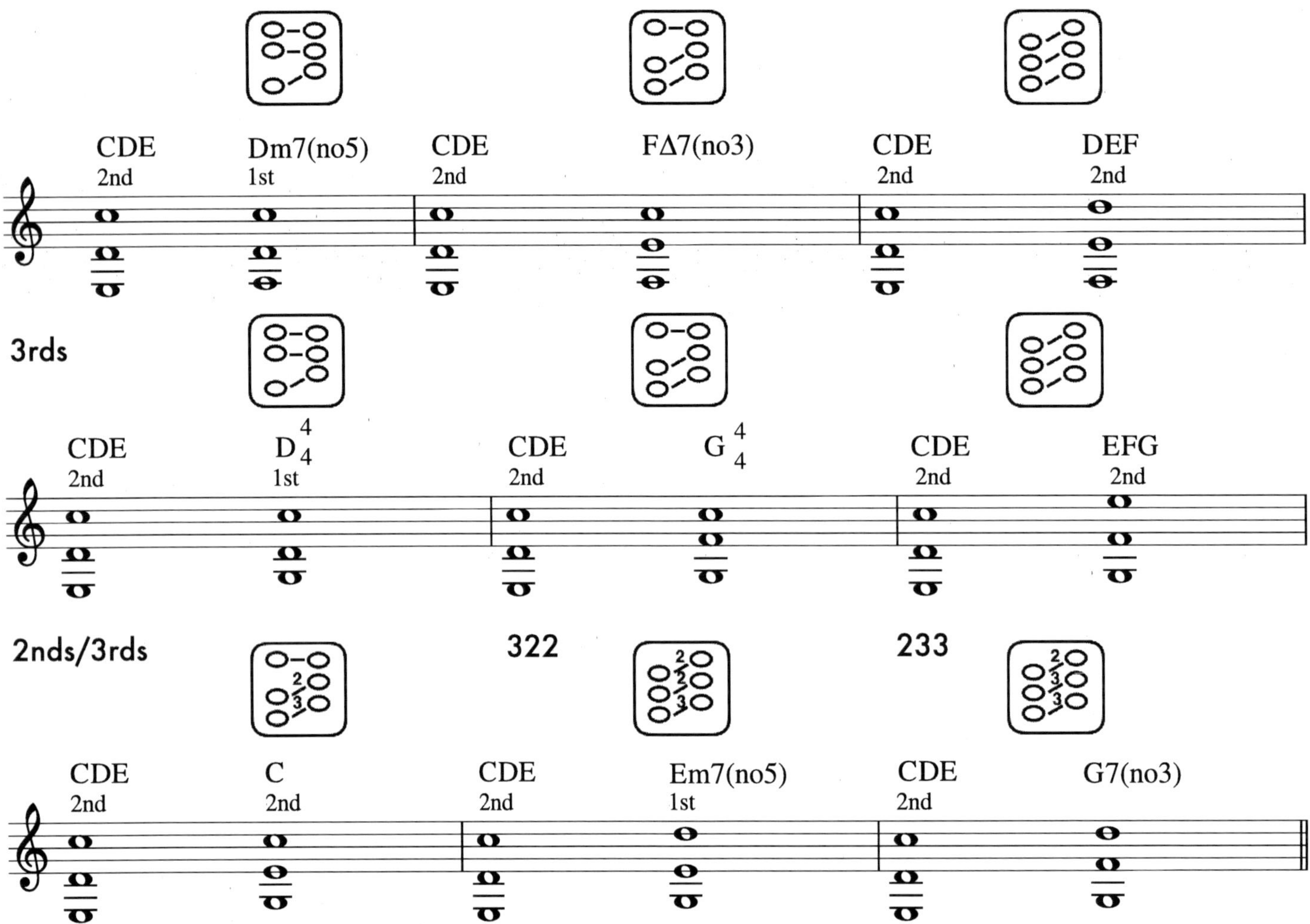

2nds

Clusters in 2nd Inversion

Using reverse/descending motion

open

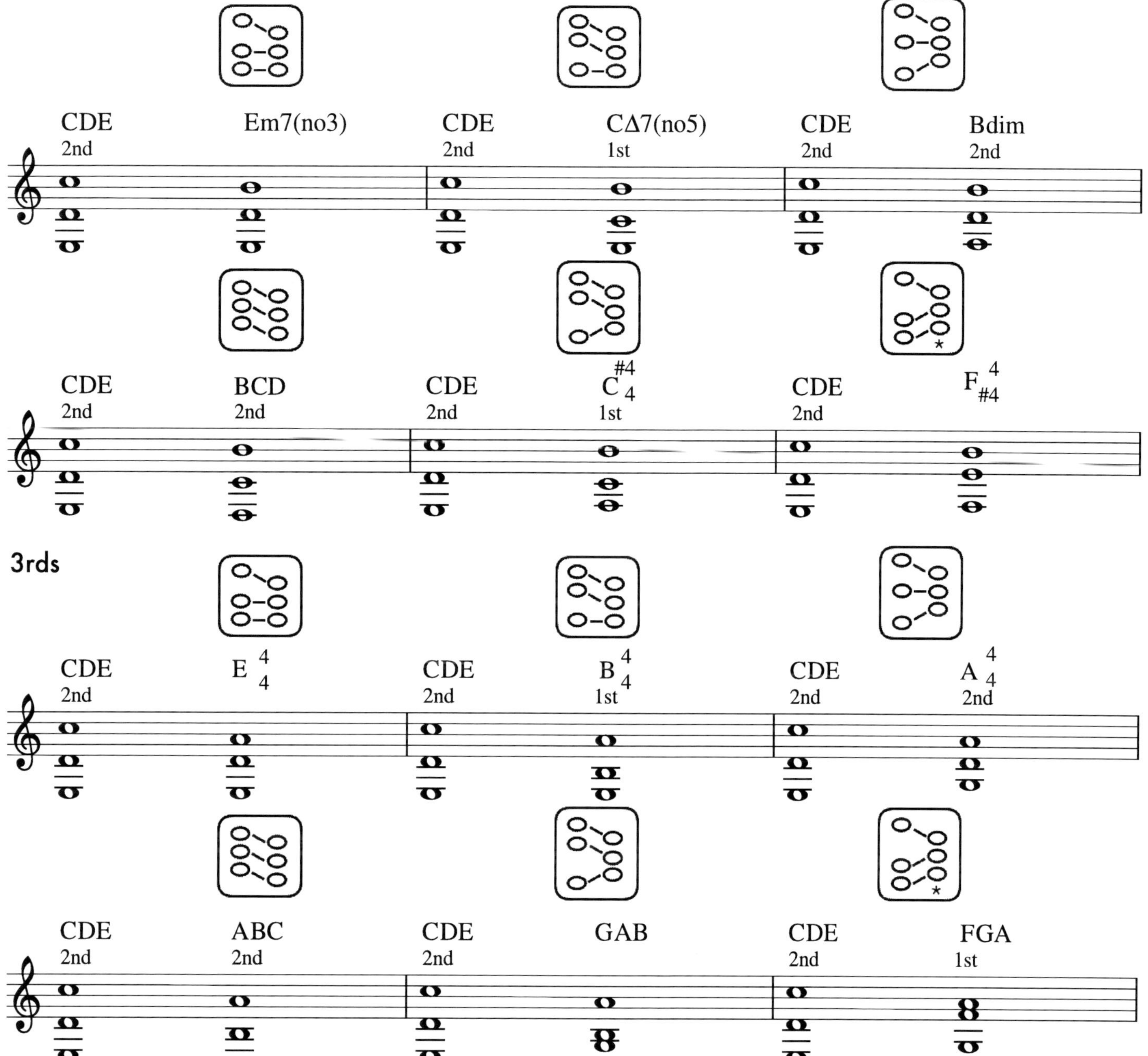

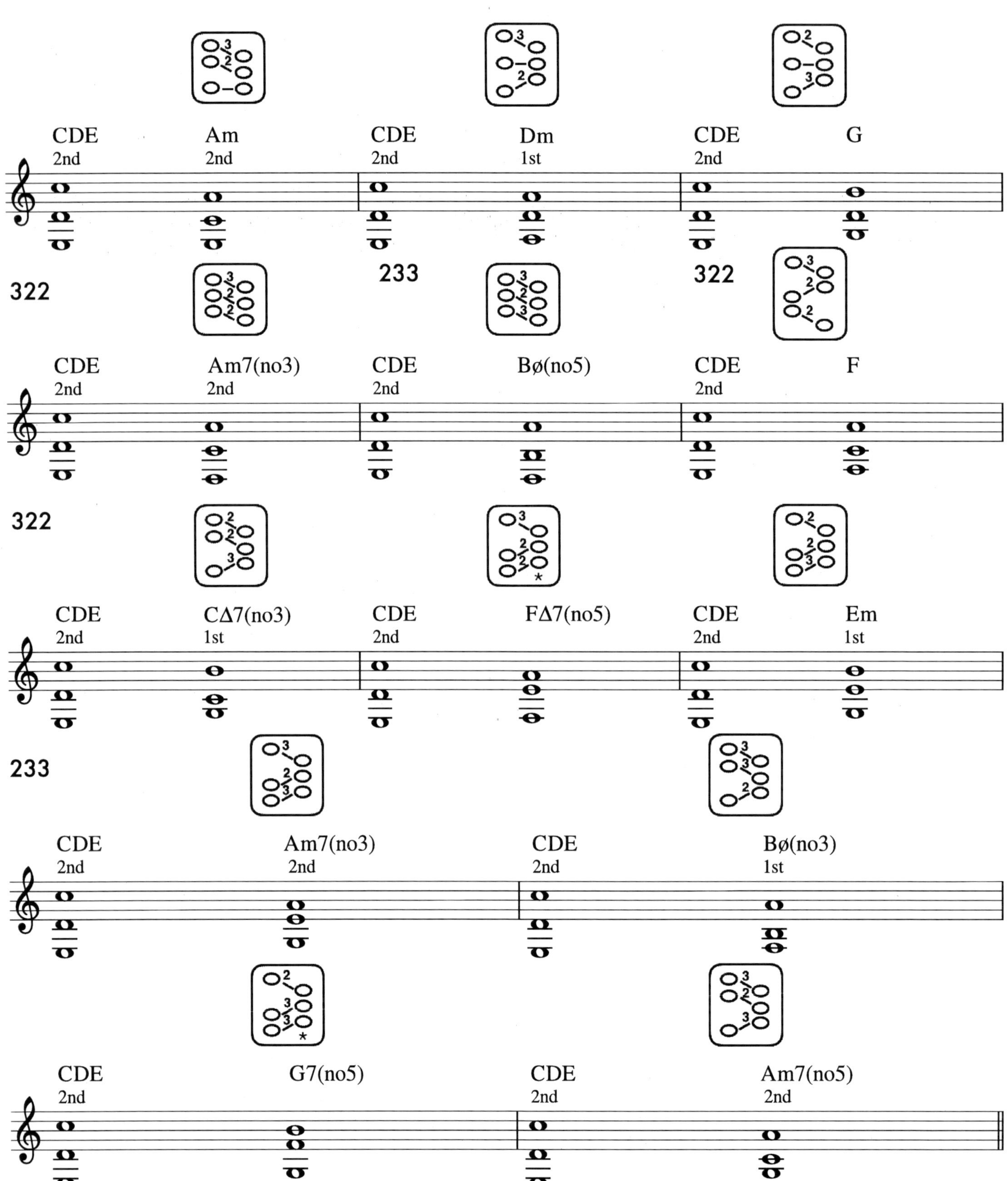
CDE
2nd
Am
2nd
CDE
2nd
Dm
1st
CDE
2nd
G
322
233
322
CDE
2nd
Am7(no3)
2nd
CDE
2nd
Bø(no5)
CDE
2nd
F
322
CDE
2nd
CΔ7(no3)
1st
CDE
2nd
FΔ7(no5)
CDE
2nd
Em
1st
233
CDE
2nd
Am7(no3)
2nd
CDE
2nd
Bø(no3)
1st
CDE
2nd
G7(no5)
CDE
2nd
Am7(no5)
2nd

2nds

Clusters in Root Position

Using regular/ascending motion

open

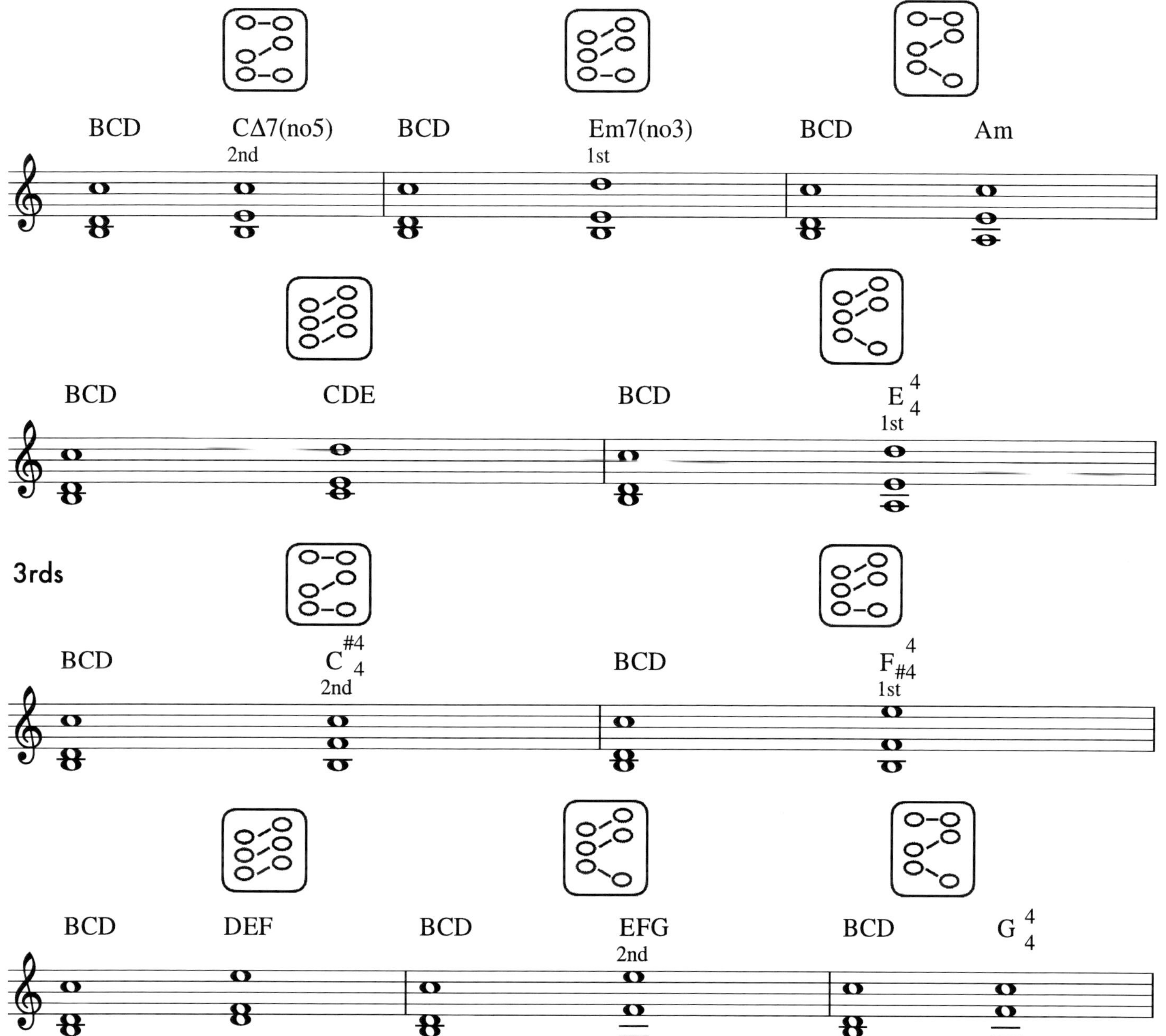

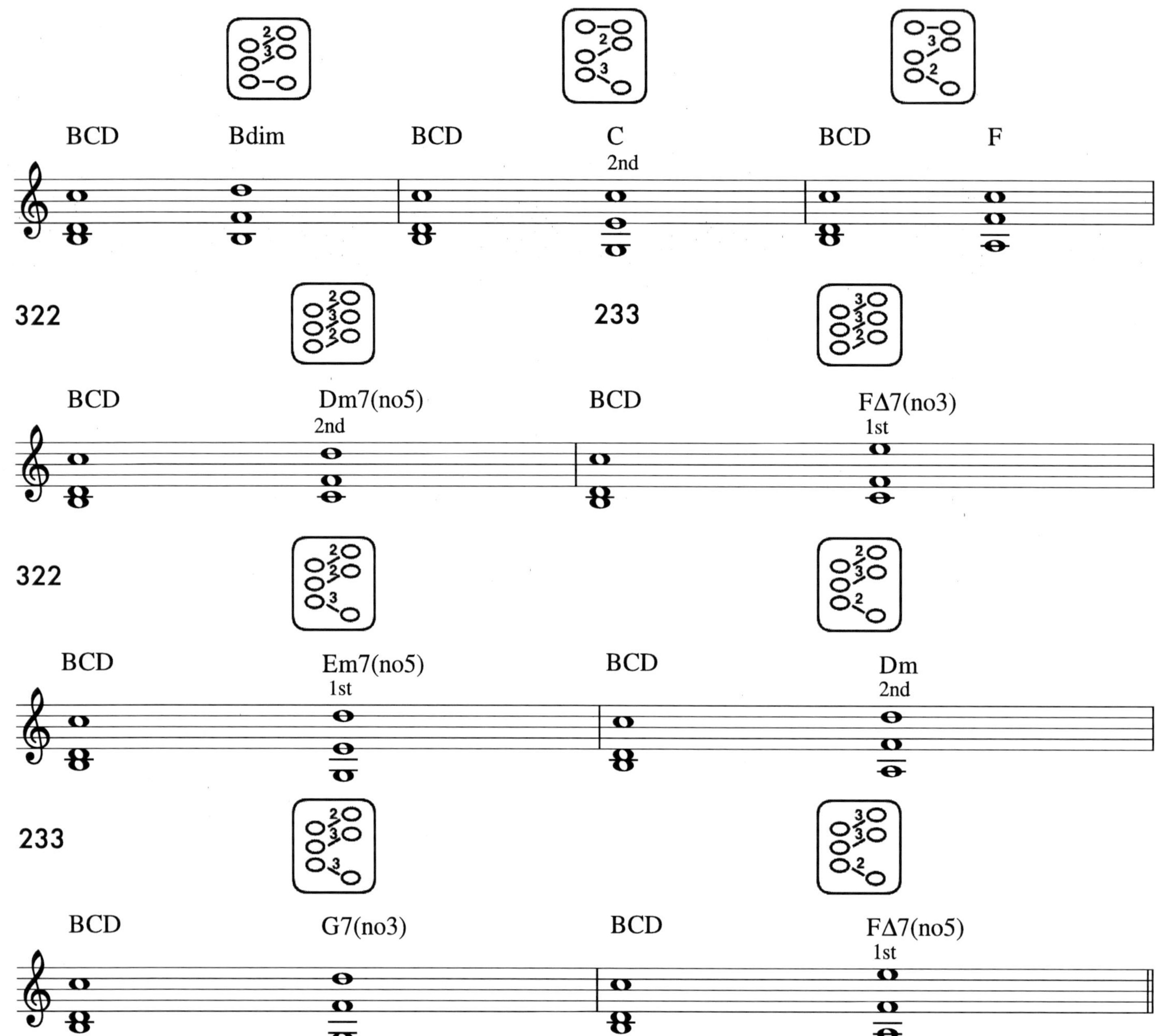
BCD
Bdim
BCD
C
2nd
BCD
F
322
BCD
Dm7(no5)
2nd
233
BCD
FΔ7(no3)
1st
322
BCD
Em7(no5)
1st
BCD
Dm
2nd
233
BCD
G7(no3)
BCD
FΔ7(no5)
1st

Clusters in Root Position

Using reverse/descending motion

open

2nds

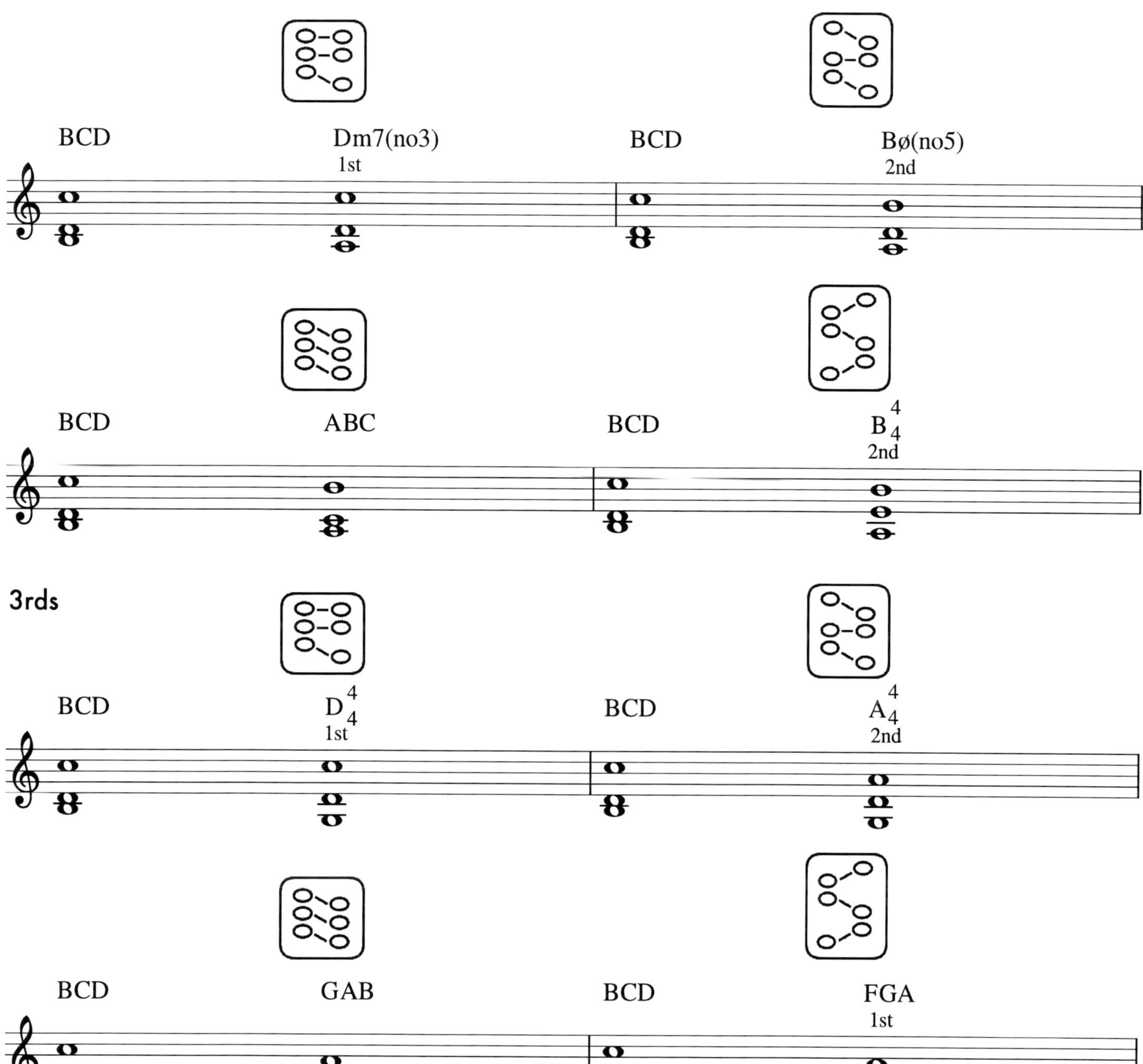

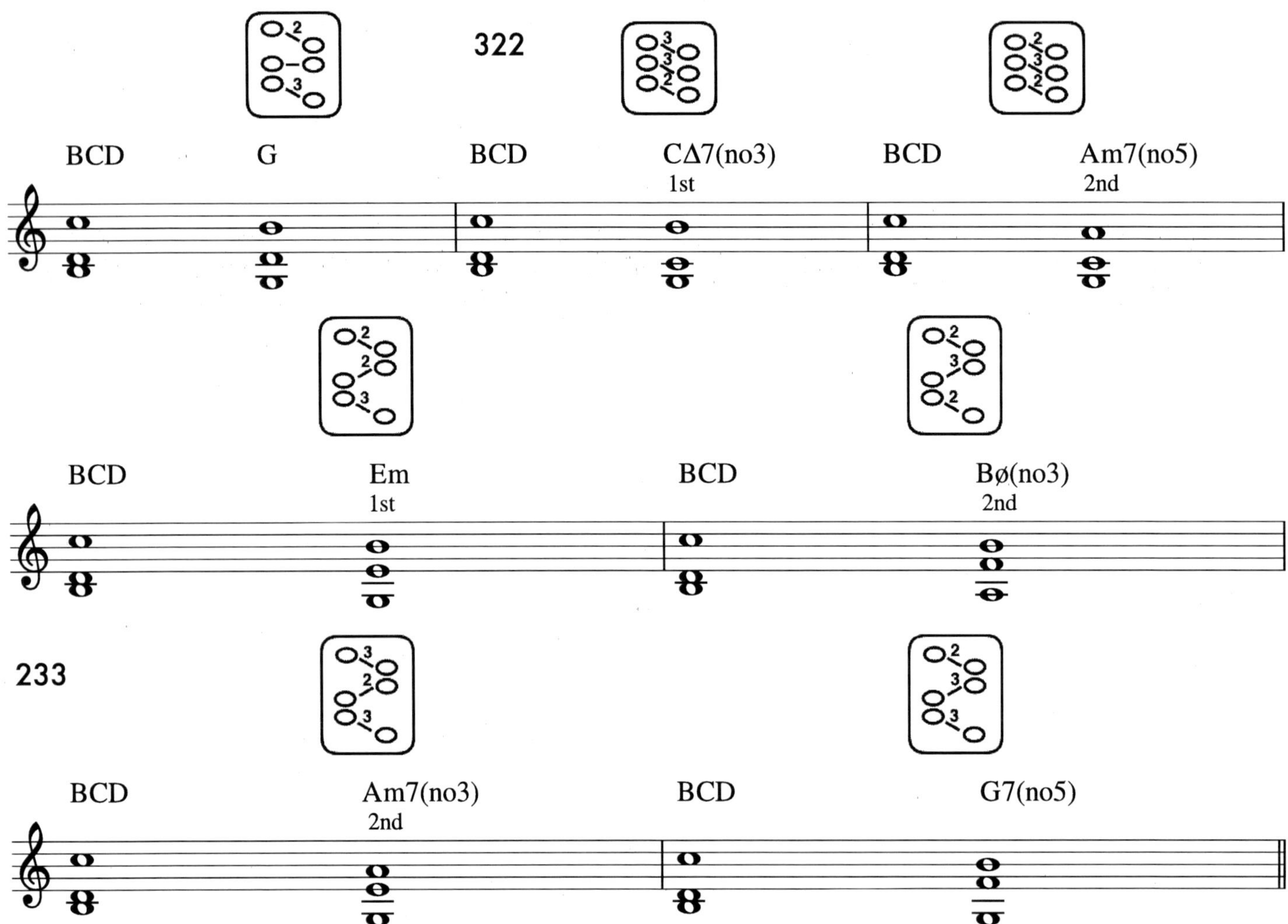
322
BCD
G
BCD
CΔ7(no3)
1st
BCD
Am7(no5)
2nd
BCD
Em
1st
BCD
Bø(no3)
2nd
233
BCD
Am7(no3)
2nd
BCD
G7(no5)

2nds

Clusters in 1st Inversion

Using regular/ascending motion

open

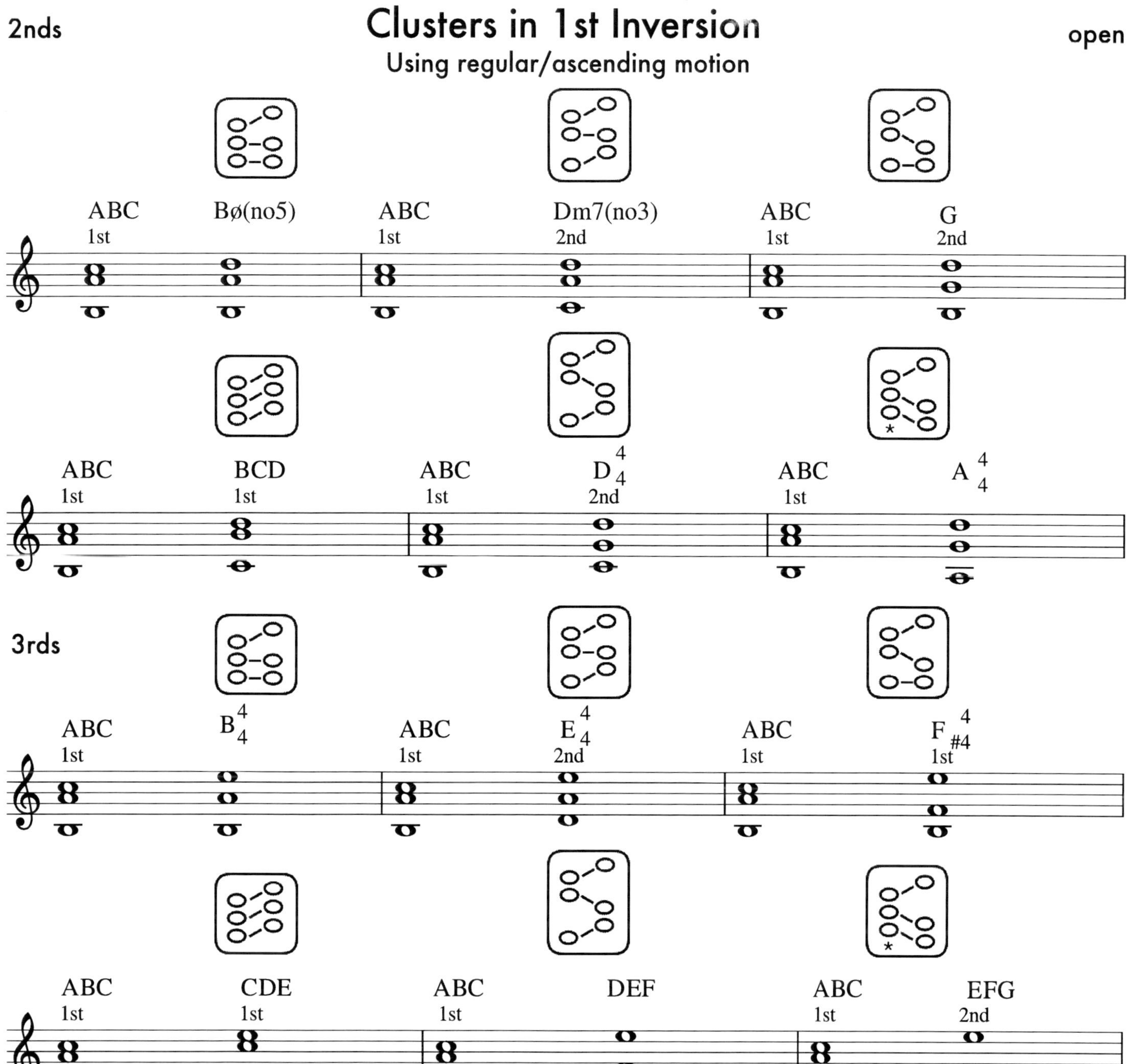

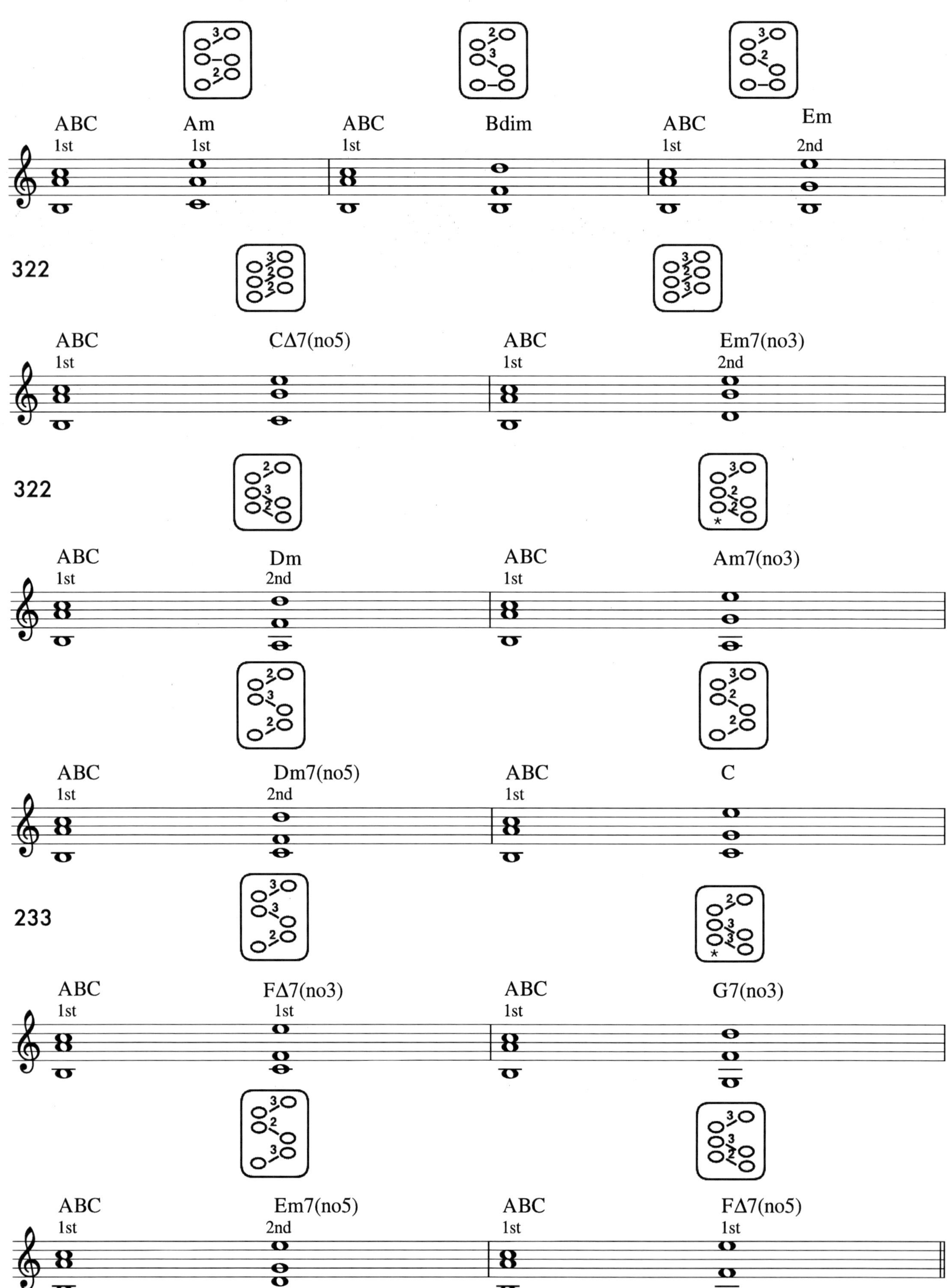
ABC
1st
Am
1st
ABC
1st
Bdim
ABC
1st
Em
2nd
322
ABC
1st
CΔ7(no5)
ABC
1st
Em7(no3)
2nd
322
ABC
1st
Dm
2nd
ABC
1st
Am7(no3)
ABC
1st
Dm7(no5)
2nd
ABC
1st
C
233
ABC
1st
FΔ7(no3)
1st
ABC
1st
G7(no3)
ABC
1st
Em7(no5)
2nd
ABC
1st
FΔ7(no5)
1st

Clusters in 1st Inversion

Using reverse/descending motion

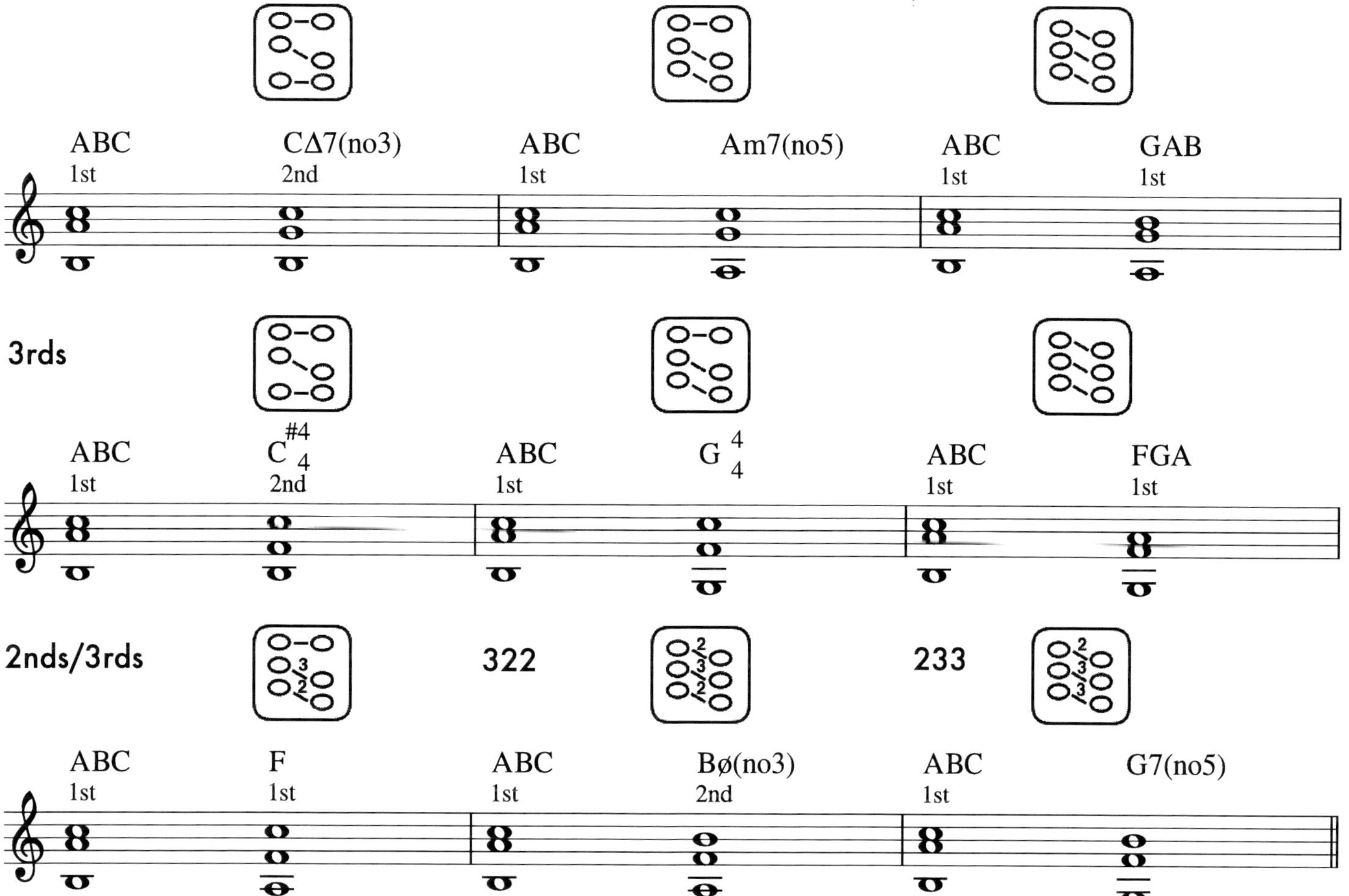

The short guitar piece on the next page marks the end of Part 2.
It is strictly composed in open three-part harmony using drop-2 voicings, and shows the application of voice motion move 40) in the context of a 12-bar blues head in the key of C.
It can be practiced unaccompanied, but it works best when played with a rhythm section and then used as a springboard for improvisation on the form.

"Spread Your Things and Try"

Guitar Part

Johannes Haage

♩ = 100
Swing

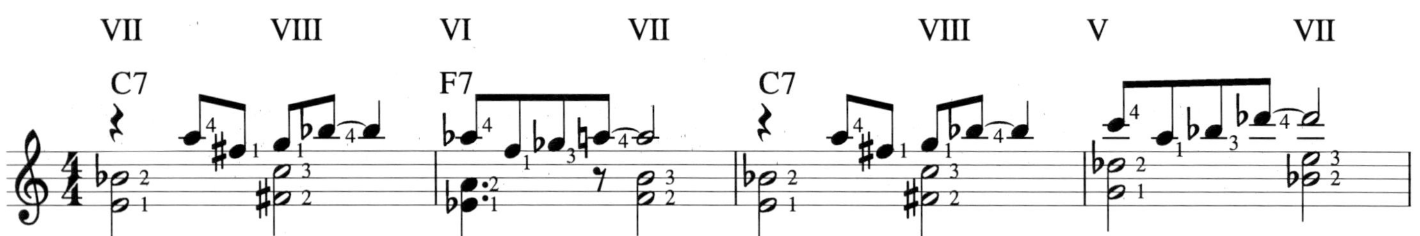

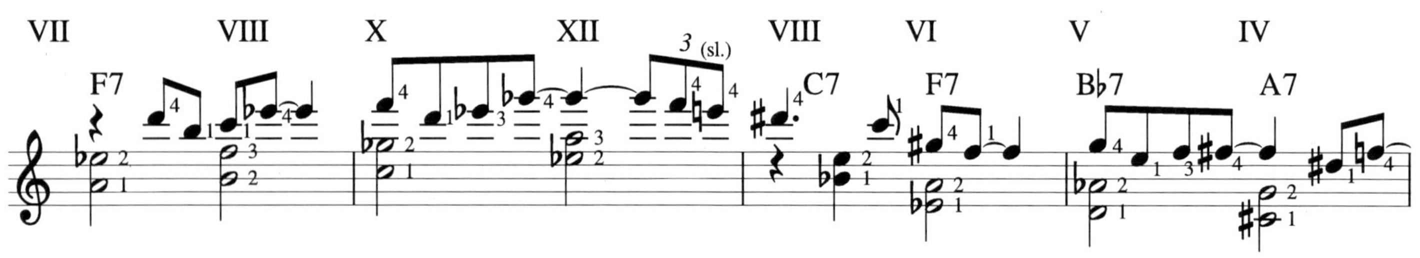

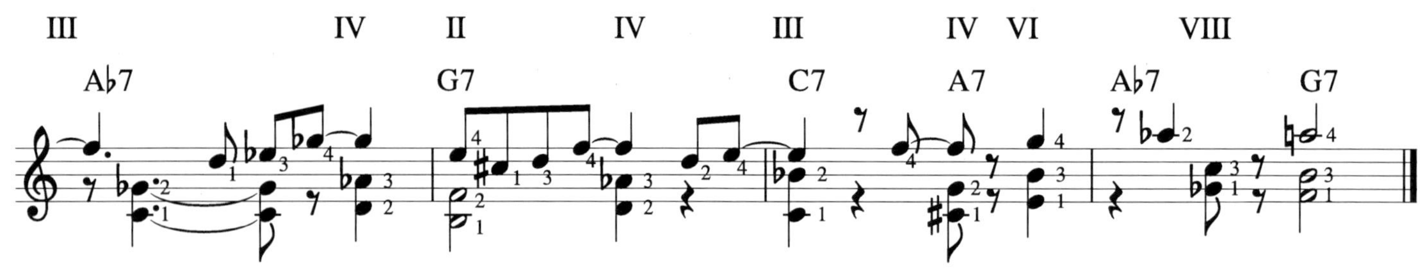

PART THREE: Application

OVERVIEW

This chapter will teach you various ways to apply the material presented in Parts 1 and 2.

It starts with a complete course on basic heptatonics, which makes the *VOICE MOTION* moves applicable to practically any harmonic situation.

Concepts, exercises and etudes are presented to effectively practice the material in Parts 1 and 2 in all keys, as well as chromatically.

Furthermore, it expands the scope of application to larger interval sizes, and all other playable three-part voicing types on the guitar.

CONTENTS

PART 3A

Heptatonics

OVERVIEW

This chapter introduces other heptatonic (7-note) scales beyond the major diatonic, to expand the possible application of the material presented in Parts 1 and 2 to a vast range of melodic and harmonic situations.

Various principles, examples and exercises are shown for practicing the *VOICE MOTION* moves within the context of heptatonics in all keys.

CONTENTS

INTRODUCTION to HEPTATONICS

The material presented in the main Parts 1 and 2 of this book uses only the notes from one specific seven-note (heptatonic) scale called the major diatonic scale.

If we compare all possible scales that can be derived as subsets from the equal-tempered chromatic 12-note scale, the diatonic holds a special place: it produces melody and harmony that seem to sound particularly interesting and pleasing to the human ear, making it the basis for most western music and for our common notation system.

One reason for this is that the diatonic represents the most even way possible to distribute seven notes in the space of an octave.
Because there are only 12 semitones available, there will always be at least two minor 2nds or half steps somewhere in any seven-note scale.
The diatonic has these two minor 2nds set as far apart from each other as possible, and uses only whole steps otherwise, making it the most balanced of all heptatonic scales.

Balanced heptatonic scales like the diatonic seem to hit a harmonic "sweet-spot" compared to scales of higher or lower order, because they produce unique and consistently built chord structures on every scale degree.
For example, if you build any of the five three-note chord types on the first degree of a diatonic and take it up the scale, it will produce a chord structure of the same inversion and chord type on all other scale degrees.
For example, a root position triad taken stepwise up the diatonic scale will produce only other root position triads on all scale degrees.

If you do the same in a pentatonic (5-note) or hexatonic (6-note) scale, not only will the number of available chord types be more limited, but the chord structures on every scale degree will differ inevitably.

Toward the other end of the chromatic spectrum, scales with more than seven notes will tend to contain more consecutive semitones, and thus produce more clustered, ambiguous chord structures, which also change in type and inversion when taken stepwise up the scale.

Therefore, the diatonic is the most widely used heptatonic scale. Nevertheless, its application is naturally limited; there are other balanced seven-note scales that are worth exploring to fit the harmonic and melodic situations not covered by the diatonic.

Out of the total 66 possible unique seven-note scales within the chromatic, 28 include intervals greater than a minor third, indicating a very uneven distribution of notes.
Of the remaining 38 scales, only six heptatonics are balanced enough not to include any consecutive half steps or semitones.

On the next page, these "Six Basic Heptatonics" are shown in order of balance,
in the key of C.

THE SIX BASIC HEPTATONICS

without consecutive halfsteps/semitones
in the key of C
in order of balance

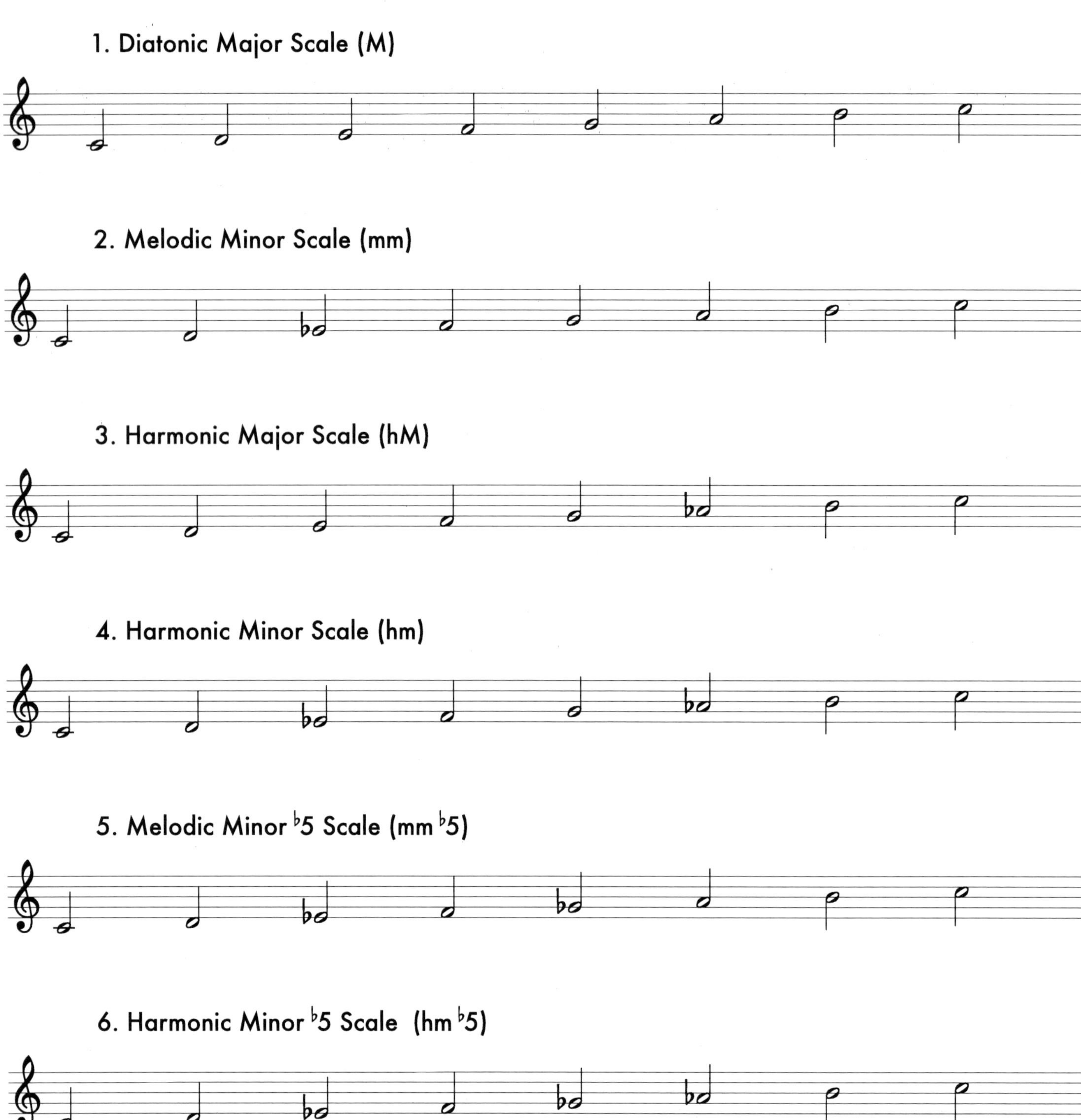

Practice all six scales the full range of your instrument, in all keys.
On the guitar, apply the exercises of the Addendum to explore and internalize their note locations on the fretboard.

HEPTATONIC HARMONIZATION

The next pages show all six basic heptatonic scales harmonized with the five three-note chord types in all inversions.
Practice throughout the full range of your instrument, in all keys - referring to the preparatory exercises in the introduction to Part 1 for variation.

As the imbalance in the distribution of notes throughout the octave increases compared to the diatonic, the five other heptatonics produce more ambiguous chord structures.
For example, the melodic minor scale introduces the augmented triad, which is intervallically identical in all three inversions.

Furthermore, diminished and augmented intervals in these scales produce enharmonic equivalent notes that cause increasing inconsistencies in the chord structures when applied to these scales:
The 4ths especially produce different chord types on higher scale degrees;
for example (in the key of C) a B7(no5) on the 7th step of the melodic minor scale,
an E7(no5) on the 3rd degree of the harmonic Major scale, or an A♭ minor triad on the 7th degree of the harmonic minor scale.

A particularly notable phenomenon occurs when triads are taken up the melodic minor (♭5) and harmonic minor (♭5) scales:
The intervallic structure of the scales causes some of the inversions to flip, and produces three different triads with the 7th scale degree as their root.
In the key of C for example, root position triads taken up these scales produce a B major triad (1st Inv.) on the 3rd step, a B minor triad (2nd Inv.) on the flat 5th step, as well as the regular B diminished triad on the 7th step.

The five increasingly imbalanced basic heptatonics provide the melodic and harmonic material to fit most situations where the diatonic and its modes fall short.

Out of the six basic heptatonics, the two minor scales with the ♭5 are the least covered as independent scale systems in other books, as they represent the two possible heptatonic subsets of the symmetrical diminished (octatonic) scale.
Apart from their unique harmonic character created by the phenomenon described above, they provide most of the missing combinations of upper structure extensions on 7th chords that are not included in the more common heptatonic scales and their modes.

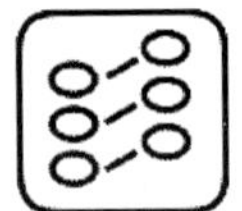

close

C Diatonic Major Scale

Harmonized with all five chord types (3 inversions)

Triple-Voice Parallel Motion

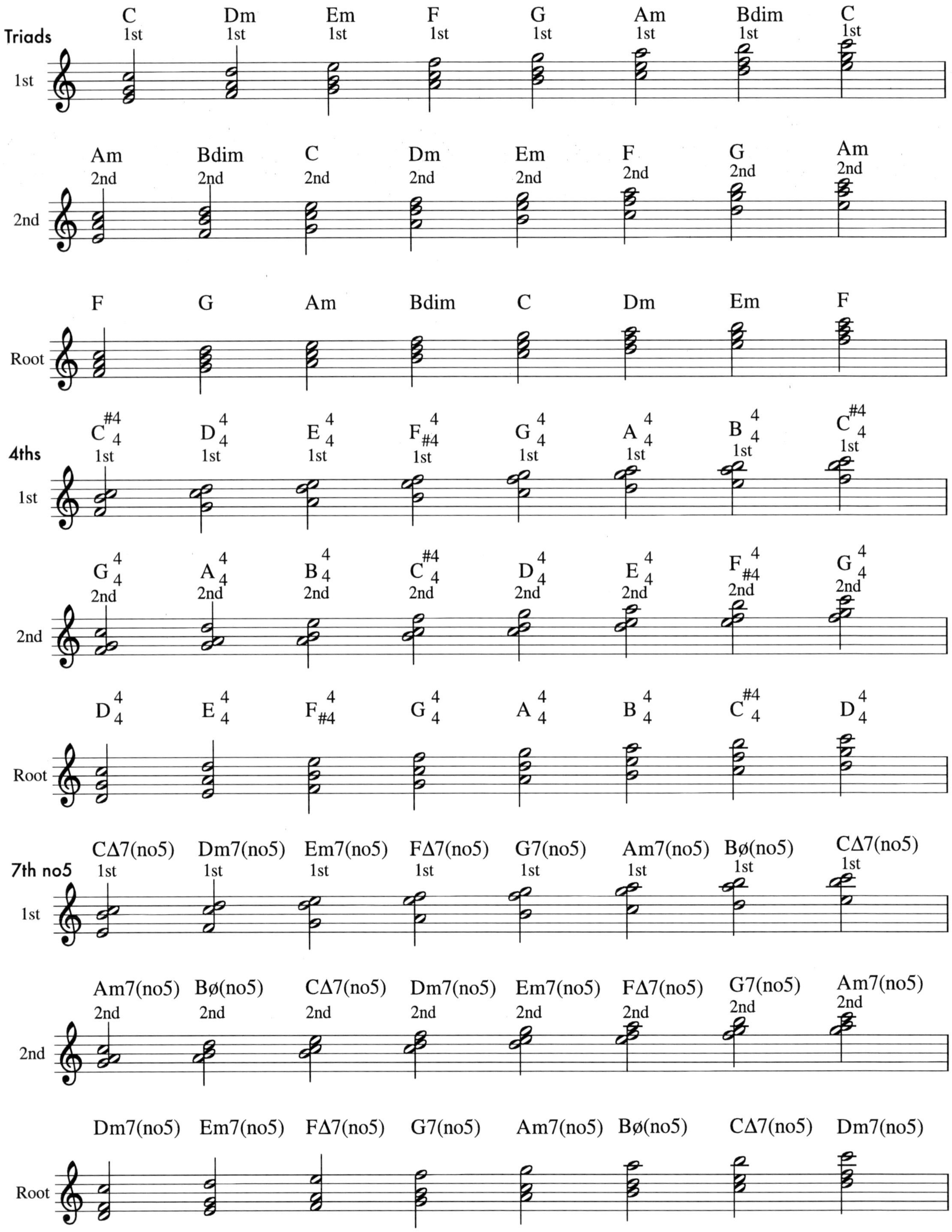

Triads

1st: C 1st · Dm 1st · Em 1st · F 1st · G 1st · Am 1st · Bdim 1st · C 1st

2nd: Am 2nd · Bdim 2nd · C 2nd · Dm 2nd · Em 2nd · F 2nd · G 2nd · Am 2nd

Root: F · G · Am · Bdim · C · Dm · Em · F

4ths

1st: $C^{\#4}_{4}$ 1st · D^{4}_{4} 1st · E^{4}_{4} 1st · $F^{4}_{\#4}$ 1st · G^{4}_{4} 1st · A^{4}_{4} 1st · B^{4}_{4} 1st · $C^{\#4}_{4}$ 1st

2nd: G^{4}_{4} 2nd · A^{4}_{4} 2nd · B^{4}_{4} 2nd · $C^{\#4}_{4}$ 2nd · D^{4}_{4} 2nd · E^{4}_{4} 2nd · $F^{4}_{\#4}$ 2nd · G^{4}_{4} 2nd

Root: D^{4}_{4} · E^{4}_{4} · $F^{4}_{\#4}$ · G^{4}_{4} · A^{4}_{4} · B^{4}_{4} · $C^{\#4}_{4}$ · D^{4}_{4}

7th no5

1st: CΔ7(no5) 1st · Dm7(no5) 1st · Em7(no5) 1st · FΔ7(no5) 1st · G7(no5) 1st · Am7(no5) 1st · Bø(no5) 1st · CΔ7(no5) 1st

2nd: Am7(no5) 2nd · Bø(no5) 2nd · CΔ7(no5) 2nd · Dm7(no5) 2nd · Em7(no5) 2nd · FΔ7(no5) 2nd · G7(no5) 2nd · Am7(no5) 2nd

Root: Dm7(no5) · Em7(no5) · FΔ7(no5) · G7(no5) · Am7(no5) · Bø(no5) · CΔ7(no5) · Dm7(no5)

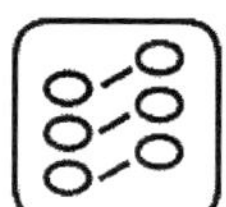

C Major Scale Harmonized cont...

close

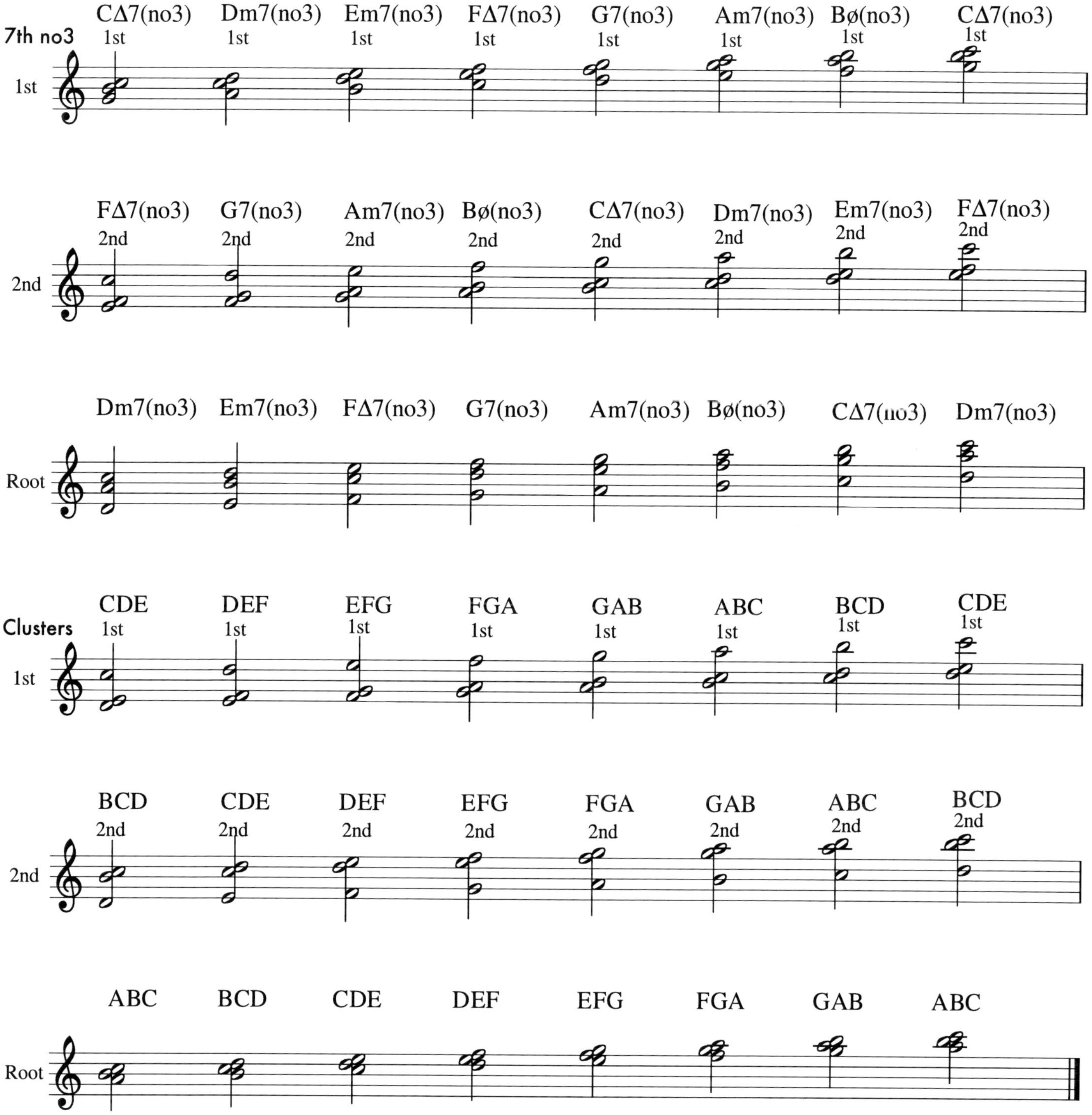

7th no3

1st

CΔ7(no3) 1st | Dm7(no3) 1st | Em7(no3) 1st | FΔ7(no3) 1st | G7(no3) 1st | Am7(no3) 1st | Bø(no3) 1st | CΔ7(no3) 1st

2nd

FΔ7(no3) 2nd | G7(no3) 2nd | Am7(no3) 2nd | Bø(no3) 2nd | CΔ7(no3) 2nd | Dm7(no3) 2nd | Em7(no3) 2nd | FΔ7(no3) 2nd

Root

Dm7(no3) | Em7(no3) | FΔ7(no3) | G7(no3) | Am7(no3) | Bø(no3) | CΔ7(no3) | Dm7(no3)

Clusters

1st

CDE 1st | DEF 1st | EFG 1st | FGA 1st | GAB 1st | ABC 1st | BCD 1st | CDE 1st

2nd

BCD 2nd | CDE 2nd | DEF 2nd | EFG 2nd | FGA 2nd | GAB 2nd | ABC 2nd | BCD 2nd

Root

ABC | BCD | CDE | DEF | EFG | FGA | GAB | ABC

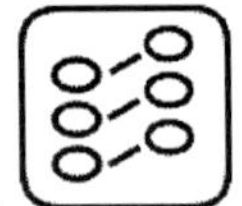

C Diatonic Major Scale

open

Harmonized with all five chord types (3 Inversions)

Triple-Voice Parallel Motion

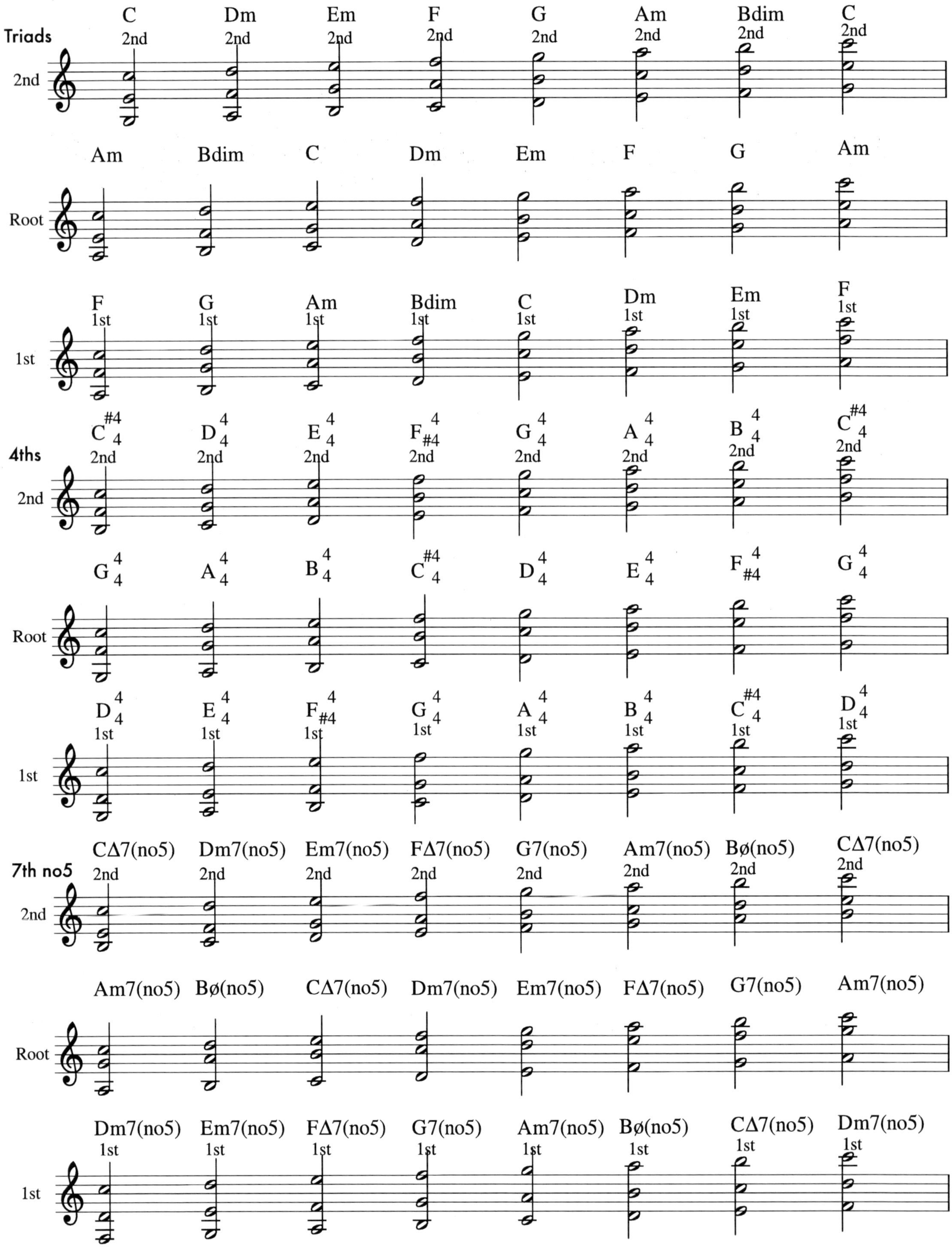

Triads

2nd: C 2nd | Dm 2nd | Em 2nd | F 2nd | G 2nd | Am 2nd | Bdim 2nd | C 2nd

Root: Am | Bdim | C | Dm | Em | F | G | Am

1st: F 1st | G 1st | Am 1st | Bdim 1st | C 1st | Dm 1st | Em 1st | F 1st

4ths

2nd: $C^{\#4}_{4}$ 2nd | D^{4}_{4} 2nd | E^{4}_{4} 2nd | $F^{4}_{\#4}$ 2nd | G^{4}_{4} 2nd | A^{4}_{4} 2nd | B^{4}_{4} 2nd | $C^{\#4}_{4}$ 2nd

Root: G^{4}_{4} | A^{4}_{4} | B^{4}_{4} | $C^{\#4}_{4}$ | D^{4}_{4} | E^{4}_{4} | $F^{4}_{\#4}$ | G^{4}_{4}

1st: D^{4}_{4} 1st | E^{4}_{4} 1st | $F^{4}_{\#4}$ 1st | G^{4}_{4} 1st | A^{4}_{4} 1st | B^{4}_{4} 1st | $C^{\#4}_{4}$ 1st | D^{4}_{4} 1st

7th no5

2nd: CΔ7(no5) 2nd | Dm7(no5) 2nd | Em7(no5) 2nd | FΔ7(no5) 2nd | G7(no5) 2nd | Am7(no5) 2nd | Bø(no5) 2nd | CΔ7(no5) 2nd

Root: Am7(no5) | Bø(no5) | CΔ7(no5) | Dm7(no5) | Em7(no5) | FΔ7(no5) | G7(no5) | Am7(no5)

1st: Dm7(no5) 1st | Em7(no5) 1st | FΔ7(no5) 1st | G7(no5) 1st | Am7(no5) 1st | Bø(no5) 1st | CΔ7(no5) 1st | Dm7(no5) 1st

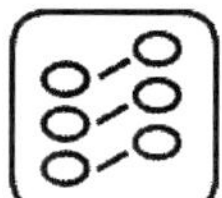

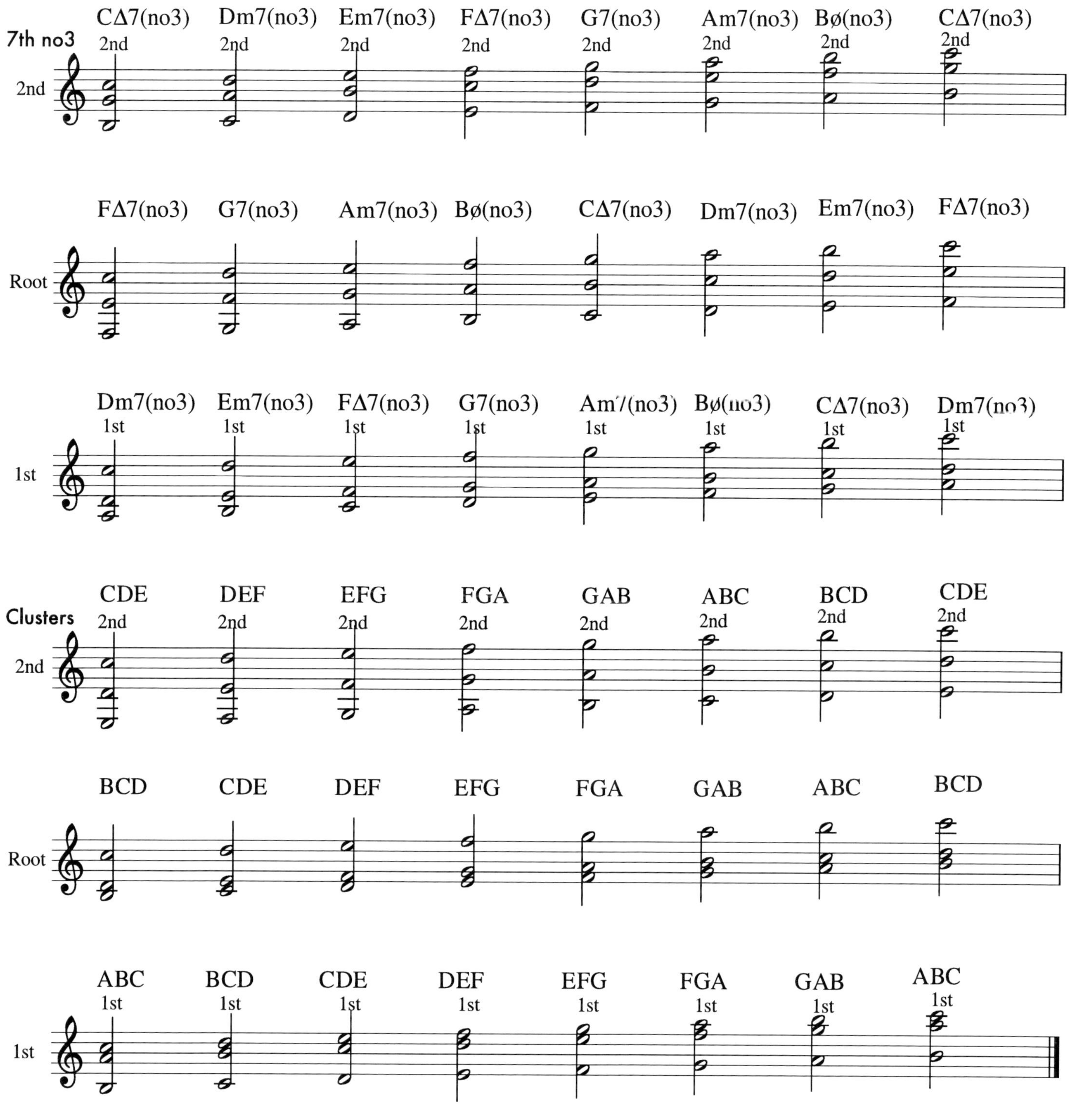

7th no3

2nd: CΔ7(no3) 2nd, Dm7(no3) 2nd, Em7(no3) 2nd, FΔ7(no3) 2nd, G7(no3) 2nd, Am7(no3) 2nd, Bø(no3) 2nd, CΔ7(no3) 2nd

Root: FΔ7(no3), G7(no3), Am7(no3), Bø(no3), CΔ7(no3), Dm7(no3), Em7(no3), FΔ7(no3)

1st: Dm7(no3) 1st, Em7(no3) 1st, FΔ7(no3) 1st, G7(no3) 1st, Am7(no3) 1st, Bø(no3) 1st, CΔ7(no3) 1st, Dm7(no3) 1st

Clusters

2nd: CDE 2nd, DEF 2nd, EFG 2nd, FGA 2nd, GAB 2nd, ABC 2nd, BCD 2nd, CDE 2nd

Root: BCD, CDE, DEF, EFG, FGA, GAB, ABC, BCD

1st: ABC 1st, BCD 1st, CDE 1st, DEF 1st, EFG 1st, FGA 1st, GAB 1st, ABC 1st

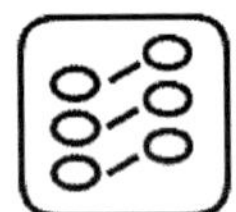

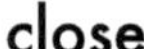

C Melodic Minor Scale

Harmonized with all five chord types (3 Inversions)

Triple-Voice Parallel Motion

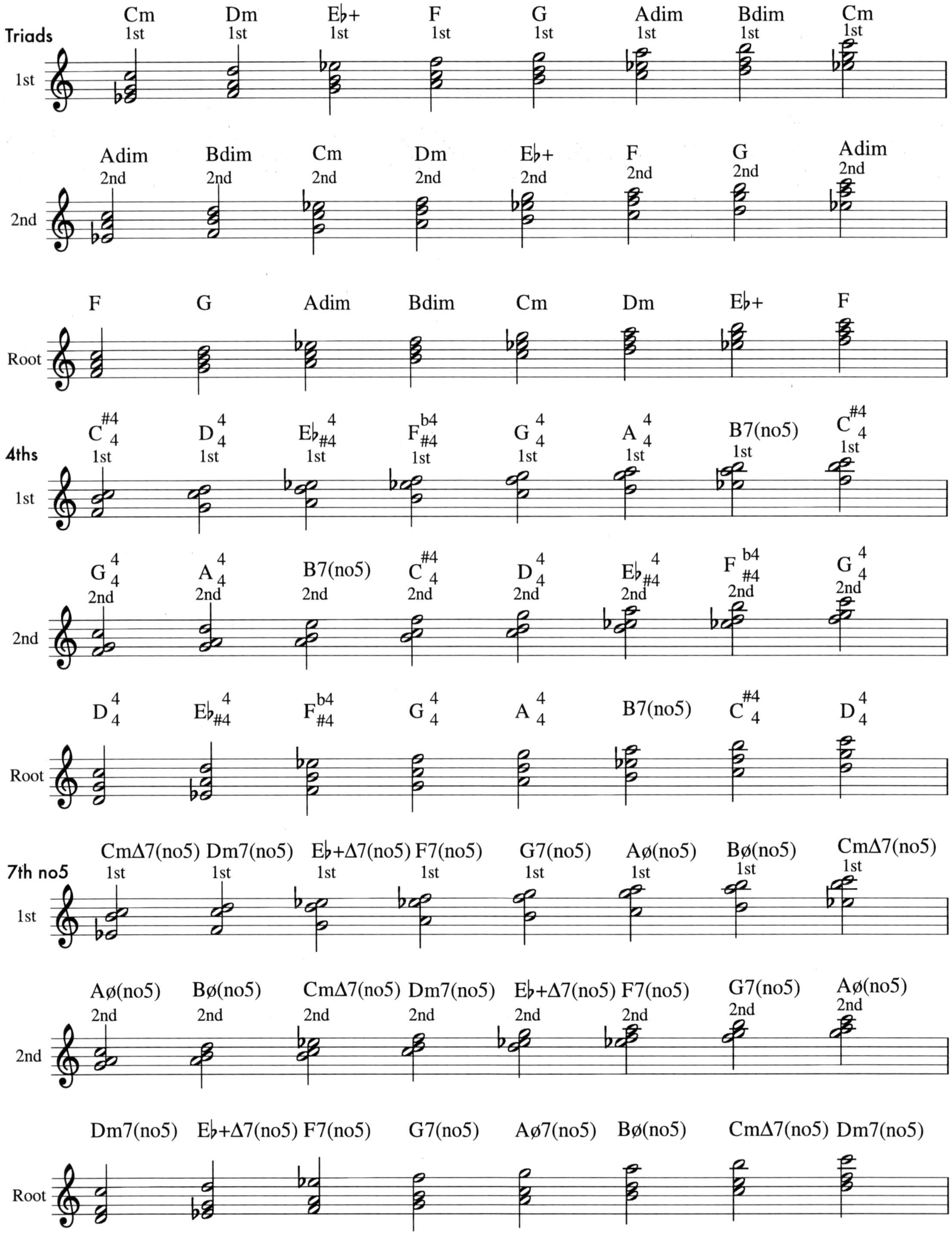

Triads

1st: Cm 1st | Dm 1st | E♭+ 1st | F 1st | G 1st | Adim 1st | Bdim 1st | Cm 1st

2nd: Adim 2nd | Bdim 2nd | Cm 2nd | Dm 2nd | E♭+ 2nd | F 2nd | G 2nd | Adim 2nd

Root: F | G | Adim | Bdim | Cm | Dm | E♭+ | F

4ths

1st: C$^{\#4}_{4}$ 1st | D$^{4}_{4}$ 1st | E♭$^{4}_{\#4}$ 1st | F$^{b4}_{\#4}$ 1st | G$^{4}_{4}$ 1st | A$^{4}_{4}$ 1st | B7(no5) 1st | C$^{\#4}_{4}$ 1st

2nd: G$^{4}_{4}$ 2nd | A$^{4}_{4}$ 2nd | B7(no5) 2nd | C$^{\#4}_{4}$ 2nd | D$^{4}_{4}$ 2nd | E♭$^{4}_{\#4}$ 2nd | F$^{b4}_{\#4}$ 2nd | G$^{4}_{4}$ 2nd

Root: D$^{4}_{4}$ | E♭$^{4}_{\#4}$ | F$^{b4}_{\#4}$ | G$^{4}_{4}$ | A$^{4}_{4}$ | B7(no5) | C$^{\#4}_{4}$ | D$^{4}_{4}$

7th no5

1st: CmΔ7(no5) 1st | Dm7(no5) 1st | E♭+Δ7(no5) 1st | F7(no5) 1st | G7(no5) 1st | Aø(no5) 1st | Bø(no5) 1st | CmΔ7(no5) 1st

2nd: Aø(no5) 2nd | Bø(no5) 2nd | CmΔ7(no5) 2nd | Dm7(no5) 2nd | E♭+Δ7(no5) 2nd | F7(no5) 2nd | G7(no5) 2nd | Aø(no5) 2nd

Root: Dm7(no5) | E♭+Δ7(no5) | F7(no5) | G7(no5) | Aø7(no5) | Bø(no5) | CmΔ7(no5) | Dm7(no5)

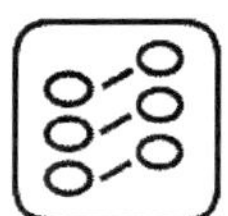

C mm Scale Harmonized cont...

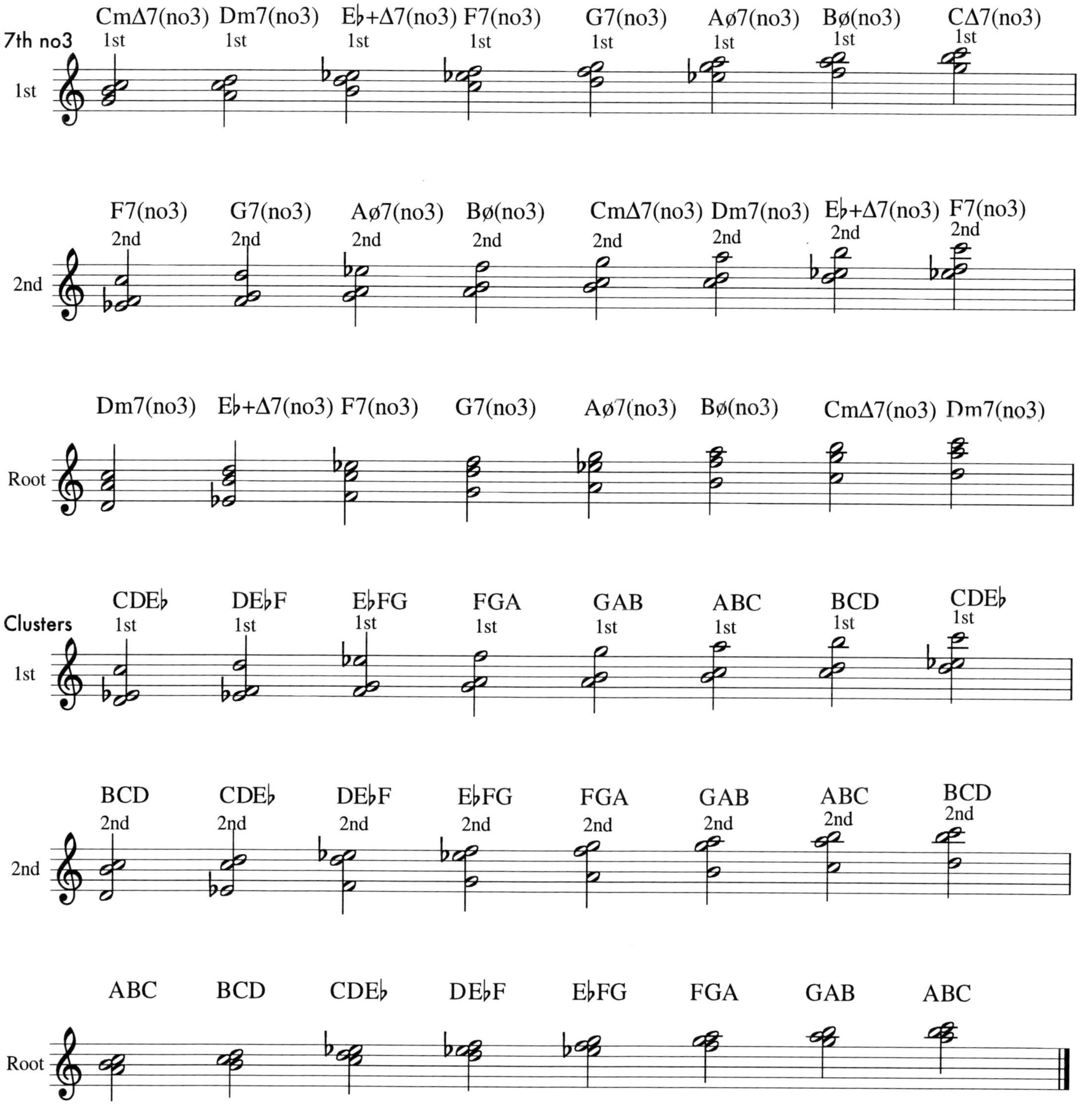

close

7th no3

1st: CmΔ7(no3) 1st, Dm7(no3) 1st, E♭+Δ7(no3) 1st, F7(no3) 1st, G7(no3) 1st, Aø7(no3) 1st, Bø(no3) 1st, CΔ7(no3) 1st

2nd: F7(no3) 2nd, G7(no3) 2nd, Aø7(no3) 2nd, Bø(no3) 2nd, CmΔ7(no3) 2nd, Dm7(no3) 2nd, E♭+Δ7(no3) 2nd, F7(no3) 2nd

Root: Dm7(no3), E♭+Δ7(no3), F7(no3), G7(no3), Aø7(no3), Bø(no3), CmΔ7(no3), Dm7(no3)

Clusters

1st: CDE♭ 1st, DE♭F 1st, E♭FG 1st, FGA 1st, GAB 1st, ABC 1st, BCD 1st, CDE♭ 1st

2nd: BCD 2nd, CDE♭ 2nd, DE♭F 2nd, E♭FG 2nd, FGA 2nd, GAB 2nd, ABC 2nd, BCD 2nd

Root: ABC, BCD, CDE♭, DE♭F, E♭FG, FGA, GAB, ABC

C Melodic Minor Scale

open

Harmonized with all five chord types (3 Inversions)

Triple-Voice Parallel Motion

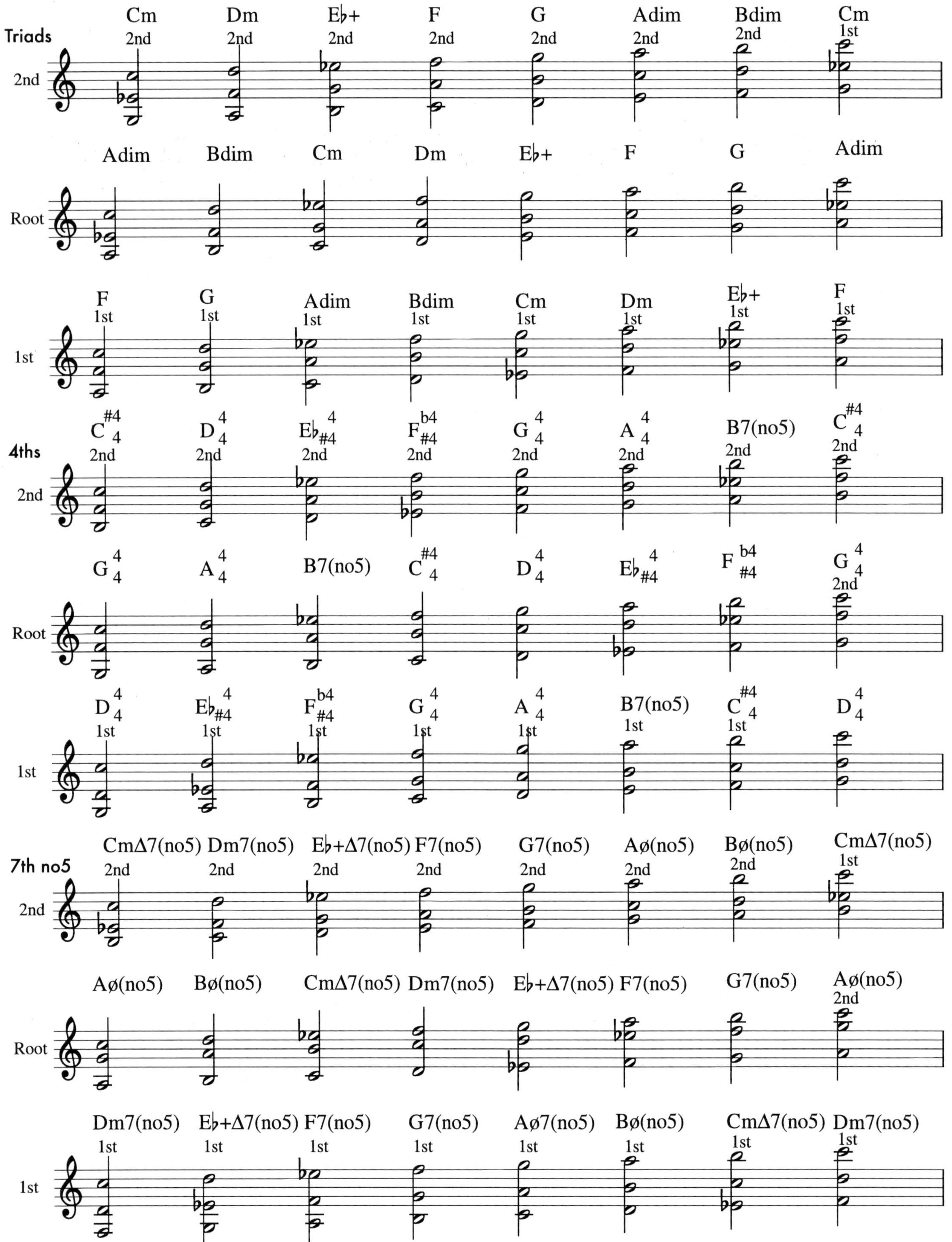

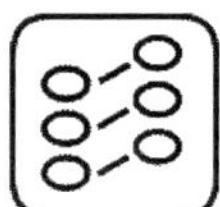

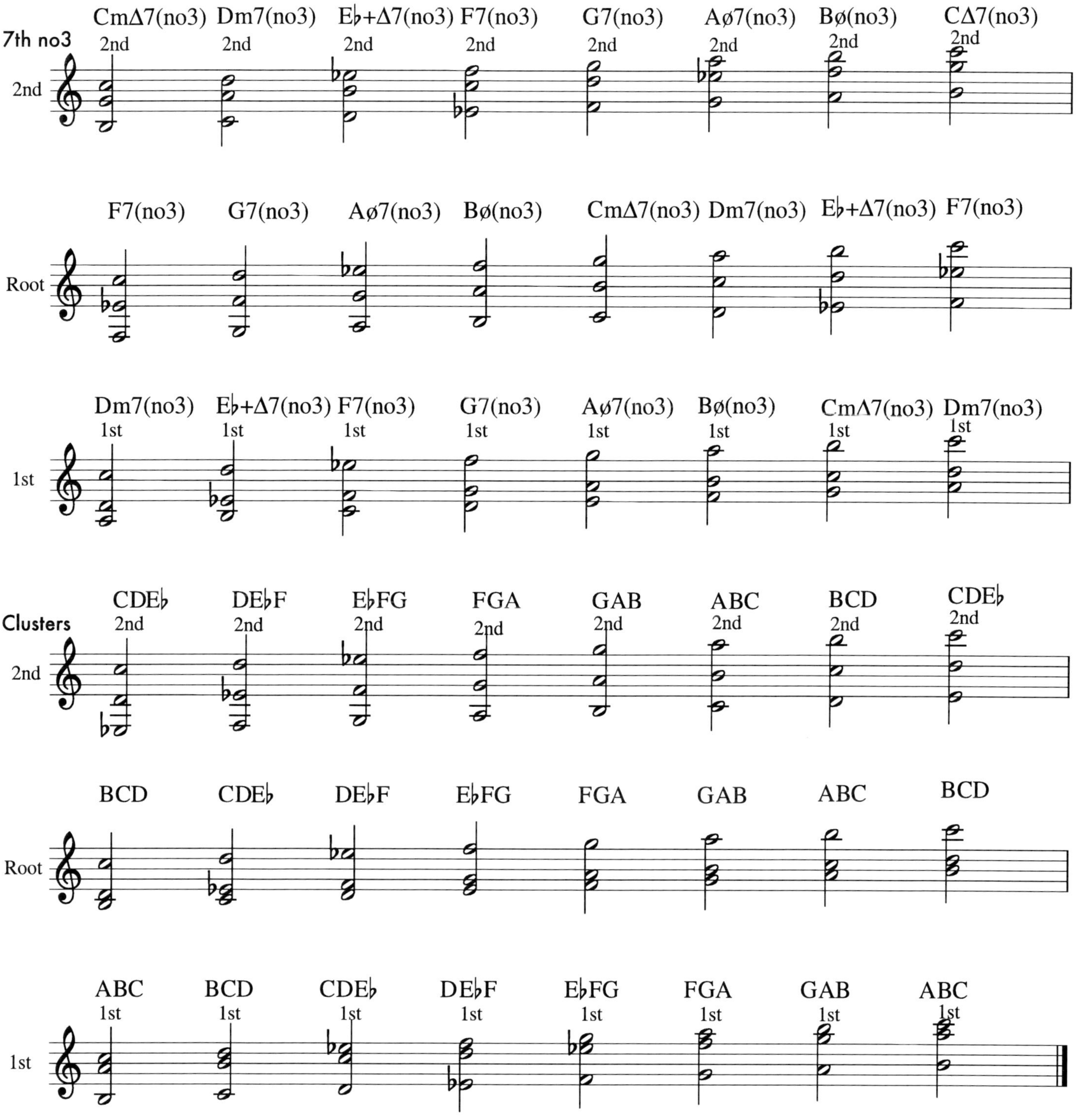

7th no3

2nd: CmΔ7(no3) 2nd, Dm7(no3) 2nd, E♭+Δ7(no3) 2nd, F7(no3) 2nd, G7(no3) 2nd, Aø7(no3) 2nd, Bø(no3) 2nd, CΔ7(no3) 2nd

Root: F7(no3), G7(no3), Aø7(no3), Bø(no3), CmΔ7(no3), Dm7(no3), E♭+Δ7(no3), F7(no3)

1st: Dm7(no3) 1st, E♭+Δ7(no3) 1st, F7(no3) 1st, G7(no3) 1st, Aø7(no3) 1st, Bø(no3) 1st, CmΔ7(no3) 1st, Dm7(no3) 1st

Clusters

2nd: CDE♭ 2nd, DE♭F 2nd, E♭FG 2nd, FGA 2nd, GAB 2nd, ABC 2nd, BCD 2nd, CDE♭ 2nd

Root: BCD, CDE♭, DE♭F, E♭FG, FGA, GAB, ABC, BCD

1st: ABC 1st, BCD 1st, CDE♭ 1st, DE♭F 1st, E♭FG 1st, FGA 1st, GAB 1st, ABC 1st

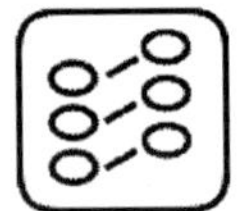

C Harmonic Major Scale

close

Harmonized with all five chord types (3 Inversions)

Triple-Voice Parallel Motion

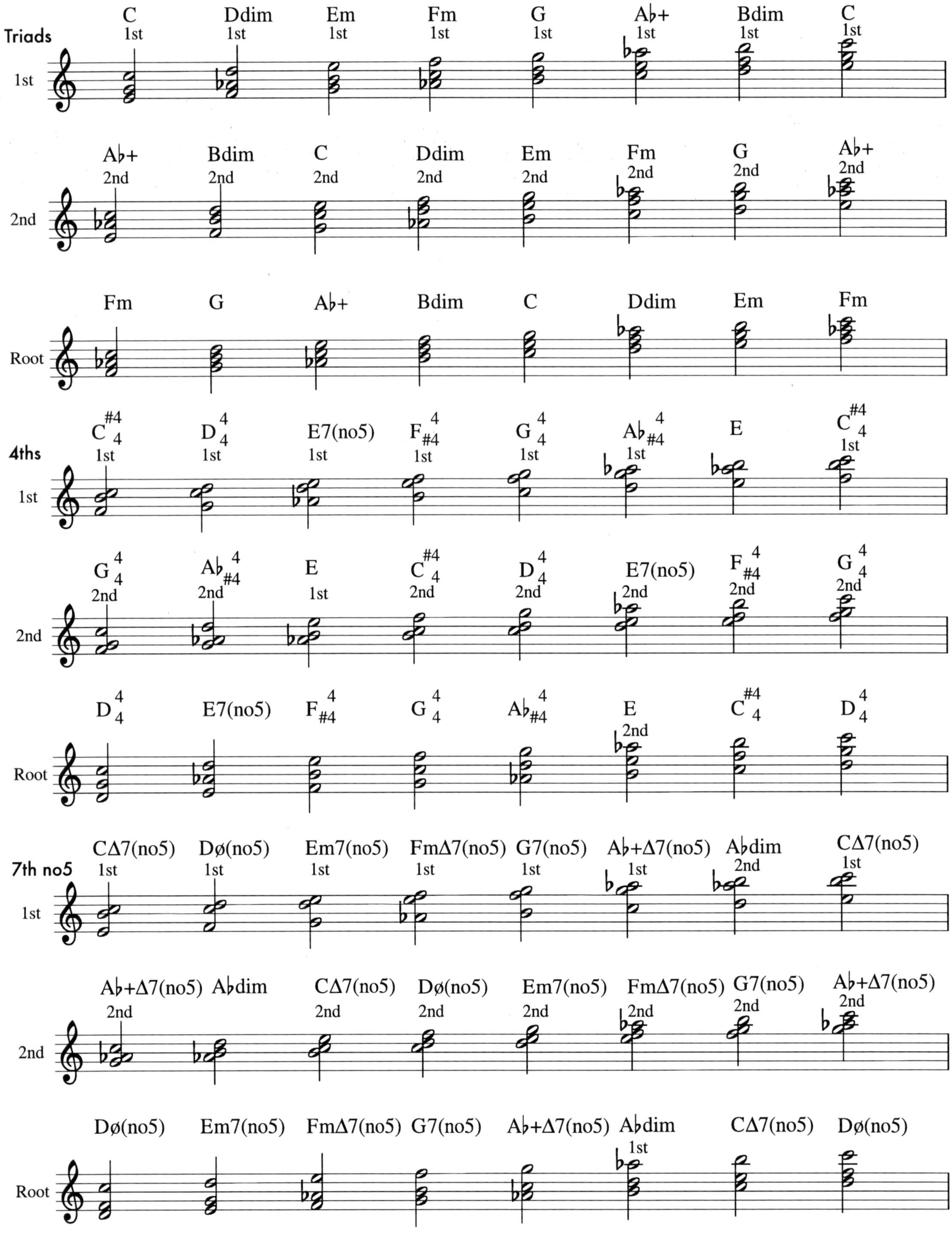

Triads

1st: C 1st | Ddim 1st | Em 1st | Fm 1st | G 1st | A♭+ 1st | Bdim 1st | C 1st

2nd: A♭+ 2nd | Bdim 2nd | C 2nd | Ddim 2nd | Em 2nd | Fm 2nd | G 2nd | A♭+ 2nd

Root: Fm | G | A♭+ | Bdim | C | Ddim | Em | Fm

4ths

1st: $C^{\#4}_{4}$ 1st | D^{4}_{4} 1st | E7(no5) 1st | $F^{4}_{\#4}$ 1st | G^{4}_{4} 1st | $A\flat^{4}_{\#4}$ 1st | E | $C^{\#4}_{4}$ 1st

2nd: G^{4}_{4} 2nd | $A\flat^{4}_{\#4}$ 2nd | E 1st | $C^{\#4}_{4}$ 2nd | D^{4}_{4} 2nd | E7(no5) 2nd | $F^{4}_{\#4}$ 2nd | G^{4}_{4} 2nd

Root: D^{4}_{4} | E7(no5) | $F^{4}_{\#4}$ | G^{4}_{4} | $A\flat^{4}_{\#4}$ | E 2nd | $C^{\#4}_{4}$ | D^{4}_{4}

7th no5

1st: CΔ7(no5) 1st | Dø(no5) 1st | Em7(no5) 1st | FmΔ7(no5) 1st | G7(no5) 1st | A♭+Δ7(no5) 1st | A♭dim 2nd | CΔ7(no5) 1st

2nd: A♭+Δ7(no5) 2nd | A♭dim | CΔ7(no5) 2nd | Dø(no5) 2nd | Em7(no5) 2nd | FmΔ7(no5) 2nd | G7(no5) 2nd | A♭+Δ7(no5) 2nd

Root: Dø(no5) | Em7(no5) | FmΔ7(no5) | G7(no5) | A♭+Δ7(no5) | A♭dim 1st | CΔ7(no5) | Dø(no5)

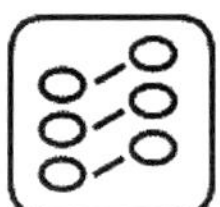

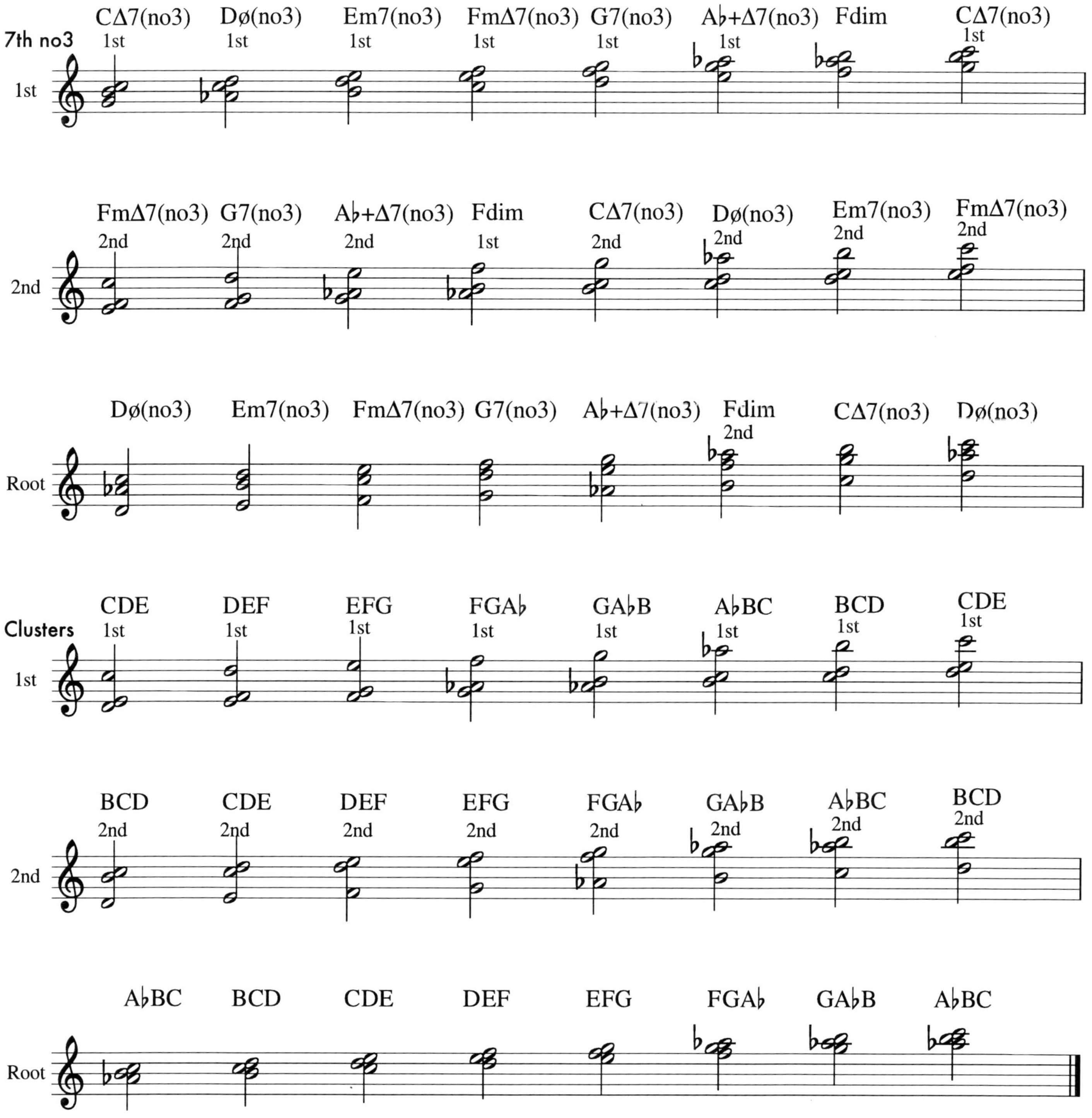

7th no3

1st: CΔ7(no3) 1st — Dø(no3) 1st — Em7(no3) 1st — FmΔ7(no3) 1st — G7(no3) 1st — A♭+Δ7(no3) 1st — Fdim — CΔ7(no3) 1st

2nd: FmΔ7(no3) 2nd — G7(no3) 2nd — A♭+Δ7(no3) 2nd — Fdim 1st — CΔ7(no3) 2nd — Dø(no3) 2nd — Em7(no3) 2nd — FmΔ7(no3) 2nd

Root: Dø(no3) — Em7(no3) — FmΔ7(no3) — G7(no3) — A♭+Δ7(no3) — Fdim 2nd — CΔ7(no3) — Dø(no3)

Clusters

1st: CDE 1st — DEF 1st — EFG 1st — FGA♭ 1st — GA♭B 1st — A♭BC 1st — BCD 1st — CDE 1st

2nd: BCD 2nd — CDE 2nd — DEF 2nd — EFG 2nd — FGA♭ 2nd — GA♭B 2nd — A♭BC 2nd — BCD 2nd

Root: A♭BC — BCD — CDE — DEF — EFG — FGA♭ — GA♭B — A♭BC

C Harmonic Major Scale

open

Harmonized with all five chord types (3 Inversions)

Triple-Voice Parallel Motion

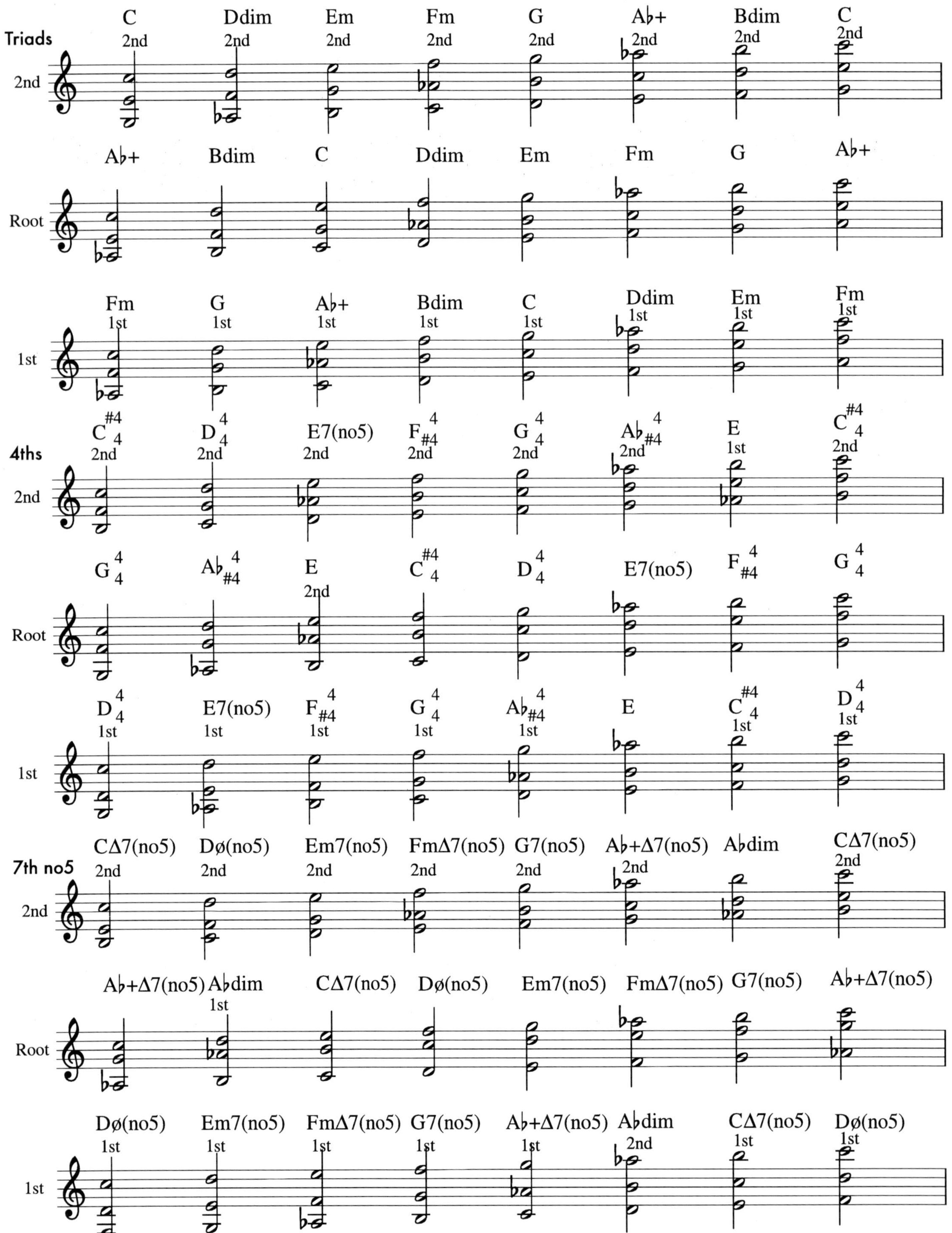

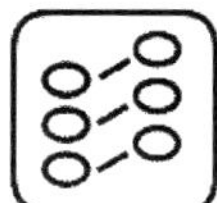

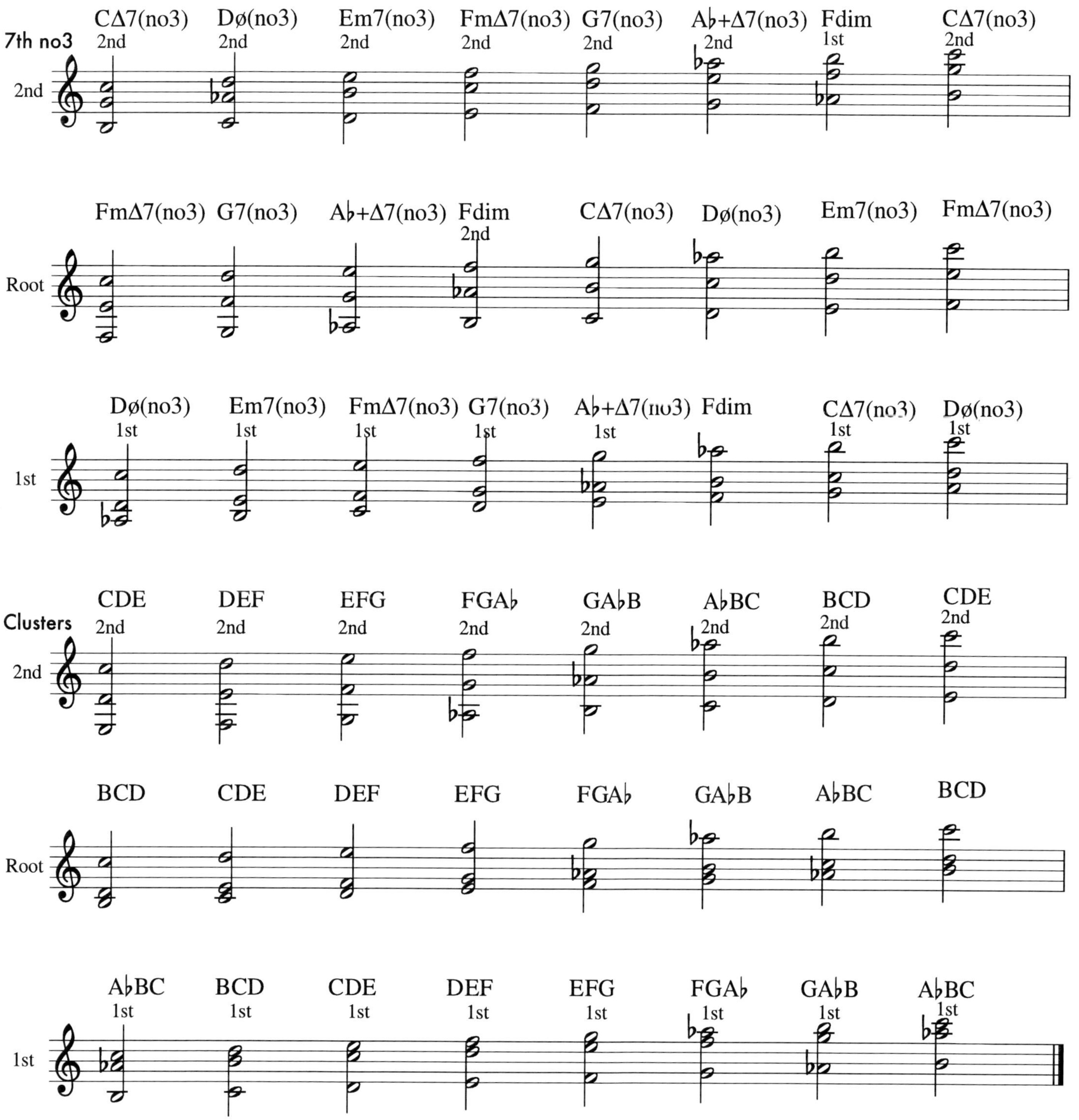

7th no3

2nd

CΔ7(no3) 2nd | Dø(no3) 2nd | Em7(no3) 2nd | FmΔ7(no3) 2nd | G7(no3) 2nd | A♭+Δ7(no3) 2nd | Fdim 1st | CΔ7(no3) 2nd

Root

FmΔ7(no3) | G7(no3) | A♭+Δ7(no3) | Fdim 2nd | CΔ7(no3) | Dø(no3) | Em7(no3) | FmΔ7(no3)

1st

Dø(no3) 1st | Em7(no3) 1st | FmΔ7(no3) 1st | G7(no3) 1st | A♭+Δ7(no3) 1st | Fdim | CΔ7(no3) 1st | Dø(no3) 1st

Clusters

2nd

CDE 2nd | DEF 2nd | EFG 2nd | FGA♭ 2nd | GA♭B 2nd | A♭BC 2nd | BCD 2nd | CDE 2nd

Root

BCD | CDE | DEF | EFG | FGA♭ | GA♭B | A♭BC | BCD

1st

A♭BC 1st | BCD 1st | CDE 1st | DEF 1st | EFG 1st | FGA♭ 1st | GA♭B 1st | A♭BC 1st

C Harmonic Minor Scale

close

Harmonized with all five chord types (3 Inversions)

Triple-Voice Parallel Motion

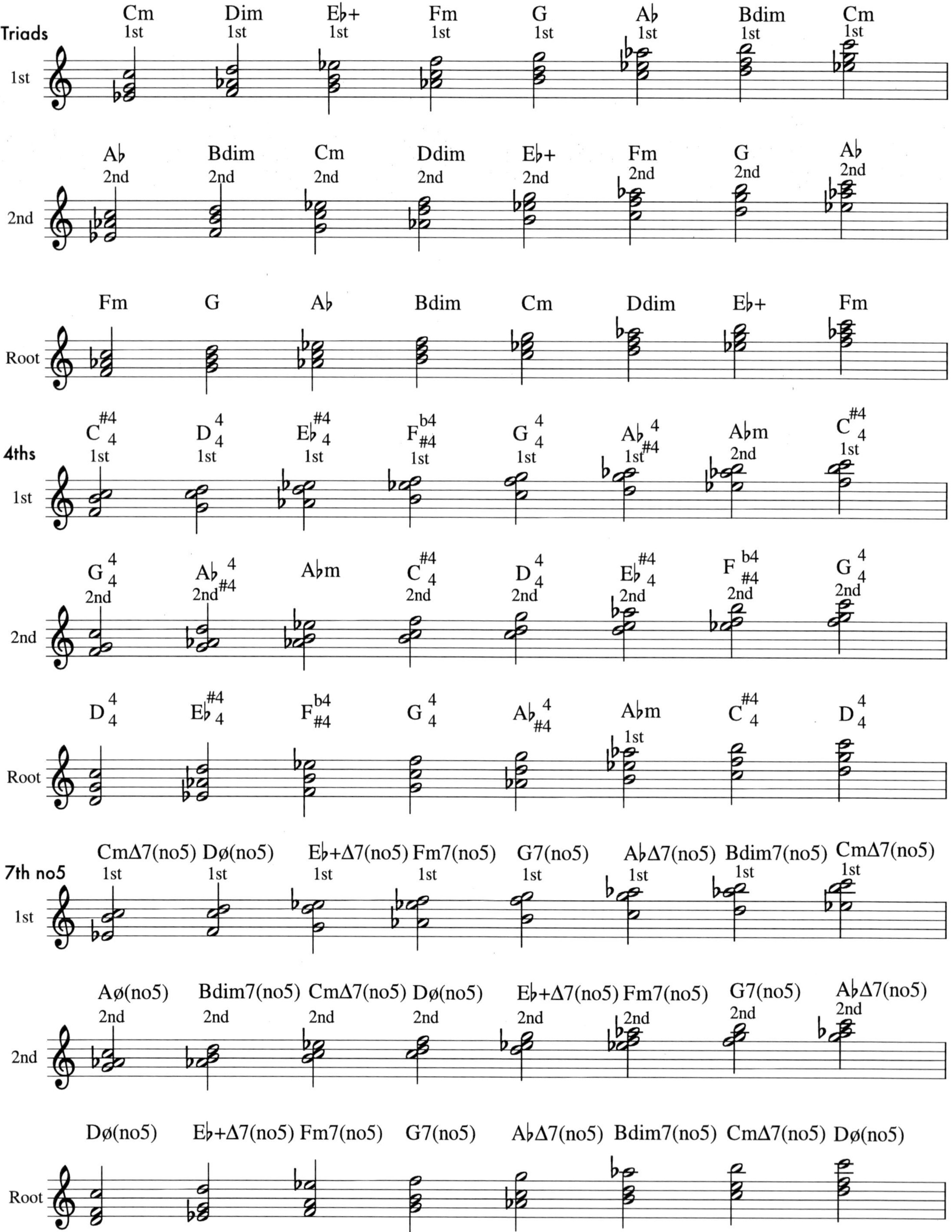

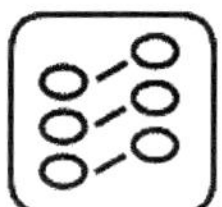

7th no3

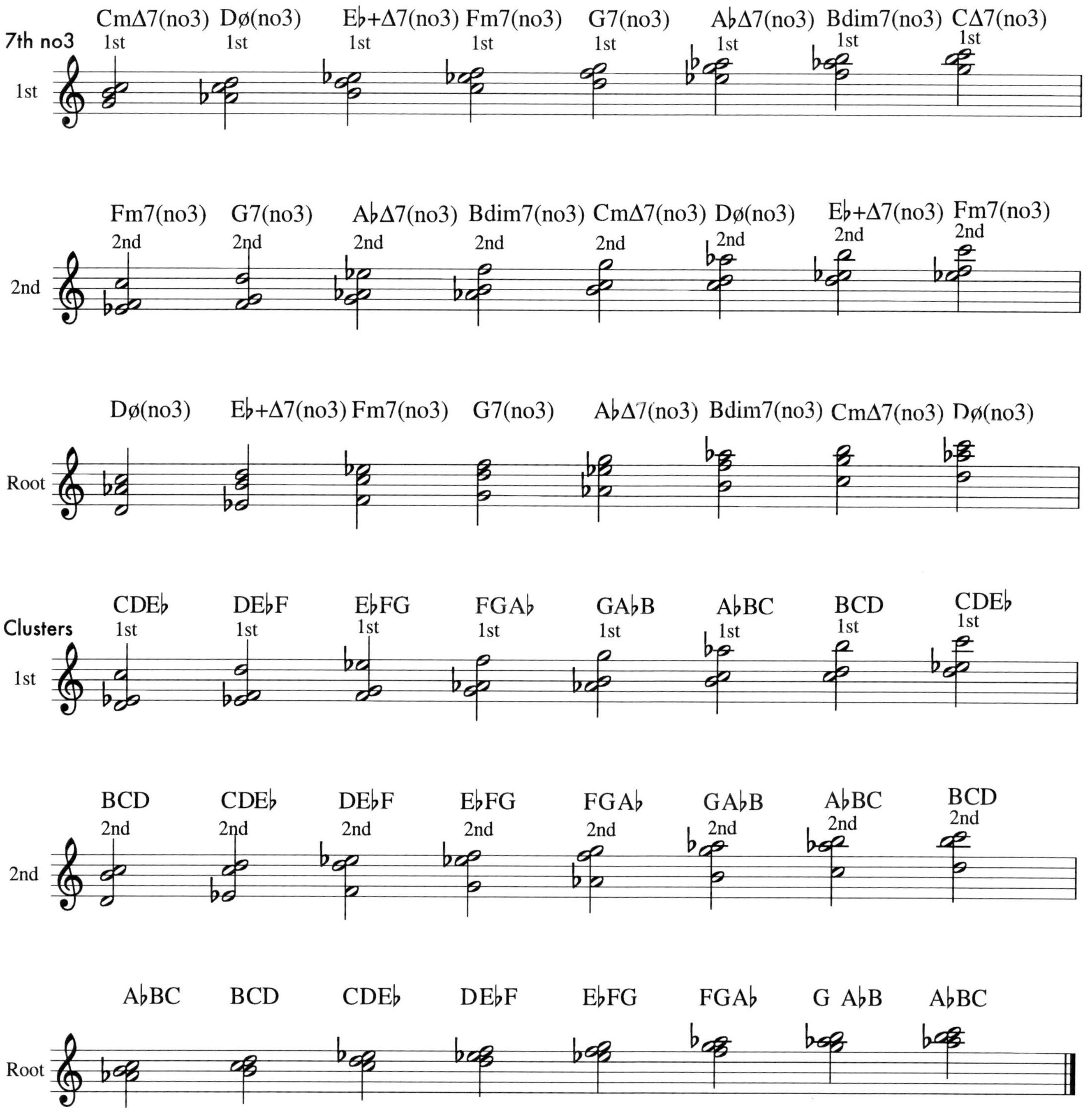

1st: CmΔ7(no3) 1st, Dø(no3) 1st, E♭+Δ7(no3) 1st, Fm7(no3) 1st, G7(no3) 1st, A♭Δ7(no3) 1st, Bdim7(no3) 1st, CΔ7(no3) 1st

2nd: Fm7(no3) 2nd, G7(no3) 2nd, A♭Δ7(no3) 2nd, Bdim7(no3) 2nd, CmΔ7(no3) 2nd, Dø(no3) 2nd, E♭+Δ7(no3) 2nd, Fm7(no3) 2nd

Root: Dø(no3), E♭+Δ7(no3), Fm7(no3), G7(no3), A♭Δ7(no3), Bdim7(no3), CmΔ7(no3), Dø(no3)

Clusters

1st: CDE♭ 1st, DE♭F 1st, E♭FG 1st, FGA♭ 1st, GA♭B 1st, A♭BC 1st, BCD 1st, CDE♭ 1st

2nd: BCD 2nd, CDE♭ 2nd, DE♭F 2nd, E♭FG 2nd, FGA♭ 2nd, GA♭B 2nd, A♭BC 2nd, BCD 2nd

Root: A♭BC, BCD, CDE♭, DE♭F, E♭FG, FGA♭, G A♭B, A♭BC

C Harmonic Minor Scale

open

Harmonized with all five chord types (3 Inversions)

Triple-Voice Parallel Motion

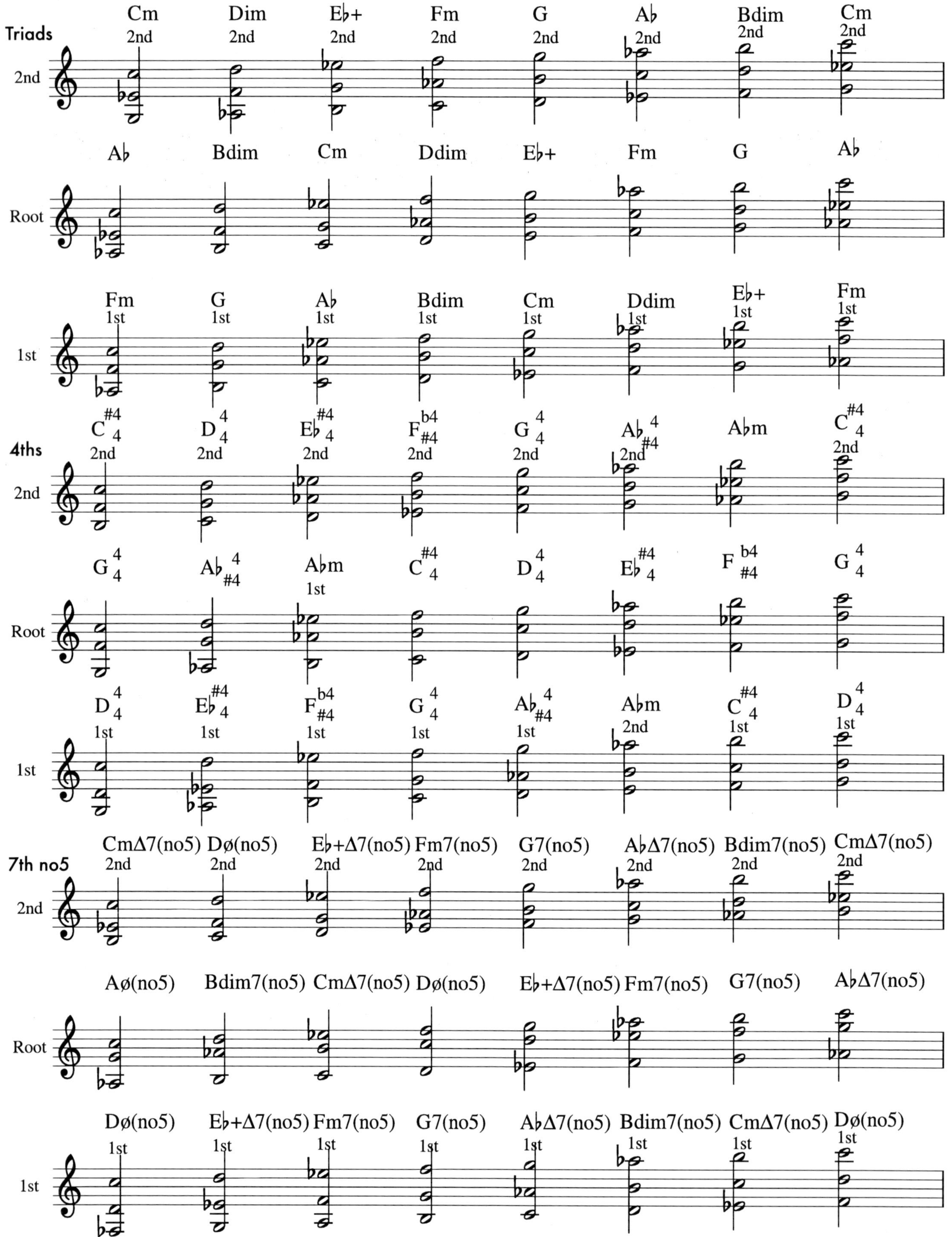

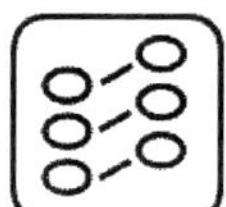

7th no3

2nd

CmΔ7(no3) 2nd | Dø(no3) 2nd | E♭+Δ7(no3) 2nd | Fm7(no3) 2nd | G7(no3) 2nd | A♭Δ7(no3) 2nd | Bdim7(no3) 2nd | CΔ7(no3) 2nd

Root

Fm7(no3) | G7(no3) | A♭Δ7(no3) | Bdim7(no3) | CmΔ7(no3) | Dø(no3) | E♭+Δ7(no3) | Fm7(no3)

1st

Dø(no3) 1st | E♭+Δ7(no3) 1st | Fm7(no3) 1st | G7(no3) 1st | A♭Δ7(no3) 1st | Bdim7(no3) 1st | CmΔ7(no3) 1st | Dø(no3) 1st

Clusters

2nd

CDE♭ 2nd | DE♭F 2nd | E♭FG 2nd | FGA♭ 2nd | GA♭B 2nd | A♭BC 2nd | BCD 2nd | CDE♭ 2nd

Root

BCD | CDE♭ | DE♭F | E♭FG | FGA♭ | GA♭B | A♭BC | BCD

1st

A♭BC 1st | BCD 1st | CDE♭ 1st | DE♭F 1st | E♭FG 1st | FGA♭ 1st | GA♭B 1st | A♭BC 1st

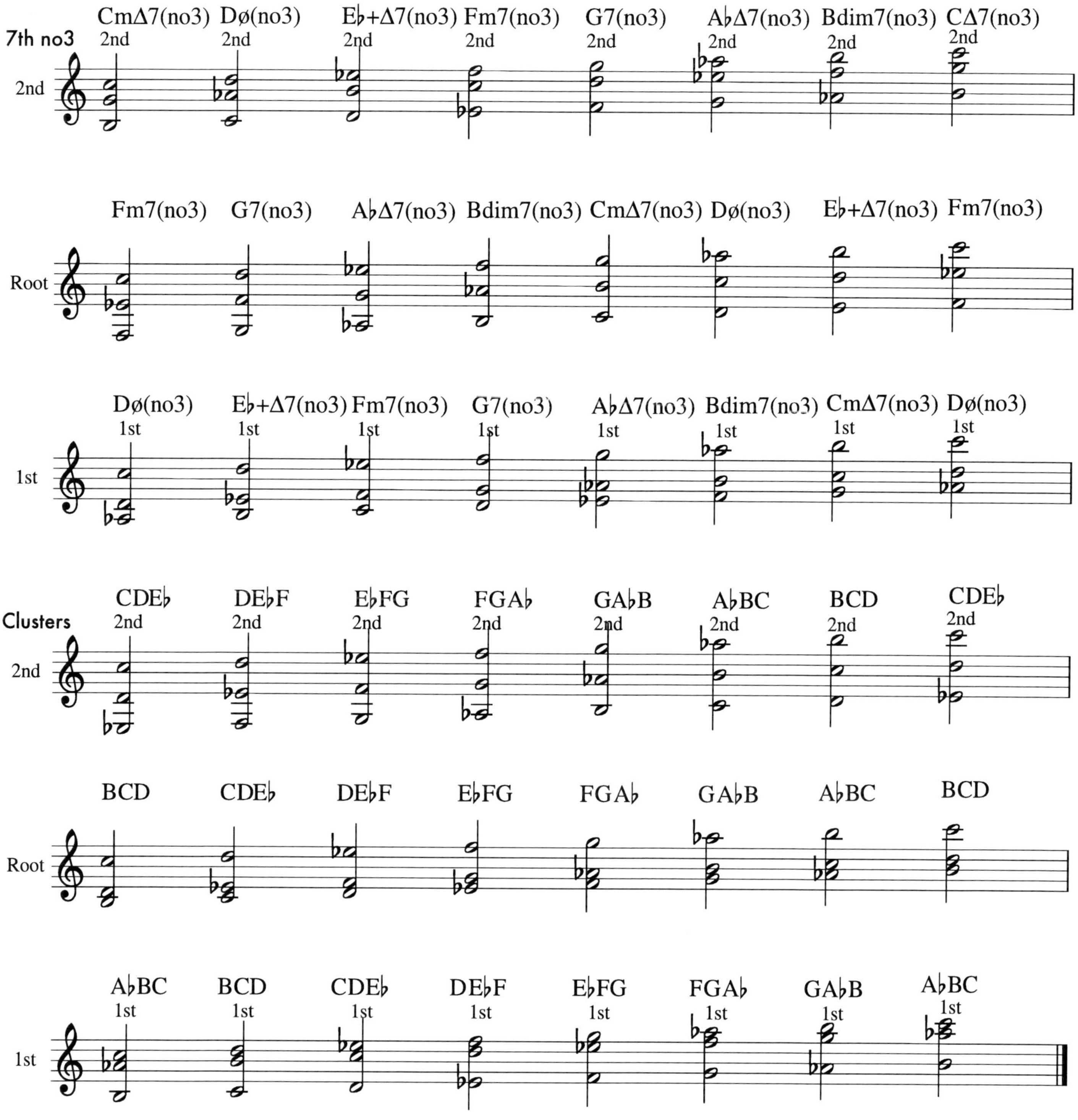

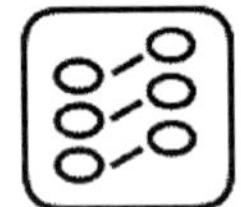

C Melodic Minor ♭5 Scale

close

Harmonized with all five chord types (3 Inversions)

Triple-Voice Parallel Motion

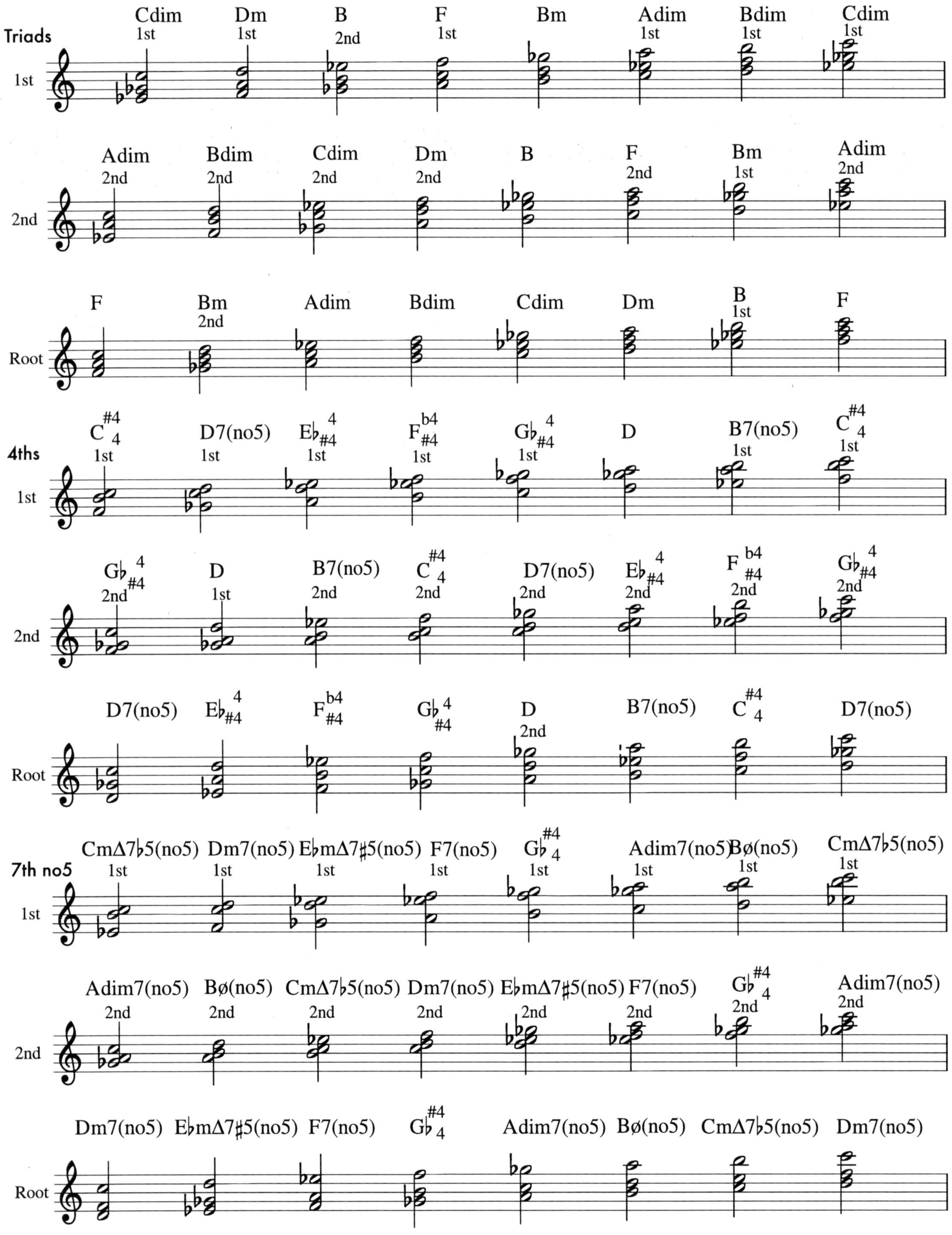

Triads

1st: Cdim 1st, Dm 1st, B 2nd, F 1st, Bm, Adim 1st, Bdim 1st, Cdim 1st

2nd: Adim 2nd, Bdim 2nd, Cdim 2nd, Dm 2nd, B, F 2nd, Bm 1st, Adim 2nd

Root: F, Bm 2nd, Adim, Bdim, Cdim, Dm, B 1st, F

4ths

1st: C#4 4 1st, D7(no5) 1st, E♭4 #4 1st, Fb4 #4 1st, G♭4 #4 1st, D, B7(no5) 1st, C#4 4 1st

2nd: G♭4 #4 2nd, D 1st, B7(no5) 2nd, C#4 4 2nd, D7(no5) 2nd, E♭4 #4 2nd, Fb4 #4 2nd, G♭4 #4 2nd

Root: D7(no5), E♭4 #4, Fb4 #4, G♭4 #4, D 2nd, B7(no5), C#4 4, D7(no5)

7th no5

1st: CmΔ7♭5(no5) 1st, Dm7(no5) 1st, E♭mΔ7♯5(no5) 1st, F7(no5) 1st, G♭#4 4 1st, Adim7(no5) 1st, Bø(no5) 1st, CmΔ7♭5(no5) 1st

2nd: Adim7(no5) 2nd, Bø(no5) 2nd, CmΔ7♭5(no5) 2nd, Dm7(no5) 2nd, E♭mΔ7♯5(no5) 2nd, F7(no5) 2nd, G♭#4 4 2nd, Adim7(no5) 2nd

Root: Dm7(no5), E♭mΔ7♯5(no5), F7(no5), G♭#4 4, Adim7(no5), Bø(no5), CmΔ7♭5(no5), Dm7(no5)

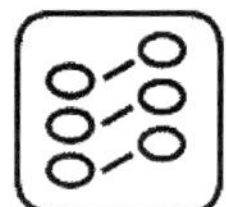

close

7th no3

1st: $C^{4}_{\sharp 4}$ (1st), Dm7(no3) (1st), E♭mΔ7♯5(no3) (1st), F7(no3) (1st), G♭+Δ7(no3) (1st), Adim7(no3) (1st), Bø(no3) (1st), CΔ7(no3) (1st)

2nd: F7(no3) (2nd), G♭+Δ7(no3) (2nd), Adim7(no3) (2nd), Bø(no3) (2nd), $C^{4}_{\sharp 4}$ (2nd), Dm7(no3) (2nd), E♭mΔ7♯5(no3) (2nd), F7(no3) (2nd)

Root: Dm7(no3), E♭mΔ7♯5(no3), F7(no3), G♭+Δ7(no3), Adim7(no3), Bø(no3), $C^{4}_{\sharp 4}$, Dm7(no3)

Clusters

1st: CDE♭ (1st), DE♭F (1st), E♭FG♭ (1st), F G♭A (1st), G♭AB (1st), ABC (1st), BCD (1st), CDE♭ (1st)

14 2nd: BCD (2nd), CDE♭ (2nd), DE♭F (2nd), E♭FG♭ (2nd), F G♭A (2nd), G♭AB (2nd), ABC (2nd), BCD (2nd)

Root: ABC, BCD, CDE♭, DE♭F, E♭FG♭, F G♭A, G♭AB, ABC

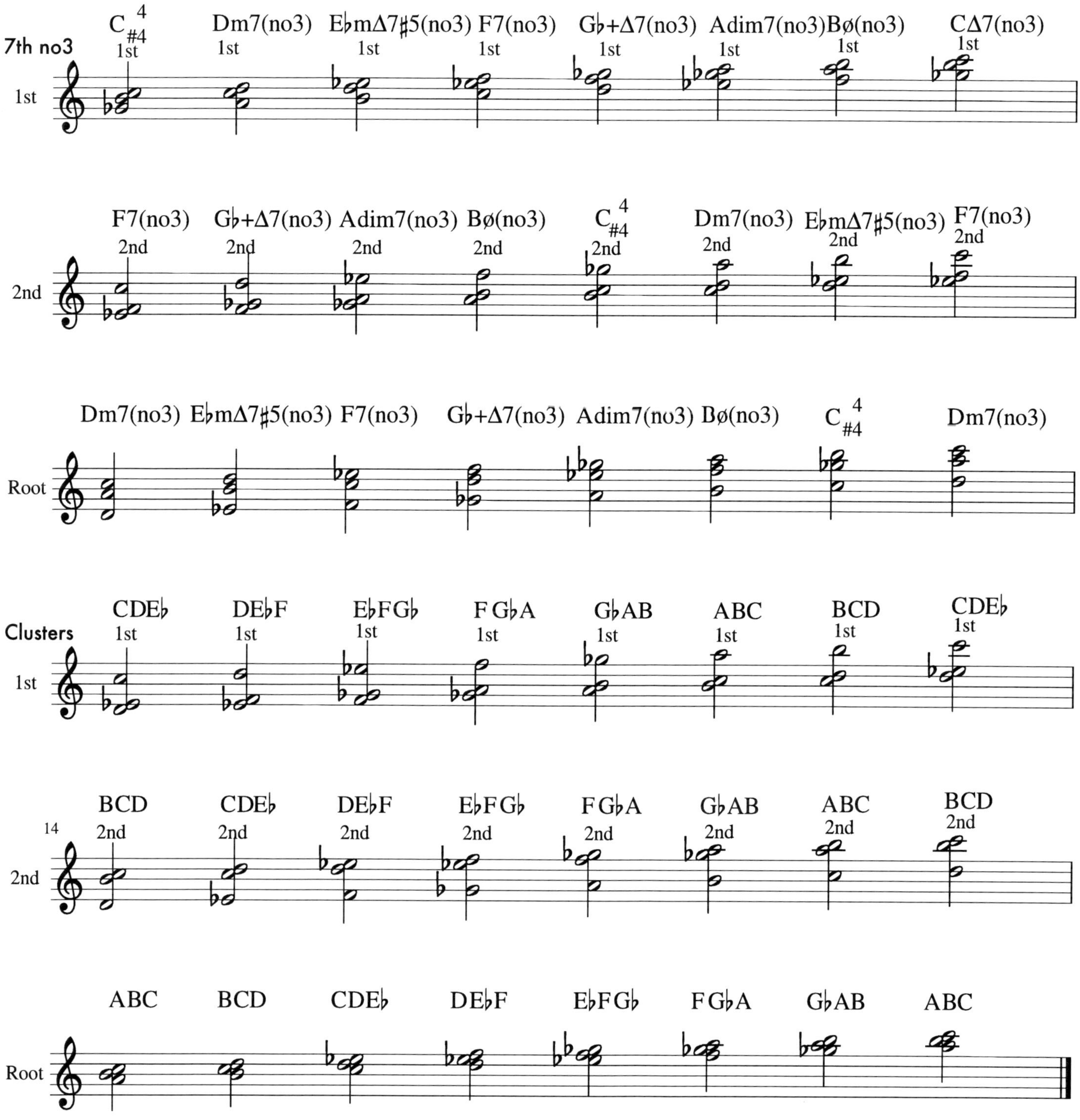

open

C Melodic Minor ♭5 Scale

Harmonized with all five chord types (3 Inversions)

Triple-Voice Parallel Motion

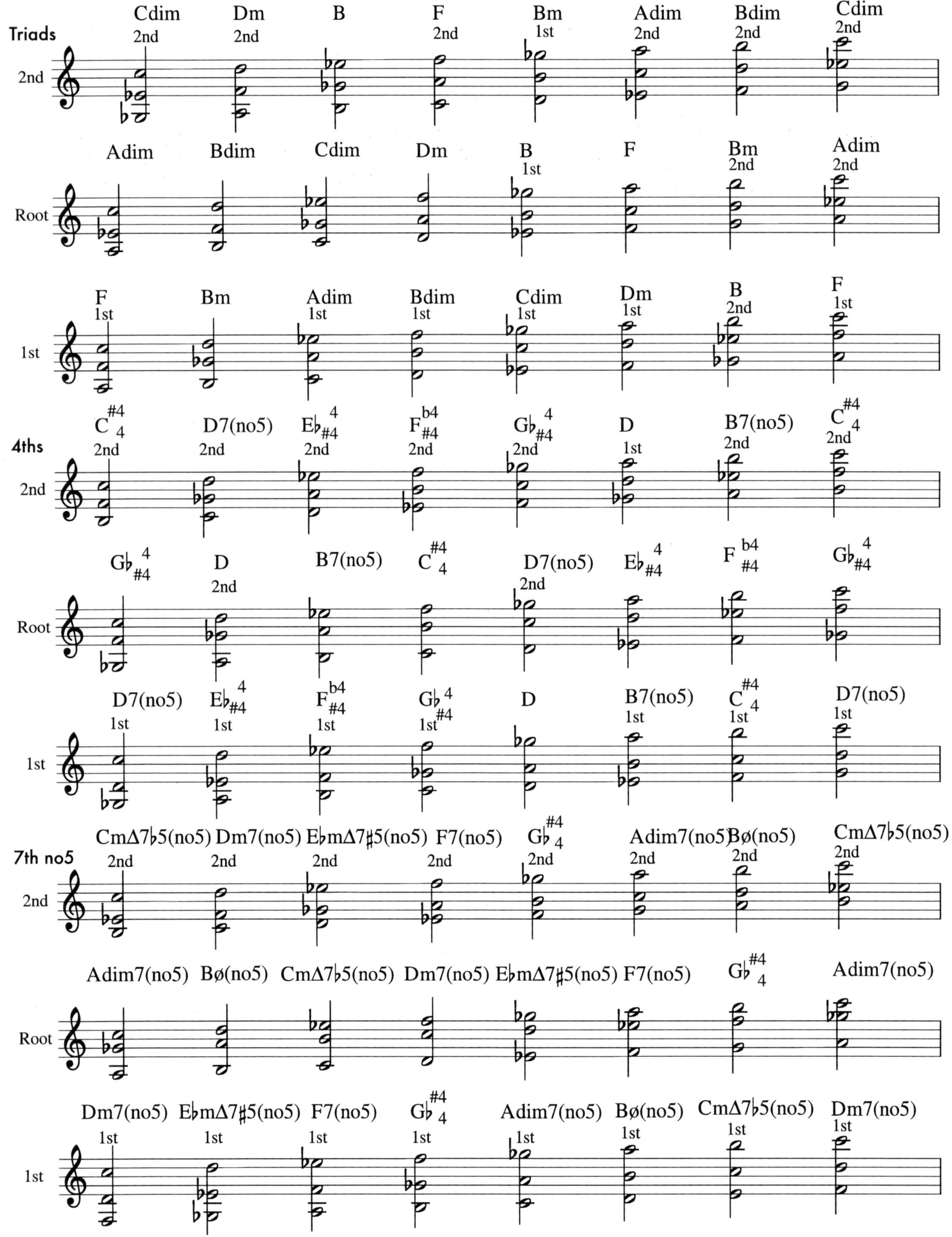

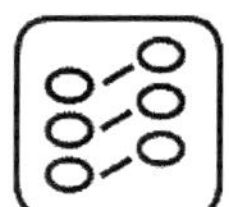

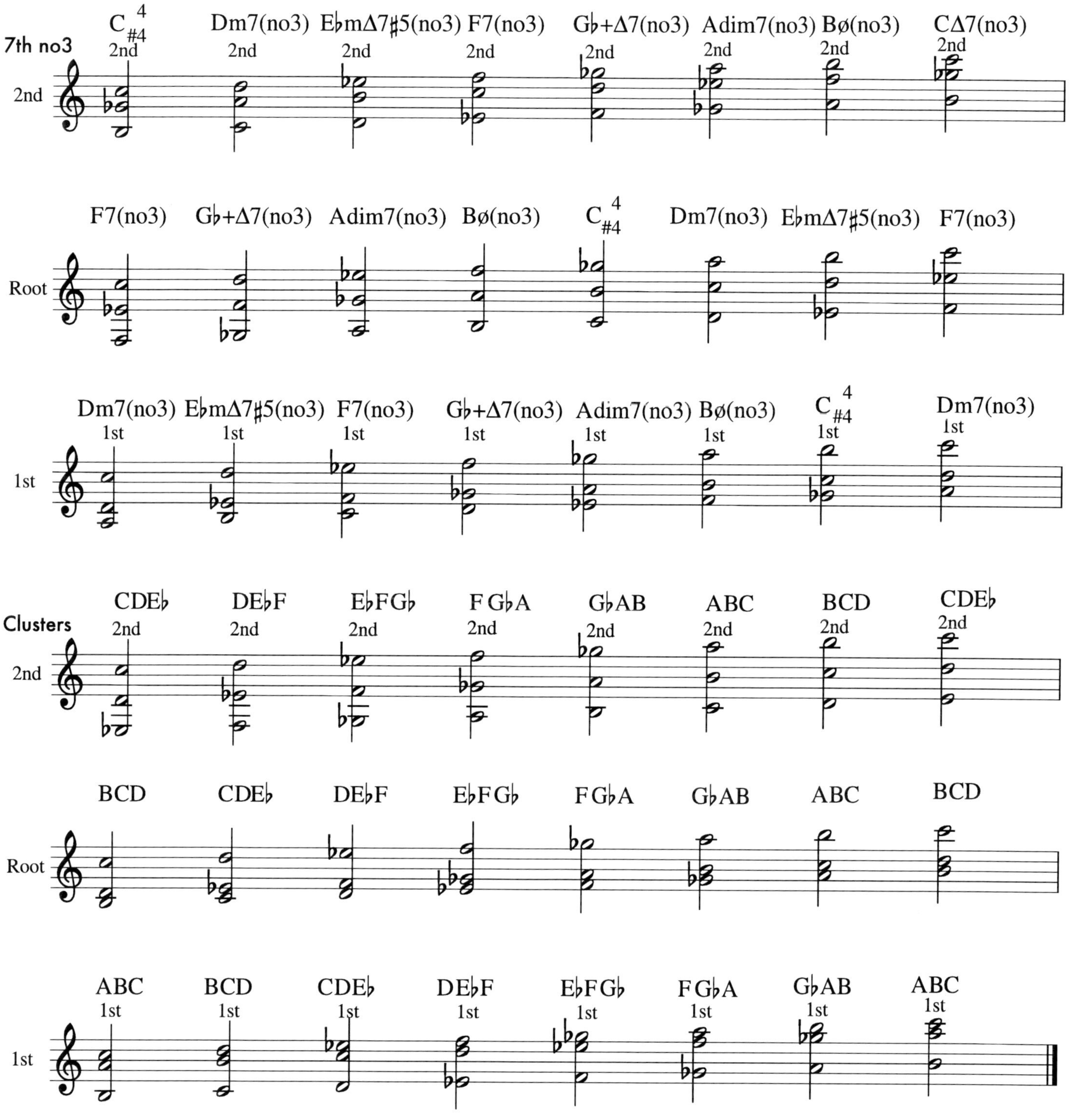

C mm ♭5 Scale Harmonized cont...

open

7th no3

2nd

C $^{4}_{\#4}$ (2nd) | Dm7(no3) (2nd) | E♭mΔ7♯5(no3) (2nd) | F7(no3) (2nd) | G♭+Δ7(no3) (2nd) | Adim7(no3) (2nd) | Bø(no3) (2nd) | CΔ7(no3) (2nd)

Root

F7(no3) | G♭+Δ7(no3) | Adim7(no3) | Bø(no3) | C $^{4}_{\#4}$ | Dm7(no3) | E♭mΔ7♯5(no3) | F7(no3)

1st

Dm7(no3) (1st) | E♭mΔ7♯5(no3) (1st) | F7(no3) (1st) | G♭+Δ7(no3) (1st) | Adim7(no3) (1st) | Bø(no3) (1st) | C $^{4}_{\#4}$ (1st) | Dm7(no3) (1st)

Clusters

2nd

CDE♭ (2nd) | DE♭F (2nd) | E♭FG♭ (2nd) | F G♭A (2nd) | G♭AB (2nd) | ABC (2nd) | BCD (2nd) | CDE♭ (2nd)

Root

BCD | CDE♭ | DE♭F | E♭F G♭ | F G♭A | G♭AB | ABC | BCD

1st

ABC (1st) | BCD (1st) | CDE♭ (1st) | DE♭F (1st) | E♭FG♭ (1st) | F G♭A (1st) | G♭AB (1st) | ABC (1st)

C Harmonic Minor ♭5 Scale

close

Harmonized with all five chord types (3 Inversions)

Triple-Voice Parallel Motion

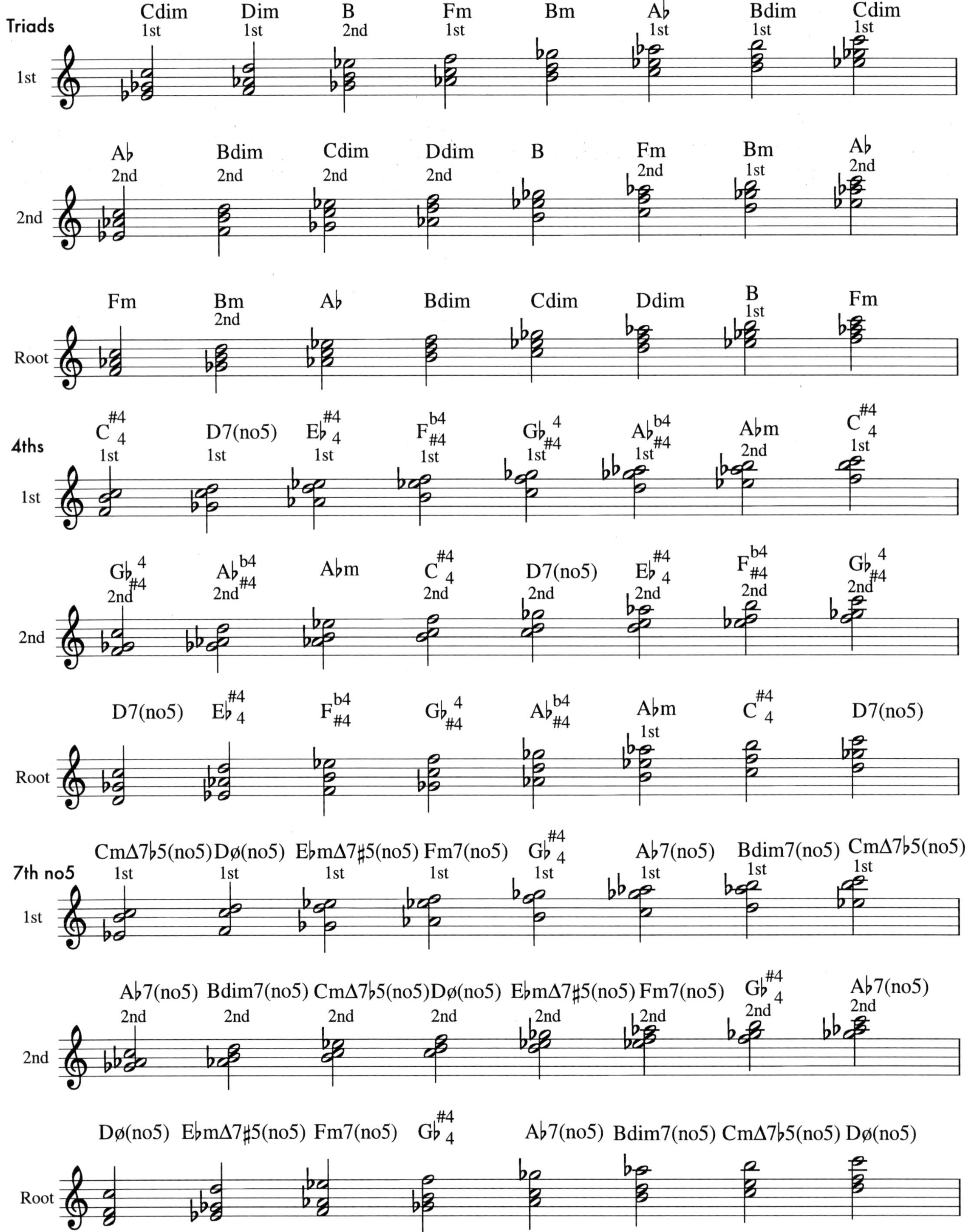

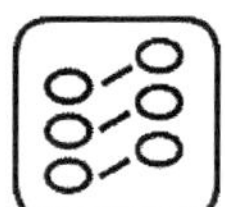

7th no3
1st
C 4 #4 1st
Dø(no3) 1st
E♭mΔ7♯5(no3) 1st
Fm7(no3) 1st
G♭+Δ7(no3) 1st
A♭7(no3) 1st
Bdim7(no3) 1st
C 4 #4 1st
2nd
F7(no3) 2nd
G♭+Δ7(no3) 2nd
A♭7(no3) 2nd
Bdim7(no3) 2nd
C 4 #4 2nd
Dø(no3) 2nd
E♭mΔ7♯5(no3) 2nd
Fm7(no3) 2nd
Root
Dø(no3)
E♭mΔ7♯5(no3)
Fm7(no3)
G♭+Δ7(no3)
A♭7(no3)
Bdim7(no3)
C 4 #4
Dø(no3)
Clusters
1st
CDE♭ 1st
DE♭F 1st
E♭FG♭ 1st
FG♭A♭ 1st
G♭A♭B 1st
A♭BC 1st
BCD 1st
CDE♭ 1st
2nd
BCD 2nd
CDE♭ 2nd
DE♭F 2nd
E♭FG♭ 2nd
FG♭A♭ 2nd
G♭A♭B 2nd
A♭BC 2nd
BCD 2nd
Root
A♭BC
BCD
CDE♭
DE♭F
E♭FG♭
FG♭A♭
G♭A♭B
A♭BC

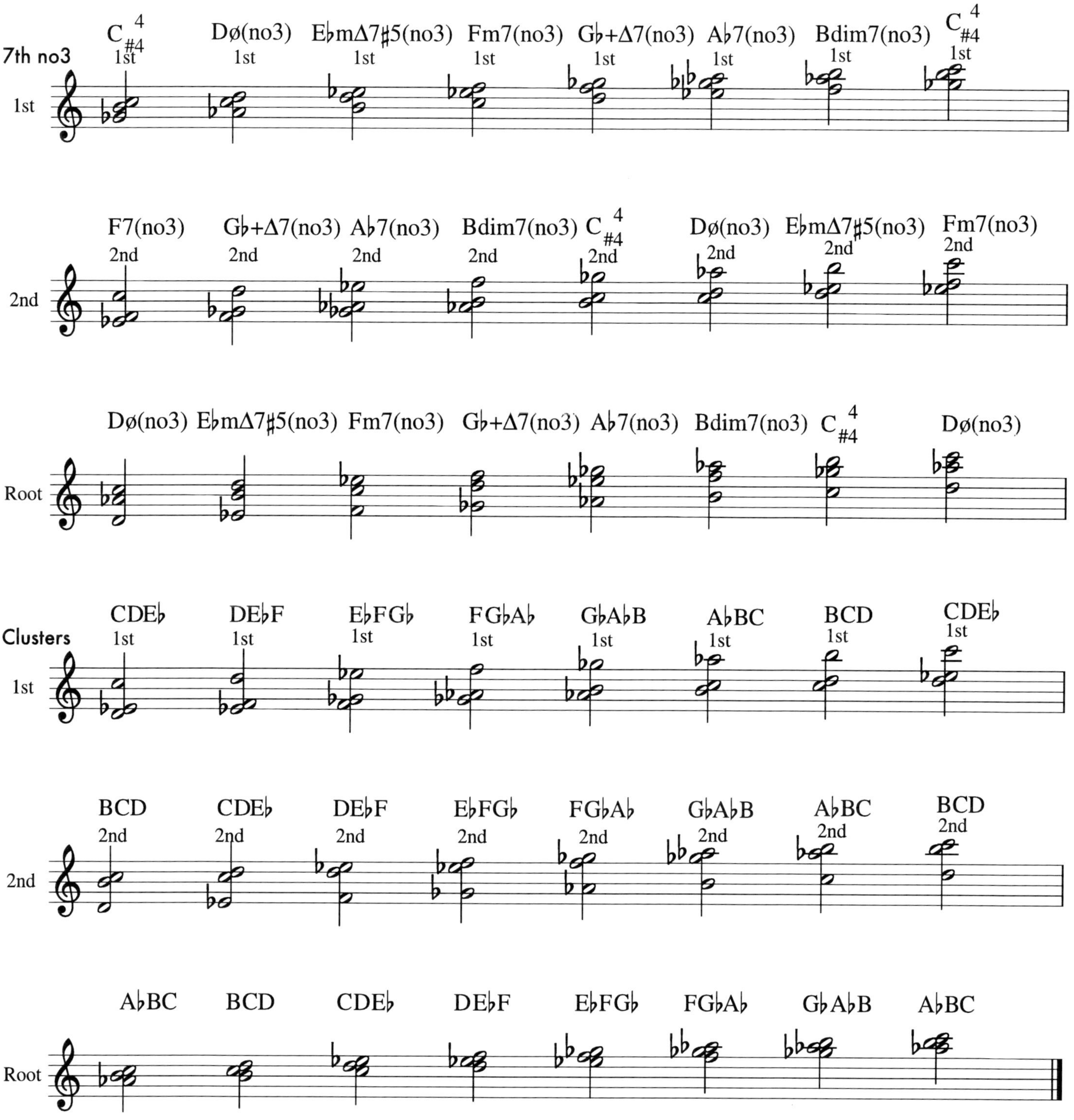

C Harmonic Minor ♭5 Scale

open

Harmonized with all five chord types (3 Inversions)

Triple-Voice Parallel Motion

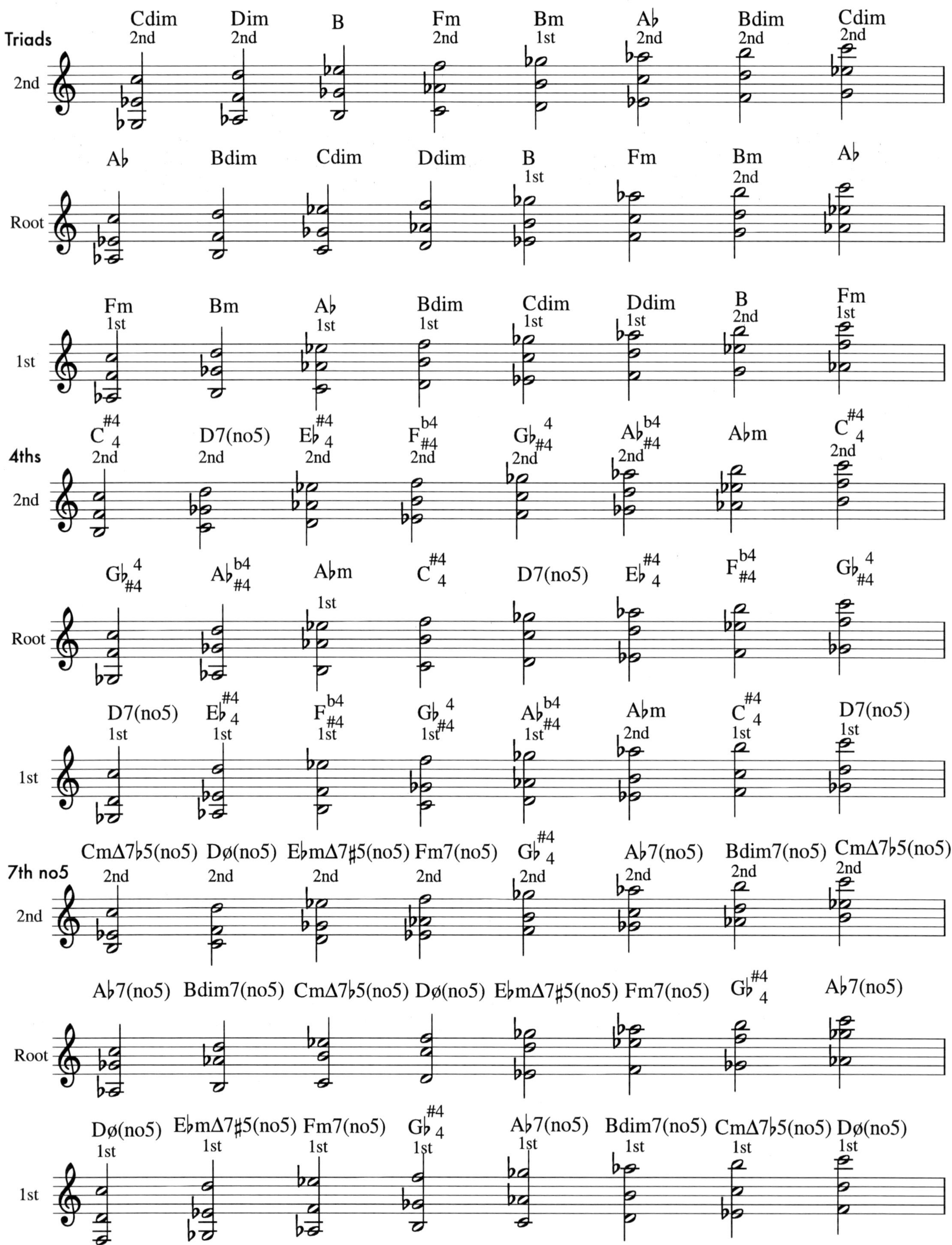

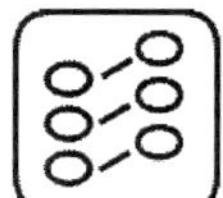

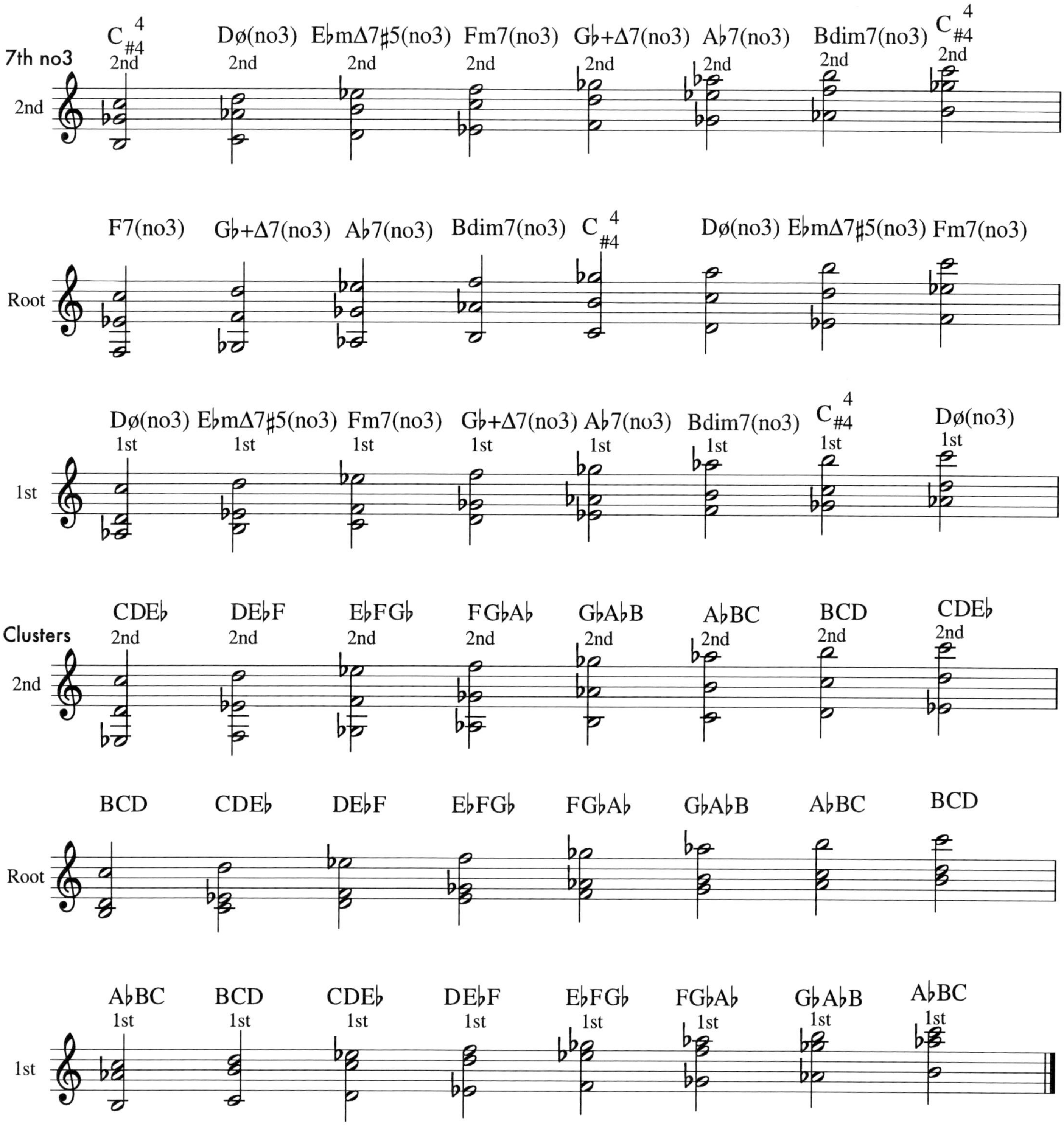

C hm ♭5 Scale Harmonized cont...

open

7th no3

2nd: C$^{4}_{\#4}$ 2nd | Dø(no3) 2nd | E♭mΔ7♯5(no3) 2nd | Fm7(no3) 2nd | G♭+Δ7(no3) 2nd | A♭7(no3) 2nd | Bdim7(no3) 2nd | C$^{4}_{\#4}$ 2nd

Root: F7(no3) | G♭+Δ7(no3) | A♭7(no3) | Bdim7(no3) | C$^{4}_{\#4}$ | Dø(no3) | E♭mΔ7♯5(no3) | Fm7(no3)

1st: Dø(no3) 1st | E♭mΔ7♯5(no3) 1st | Fm7(no3) 1st | G♭+Δ7(no3) 1st | A♭7(no3) 1st | Bdim7(no3) 1st | C$^{4}_{\#4}$ 1st | Dø(no3) 1st

Clusters

2nd: CDE♭ 2nd | DE♭F 2nd | E♭FG♭ 2nd | FG♭A♭ 2nd | G♭A♭B 2nd | A♭BC 2nd | BCD 2nd | CDE♭ 2nd

Root: BCD | CDE♭ | DE♭F | E♭FG♭ | FG♭A♭ | G♭A♭B | A♭BC | BCD

1st: A♭BC 1st | BCD 1st | CDE♭ 1st | DE♭F 1st | E♭FG♭ 1st | FG♭A♭ 1st | G♭A♭B 1st | A♭BC 1st

The harmonic minor ♭5 scale is the most imbalanced, thus "weird" of the six basic heptatonics, so the harmonizations sound the most unusual of them all.
Depending on your personal interest, use them to expand your active harmonic palette, or come back to them later if they seem too foreign to you at the moment.

APPLYING THE VOICE MOTION MOVES

Try to use all of the material found in Parts 1 and 2 regarding three-part harmony within the six basic heptatonics, throughout the full range of your instrument, in all keys and inversions.

Below is an example of applying move 21) to the melodic minor scale, variations a) to d) with upper voice motion analogous to the example in the introduction to Part 1.
Try applying other motions with the top note moving up/down a 2nd in the same way, in close as well as open voicing (d2).

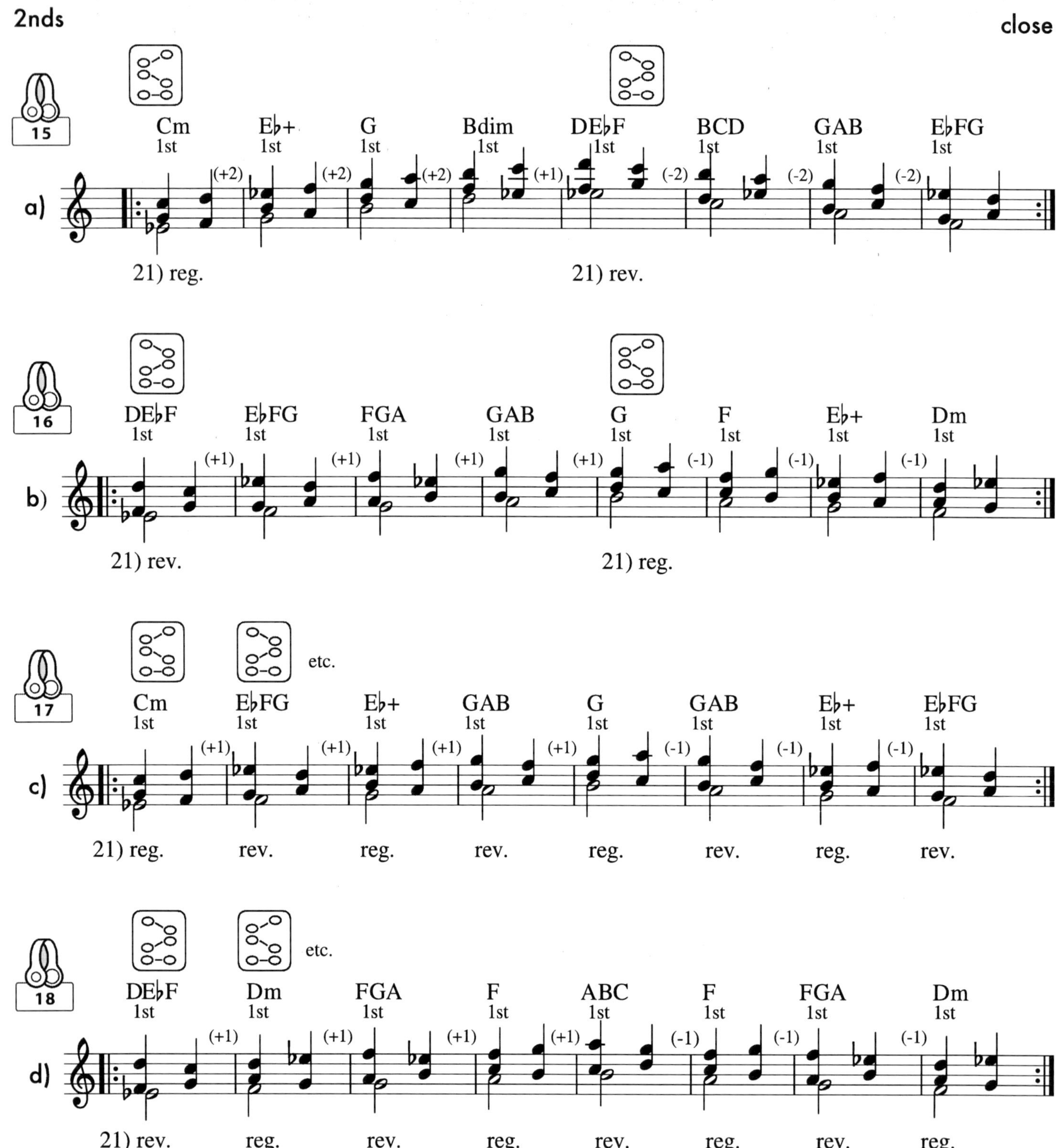

In this example, move 38) is applied to the melodic minor ♭5 scale, in open voicing (d2).

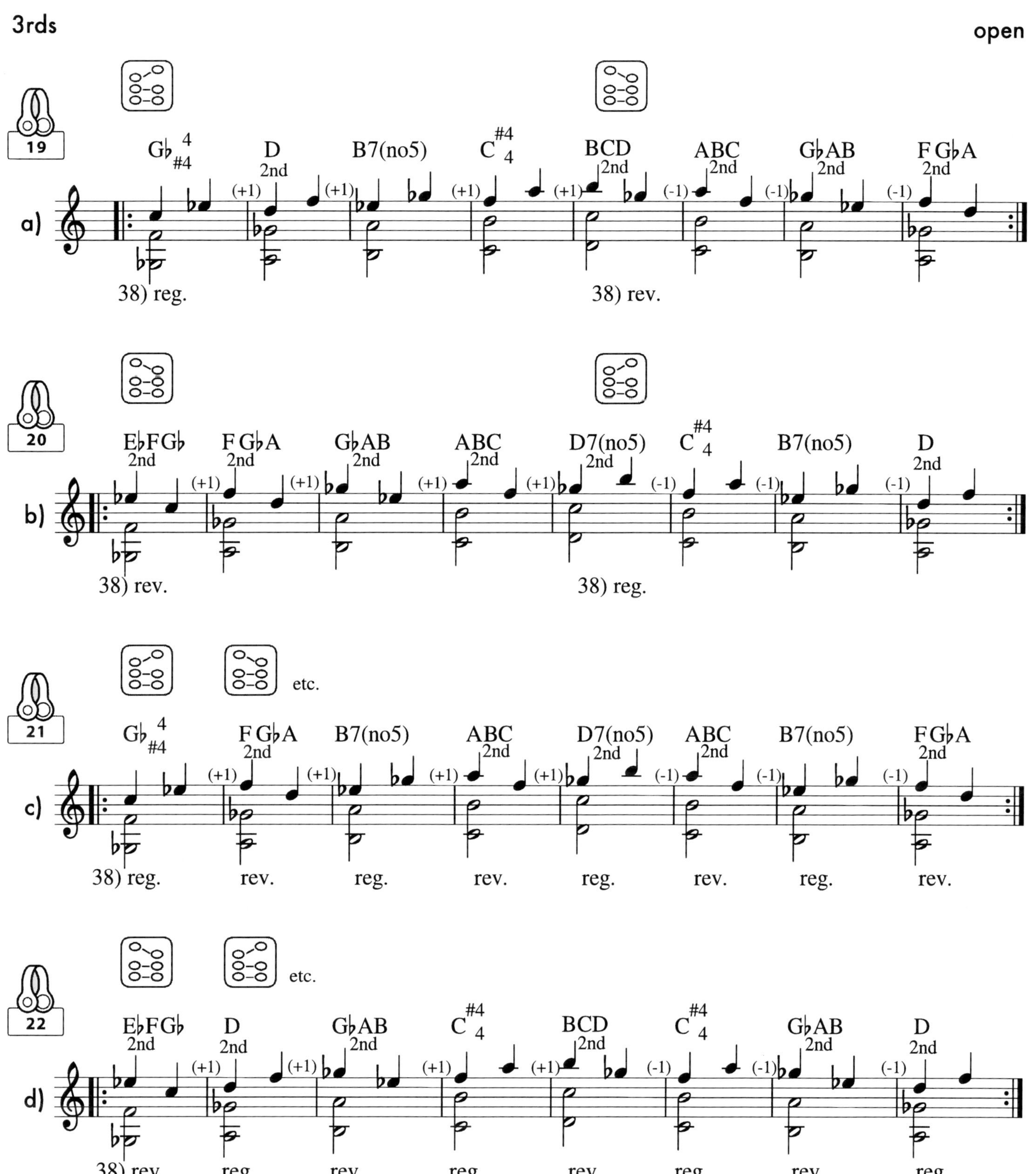

Try applying other moves with the top note moving up/down a 3rd as in a) to d) above, to the six heptatonic scales in all keys and the full range of your instrument - both in close and open voicing.

In this example, move 59) is applied to the harmonic minor ♭5 scale, in open voicing (d2).

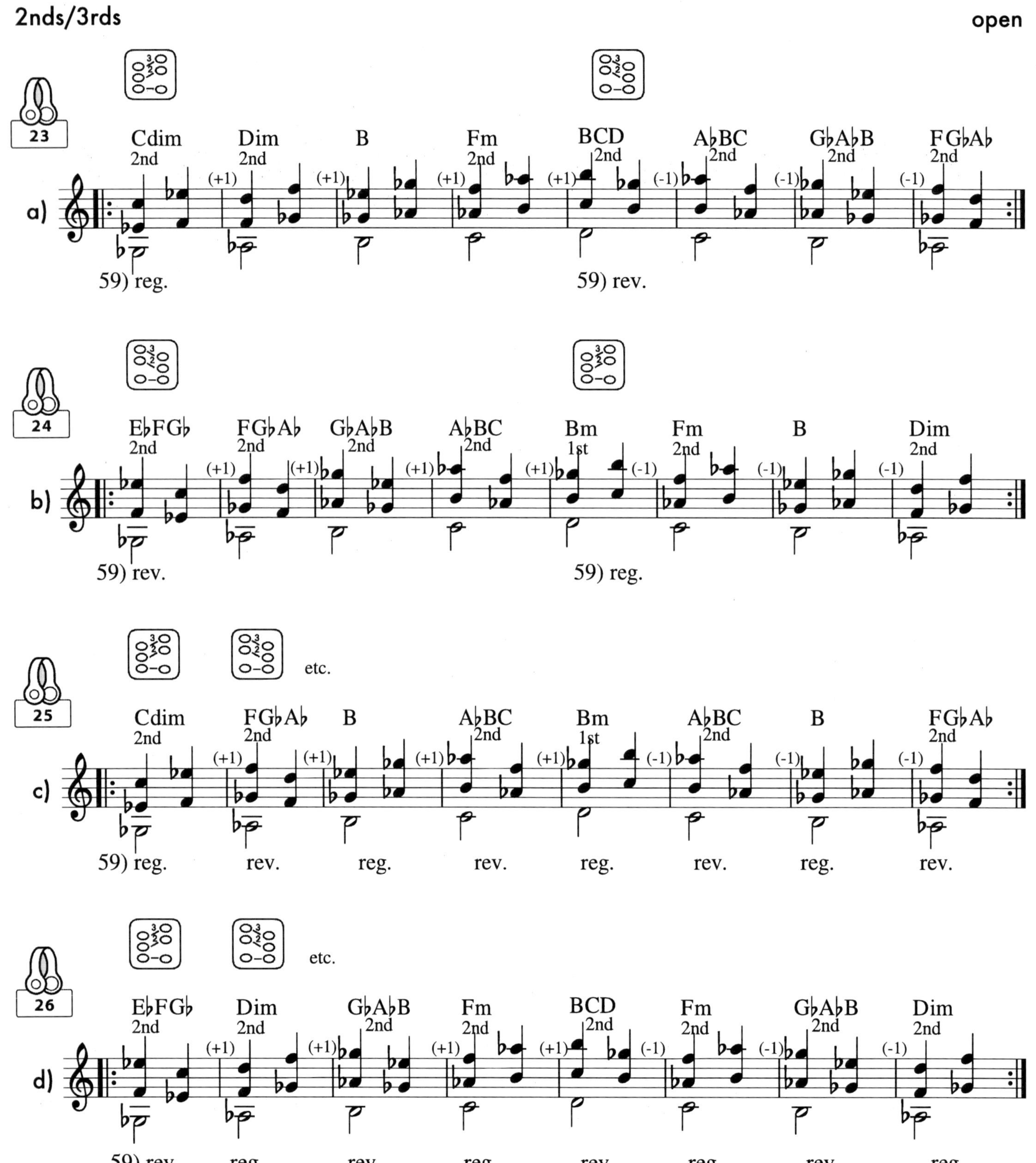

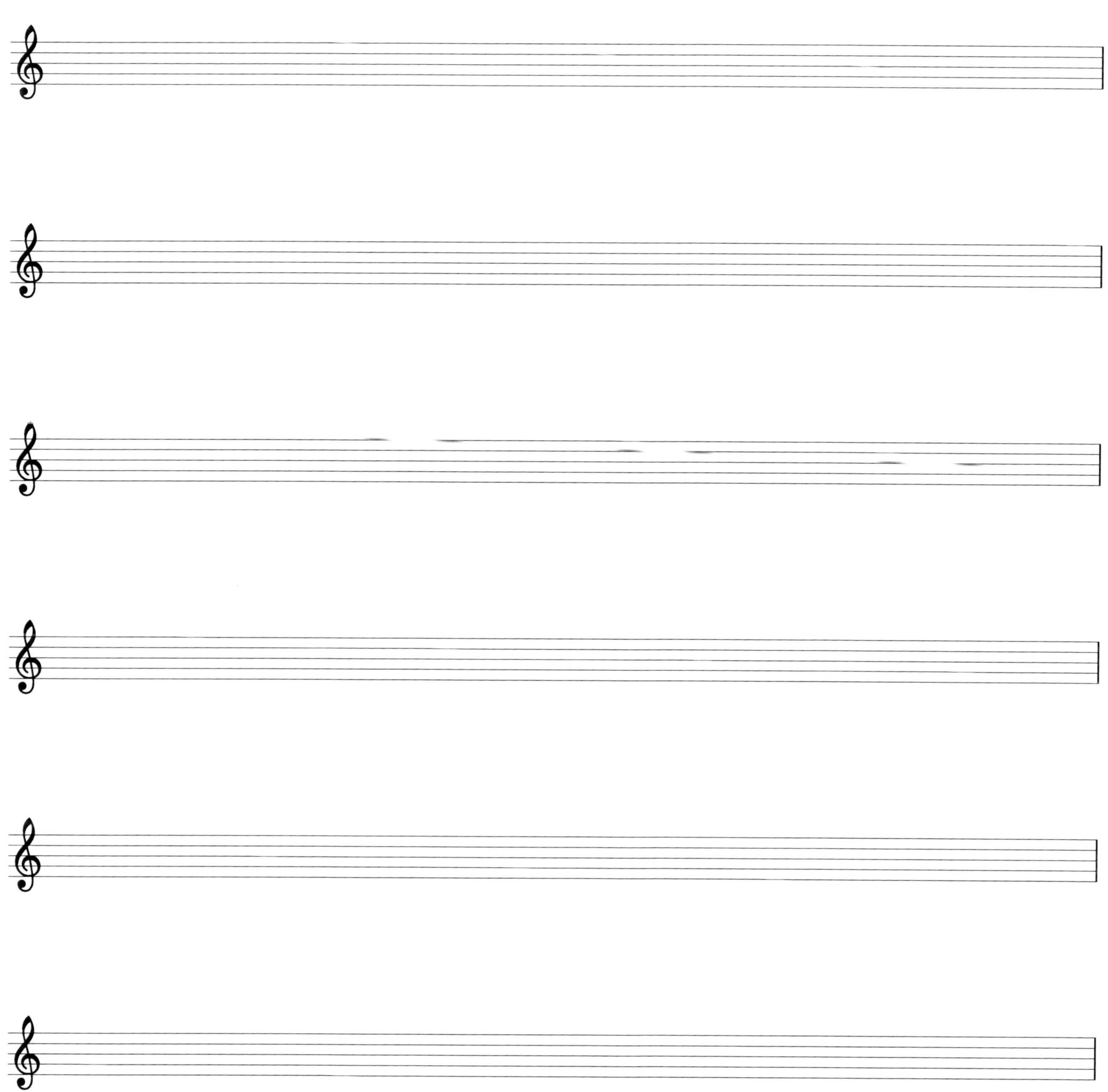

Page left blank for layout purposes and your personal notes

NARROW-RANGE VOICE LEADING

The next pages show the five close-voiced chord types taken stepwise up the diatonic major scale, changing inversions every other step to stay close to the range of the starting chord voicing.

Each harmonization is followed by an example of one of the 108 moves applied to it.
Read and play each line backwards (right to left) as well, and apply them to all six heptatonic scales and their modes throughout the full range of your instrument in all keys.
Explore this concept to find your own ways to apply the *VOICE MOTION* moves in Parts 1 and 2.

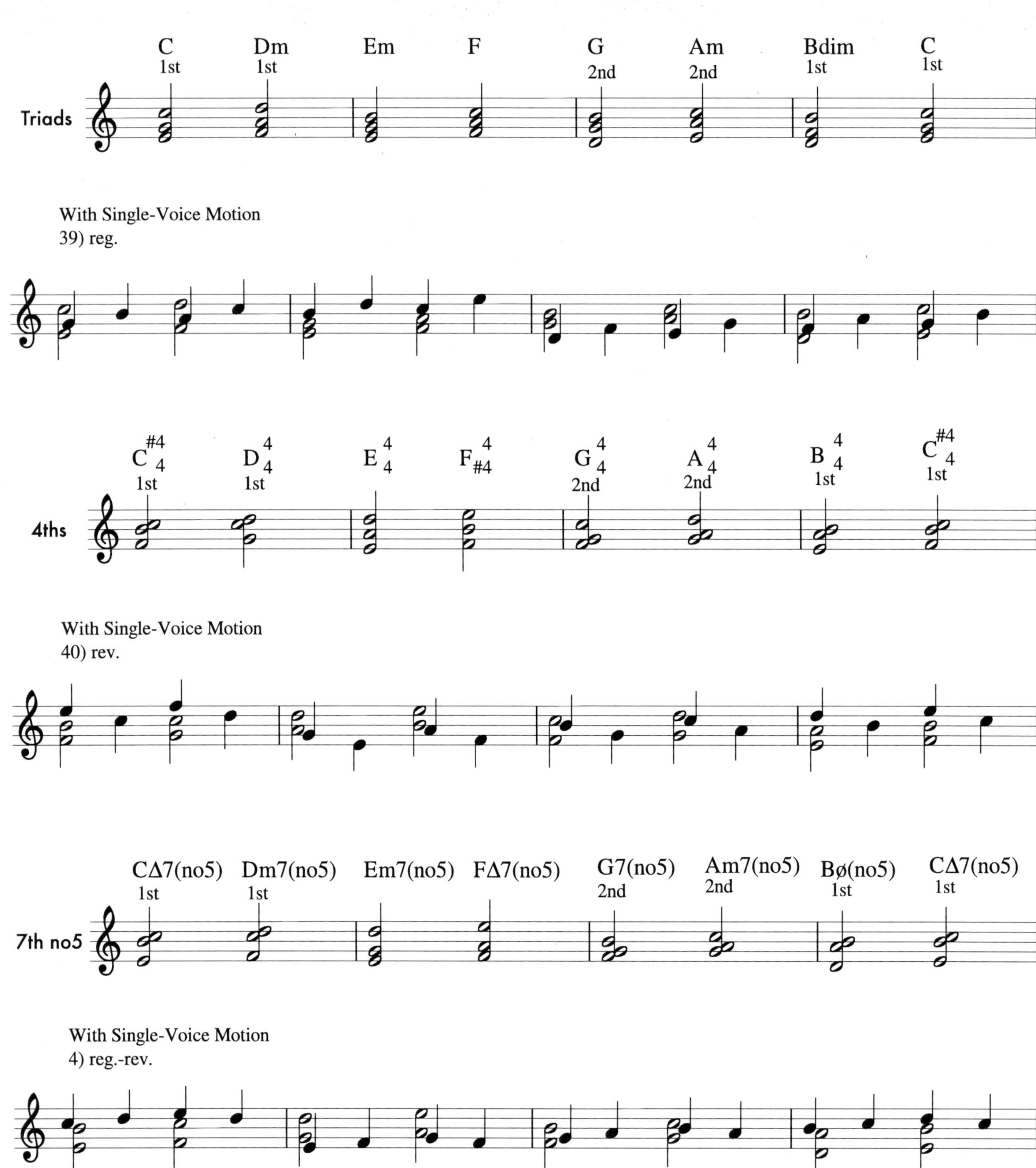

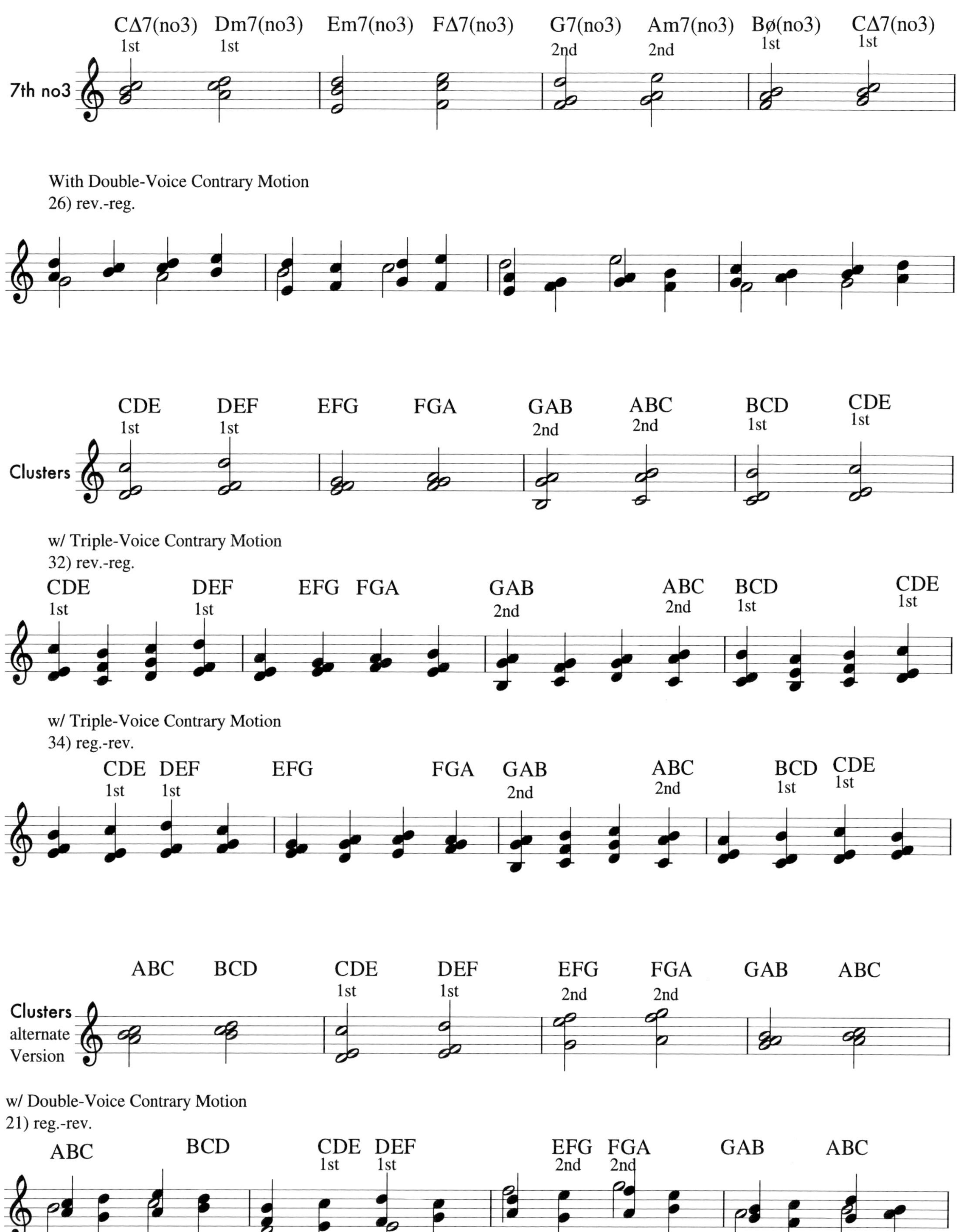
CΔ7(no3) Dm7(no3) Em7(no3) FΔ7(no3) G7(no3) Am7(no3) Bø(no3) CΔ7(no3)
1st 1st 2nd 2nd 1st 1st
7th no3
With Double-Voice Contrary Motion
26) rev.-reg.
CDE DEF EFG FGA GAB ABC BCD CDE
1st 1st 2nd 2nd 1st 1st
Clusters
w/ Triple-Voice Contrary Motion
32) rev.-reg.
CDE DEF EFG FGA GAB ABC BCD CDE
1st 1st 2nd 2nd 1st 1st
w/ Triple-Voice Contrary Motion
34) reg.-rev.
CDE DEF EFG FGA GAB ABC BCD CDE
1st 1st 2nd 2nd 1st 1st
ABC BCD CDE DEF EFG FGA GAB ABC
1st 1st 2nd 2nd
Clusters alternate Version
w/ Double-Voice Contrary Motion
21) reg.-rev.
ABC BCD CDE DEF EFG FGA GAB ABC
1st 1st 2nd 2nd

NARROW-RANGE VOICE LEADING

in Open Harmony (drop-2)

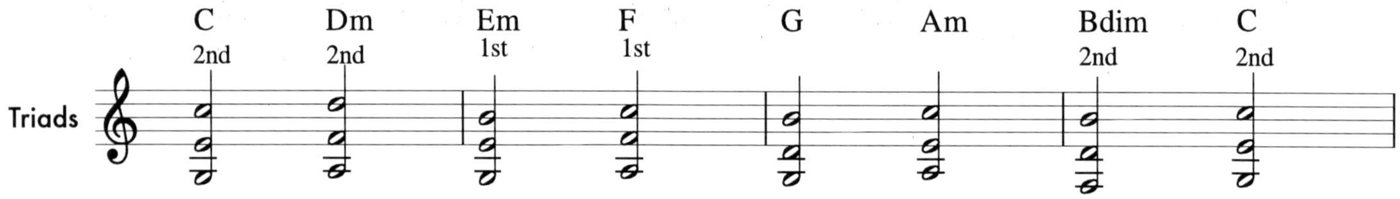

Triads

C 2nd | Dm 2nd | Em 1st | F 1st | G | Am | Bdim 2nd | C 2nd

With Single-Voice Motion
6) reg.-rev.

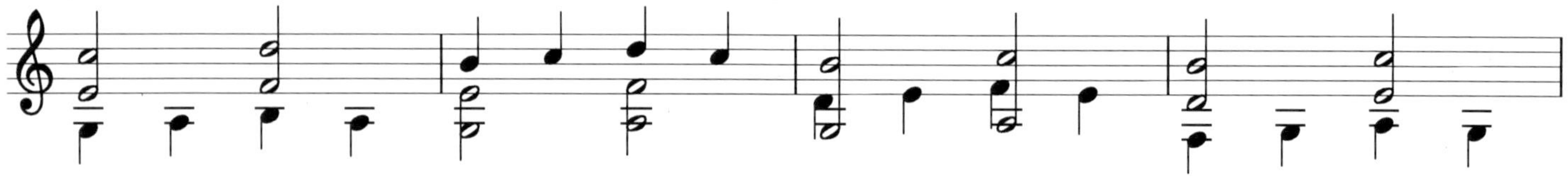

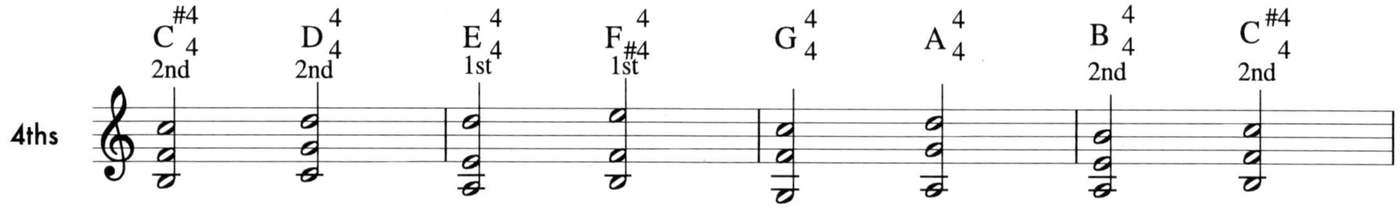

4ths

C #4 4 2nd | D 4 4 2nd | E 4 4 1st | F 4 #4 1st | G 4 4 | A 4 4 | B 4 4 2nd | C #4 4 2nd

With Single-Voice Motion
43) rev. with passing tone

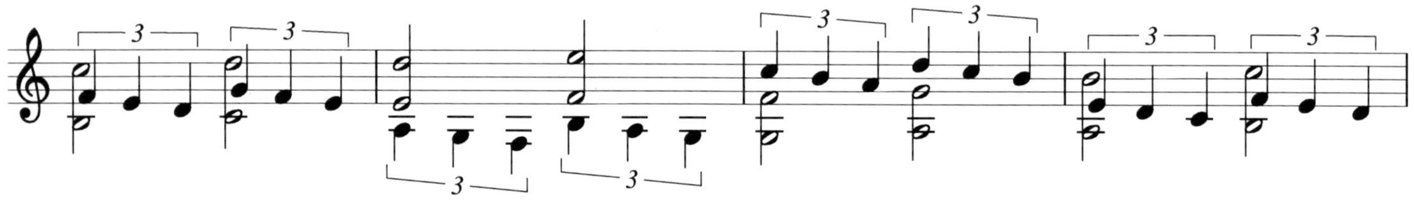

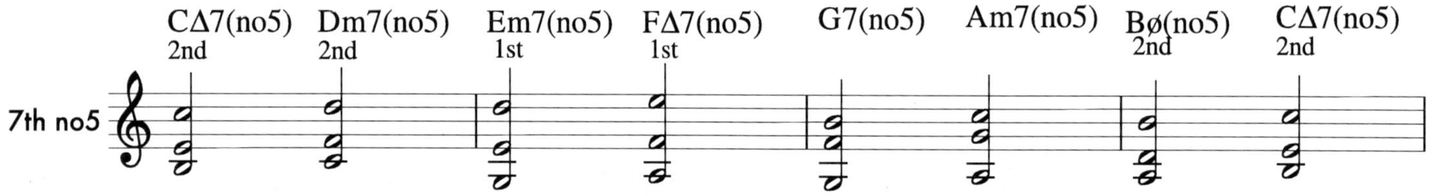

7th no5

CΔ7(no5) 2nd | Dm7(no5) 2nd | Em7(no5) 1st | FΔ7(no5) 1st | G7(no5) | Am7(no5) | Bø(no5) 2nd | CΔ7(no5) 2nd

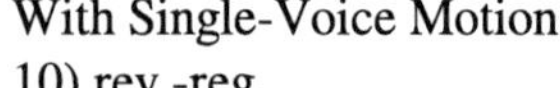

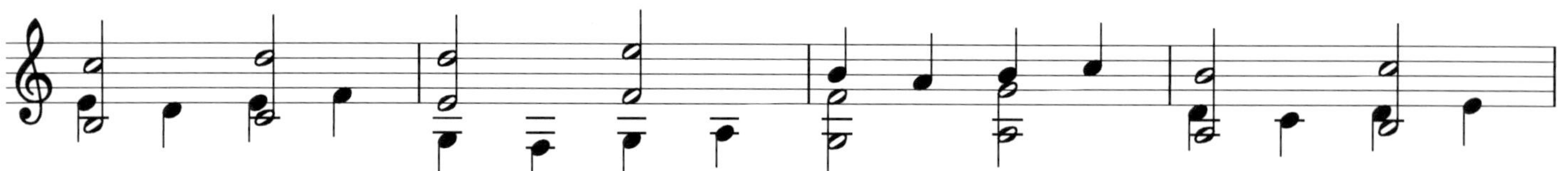

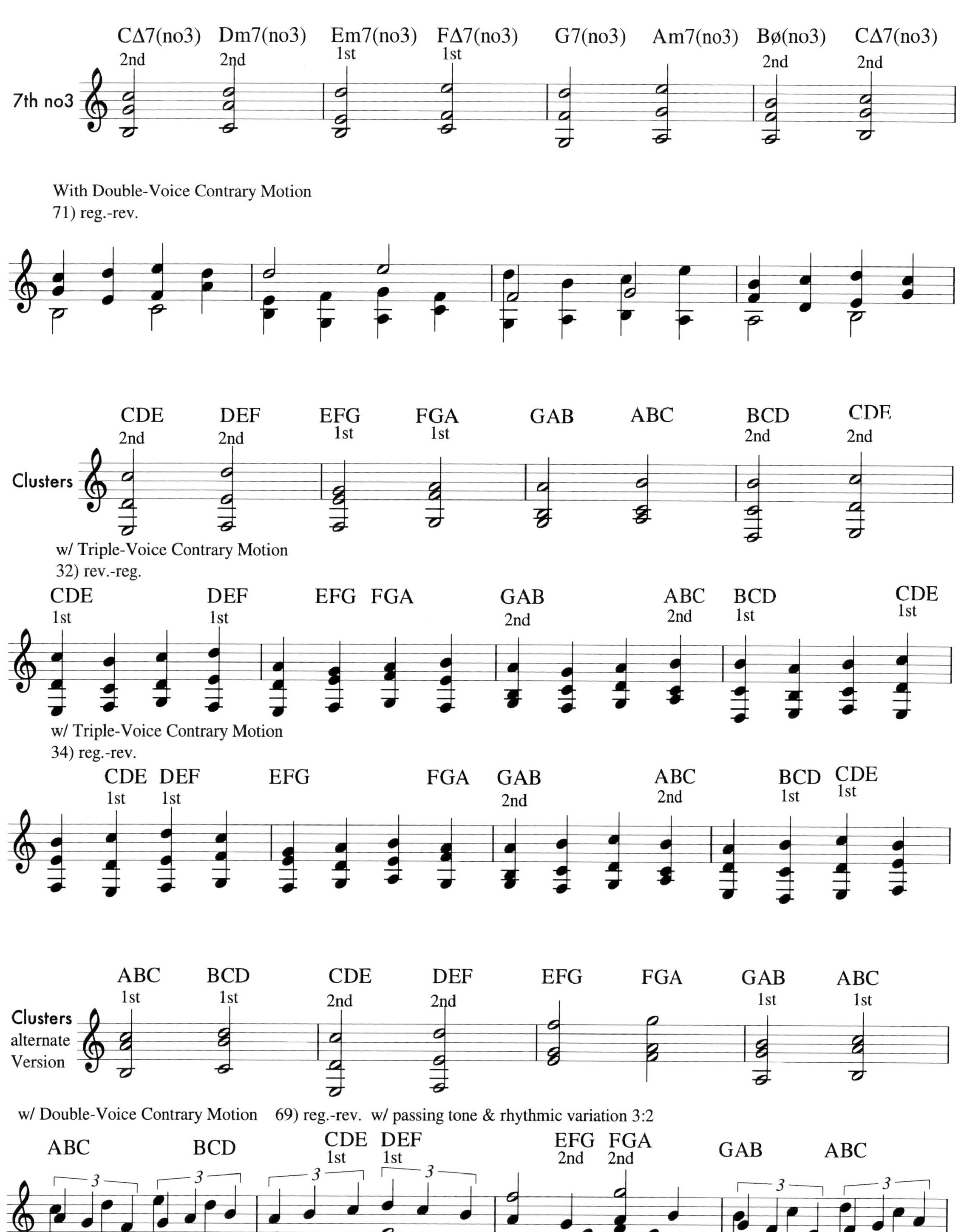
CΔ7(no3) Dm7(no3) Em7(no3) FΔ7(no3) G7(no3) Am7(no3) Bø(no3) CΔ7(no3)
2nd 2nd 1st 1st 2nd 2nd
7th no3
With Double-Voice Contrary Motion
71) reg.-rev.
CDE DEF EFG FGA GAB ABC BCD CDE
2nd 2nd 1st 1st 2nd 2nd
Clusters
w/ Triple-Voice Contrary Motion
32) rev.-reg.
CDE DEF EFG FGA GAB ABC BCD CDE
1st 1st 2nd 2nd 1st 1st
w/ Triple-Voice Contrary Motion
34) reg.-rev.
CDE DEF EFG FGA GAB ABC BCD CDE
1st 1st 2nd 2nd 1st 1st
ABC BCD CDE DEF EFG FGA GAB ABC
1st 1st 2nd 2nd 1st 1st
Clusters
alternate
Version
w/ Double-Voice Contrary Motion 69) reg.-rev. w/ passing tone & rhythmic variation 3:2
ABC BCD CDE DEF EFG FGA GAB ABC
1st 1st 2nd 2nd
3 3 3 3 3 3 3 3

USING HARMONIC CYCLES TO CHANGE KEYS

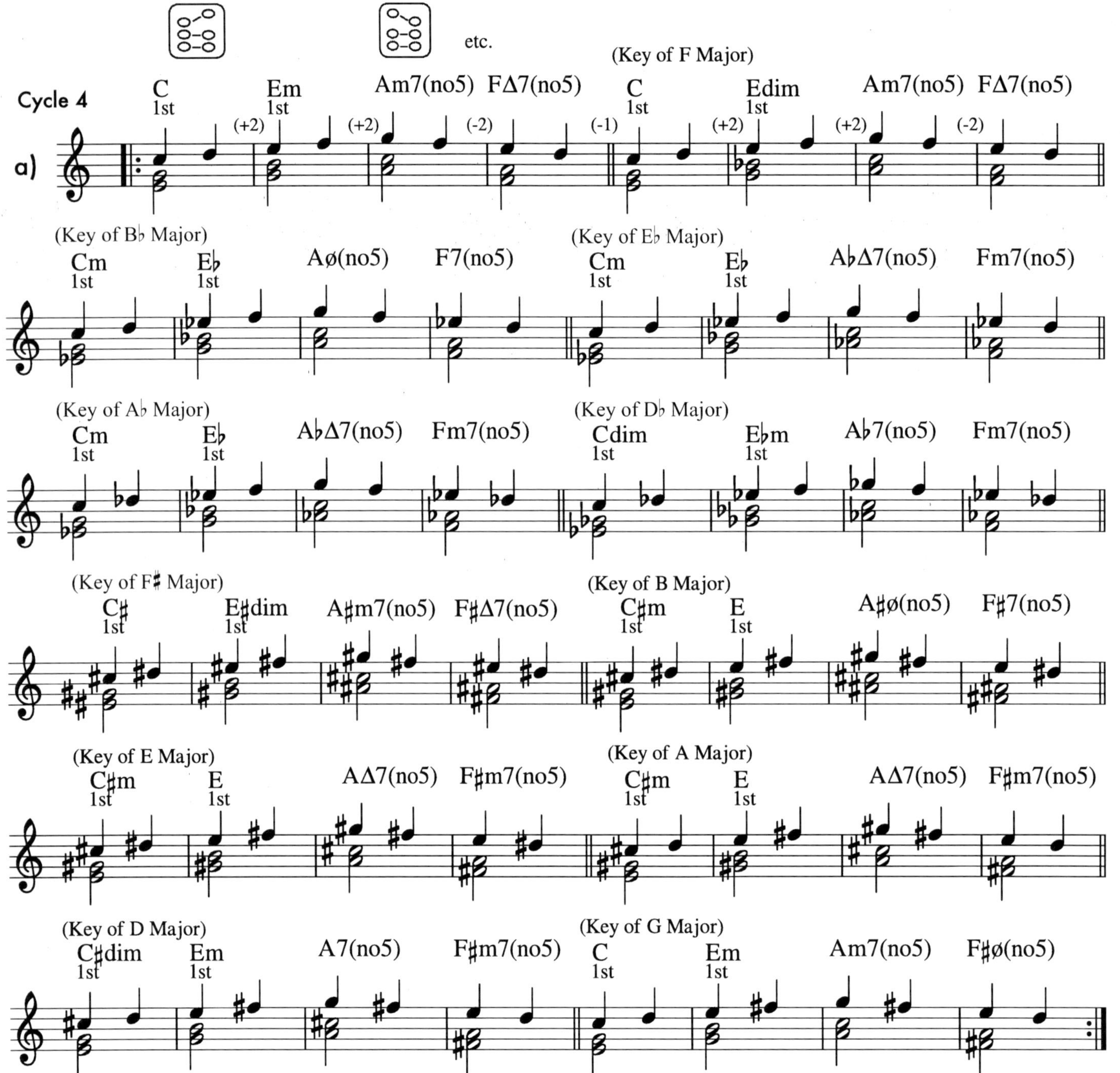

This page shows an ascending/descending four-measure scale excerpt created by exercise variation a) as presented earlier (see p.16), applied to move 2) with upper-voice motion.

Every four bars the key changes up a perfect 4th (Cycle 4), until all 12 keys are covered, before cycling back to the key of C.
The scale excerpt itself does not get moved up or down, only the accidentals change according to the keys, keeping all chords and motions in the same range.
Observe how the changing keys affect the chord qualities and the melody of the leading voice, which resembles the different modes of the scale.

Refer to exercise variations b) to d) as well, and practice any other motion, melody, scale excerpt, or whole scale through all keys and inversions in the same way.

Proceed to practice all other cycles to change keys:

Cycle 5 (up a perfect 5th / all 12 keys per cycle)
Cycle 2 (up a major 2nd / 6 keys per cycle) / Cycle ♭7 (up a minor 7th / 6 keys per cycle)
Cycle ♭3 (up a minor 3rd / 4 keys per cycle) / Cycle 6 (up a major 6th / 4 keys per cycle)
Cycle 3 (up a major 3rd / 3 keys per cycle) / Cycle ♭6 (up a minor 6th / 3 keys per cycle)
Cycle ♯11/♭5 (up/down a tritone / 2 keys per cycle).

In the next two exercises, the same scale excerpt from the previous page is used.
With each new key, the melody is transposed so it keeps the same intervallic structure as the original, using the same scale degrees. A new inversion of the move is used for every new key, keeping all chords and motions in the same range, and moving the melody to a different voice.

Practice any other applicable material in the same way, experimenting with all kinds of cycles.

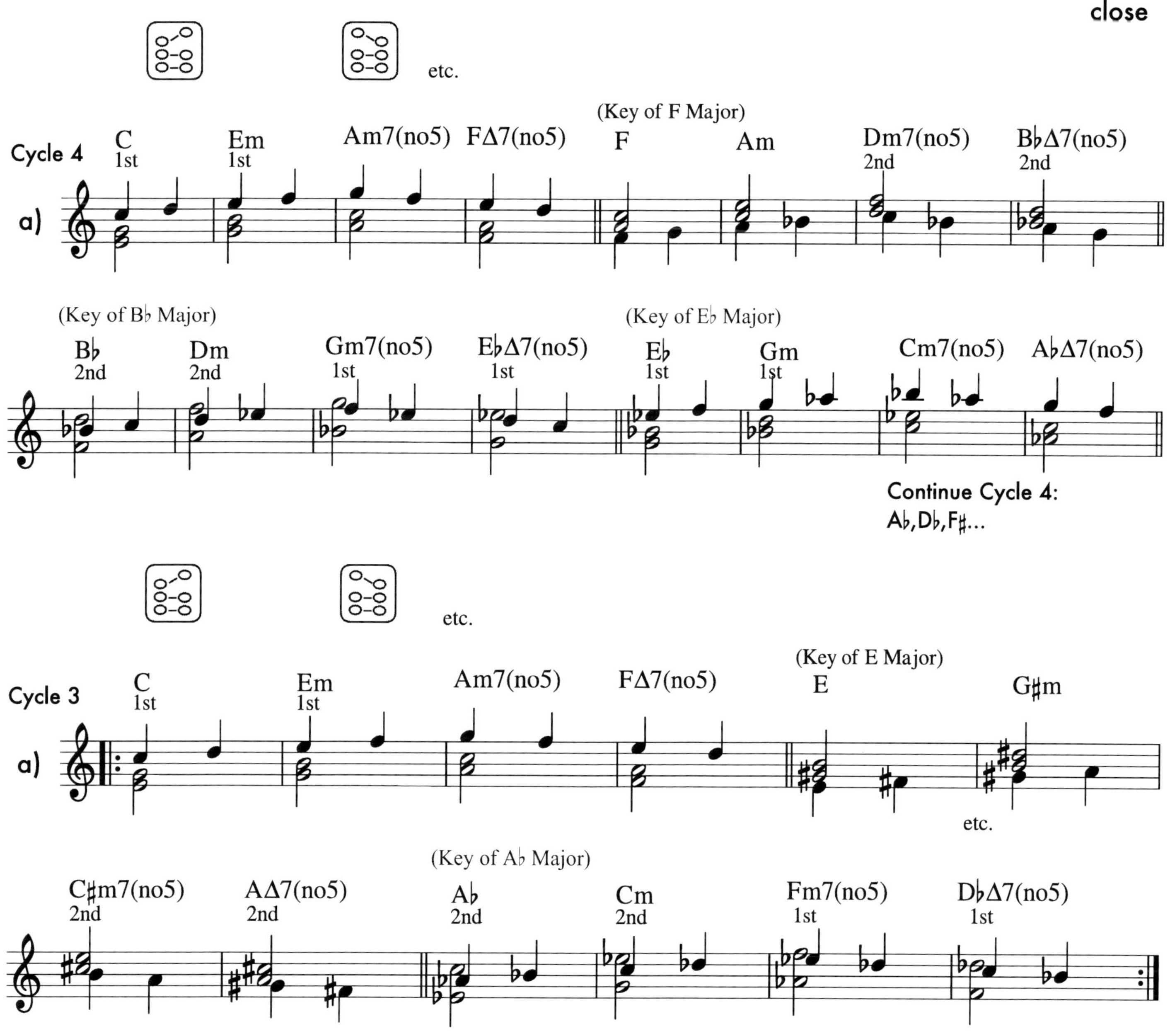

HEPTATONIC MODES

All heptatonic scales naturally have seven modes starting from each of the scale degrees. The six basic heptatonics with their 7 modes in all 12 keys thus give you (6x7x12=) 504 unique harmonic situations to which all of the material in this book can be applied.

To gradually explore all of these situations including the less common ones, and to avoid practicing the same combinations of scales, modes and keys repetitively, try randomly choosing one combination per day or practice session, physically rolling an ordinary 6-sided die - once for the heptatonic (1 out of 6), and twice for the key (1 out of 12).

Then choose the harmony, i.e. the 7th chord of the basic heptatonic (Δ7,mΔ7, or mΔ7♭5) that you will play over, or roll the die once again to choose one of the other six modes/chord qualities.

See below for a list of all modes of each of the six basic heptatonics, including their 7th Chord and the resulting upper structure extensions.

Try to get to know each of these 42 scales individually, as they all represent their own unique harmolodic universe...

THE SIX BASIC HEPTATONICS AND THEIR MODES

With Corresponding 7th Chords and Extensions

Mode	Scale Name	7th Chord	Upper Structure Extensions
I	Ionian (M)	Δ7	9, 11, 13
II	Dorian	m7	9, 11, 13
III	Phrygian	m7	♭9, 11 , ♭13
IV	Lydian	Δ7	9, ♯11, 13
V	Mixolydian	Dom7	9, 11, 13
VI	Aeolian	m7	9, 11, ♭13
VII	Locrian	ø7	♭9,11, ♭13

I	Melodic Minor (mm)	mΔ7	9, 11, 13
II	Dorian ♭9	m7	♭9, 11, 13
♭III	Lydian Augmented	Δ7♯5	9, ♯11, 13
IV	Mixolydian ♯11	Dom7	9, ♯11, 13
V	Mixolydian ♭13	Dom7	9, 11, ♭13
VI	Locrian ♮9	ø7	9, 11, ♭13
VII	Altered	ø7	♭9, ♭11, ♭13

Mode	Scale Name	7th Chord	Upper Structure / Tensions
I	Harmonic Major (hM)	Δ7	9, 11, ♭13
II	Dorian ♭5	ø7	9, 11, 13
III	Altered ♮5	m7	♭9, ♭11, ♭13
IV	Melodic Minor ♯11	mΔ7	9, ♯11, 13
V	Mixolydian ♭9	Dom7	♭9, 11, 13
♭VI	Lydian Aug. ♯9	Δ7♯5	♯9, ♯11, 13
VII	Locrian dim7	dim7	♭9,11, ♭13

I	Harmonic Minor (hm)	mΔ7	9, 11, ♭13
II	Locrian ♮13	ø7	♭9, 11, 13
♭III	Ionian Augmented	Δ7♯5	9, 11, 13
IV	Dorian ♯11	m7	9, ♯11, 13
V	Mixolydian ♭9 ♭13	Dom7	♭9,11, ♭13
♭VI	Lydian ♯9	Δ7	♯9, ♯11, 13
VII	Altered dim7	dim7	♭9, ♭11, ♭13

I	Melodic Minor ♭5 (mm ♭5)	mΔ7♭5 (major / ♭9)	9, 11, 13
II	Altered ♮5 ♮13	m7	♭9, ♭11, 13
♭III	Melodic Minor ♯11 ♯5	mΔ7♯5 (major♯9 /3)	9, ♯11, 13
IV	Mixolydian ♭9 ♯11	Dom7	♭9, ♯11, 13
♭V	Octatonic WT/HT no 9	minor(add ♯11) /5	(♯9, ♯11, 13)
VI	Locrian ♮9 dim7	dim7	9, 11, ♭13
VII	Altered 𝄫6	ø7	♭9, ♭11, 𝄫13

I	Harmonic Minor ♭5 (hm ♭5)	mΔ7♭5 (major / ♭9)	9, 11, ♭13
II	Altered ♮13	ø7	♭9, ♭11, 13
♭III	Melodic Minor ♯5	mΔ7♯5 (major♯9 /3)	9, 11, 13
IV	Dorian ♭9 ♯11	m7	♭9, ♯11, 13
♭V	Octatonic WT/HT no ♭3	(minor add ♯11 /5)	(9, ♯11, 13)
♭VI	Mixolydian ♯9 ♯11	Dom7	♯9, ♯11, 13
VII	Altered dim7 𝄫6	dim7	♭9, ♭11, 𝄫13

PART 3B

Symmetrical Application

OVERVIEW

This chapter focuses on the application of the *VOICE MOTION* moves outside of a particular key, and how to move any individual chord structure or motion symmetrically, through the chromatic space.

All 19 possible three-note structures within the chromatic scale are presented in close and open (d2) voicing, along with exercises to practice inverting them individually with and without voice motion.

In the end of the section, as a brief glimpse beyond three-part harmony, a simple method is shown for adding an additional pitch to any three-part chord structure to attain and discover four-part chords.

CONTENTS

SYMMETRICAL CYCLES

Examples and Exercises

The following exercises show how to use cycles to move a single motion symmetrically up and down, while keeping its intervallic structure constant.
Depending on which cycle is being used, it takes 2 to 4 moves/transpositions to cycle back to the original chord. Apply this concept to single chord structures as well as more complex motions, and use it to weave in and out of any key or harmonic situation. Practice exercise variations b) to d) as introduced before (see p.16), mixing ascending and descending voice motion.

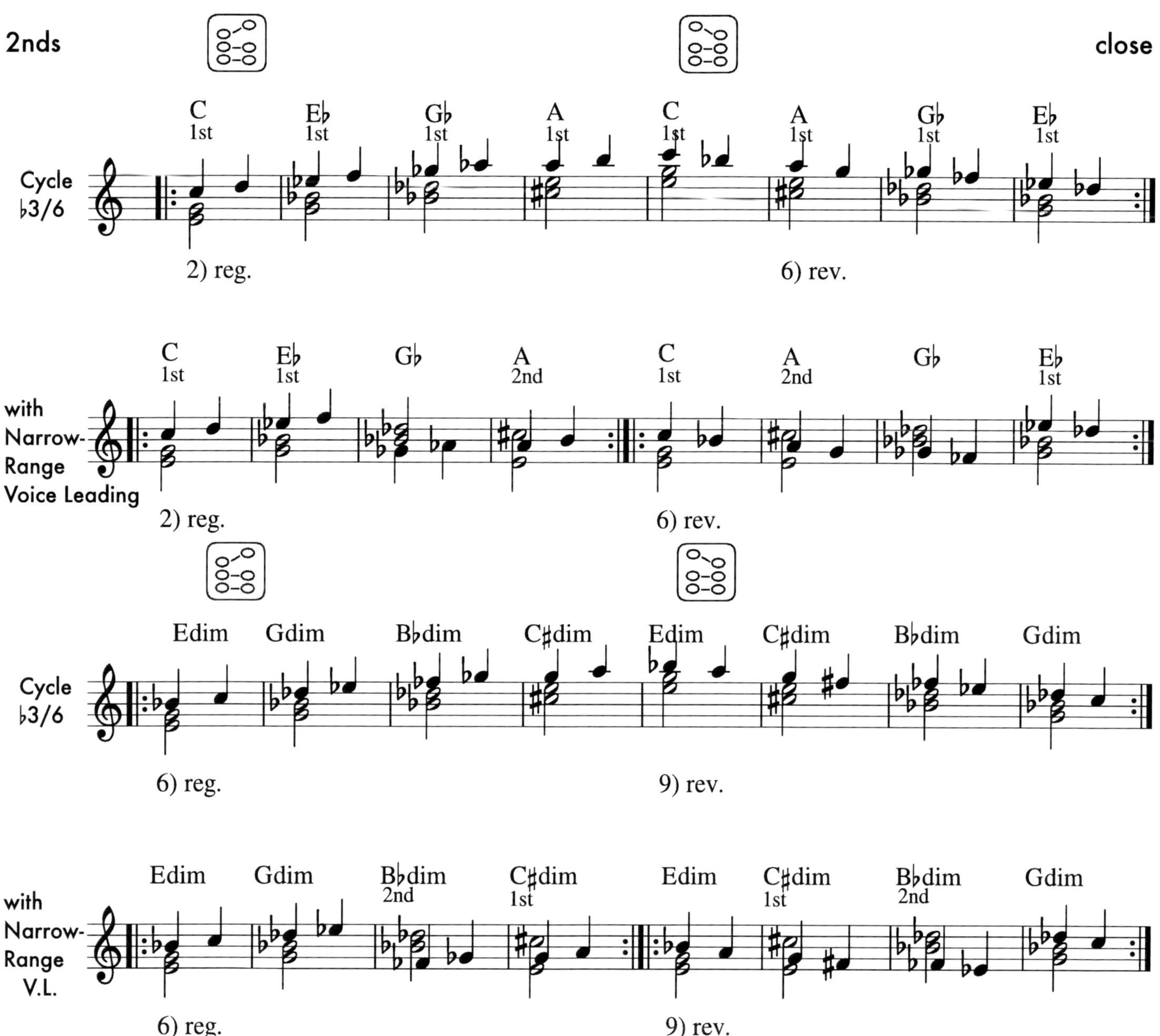

Note that the cycle ♭3/6 tends to produce the notes of a symmetrical diminished octatonic scale when applied to motions with the leading voice moving up or down a 2nd,
while cycle 3/♭6 produces a symmetrical wholetone hexatonic scale.

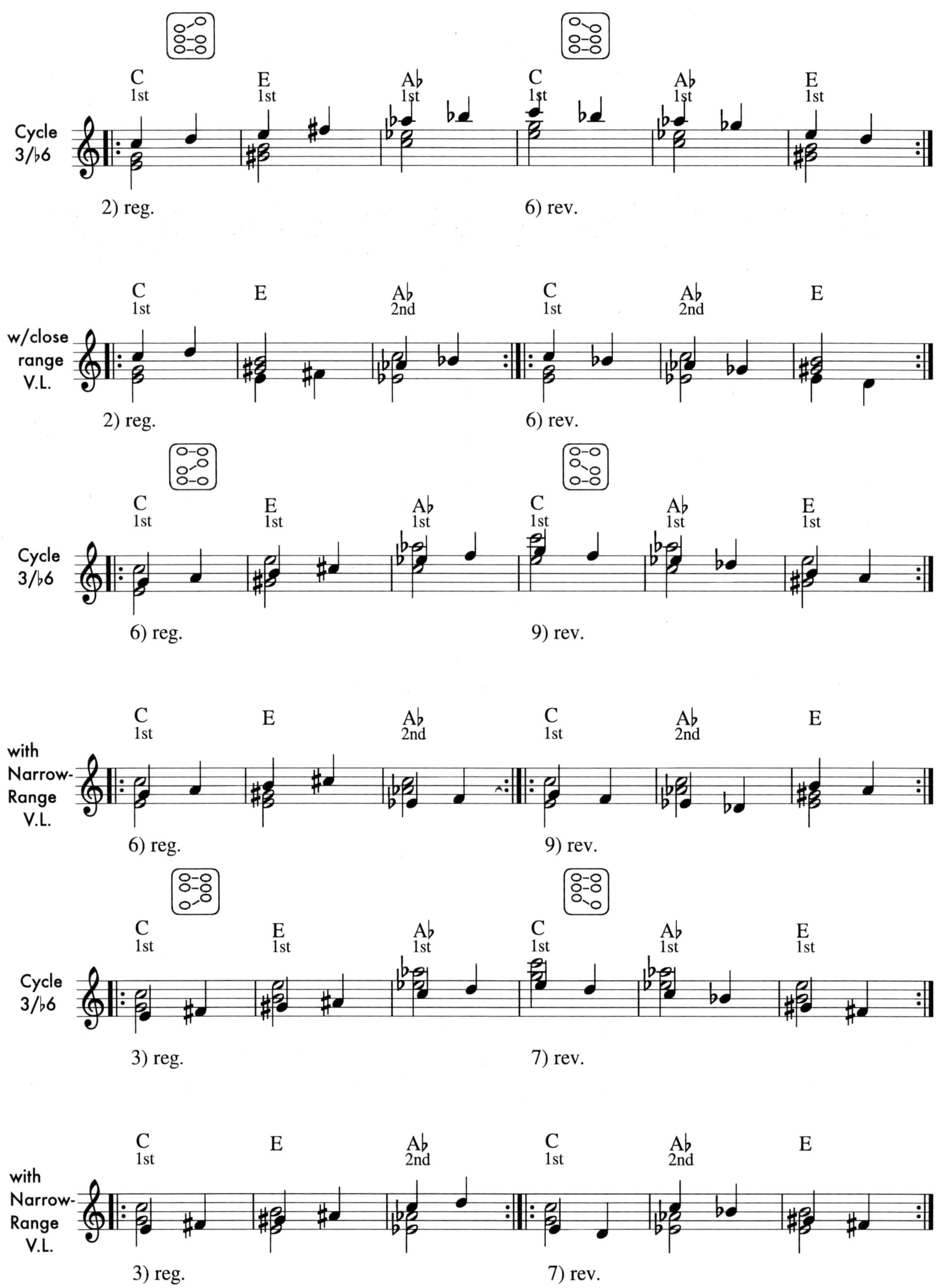
C
1st
E
1st
A♭
1st
C
1st
A♭
1st
E
1st
Cycle
3/♭6
2) reg.
6) rev.
C
1st
E
A♭
2nd
C
1st
A♭
2nd
E
w/close
range
V.L.
2) reg.
6) rev.
Cycle
3/♭6
6) reg.
9) rev.
with
Narrow-
Range
V.L.
6) reg.
9) rev.
Cycle
3/♭6
3) reg.
7) rev.
with
Narrow-
Range
V.L.
3) reg.
7) rev.

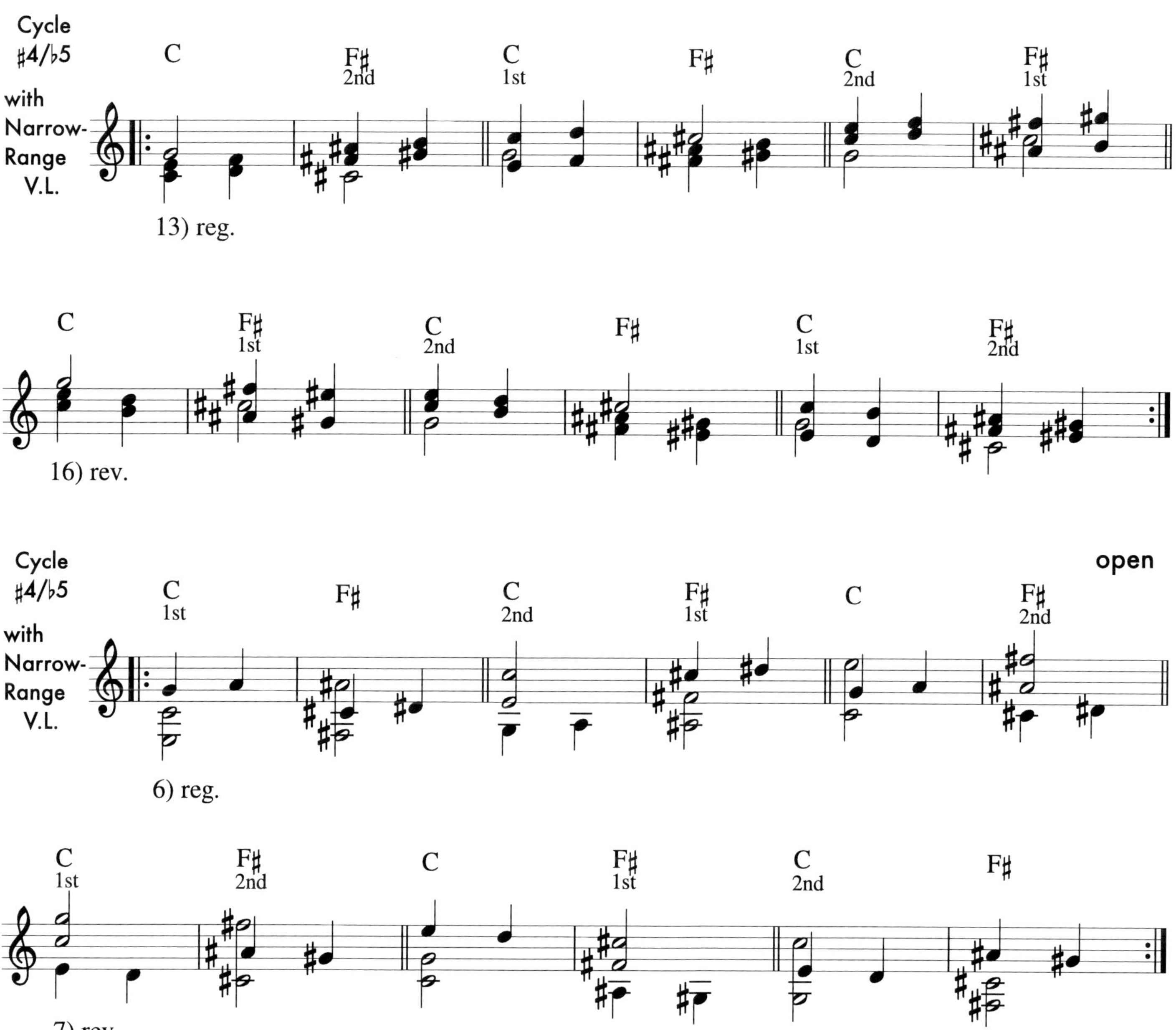

All of the examples above are based on the major triad.
Independent of their scale origin, practice moving all possible three-part chords symmetrically, with and without voice motion using the cycles ♭3, 3, ♭6, 6 and ♯4/♭5; either keeping the inversion constant, or with Narrow-Range Voice Leading.

19 THREE-PART CHORDS

close

Bottom Note C'

All Possible Three-Note Structures Within the Chromatic Scale

There are 19 possible unique three-part chords that can be built with the notes of the chromatic scale - all except one (a cluster of two consecutive semitones) are contained within the six basic heptatonic scales.
The next pages show all 19 of these three-part chords and their two inversions moved into the same range so that C' is the lowest note, in close and open voicing (19x3x2=114 total). The numbers to the right of the chord symbols show the two intervals that make up the respective chord, and how these intervals are stacked on top of each other to produce the unique sound of the specific voicing. Study and identify the voicings individually in all keys and examine which cycles work best for each. Then, add voice motion; refer to Parts 1B and 2B for all motions departing from each chord type.

Triads

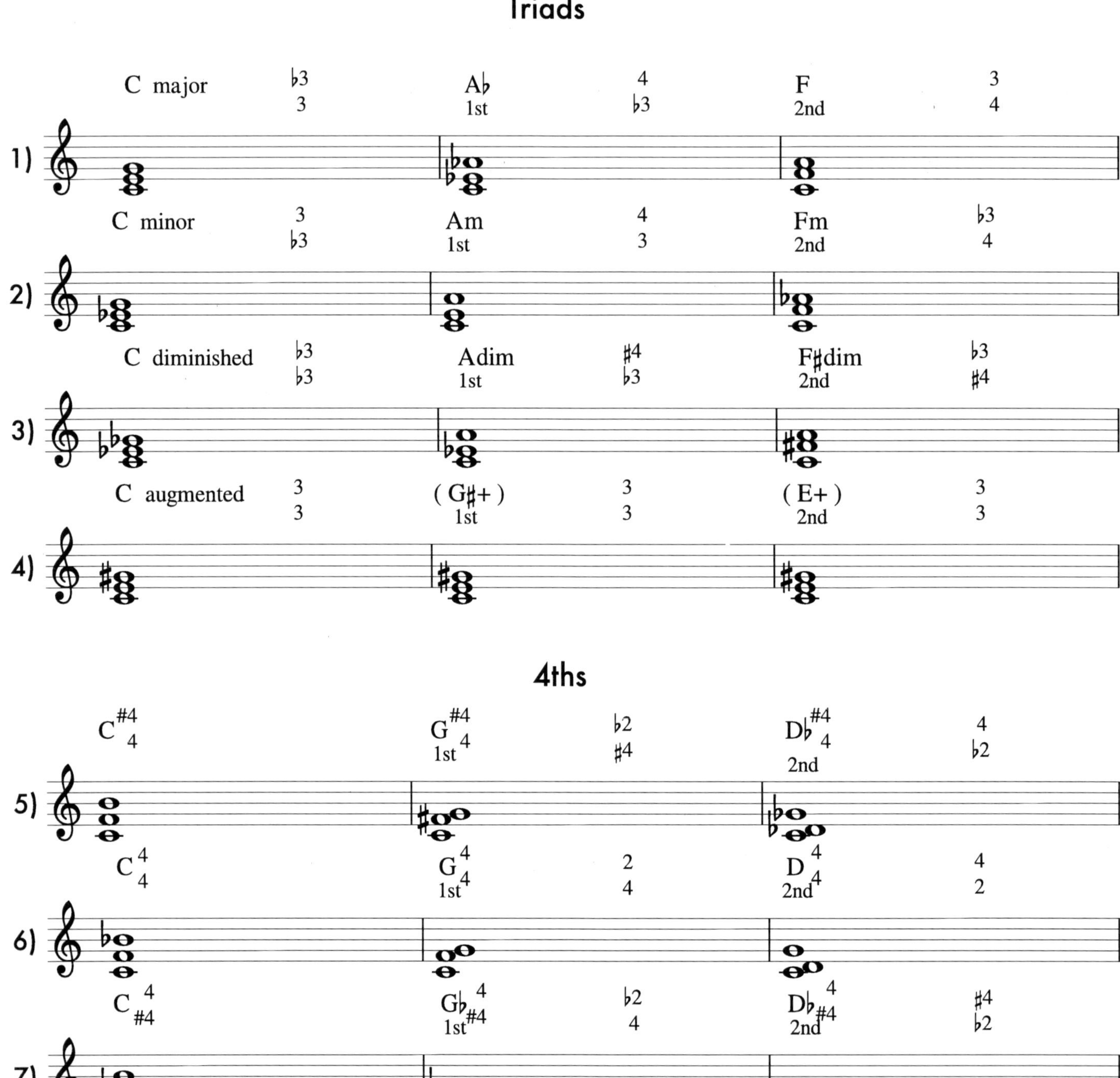

close

7th no5

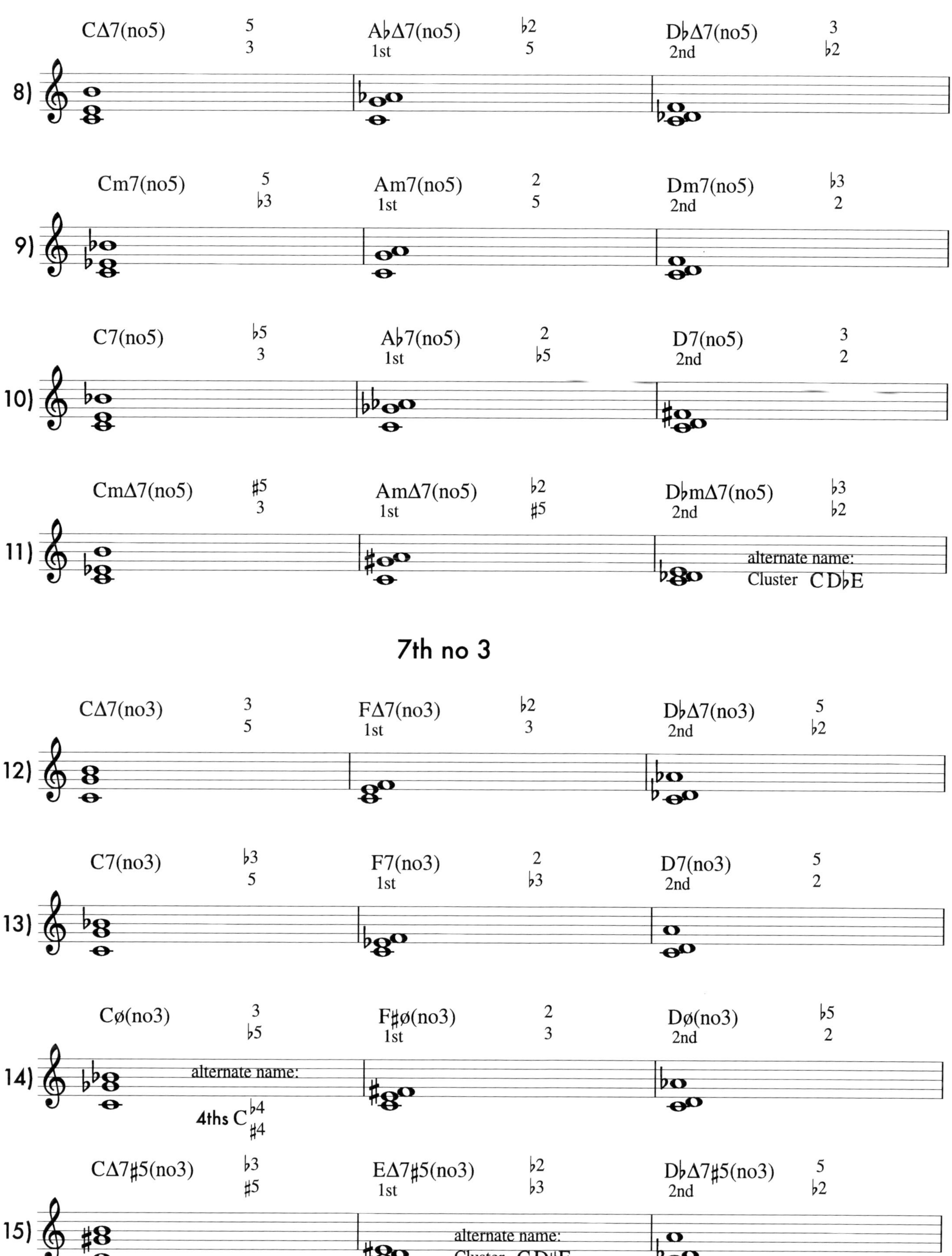

Clusters

16)
CDE
2
2
B♭CD
1st
♭6
2
A♭B♭C
2nd
2
♭6
17)
CDE♭
♭2
2
B♭CD♭
1st
6
♭2
ABC
2nd
2
6
18)
CD♭E♭
2
♭2
BCD
1st
6
2
AB♭C
2nd
♭2
6
19)
CD♭E𝄫
♭2
♭2
BCD♭
1st
♭7
♭2
A♯BC
2nd
♭2
♭7

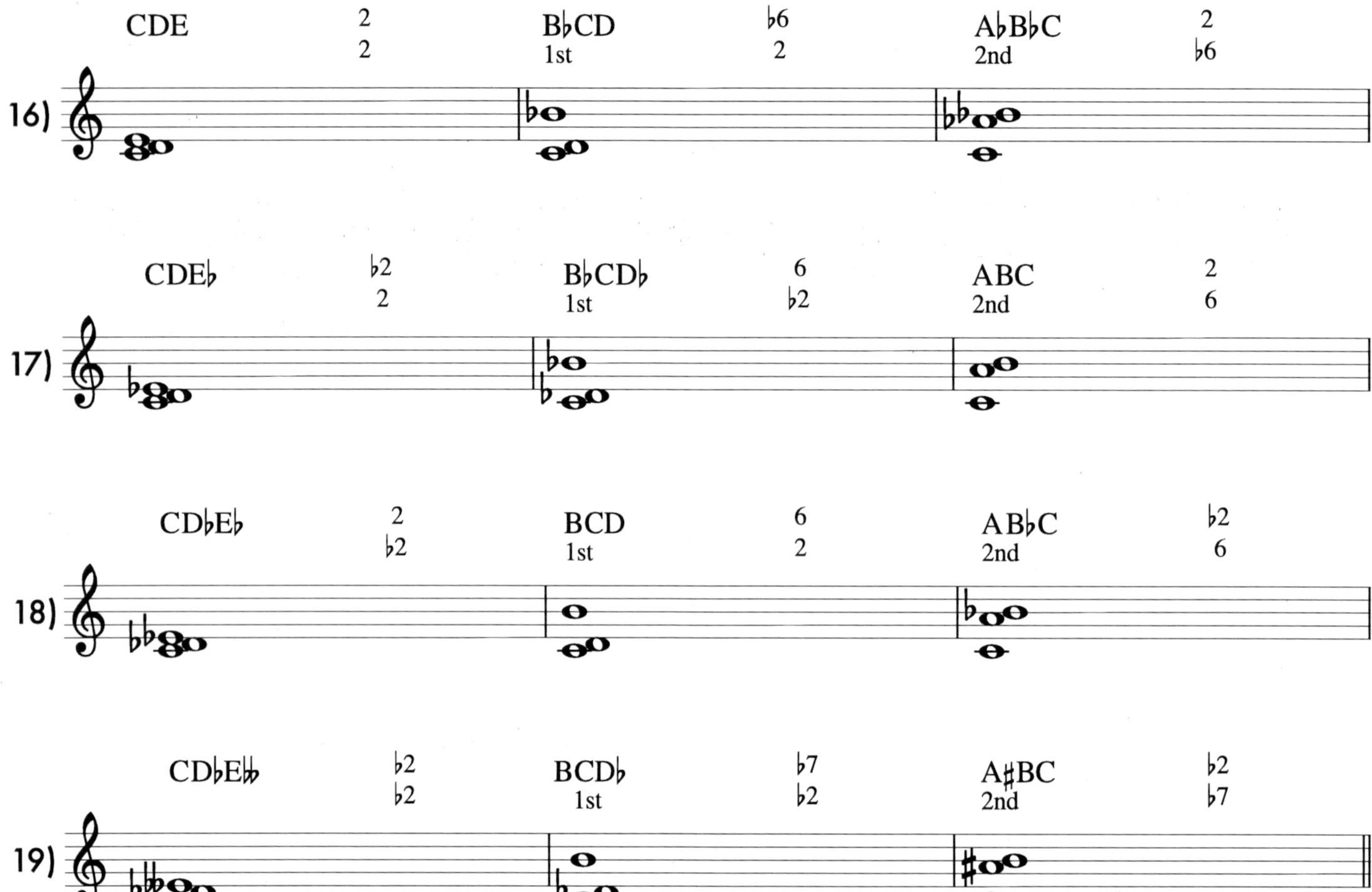

19 THREE-PART CHORDS

open

Bottom Note C'

All Possible Three-Note Structures Within the Chromatic Scale in Drop-2 Voicing

Triads

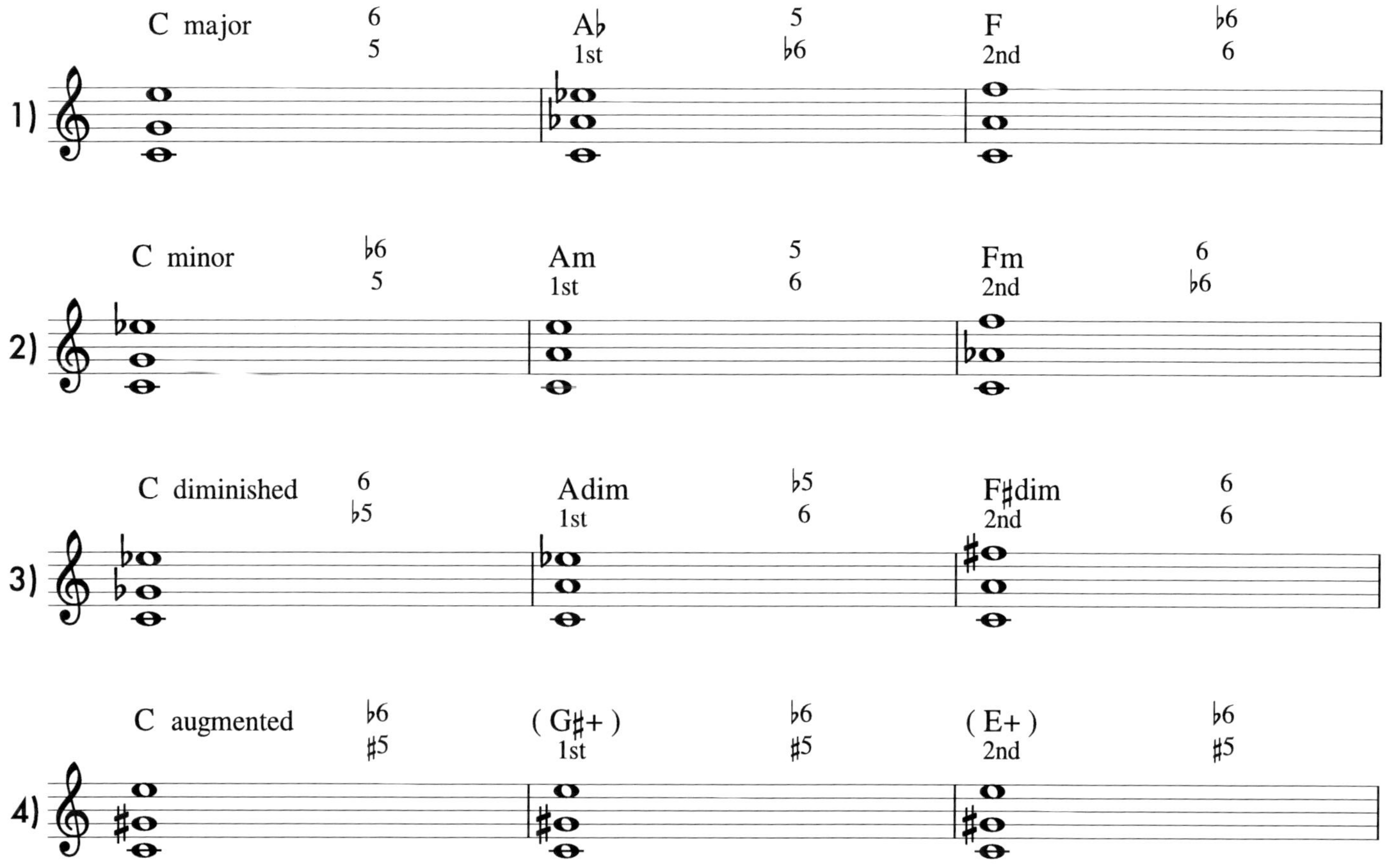

1) C major 6 5 | A♭ 1st 5 ♭6 | F 2nd ♭6 6

2) C minor ♭6 5 | Am 1st 5 6 | Fm 2nd 6 ♭6

3) C diminished 6 ♭5 | Adim 1st ♭5 6 | F♯dim 2nd 6 6

4) C augmented ♭6 ♯5 | (G♯+) 1st ♭6 ♯5 | (E+) 2nd ♭6 ♯5

4ths

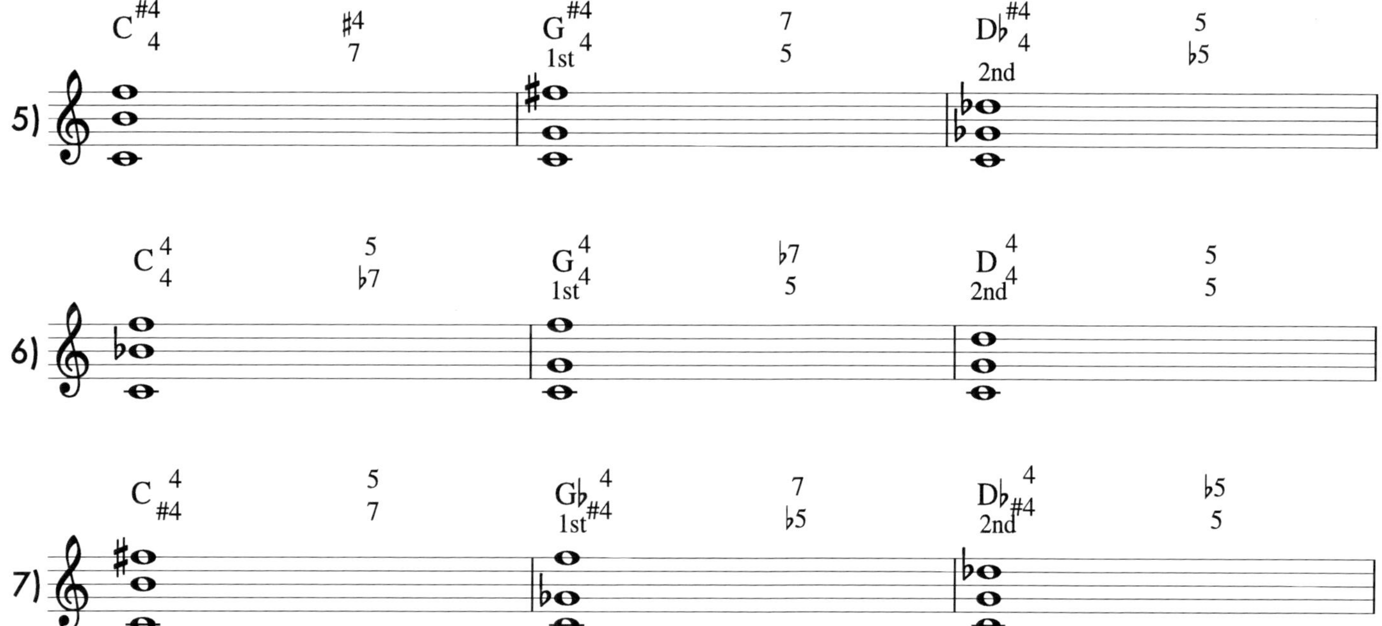

7th no5

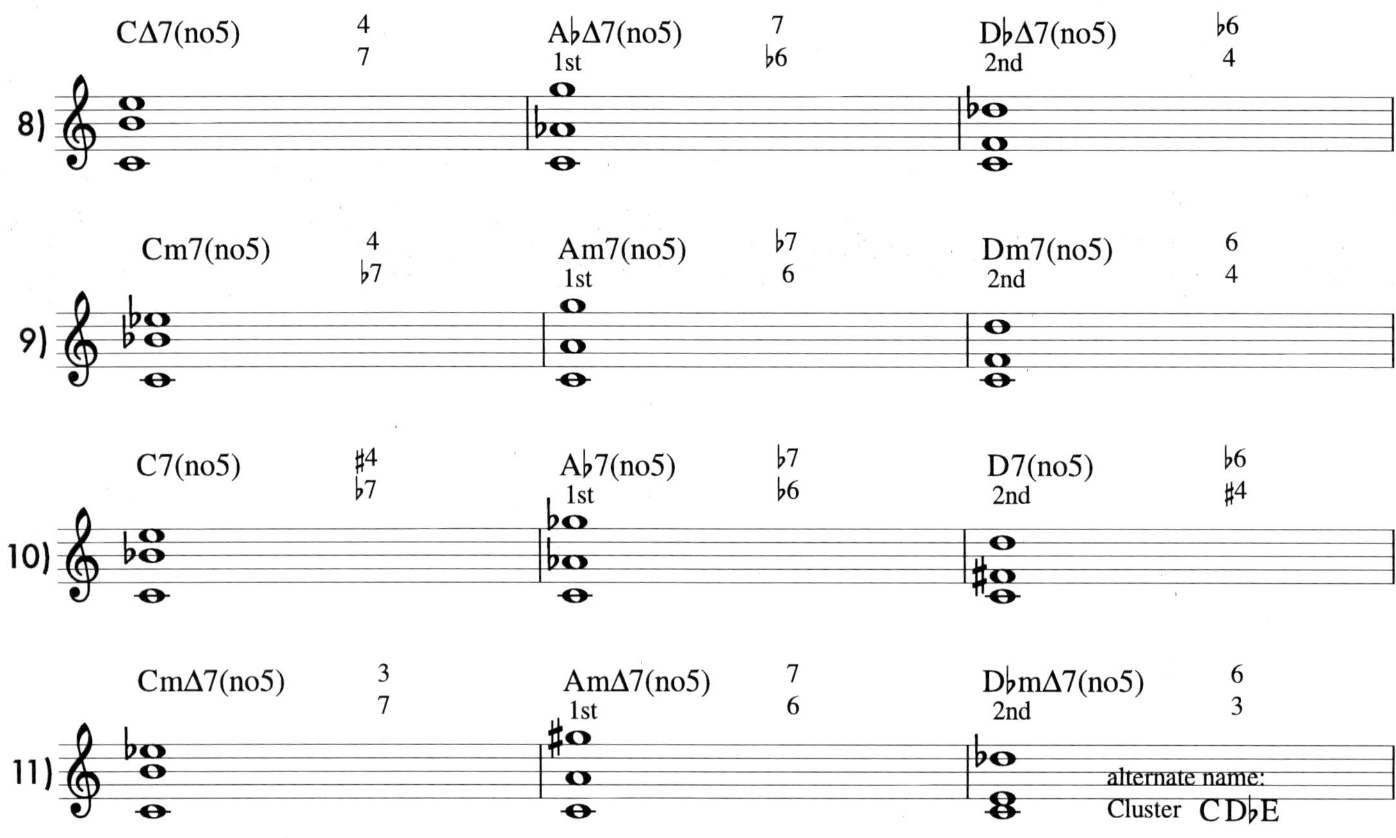

7th no3

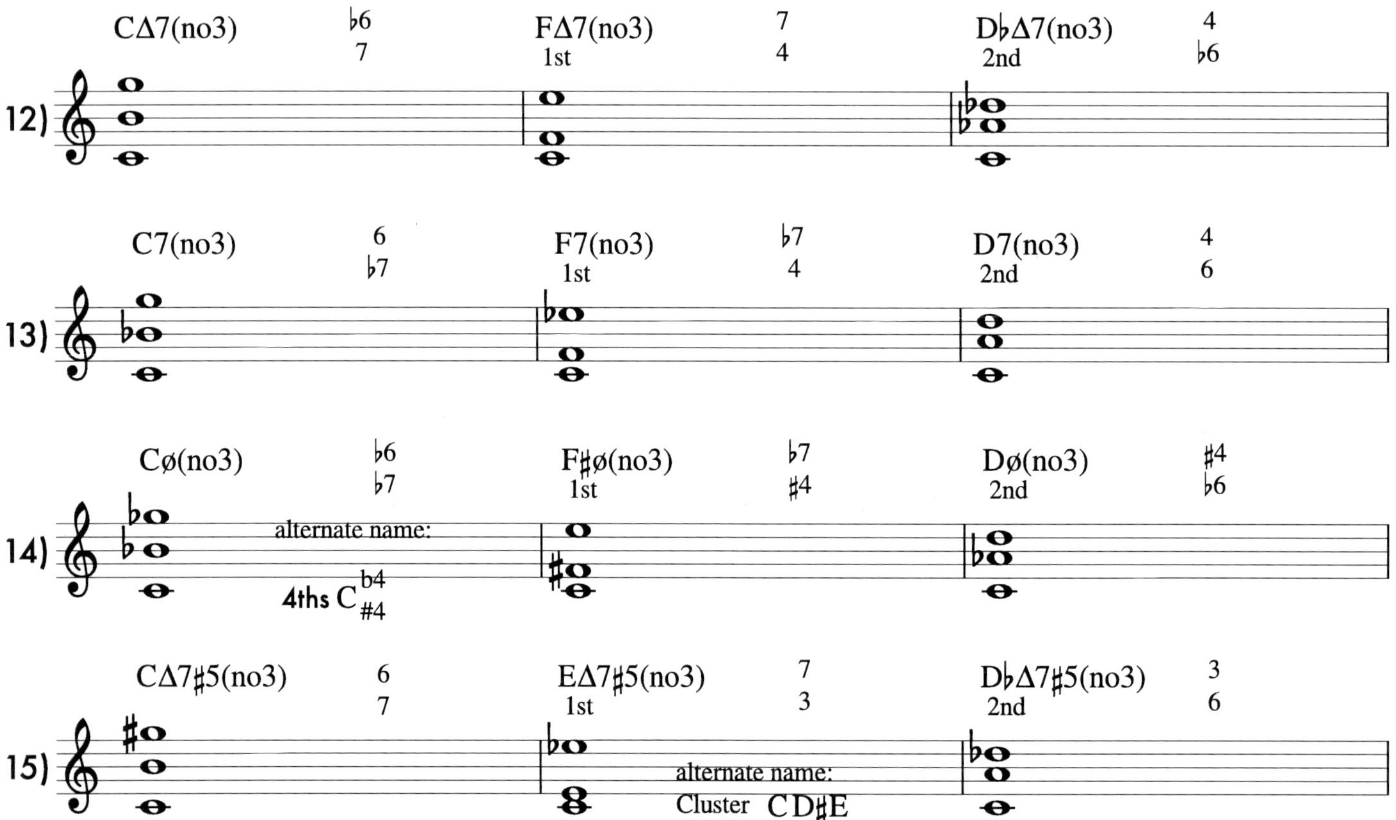

Clusters

CDE
♭7
3
B♭CD
1st
3
♭7
A♭B♭C
2nd
♭7
♭7
16)

CDE♭
7
♭3
B♭CD♭
1st
♭3
♭7
ABC
2nd
♭7
7
17)

CD♭E♭
b7
b3
BCD
1st
b3
7
AB♭C
2nd
7
b7
18)

CD♭E𝄫
7
2
BCD♭
1st
2
7
A♯BC
2nd
7
7
19)

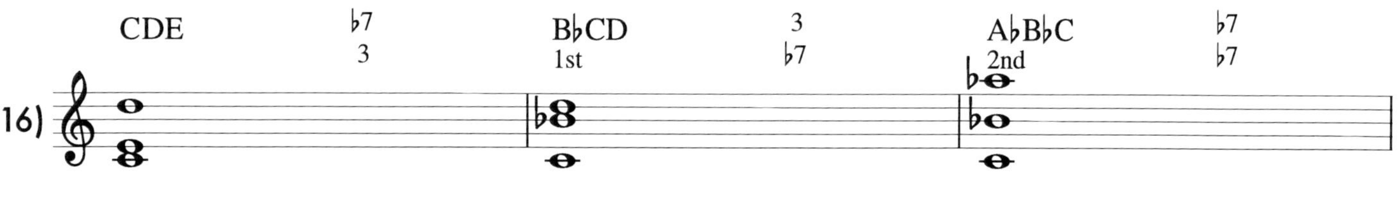

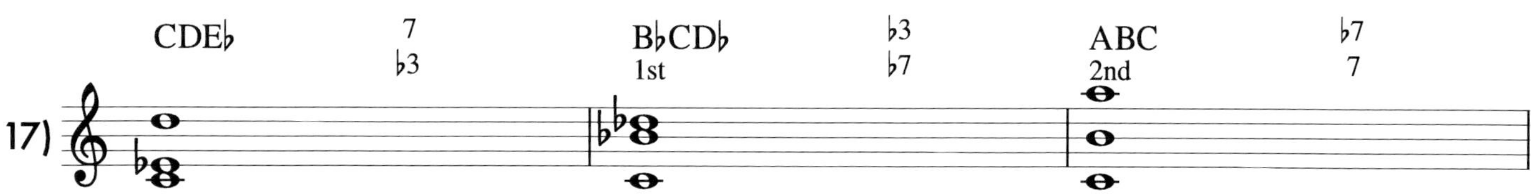

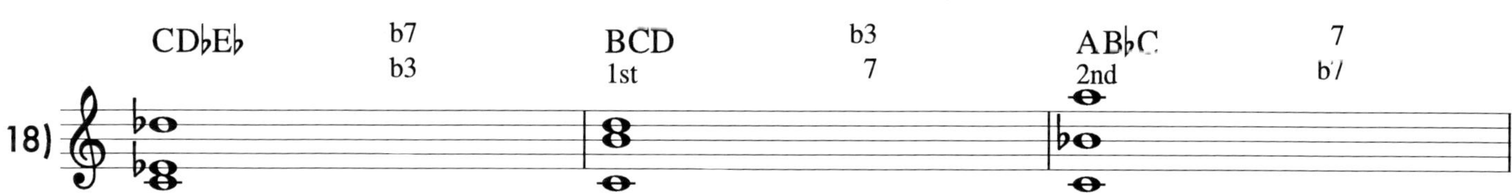

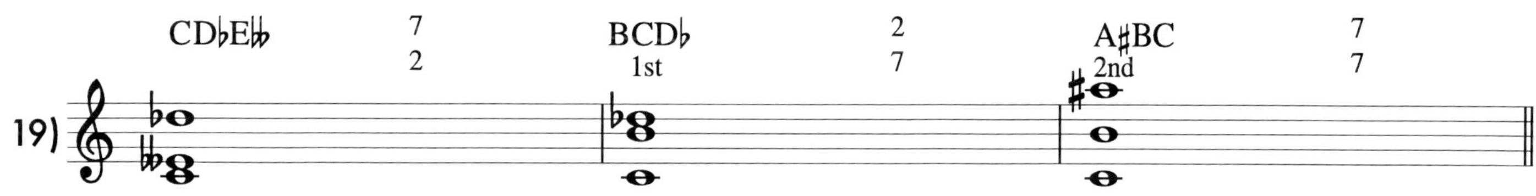

INVERSION EXERCISES

To internalize each chord structure and its shape on the entire guitar fretboard, take any of the 19 close-voiced three-part chords, and play all possible inversions from lowest to highest and back down on one constant set of three strings.
Use cycle 4 or 5 to play through all 12 possible keys/roots, with 8 chord locations per key, keeping a consistent, slow tempo.

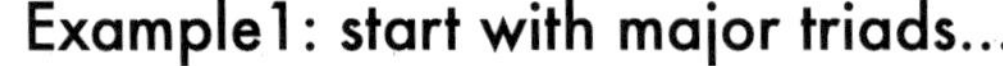

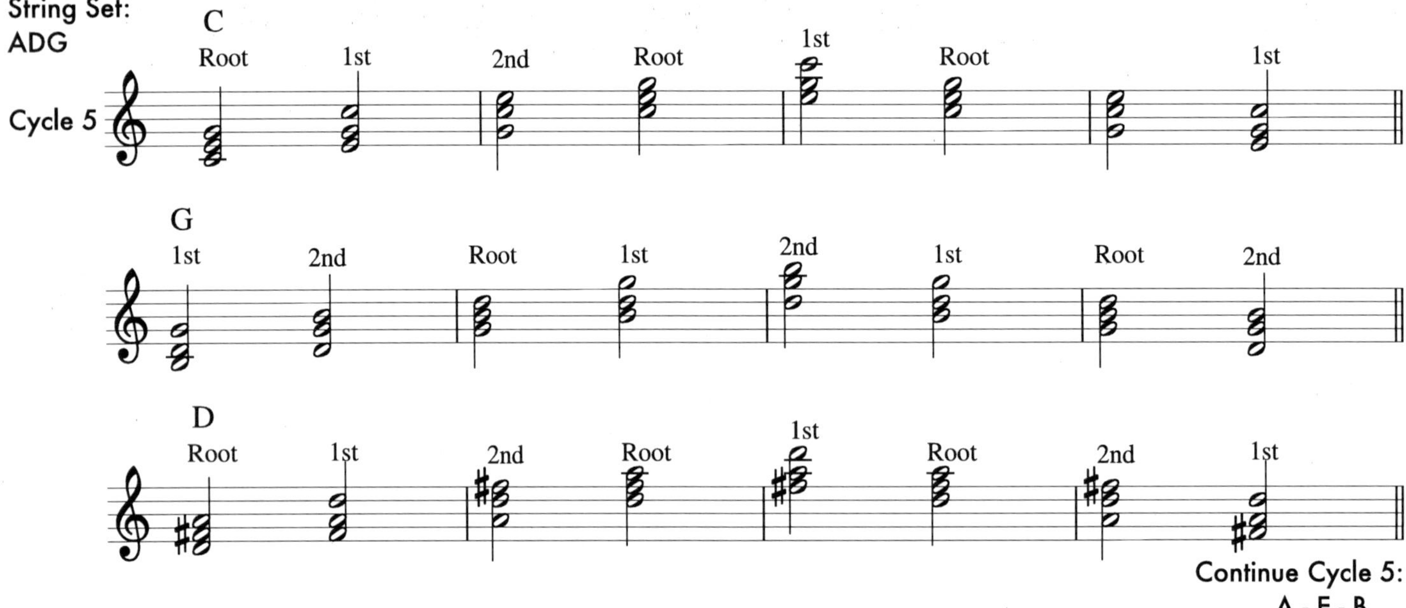

....then add voice motion:

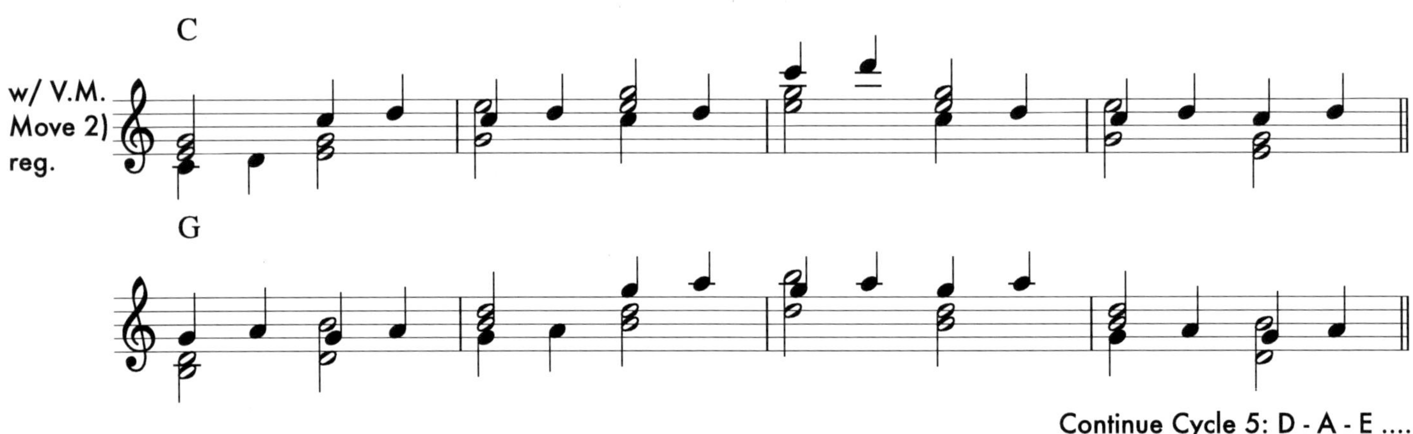

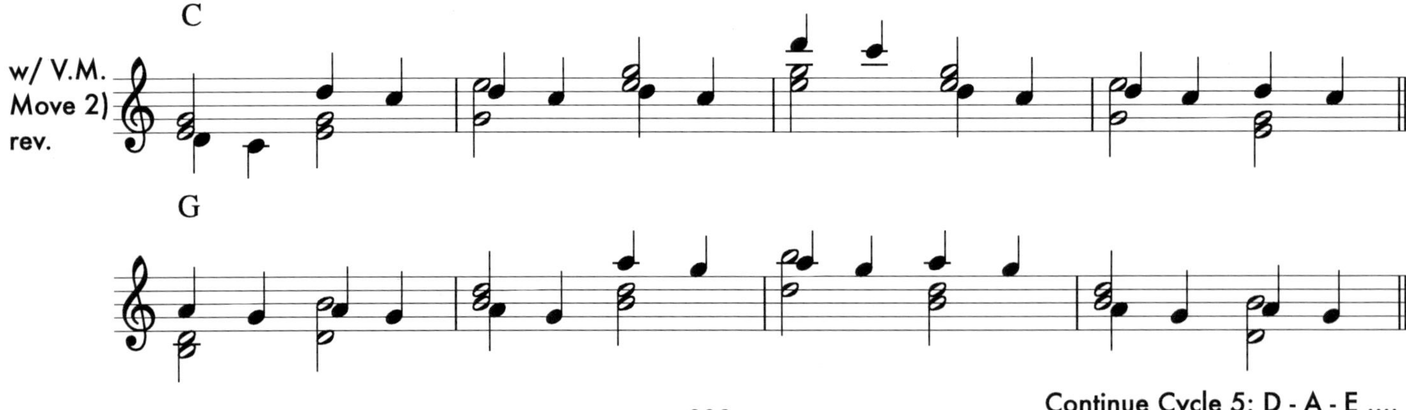

Experiment with other applicable moves.
Also try cycles ♭3, 3, ♭6, 6 and ♯4/♭5 for practicing less than 12 keys per exercise.

Example 2: minor triads on a different string set.

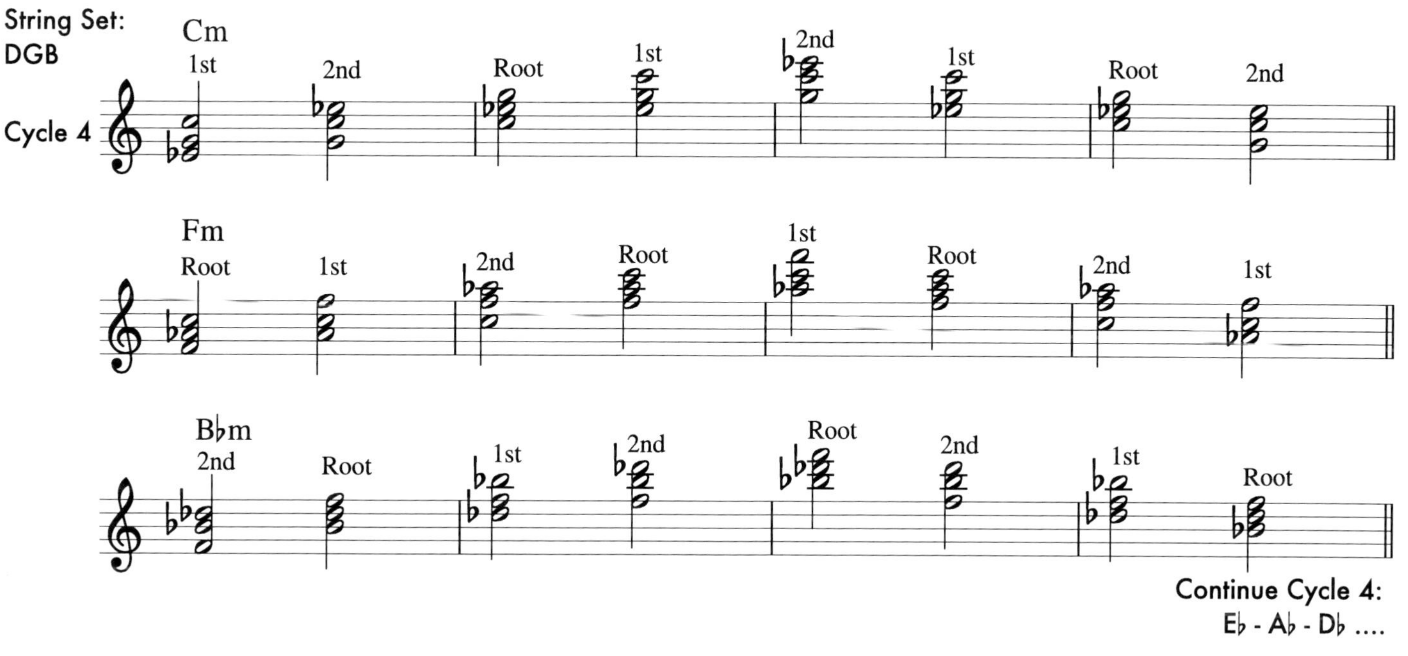

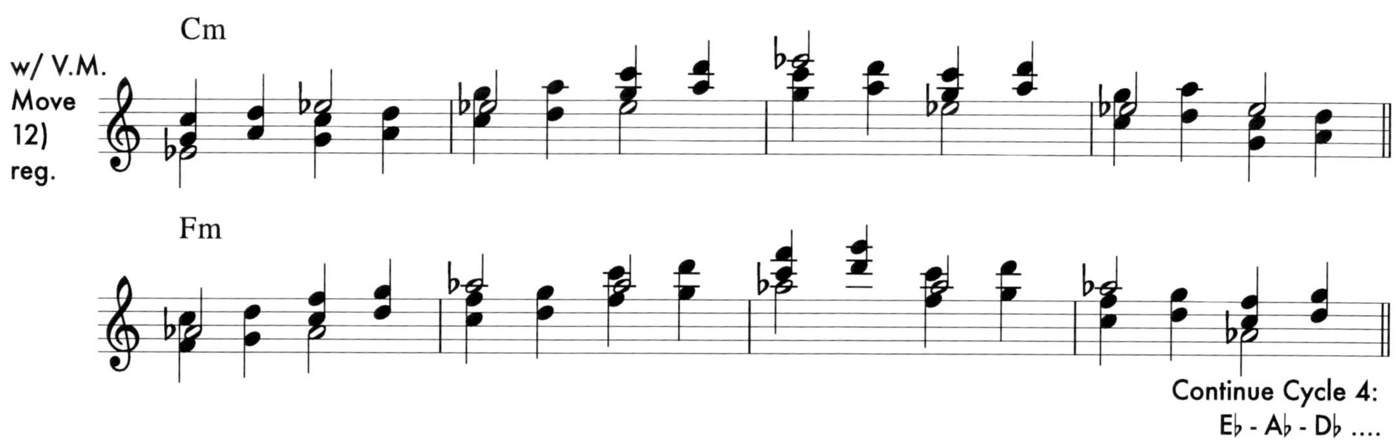

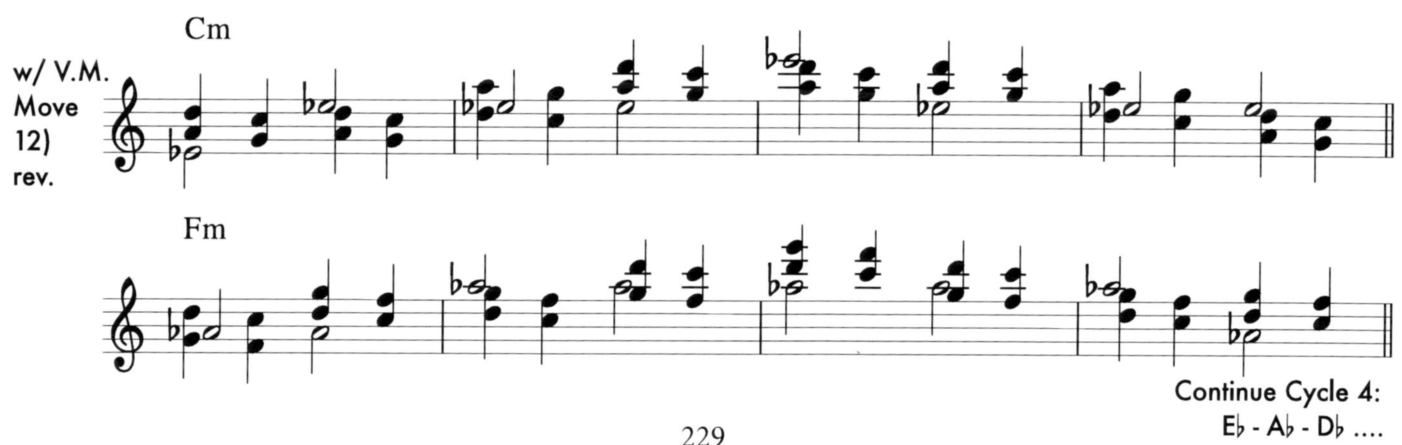

INVERSION EXERCISES

open

in Drop-2 Voicing

For any of the 19 open-voiced three-part chords, use multiple string sets, lowest to highest. The number of different possible inversions may differ per key.

Example 3: mΔ7(no5)

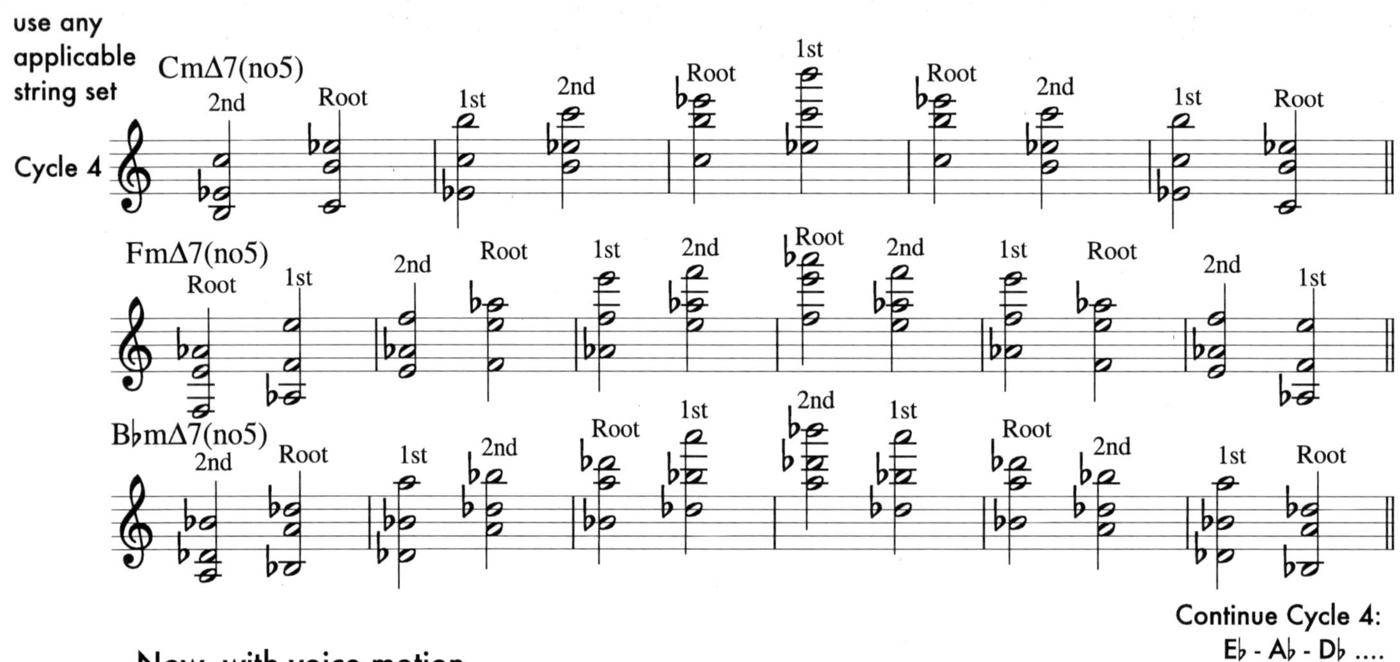

Continue Cycle 4: E♭ - A♭ - D♭ ....

Now, with voice motion....

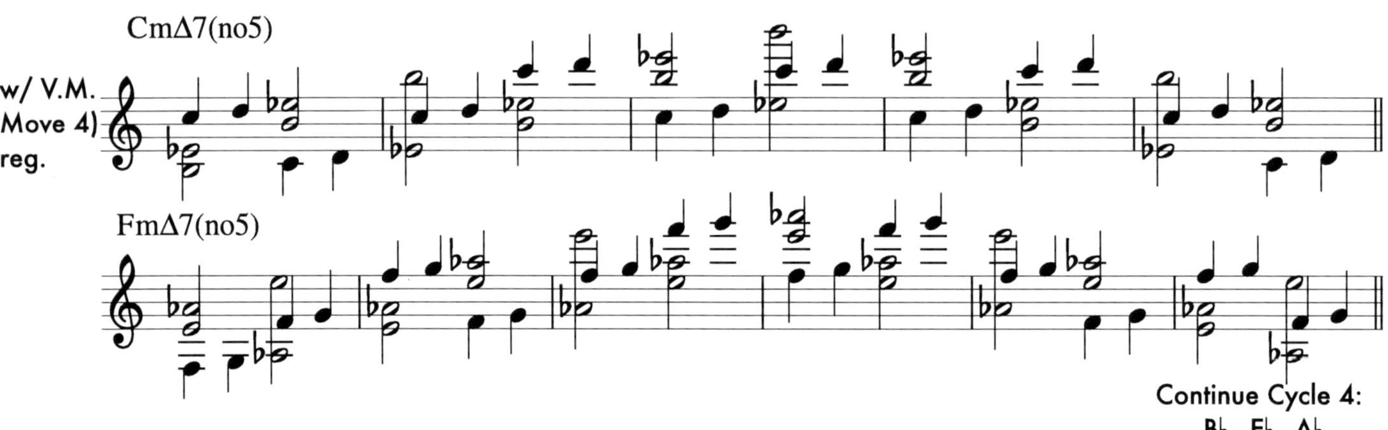

Continue Cycle 4: B♭ - E♭ - A♭ ....

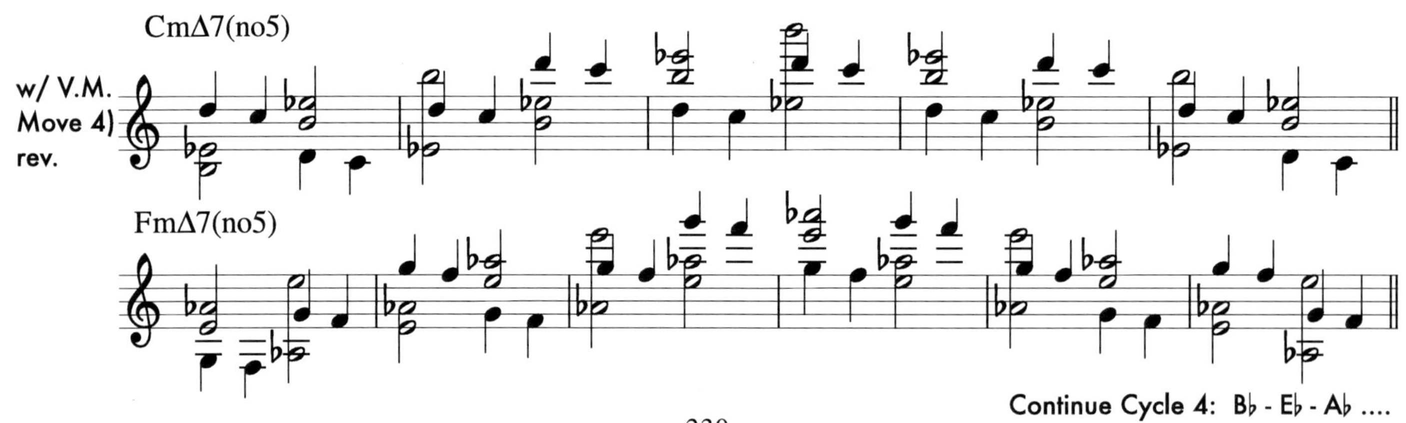

Continue Cycle 4: B♭ - E♭ - A♭ ....

BUILDING FOUR-PART CHORDS

A Brief Glimpse Beyond Three-Part Harmony...

One additional pitch can be added to any of the 19 possible three-part chords to attain a four-part chord structure.
Start by adding any of the four other notes from a basic heptatonic scale which may contain the three-part chord, then try using the remaining five notes left in the chromatic scale.
All common 7th-chords can be found this way (i.e., C major triad +A= Am7 etc.), as well as more exotic structures.

In the following example, each of the chromatic notes **not** contained in the C major triad is added individually to the chord to create nine different four-part structures.
Try all possible voicings and inversions.

Add the notes contained in the C diatonic scale first:

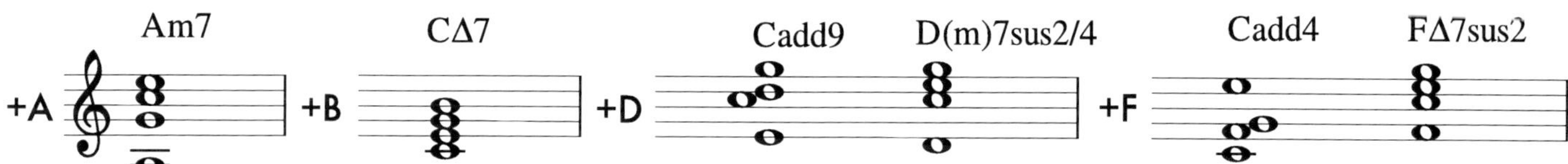

Then add the rest of the chromatic notes:

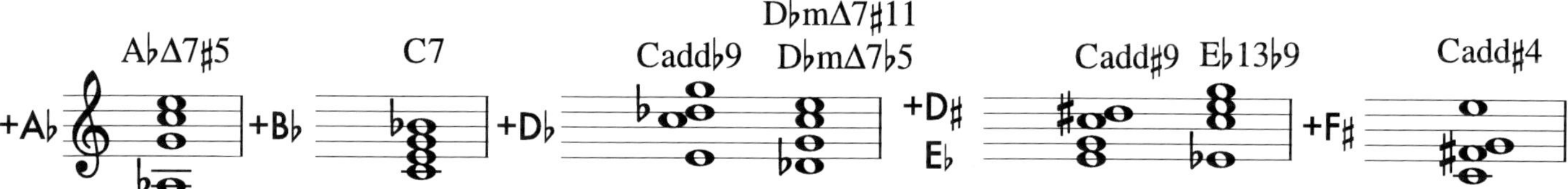

Apply this procedure to any other one of the 19 three-part chords, and take each of the nine resulting four-part structures up and down any heptatonic scale that may contain it.

Experiment with this method to discover four-part chords, and to find new harmonic situations in which the three-part chords and their respective moves might be used.

PART 3C

Voice Motion Etudes

OVERVIEW

This section presents three etudes as examples of how to apply the moves of the main part of this book to existing melodic material in the harmonic context of a common chord progression.

Etudes 1 and 2 show the application of the moves to harmonize a melody consisting of constant quarter notes, using the intervallic movement of that pre-existing melody as a moving voice within a three-part harmonization in many variations.

Etude 3 shows how voice motion can embellish a slower moving melody or harmonic guideline, by adding movement to the two additional harmony voices.

Throughout this section, various principles of variation and rhythmic reduction are introduced to help with the practical application of the material presented.

Do your best to play all all of the etudes on the guitar even though some may prove extremely challenging when multiple-voice motion is required.

CONTENTS

INTRODUCTION to ETUDE 1

This etude is based on a simple melody moving in intervals of 2nds and 3rds and consisting only of quarter notes, set over a standard 8-bar chord progression in the key of C major:

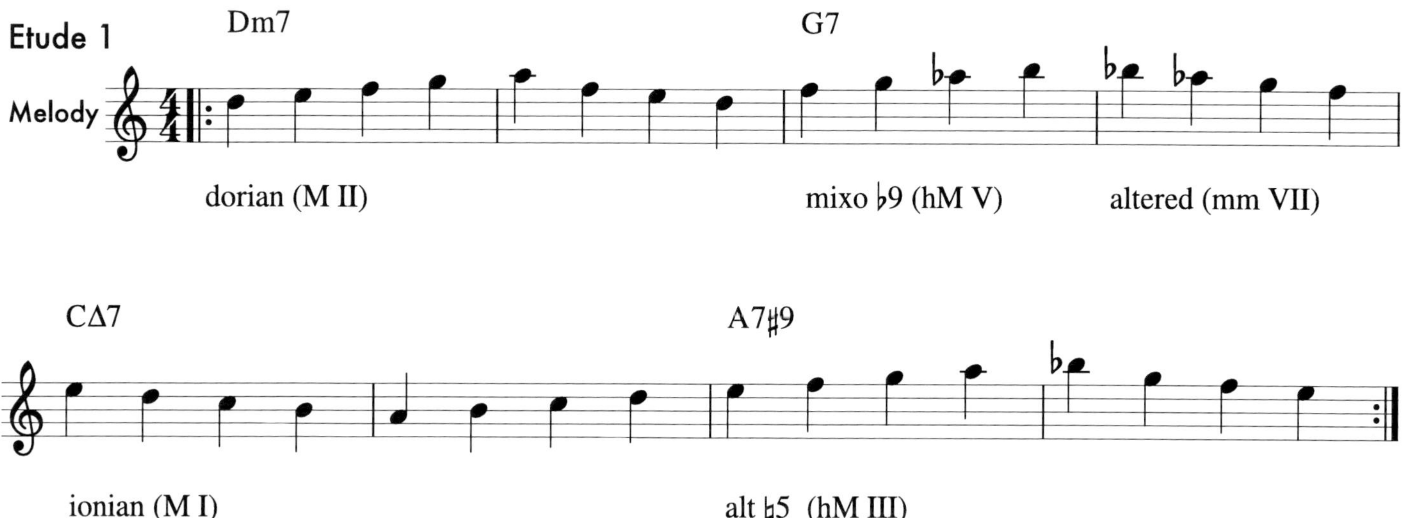

The names of the heptatonic scales used are shown below each bar.
(see "Heptatonic Modes" p.216)

Play the melody repeatedly and slowly with an even rhythmic feel.
Note how the melody corresponds with the chords, and how it is constructed intervallically.

To prepare for the etude variations involving various voice motion moves that were introduced in Parts 1 and 2 of this book, harmonize the melody with any common three-part chord structures, creating consistent triple-voice parallel motion.

The next few pages show a few preparatory exercises harmonizing the melody of "Etude 1" with the chord structures that are most frequently used later in the variations.

Play through the following harmonizations slowly, being aware of all chord names and types being used, and how they change and move according to the specific scales and underlying harmonies.
Refer to Part 3A "Heptatonics" for identifying the chords and harmonizing the six basic heptatonics with the five three-part chord types.
Try to learn the melody by heart so you can practice harmonizing it without looking at the page or even having to read the preparatory exercises.

Preparatory Exercises for "Etude 1"

close

Melody Harmonized with 4ths in 3 Inversions

Triple-Voice Parallel Motion

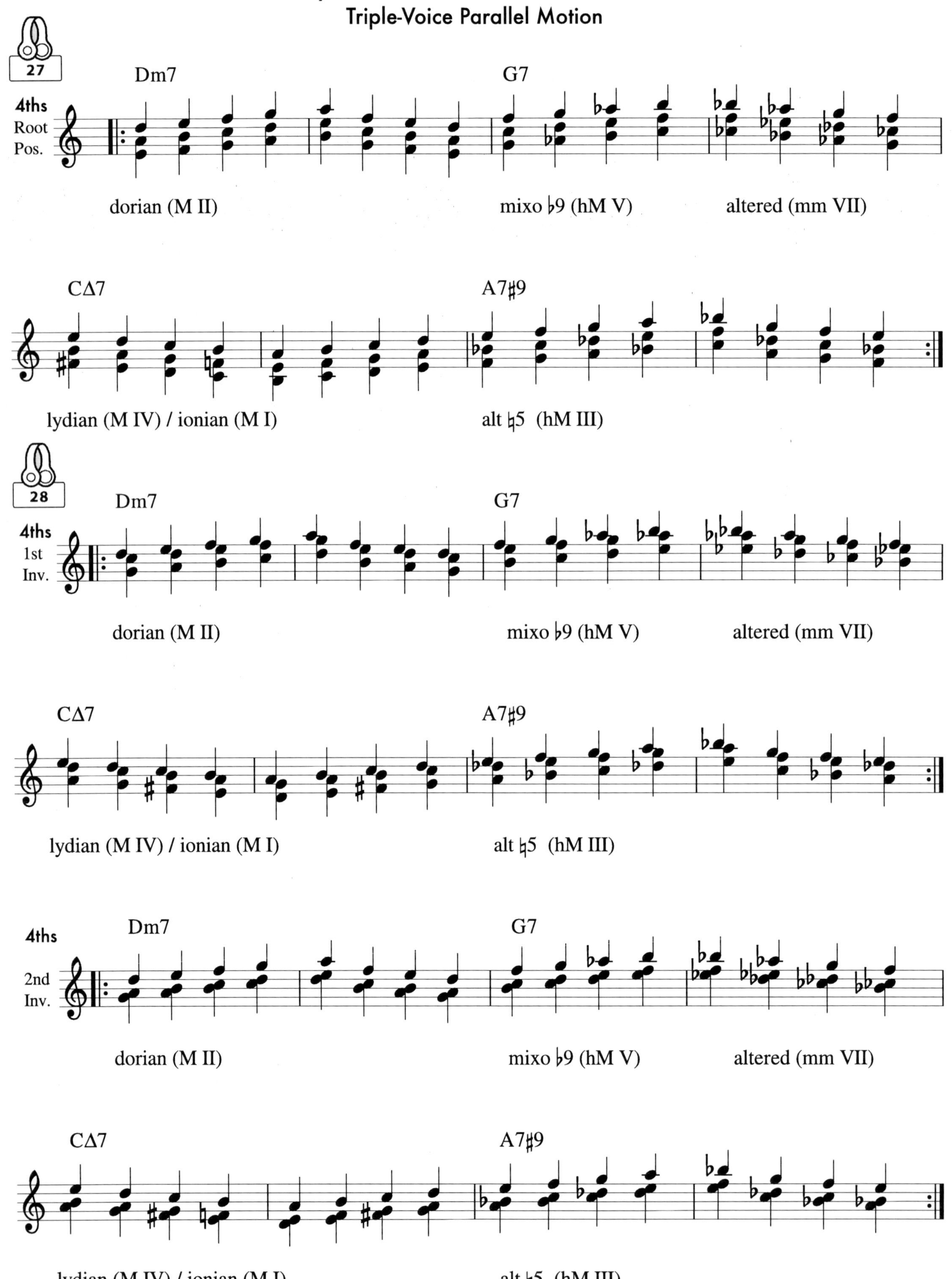

Preparatory Exercises for "Etude 1"

open

Melody Harmonized with 4ths in 3 Inversions
Triple-Voice Parallel Motion

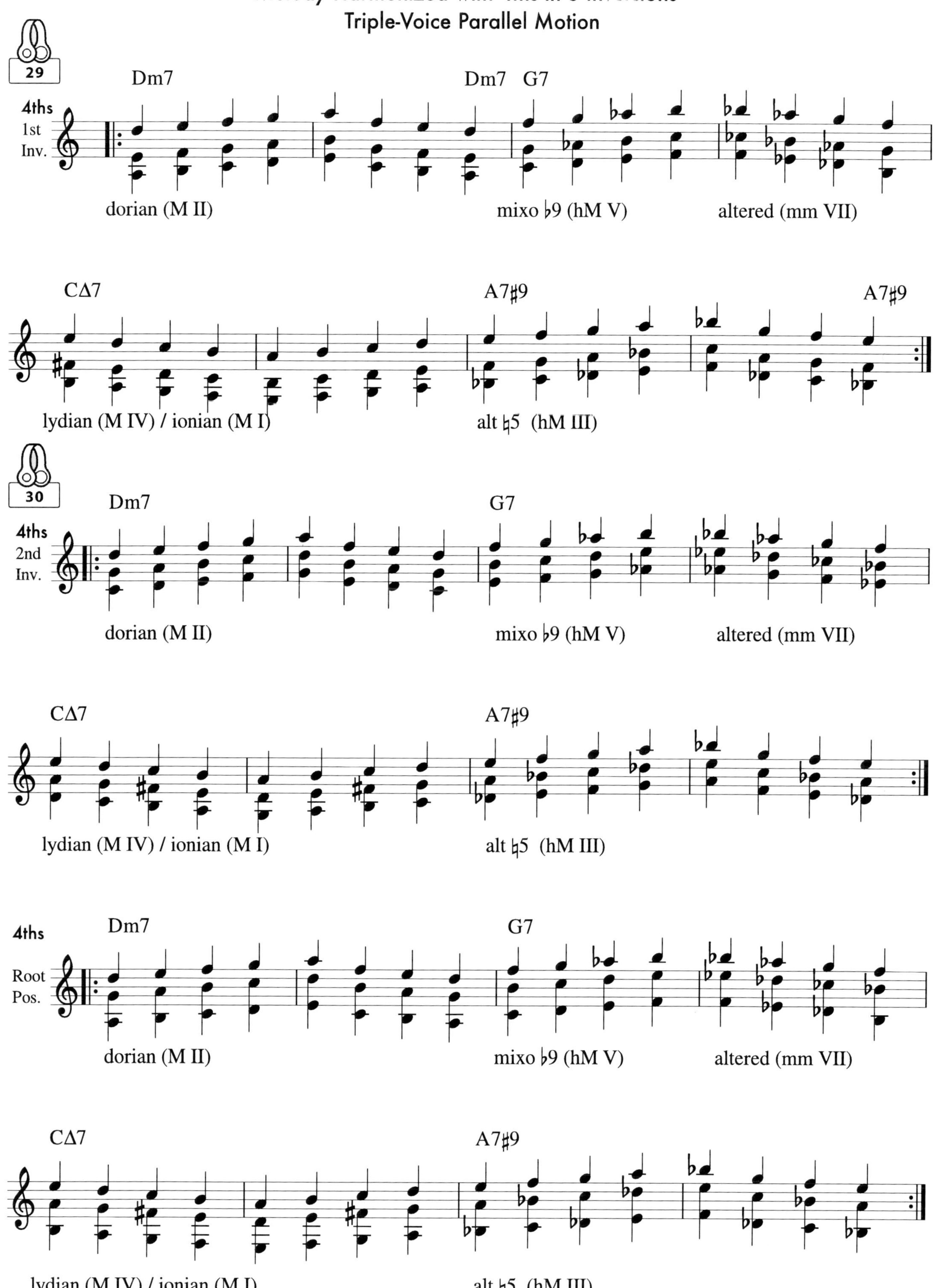

Preparatory Exercises for "Etude 1"

close

Melody Harmonized with Triads & 7th no3 Chords

Triple-Voice Parallel Motion

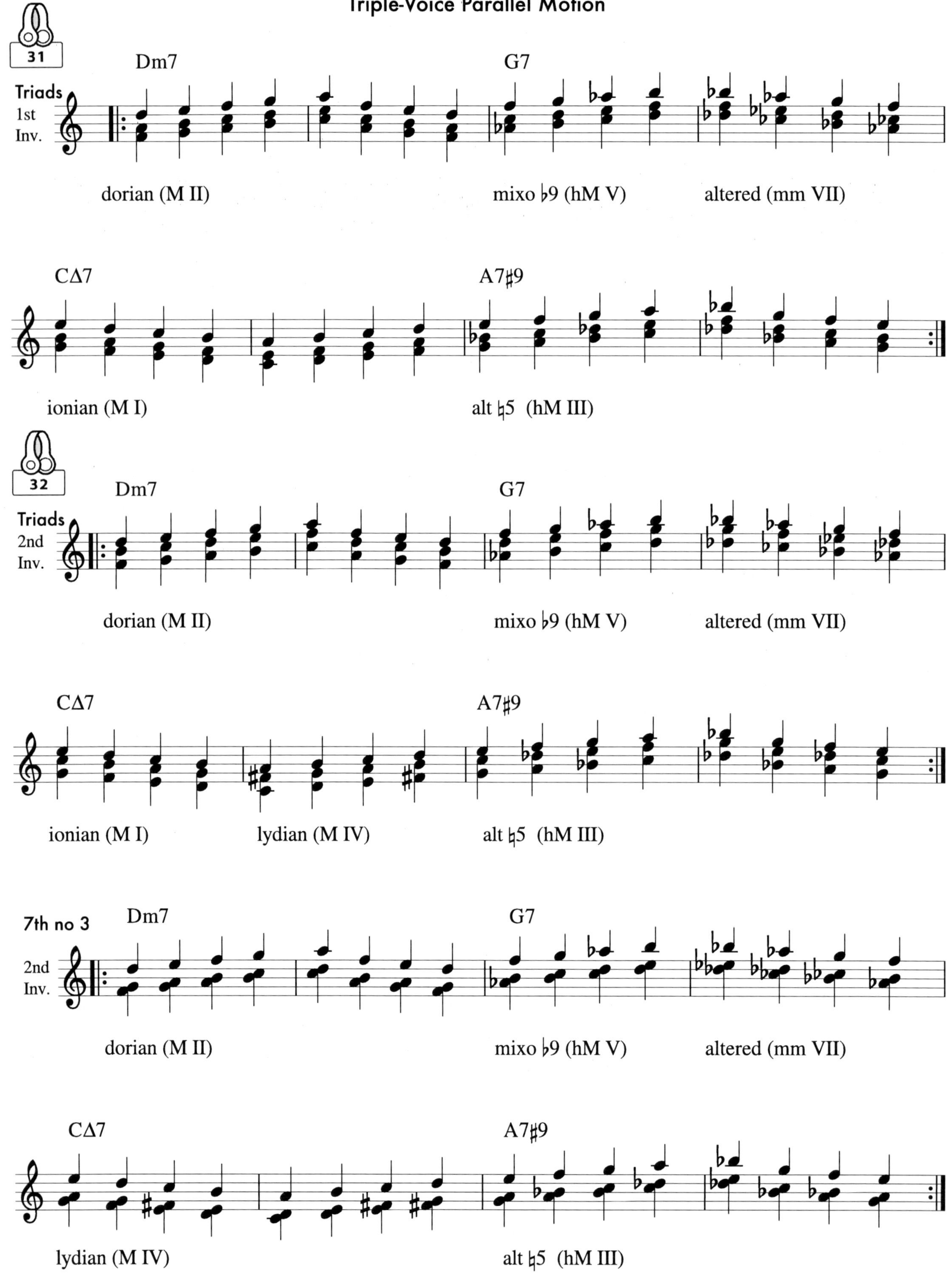

Preparatory Exercises for "Etude 1"

open

Melody Harmonized with Triads & 7th no3 Chords

Triple-Voice Parallel Motion

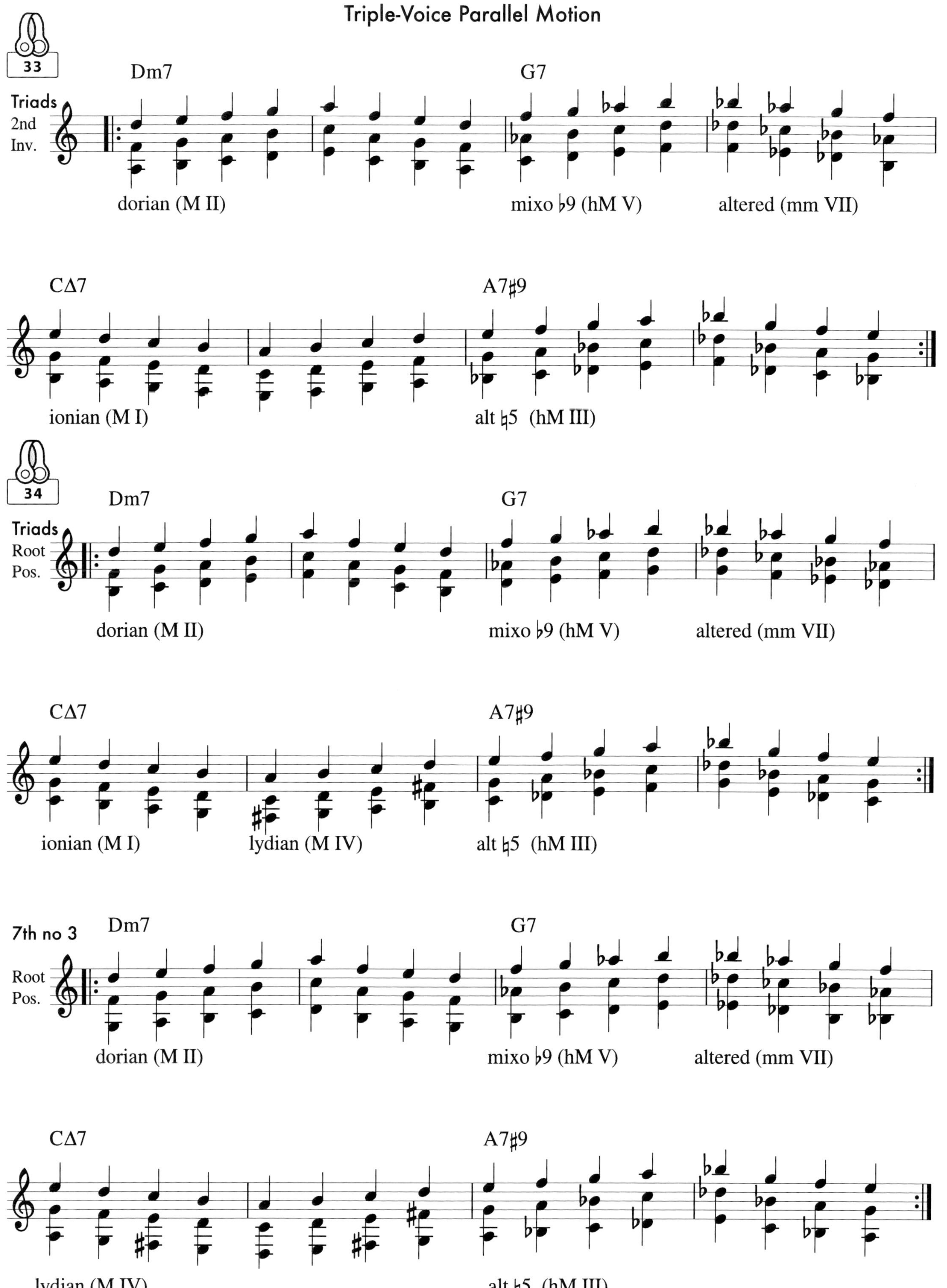

Preparatory Exercises for "Etude1"

close

Melody Harmonized with 7th no5 Chords
Triple-Voice Parallel Motion

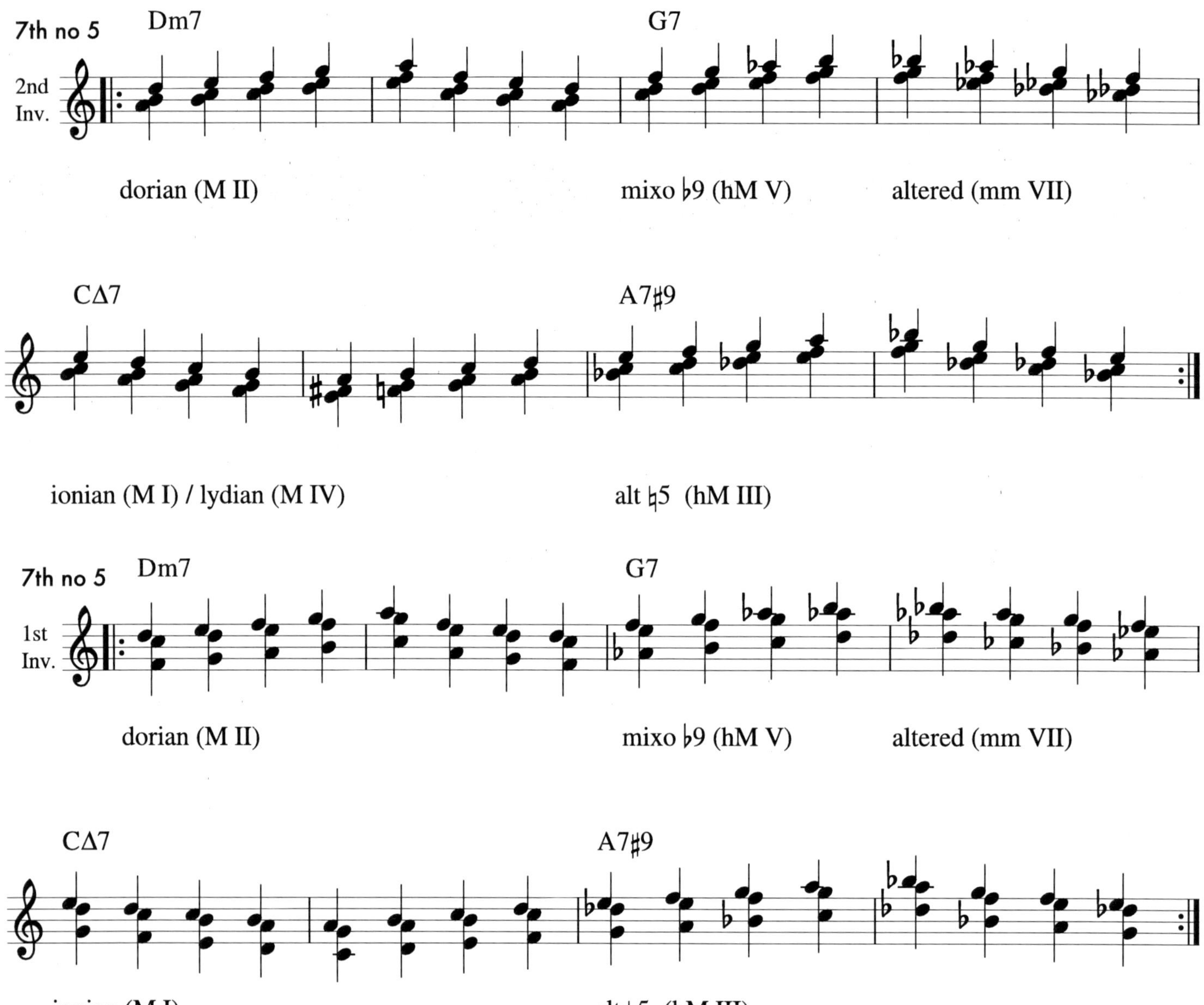

Preparatory Exercises for "Etude1"

open

Melody Harmonized with 7th no5 Chords

Triple-Voice Parallel Motion

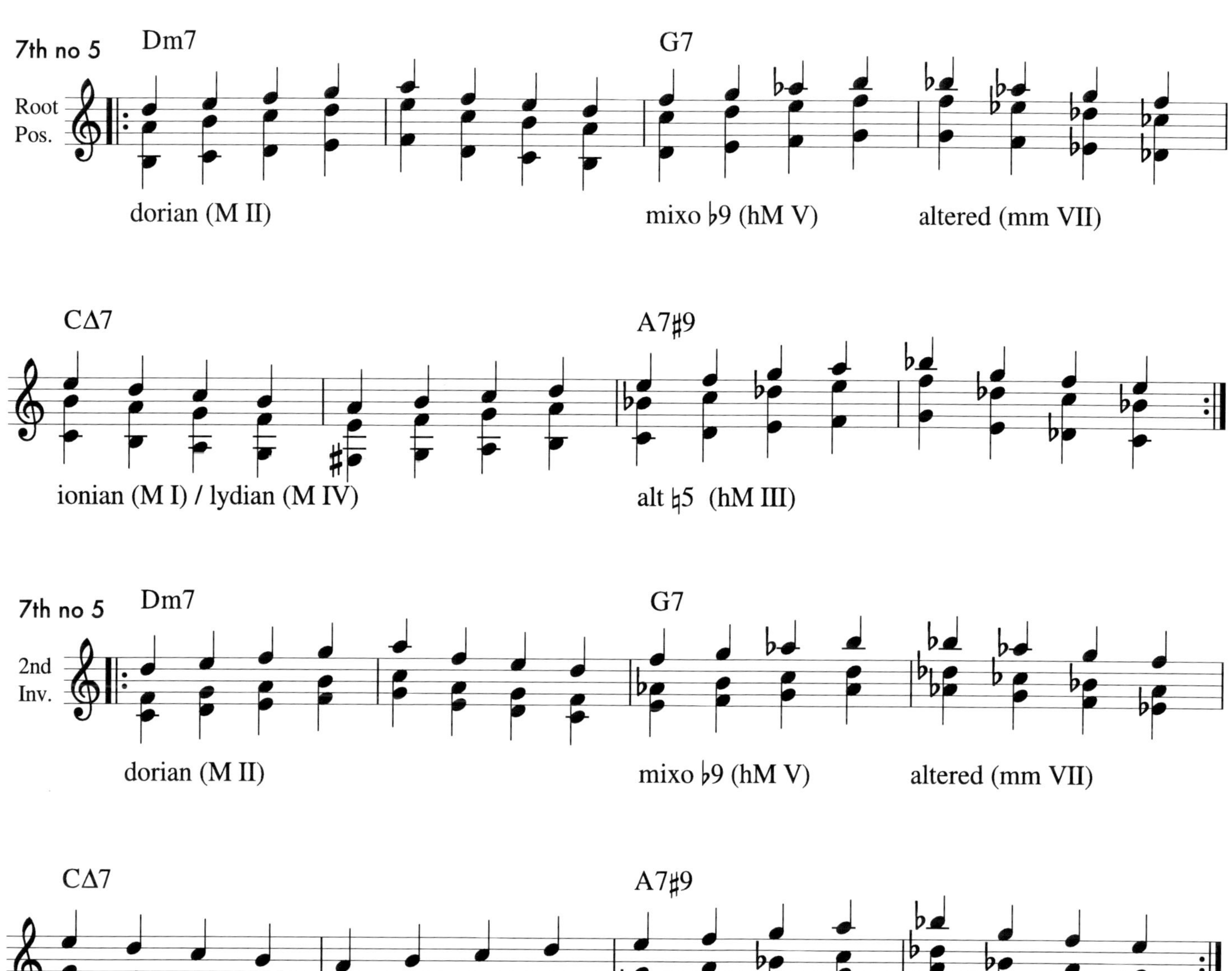

APPLYING VOICE MOTION TO THE MELODY
Etude 1

The 108 moves in Parts 1 and 2 of this book represent pairs of three-note chords connected by voice motion of 2nds and/or 3rds, so each of the moves can be applied to any pair of two consecutive notes moving a 2nd and/or 3rd to harmonize them in a specific way.

When evenly applying voice motion moves to the consistent melodic quarter notes of "Etude 1", a move will start on every other note.

"Etude 1.1" variations have the moves starting on the odd beats 1 and 3 (from page 242):

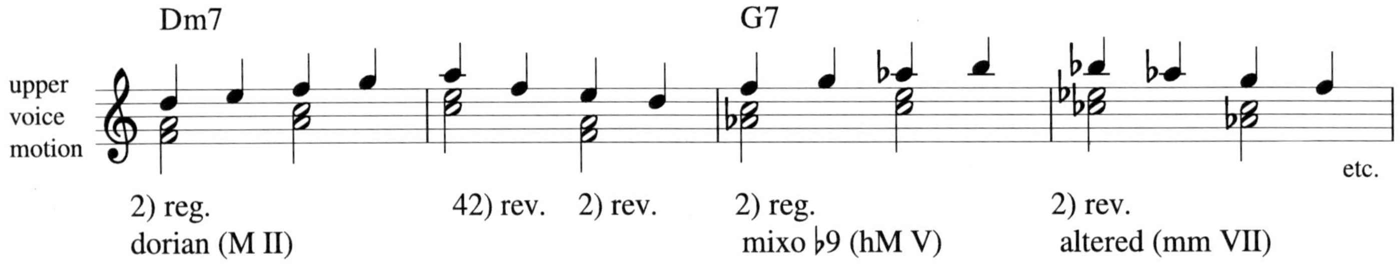

In "Etude 1.2" variations, the moves start on the even beats 2 and 4 (from page 258):

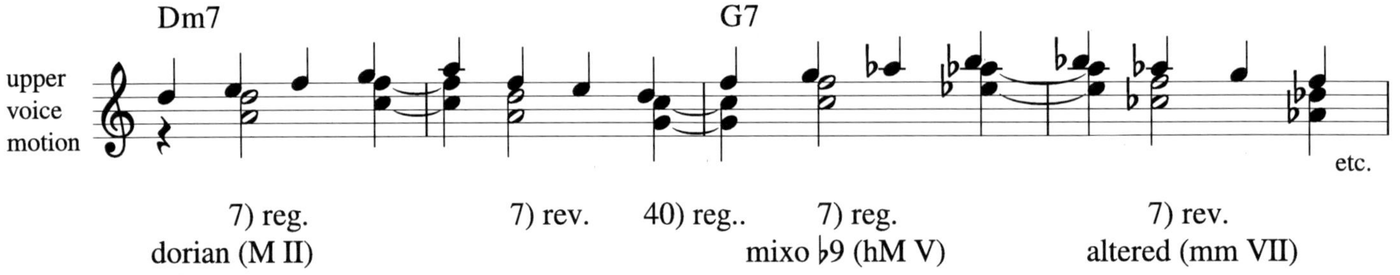

"Etude 1.3" has moves starting on alternating odd **and** even beats (page 270):

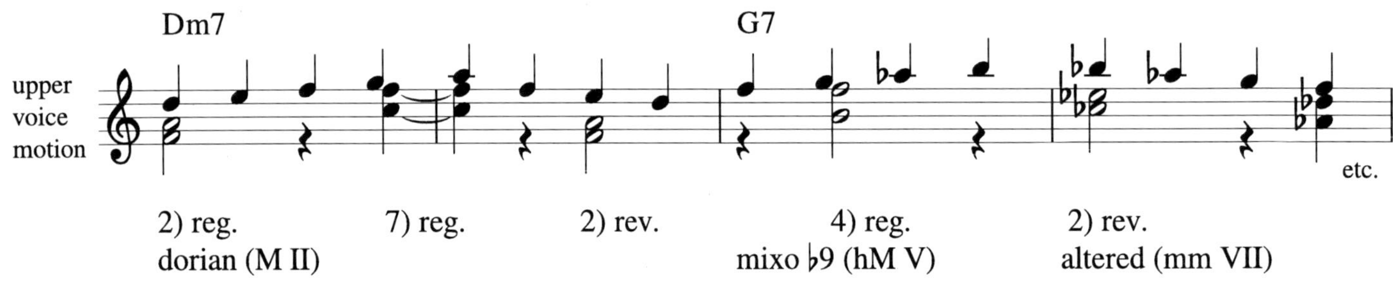

Observe the harmonic and rhythmic differences caused by starting the moves in different places within the bar.

ETUDE VARIATIONS

The variations of "Etude 1" on the next pages are presented in order of complexity, starting with single-voice motion, up to triple-voice contrary motion.
Each variation is shown both in close and open voicing, in all inversions.
The purpose of this approach is to present the material in a complete and conclusive way so it is available as a resource for thorough study.

If possible, practice transposing these etudes to all keys and try applying them to minor keys as well.

Depending on your personal level and interest, the relevance of each variation may vary; on the guitar, some inversions are very difficult to play, with some being almost unplayable, especially the lowest inversions on each page.
In that case, try transposing them up or down an octave, leaving out the least relevant voice of a move to make it playable, or only playing the parts that seem possible to you.
There is a lot to be learned technically by trying to find ways to play these more difficult voicings and motions. As with all the material in this book, use caution, play slowly and stop immediately should any pain occur.

The melody of "Etude 1" is constructed so it is largely neutral from a rhythmic and stylistic perspective, using only quarter notes of widely used heptatonic scales over a common set of chords.
This melody should not be confused with something to be played unchanged in an actual real-life musical situation in which a similar chord progression might occur.
Practice these etudes in oder to study the application of different moves to the same melodic material and how they work within the given harmonic context.
Use only those excerpts of the variations which personally seem most interesting to you and apply/adapt them to your own melodic ideas and improvisations.
Later in this section, a number of examples show how to systematically reduce the melodic material of the etudes, and extract shorter rhythmic phrases from them (rhythmic reduction).

All variations use the same set of scales in order to better compare them.
In the two bars of G7, a different scale/sound is used for each: mixolydian ♭9 for the first bar, often times with a suspended sound, leading into an altered dominant sound for the second bar.
For the two bars of CΔ7, either ionian or lydian scales are used, depending on where the motions fall rhythmically when the 4th degree of the respective scale gets involved.

Etude 1.1

close

Moves start on beats 1 and 3
Variation A with Single-Voice Motion in 3 Inversions

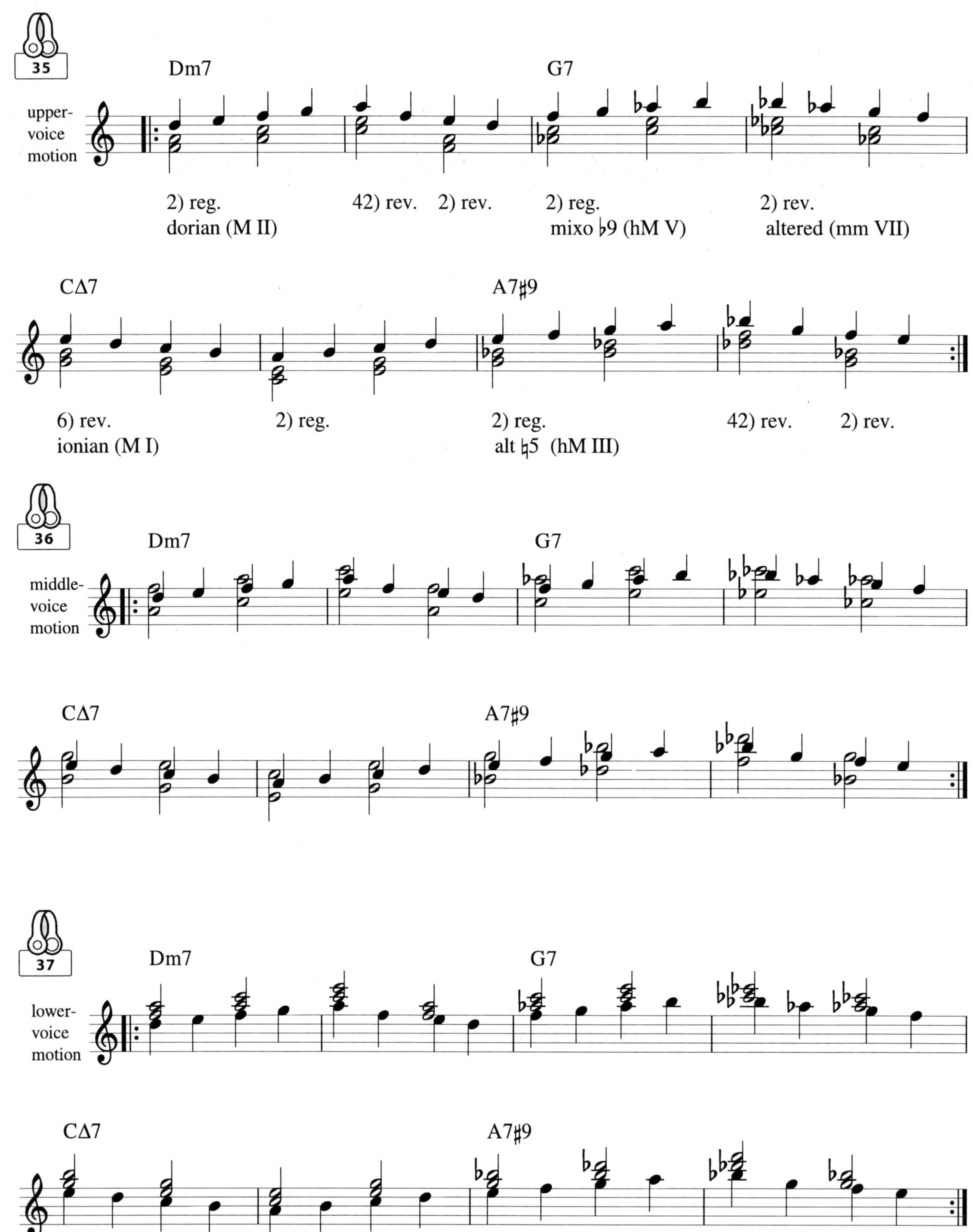

Etude 1.1

open

Moves start on beats 1 and 3

Variation A with Single-Voice Motion in 3 Inversions

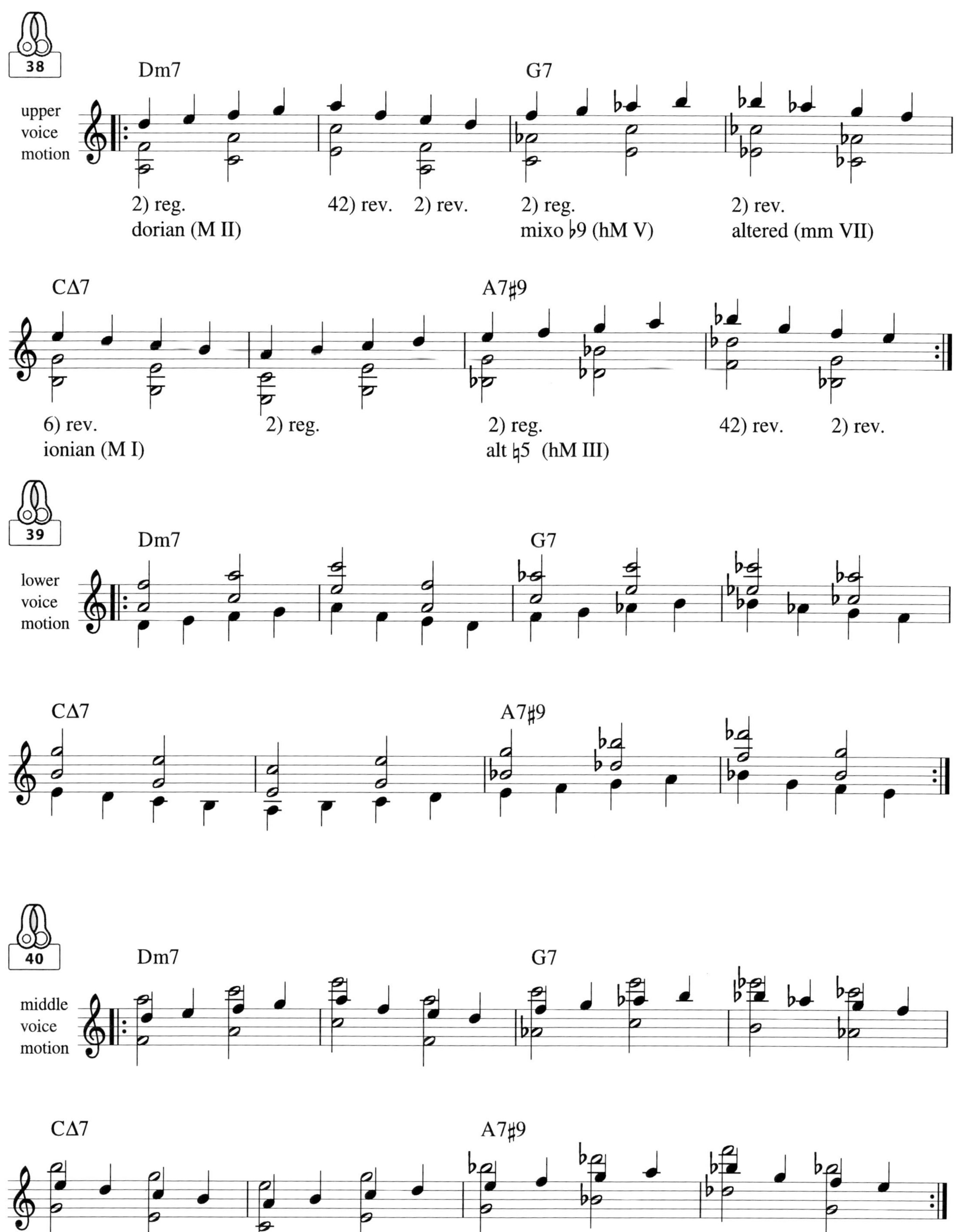

Etude 1.1

close

Moves start on beats 1 and 3

Variation B with Single-Voice Motion in 3 Inversions

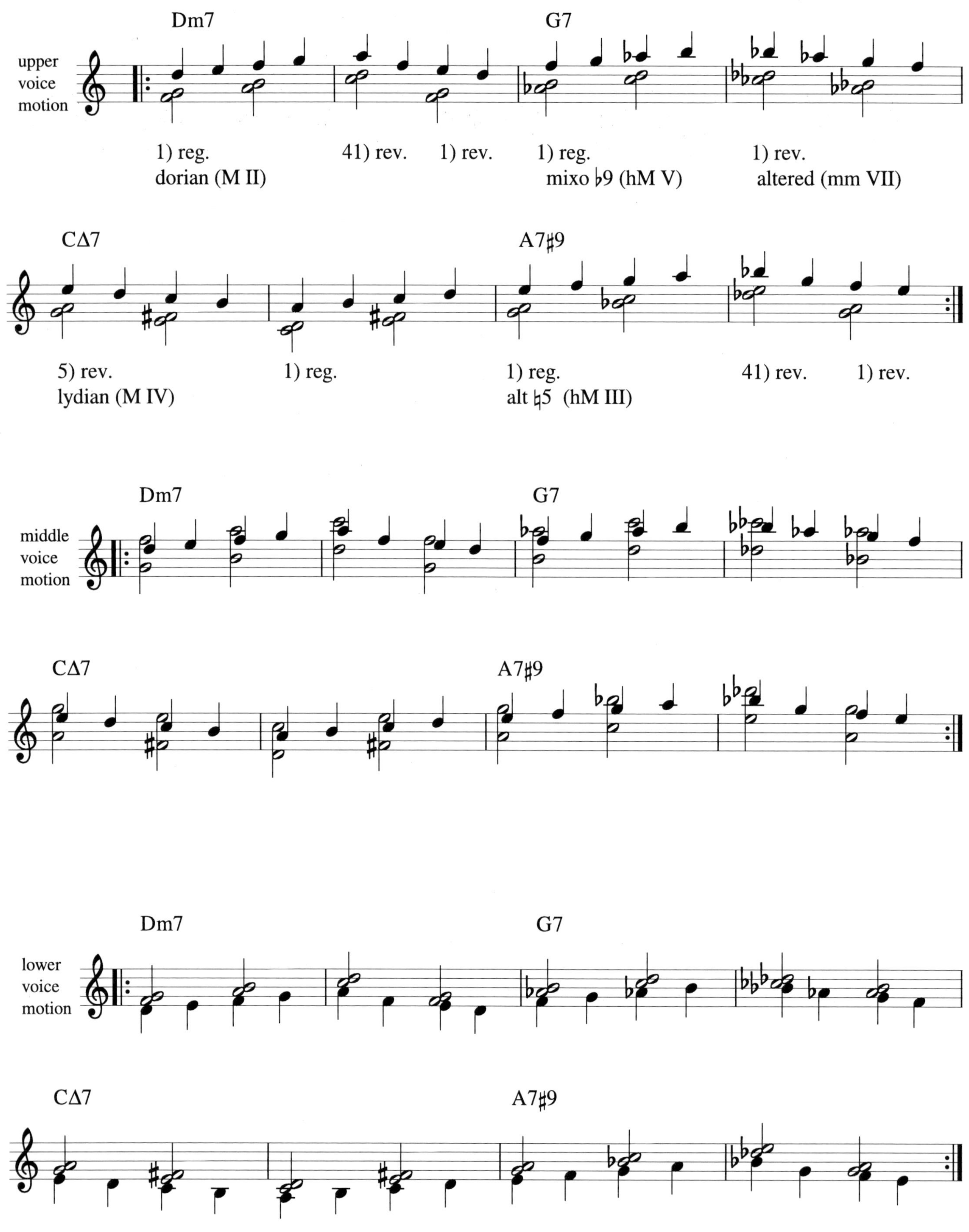

Etude 1.1

open

Moves start on beats 1 and 3

Variation B with Single-Voice Motion in 3 Inversions

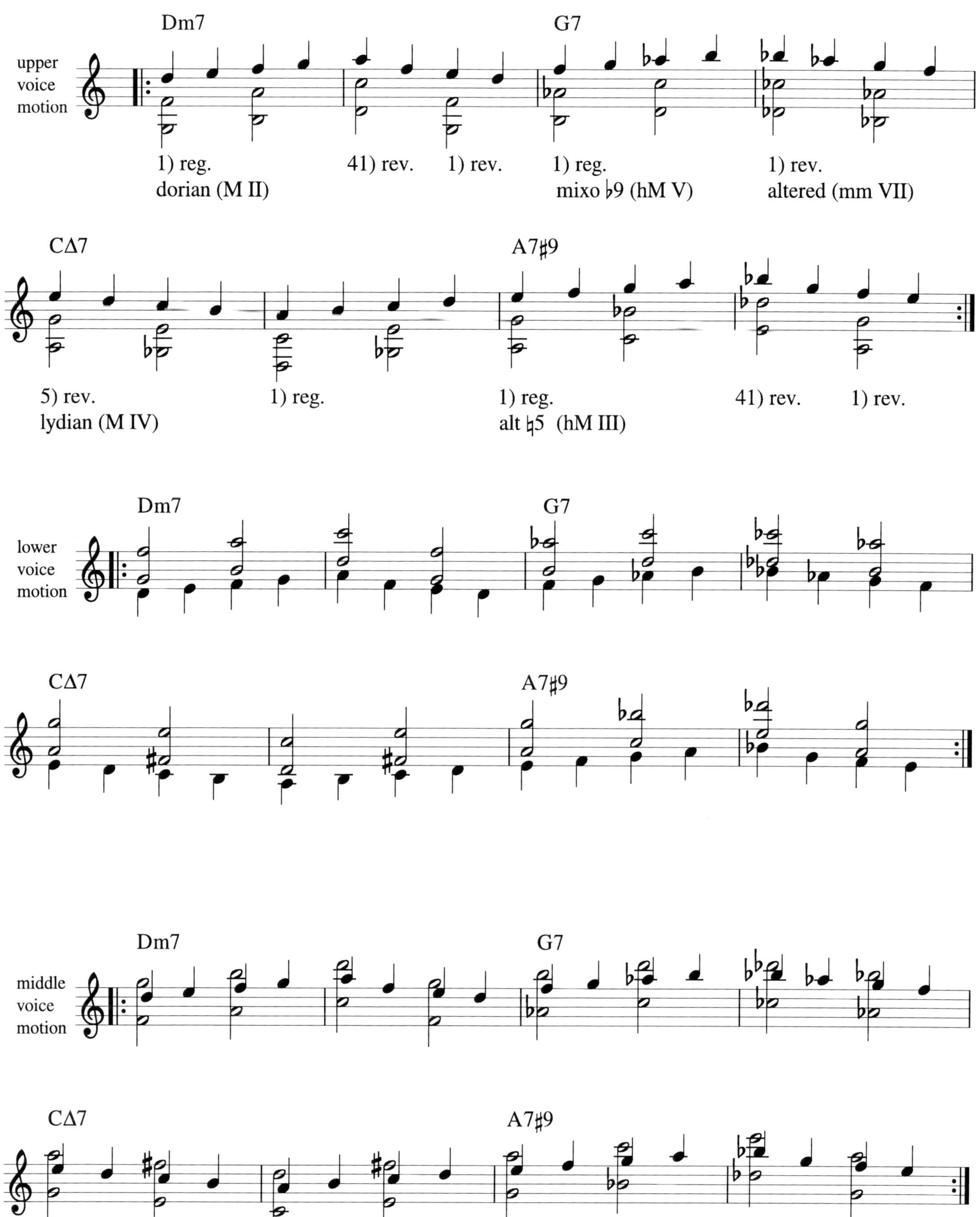

Etude 1.1

close

Moves start on beats 1 and 3

Variation C with (mostly) Single-Voice Motion in 3 Inversions

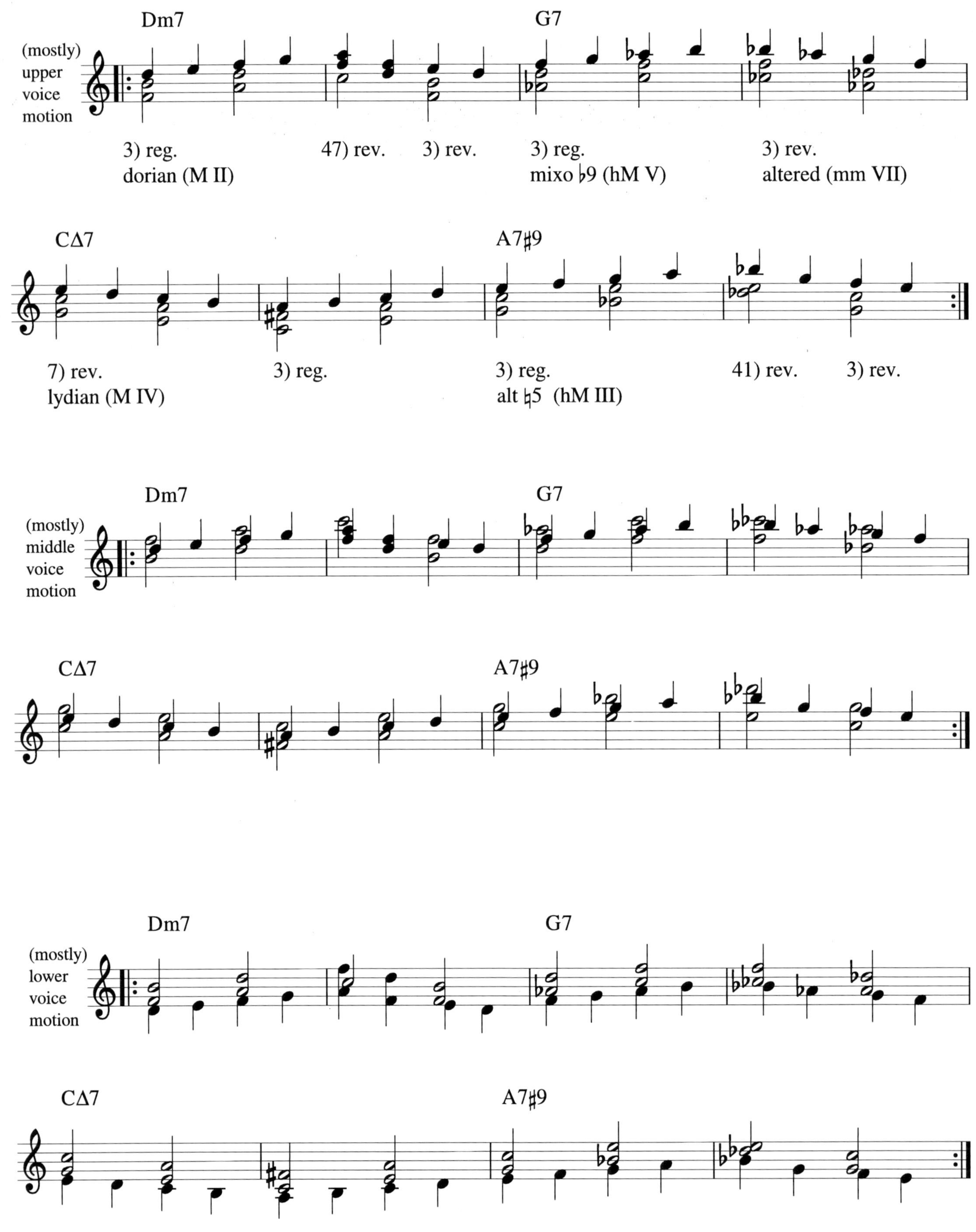

Etude 1.1

open

Moves start on beats 1 and 3

Variation C with (mostly) Single-Voice Motion in 3 Inversions

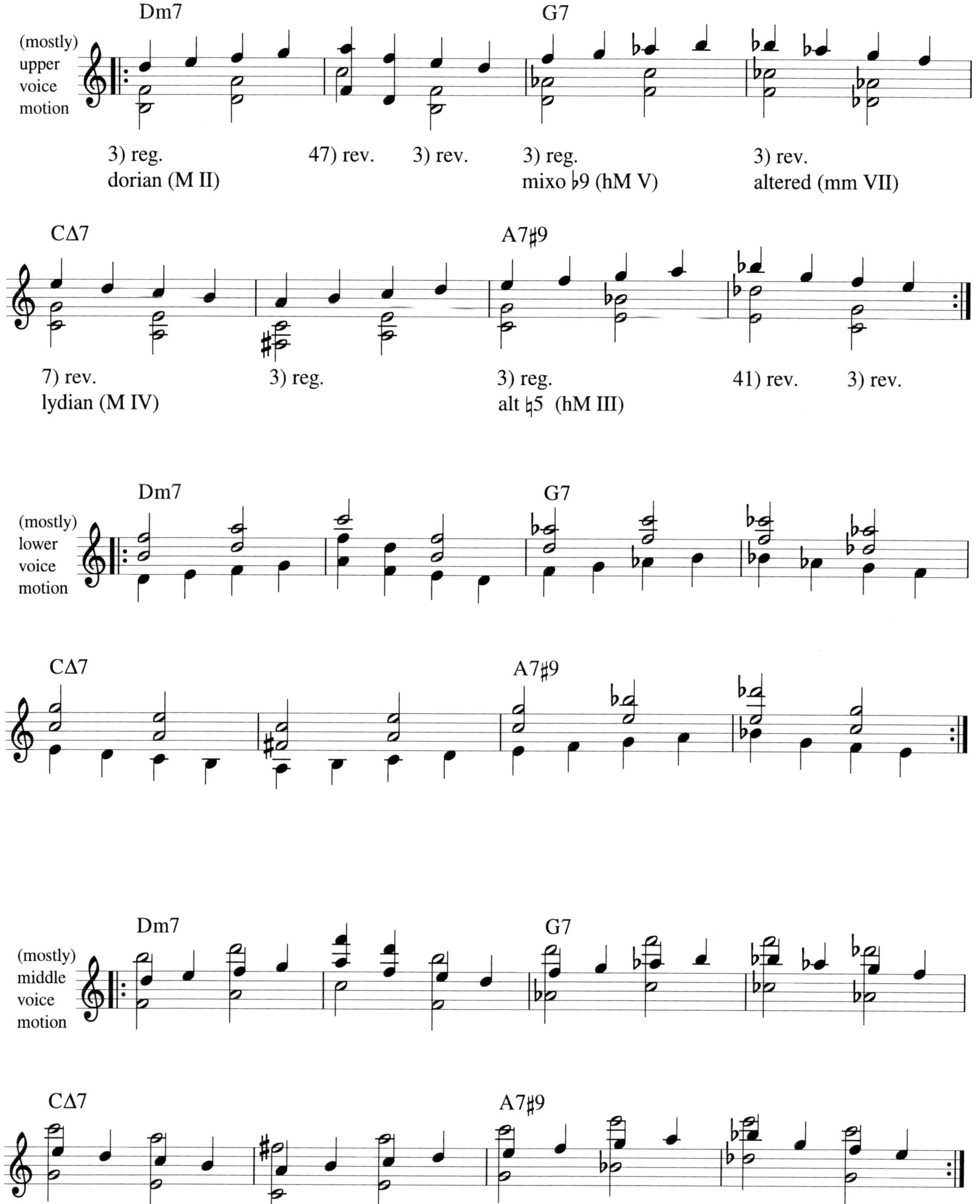

Etude 1.1

close

Moves start on beats 1 and 3

Variation D with (mostly) Single-Voice Motion in 3 Inversions

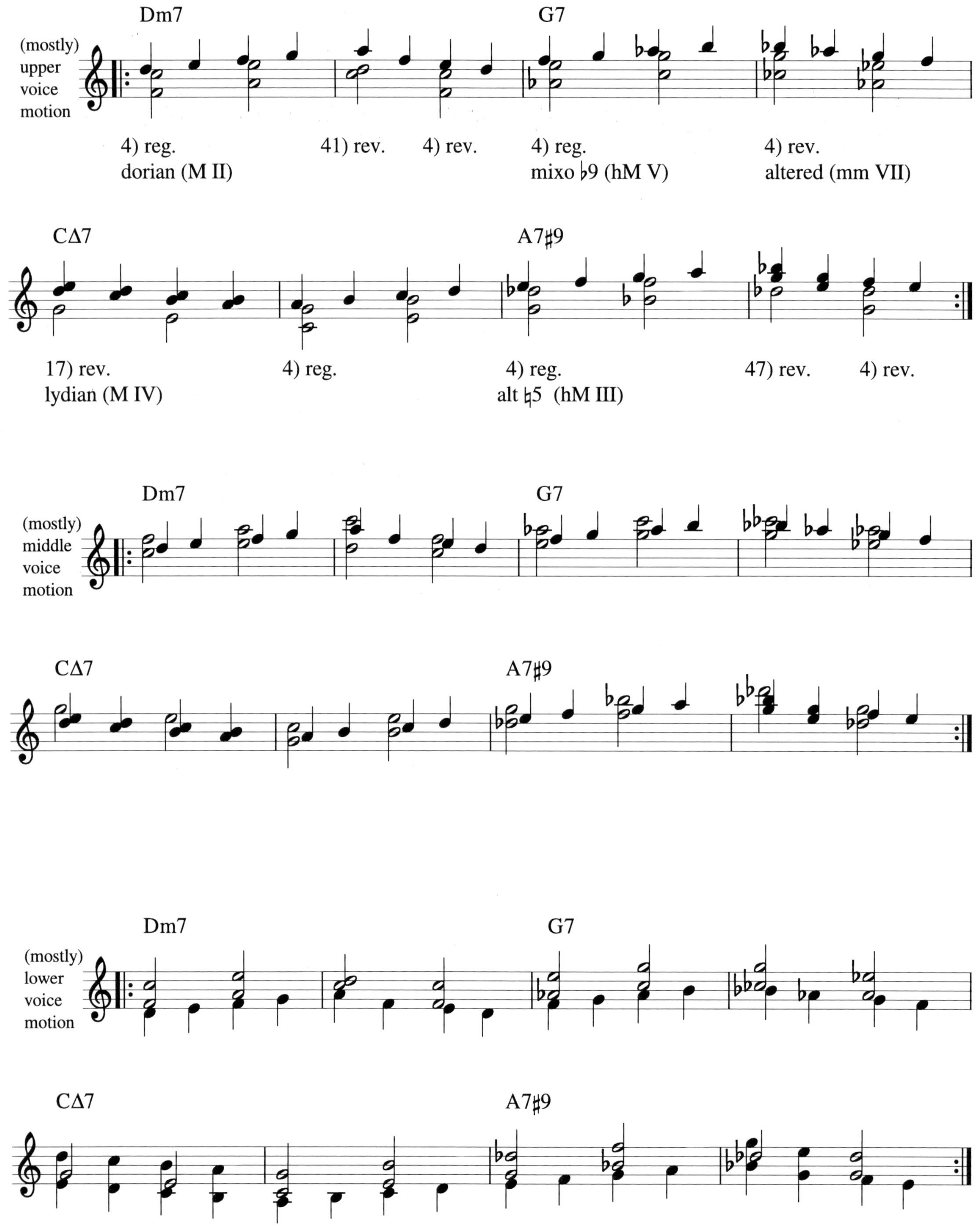

Etude 1.1

open

Moves start on beats 1 and 3

Variation D with (mostly) Single-Voice Motion in 3 Inversions

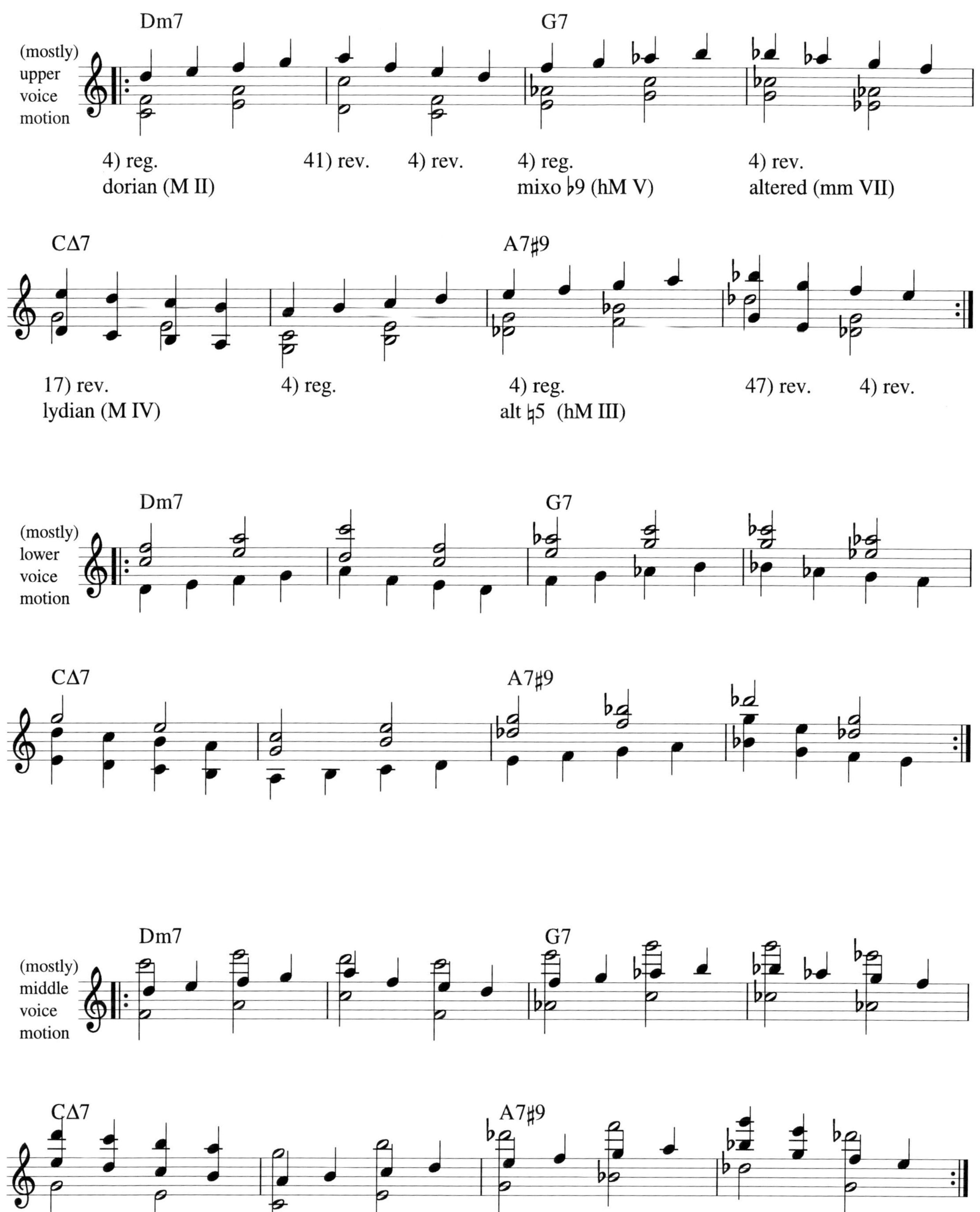

Etude 1.1

close

Moves start on beats 1 and 3

Variation E with Double-Voice Contrary Motion in 3 Inversions

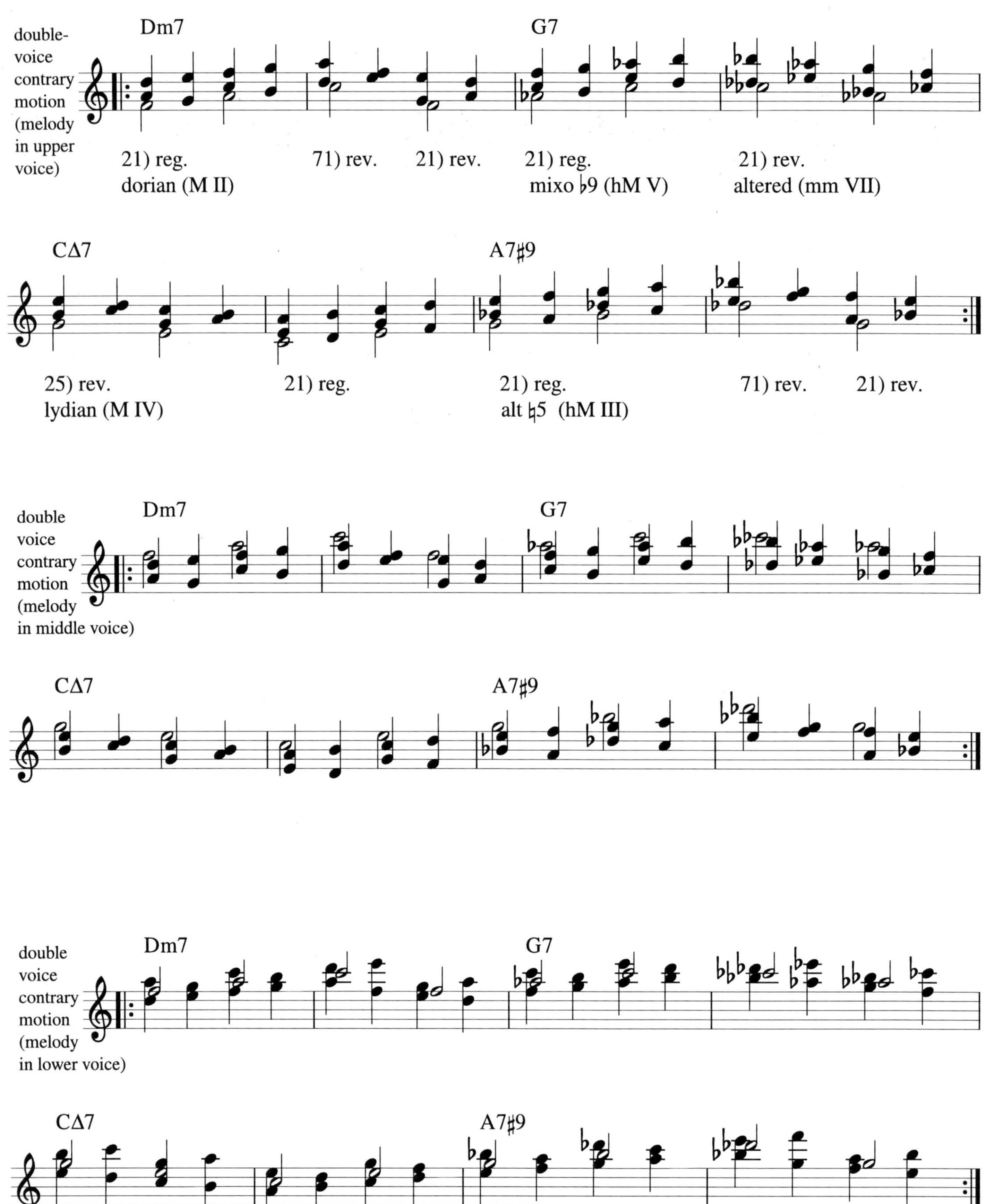

Etude 1.1

open

Moves start on beats 1 and 3

Variation E with Double-Voice Contrary Motion in 3 Inversions

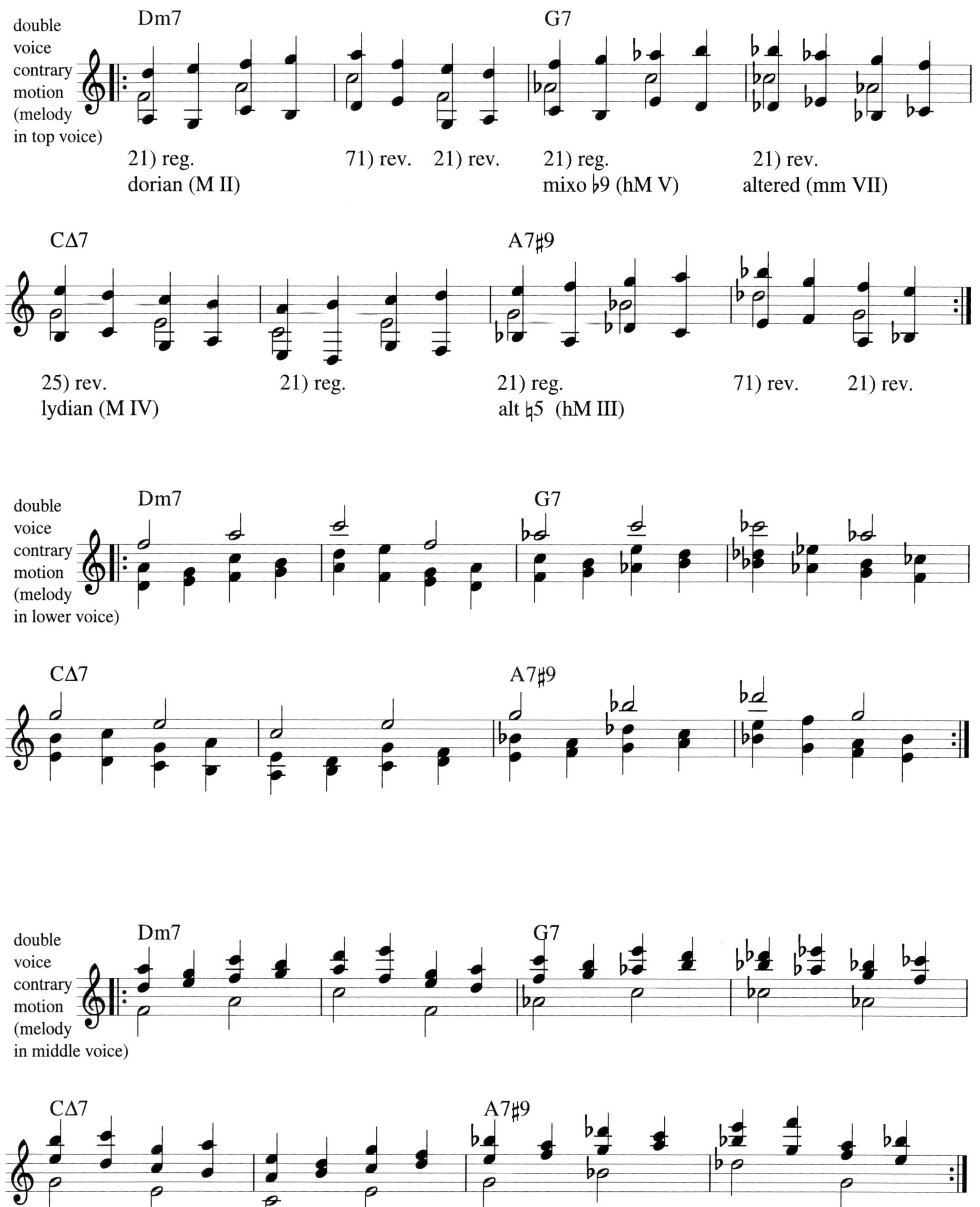

Etude 1.1

close

Moves start on beats 1 and 3

Variation F with Triple-Voice Contrary Motion in 3 Inversions

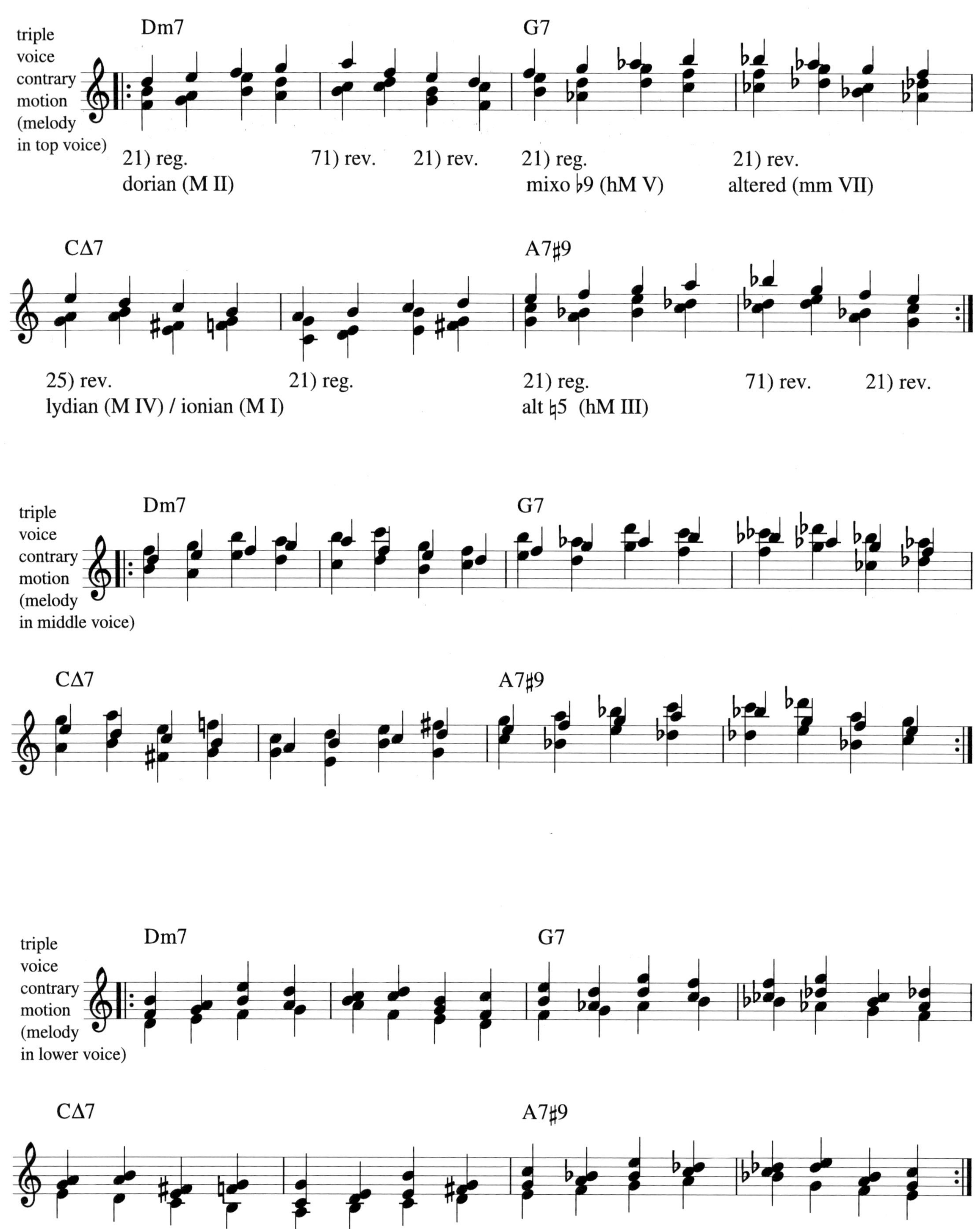

Etude 1.1

open

Moves start on beats 1 and 3

Variation F with Triple-Voice Contrary Motion in 3 Inversions

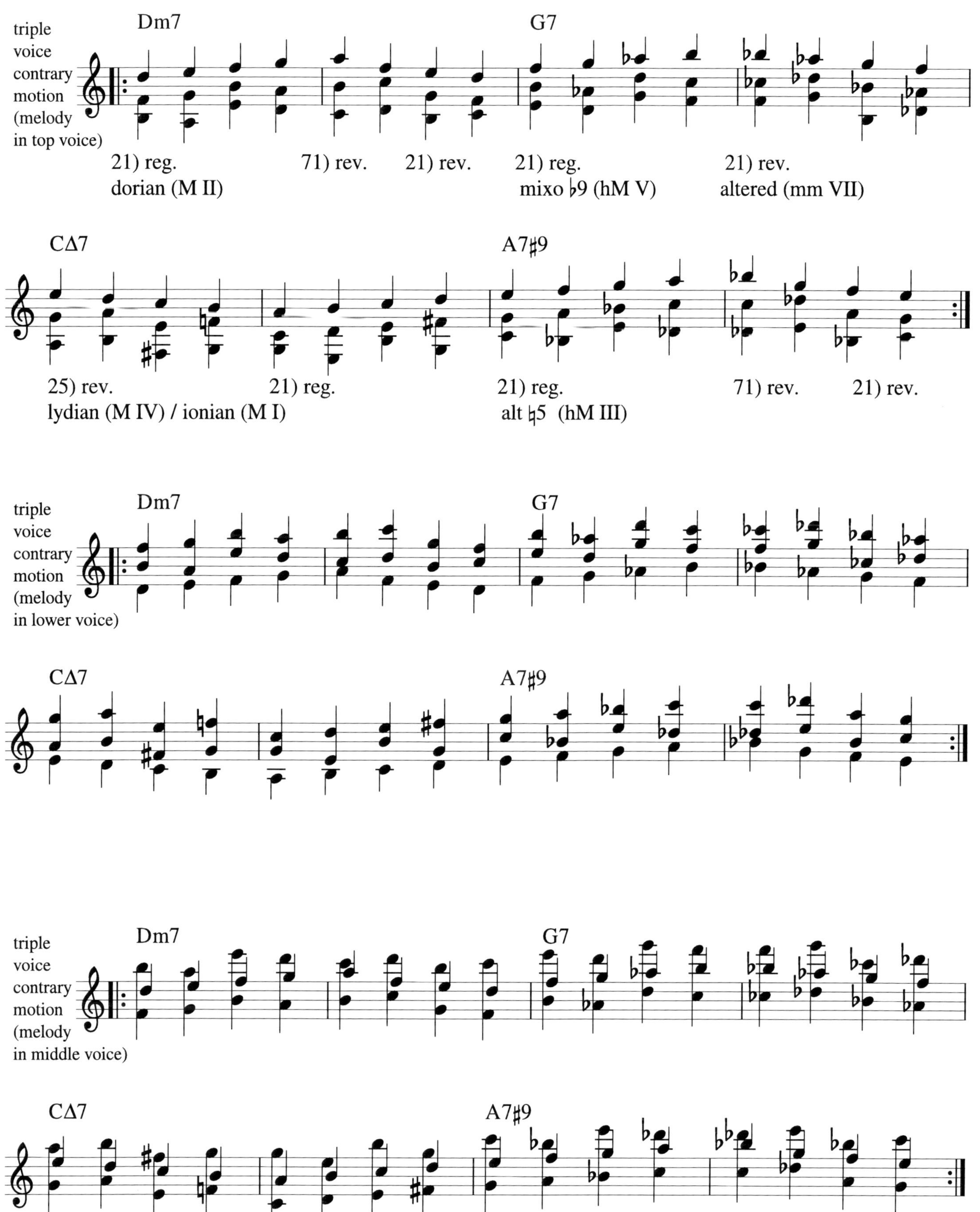

Etude 1.1

close

Moves start on beats 1 and 3

Variation G with Triple-Voice Contrary Motion in 3 Inversions

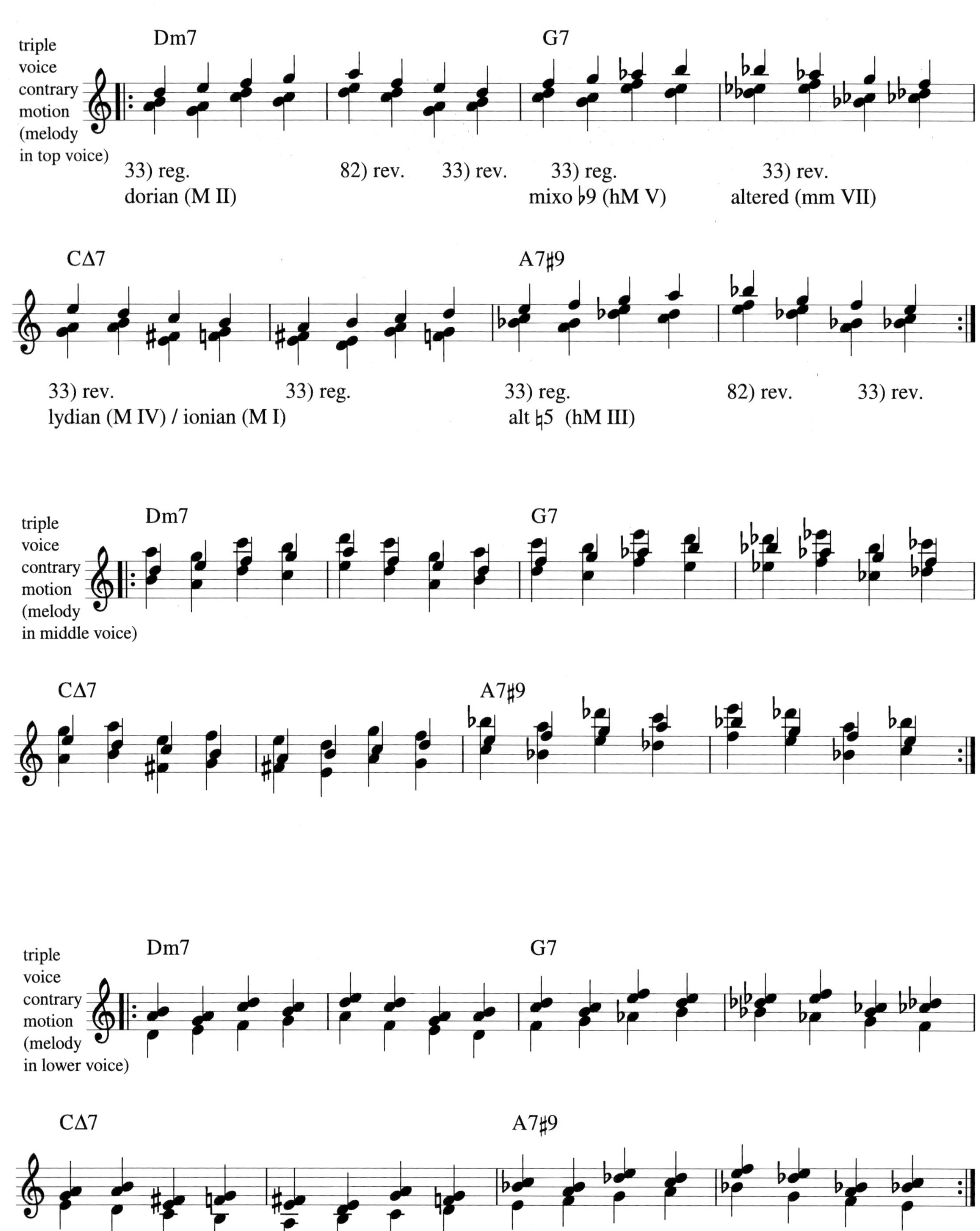

Etude 1.1

open

Moves start on beats 1 and 3

Variation G with Triple-Voice Contrary Motion in 3 Inversions

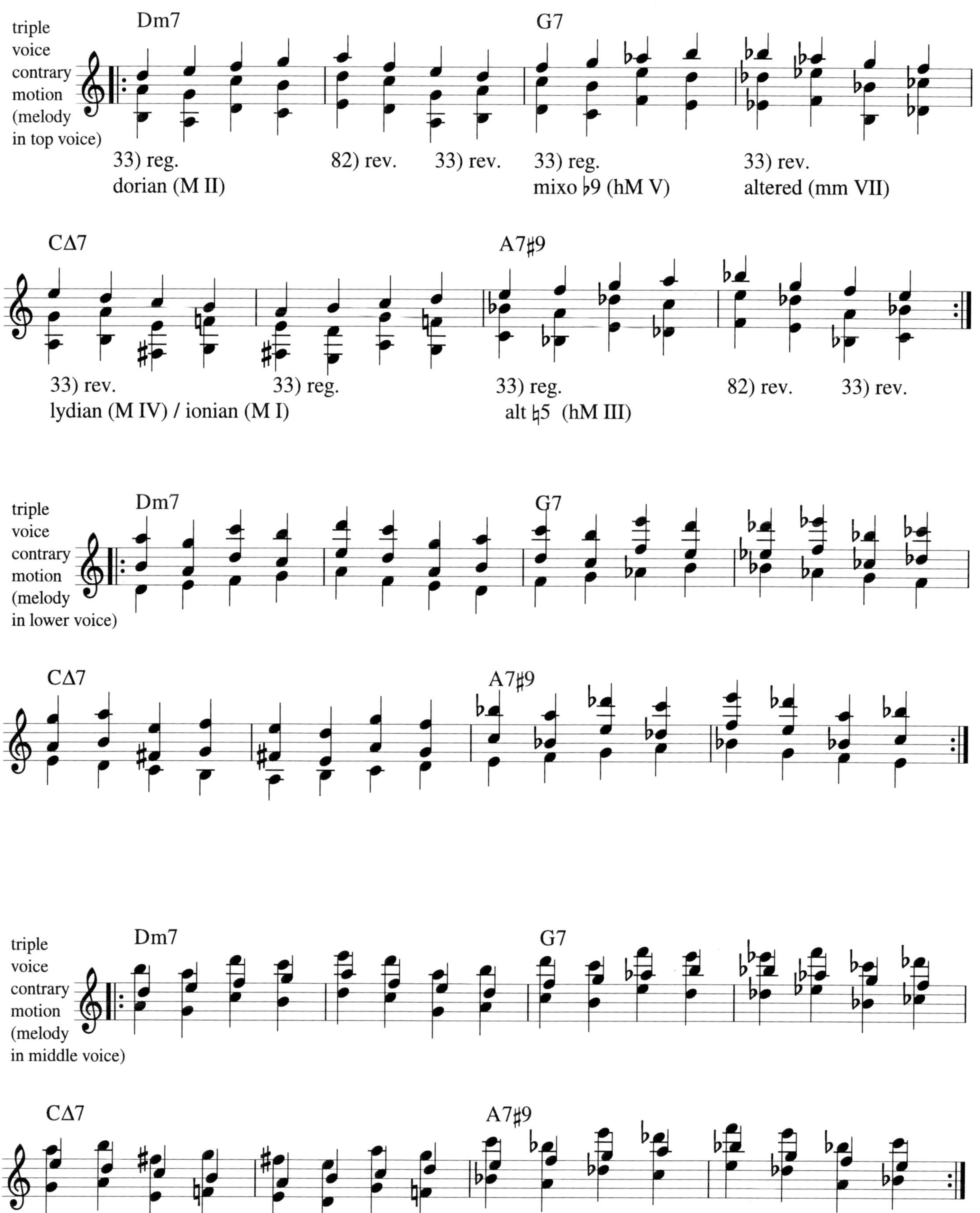

Etude 1.1

Moves start on beat 1 and 3
With Six Rhythmic Reductions of the Melody

These two pages show different ways to rhythmically reduce or thin-out the melody of the etude to single-out phrases and sets of moves from it, making them more accessible for application. Start by learning one of the preparatory exercises or variations of Etude 1.1 by heart, and then use its harmonization to play through the following rhythmic reductions of the melody.

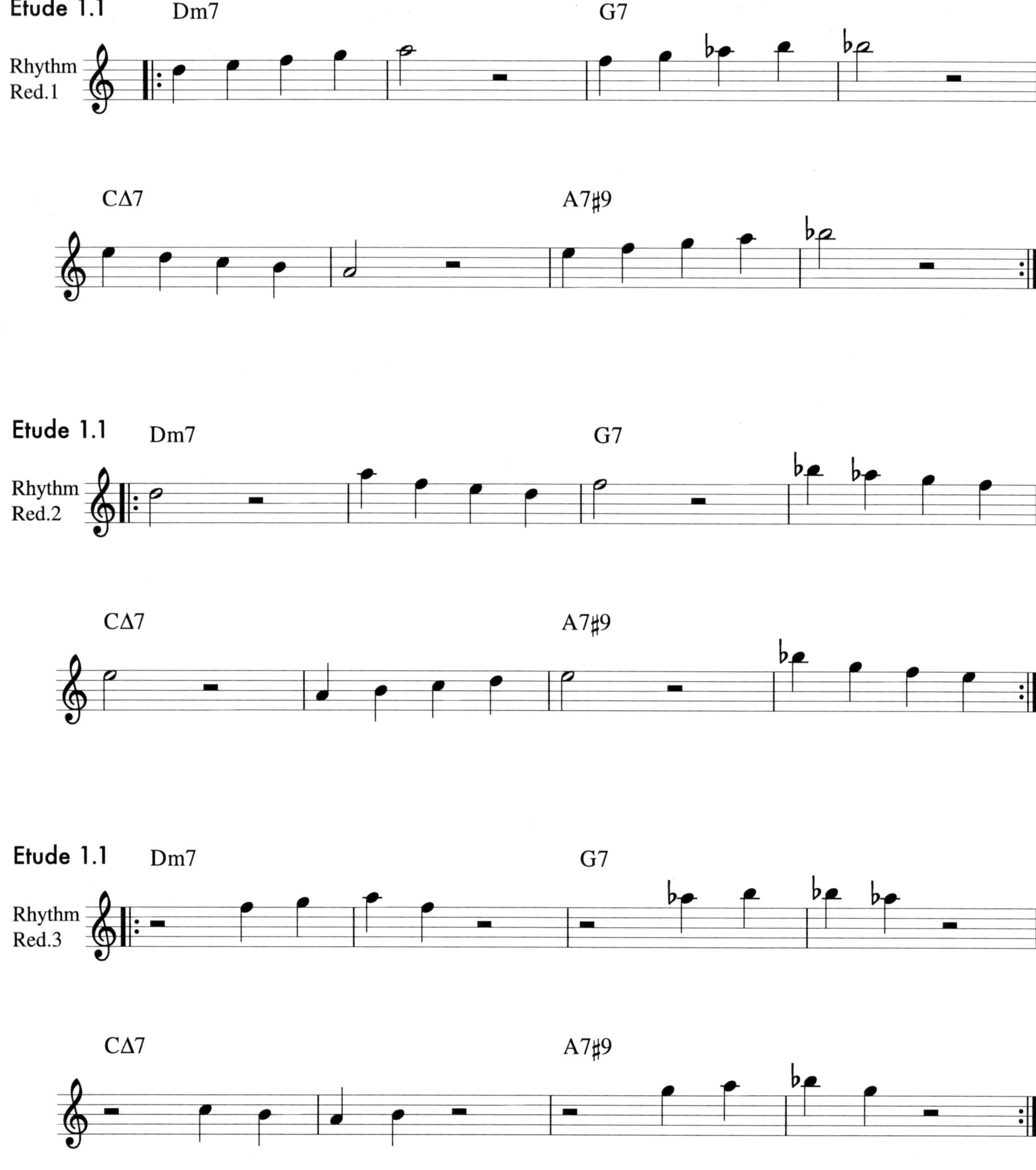

Etude 1.1
Six Rhythmic Reductions cont...

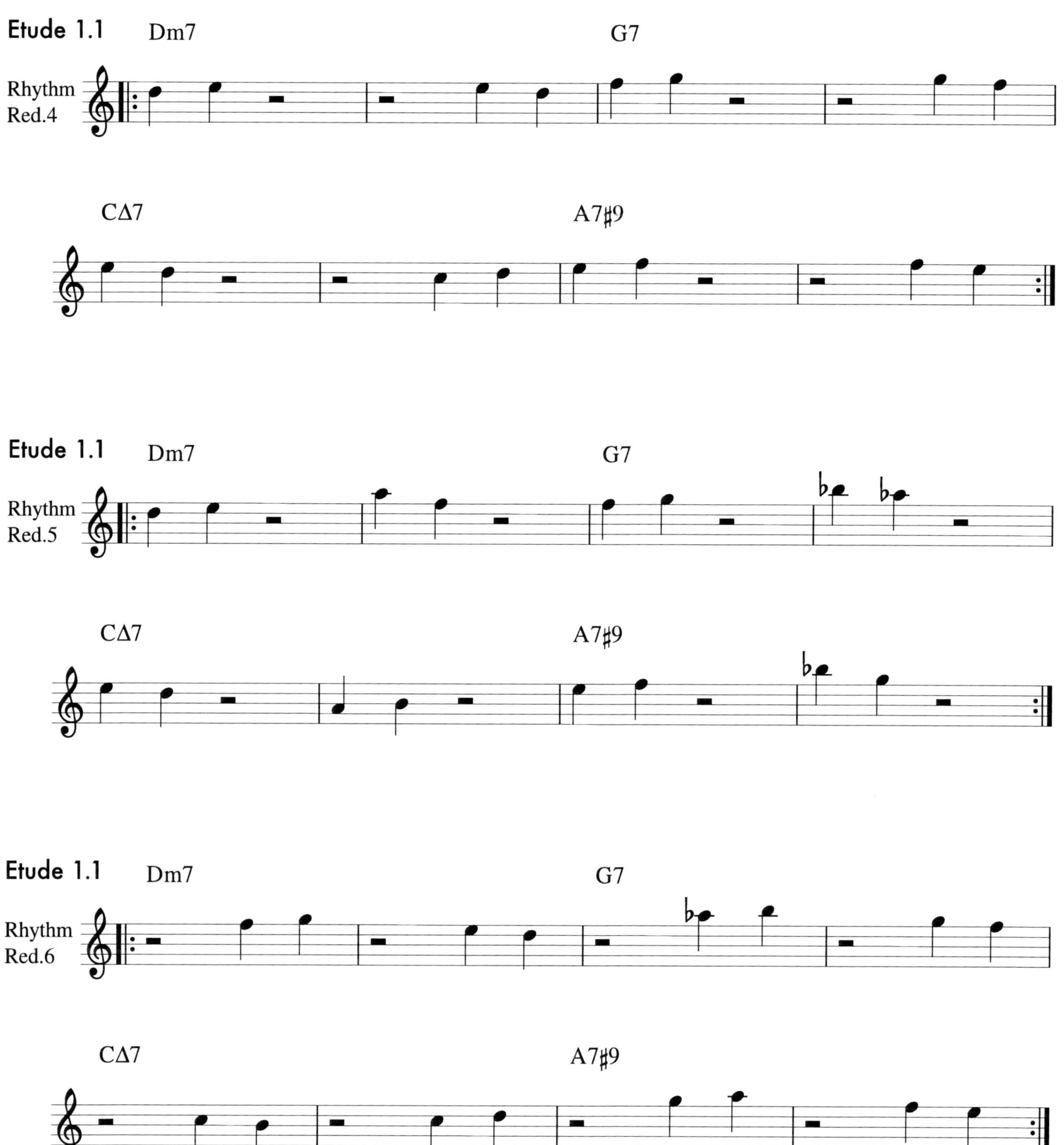

Etude 1.2

close

Moves start on beats 2 and 4
Variation A with Single-Voice Motion in 3 Inversions

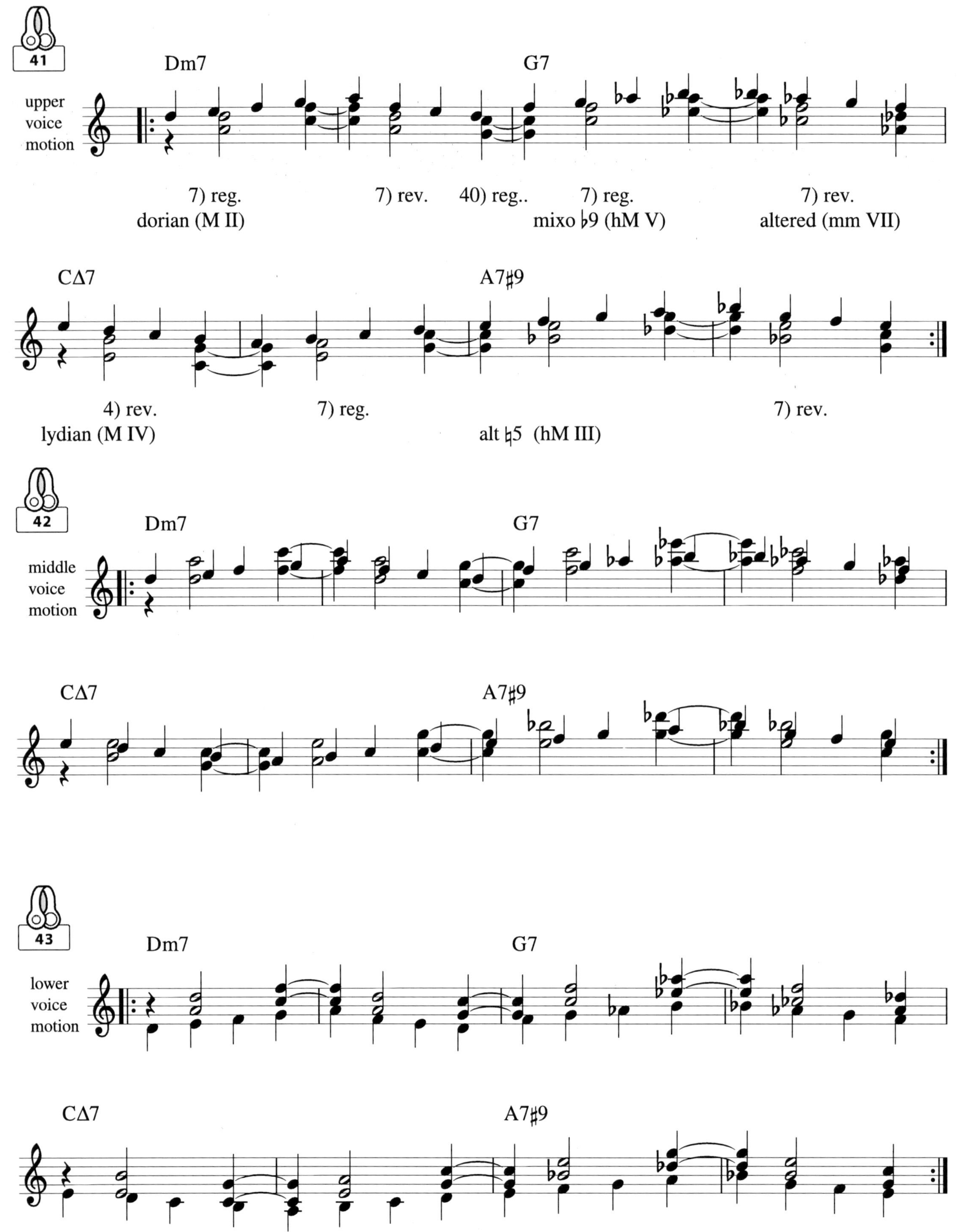

Etude 1.2

open

Moves start on beats 2 and 4

Variation A with Single-Voice Motion in 3 Inversions

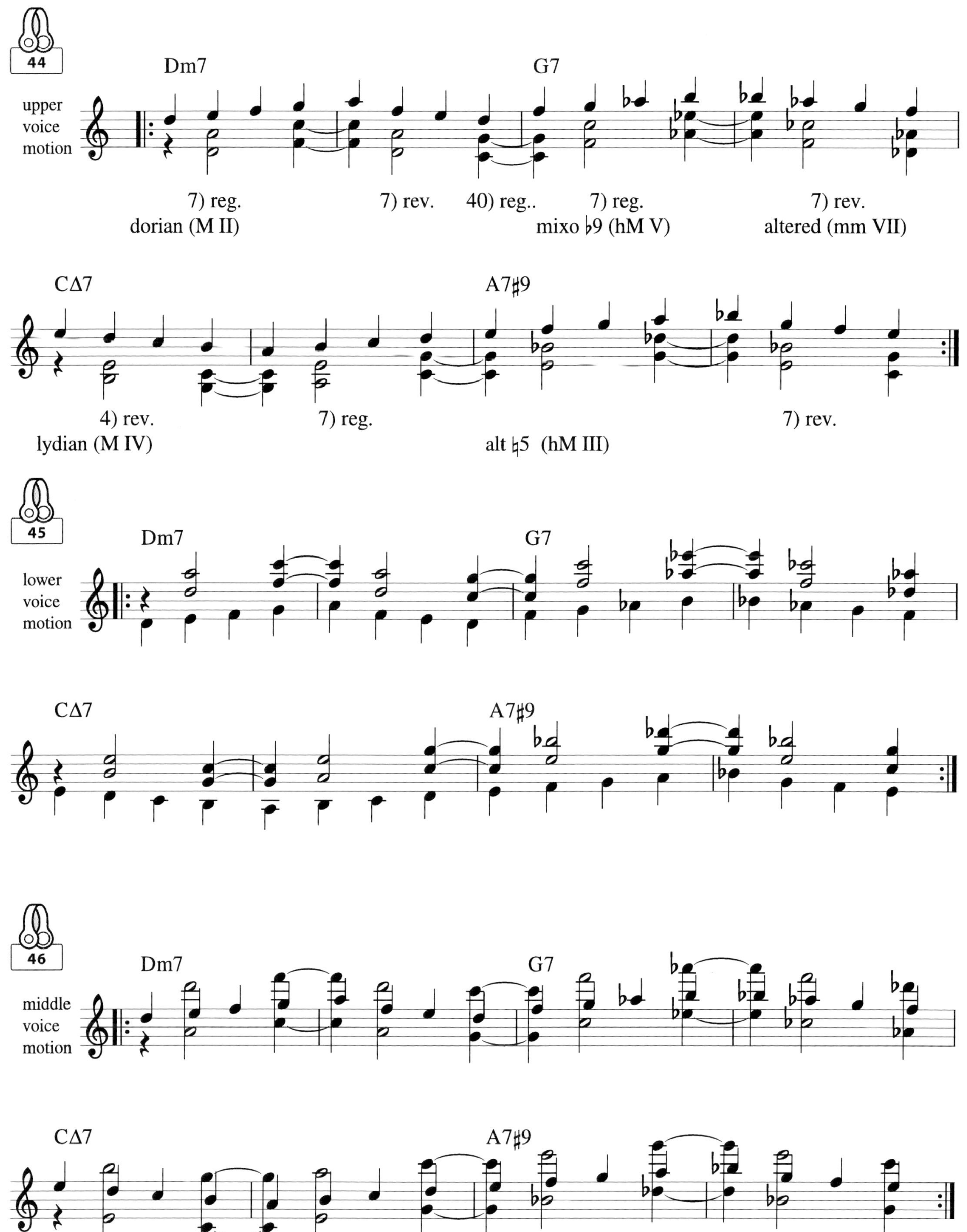

Etude 1.2

close

Moves start on beats 2 and 4

Variation B with Single-Voice Motion in 3 Inversions

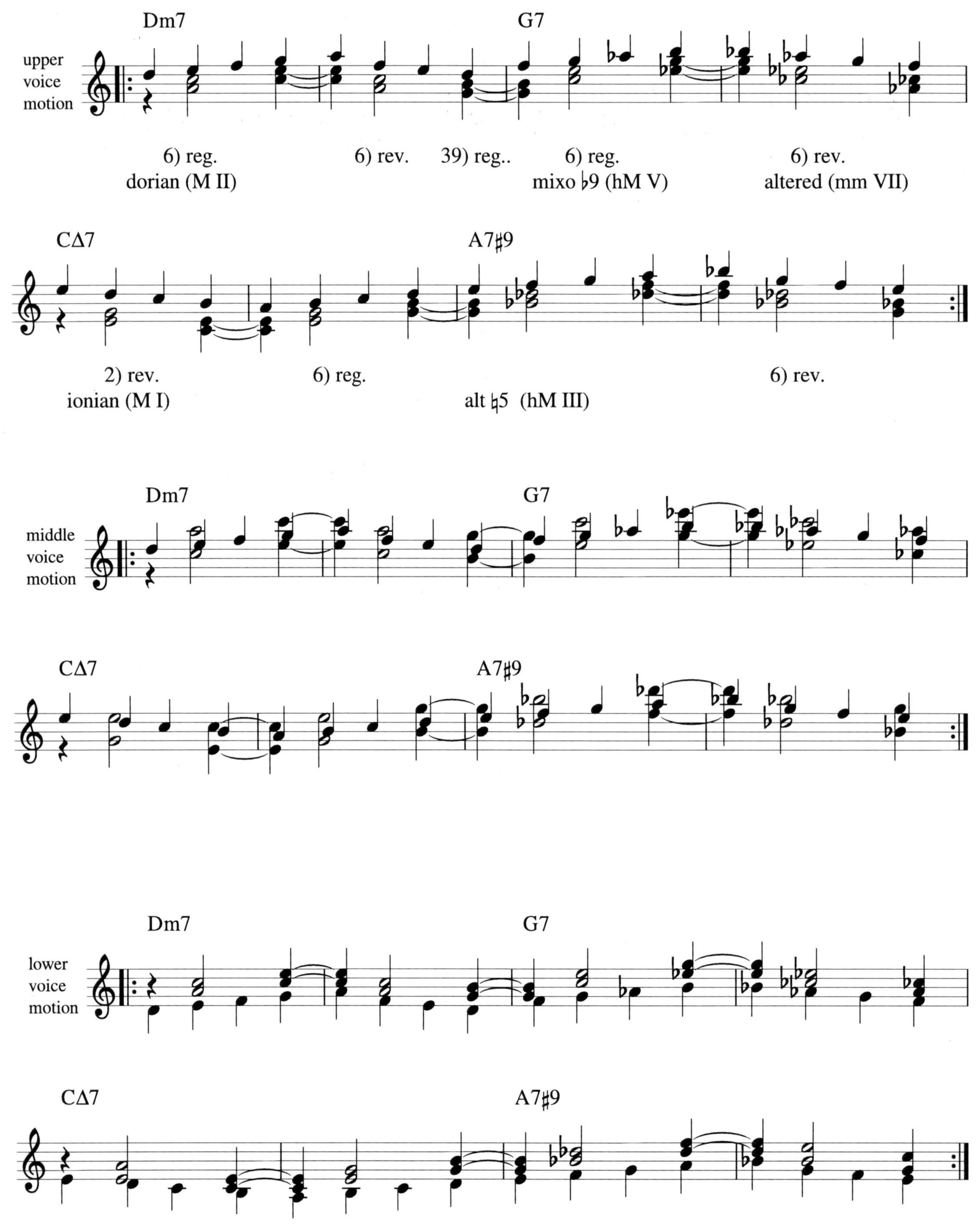

Etude 1.2

open

Moves start on beats 2 and 4

Variation B with Single-Voice Motion in 3 Inversions

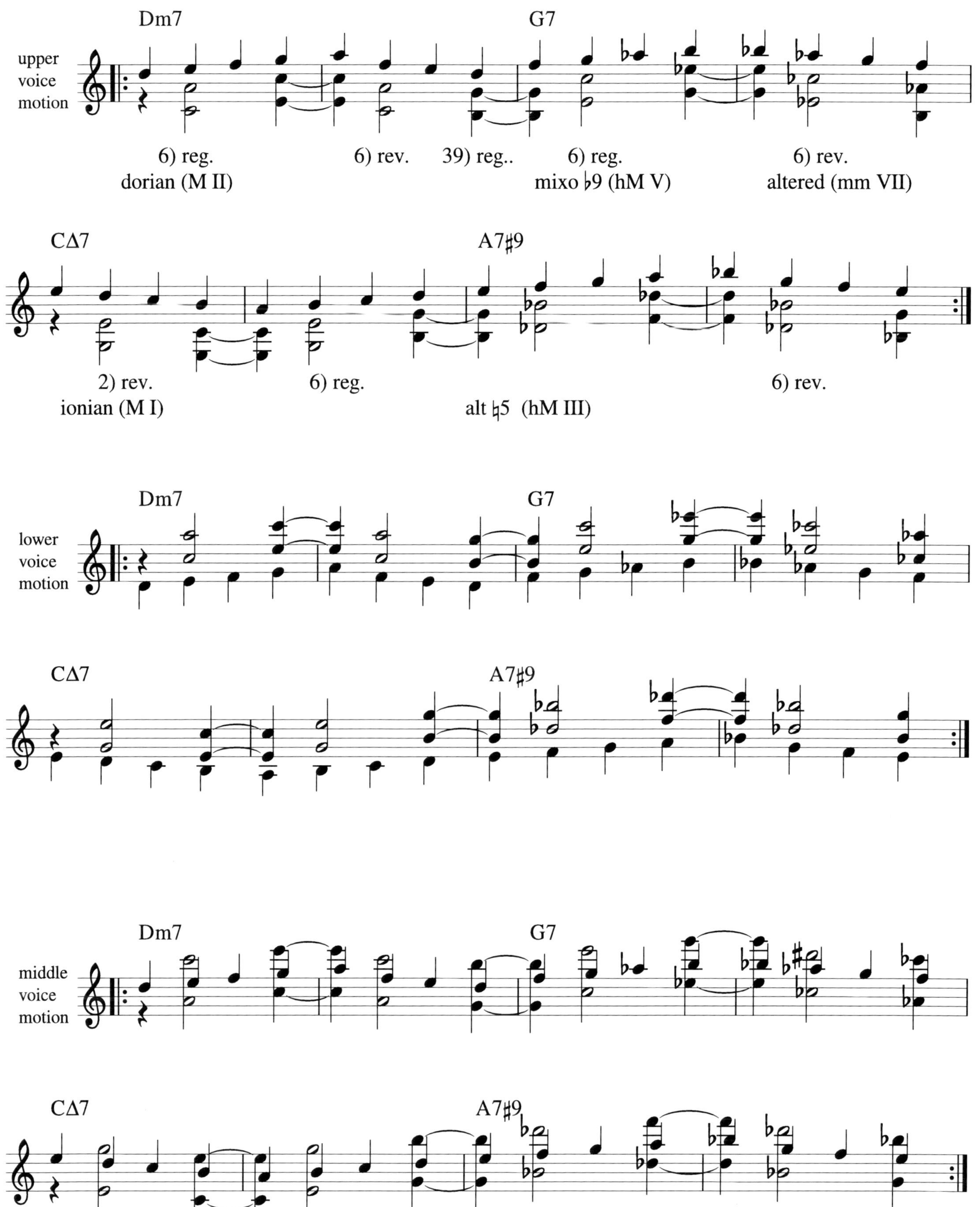

Etude 1.2

close

Moves start on beats 2 and 4

Variation C with (mostly) Single-Voice Motion in 3 Inversions

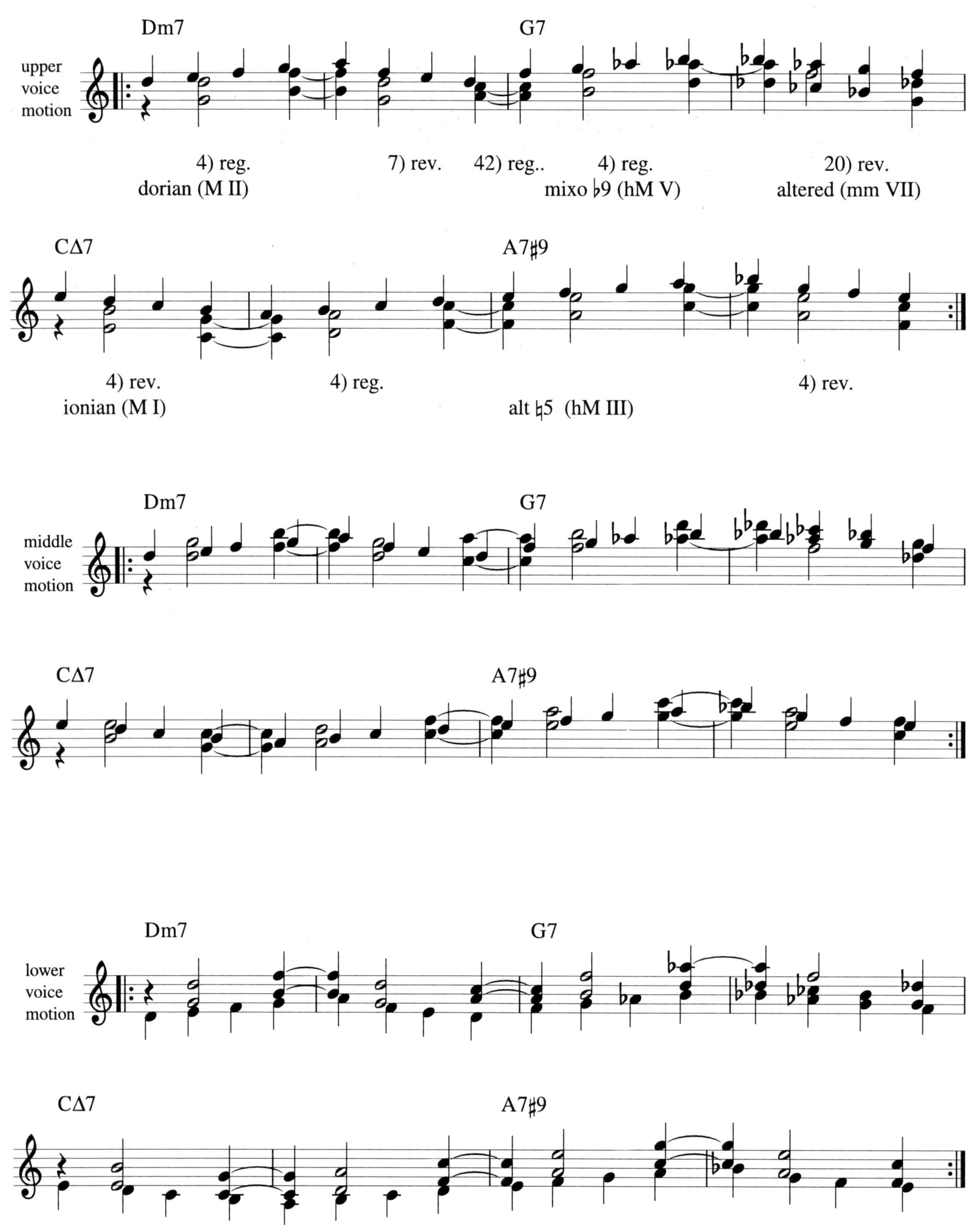

Etude 1.2

open

Moves start on beats 2 and 4

Variation C with (mostly) Single-Voice Motion in 3 Inversions

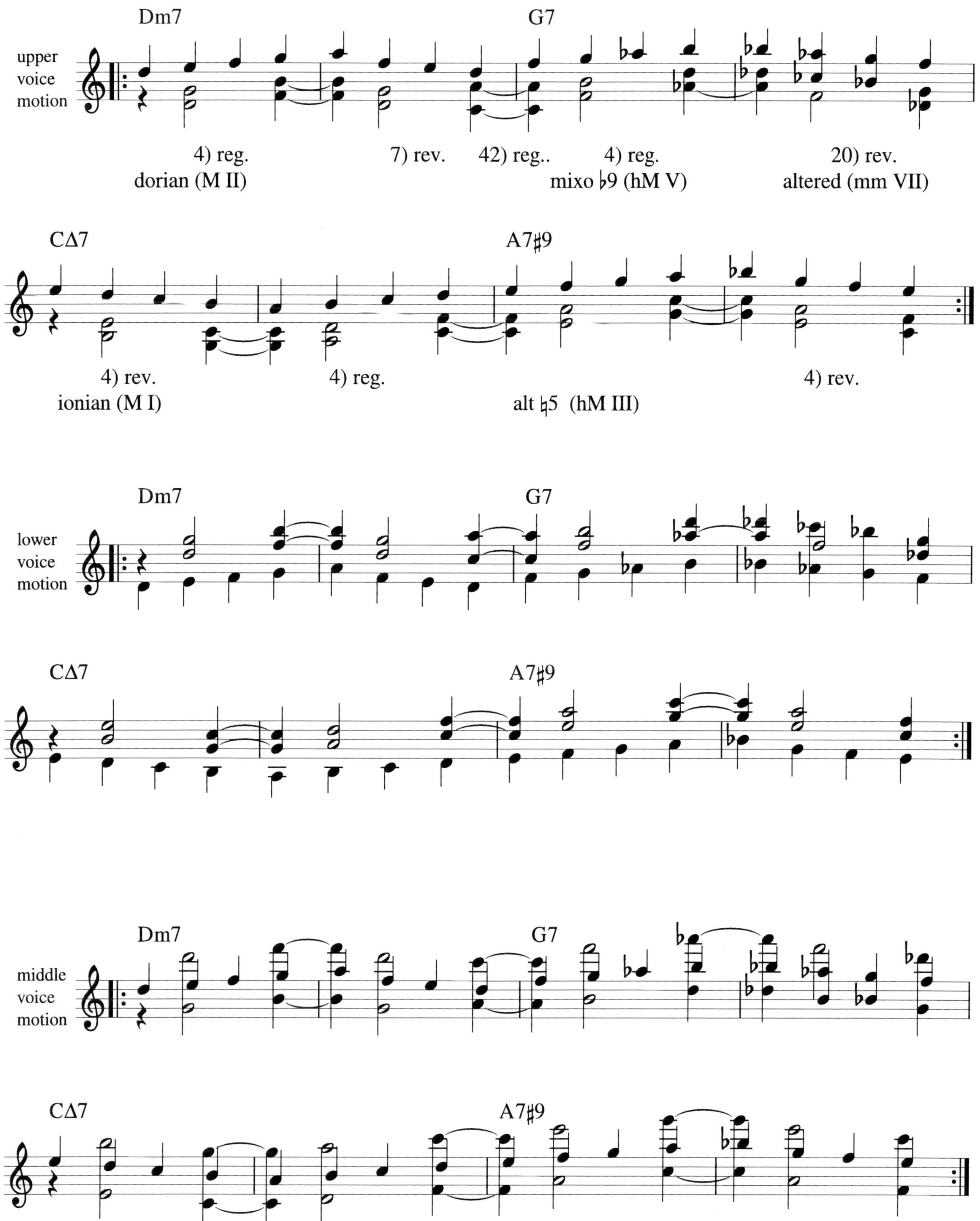

Etude 1.2

close

Moves start on beats 2 and 4

Variation D with Double-Voice Contrary Motion in 3 Inversions

double voice contrary motion (melody in upper voice)

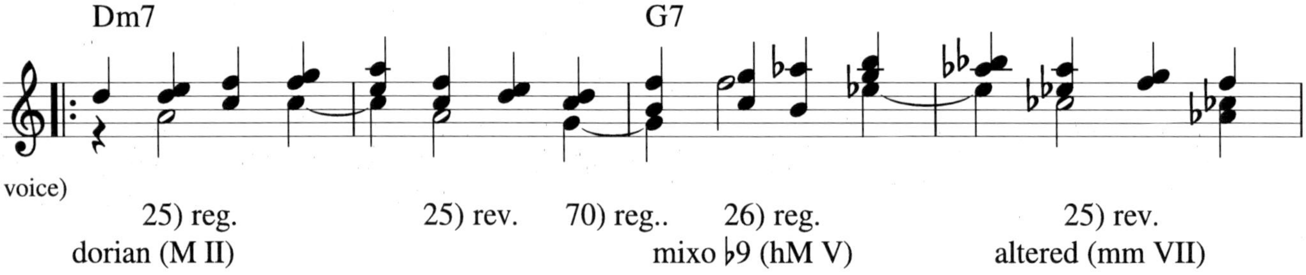

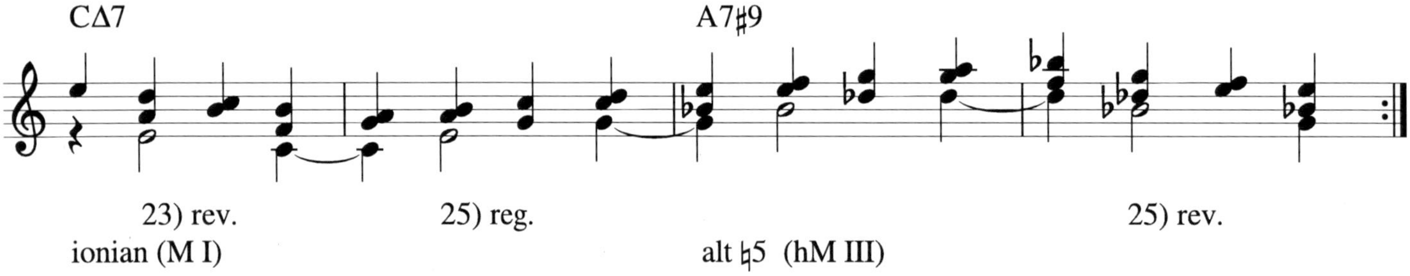

Dm7 G7

25) reg. 25) rev. 70) reg.. 26) reg. 25) rev.

dorian (M II) mixo ♭9 (hM V) altered (mm VII)

C∆7 A7♯9

23) rev. 25) reg. 25) rev.

ionian (M I) alt ♮5 (hM III)

double voice contrary motion (melody in middle voice)

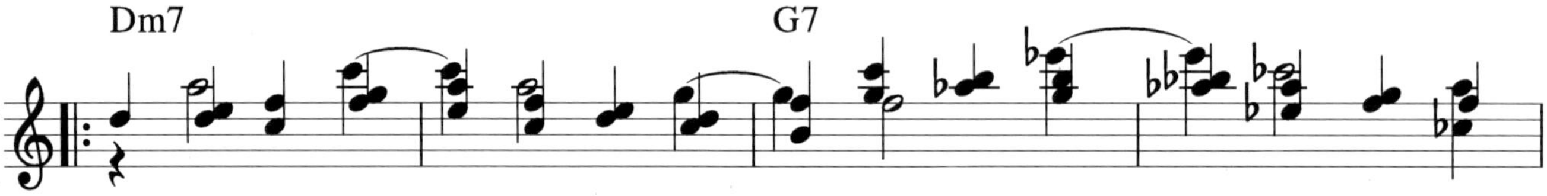

Dm7 G7

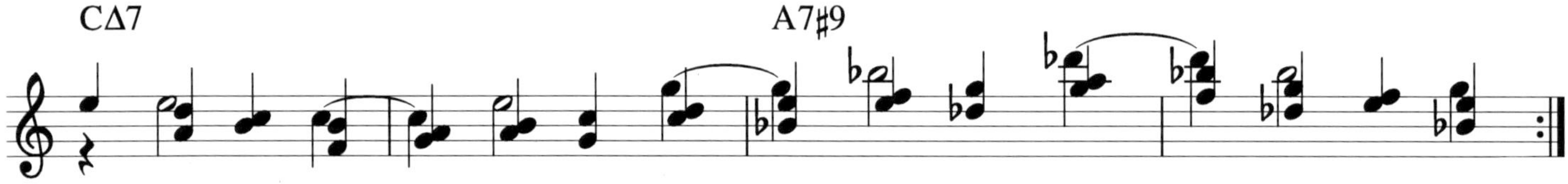

C∆7 A7♯9

double voice contrary motion (melody in lower voice)

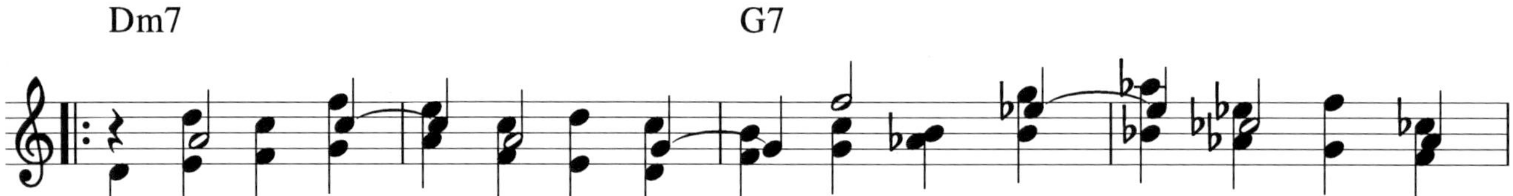

Dm7 G7

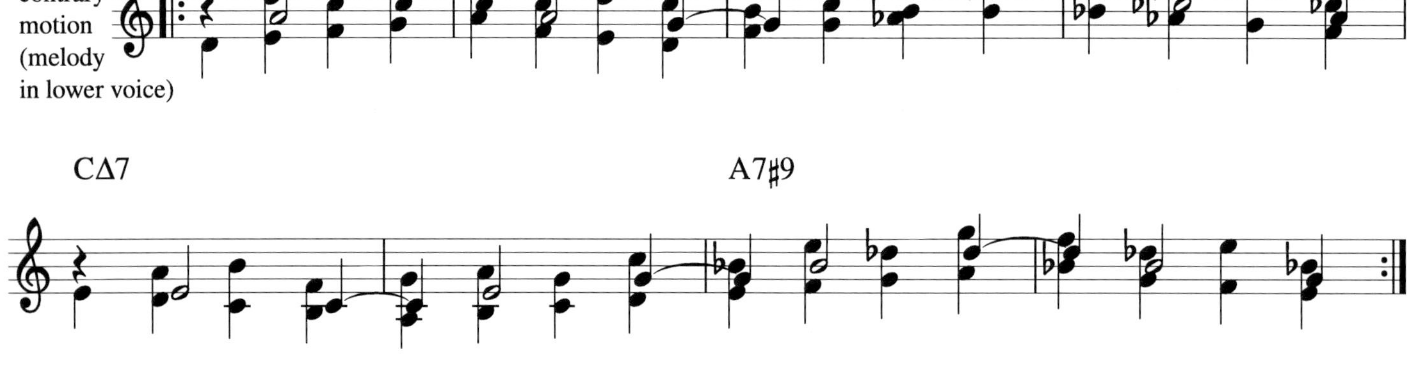

Etude 1.2

open

Moves start on beats 2 and 4

Variation D with Double-Voice Contrary Motion in 3 Inversions

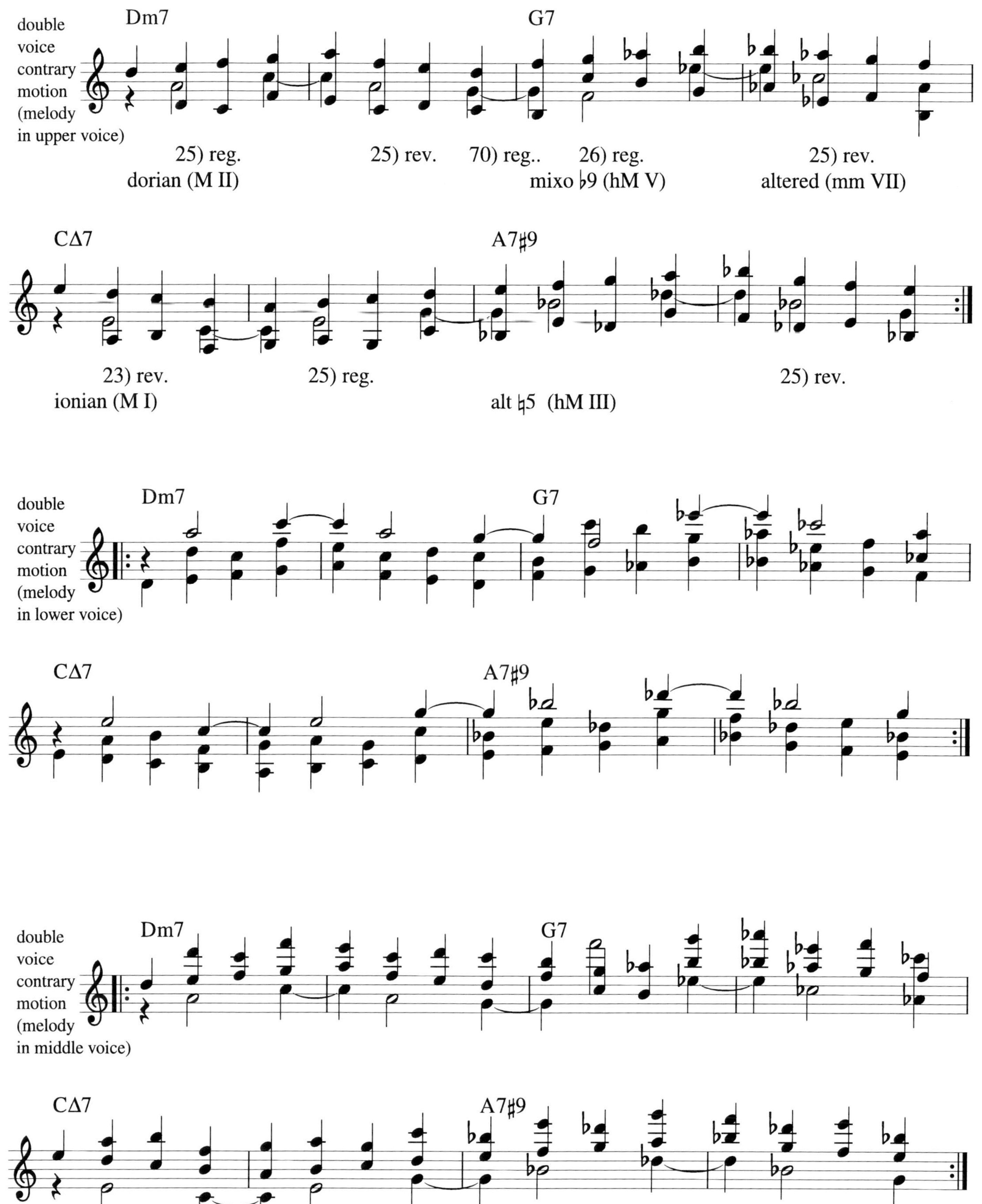

Etude 1.2

close

Moves start on beats 2 and 4

Variation E with Triple-Voice Contrary Motion in 3 Inversions

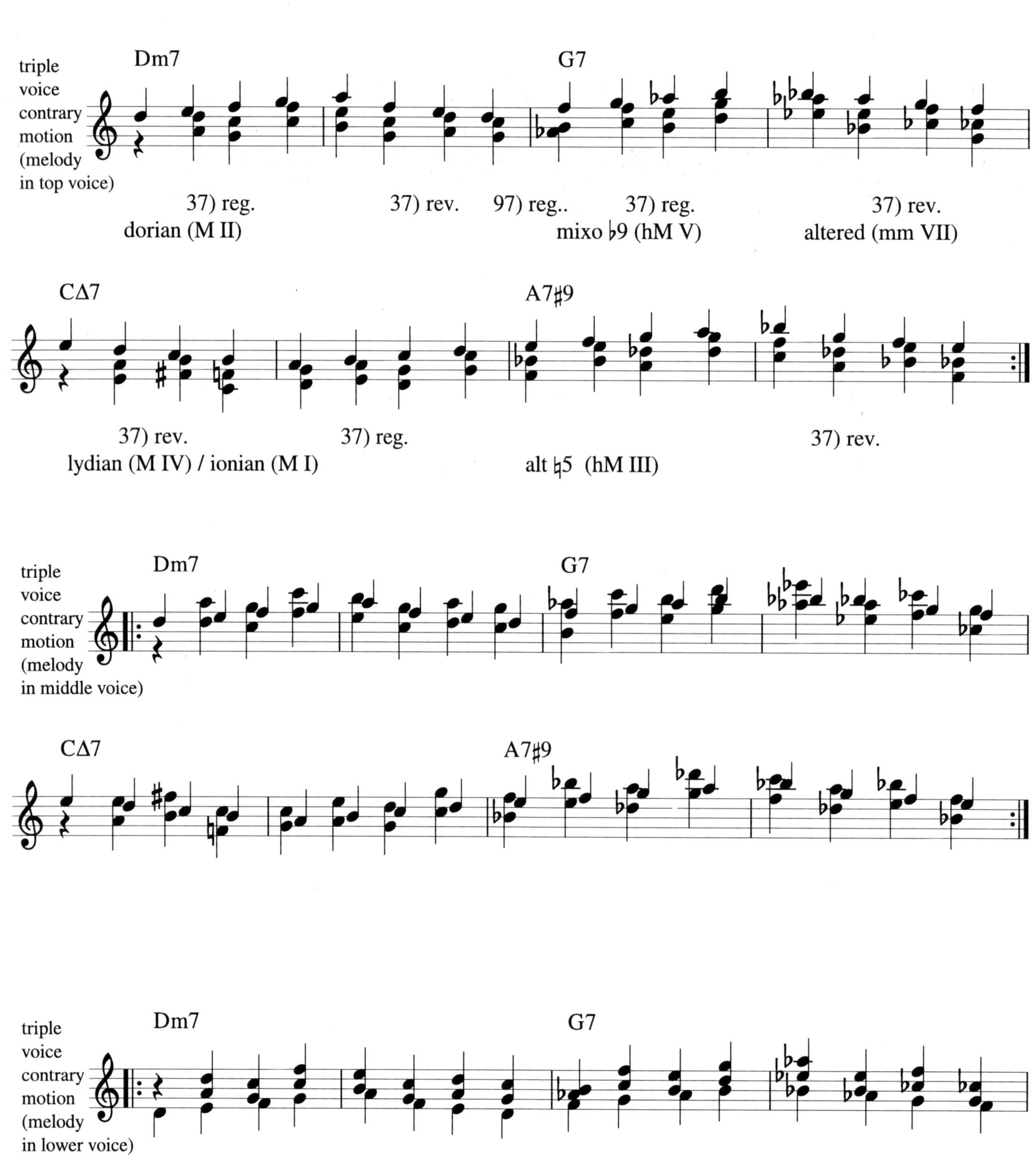

Etude 1.2

open

Moves start on beats 2 and 4

Variation E with Triple-Voice Contrary Motion in 3 Inversions

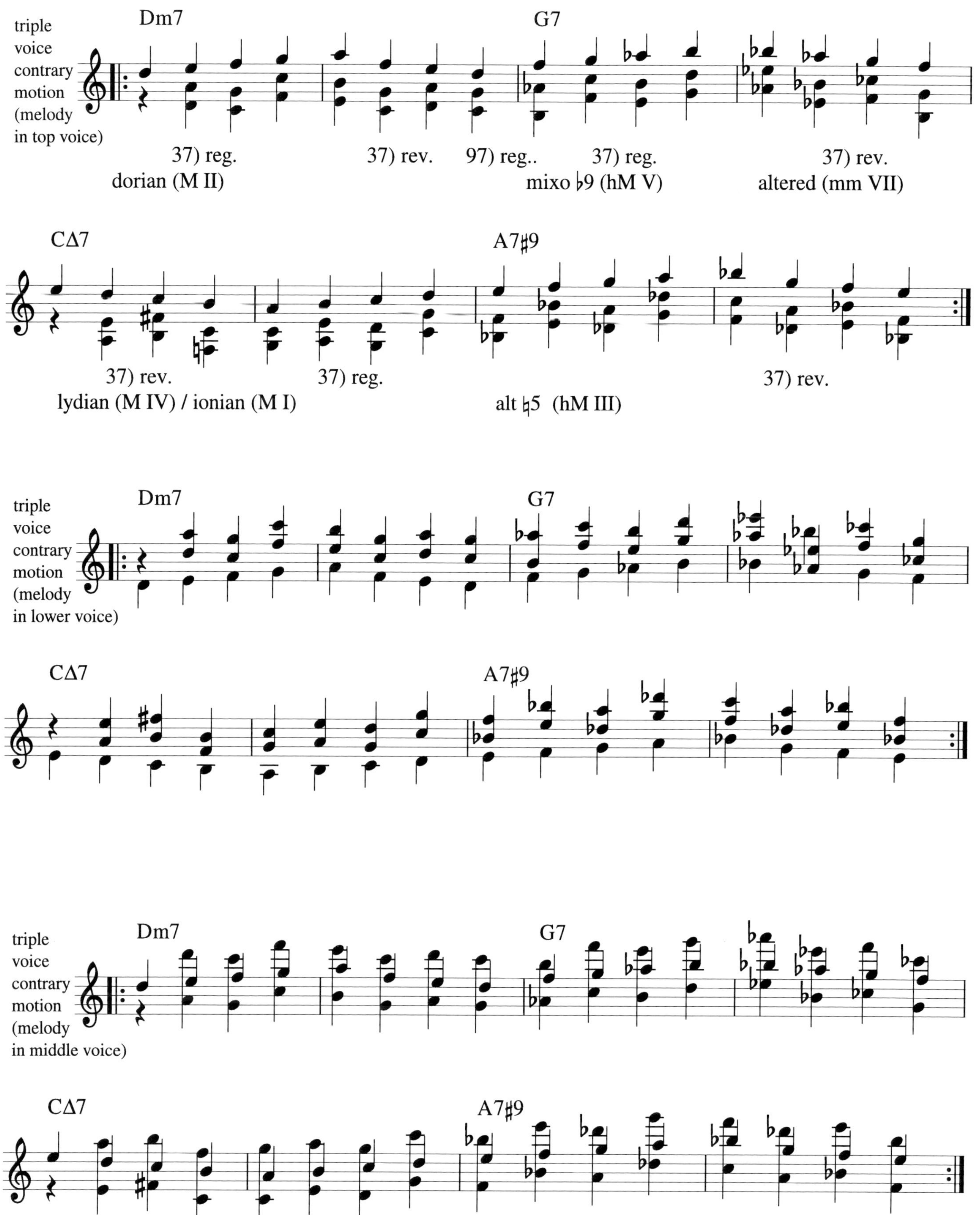

Etude 1.2

Moves start on beat 2 and 4

With Six Rhythmic Reductions of the Melody

Apply to all variations and preparatory exercises.

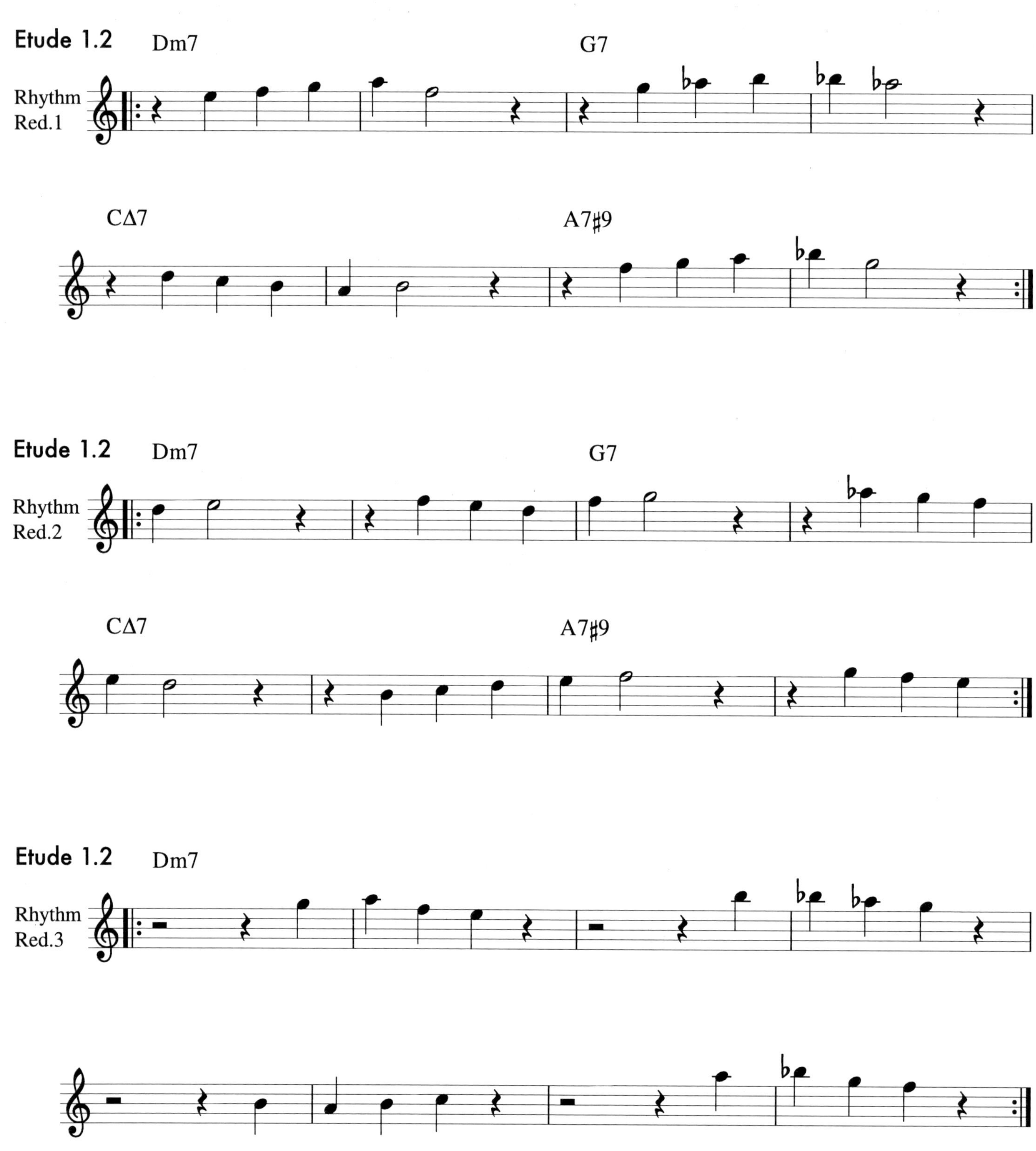

Etude 1.2
Six Rhythmic Reductions cont...

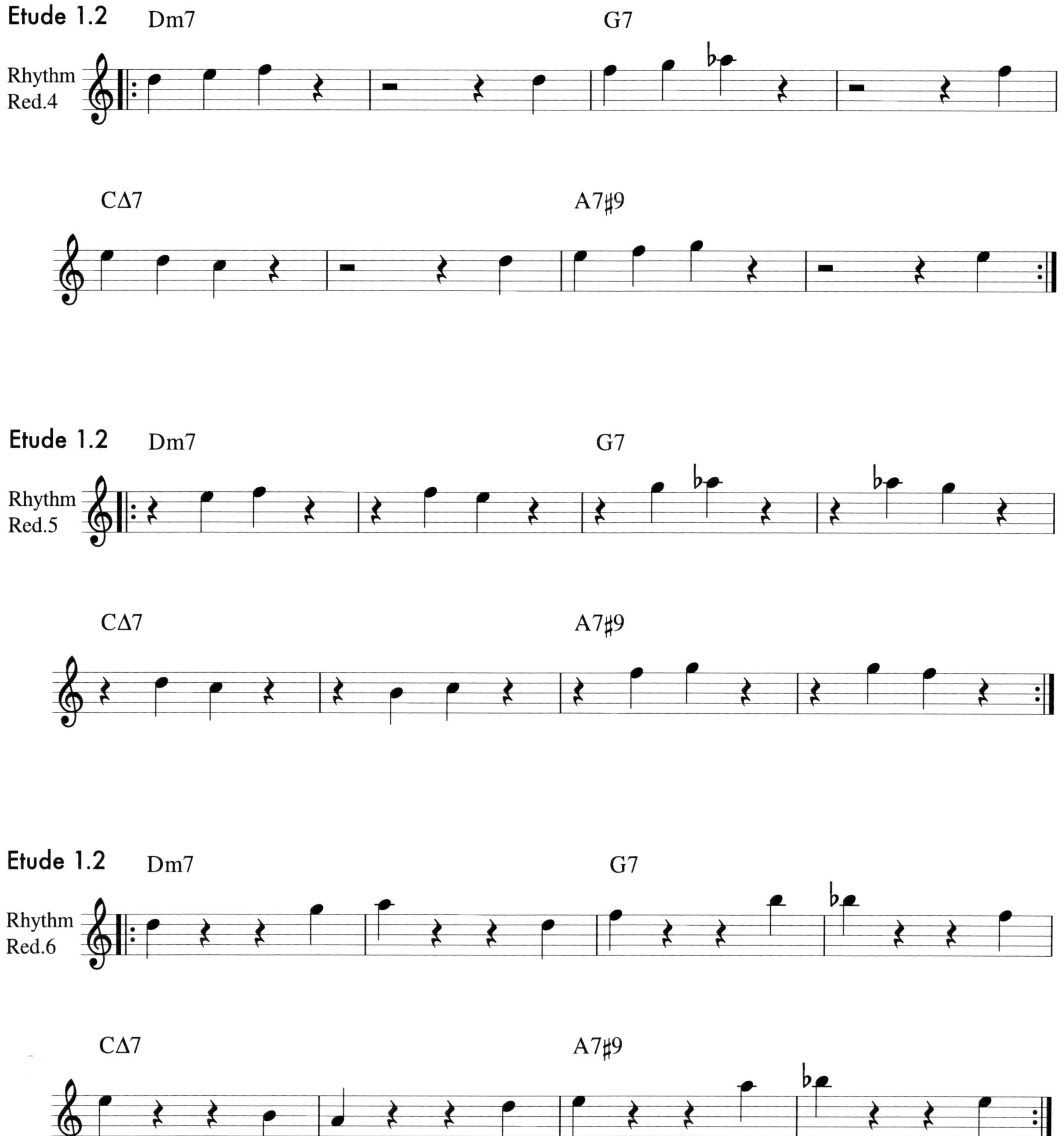

Etude 1.3

close

Moves start on alternating odd and even beats in single-voice motion.
Apply other moves if applicable, and try inversions as well.

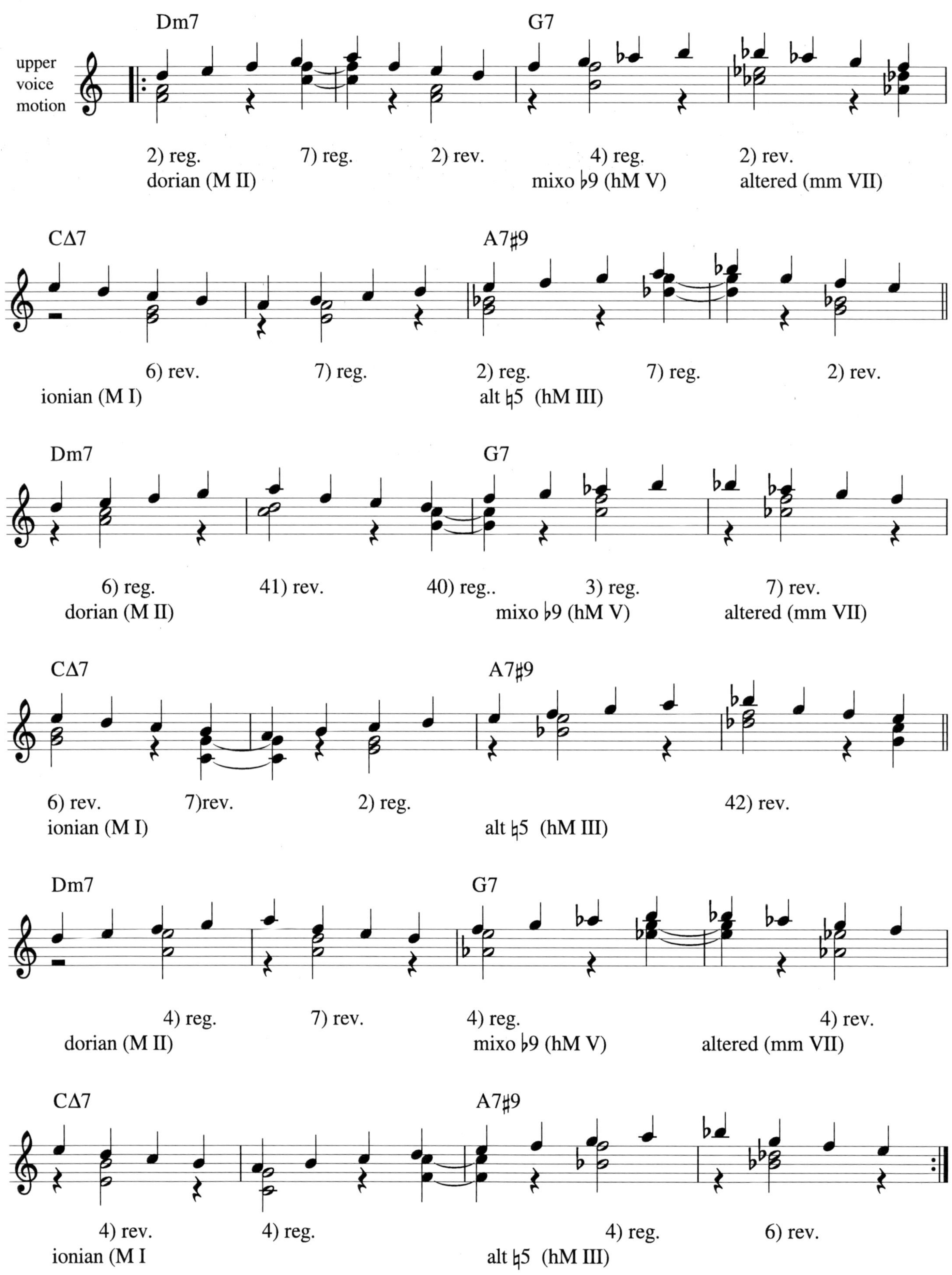

Etude 1.3

open

Moves start on alternating odd and even beats in single-voice motion.

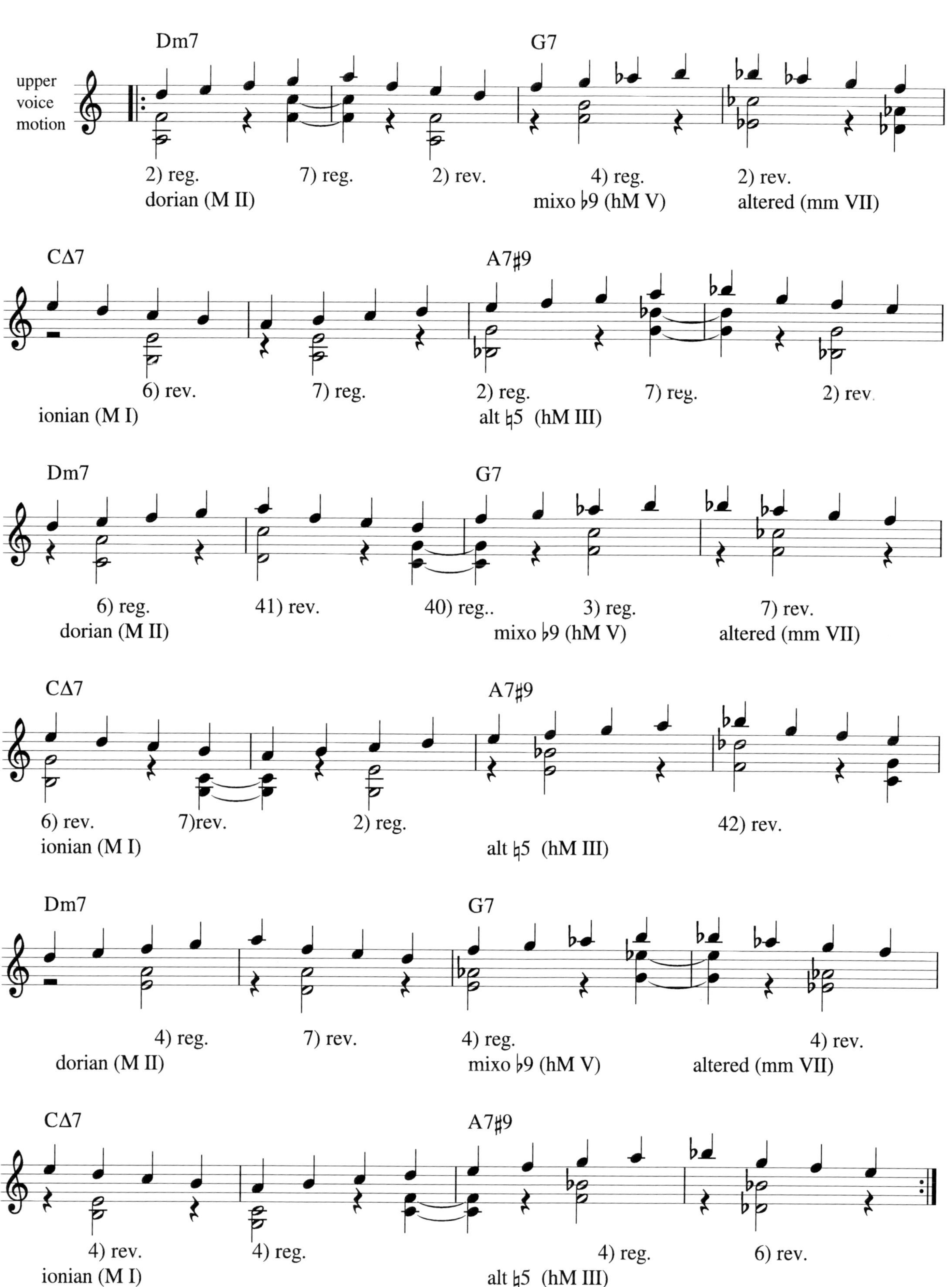

Etude 1.3

Moves/phrases start on odd and even beats, alternating.
Two rhythmic reductions of the melody.
Apply to preparatory exercises and experiment with all applicable voice motion moves.

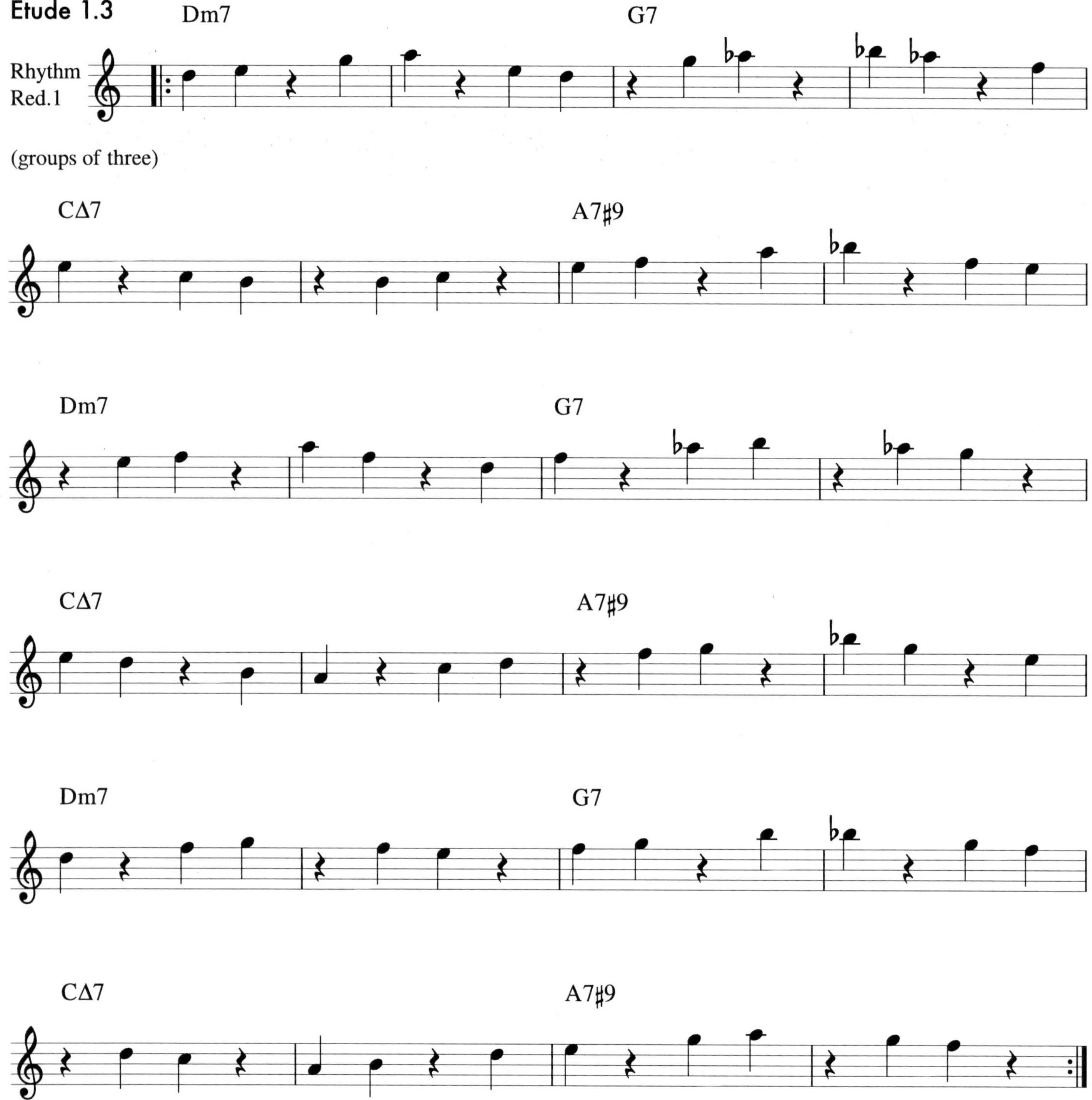

Etude 1.3

This second rhythmic reduction does not exactly reflect the way the moves start in the etude. Apply the rhythm anyways and study how it relates to the placement of the moves, adding another rhythmic layer; or use any applicable move employing the note pairs as you read through the piece.

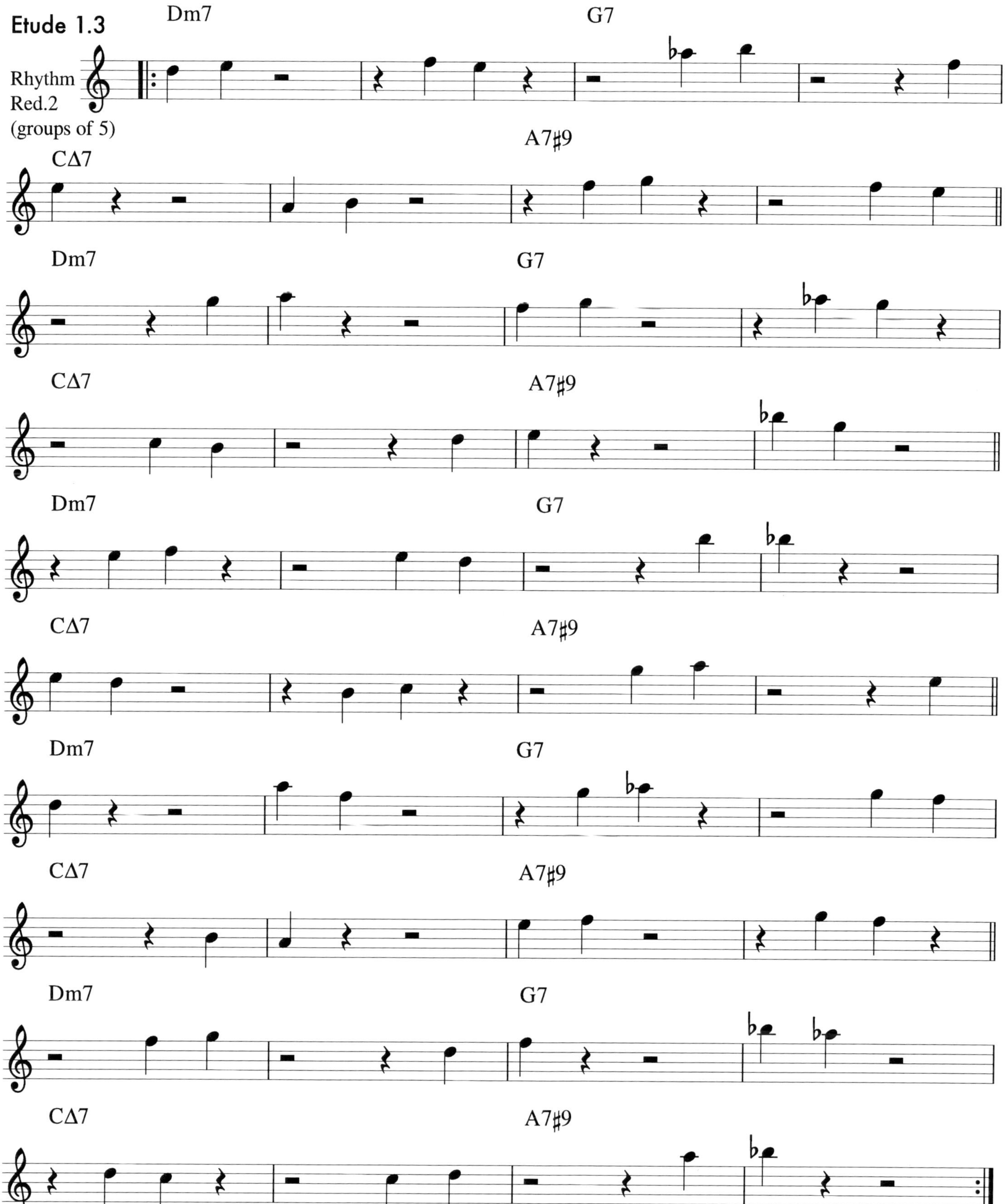

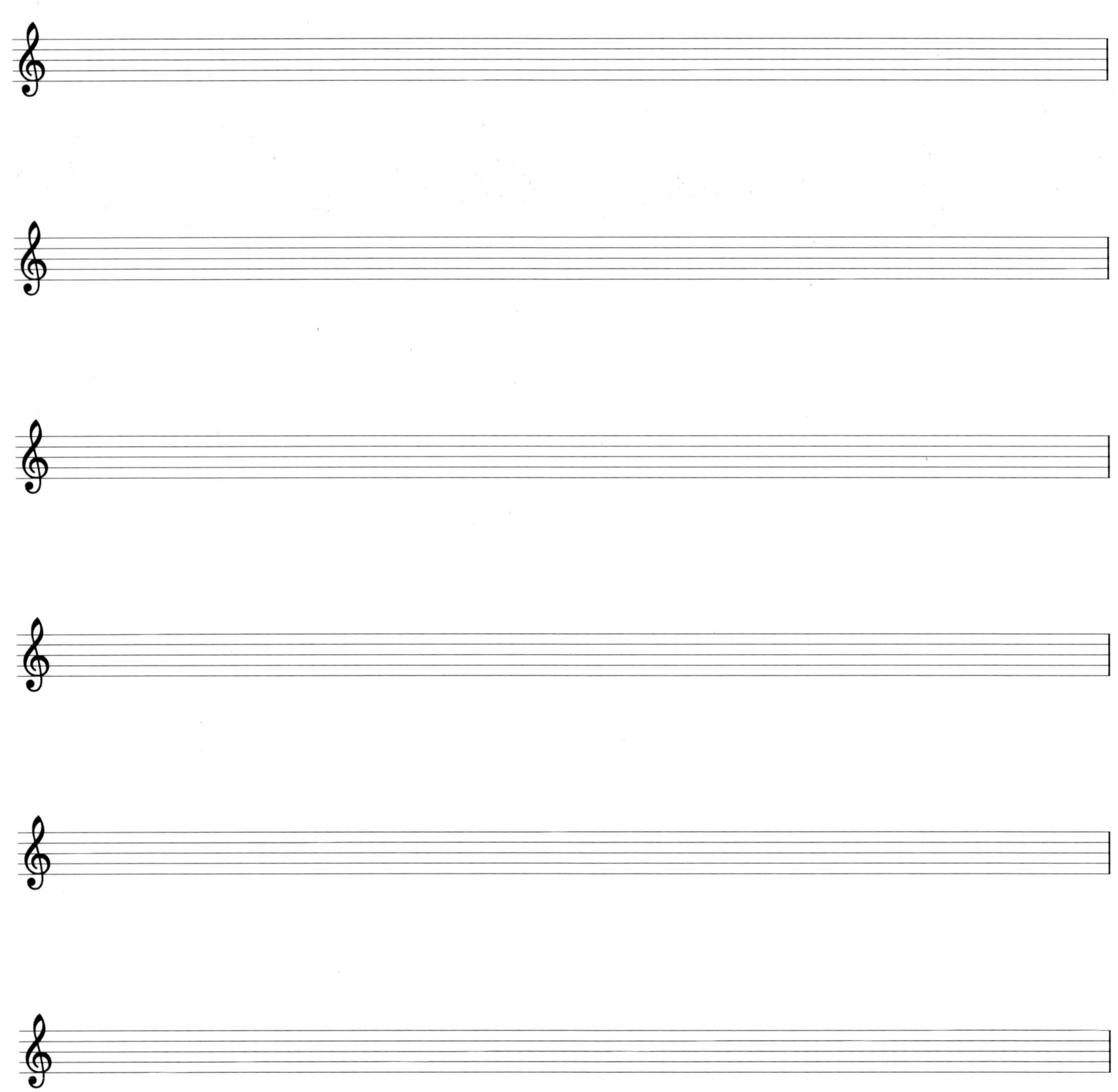

Page left blank for layout purposes and your personal notes

INTRODUCTION to ETUDE 2

"Etude 2" uses the same scales and set of chords as "Etude 1".
The melody is constructed in the same way intervallically, but starts an interval of a 3rd higher:

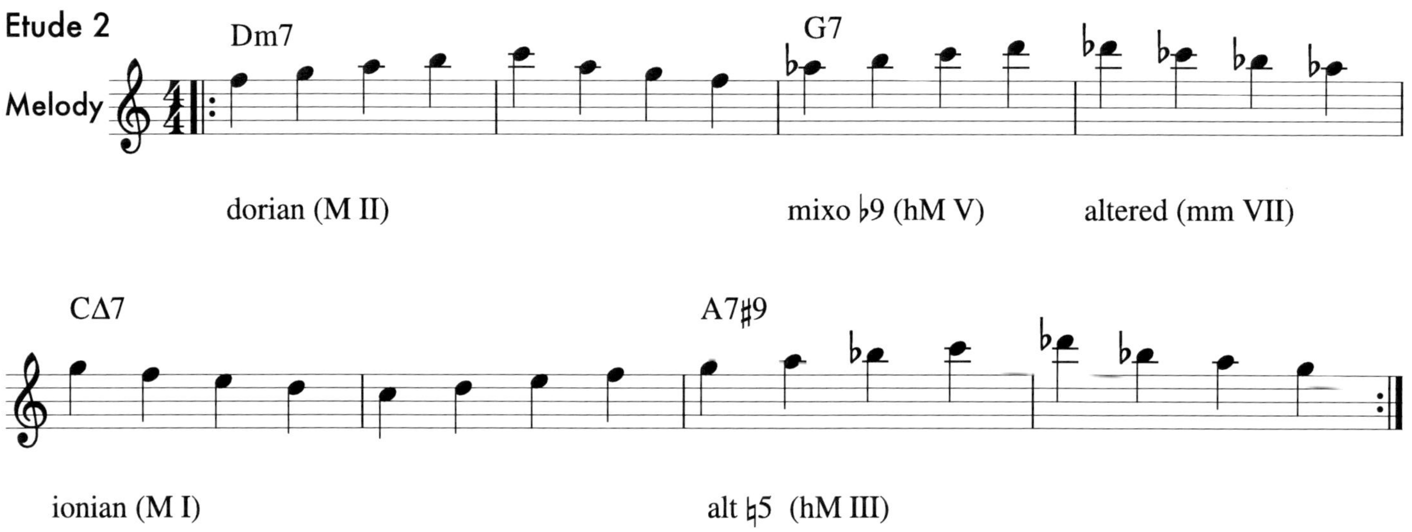

Play the melody repeatedly and slowly in an even tempo.
Note how it correlates differently with the chords, compared to the melody of Etude 1.

To prepare for the etude variations involving voice motion, harmonize the melody with any common three-part chord structure, similar to "Etude 1":

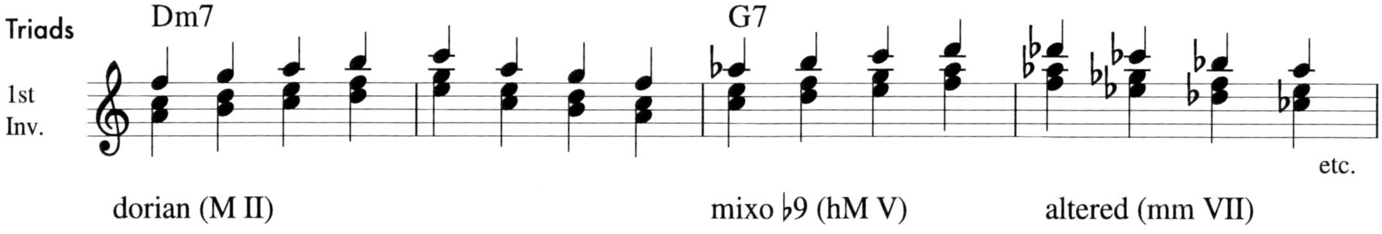

Refer to the Preparatory Exercises for "Etude 1" to harmonize the melody of "Etude 2" in the same way, creating consistent triple-voice parallel motion with the chord structures most frequently used in the variations.

For "Etude 2.1" and "2.2", only variation A is written out on the following pages.
Based on the other, more complex variations introduced for "Etude 1",
construct similar ones for "Etude 2" yourself, using the same sets of voice motion moves,
but starting a third higher up the respective scale.
If possible, apply the various rhythmic reductions of "Etude 1" to "Etude 2" as well.

Etude 2.1

close

Moves start on beats 1 and 3

Variation A with Single-Voice Motion in 3 Inversions

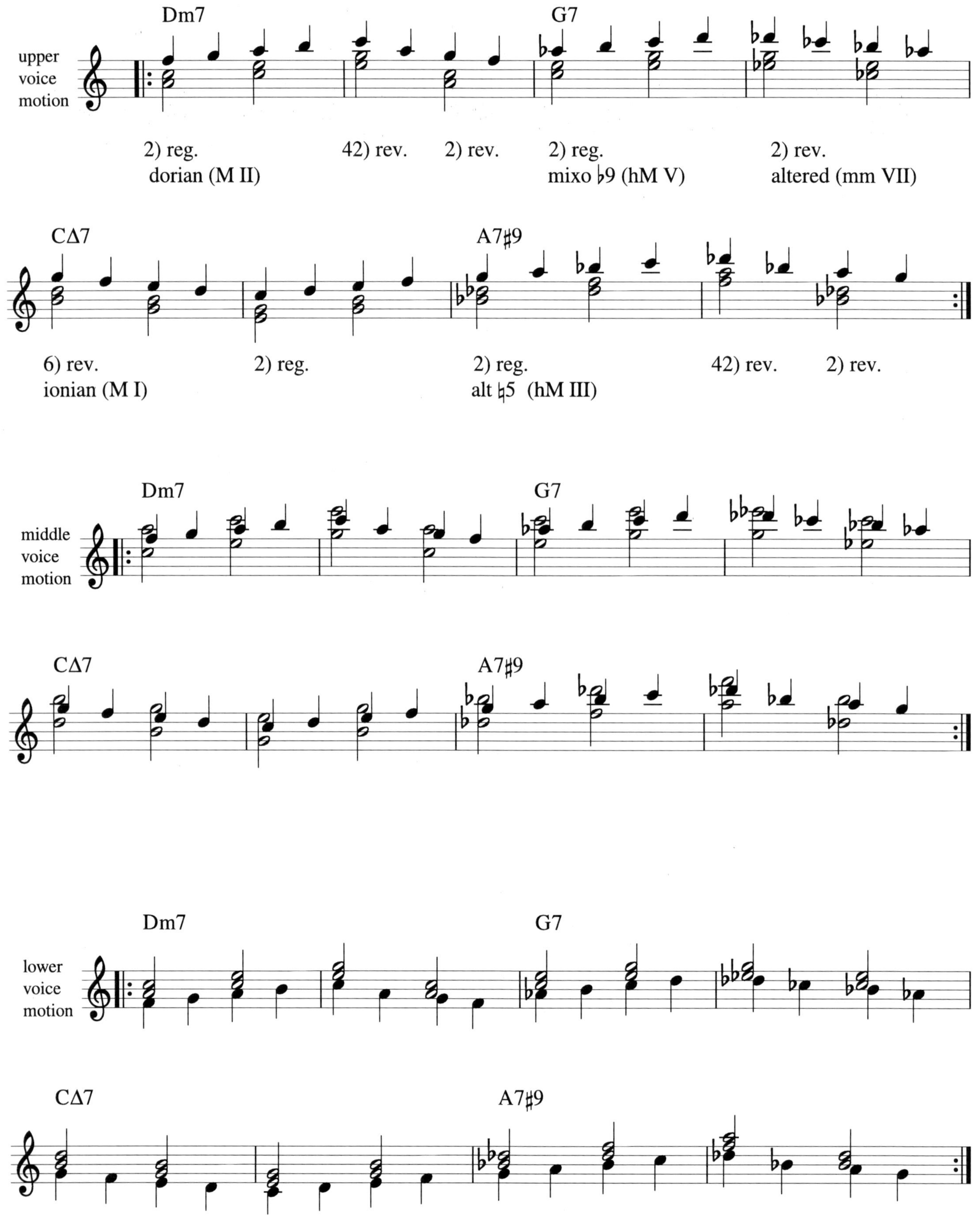

Etude 2.1

open

Moves start on beats 1 and 3

Variation A with Single-Voice Motion in 3 Inversions

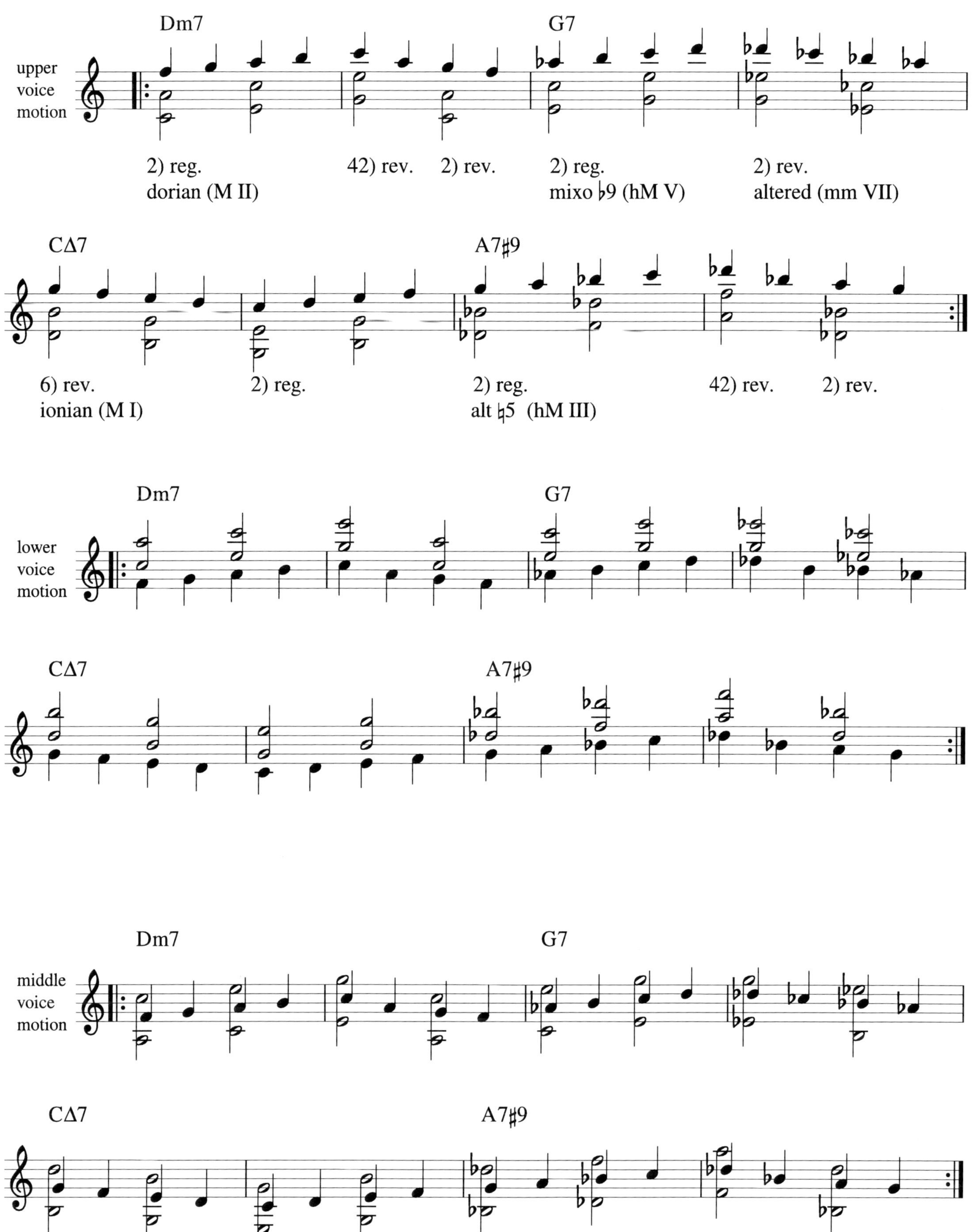

Etude 2.2

close

Moves start on beats 2 and 4

Variation A with Single-Voice Motion in 3 Inversions

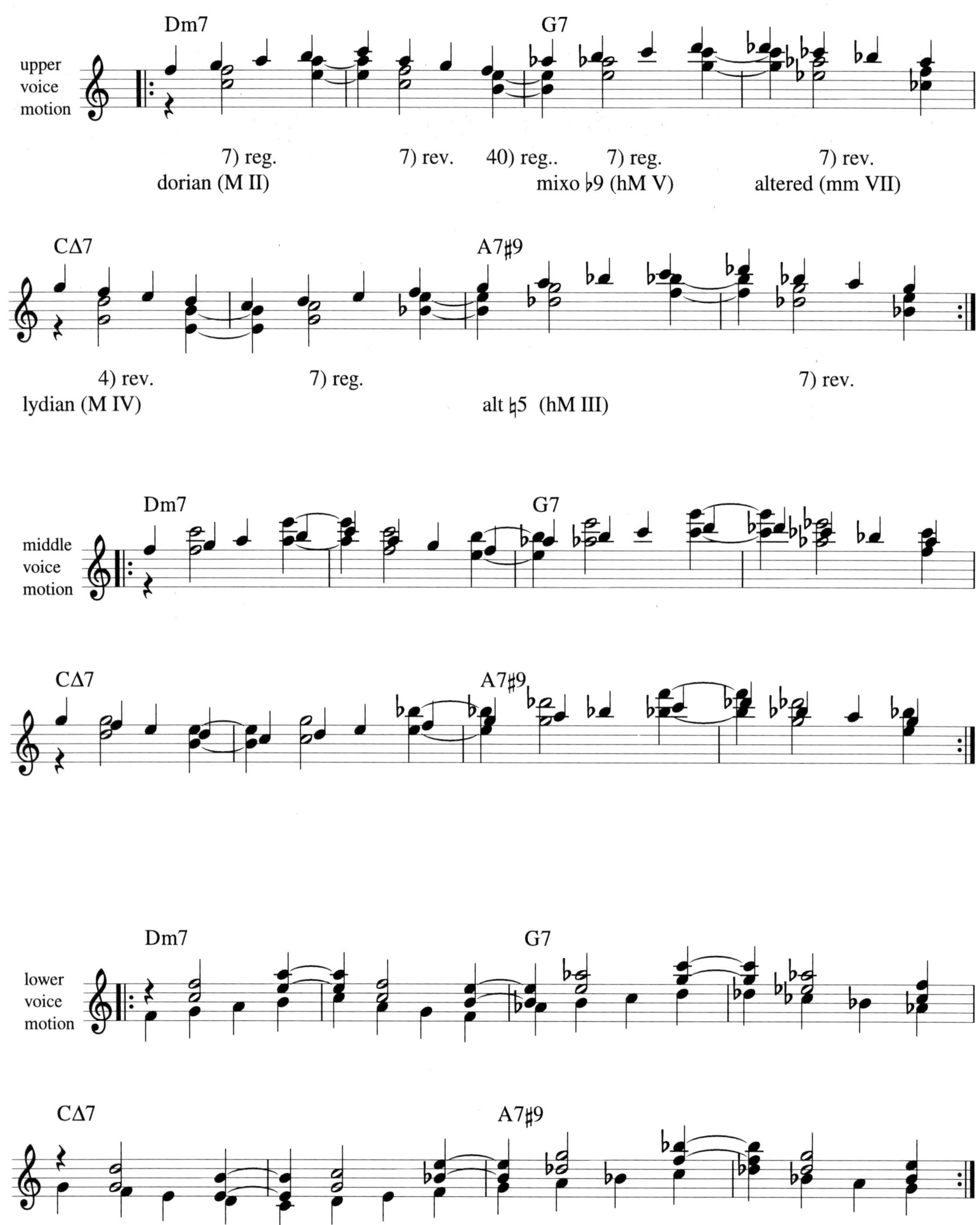

Etude 2.2

open

Moves start on beats 2 and 4

Variation A with Single-Voice Motion in 3 Inversions

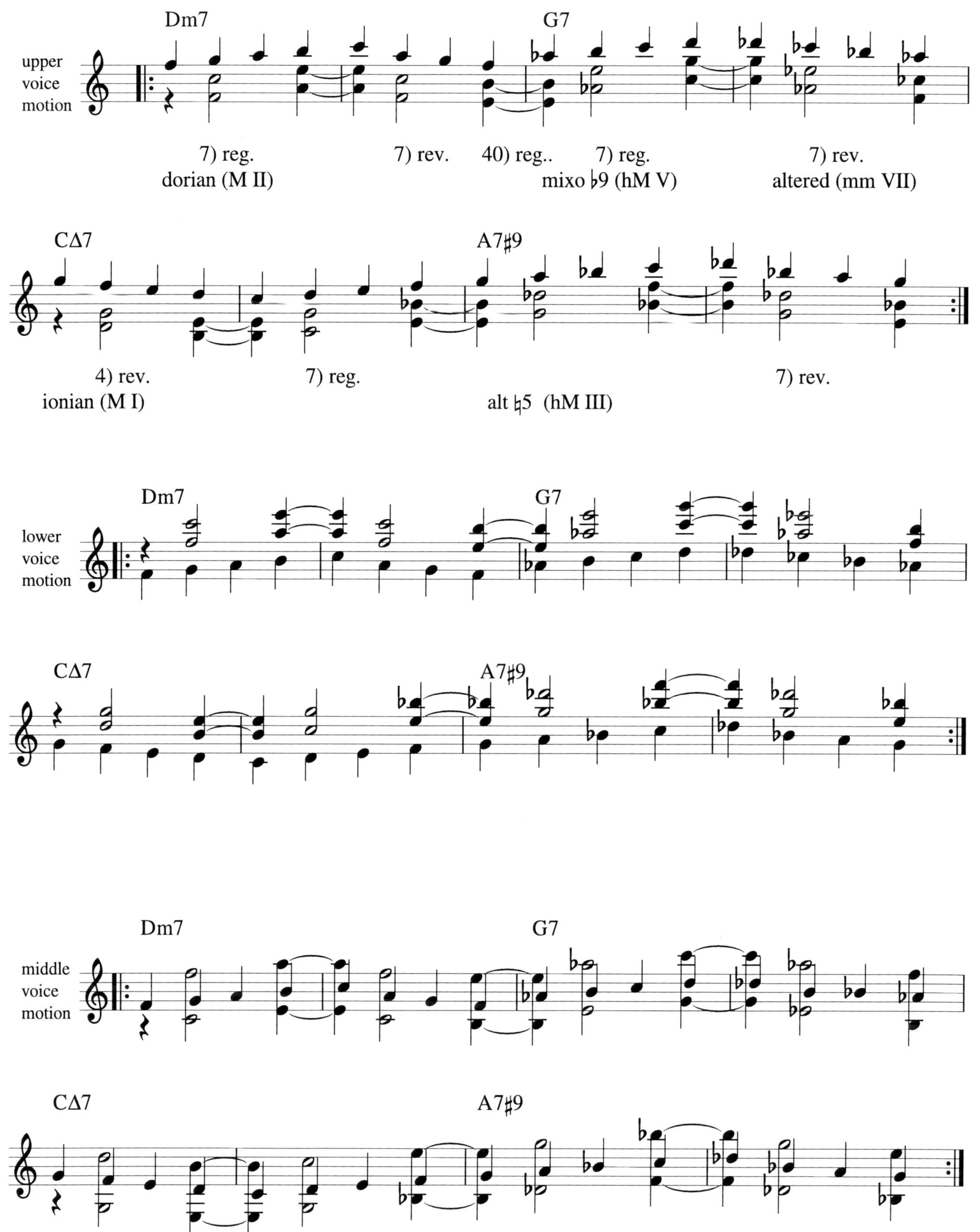

Etude 2.3

close

Moves start on alternating even and odd beats in Single-Voice Motion

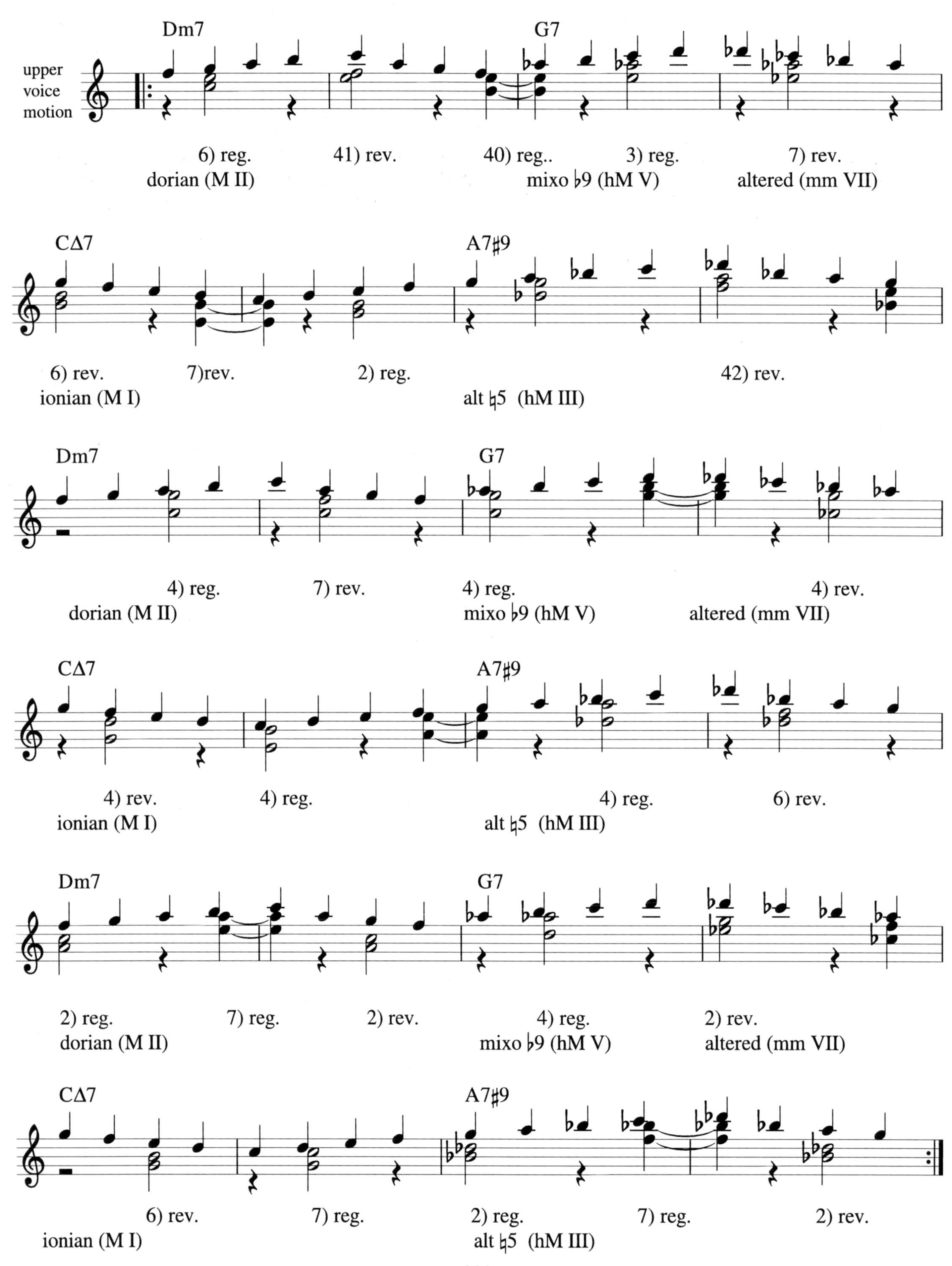

Etude 2.3

open

Moves start on alternating even and odd beats in Single-Voice Motion

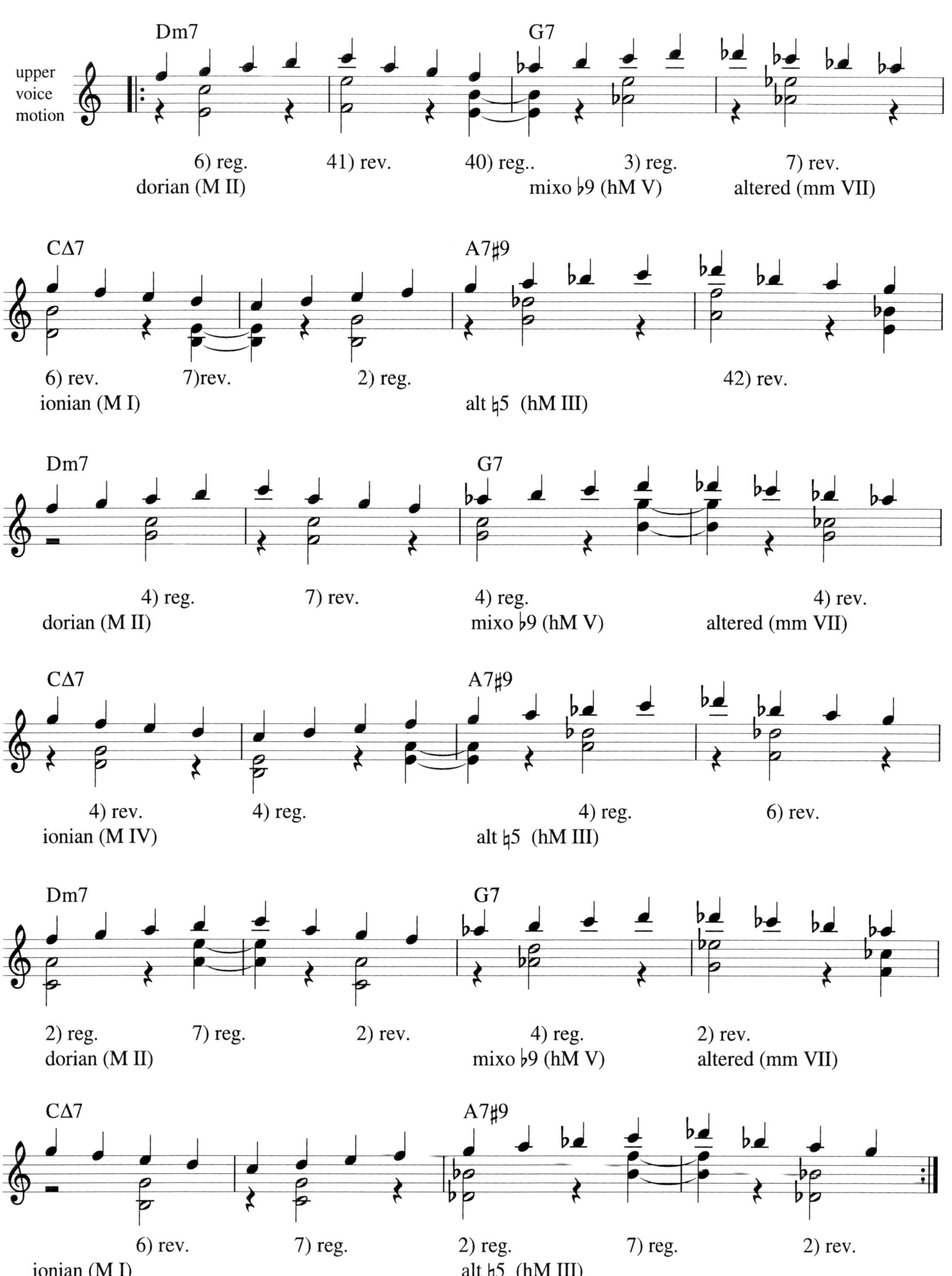

USING ALTERNATIVE SCALES on VOICE MOTION ETUDES close

Variation A with Single-Voice Motion

Apply to all other variations, inversions etc.

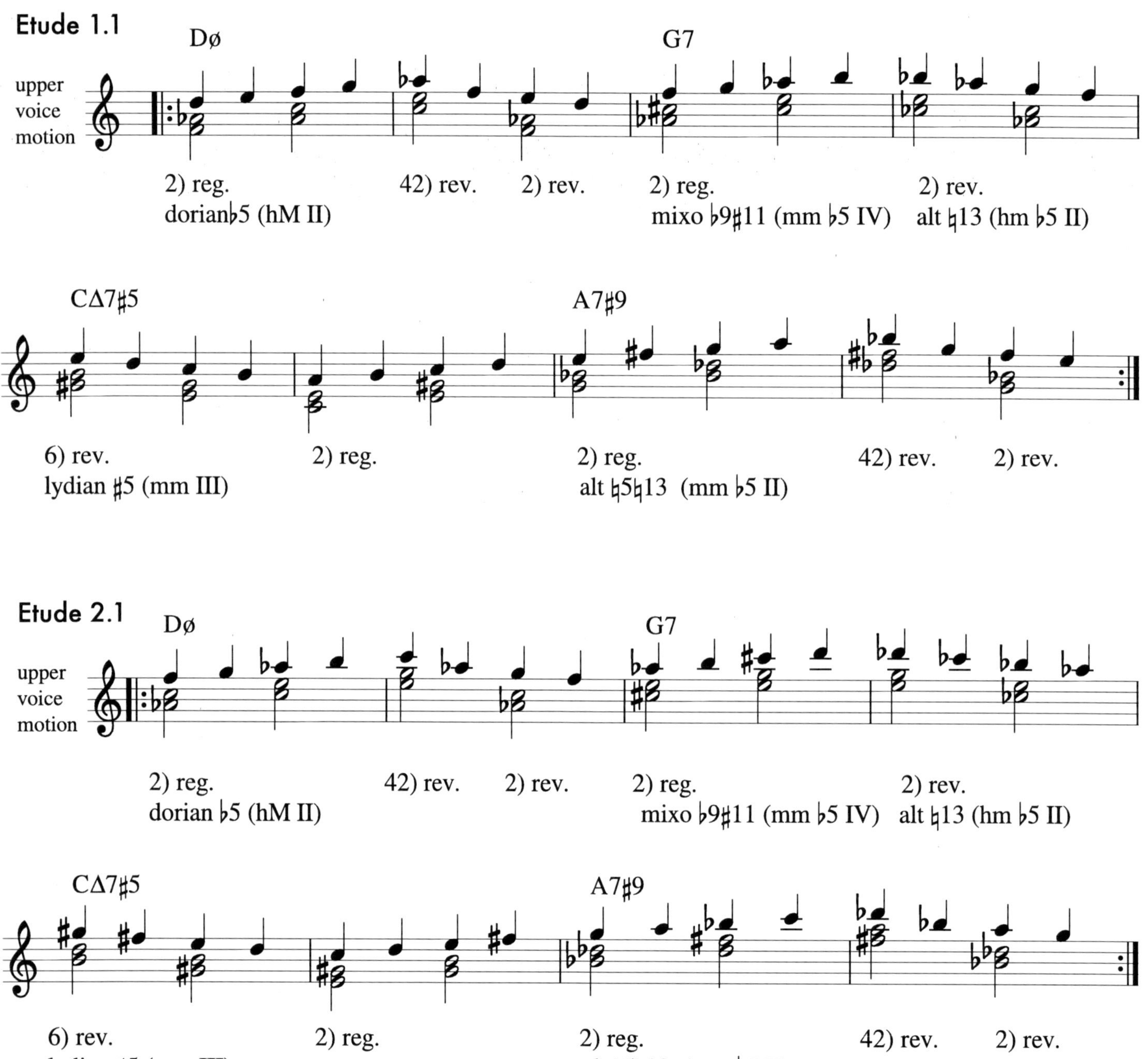

Try other scales and chord substitutions; refer to Part 3A "Heptatonics" for options.
To put any regular variation into the key of C minor, start by changing all E notes to E♭ , and study how it affects the chords and scales - then change any other note to your liking.

Variation A with Single Voice-Motion in Drop-2 Voicing using alternative scales

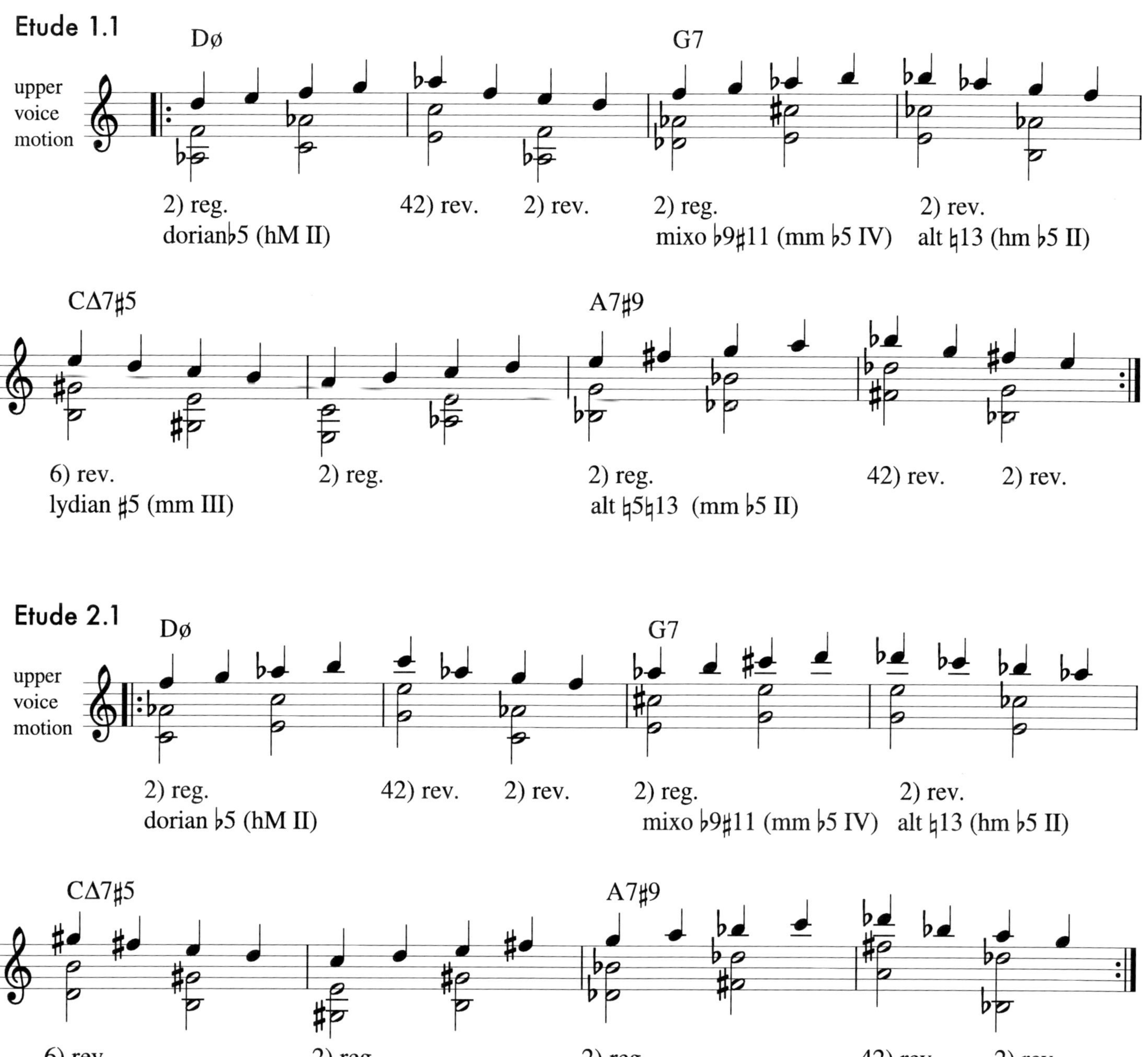

INTRODUCTION to ETUDE 3

In the Etudes 1 and 2, the melody was rhythmically moving in quarter notes, and the moves were applied using the pre-existing melody as a moving voice within the three-part harmonization.

"Etude 3" illustrates the application of the voice motion moves in a different but equally important context: The chord progression is the same, but the melody consists entirely of whole notes, forming a simple scale-guideline with one note per chord. Voice motion will be applied to embellish the melody by adding movement to the two additional voices used to harmonize this guideline.

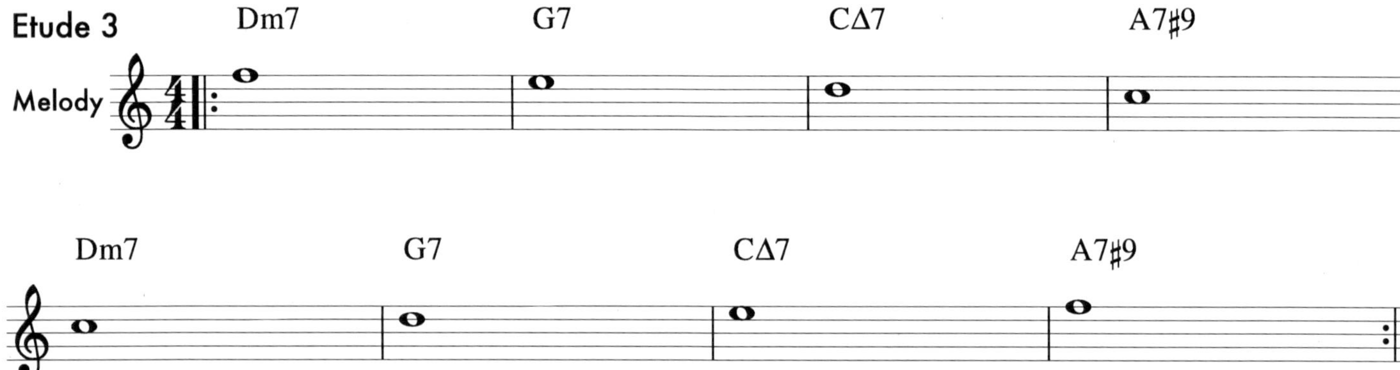

Practice playing the melody over the chord progression, or play the roots of the chords at the same time on the guitar. Observe how the melody moves over the root movement, being aware of the functions of the melody notes within each chord.

Before adding motion of smaller note values to any additional lower voices, start by harmonizing each melody note individually with three-part chord structures reflecting the harmonies, as in a musical situation in which the roots of the chords are being played by another instrument.

Play through the following two examples of such static harmonizations, observing the resulting linear movement of each voice as well as the chord types and names of each individual three-part chord structure, and how they work in relation to the harmonies of the chord progression.

Static Harmonization 1 close

Etude 3

Static Harm. 1

Dm7 G7 CΔ7 A7♯9

Dm7 G7 CΔ7 A7♯9

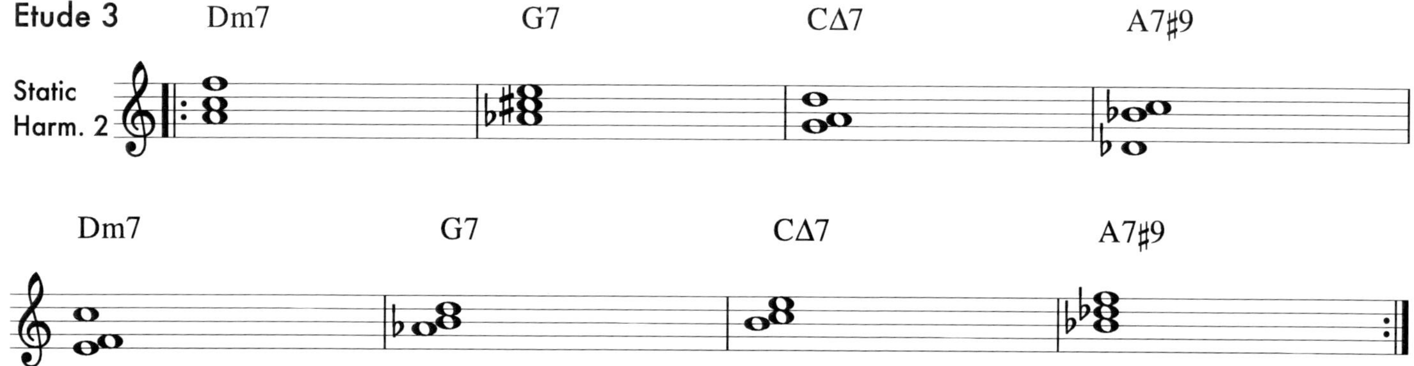

By splitting the two harmonizing voices from the melody and playing them on a different beat, the static harmonizations can be varied without even applying additional voice motion, while still producing melodic movement.
Play through the following rhythmic variations of the Static Harmonization 1, and observe the emerging rhythmic and melodic structures:

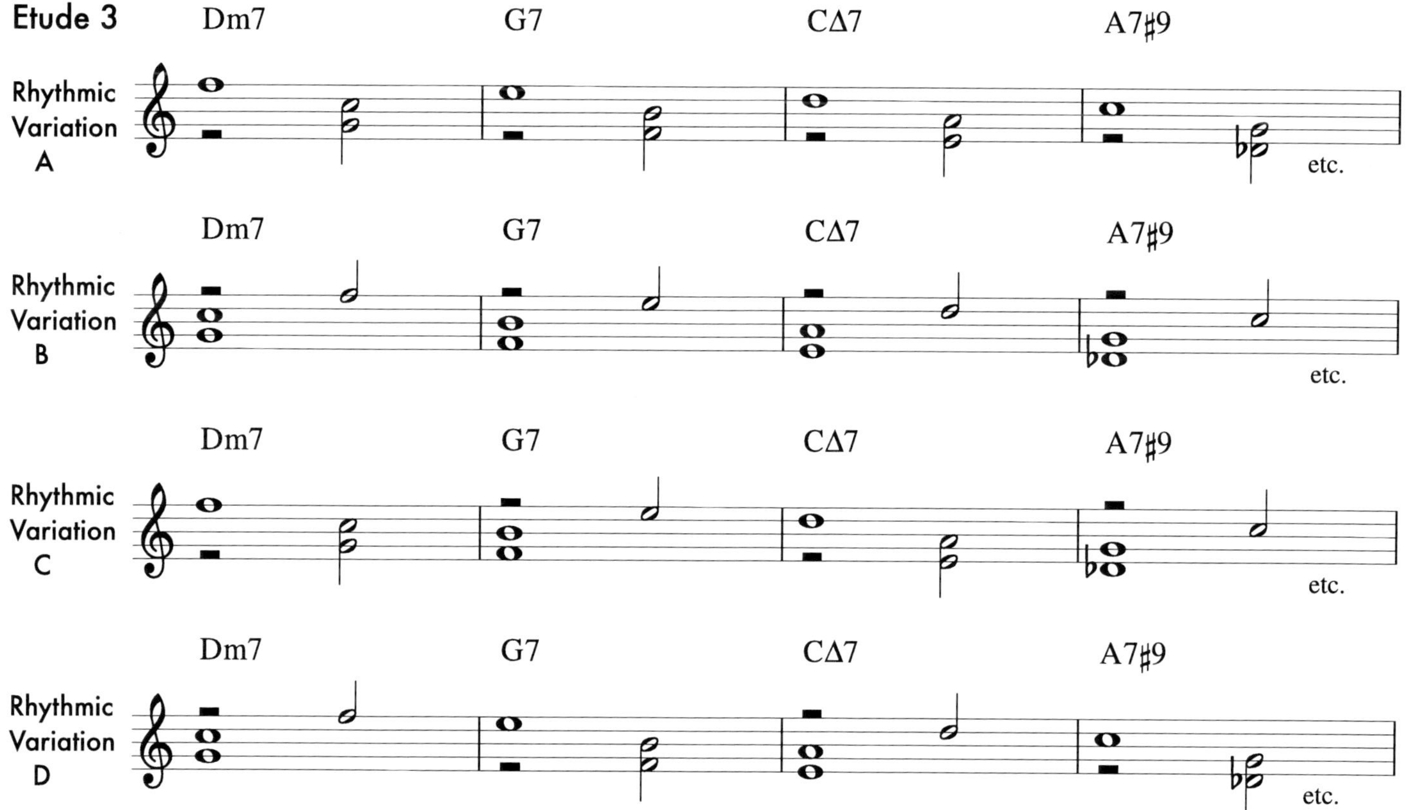

Apply these variations to Static Harmonization 2 as well.

Experiment with different note values, and start each event on different beats to extract shorter melodic phrases from the otherwise static chord structures.

APPLYING VOICE MOTION TO THE MELODY
Etude 3 Variations

The following two pages show three examples of how to apply voice motion moves to the long melody notes, adding melodic and rhythmic movement.

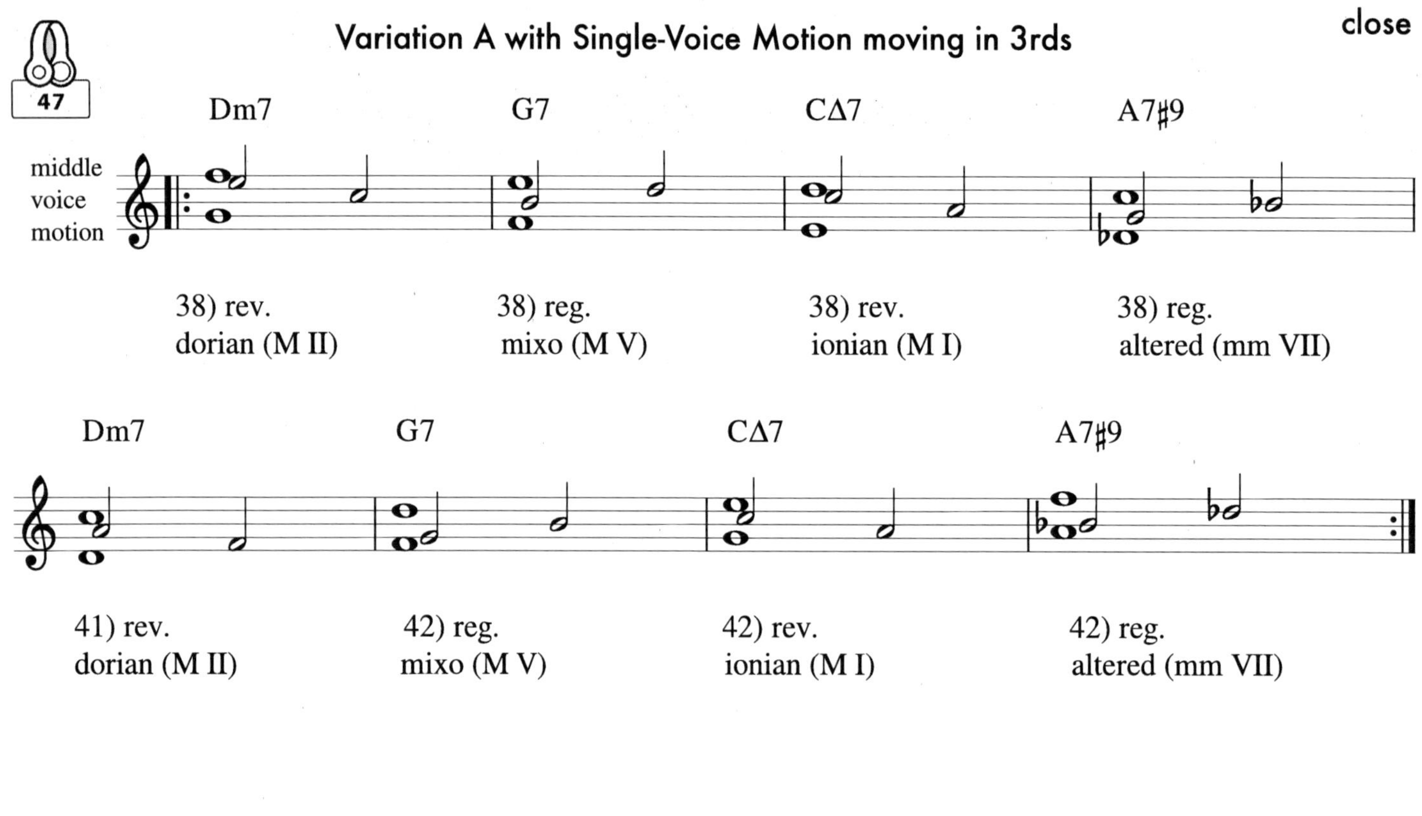

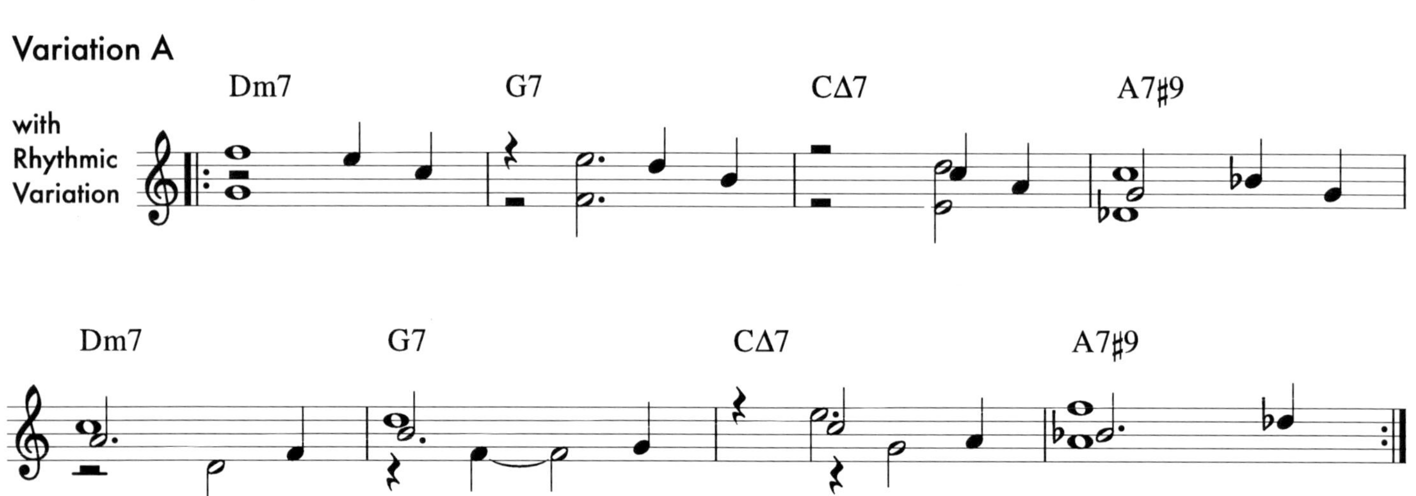

In this example, each bar represents a unique rhythmic variation of the respective move used in variation A above. Apply each pattern to all bars for the whole etude; find your own rhythmic variations and combine them to produce longer improvisational melodic phrases.

Variation B with Single-Voice Motion moving in 2nds

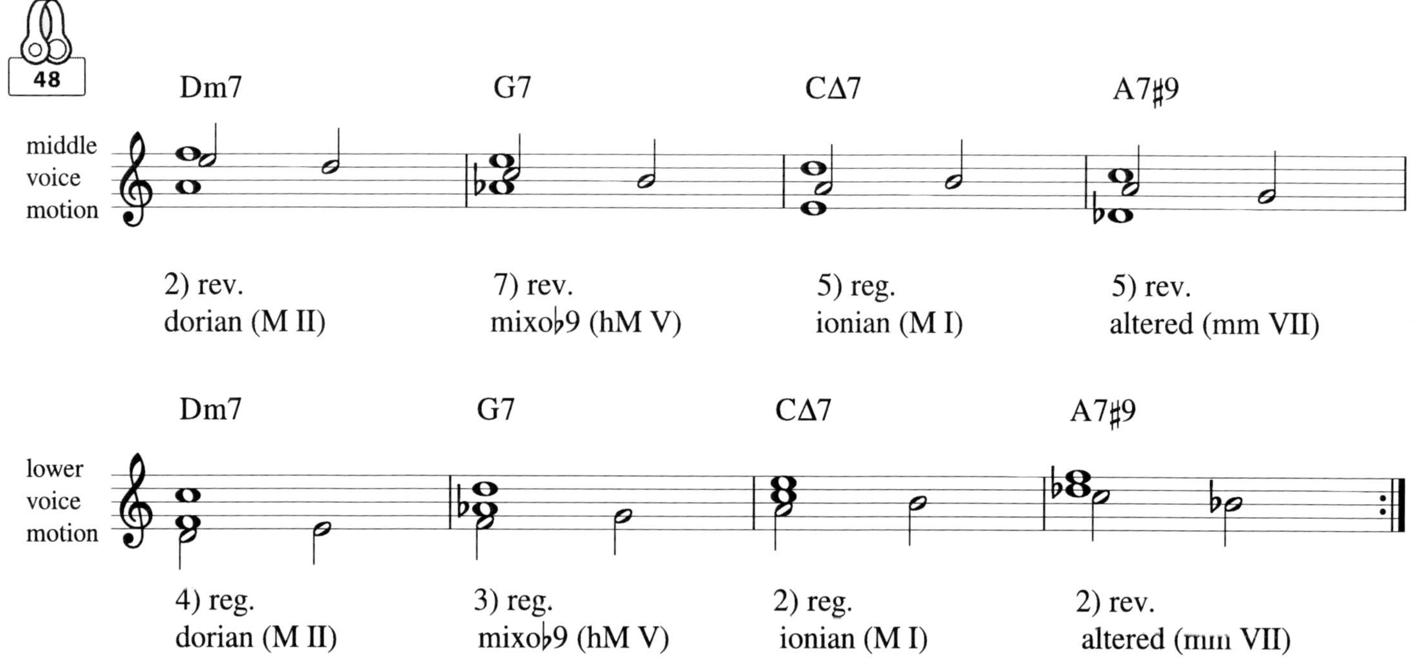

Variation C with Single-Voice Motion

This last variation is based on Static Harmonization 2 (see p.285).
The number of the moves are not shown below, as the melodic movement is added rather freely to the pre-existing chord structures.
Depending on your personal interest, analyze the resulting chord structures and scales in use.

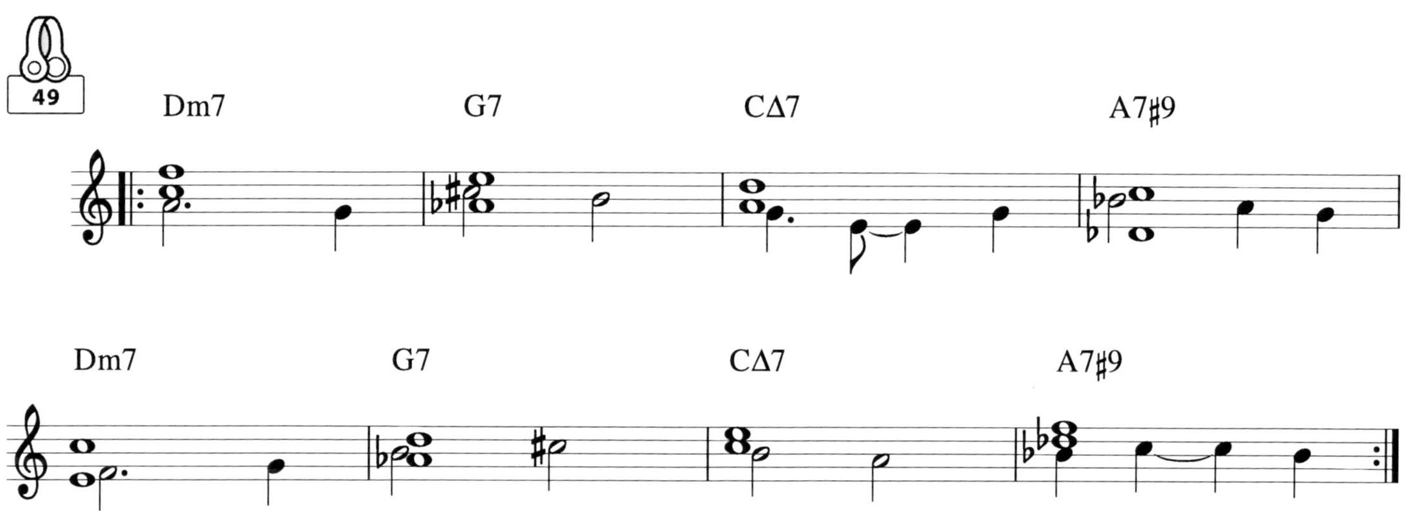

Experiment with the rhythmic variations, and play with the starting point of each move within the bar.
Use the various principles presented in this section to embellish any linear guideline in accompaniment, or to add motion to any applicable melody constructed of longer notes.
If interested, try other inversions to move the melodic guideline to the middle or lower voice, and experiment with open voicings as well.

PART 3D

4ths and 5ths

This chapter displays all possible moves involving the intervallic steps of 4ths and 5ths within the limitations established in the Introduction to Part 1.

This material goes somewhat beyond the scope of this book, which focuses mainly on melodic movement in 2nds and/or 3rds.

These moves are included nevertheless for completeness sake, and for the rich harmolodic possibilities they contain.
Depending on your personal interest, explore any other move that combines these wider intervals of 4ths and 5ths with 2nds and/or 3rds as well.

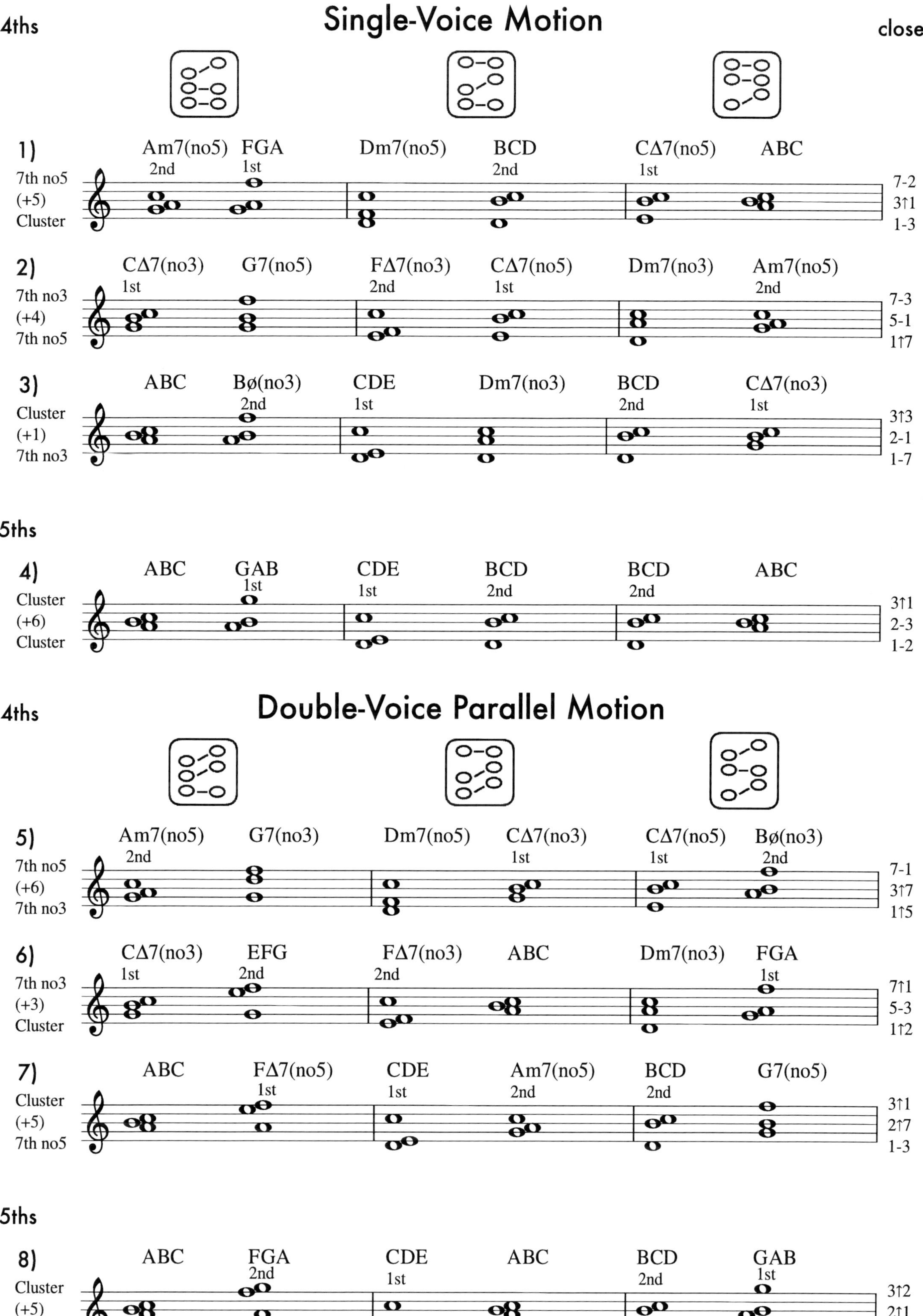
4ths
Single-Voice Motion
close
1)
7th no5
(+5)
Cluster
Am7(no5) FGA Dm7(no5) BCD CΔ7(no5) ABC
2nd 1st 2nd 1st
7-2
3↑1
1-3
2)
7th no3
(+4)
7th no5
CΔ7(no3) G7(no5) FΔ7(no3) CΔ7(no5) Dm7(no3) Am7(no5)
1st 2nd 1st 2nd
7-3
5-1
1↑7
3)
Cluster
(+1)
7th no3
ABC Bø(no3) CDE Dm7(no3) BCD CΔ7(no3)
2nd 1st 2nd 1st
3↑3
2-1
1-7
5ths
4)
Cluster
(+6)
Cluster
ABC GAB CDE BCD BCD ABC
1st 1st 2nd 2nd
3↑1
2-3
1-2
4ths
Double-Voice Parallel Motion
5)
7th no5
(+6)
7th no3
Am7(no5) G7(no3) Dm7(no5) CΔ7(no3) CΔ7(no5) Bø(no3)
2nd 1st 1st 2nd
7-1
3↑7
1↑5
6)
7th no3
(+3)
Cluster
CΔ7(no3) EFG FΔ7(no3) ABC Dm7(no3) FGA
1st 2nd 2nd 1st
7↑1
5-3
1↑2
7)
Cluster
(+5)
7th no5
ABC FΔ7(no5) CDE Am7(no5) BCD G7(no5)
1st 1st 2nd 2nd
3↑1
2↑7
1-3
5ths
8)
Cluster
(+5)
Cluster
ABC FGA CDE ABC BCD GAB
2nd 1st 2nd 1st
3↑2
2↑1
1-3

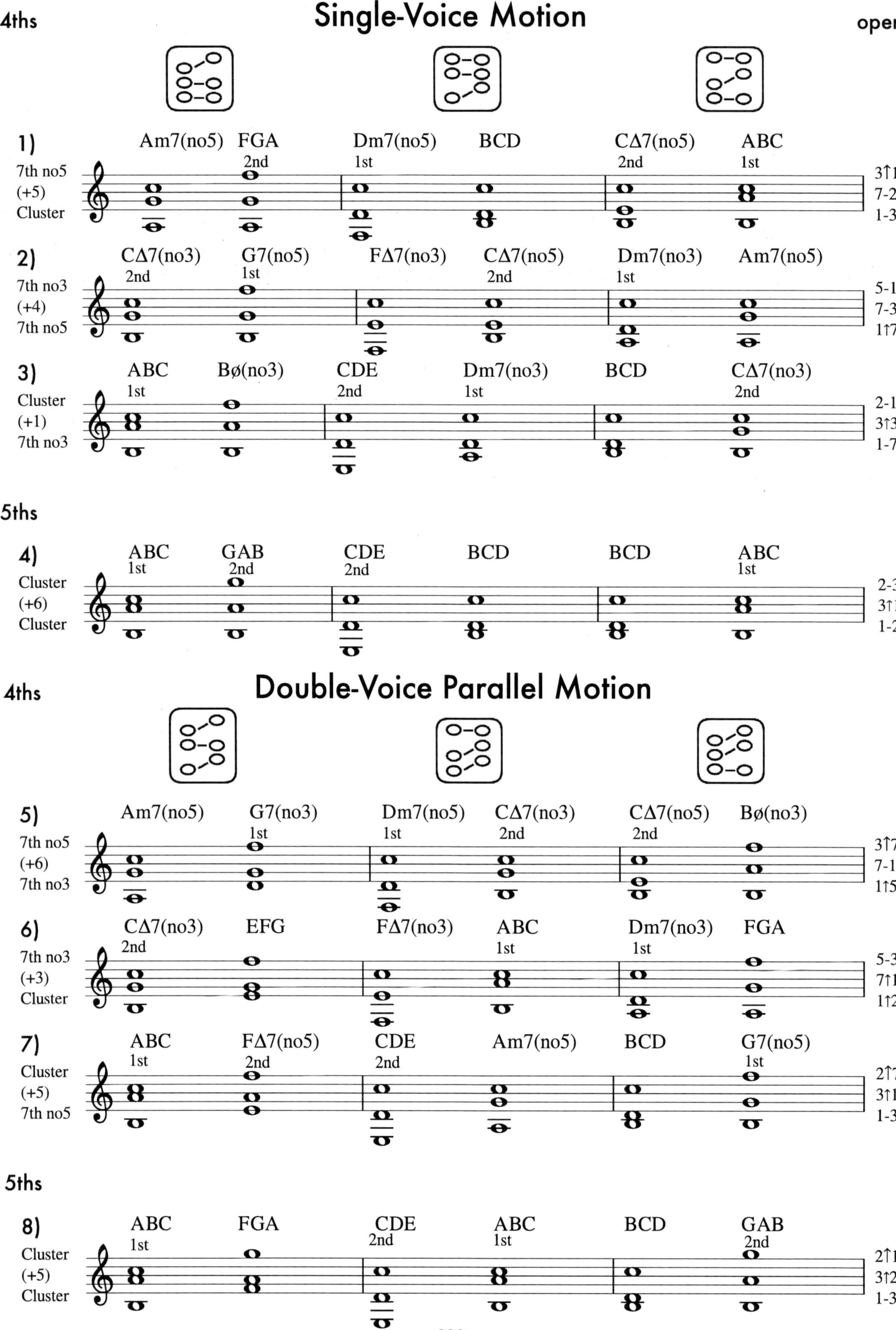
4ths
Single-Voice Motion
open
1)
7th no5
(+5)
Cluster
Am7(no5) FGA Dm7(no5) BCD CΔ7(no5) ABC
2nd 1st 2nd 1st
3↑1
7-2
1-3
2)
7th no3
(+4)
7th no5
CΔ7(no3) G7(no5) FΔ7(no3) CΔ7(no5) Dm7(no3) Am7(no5)
2nd 1st 2nd 1st
5-1
7-3
1↑7
3)
Cluster
(+1)
7th no3
ABC Bø(no3) CDE Dm7(no3) BCD CΔ7(no3)
1st 2nd 1st 2nd
2-1
3↑3
1-7
5ths
4)
Cluster
(+6)
Cluster
ABC GAB CDE BCD BCD ABC
1st 2nd 2nd 1st
2-3
3↑1
1-2
4ths
Double-Voice Parallel Motion
5)
7th no5
(+6)
7th no3
Am7(no5) G7(no3) Dm7(no5) CΔ7(no3) CΔ7(no5) Bø(no3)
1st 1st 2nd 2nd
3↑7
7-1
1↑5
6)
7th no3
(+3)
Cluster
CΔ7(no3) EFG FΔ7(no3) ABC Dm7(no3) FGA
2nd 1st 1st
5-3
7↑1
1↑2
7)
Cluster
(+5)
7th no5
ABC FΔ7(no5) CDE Am7(no5) BCD G7(no5)
1st 2nd 2nd 1st
2↑7
3↑1
1-3
5ths
8)
Cluster
(+5)
Cluster
ABC FGA CDE ABC BCD GAB
1st 2nd 1st 2nd
2↑1
3↑2
1-3

PART 3E

The Big Picture

This final chapter gives a complete overview of all playable 3-part chord voicings on the guitar within reach of the fretting hand.
Up to this point in the book, all chords were either in close voicing, or in one specific type of open voicing (drop 2).
All voice motion took place within these two voicing types, which are arguably the most versatile and widely used.
An average-size fretting hand can however span two octaves plus an interval of a 3rd, which means that beyond the 30 different close and drop-2 chord structures introduced in Parts 1 and 2, many more open chord structures are possible to play on the guitar.
Similar to the drop-2 voicings presented in Part 2, these other open voicings can be derived from the 15 possible close-voiced chord structures by dropping one or two of their lower voices (voice 2 and/or 3) down an octave, or even two octaves ("double drop").

This is the complete list of all possible spread 3-part chord voicing types on the guitar:

drop-2 (d2)
drop-3 (d3)
drop-2 & drop 3 (d2&d3)

double drop-2 (dd2)
double drop-2 & drop-3 (dd2&d3)
double drop-3 & drop-2 (dd3&d2)

If we examine all of the 3-note structures within the reachable range on the guitar, in the harmonic context of any heptatonic scale, we find a total of 79 chord voicings that share a common note in the same voice.
Note that the 30 close and drop-2 chord structures used throughout the book make up only around 38% of these 79 possible chord voicings, and that any and all of them are versions of the 15 basic chord structures presented in the introduction to Part 1.

On the next pages, these 79 chord voicings are presented within the diatonic major scale in the key of C, parallel to the introductions of Parts 1 and 2.
Throughout each page, all voicings will share one common note, either C''' on top, C'' in the middle, or C' in the low voice.
Play through each page horizontally, vertically, and diagonally, in both directions.
Note any common notes and resulting voice movement.
Take any of the new and less common open chord structures up and down the diatonic scale, and try other heptatonic scales as well. Then add voice motion and apply cycles to change keys, etc.

Use these pages to expand your ears and to mine for new, less common chord voicings and sounds. Come back to them later if they do not seem interesting or accessible at this point.

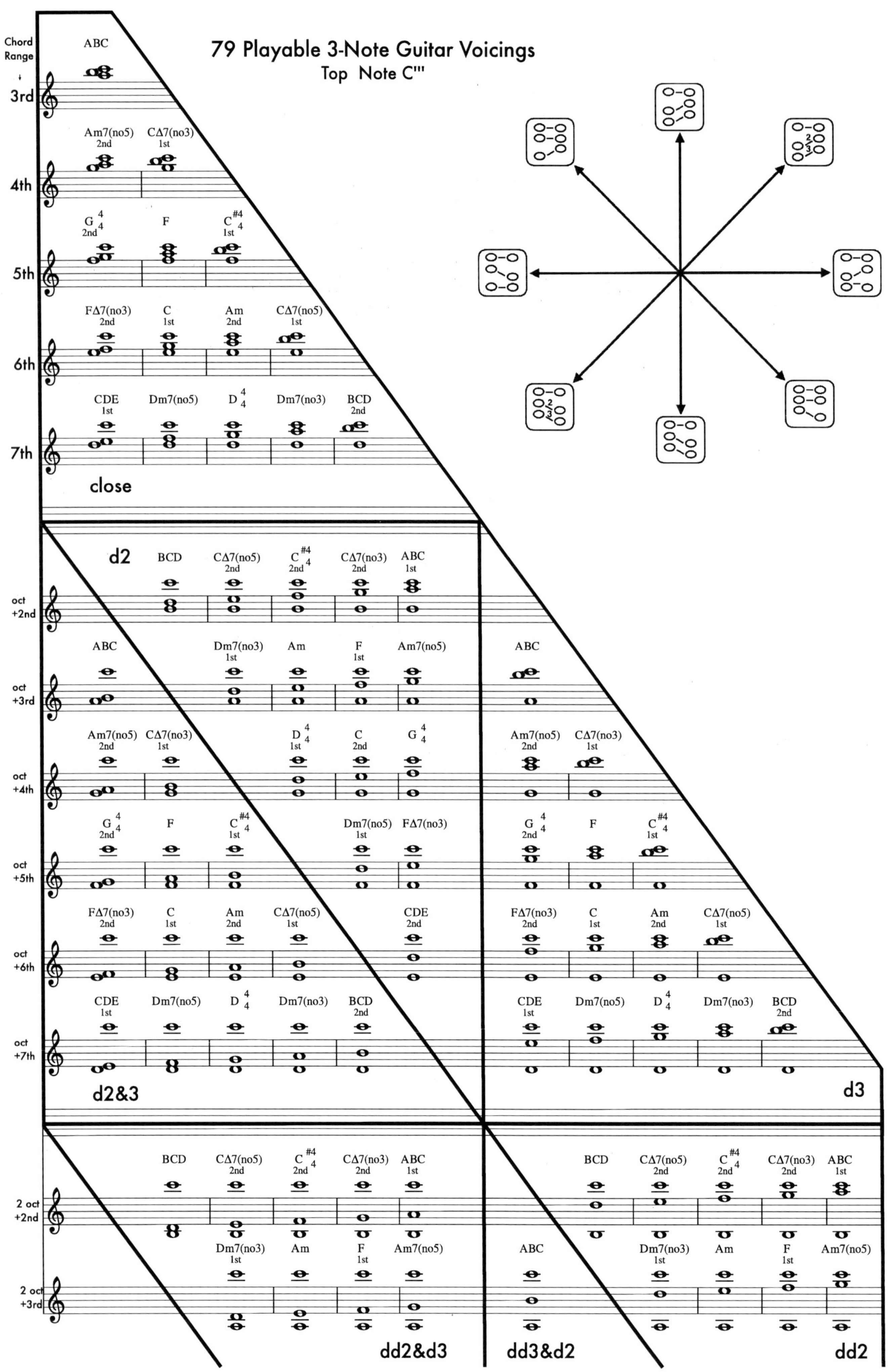
79 Playable 3-Note Guitar Voicings
Top Note C'''
Chord Range
3rd
4th
5th
6th
7th
ABC
Am7(no5) 2nd
CΔ7(no3) 1st
G 4 4 2nd
F
C #4 4 1st
FΔ7(no3) 2nd
C 1st
Am 2nd
CΔ7(no5) 1st
CDE 1st
Dm7(no5)
D 4 4
Dm7(no3)
BCD 2nd
close
d2
CΔ7(no5) 2nd
C #4 4 2nd
CΔ7(no3) 2nd
ABC 1st
oct +2nd
oct +3rd
oct +4th
oct +5th
oct +6th
oct +7th
Dm7(no3) 1st
F 1st
Am7(no5)
D 4 4 1st
C 2nd
G 4 4
Dm7(no5) 1st
CDE 2nd
d2&3
d3
2 oct +2nd
2 oct +3rd
dd2&d3
dd3&d2
dd2

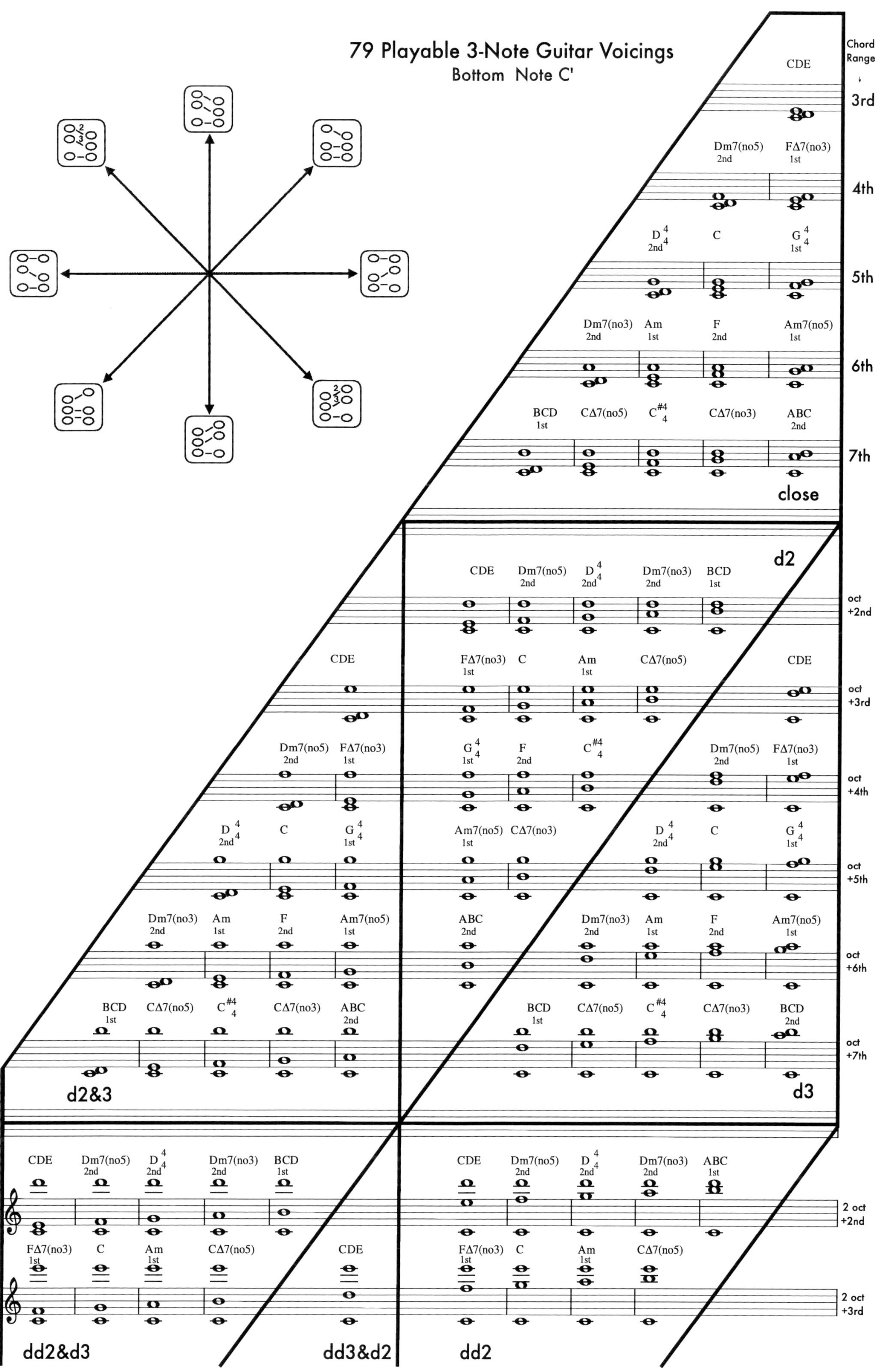
79 Playable 3-Note Guitar Voicings
Bottom Note C'
Chord Range
CDE
3rd
Dm7(no5) 2nd
FΔ7(no3) 1st
4th
D 4 4 2nd
C
G 4 4 1st
5th
Dm7(no3) 2nd
Am 1st
F 2nd
Am7(no5) 1st
6th
BCD 1st
CΔ7(no5)
C #4 4
CΔ7(no3)
ABC 2nd
7th
close
d2
CDE
Dm7(no5) 2nd
D 4 4 2nd
Dm7(no3) 2nd
BCD 1st
oct +2nd
FΔ7(no3) 1st
C
Am 1st
CΔ7(no5)
CDE
oct +3rd
G 4 4 1st
F 2nd
C #4 4
Dm7(no5) 2nd
FΔ7(no3) 1st
oct +4th
Am7(no5) 1st
CΔ7(no3)
D 4 4 2nd
C
G 4 4 1st
oct +5th
ABC 2nd
Dm7(no3) 2nd
Am 1st
F 2nd
Am7(no5) 1st
oct +6th
BCD 1st
CΔ7(no5)
C #4 4
CΔ7(no3)
BCD 2nd
oct +7th
d3
d2&3
dd2&d3
dd3&d2
dd2
2 oct +2nd
2 oct +3rd

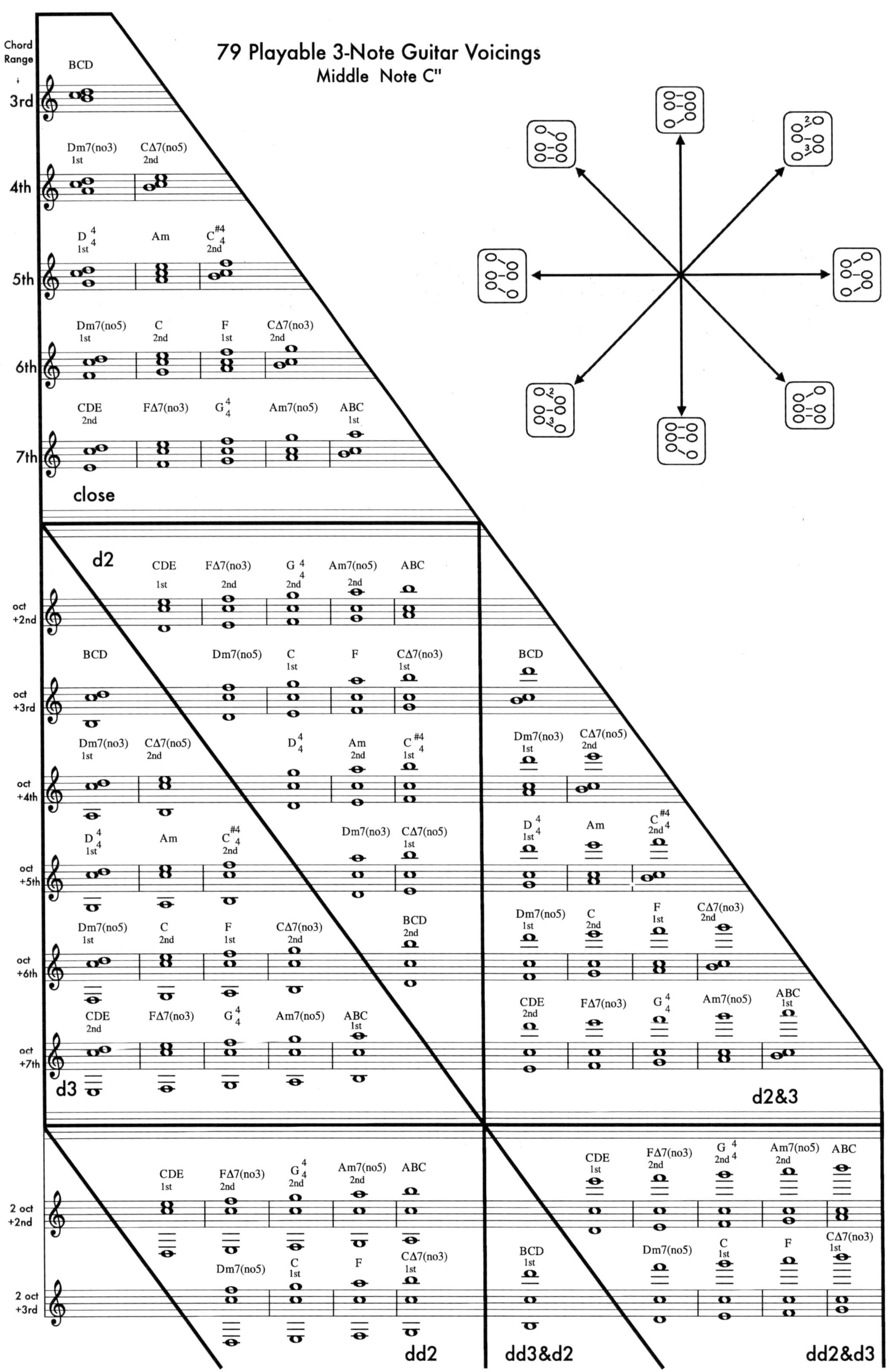
79 Playable 3-Note Guitar Voicings
Middle Note C"
Chord Range
3rd
BCD
4th
Dm7(no3) 1st
CΔ7(no5) 2nd
5th
Am
6th
Dm7(no5) 1st
C 2nd
F 1st
CΔ7(no3) 2nd
7th
CDE 2nd
FΔ7(no3)
Am7(no5)
ABC 1st
close
d2
CDE 1st
FΔ7(no3) 2nd
Am7(no5) 2nd
ABC
oct +2nd
oct +3rd
oct +4th
oct +5th
oct +6th
oct +7th
BCD 2nd
d3
d2&3
2 oct +2nd
2 oct +3rd
dd2
dd3&d2
dd2&d3

The solo guitar piece on the next page concludes Part 3.
It is composed rather freely with no restriction on any particular voicing type, moving the three voices independently and often chromatically.
For the first time in this book, natural harmonics (all at the 12th fret) are used here as a technique to broaden the possibilities for voice movement and for making wider chord voicings possible.
Experiment with all natural harmonics on the guitar and discover how to incorporate them into your own playing along with the material presented in this book.

Depending on your interest, analyze this last composition to identify the specific moves, chord structures, scales, keys and other elements in play.
But more importantly, use the piece as an example of a moving harmony which is simply created by three independent melodic voices.
Try playing and/or composing improvisationally; without thinking about voicings, chord types, keys etc., just letting the individual voices lead you where they want to go.

Congratulations and thank you to any reader who has taken this intensive harmonic journey with me. The information in this book will become increasingly more meaningful as you begin to use it in your own compositions, arrangements and improvisations, progressing on your musical path.
I hope it opens new doors for you.

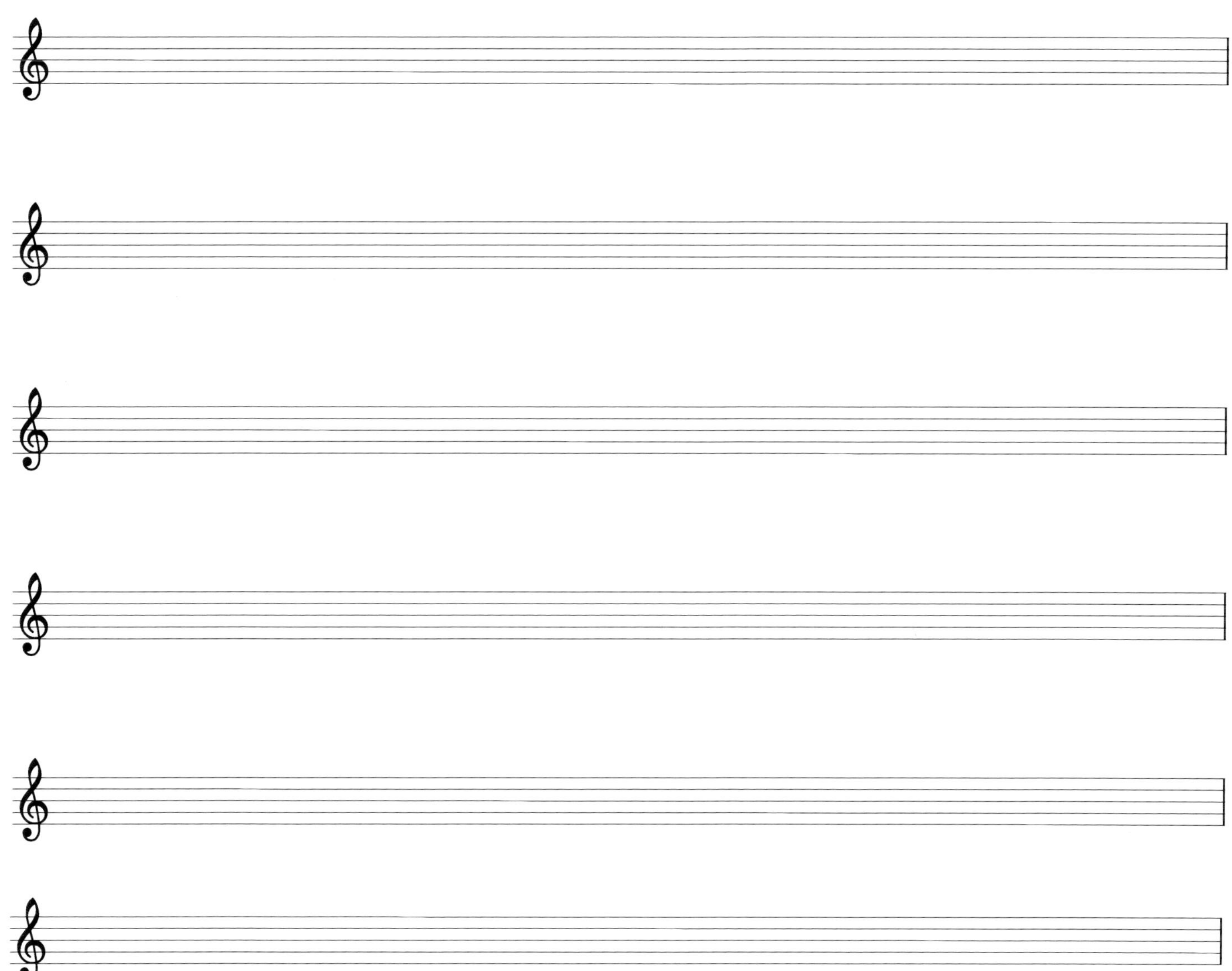

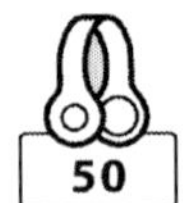

"Holy Freedom"

Guitar Solo

Johannes Haage

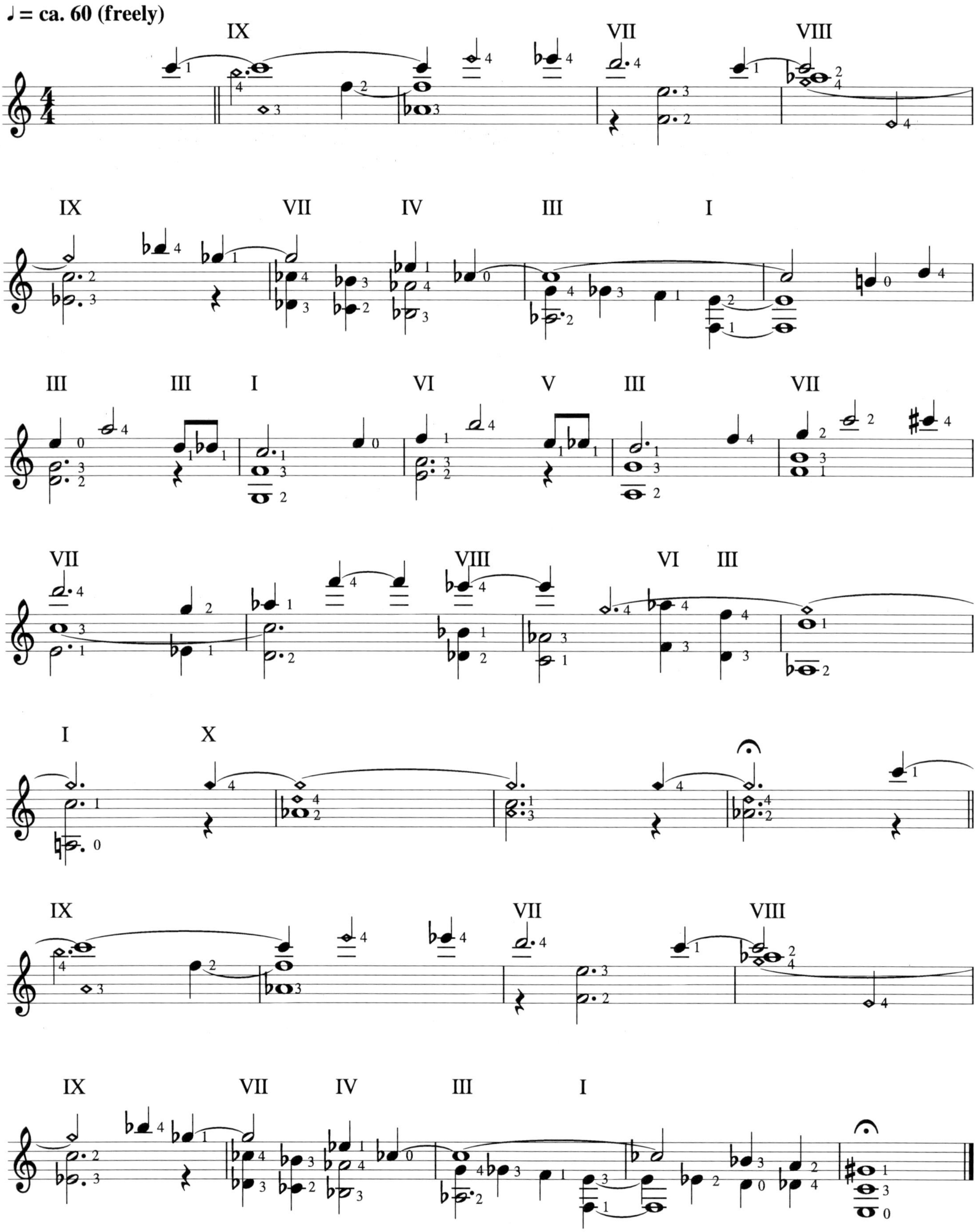

♩ = ca. 60 (freely)

IX VII VIII

IX VII IV III I

III III I VI V III VII

VII VIII VI III

I X

IX VII VIII

IX VII IV III I

APPENDIX FOR GUITARISTS

NAVIGATING THE FRETBOARD
Learning to locate and read all available notes on the guitar

OVERVIEW

This chapter will teach you to identify the natural notes in standard notation, and to find and play all of their possible locations within the full range of your instrument; this is a key requirement to successfully learn with this book as a guitarist.
Furthermore, you will learn to locate the rest of the notes which complete the whole chromatic range of our western equal tempered system.

Although quite helpful of course, good/fast sight reading is not necessary to work with this book.
All you need to know to start working is how to identify and locate the notes on your instrument, which you will learn on the following pages with a clear method in a very concentrated way.
Please refer to outside sources for further sight-reading material.

More advanced players may be inclined to skip this chapter.
Nevertheless, they are advised to try out the exercises and concepts presented here, as they tend to reveal the "blind spots" most players encounter at higher frets, among other things.
Furthermore, the diagonal octave zones may provide a new insight and a fresh angle from which to view and better understand the general architecture of the fretboard.

FINDING THE NOTES ON THE FRETBOARD

In the main Parts 1 and 2 of this book, all voice motion is shown using the diatonic major scale in the key of C. The notes of this seven-note (heptatonic) scale are also often referred to as the "natural notes". They form the basis of both our Western music notation system and the design of the piano keyboard - they are what you hear when you press the white keys. These seven notes are distributed as evenly as possible across the octave, using five whole steps and two half steps, and are named using the first seven letters of the alphabet.
In the illustration below, one octave of the diatonic on the piano keyboard is shown, starting from the middle C (or C''), with standard notation below the white keys as well as the locations of the corresponding notes on the B-String.

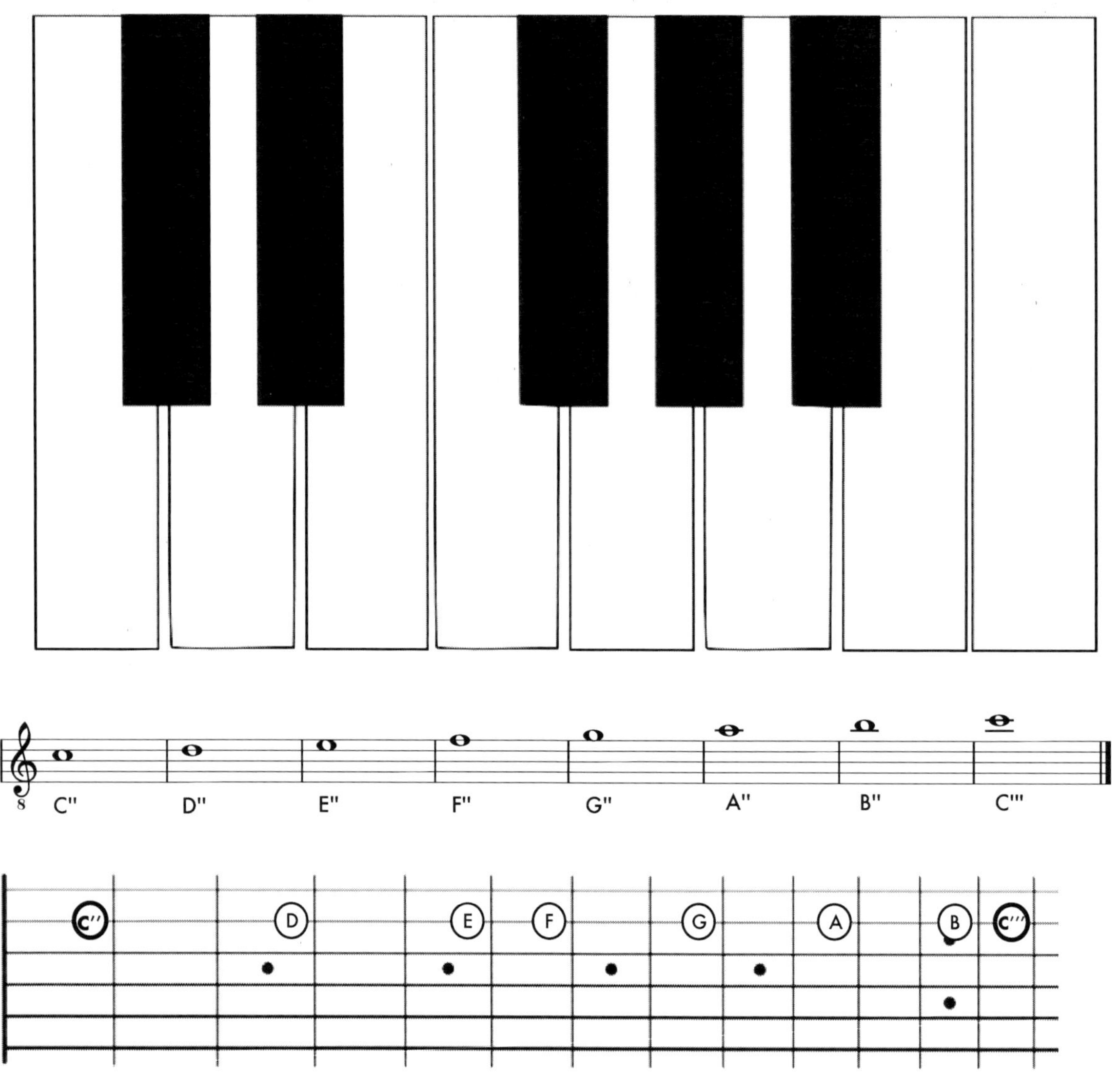

Seeing the diatonic scale horizontally on a single string as a straight line clearly reveals its intervallic design, with the half steps between the 3rd and 4th note (E-F) and between the 7th note leading to the 8th note, which is the root in the next higher octave (B-C).
All diatonic major scales have this intervallic design of wholesteps (W) and halftsteps (H) in every octave:
WWHWWWH (in the key of C: C D EF G A BC D EF G A BC D EF G A B etc.)
Learn the notated notes as well as their locations on the B-string, saying the note names out loud as you play. Improvise, find common diatonic melodies, arpeggios etc.

HORIZONTAL OCTAVE RANGES
on Single Strings

The common 22-fret guitar in standard tuning has a total range of nearly four octaves. This page shows the nearly four-octave range of the C major diatonic scale as it might be played on single strings across the entire fretboard.
For example, the full scale previously covered on the B string can be played on the G and the D string as well; but note the difference in feel, timbre and accessibility. Play through all four octaves on each applicable string individually, learning the note names and locations both on the fretboard as well as in the notation system. Improvise using a broad range of natural notes. Play any simple melody, phrase, or arpeggio within the range of one octave, and find them on all strings individually.

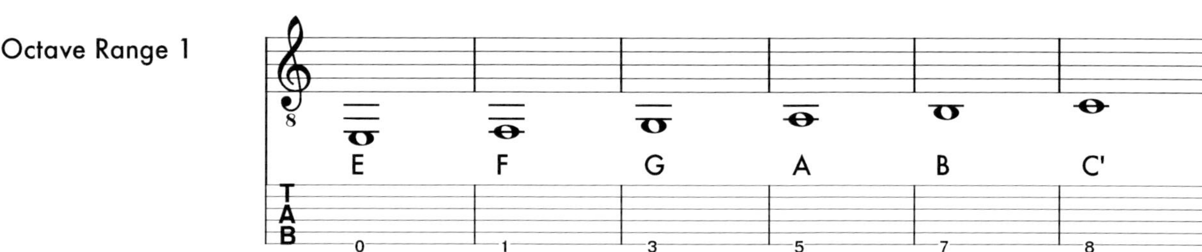

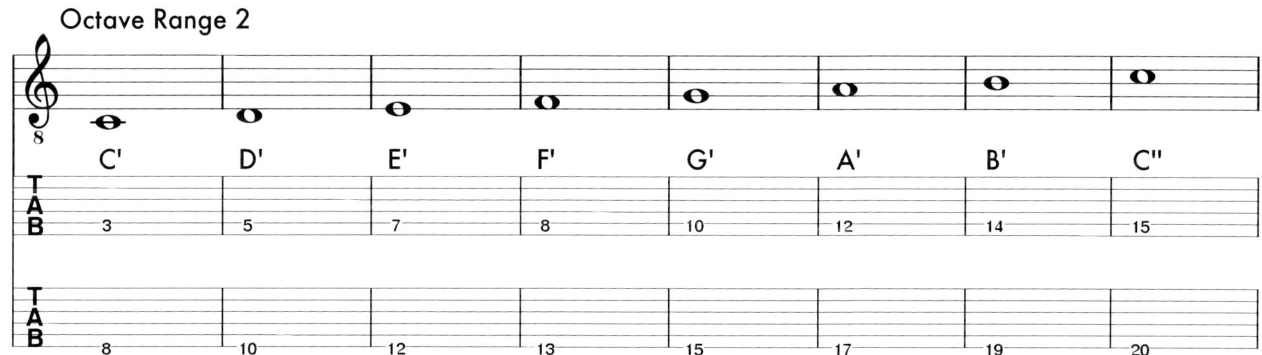

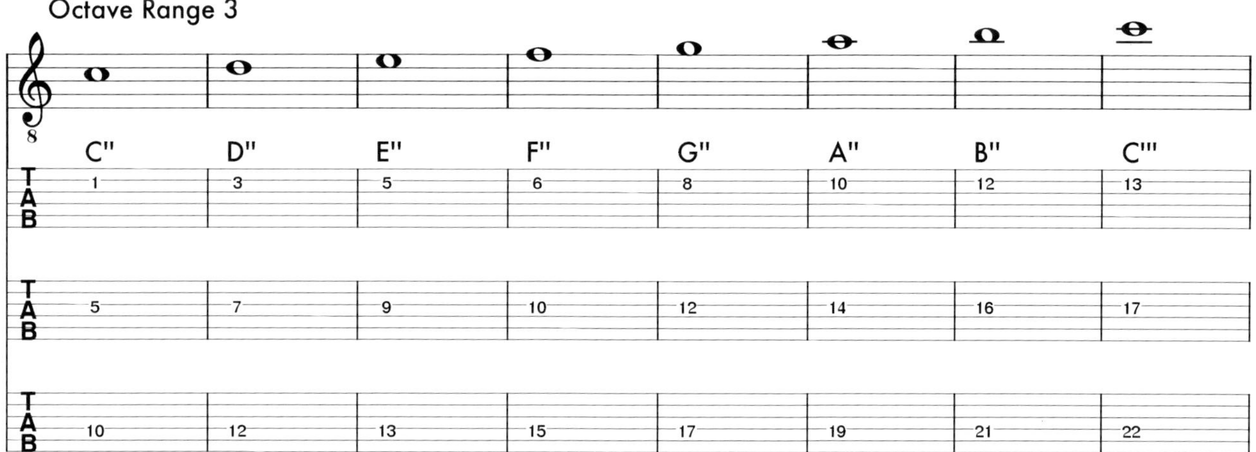

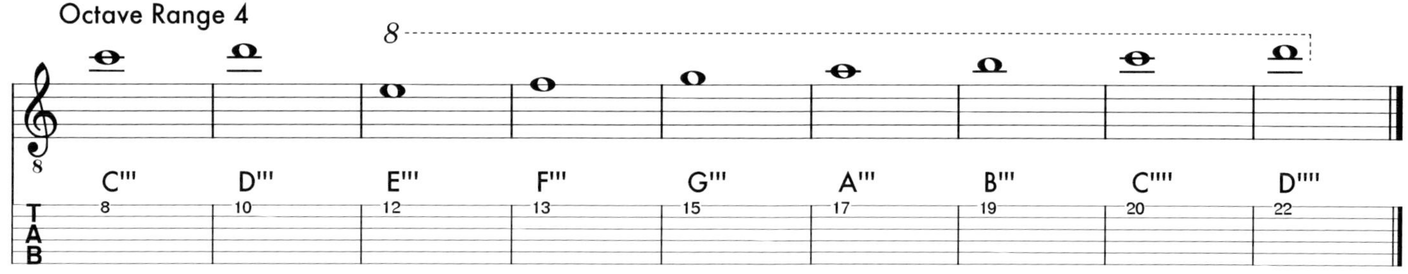

DIAGONAL OCTAVE ZONES

There are 28 different natural note pitches within the regular range of the guitar between E and D''''. When we map them all out on the fretboard, we find them in 84 locations (14 on each string), which means that, on average, there are three different locations for any natural note. This math may give us an idea of the non-linear, multidimensional design of the guitar.
In comparison, though no less complex, the piano keyboard is linear and one-dimensional, as there is only one key for any single pitch, and moving to a higher or lower note is always directly correlated to moving right (up) or left (down) on the keyboard.

When we look again individually at the different octave ranges as before, but taking into account all possible note locations on multiple strings, we see that these octave ranges run diagonally across the fretboard as virtual diagonal octave zones or corridors.
It is very important to understand that these diagonal lines reveal the true nature of the fretboard.
It is also important to play up and down along strings horizontally and to study vertical position playing, but in the end everything played on the guitar has to follow these diagonal lines and zones.
When playing in different keys or modes, these virtual diagonal zones shift right or left, but always keep their shape and direction.

On the right, you can see all 84 of the natural note locations on the fretboard; the diagonal octave zones appear in different shades of grey. Explore each zone individually by improvising. Be aware of the note names and their notation, as well as the multiple locations for any single pitch.

The exercise on the next page will help you locate and play all natural notes on the fretboard, and experience the diagonal shape of the octave zones.
Set your metronome to a slow tempo, and play through the whole page, one note per click.
When you move from one note to the next, be aware of the note name and location; for the best learning experience, say the name of each new note out loud while playing.
Some notes have only one location, others have up to five. Make sure to set the metronome at a comfortably slow speed, so you are able to play all note locations evenly without a break.
By the end of the page, you will have played all 84 natural note locations on the fretboard, always moving along the diagonal octave zones, ascending the diatonic. Play this exercise backwards as well, starting on the highest note, and descending - reading the page in reverse.

If you cannot physically reach a note on a high fret on one of the lower strings on your instrument, simply omit that note location and move on.

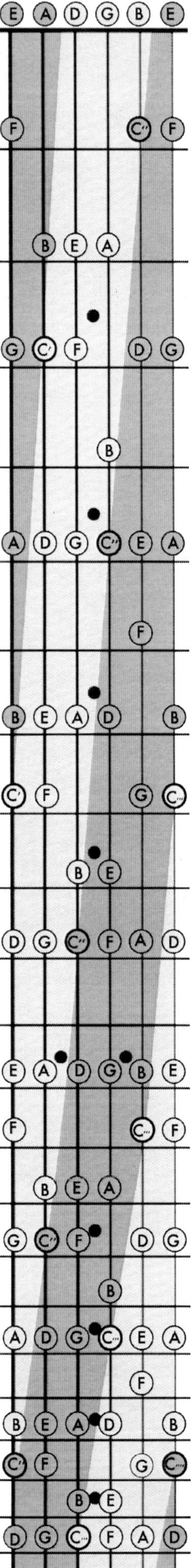

NOTE LOCALIZATION EXERCISE

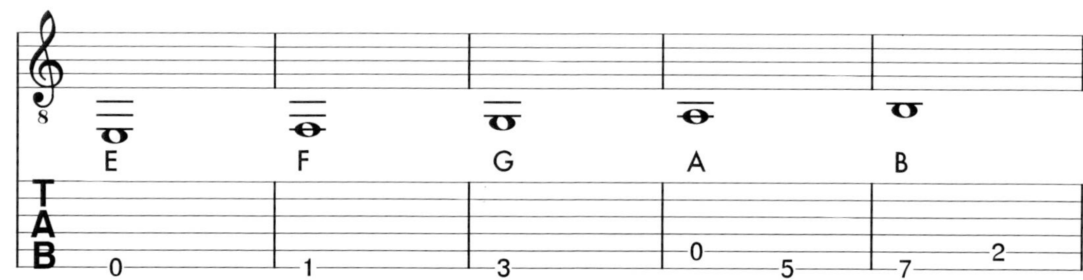

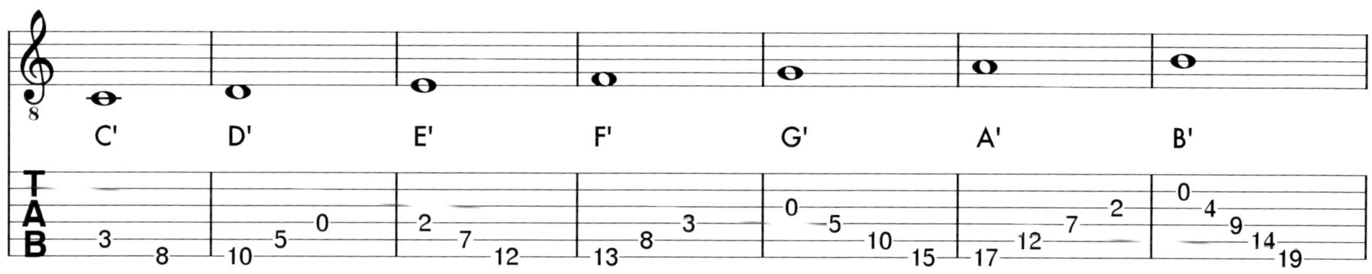

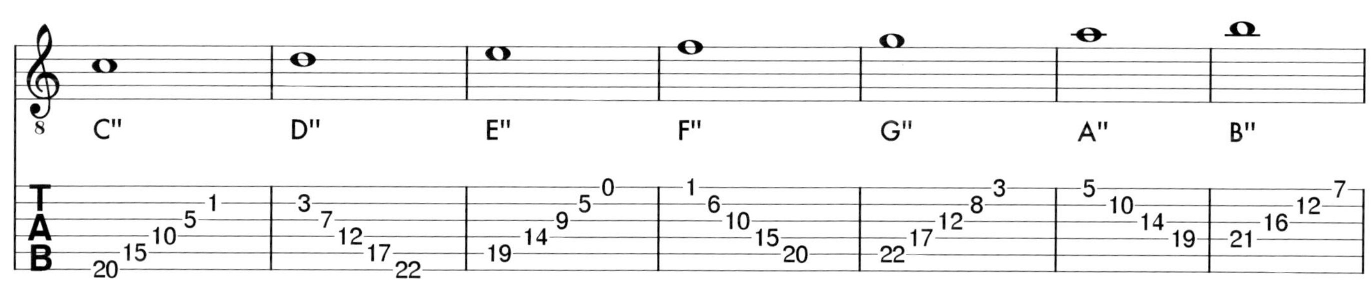

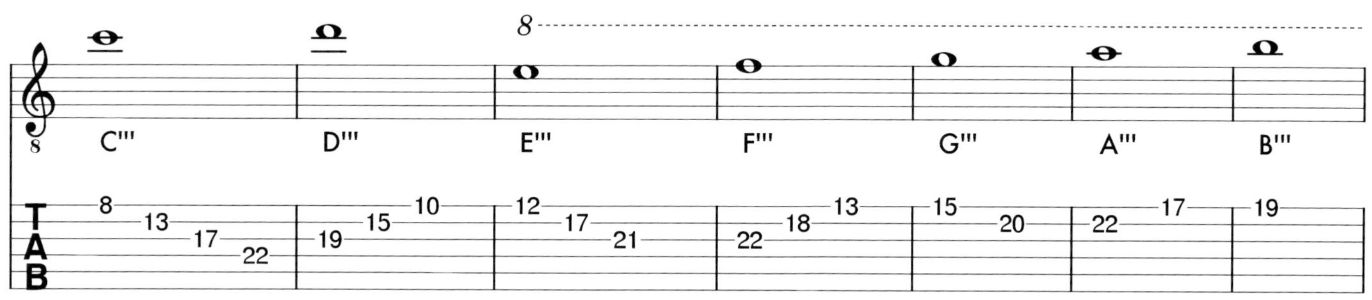

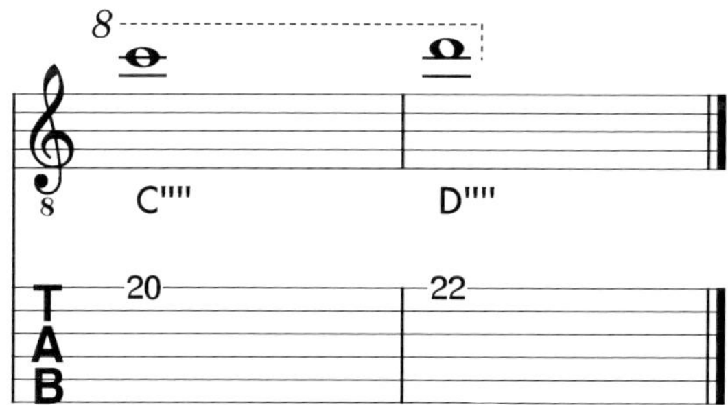

ADDING ACCIDENTALS / COMPLETING THE CHROMATIC SPACE

This page shows the same octave of the piano keyboard as before, but this time adding the black keys, or the five missing notes not covered by the diatonic, to complete the chromatic scale. Note that every one of these five new notes can be named by either raising the lower neighbouring natural note with a sharp (♯) or lowering the higher one with a flat (♭).

Study the location of these notes in the notation system as well as within the chromatic scale on the B-string. Then move on to the other five strings and add them to the horizontal octave ranges as well. When you play within the diagonal zones, study the location of all pitches of the chromatic scale, but try to keep an awareness of the diatonic key of C you are still in. Keeping a harmonic loop or drone of the root note going can help.

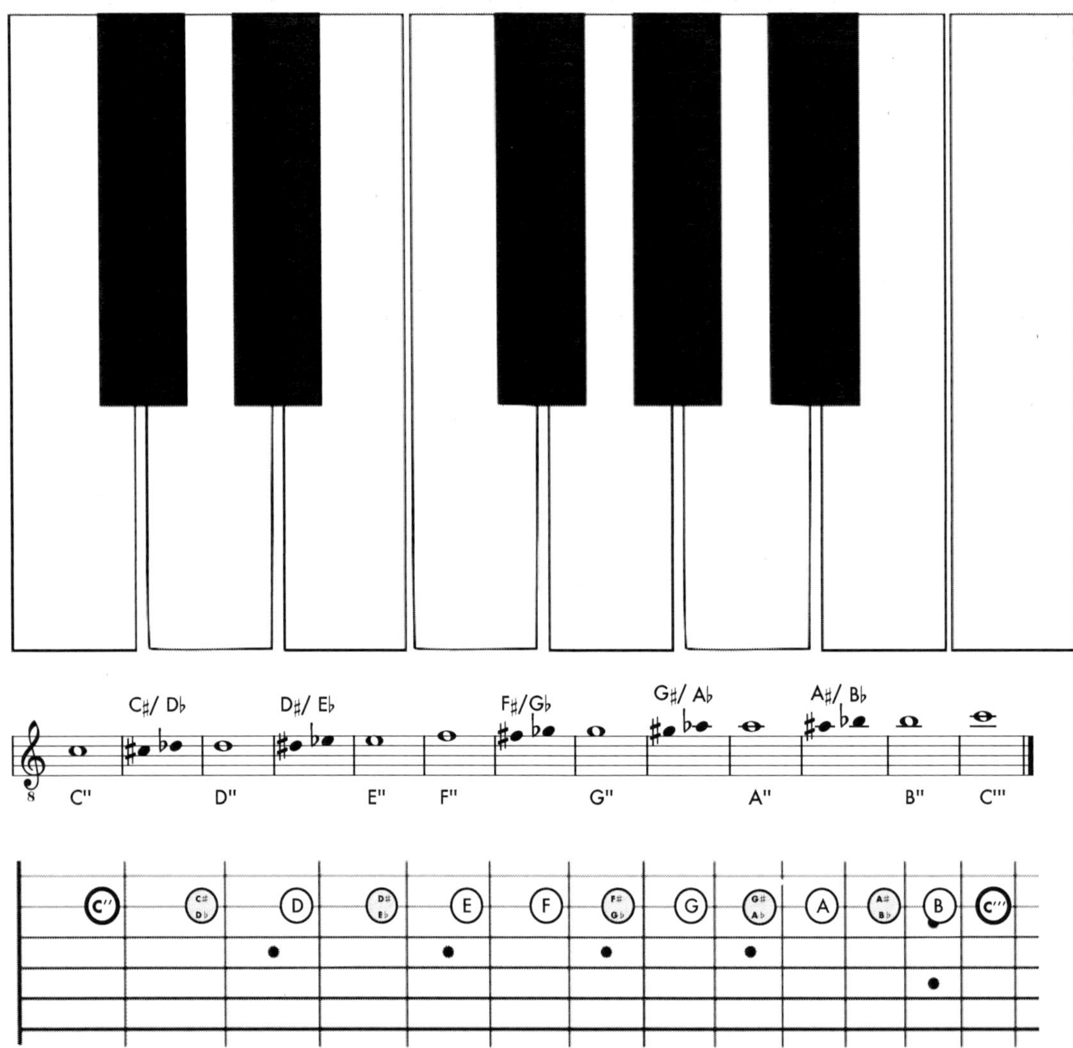

Depending on your personal level, use the new pitches to play in other keys, following the aforementioned intervallic design (WWHWWWH) to form a diatonic major scale from any root.
Go back to the note localization exercise on the previous page, and play it in different keys, from the lowest to highest note of the given diatonic scale and back down.
Of the 12 notes of the chromatic scale, there are 138 different locations on the fretboard, or an average of 11.5 locations for every chromatic note across the full four-octave range.
The exercise on the next page is related to the previous diatonic note localization exercise, but covering the whole chromatic scale using a 12-tone row. Set the metronome to a slow and comfortable speed, and play every possible location of a note in all octaves before moving to the next note of the row. Keep a steady and even tempo - always moving along the diagonal zones to the next available location, ascending and descending. After completing the row, you will have played all 138 chromatic note locations on the fretboard once.
Try this with any other 12-tone row, being aware of the note names and locations at all times.

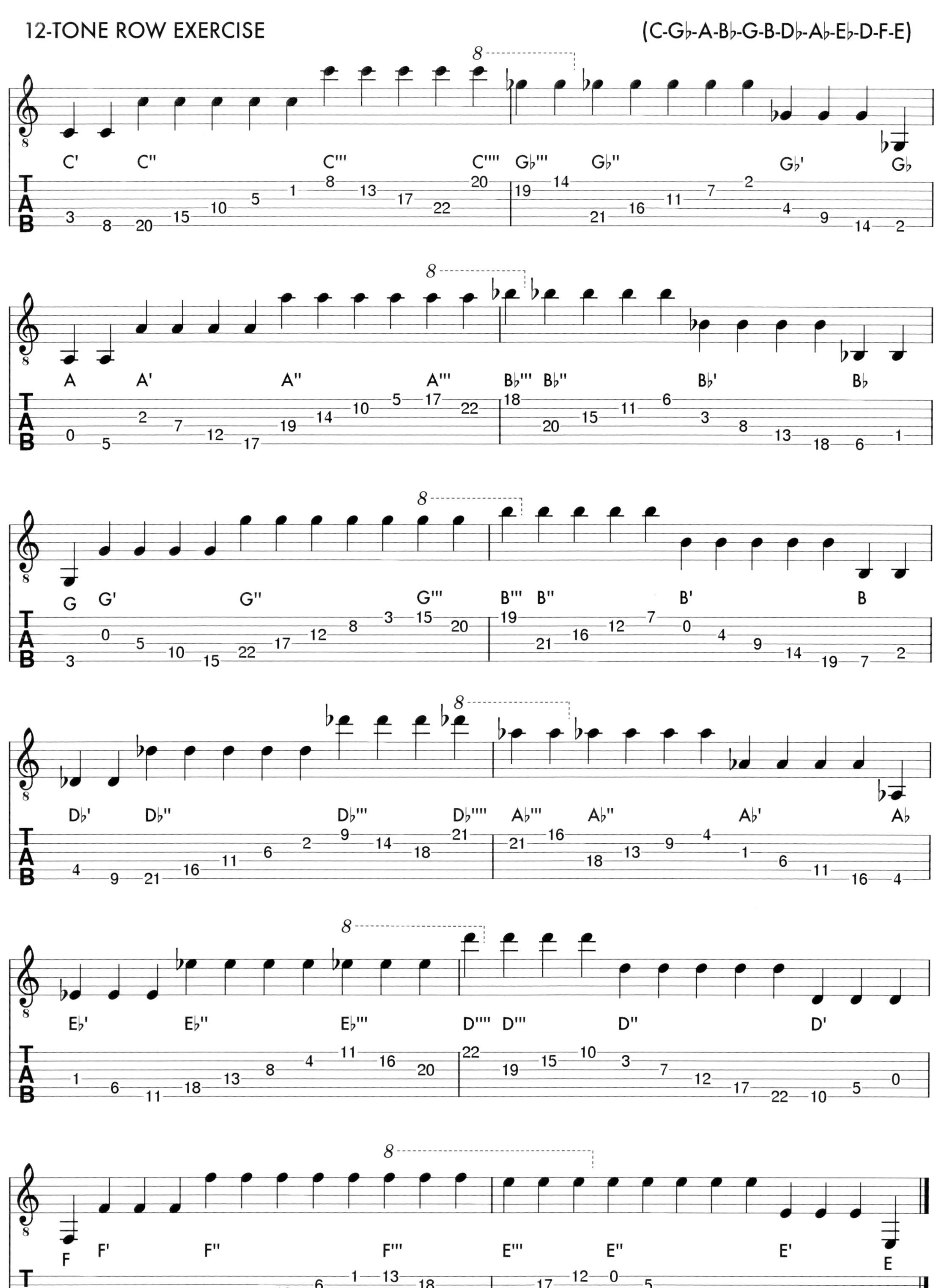
12-TONE ROW EXERCISE
(C-G♭-A-B♭-G-B-D♭-A♭-E♭-D-F-E)
C' C'' C''' C'''' G♭''' G♭'' G♭' G♭
3 8 20 15 10 5 1 8 13 17 22 20 | 19 14 21 16 11 7 2 4 9 14 2
A A' A'' A''' B♭''' B♭'' B♭' B♭
0 5 2 7 12 17 19 14 10 5 17 22 | 18 20 15 11 6 3 8 13 18 6 1
G G' G'' G''' B''' B'' B' B
3 0 5 10 15 22 17 12 8 3 15 20 | 19 21 16 12 7 0 4 9 14 19 7 2
D♭' D♭'' D♭''' D♭'''' A♭''' A♭'' A♭' A♭
4 9 21 16 11 6 2 9 14 18 21 | 21 16 18 13 9 4 1 6 11 16 4
E♭' E♭'' E♭''' D'''' D''' D'' D'
1 6 11 18 13 8 4 11 16 20 | 22 19 15 10 3 7 12 17 22 10 5 0
F F' F'' F''' E''' E'' E' E
1 3 8 13 20 15 10 6 1 13 18 22 | 21 17 12 0 5 9 14 19 12 7 2 0

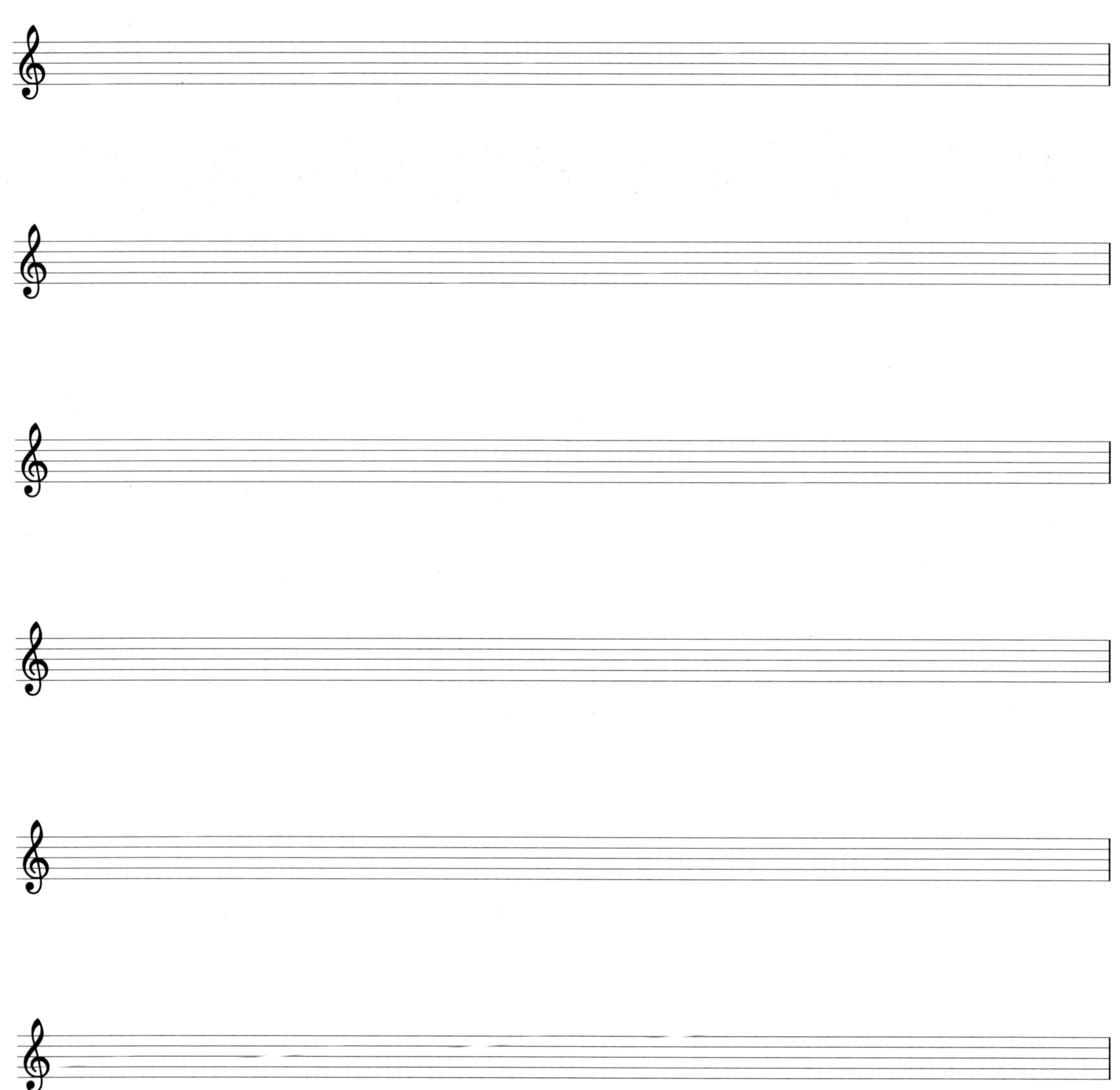

Page left blank for layout purposes and your personal notes

APPENDIX FOR PIANISTS

APPLYING VOICE MOTION TO THE KEYBOARD

OVERVIEW

This chapter will help pianists apply the content of this book to their instrument.

All musical examples in this book are shown in treble clef, primarily with the guitar in mind - but all material herein is easily accessible on the piano keyboard as well. In fact, the piano can be very useful for exploring and studying the different voice motion types for all readers.
On the next few pages, examples are presented in standard piano notation on the grand staff. These examples show basic ways to distribute the three-note harmony notes between the two hands.
Pianists should work through the book from the beginning, applying the material to the keyboard using the principles outlined in the following pages.

With ten fingers available, pianists can easily play more than three notes simultaneously; certainly more than any guitarist. Nevertheless, pianists are encouraged to explore strictly three-part harmony in depth with the tools presented in this book, as this kind of playing yields deep, possibly untapped harmonic riches and establishes a firm foundation on which to add more notes and build denser harmonies. Refer to "Building 4-part Chords" in Part 3B (p. 233) for a method to add an additional voice to any chord or voice motion in the book.

At the end of this section, the principle of **doubling** is introduced, which is a particularly valuable and useful tool for pianists when applying the material in this book to the keyboard. By duplicating any of the three notes either an octave higher or lower, a fourth note can be added without leaving the sphere of three-part harmony, offering subtle ways of altering the sound of any chord or voice movement.

PLAYING THREE-PART HARMONY on PIANO

Close Voicing

All close-voiced chords and moves in the book can easily be played on the piano, in four ways: Either hand can play all three notes, or the voices can be split between the hands, with one hand playing one voice and the other hand playing the remaining two voices.

Example: Move 2) close

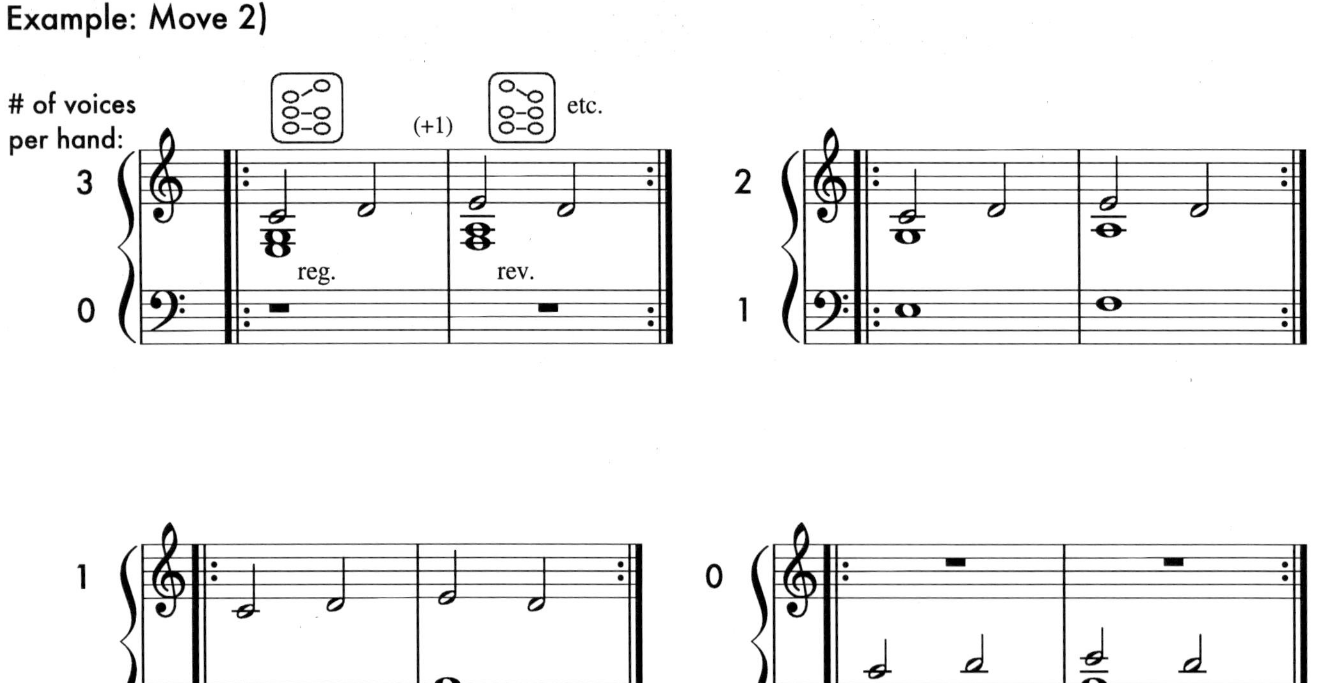

Play any of the 15 close-voiced chord forms, or any of the 108 possible voice motion moves presented in Part 1 in all inversions, and move them up and down the diatonic or other heptatonic scales (using the examples presented in the introduction to Part 1) in all keys.

Experiment with the four ways of note distribution to find out which works best for each chord structure on the piano.

When playing close-voiced three-part harmony with the right hand, the left hand is free to play additional notes or a melody in the lower register.
A good entry point for application is to play through the close-voiced etudes presented in Part 3C with the right hand, while playing the root and 7th of the harmony with the left hand:

Example: Etude 1.1 Variation A

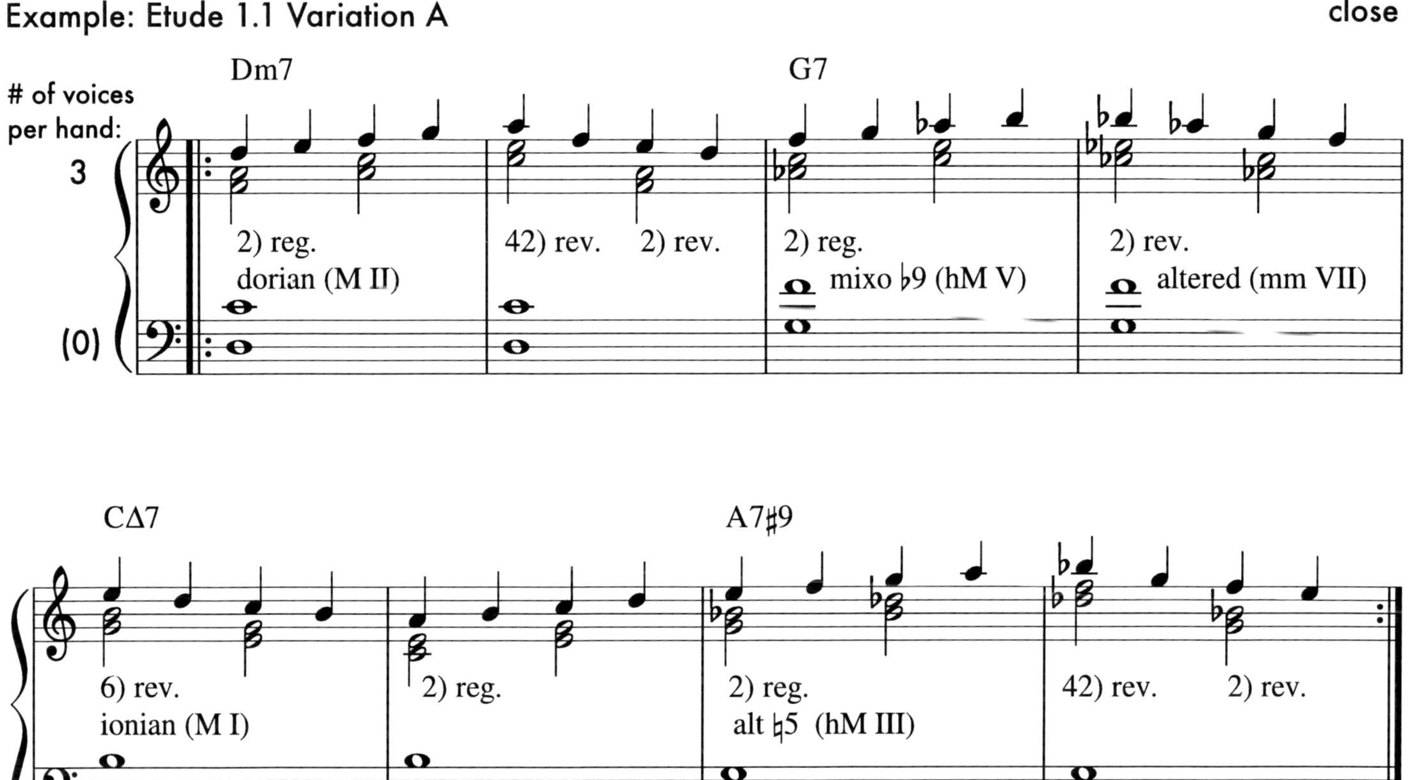

The following two examples show different moves played with both hands, taken up and down heptatonic scales. Apply any other move presented in Part 1 in a similar way.
Experiment with all six of the basic heptatonics in all keys and inversions.

Example: Move 26)
C melodic minor

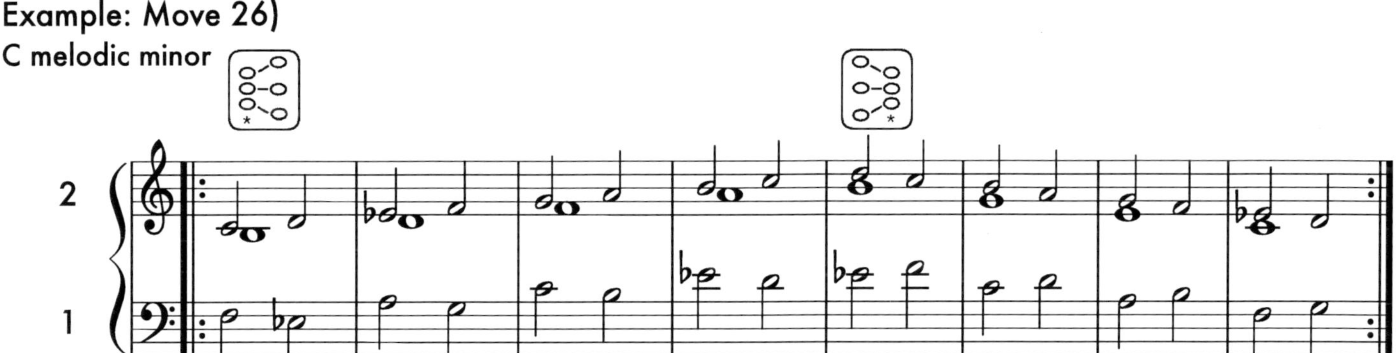

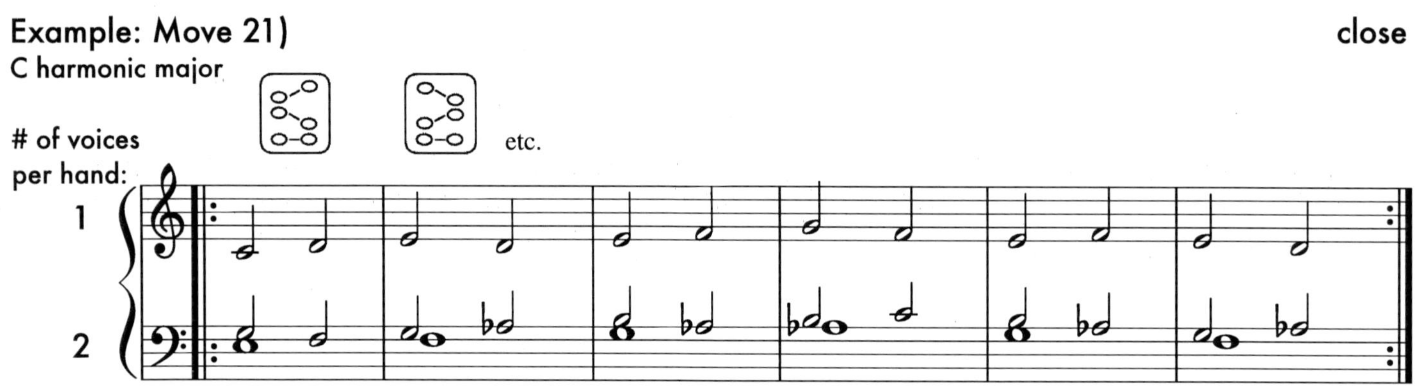

Similarly, when playing close-voiced three-part harmony with the left hand, the right hand is free to play additional notes or a melody in the higher register.
Experiment with any guideline or melodic idea with long notes, or improvise with your right hand against any set of voice motion moves:

close

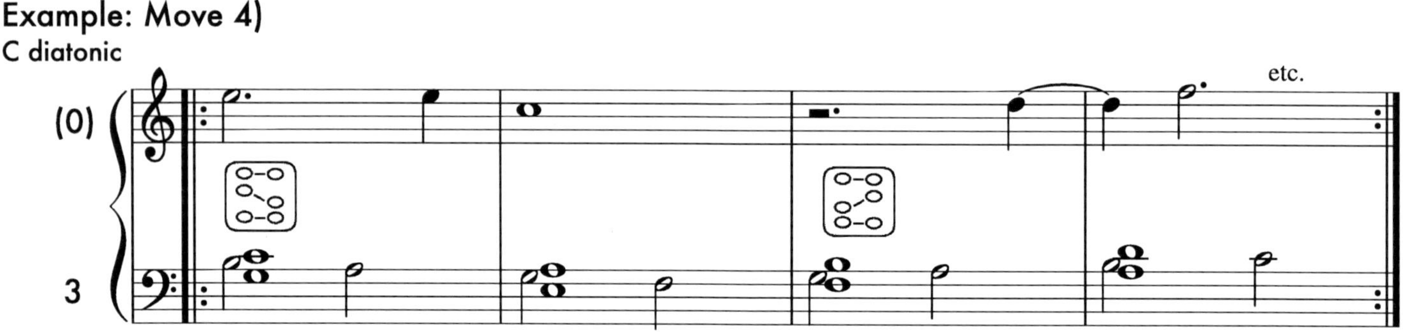

PLAYING THREE-PART HARMONY on PIANO

Open Voicing (Drop-2)

The three notes of any open chord or move can be split between the hands in two ways, in which one hand plays one, and the other hand plays the two remaining notes:

open

Example: Move 2)

# of voices per hand:

2 / 1 — reg. (+1) rev. etc.

1 / 2 — reg. rev.

Experiment with any of the 15 open (d2) chords or any of the 108 moves presented in Part 2, using the full range of the piano, all inversions and keys. Note which of the two ways of note distribution works best for each situation.

In the following example, the first eight bars of "Etude 1.3" are set in a minor key, and the bassnote of each chord is added on the first beat of each measure.
Continue to change the rest of the etude to C minor, or leave out the bassnotes for a direct transcription of the original etude.

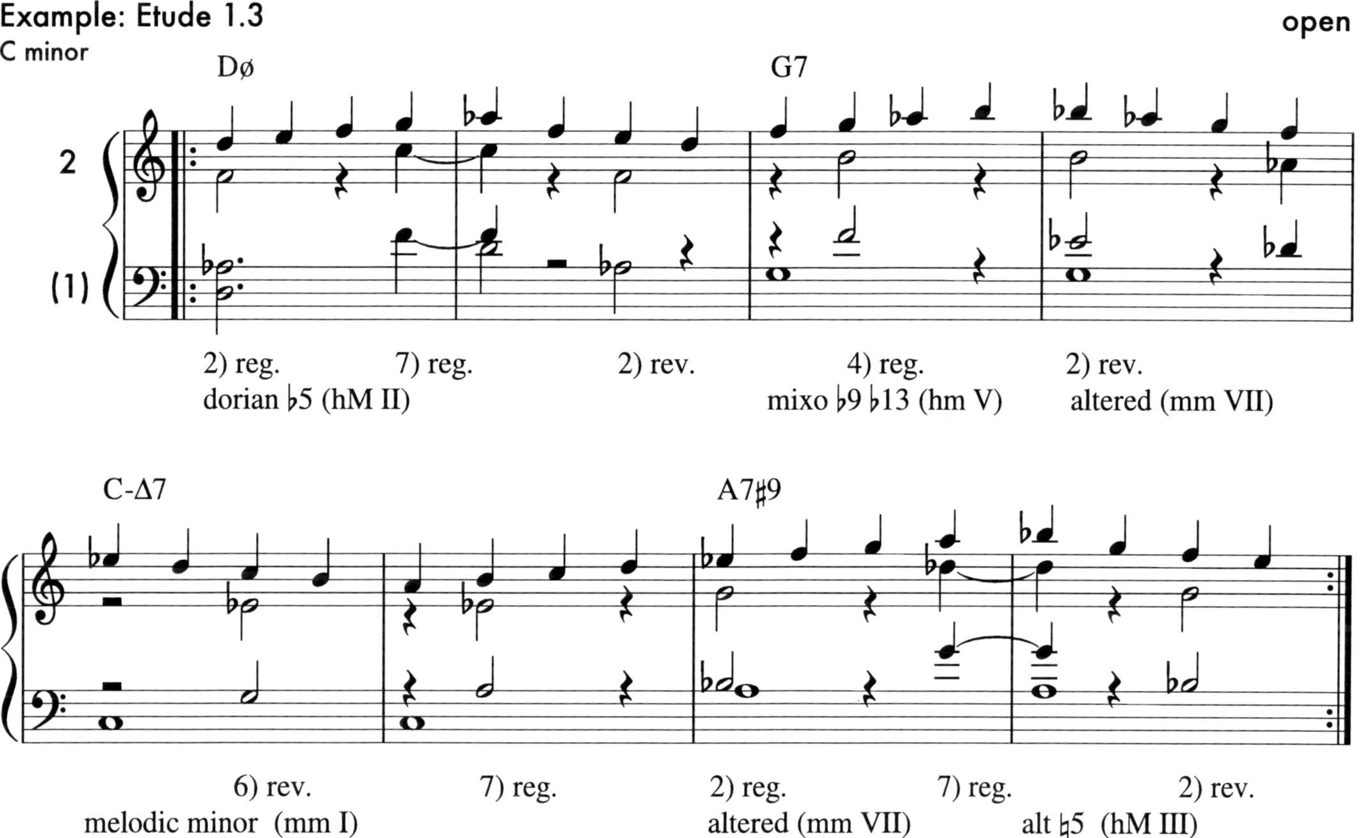

DOUBLING NOTES

Doubling any of the three notes an octave up or down is a very useful tool on the piano when working with the material in this book.
Three-part harmony offers six options to double any single voice.
If the moving voice gets doubled, either hold it (a), or move it as well (b).

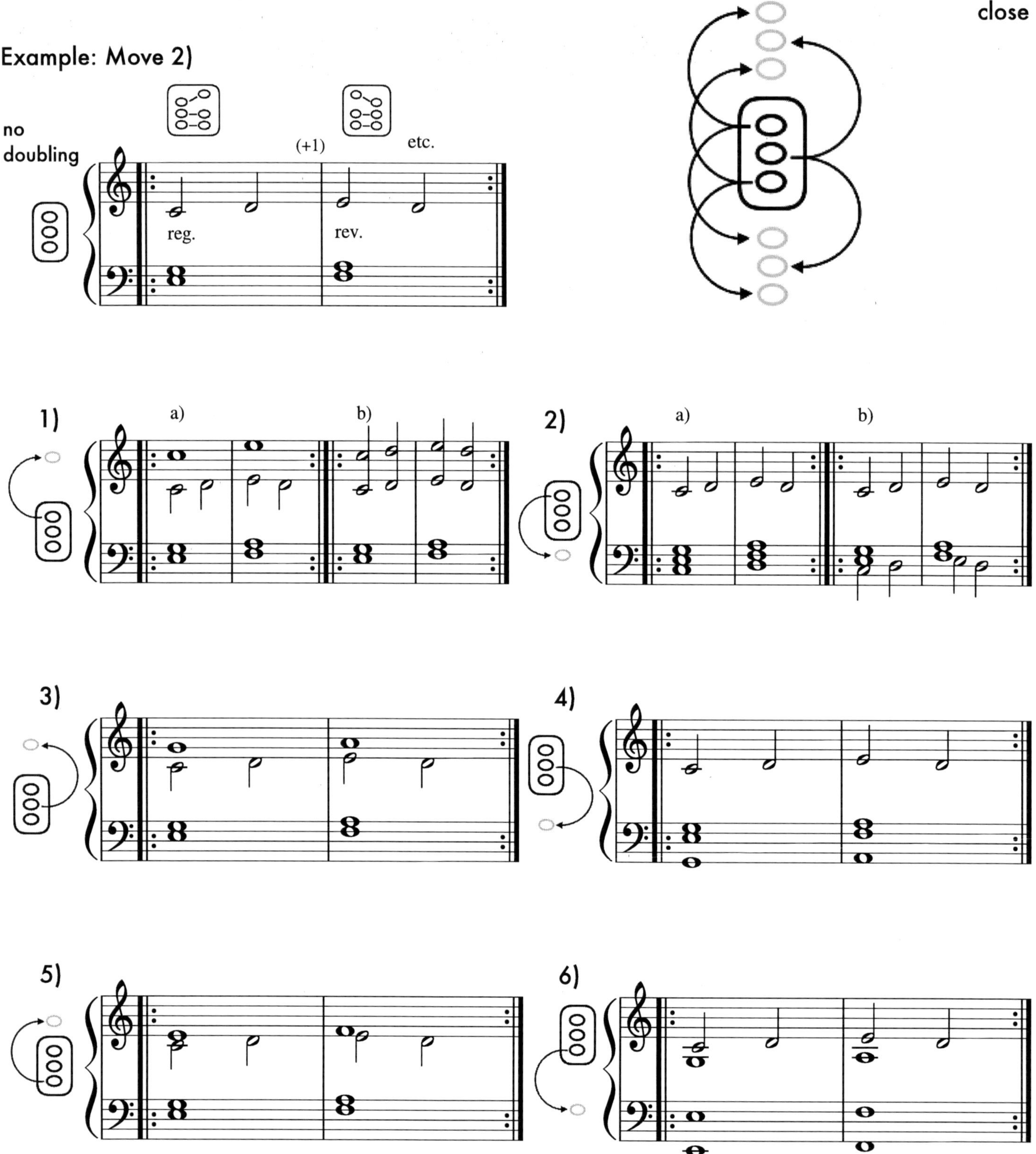

On the piano, experiment with the six ways of doubling, and apply them to any of the material presented in this book, in close and open (drop-2) voicing.

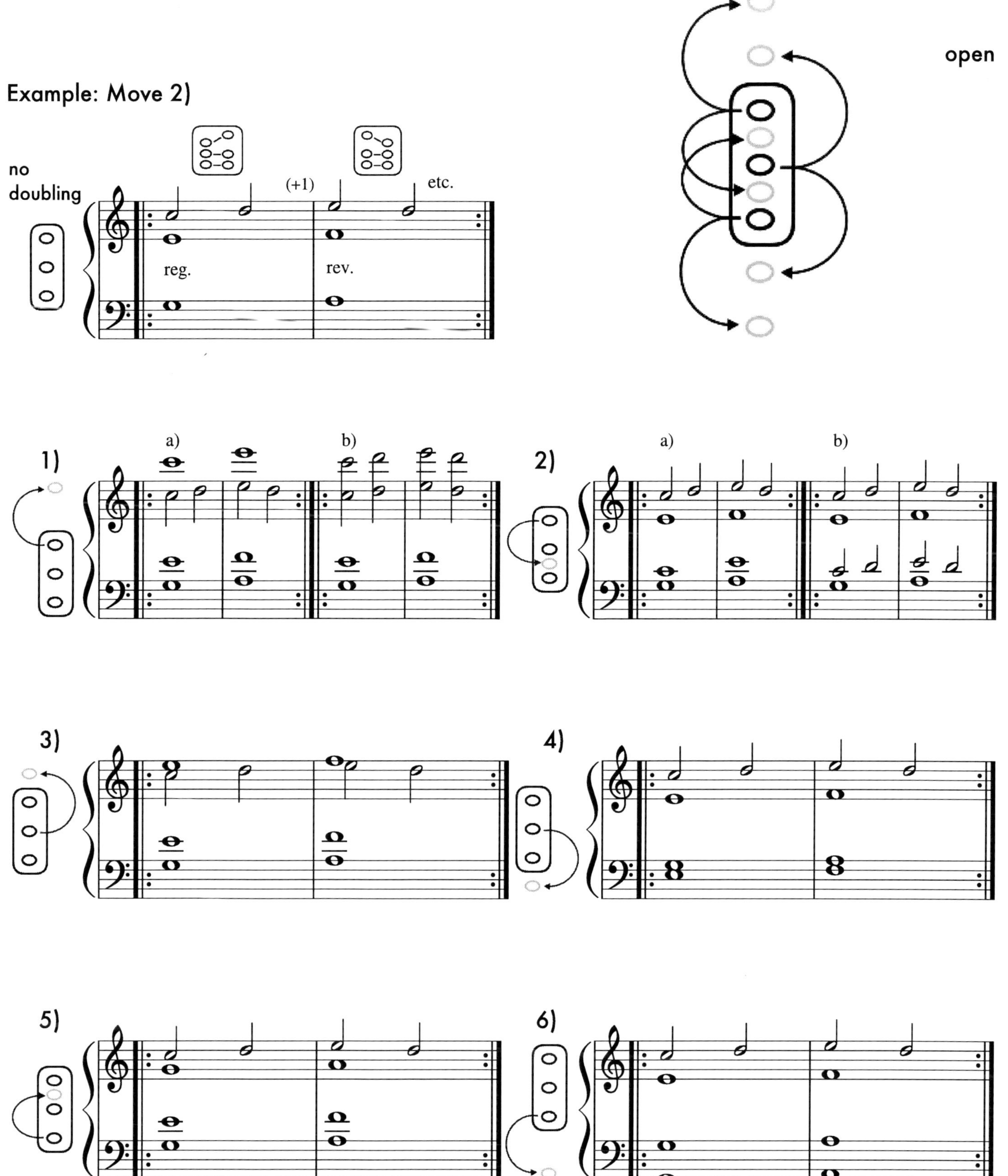

GLOSSARY

1st: Abbreviation for "First Inversion"; an inversion of a three-part chord structure which has the middle voice of its close-voiced root position chord as its lowest note.

2nd: Abbreviation for "Second Inversion"; an inversion of a three-part chord structure in which the upper voice of its close-voiced root position chord serves as the lowest note. Alternatively, it may refer to the *interval of a second*, which is the distance from one note to the next in any of the basic heptatonic scales. A *second* may encompass one, two or three semitones.

322/223: Specific intervallic combination of 2nds and 3rds within moves employing triple-voice motion.
322 = One voice moving in an interval of a 3rd, while the remaining two voices move in intervals of 2nds.
233 = One voice moving in an interval of a 2nd, while the two other voices move in intervals of 3rds.

3rd: Interval of a third, which is the distance from any note by two scale degrees in either direction within any of the basic heptatonic scales, usually three semitones (minor 3rd) or four semitones (major 3rd).

4ths: Refers to intervals of a 4th, or to three-part chord structures built by stacking two 4th intervals on top of each other, with the scale degrees 1-4-7 from any note.
The chord symbols used in this book to describe the chords of this type show the specific kind of 4th intervals as they are stacked to form the root position of the respective chord:
4 = perfect 4th with five semitones, ♭4 = diminished fourth with four semitones ,
♯4 = augmented fourth with six semitones.

7th no 3: Three-part chord structure attained by omitting the 3rd degree of any four-part 7th chord, with the resulting scale degrees 1-5-7 from any note of a heptatonic scale.

7th no 5: Three-part chord structure attained by omitting the 5th degree of any four-part 7th chord, with the resulting scale degrees 1-3-7 from any note of a heptatonic scale.

alt.: Abbreviation for "altered"; refers to the altered scale, which is the seventh mode of the melodic minor scale ("mm VII").

asc.: Abbreviation for "ascending", or moving higher within a scale.

C' / C" etc.: The apostrophes indicate the octave location of the respective note; C' is the middle C (sometimes called C4), which is the tone represented by a note on the first ledger line below the treble clef. C" is one octave higher, C"' two octaves higher and so forth.

close: Indicates close voicings, or close-voiced chords, in which all of the notes of a chord structure move within a range of one octave, so in terms of intervals, they are as close together as possible.

clusters: Three-part chord structures built by stacking two 2nds, or by playing three adjacent notes of a scale simultaneously.

cycle: The concept of moving any chord structure through the harmonic space using a specific interval, either within a certain scale and key, or symmetrically/chromatically. See pages 214 and 219 for further explanation.

desc.: Abbreviation for "descending", or moving lower within a scale.

diatonic: Refers to the diatonic major scale and its modes, which represent the most even way possible to distribute seven notes in the space of an octave in equal temperament, with the necessary two half steps set as far apart from each other as possible.

heptatonic: A scale with seven pitches per octave.

hexatonic: A scale with six pitches per octave.

hM: Harmonic major scale. The heptatonic scale that can be derived from the diatonic major scale by lowering its 6th degree by a half tone.

hm: Harmonic minor scale. The heptatonic scale that can be derived from the diatonic major scale by lowering its 3rd and its 6th degrees by a half tone.

hm ♭5: Harmonic minor ♭5 scale. The heptatonic scale that can be derived from the diatonic major scale by lowering its 3rd, 5th, and 6th degrees by a half tone.

I -VII: Roman numerals refer to the seven modes of a heptatonic scale. For example, "M IV" is the **Lydian** scale, the fourth mode of the major scale; "mm VII" is the **altered scale** (aka: *diminished whole-tone* or *super Locrian* scale), based on the seventh degree of the melodic minor scale, etc.
In the three guitar solo pieces, Roman numerals are used to indicate playing positions on the guitar.

M: Diatonic major scale (see **diatonic** above)

mixo: A mixolydian scale, the fifth mode of the diatonic major scale ("M V")

mixo ♭9: A mixolydian ♭9 scale, fifth mode of the harmonic major scale ("hM V")

mm: Melodic minor scale. The heptatonic scale that can be derived from the diatonic major scale by flattening its 3rd degree. In the more contemporary conception of scale theory used here, the term *melodic minor* refers only to the ascending half of the classical melodic minor scale.

mm ♭5: Melodic minor ♭5 scale. The heptatonic scale that can be derived from the diatonicmajor scale by lowering its 3rd and 5th degrees by a half tone.

motion: Refers to any melodic movement from one three-part chord structure leading into the next three-part structure, i.e. single upper-voice motion, or triple-voice contrary motion etc.

move: Refers to the 108 possible voice motion moves (see p. 14). Each move represents a unique pair of chord types connected by melodic voice movement. Like any chord structure in three-part heptatonic harmony, each move has three inversions which produce distinct voice motions and can be performed on any scale degree.

narrow-range voice leading: The concept of taking a move up or down a scale or through a symmetrical cycle, while changing the inversions usually every other step, to stay close to the range of the starting chord voicing.

octatonic: A scale with eight pitches per octave.

open: Indicates open voicings, or open-voiced chords. Compared to close voicings, the notes of open chords consist of wider intervals which collectively exceed one octave. The open chords in Part 2 are all in drop-2 voicing, which can be derived from the close-voiced chords of Part 1 by dropping down the middle voices down one octave.

pentatonic: A scale with five pitches per octave.

reg.: Abbreviation for "regular"; reading any of the voice motion moves regularly from left to right will produce ascending voice motion.

rev.: Abbreviation for "reverse"; reading any of the voice motion moves backwards from right to left will produce descending voice motion.

root: Abbreviation for "Root Position"; an inversion of a three-part chord structure that uses the root of the chord as the bottom note.

triads: Three-part chord structures built by stacking two intervals of a 3rd on top of one another, consisting of scale degrees 1-3-5 from any note of a heptatonic scale.